The Classical Liberal Constitution

THE CLASSICAL LIBERAL CONSTITUTION

The Uncertain Quest for Limited Government

RICHARD A. EPSTEIN

HARVARD UNIVERSITY PRESS

Cambridge, Massachusetts

London, England

2014

Publication of this book has been supported through the generous
provisions of the Maurice and Lula Bradley Smith Memorial Fund.

Library of Congress Cataloging-in-Publication Data
Epstein, Richard Allen, 1943–
The classical liberal constitution : the uncertain quest for limited
government / Richard A. Epstein.
pages cm
Includes bibliographical references and index.
ISBN 978-0-674-72489-1
1. Constitutional law—United States.   2. Liberalism.   I. Title.
KF4550.E69 2013
342.73—dc23   2013015767

To Eileen again, for everything,

and

To the Memory of David Currie (1936–2007)
constitutionalist extraordinaire

Contents

Preface: My Constitutional Odyssey

The Classical Liberal Constitution represents the culmination of my lifetime project of developing a distinctive synthesis of constitutional law that does not fall squarely within either the conservative or progressive camp. I started work on this volume in 2006, finished a first draft in 2010, and have done extensive revision and expansion of the book to prepare it for publication in late 2013. At one level, my ambition has been to give a comprehensive account of how the various provisions of the United States Constitution, dealing as they do with both structural issues and individual rights, can best be explained in light of classical liberal theory. That theory in turn starts from the twin pillars of private property and limited government, and seeks to make sure that each and every government action improves the overall welfare of the individuals in the society it governs. It is no part of the theory to extol any version of philosophical egoism that allows any individual to do what he or she will no matter what the consequences to others. Classical liberalism is a social theory, not the magic paean of radical individualism with which it has often been conflated, especially by its detractors on all sides of the political spectrum.

In the course of my thinking on this subject, it became increasingly clear that an examination of constitutional law principles must start with the text of the Constitution. But that truism is not a full-throated endorsement of the strong modern defenses of constitutional originalism. The harder one probes, the more apparent it becomes that analysis must go quickly beyond that starting point in order to fill in the details of the larger picture of which the text is an indispensable part. In particular, the Constitution makes liberal use of such terms, taken in alphabetical order, as "citizen," "commerce," "contract," "cruel and unusual punishments," "due process," "freedom," "general welfare of the United States," "judicial power," "law and equity," "necessary and proper," "private property," "religion," and many more. Yet at the same time the document, self-consciously, does not contain a glossary of what these vital terms mean. We know, however, that their use long antedates their inclusion in the Constitution, so that in a deep sense no one can understand how these terms operate without understanding their historical context in relation to both institutional arrangements and private transactions. Many of these terms have received extensive elaboration in private law disputes between ordinary persons. Others were in constant use in public law contexts prior to the drafting of the Constitution. A full analysis must take both these developments into account.

At the same time, the Constitution does not contain such vital terms as "police power," "privacy," "race," "sex," and "standing" that have become critical to complement the exposition of those provisions found in the Constitution. Any constitutional analysis must explain why and how these additional elements play an essential role in constitutional interpretation. A general theory of constitutional interpretation therefore deals with at least two levels of integration: first, public and private law, and second, the written and implied provisions in the constitutional structure.

Constitutional interpretation also contains a third organizing principle—what I call constitutional prescription. In ordinary private disputes, notions like prescription, statutes of limitation, and the doctrine of laches play an essential role in legitimating through the passage of time actions and behaviors that were regarded as wrongful when committed. Thus long use allows a party to obtain a prescriptive easement over the lands of a neighbor even though that right originates in a wrongful trespass against the original owner. Constitutional law has its own doctrine of prescription whereby some (but not all) doctrines that have been in play for long periods of time become part of the constitutional culture even though they were incorrect constructions of the original text under the first two interpretative principles dealing with textual interpretation and implication respectively. The issue is of immense importance because many of our most entrenched constitutional doctrines, including that of judicial supremacy, are incorrect under normal interpretive principles.

In working through these puzzles, I should state at the outset that in a conventional sense I am not a teacher of constitutional law, having taught the structural course and the First Amendment course once each, and over a decade ago. But by the same token I count as a constitutional lawyer because I have taught a wide range of courses in which constitutional issues play an integral role. These include basic first-year courses in civil procedure, contracts, property, and torts. These also include upper-level courses in subjects like antitrust law, conflicts of law, employment discrimination law, environmental law, food and drug law, labor law, land use planning, political theory, taxation, telecommunications law, and especially jurisprudence, legal history, political theory, and Roman law. All of these courses shed light on topics that are normally overlooked or disparaged by more conventional constitutional scholars who have scant interest or knowledge in many of these areas. It is also significant that my initial legal education was at Oxford in the mid-1960s, where my common law education contained no serious discussion of either federalism or the basic structure of the United States Constitution.

The consequences of my distinctive intellectual background should be evident in this book, which defends with a passionate intensity the classical liberal vision of the Constitution against its rival, and ascendant, progressive alternative. Any close reading of the historical materials shows that the Constitution is grounded in the work of such great Enlightenment thinkers as Hobbes, Locke, Hume, Madison, and Montesquieu. There is always slippage between the world of ideas and the world of practical politics, so that it would be a mistake to posit any perfect correspondence between what the original Constitution prescribes and what a classical liberal theory demands. In part this is due to the fact that the standard social contract theory that undergirds the classical liberal approach thinks of compacts among individuals that form a state, and not compacts between states to form a federal nation. In part this is because of the inability of the Founders to deal decisively with slavery, which introduced major blemishes into the original structure that only a blood-soaked Civil War could remove. And it is in part because the Founders, in sailing uncharted waters, made many serious errors, both of omission and commission, in designing the Electoral College, the structure of federal courts, the institution of judicial review, and the relations between dual state and federal sovereigns.

But what is striking about the whole package is this firm proposition. Whenever the Supreme Court takes any constitutional claim seriously, it reverts back to classical liberal principles, often without acknowledging the close resemblance between that theory and its own judicial decisions. Basic rights are defined broadly to prevent political evasion; police power justifications for the use of state or federal power tend to be narrowly confined to such objects as the control of force and monopoly. That trend of classical liberalism is equally evident in dealing with judicial efforts to maintain open trade across state borders in connection with the dormant Commerce Clause and to protect political dissent through freedom of speech under the First Amendment. The difference in subject matters should never be allowed to conceal the unity of approach.

The tenor of judicial decisions, however, changes rapidly once specific constitutional protections are watered down by a low "rational basis" standard of review. In this new environment, rights are narrowly constructed; state justifications for the limitation of these rights are broadly stated. The relentless application of the lax "rational basis" test in the treatment of contract, property, the commerce power, and the power to tax and spend has left such rights and powers twisted from their original meanings. There is, to be sure, a critical place in the overall analysis for some deference to government, but it should—to use the appropriate corporate law analogy—involve the acceptance of a business judgment rule. To the extent that the government runs major social institutions, including the military, the courts, and the schools, it receives the benefit of the doubt in making hard choices so long as it acts reasonably and in good faith. But by the same token, no government should receive that level of deference when it uses its political muscle to tax, to regulate, or to change liability rules in ways that limit the protection of both liberty and property. At that point, deference is an open invitation to the faction and intrigue that have done so much in recent years to sap the strength and the focus of the nation, so much so that all too many people today rightly see the United States as a great power in decline.

In taking this position, I know that my outspoken views run against the grain of both conservative and progressive constitutional approaches. But in light of the massive disarray of modern American culture, I regard this conscious departure from conventional wisdom as a point of strength and not of weakness. I leave it to the reader to judge whether I have made the right choice.

I have spent a long time pursuing this unorthodox path in my legal writings. My engagement with constitutional law took explicit form in the mid-1980s with the publication of my 1985 book, *Takings: Private Property and the Power of Eminent Domain* (Harvard), which took dead aim at the New Deal jurisprudence on the Takings Clause. Two years later I wrote an article in the *Virginia Law Review,* "The Proper Scope of the Commerce Power," that defended the pre-1937 view of that power against the modern synthesis. In 1993, I wrote a book entitled *Bargaining with the State* (Princeton). In it, I articulated the doctrine of unconstitutional conditions, which imposes principled limitations on how the government uses its monopoly power to restrict private parties who receive grants or licenses from the government. In 2006, I wrote a short book entitled *How Progressives Rewrote the Constitution* (Cato Institute), which took that movement to task for its views on private property and the federal commerce power. And most recently in 2011, I wrote a short book, *Design for Liberty: Private Property, Public Administration, and the Rule of Law* (Harvard), which sought to explain why systems of private property and limited government are, as an empirical matter, best able to preserve the level of independence and evenhandedness associated with the rule of law. In some sense, *The Classical Liberal Constitution* should be regarded as both a summation and an expansion of these earlier works on constitutional law.

I owe thanks to the many colleagues and institutions that have, over the past several years, and often with disbelief, heard me present the main arguments of this book. On countless occasions, I have benefited from both casual encounters and detailed conversations on various issues discussed in this book with Larry Alexander, Rachel Barkow, Randy Barnett, Paul Brest, Gerhard Casper, Adam Cox, Barry Friedman, Jacob Gersen, Michael Greve, Don Herzog, Samuel Issacharoff, Andrew Koppelman, Larry Kramer, John Manning, Michael McConnell, John McGinnis, Frank Michelman, Trevor Morrison, Richard Pildes, Sai Prakash, Michael Rappaport, Adam Samaha, Geoffrey Stone, Cass Sunstein, and surely others. Many of these eminent scholars were doubtless unaware of their unwitting role in the evolution and formulation of the ideas that eventually came to fruition in this book, but their influence is evident throughout this work.

In addition, this book is markedly stronger than it would ever have been without the comprehensive and insightful comments of my good friend Steven Calabresi, who went far beyond the requirements of a referee in giving a detailed account of arguments that I had overlooked or misunderstood, or cases that I had ignored. I have also benefited greatly from some comments on particular texts of the book from Aziz Huq at the University of Chicago and Daniel Ho of Stanford University, on the First Amendment and standing, respectively.

I have lost track of all the institutions that have hosted me for talks on one or another part of this volume, but they include at the very least both the University of Chicago, where I was a regular member of the faculty from 1972 to 2010, and New York University School of Law, where I have been a member of the full-time faculty since 2010. They also include Berkeley Law School, Boston University Law School, Columbia Law School, DePaul Law School, Duke Law School, Harvard Law School, Michigan Law School, Northwestern Law School, Stanford Law School, and Yale Law School. I have also benefited from the ability to present various arguments at many meetings of the Federalist Society, the American Constitution Society, the Southern Economics Association, and the Canadian Law and Economics Association, as well as from speeches and events at the Cato Institute, the Manhattan Institute, the American Enterprise Institute, and other gracious hosts both inside and outside the academy.

The actual preparation of this book was a huge effort, which could not have been done without the incredible assistance, devotion, and excellence of my research assistants who spanned several generations of law students at NYU Law School: Melissa Berger, Jean Bisnar, Mikalya Consalvo, Thomas Coyle, Jordana Haviv, Matthew Holbreich, Peter Horn, Benjamin Margo, Hannah Menda, Amber Rudolphi, Daniel Schwartz, and Joshua Stanton, and also Graham Safty of the University of Chicago. The constant iterations of the manuscript; their detailed comments on each word and phrase; the endless marginal questions forced me time and again to expand the basic text to respond to their objections as best I could. They spared me many errors and infelicities. They are obviously not responsible for those that remain.

In addition, I owe a debt of special thanks to the unwavering institutional support that I have received from the University of Chicago under Deans Saul Levmore and Michael Schill; from the Hoover Institution, whose Director John Raisian welcomed me into the ranks of the Hoover Scholars in 2000 and has provided me with generous support ever since; and of course from Richard Revesz, who recruited me to NYU after I took emeritus status at Chicago and has been a strong supporter of my work ever since. All three institutions have prospered under their able leadership. I have also received invaluable help from my longtime personal assistant, Kathryn Kepchar, and from Marjorie Holme, who often ventured beyond her work administering the Law and Economics Program at the University of Chicago to help out in a pinch. The University of Chicago reference librarian, Margaret Schilt, never failed to find obscure historical information in record time. I owe a debt of gratitude to my two NYU assistants, first Jeremy Heilman and then Jennifer Canose, who guided the traffic from the New York end. In addition, I am thankful for the support that I received from the Hoover Institution's John and Jean De Nault Task Force on Property Rights, Freedom, and Prosperity. It was at an early meeting of that group that I was prompted to write a short and snappy introduction to constitutional law. Somehow that venture spun out of control to morph into this far more ambitious project that I hope does indeed show how property rights, freedom, and prosperity are inextricably linked together in deep and profound ways that our Founders understood, but which our modern lawyers, thinkers, and judges all too often have forgotten.

PART ONE

PRELIMINARIES

Introduction

Our Two Constitutions

T HE UNITED STATES CONSTITUTION must, on any neutral evaluation, count as the greatest triumph of political statecraft in the history of the world. That achievement is all the more remarkable because it came in the face of immense practical and theoretical difficulties. The Constitutional Convention in Philadelphia was called together to remedy the manifest ills of the Articles of Confederation that had governed the United States since 1781. But the Founders quickly went beyond their original mandate, with obvious misgivings, after concluding that the basic structure of the Articles, with its ineffectual national government, was beyond repair. Their self-imposed task of nation-building, moreover, did not align itself neatly with the major classical political theory teachings of Thomas Hobbes, John Locke, Montesquieu, or David Hume. The Framers did not seek to forge a government for individuals living together in uneasy harmony in the state of nature. Rather, they sought to form a federal government consisting of individual states, which were already full-fledged sovereigns and signatories to the now-imperiled Articles.

The obstacles encountered in Philadelphia were sufficient to ward off any utopian beliefs in the perfectibility of man or civil society. The Articles of Confederation had achieved some major triumphs, including the passage of the Northwest Ordinance in 1787. But the structure had proved weak insofar as it did not provide for any executive authority or give the national government the direct power to tax. Both of these structural features touched a sensitive historical nerve, for the former raised the specter of arbitrary royal power, while the latter recalled fierce colonial objections to British taxes in the run-up to the Revolutionary War. Working their way through these difficulties required the Framers to correct the disadvantages of weak central government, while heeding the somber warnings of their intellectual heroes who, for all their differences, agreed with Thomas Paine when he wrote: "[G]overnment even in its best state is but a necessary evil in its worst state, an intolerable one."[1]

The point is worth some explication. The basic dilemma in theory and constitutional design was, and is, just this: to maintain order without destroying liberty. A government that is too strong can become tyrannical and oppress its citizens; yet a government that is too weak cannot withstand a succession of internal upheavals or external attacks, which eventually take their toll on the well-being of its citizens, with catastrophic loss of liberty and destruction of property. The key challenge was to determine how best to navigate between these two perils. Michael McConnell has succinctly summarized the Framers' basic position: "The classical liberal tradition emphasizes limited government, checks and balances, and strong protection of individual rights."[2] What rights? Strangely enough, that probing question had, for the Framers, clear answers: their conception of rights embraced the liberty of action, the ownership of private property, and the freedom from arbitrary arrest and prosecution. A right to housing, health care, or a decent income—or indeed any positive entitlement against government—was not on their list, or even a distant image on their intellectual horizon.

Implementing their middle road was no easy matter given the Framers' precarious legal position. It is no wonder that their deliberations produced awkward compromises, omissions, and redundancies—not to mention major blunders of historical proportion, some of which became painfully evident shortly after the ink on the Constitution was dry. Still, the Constitution has survived these bumpy patches—and one deadly Civil War—because of its core commitment to a coherent set of political principles. Even so, the tread-wear is obvious because more than two centuries of continuous pounding has inevitably led to major revisions. Some of these were conscious efforts to fix glitches in the original structure, such as the Twelfth Amendment, which radically altered the rules for selecting the vice president. Other changes, like the removal of the odious and oblique acceptance of slavery (a word not used in the Constitution) and the extension of suffrage to women, became irresistible with time. These major modifications came by two constitutional amendments: the Thirteenth Amendment (1865) abolished slavery in the United States and the Nineteenth Amendment (1920) guaranteed women the right to vote. The Constitution has also been transformed by judicial reasoning through sensible analogies that have preserved and extended the original classical liberal position. Freedom of the press, reasonably enough, covers the broadcast media that were unknown in 1791. The commerce power covers all modern modes of transportation, not just horses and buggies.

The greatest challenge to the original constitutional plan comes not from these inevitable and salutary historical adaptations, but from a conscious reversal of philosophical outlook on the proper role of government. It is often tempting to paper over the depth of these philosophical conflicts by claiming various kinds of ongoing disputes are amenable to "incompletely theorized agreements"[3] that allow people with fundamentally different views to find common ground in deciding concrete cases. That argument may work when supporters of abortion cannot decide whether to rest their case on a woman's right to privacy or on a theory of sex discrimination. But that benign compromise does not work to broker the difference between pro-choice and pro-life groups. The people who think that life begins at conception will not take kindly to their opponents who are hard-pressed to see or respect any difference in ontological status between an embryo and a lock of hair.

The more accurate description of the present impasse is that the recurrent and sharp splits on constitutional law come from what are more accurately described as "completely theorized disagreements" on all fundamental legal questions. These current disputes start with basic disagreements about human nature, language, knowledge, and institutions. On this score, the differences between the Federalists and the Anti-Federalists were less important than their shared assumptions. Their entire debate rested on a sober and shared appreciation of the potentially corrosive effects of self-interest on human affairs, a modest confidence that our collective capacities with language and cooperation allow us to devise institutions capable of coping with these ever-present risks without bringing government to a standstill, and a deep suspicion of government monopolies of all sorts and descriptions. At root, the classical view of American constitutionalism examined all legal interventions under a presumption of error. The structural protections of the separation of powers, checks and balances, federalism and the individual rights guarantees built into the basic constitutional structure were all part of combined efforts to slow down the political process that, left to its own devices, could easily overheat.

Starting with the rise of industrialization in the post–Civil War period and gaining traction after 1900, the pendulum on political philosophy and constitutional theory swung sharply away from these twin verities of private rights and limited government. In their place arose a different understanding of the relationship of the individual to the state. That new vision rested on an intellectual worldview that dominated the Progressive Era, which ran from about 1900 to 1932. Under President Franklin Delano Roosevelt, that philosophy quickly formed the foundation for the modern New Deal constitutional order, which received its whole-hearted judicial blessing during the momentous October 1936 Term of the United States Supreme Court. In that Term, a sharply divided Court decisively repudiated what remained of the classical liberal synthesis, which prized both federalism and the strong protection of economic liberties. The progressives did not view government as a necessary evil, but rather as a positive force for good in a wide range of social situations where the comparatively minimalist classical liberal view was said to have faltered.

The central thesis of this book is that the older view of the Constitution was correct, not only for the conditions of 1787 but also, most emphatically, for vastly more complex conditions today. The book is offered in the spirit of explaining how matters should have evolved and why the original classical liberal constitutional order would have served this nation better than the progressive order that remains ascendant today. The analysis covers both halves of the constitutional enterprise— its structural safeguards and its account of individual rights.

In order to make out this case, I shall compare the classical liberal and the modern progressive, or social democratic, accounts along two parallel tracks. The first of these deals with the political presuppositions used to justify the modern social democratic state that the progressives championed, and the second deals with the thorny issue of textual interpretation.

On the philosophical level, the shift to a social democratic model during the New Deal period was anchored in two central premises. The first is that individual rights are not just protected by state power, but are in some deep sense created by the very government agencies whose power our Constitution is intended to limit. Any theory of natural law in the tradition of John Locke's *Second Treatise of Government*[4] that posits rights of liberty and property antecedent to the state had to be rejected as philosophical mumbo-jumbo or political naiveté. The second is that the benevolent force of state power, exercised by dedicated and impartial administrative experts, can eliminate the chronic economic imbalances wrought by the unprecedented scale of industrialization that untamed market forces had driven. These new historical imbalances were said to falsify the premises of laissez-faire, which one of the prime defenders of the modern administrative state, James M. Landis, defined in 1938 as "the simple belief that only good could come by giving economic forces free play."[5] The progressive spirit of the early twentieth century sought to keep the Constitution in tune with the times. It did not believe, as Walter Berns once famously quipped, that the proper social goal is not "to keep the Constitution in tune with the times but, rather, to keep the times, to the extent possible, in tune with the Constitution."[6]

Put otherwise, to the progressive mindset, the traditional safeguards against excessive state power that animated early constitutional theory on both structural issues and property rights were perceived as pointless roadblocks that the modern technological state should overcome through a greater concentration and use of government power at all levels. The progressive prescription called for expert modern planners to exercise this power through administrative agencies that derive their authority from the legislature and typically displace the ordinary courts of justice as the major arena for dispute resolution. In effect, the giant social exchange wrought by the administrative state requires all persons to cede a large portion of their common law property rights (especially as they relate to the ability to enter and exit markets) in exchange for the rights, first, to participate in the democratic procedures that set the rules of the game and, second, to appear before the administrative agencies that carry out the legislative mandate. The Administrative Procedure Act of 1946 represented the solidification of this view in the decade after the New Deal.[7]

Once the progressives laid out their views on the proper social role for government action, their second challenge was to square that vision with a constitutional text that on its face did not cede all control over major economic and social issues to the legislature. That attack on the Constitution took place on multiple levels simultaneously. The first of these was their claim that the key terms of the Constitution—legislative, executive, and judicial power, or commerce, property, freedom of speech, and so on—were subject to deep and inescapable definitional ambiguities. These uncertainties sapped key constitutional terms of the intellectual clarity and power needed to block the changes in governance structure that modern thinkers thought desirable on substantive grounds.[8] There is no deviation from the rule of law and no usurpation of power if all constitutional commands are clouded by cognitive or linguistic deficits that wise progressive justices could overcome with astute textual interpretation. It is as though the progressives thought they exposed some deep conceptual incoherence in an effort to draft a Constitution that was faithful to the classical liberal ideals. Second, modern interpretivists have tirelessly trumpeted the claim that it is not now, and probably never was, possible to develop a coherent "originalist" interpretation of any constitutional text. No one can achieve the thankless task of sifting through the manifold intentions of the many individuals who participated in drafting or ratifying particular constitutional provisions. Third, the modern progressives insist that the huge changes in social circumstances from the time of the original Constitution to the present require a fresh solution that depends on expanded governments, both federal and state, to manage the constant individual and group conflicts that necessarily arise in an ever more complex and interdependent social environment. Fourth and finally, they claim that major issues concerning the public welfare should not be decided by unelected judges, but instead by the people acting collectively and responsibly through their elected officials, under the systems as they now exist at both the federal and state levels. The bottom line is that the progressives thought, and their contemporary disciples continue to think, that the plasticity of the constitutional text in the face of a radically new social environment leaves far greater running room for government action than any classical liberal conception could ever tolerate.[9]

I believe that this alluring constellation of theoretical and linguistic arguments is wrong at every point. Any counterattack, however, must guard against the risk of overclaiming in favor of the earlier classical liberal position. Most emphatically, there is no perfect correspondence between the classical liberal theory and the constitutional text: its backhanded acceptance of slavery alone is a devastating refutation of that position. Nonetheless, the constitutional provisions with the longest staying power have consistently drawn their strength from classical liberal theory. Surely the protection of freedom of speech, religion, and contract (in no particular order) have greater appeal than the reviled provisions dealing with the Three-Fifths Rule[10] and the Fugitive Slave Clause,[11] both of which were introduced as a matter of political compromise, not political principle. To be sure, in any normative inquiry the political theory should dominate, even as it is informed by the constitutional text. On the other hand, in judicial contexts, the interpretive issues should dominate, at least in relatively clear cases. Yet legitimate ambiguity is sometimes unavoidable, and on those matters constitutional text and political theory no longer fall into watertight compartments. At this juncture our basic conception of the proper scope of government action will, and should, influence the resolution of key interpretive disputes. Filling in those lacunae fully reveals the profound differences in attitude between the classical liberal and the modern progressive.[12] The classical liberal is far more likely to undertake a detailed textual analysis before making appeals to changed circumstances or contemporary mores. The modern progressive is much more likely to adopt the opposite strategy.

These differences matter, for my full-throated defense of classical liberal positions leads me to conclusions on many issues that are at sharp variance from those of *both* modern liberals and conservatives. For all their differences on social policy, the two dominant groups gravitate toward a shared progressive outlook on key constitutional questions. Thus, on the question of government regulation of economic liberties, including such hot button topics as wages and hours laws, all of the conservative justices, with the possible exception of Justice Clarence Thomas, think that the courts should show extreme deference to legislative judgments on the proper way to regulate the economy. Similarly, on questions of federalism, it is only Justice Thomas, again, who rejects the modern synthesis that gives the federal government, under the Commerce Clause, the full power to regulate all economic activities within as well as among the several states.[13] The cleavages between large and small government types are not only confined to these economic issues, but also embrace matters that deal with executive power and individual rights. On the former issue, my small government instincts place me in the company of the opponents of presidential power. Yet the alliances shift again on questions such as freedom of speech, where the small government position is often taken by liberals on some matters, such as political protest, but not on others, like campaign finance, which is often viewed more as a matter of economic power and less as one of free speech. Many conservatives would flip-flop on these issues. My view deviates from both camps to the extent that it adopts a consistently small government approach.

Fully aware of the many bends in the road, this book explores the tension between these two outlooks in successive chapters. Part One, dealing with Preliminaries, opens in Chapters 1 and 2 by explicating and contrasting the classical constitutional synthesis with the modern progressive or social democratic alternative that came of age in the New Deal. That vision moves in a grand arc that starts with a conception of human nature and ends with a constitutional design intended to control its excesses. Chapter 3, dealing with constitutional interpretation, then asks how best to interpret an iconic but laconic document that, as noted, contains its fair measure of undefined terms. Even if courts could derive unambiguous meanings for each of these terms, they still face the daunting task of breathing life into a document, many of whose key principles are left unmentioned in the text: preservation of the union, judicial review, sovereign immunity, the police power, and the creation of administrative agencies head an incomplete list. The joinder of these two challenges requires an integration of text with context in light of background political theory and overall constitutional structure. Nor do these two questions exhaust the challenges, for a third question looms ominously behind them. Interpretive mistakes are easy to make but hard to correct. Yet once error creeps in, should further interpretation continue down the same dubious path, abruptly turn back, or map out some intermediate, if unprincipled, course?

Part Two then deals with Constitutional Structures. That initial task of *how* to interpret our Constitution is necessarily paired with the question of *who*, if anyone, has the last word on interpretation, which is the subject of Section I dealing with the judicial power. That Section explores the excruciating tension that arises when commentators first lament the excesses of democratic majorities, only to bemoan the arrogance of unelected justices. Both criticisms are true, but neither can be honored in full. We must understand how our collective unhappiness with all branches of government guides, or frustrates, constitutional interpretation. That question sets up a discussion of the alternative conceptions of judicial review that vacillate between imposing exacting standards of review to avoid political unrest and using technical doctrines of standing and ripeness to impose self-limitations on any claim to judicial supremacy. That analysis always reads particular texts in light of the original classical liberal theory of government, given the unavoidable overlap between the normative efforts to articulate the law as it should be and the positive efforts to explain what the law is, whether one likes it or not.

The divisions on this issue are deep. The classical liberals are strong supporters of a system of judicial supremacy on all areas touched by the Constitution. The modern defenders of the progressive tradition, wholly apart from their massive disenchantment with the Rehnquist and Roberts Courts, are deeply suspicious of this settled practice and tend strongly in the opposite direction. Thus, Mark Tushnet would junk the doctrine of judicial review entirely and replace it with a version of "populist constitutional law," in which the courts are bystanders to the true business of constitutional interpretation via a populist manifesto in which "the" people take over the business of government, "whether we act in the streets, in the voting booths, or in the legislatures as representatives of others."[14] A similar theme is echoed (with far more emphasis on the historical materials) by Larry Kramer, whose deep distrust of judicial review is found in the title of his book *The People Themselves*.[15] The same theme is taken up by two individuals who are somewhat more receptive of judicial review: Justice Stephen Breyer, writing in defense of "active liberty," sees only a limited role for judicial review.[16] Cass Sunstein has waded into the fray on multiple occasions, insisting on a brand of "judicial minimalism,"[17] which at its core follows James Bradley Thayer's original insight that the Courts "follow a rule of administration" under which a court can "only disregard the Act when those who have the right to make laws have not merely made a mistake, but have made a very clear one, — so clear that it is not open to rational question."[18] In other words, judicial invalidation should be reserved for cases where there is an extreme breakdown in democratic politics. The lack of specificity as to when this approach might work, and when it might not, is in itself reason to doubt whether any mileage can be obtained from a theory that necessarily works only at a high level of abstraction. For all their political differences, Sunstein's minimalist approach is largely anticipated—albeit with a very different political valence—in the writings of Robert Bork, who offers a strong defense of modern democratic politics against judicial activism of all political stripes.[19] In fact, however, all these positions founder for one common reason: their excessive faith in democratic politics, which is inconsistent with the Framers' guarded view of the subject and which offers, on its own terms, an overly optimistic account of the political performance of legislative bodies that find it difficult to withstand the temptations of factional intrigue.

After these preliminaries, Section II deals with the legislative power addressing the full range of questions that surround our federalist enterprise that divvies up power between the federal and state governments. That inquiry has three essential components. The first examines those issues that are properly subject to congressional control. In 1787, the state delegates to the Constitutional Convention knew that they had to surrender more power to the central government to make the revised Articles of Confederation work. Hence, Article I, Section 1 of the Constitution starts by saying that all legislative powers "herein granted" shall be vested in the Congress[20]—without telling the reader who that grantor is. Relative to the Articles of Confederation, the powers located in the new national government were vast even under their narrowest reading. Nonetheless, more power at the national level is not tantamount to inexhaustible power at the center. In keeping with the classical liberal desire to fragment power, the basic constitutional plan limited the legislative power of Congress to certain listed or "enumerated" categories. Consistent with this scheme, Article I, Section 8 lists powers that by no stretch of the imagination are sufficient to cover the entire waterfront, even though Congress is given the power to tax, borrow, and regulate commerce with foreign nations, among the states, and with the Indian tribes. Control over naturalization clearly works better at the national than at the state level, and the same can be said for a uniform monetary system and the power to prevent counterfeiting. The national control over bankruptcy has a less clear rationalization and in practice was shared with the states, which retained power to regulate insolvency. The enumerated list also includes the power to establish post offices and post roads, which could either mean the ability to build them or to designate existing facilities to fulfill that function. Yet, as intellectual property knows no physical boundaries, it made sense to put patents and copyrights under national control. Congress also receives extensive powers to regulate both military and foreign affairs, including the power to declare war, support the army and navy, and regulate the operations of the armed forces. The residual power of the "police," however, was left to the states to exercise as they saw fit, subject, of course, to their own constitutional limitations, which at the Founding typically showed a real solicitude for the rights of life, liberty, and property that lay at the core of the natural rights tradition.

In light of the peculiar history of American constitutionalism, virtually all of the huge movement from the classical liberal to the social democratic Constitution took place under the Commerce Clause, which is important not only for the direct power that it gives Congress over the economy, but also in connection with what is commonly called the dormant Commerce Clause. When Congress does *not* act pursuant to its Commerce Clause powers, to what extent does the Constitution by its own force limit the power of individual states to disrupt commerce? Today's answer is questionable on textual grounds, given that the grant of power to the federal government does not in and of itself exclude operations of the states in the same area. It could be argued, therefore, that state protectionism of local economic interests should be given free rein in the absence of congressional action to the contrary. On this issue, however, the Supreme Court has for the most part adhered to a regime that is consistent with the original classical liberal synthesis by knocking down anticompetitive state barriers in order to preserve a national common market (in which Congress can regulate at will). More than any other judicial creation, the dormant Commerce Clause has resisted state parochialism to the immense benefit of us all.

The federal control over state laws is also addressed by a specialized doctrine that is now called "preemption," a term that entered the legal lexicon only in 1917.[21] Our Constitution states that it and the laws and treaties enacted pursuant to it are the supreme law of the land, no state law withstanding.[22] Under this rule, any lofty state constitutional command has to give way to the lowliest federal regulation. How should preemption be understood in the classical constitution? How should it be understood today in a world with vastly expanded federal power?[23]

Section III then deals with the executive power, which starts with an examination of the role of the president in domestic affairs. It then covers the doctrine of delegation and the rise of the administrative state, and concludes with a discussion of the role of the executive in foreign and military affairs. This Section first examines the role of the executive in the American system of checks and balances. It then turns to the many issues raised by the creation of independent administrative agencies, often called the "fourth branch" of government, that exercise in varying proportions all the functions that the original Constitution uniquely assigns to one of the three branches. As before, it is critical to assess these agencies under both classical liberal theories, where they are found sorely wanting, and modern social democratic theories, where they are viewed as an indispensable fount of government power. Last, in a problem of ever greater contemporary importance, it is critical to look at the relationship among the three branches of government in connection with both foreign affairs and war, where the major struggle takes place between Congress and the executive, with the courts playing an important but subordinate role. The issues here affect everything from the question of who controls the military and the ability of the nation to make war, to the power of Congress or the president to suspend traditional individual rights, including, most critically, the ability of persons detained under presidential order to bring the ancient writ of habeas corpus, which allows them to challenge the legality of their detention before an independent tribunal. On this point, many individuals who champion the rise of the New Deal state embrace the classical liberal vision of limited government with multiple checks and balances. However, let us be clear that even with this notable example of ideological convergence, it is the progressives who have reverted to classical liberal principles of political theory and constitutional interpretation, not the classical liberals who have accepted the progressives' expansionist view of government power. Meanwhile, many conservatives with only weak libertarian sympathies have tended to champion what I regard as an extravagant vision of presidential power.

Once the structural issues are analyzed, I shall turn our attention in Part Three to matters of the individual rights that the Constitution secures to various persons against both the national government and the states. The original Constitution contained some limited protection of these individual rights, including prohibitions against ex post facto laws, bills of attainder, and, most notably, the impairment of obligation of contracts. None of these protections was spelled out with any particularity, and this set of prohibitions was directed solely at the states and not at the federal government. The sentiment at the time of ratification was divided on the question of whether the federal Constitution should be amended to include a Bill of Rights similar to those prominently featured in state constitutions. The dispute did not turn on which rights were worthy of protection but instead on matters of approach and technique. On the former, Alexander Hamilton's position was that a substantive bill of rights was apt to do more mischief than good because structural protections were sufficient to protect against major invasions of individual rights—an overoptimistic conclusion that ignored how factional politics could, and often do, overwhelm democratic deliberation. On the latter, many defenders of a bill of rights were troubled by the technical objection that the enumeration of any finite set of rights could be read to exclude other rights that were not specifically enumerated. In the end, the structural objections failed to persuade, and the incorporation of the Ninth Amendment—largely a dead letter in American constitutional law—was introduced to meet the technical objection, which turned out to be overstated in any event.[24] The Bill of Rights, ratified in 1791, supplied, albeit in bare-bones fashion, comprehensive protections for both liberty and property. Some of these protections dealt with criminal prosecutions and others concerned speech, the press, religion, and private property. A second layer of protection, now against the states, was added to the Constitution in the aftermath of the Civil War and included, most notably, the three major guarantees of the Fourteenth Amendment. The first of these provided to all *citizens* of the United States an unspecified set of privileges and immunities against state interference. The last two offered all *persons* protections against the deprivation of life, liberty, or property without due process of law and a guarantee of the equal protection of the laws. The protections against government action are outlined in skeletal form, with no indication of the limitations that might be properly placed on their exercise.

Sorting out this tangle is not easy, especially since the Supreme Court has not maintained a uniform attitude over time regarding the various rights that receive explicit constitutional protection. The classical liberal period gave rise to relatively strong property and contract rights but recognized several broad exceptions, all of which are to some degree consistent with the classical liberal vision of good government. Thus, the "police power"—a term nowhere found in the text of the Constitution—limits the guarantees of liberty and property on matters customarily defined as touching the "safety, health, morals and the general welfare."[25] At the very least, this conception of the police power allows the state to deal with the problems that call for government intervention even under the classical liberal view: the use and threat of force; fraud in all its manifold forms; incompetence, as from infancy and insanity; the regulation of monopoly; and the creation and maintenance of public infrastructure. The modern social democratic outlook does not reject any of these uses of the police power but in some, though not all, cases its reach extends to matters that lie far beyond the original classical liberal framework, such as the equalization of wealth and the elimination of private forms of (invidious) discrimination. In those areas in which the strong progressive presumption of constitutionality has not overwhelmed the judicial system, such as political protest and dissent, the case law to this day conforms closely to the classical liberal pattern. But on matters of contract and property rights, the police power (now expansively renamed a "legitimate" state interest) has largely eviscerated the underlying constitutional guarantees. In an odd reversal of fate, the older and narrower account of the police power has seen a strong resurgence in such areas as race, privacy, abortion, and sexual preferences. The verdict on religion has been mixed, as courts have struggled to protect the free exercise of religion on the one hand, without giving religious activities the undue protection that might count as a forbidden establishment on the other. The last section of the book addresses these questions, both as a matter of textual interpretation and as a matter of principle, as seen through the classical liberal lens of strong private rights and limited government. Thus Section I turns to the many issues that deal with property, contract, and liberty, chiefly in the economic sphere. It starts with the extent to which the constitution's structural features offer protection for individual rights, and it then turns to key issues of procedural due process, the protection of freedom of contract and economic liberties, the issue of takings, both physical and regulatory, and concludes with a discussion of the role of the police power as it relates to questions of public morals. Section II then turns to the many issues relating to the protection of freedom of speech. Section III covers the issues that arise in dealing with both the free exercise and establishment provisions of the First Amendment. Section IV then concludes with a discussion of the Equal Protection Clause as it relates to race, citizenship, and sex. Part Four concludes with final observations.

1

The Classical Liberal Synthesis

THE CLASSICAL LIBERAL TRADITION of the founding generation prized the protection of liberty and private property under a system of limited government. That tradition also rejected the optimistic view that self-interested individuals could through an ingenious array of private voluntary agreements preserve public order against civil strife. The determined aggressor had to be suppressed by fines, imprisonment, exile, or even death, if he could not be persuaded to cooperate by lesser means. Governments, moreover, needed at the very least the powers of taxation and eminent domain to obtain both financial resources and particular assets in order to maintain both liberty and political order against random violence and unregulated militias. Anarchy is not a viable option in the long term. Power always enters to fill a void. The people who fail to form a government, whether by custom, as under the British constitution, or conscious deliberation, as with ours, will have rulers thrust upon them who will not be to their liking. The preemptive strike by decent people in search of what Justice Benjamin Cardozo once termed "ordered liberty" offers the only path for beating back the obnoxious intruder.[1]

Yet by the same token, organized governments can easily turn, as they all too frequently have done, into instruments of evil, precisely because no ordinary person can stand up to government officials backed by public force. Contemporary Americans tend not to worry about the threat of insurrection or turmoil because our nation has happily mastered the orderly succession of political power, a matter that was very much on the minds of the Framers in Philadelphia who devoted much effort to coordinating the actions of state militias and federal power to guard against invasion, insurrection, disunion, and rebellion.[2] Virtually no one remembers this constitutional provision: "No State shall, without the consent of Congress, . . . engage in war, unless actually invaded, or in such imminent danger as will not admit of delay."[3] Note that the clause does not specify, invaded by whom? But the best efforts of the Framers' all-star cast could not prevent a destructive Civil War over the issue of slavery that was finessed but not resolved at the Constitutional Convention.[4] Our constant preoccupation with current events, moreover, obscures the dismal record over most of recorded history of the "simple" task of maintaining the security of the person and property against private aggression, without inviting state-sponsored death, imprisonment, and expropriation. Truth be told, most political efforts to run the gauntlet between anarchy and tyranny have ended in disappointment and disaster. The societies best able to navigate that narrow channel are ever conscious of the lurking perils on both sides. Their odds of success improve greatly if they greet warily any extension of government power. Gerald Ford pithily explained why political power is always a double-edged sword: "A government big enough to give you everything you want is a government big enough to take from you everything you have."[5] The Founders would have agreed.

This deep ambivalence toward state power is evident in the classical liberal tradition. Its central Lockean premise, the evils of slavery notwithstanding, was that governments were created by individuals who were free, equal, and independent in the state of nature. The opening passage in the Massachusetts Constitution of 1780 faithfully tracks this synthesis:

> Article I: All men are born free and equal, and have certain, natural, essential, and unalienable rights; among which may be reckoned the right of enjoying and defending their lives and liberties; that of acquiring, possessing, and protecting property; in fine, that of seeking and obtaining their safety and happiness.[6]

The protection of these rights was said to rest in the words of the Declaration of Independence. The basic message is, oddly enough, a positive one. It assumes, correctly, that an institutional framework that allows most people to act in ways that benefit themselves and the larger society through enterprise, loyalty, cooperation, charities, and thrift will develop those positive personal characteristics that lead to fruitful social interactions on matters political, social, and commercial. The classical writers assumed that this class of sociable behaviors was embedded in human nature. Thus, "[one] recent review suggests that similarities result from the existence of four basic sets of intuitions involving: (a) suffering, harm, and violence; (b) reciprocity and fairness (including revenge); (c) hierarchy, duty, respect, and related intuitions about the social order and one's place in it; and (d) purity and related intuitions about chastity and piety."[7]

This naturalist approach boosts the case for thinking that all social organizations face much the same problems. Modern moral psychology has given that point of view a big boost by stressing the dual norms against the infliction of harm and the reciprocity of exchange, as augmented by a respect for authority and concerns with disgust. Thus, the first of these elements explains the persistence of the law of tort, and the second the law of contract. The concerns about hierarchy make families, private associations, and governments plausible, and the concern with purity and chastity tie into what is commonly called the morals head of the police power, in which the state was given, at least in the nineteenth century, extraordinary latitude to regulate sexual behavior, gambling, and other forms of sinful behaviors.

It should not, of course, be assumed that all individuals share all these propensities in the same degree. Some have more of one trait than another. Indeed it is precisely because enough people act on these four intuitions that some form of durable social organization, while not guaranteed, is at least possible. The stress on these four factors, moreover, also serves as a useful reminder of the fragility of social relations, which in turn makes it clear why, generally speaking, political theory does not worry about the good guys. Rather, in its most accurate form, it assumes a natural variation in the moral qualities and temperaments of individuals. Its concern is how best to deal with the bottom tail of the distribution—that minority of individuals, often tiny, who exhibit powerful antisocial tendencies. Unfortunately, buying them off is worse than useless, for rewarding bad actors surely encourages a long line of fence-sitters to follow in their path. So political theory, not economics, becomes the true dismal science as it works to find some way to protect the many from the aggression of the few.

Yet how is that mission justified? One appeal that finds voice in the Declaration of Independence is the "consent of the governed," which could not, of course, be individually and freely given. There are too many people, some unborn, separated by time, place, and sentiment, to find any historical contract worthy of its name. But that obvious and oft-repeated objection does not make social contract theory either empty or idle. The unifying vision of classical liberal theory insists that all individuals must somehow leave the state of nature, in which all rights of life, liberty, and property are perpetually at risk. But how? Voluntary coordination will not work when antisocial defectors could bring down the entire structure. The fatal weakness of the modern hard-line libertarian views, such as those advanced by the late Robert Nozick,[8] is that they cannot explain how states rightly gain the legitimacy and the resources needed to prevent violence, enforce contractual promises, and supply needed social infrastructure. The key to solving these problems lies in the domestication of coercion. Government works best when it *forces* each individual to surrender some of his or her own liberty and property to government in exchange for greater security for those rights that are retained. The grand social contract is no actual agreement, which is why it is called "social." But at every stage it is meant to produce the same win/win outcomes, just like ordinary contracts, and to do so in settings where huge numbers of individuals are forced to participate in this joint social venture.

Given this conception, any individual who seeks unilaterally to deviate from the sound social contract is either a menace or a freeloader. He is the former if he is willing to use force. He is the latter if he refuses to contribute his share to the joint defense, thereby forcing it on others. On controlling force, consistency is key. Allow one to deviate, and all will follow until the state unravels. State coercion for one's own good is not some code word for misguided paternalism. Nor is it a contradiction in terms. Rather, it is the minimum condition for the public provision of certain collective goods.

Fear of Faction

The ability to create a government that meets this objective is driven by the need to control the dangerous human tendencies that do not disappear even after civil society is formed. To the contrary, the anti-social individuals in a state of nature can rely on guile, intrigue, and coercion within the new political order. The modern rubric for analyzing these problems is public choice theory,[9] which asks how self-interested behaviors of both individuals and groups undermine public welfare while playing within the imperfect rules of the political game. In the crudest terms, each individual or faction will work overtime for a larger slice of a smaller pie—leaving a smaller share of a smaller pie for everyone else.

One constant danger is that the political structure may easily unravel, even though all individuals do not fit this selfish description. Once some people work the political process for partisan advantage, others will follow suit, if only in self-defense. The worst actors within the system can dictate the tempo for all through rhetoric, coalition building, committee hearings, horse-trading, agenda setting, and smear campaigns. This rough-and-tumble process will yield some public-regarding legislation, but frequently it will generate outcomes that satisfy only narrowly partisan interests. James Madison used the term "faction" to describe these risks in *Federalist No. 10*:

> By a faction, I understand a number of citizens, whether amounting to a majority or a minority of the whole, who are united and actuated by some common impulse of passion, or of interest, adverse to the rights of other citizens, or to the permanent and aggregate interests of the community.[10]

The breadth of Madison's definition tracks the magnitude and persistence of the problem. As Madison recognized, factions come in all shapes and sizes, which is why either "a majority or a minority of the whole" can be the dominant, i.e. prevailing, faction. These factions, moreover, can organize along any natural fault lines: occupation, region, race, religion, or sex. They can coalesce around any issue: war, tariffs, or national expansion. Sufficiently emboldened, adroit politicians can broker deals across coalitions over unrelated questions by invoking the time-honored principle "if you scratch my back, I will scratch yours." In the absence of any strong social or institutional constraints, a dominant faction could use its voting power or political clout to confiscate the wealth of the political losers, or, more subtly, to hobble their economic activities with legal restrictions. Nor will the propertied classes, often a minority in number, necessarily come out on top, especially if the vast majority of the population is allowed to vote transfer payments to itself from, as they are now called, the top 1 percent. That is why Madison declaimed that people were "weary" of the "long chain of repetitions," in particular, of debtor relief statutes that necessarily compromised "personal security and private right."[11] That problem has not dissipated in today's modern mortgage crisis, where we have seen repeated government efforts to prevent, without visible success, the foreclosure of home mortgages in default, which undermines long-term credit markets by creating an involuntary wealth transfer from creditors to debtors while simultaneously reducing the value of real estate once it is underwater.[12] *The Federalist Papers* knew how to accentuate the negative.

Unfortunately, this problem cannot be cured by requiring unanimous consent for political action. Let every political actor have a veto right, and political paralysis will follow. The challenge, therefore, is to develop some way to avoid the twin perils of paralysis and exploitation. Madison's own proposal, as outlined in *Federalist No. 10*, was woefully inadequate. His optimistic claim was that the "extended republic"—i.e., the national government—provided adequate protection against the operation of factions. Either he or Alexander Hamilton put the point baldly in *Federalist No. 51*: "In the extended republic of the United States, and among the great variety of interests, parties, and sects which it embraces, a coalition of a majority of the whole society could seldom take place on any other principles than those of justice and the general good. . . ."[13]

This passage suggests that national governments with built-in checks and balances are more impervious to factions for two reasons. First, a national government attracts a higher caliber of men to run for public office, who in turn would be willing to resist factional temptation. Second, the cost of organizing factions at a distance is higher than it is at the state level. But Madison was unduly optimistic on both counts, as he himself subsequently recognized. No political body is immune to the risk of political intrigue. The relative performance at different government levels depends on such evanescent factors as the mix of people and issues at any given time. Thus, once power migrates to the national government, the political hacks will follow the scent to its new abode, urged on by local electors who want their representatives in Congress to look after the interests of the home state. (Back in 1787, state legislatures wanted their appointed senators to take their cues from the local politicians.) On the second point, the greater costs of organizing national coalitions are often offset by the greater gains to be obtained. That said, important questions over the proper division between national and state authority remain: uniform national laws work better for trade, but local governments are better able to respond to variations in local conditions, as with land use regulation. In the end, no single strategy can deal with this hydra-headed problem. Redundancy and multiple safeguards are needed at all levels of government, and the Constitution provides them.

Anti-Federalists and Republicans

The drafters of the Constitution, rightly then, did not take a sunny view of political man. Their classical liberal concerns, moreover, forged the common link between the Federalists who supported the new Constitution and the Anti-Federalists who were united in opposition to it. As the late Herbert Storing accurately stressed, theirs was a family squabble "of men agreed that the purpose of government is the regulation and thereby the protection of individual rights and that the best instrument for this purpose is some form of limited, republican government."[14] That agreement over ends, with disagreement on means, led the two sides to join on the issue of the desirability of what Madison called in *Federalist No. 10* "the extended republic," which embraced the entire United States. The Anti-Federalists' opposition to the Constitution depended on their own paean to the small republic, which they thought was more in touch with local interests, and thus more likely to inculcate the civic virtue that allows citizens to resist factional temptations.[15] They made the same mistake as the Federalists in reverse, by underestimating the possibility that local majorities could exploit local minorities for whom the exit option is too expensive—a problem that plagues local land use regulation to this day. Quite bluntly, no matter how the Constitution parcels out tasks between state and national governments, the risk of faction remains endemic. Both the Federalists and the Anti-Federalists overclaimed for their respective national and local preferences. Their disputes over system design do not square with modern political conceptions. All sides of the debate couched their arguments in terms of natural rights to liberty and property, and structural protections against government abuse. None of the participants in this historical intellectual fray were social democrats or progressives, let alone socialists.

Storing also notes that the Anti-Federalists shared the Federalists' affection for limited and republican government.[16] In his formulation, the word "limited" is evident enough: the powers that are given to the government are limited, so that it could not extend its reach into all areas of human life. That understanding was part of Hamilton's defense of judicial review in *Federalist No. 78*: "The complete independence of the courts of justice is peculiarly essential in a limited Constitution. By a limited Constitution, I understand one which contains certain specified exceptions to the legislative authority; such, for instance, as that it shall pass no bills of attainder, no *ex post facto* laws, and the like."[17] On this issue, again, there was no intellectual divide between the Federalists and their opponents.

The term "republican" requires more explication in light of persistent confusion about its meaning. Historically, "republican" was a sensible, if imperfect, response to the purified and restrained form of popular government, the sort against which Madison inveighed in *Federalist No. 10*: "The instability, injustice, and confusion introduced into the public councils, have, in truth, been the mortal diseases under which popular governments have everywhere perished."[18] Manifestly, republicans opposed the monarchical, English-style regime. Historically, however, a *republic* was also defined in opposition to a *democracy*, in particular a popular democracy, which to them connoted demagogic rule by the masses, whose political power could easily trample on the very rights of liberty and property that government was sworn to preserve. Indeed, on this issue, Madison was far from alone, as other writers of the time also chimed in on the dangers of wayward state governments. At the Constitutional Convention, Hamilton was explicit: "The members most tenacious of republicanism," he observed, "were as loud as any in declaiming agst. the vices of democracy."[19] Similarly, Elbridge Gerry from Massachusetts spoke at the Constitutional Convention of "The evils we experience from the excess of democracy."[20] As early as the 1800 presidential election, earlier meanings had been transformed when Thomas Jefferson defeated the Federalist John Adams as the candidate of the Democratic-Republican Party.[21] But in 1787 the terms "democracy" and "republicanism" were used as opposites, not synonyms.

These concerns with popular democracy date back at least to Aristotle's *Politics*, which lists democracy, along with tyranny and oligarchy, as one of the three "perversions" of governments, whose "right"[22] forms are Polity (or the Republic), Kingship, and Aristocracy. The same fear of popular majorities is also evident in much of the English historical writing in the pre-revolutionary period, when authors who opposed monarchy were equally troubled with the dominant patterns of democratic politics.[23]

Historically, therefore, it is not just for stylistic reasons that the Constitution says that the "United States" (not just one branch of it) "guarantees to each state a republican form of government."[24] The fear was that state governments could become monarchies *or* degenerate into popular democracies, which the United States was duty-bound to forestall, by the use of force if necessary. The risk of monarchy is of course easier to guard against than the risk of democracy, for the line between a desired republic and its degenerate democratic twin is hard to draw in the face of the countless permutations of government structures. But the Guarantee Clause does (or at least should) call into question the use of popular initiatives and referenda on particular issues—the former allows individuals to propose legislation and the latter allows them to vote on it—precisely because the classical theory regarded reliance on direct popular decisions as the hallmark of unsound democratic practice. Nonetheless, the point was lost on the Supreme Court, which has deemed the Guarantee Clause nonjusticiable,[25] even though it obligates the United States and not just Congress to make good on this guarantee.[26]

But whatever the historical ambiguities on this matter, the Anti-Federalists did not embrace the now fashionable "republicanism" that allows the government to demand personal sacrifice or even individual valor in the service of some higher, overriding vision of community good.[27] Apart from the first three words of the Preamble—"We the People"—the Constitution is utterly devoid of stirring aspirational rhetoric. Rather, the term "republican" had a more modest office in the historical debates. Under a republican regime, only a legislature—one whose members were always selected by complex procedures—could pass laws. An important correlative was that deliberation was limited to *"res publicae"*—literally, "public affairs." Matters of war and peace fit that bill, as do the creation of systems of public roads and courts. But there is nothing in the republican view of political deliberation that treated individual decisions on what property to own, food to buy, jobs to offer or accept, or wages to pay or receive as matters properly falling into the public domain. Finally, the Constitution consciously refused to allow the direct election of key public officials, as discussed further on.

Deliberation, Incentives, and Votes

None of these structural concerns meant that the Founders were opposed to deliberation and debate among public officials or the public at large. Deliberation is the hallmark of every private board of directors for businesses and nonprofit organizations alike. Without deliberation, public bodies would be forced into making uninformed collective decisions on matters of life and death that bind even dissenters. No nation can declare war for only some of its people. The inability of a collective body to first ascertain and then express the often divergent desires of its constituent members drives the need for extended deliberative processes in corporations and other private bodies. The same requirements are even more imperative in public bodies, where dissenters can no longer exit the project by selling their individual shares. It would be inconceivable for any effective system of political governance to function in its absence. Never forget that the Constitution itself is the quintessential deliberative doctrine. Hamilton opens *Federalist No. 1* with a reminder that the people of the United States had to ask themselves "whether societies of men are really capable or not of establishing good government from reflection and choice, or whether they are forever destined to depend for their political constitutions on accident and force."[28] (He conveniently omitted the customary, but stable, English constitution, which relies on neither.)

Nonetheless, the Framers did not think that participation and deliberation, either alone or together, were sufficient to counteract the dangers of faction, as many modern republicans are inclined to believe.[29] The Framers' skepticism was not misplaced. In political institutions, the quality of leadership and deliberation is never constant. Hence Madison's famous observation in *Federalist No. 10*: "Enlightened statesmen will not always be at the helm."[30] And even if they were, they must make hard life and death decisions even under ideal institutional circumstances. But it would be a mistake to assume that the only obstacles to effective deliberation are the inevitable fluctuations in the quality of elected officials or the inherent difficulties of key policy choices. Now as then, political speech is always a double-edged sword, which can be used to inflame as well as inform. Astute politicians will choose to inflame when it paves the path to their own electoral success. The IQ of public officials of all persuasions always rises when they speak in private.

Powerful forces account for the behavioral shifts. Political deliberation never takes place in a vacuum. Private incentives thus influence rhetoric. If confiscation and arbitrary imprisonment are permissible options, deliberation could easily muster support for those ends. Witness the recent (and indefensible) suspension of habeas corpus under the Military Commissions Act of 2006, notwithstanding the serious doubts about the constitutionality of the act entertained by its supporters.[31] It is false optimism to assume that public deliberation will routinely purify discourse no matter what the rules of the game. That point became clear to Madison in his role as Thomas Jefferson's incoming secretary of state. Madison was caught up in the venomous political dispute between the outgoing Federalists and the incoming Republicans over the passage of the Judiciary Act of 1801, which enabled the departing President John Adams to appoint sixteen Federalist circuit judges and forty-two justices of the peace two days before his term ended. That blatant court-packing plan precipitated the litigation in *Marbury v. Madison*,[32] which established the power of judicial review, but not before much political blood was spilled. "[O]verwrought Federalists ranted," and "Republicans shrieked" in a knock-down brawl that exhibited none of the elegance, restraint, and decorum that Madison hoped to find in an extended republic just fourteen years before.[33]

This attitude toward deliberation had profound influences on the Framers' attitude toward voting. They consciously adopted highly restrictive rules for selecting officials for various public positions. Today we regard universal suffrage as one of the unquestioned pillars of democratic theory. The Framers, however, rejected any such moral imperative, as they sharply limited the opportunities for ordinary people to participate in public elections. Only the House of Representatives had direct elections, and in these elections the Framers did not insist on universal suffrage or indeed any uniform set of rules. Instead, fearful of discord, they prudentially punted that question back to the states such that the electors in each state "shall have the Qualifications requisite for Electors of the most numerous Branch of the State Legislature."[34] No aspiration for eternal justice here. State citizens who were shut out of the franchise by a maze of local requirements—property requirements and poll taxes, for example—found no helping hand at the federal level. Similarly, our patrician Senate was chosen by the state legislatures, as their check against national power, and its members sat for six-year terms, as a check against their political accountability. Next, the president was chosen by an Electoral College, whose members were chosen in state elections. As the name suggests, at the time the College was supposed to be a deliberative body, much like the College of Cardinals is today. As Hamilton put the matter, the process had two stages, whereby the "general mass" chooses the electors on the understanding that "the immediate election should be made by men most capable of analyzing the qualities adapted to the station, and acting under circumstances favorable to deliberation, and to a judicious combination of all the reasons and inducements which were proper to govern their choice."[35] Evidently, the entire purpose of that indirect form of election was to mute popular control over the selection of the nation's most powerful officer. Finally, members of the judicial branch were not elected at all. They were nominated by the president and had to be confirmed by a majority of the Senate. The Framers consciously cut the House of Representatives out of the loop when it came to choosing the judges and key officials to whom the constitutional Framers looked to protect individual liberty and private property.

On these matters of institutional structures, the Founders were prisoners of their own age. Their overt hostility to democratic institutions has not stood the test of time in all of its particulars. The movement toward near universal suffrage (prisoners and incompetents excepted, for example) has proved inexorable. In 1870, the Fifteenth Amendment prevented both the national and state governments from denying the right to vote on account of "race, color, or previous condition of servitude."[36] In 1920, the Nineteenth Amendment did the same "on account of sex."[37] And last (and surely less consequential), the Twenty-Sixth Amendment of 1971 did the same on account of age, for all persons eighteen and over.[38] In addition, the Seventeenth Amendment in 1913 shifted power toward the federal government by requiring the direct election of senators, subject to a rule that stipulated: "The electors in each State shall have the qualifications requisite for electors of the most numerous branch of the State legislature."[39] Finally, in 1964, the Twenty-Fourth Amendment abolished the poll tax in primaries and federal elections only, in an obvious reaction to its sorry history in excluding African-Americans from the electoral process.[40]

One worthwhile inquiry asks whether any of the constitutional limitations imposed on the franchise should be regarded as proper today in light of the Framers' widespread concern with the excesses of popular democracy. There are, of course, many reasons to impose serious constitutional limitations on what citizens and their representatives may do by simple majority. Nonetheless, the problem of faction is not solved but only exacerbated if some citizens are wholly excluded from electoral politics, even if they remain free to speak openly about those questions. The exclusion of women (let alone slaves) from the franchise is wholly indefensible on either republican or democratic principles, especially to anyone who accepts the classical liberal baseline that all individuals are free and equal in the state of nature. So much of what government does affects the lives and liberty of all persons that it takes heroic arguments to argue for the total exclusion of any group from the processes that determine the rules of the game. To be sure, keeping propertyless individuals out of government may reduce the risk of debtor relief laws or outright confiscation. However, it simultaneously increases the risk of petty legislation that could explicitly block the ability of vulnerable people to enter into various trades and professions. Universal suffrage helps mend that difficulty. At the same time, however, the broad franchise increases the majoritarian pressures on the existing constitutional protections for property and contract, both of which found their way into the United States Constitution. So long as people tend to vote in their interest, the few are at the mercy of the many within any electoral process.

This same cautious attitude toward voting is reflected in the conscious obstacles that any bill must negotiate before it can become law. One of those obstacles is that any new law must secure the approval of both houses of Congress, whose members were selected in different ways. The clear opposition featured even representation of states in the Senate, whose members are chosen for longer periods of time, against the more numerous House, whose members are elected for shorter terms. The driving force behind this view was that errors of too much legislation were of graver consequence than those of too little. This institutional design made sure that the two houses could not easily get into sync on the great matters of the day. Thereafter, legislation has to be signed by the president, whose interests are often at loggerheads with the Congress, which of course has the right to override the veto, but only if it can muster two-thirds of the vote of both houses, starting with the one in which the bill originated.[41] This complex process tends to reduce the volatility of government decisions below that of the swings in public opinion.

Why Did Our Constitution Succeed?

This recital of the well-understood vagaries of the political process gives rise to this question: how do we account for the Constitutional Convention at Philadelphia? Part of it was fortuitous. Enlightened men, none of whom were chosen by direct election, were for the most part at the helm. Indeed, it is highly doubtful that this nation of over 300 million people could assemble a roster for a constitutional convention that could come close to matching the one that met in Philadelphia over 220 years ago. Proposals to redo the Constitution in order to bring it in tune with the times would likely produce a grotesque and faddish document whose half-life would be measured in years, not decades.[42] But the confluence of two fortunate factors also helped make the Constitution the success that it was. First, the Founders' common political philosophy meant that much of their deliberations were about means and not ends. Second, on most issues, they operated behind a veil of ignorance, which, as John Rawls so famously argued,[43] sets up background conditions that make it more difficult for anyone to act on parochial motivations.

Rawls's basic theory is simplicity itself. Take any choice in which all persons are similarly situated, such that everyone can win or lose 50 percent of the time. On those assumptions, the *only* way to advance your narrowest interest is to pick that alternative offering the maximum social gain. By way of example, think of a potential trader who has no knowledge whether he will be a buyer or seller in some market. If selective restrictions on imports reduce the value to future buyers by twenty but increase those of future sellers only by ten, then any person (ignorant of his role) who votes for the restriction suffers a twenty-unit loss half of the time and receives a ten-unit gain half of the time, for a net *loss* of five. So situated, that person's private interest is to vote for the socially desirable solution that rejects the import restriction. But once future sellers can peek out from behind that veil at their own actual prospects, they are likely not only to vote for the restriction, but also to campaign on its behalf, as happened with the 1930 Smoot-Hawley Tariff[44] or the recent disgraceful ethanol subsidies, which at long last are being challenged.[45] The situation is still more difficult because the defenders of trade subsidies and restrictions often fail to perceive that they will lose on net, once indirect effects are taken into account, as surely happened with Smoot-Hawley. Within politics, both greed and incomplete knowledge are hard to avoid. But a constitutional convention reduces both risks because delegates cannot tailor their views on general provisions to suit their own perceived interests. At this point, the incentives are better (though not perfectly aligned).

In this setting, the firmer the knowledge of history and general social theory, the further back in time it is possible to go to attain the ideal governance structure. It was therefore most fortunate that few particular matters were before the Constitutional Convention, forcing delegates to make more decisions from behind the veil. It is thus wrong to condemn the Framers of favoritism to their own class, as Charles A. Beard did in 1913, arguing for that mistaken position in his well-known *Economic Interpretation of the Constitution*,[46] which saw in the Constitution a concerted effort of landholders to protect their own provincial interests. The Constitution contains little, if any, textual evidence of special interest provisions that are tied to particular groups. The strongest evidence, perhaps, of the Beard position was the willingness of the Framers to allow Congress to introduce economic protection against foreign commerce and trade, but that regrettable position does not consistently favor any particular interest group. Any effort to read into the Constitution a simple conflict between landowners and commercial traders seriously underestimates the complexity of that relationship, for then as now, it is as common to find deep divisions on such large issues within economic groups as across them.[47] Steel producers may well favor tariffs on steel imports, but such tariffs will be opposed by manufacturing firms for which steel is an input in production. The most that can be said against the Constitution is that it did not block the risks of economic protectionism, at least in the area of international trade. But it can hardly be said to have fostered it for partisan advantage. And that mercantilist attitude is in marked contrast to the strong efforts to create an internal common market that operates free of various trade restraints, which is reflected in the tightly worded prohibition against state taxes on imports or exports[48] and the guarantees to citizens of one state of the privileges and immunities, chiefly related to trading, of another.[49]

To that general rule, there was one glaring exception. The impending struggle over slavery could not be circumvented in this fashion, as the delegates from free and slave states alike knew of the gulf that separated them going in, given that the abolitionist movement had gained steam first in England and later in the United States. But on this question, their need to make a deal forced a regrettable three-fifths compromise whereby black slaves, who were denied the franchise, were each counted as three-fifths of a person for the purposes of allocating direct taxes and members of Congress across the several states.[50] Fittingly enough, Madison, who knew better, did not seek to defend that awkward compromise in his own words in *The Federalist Papers*. Coyly, he used the indirect voice, as "might one of our Southern brethren observe"—who, being only hypothetical, could not be forced to atone for his sins.[51] The same of course must be said about the delicately worded provision dealing with slaves who escaped from their home states. The Fugitive Slave provision, which followed on the heels of the Northwest Ordinance, delicately provided for the return at the insistence of his owner any person "held to service or labour in one state" who escaped to another state.[52] It is painfully clear that this provision cannot be reconciled with general classical liberal principles.

On a more principled level, the veil of ignorance was fully removed in the conflict between large and small states over their respective powers in Congress. That dispute led to that most political of compromises between the Virginia Plan, which contemplated two houses of Congress, both based on population, but selected by different means (one by the legislature and the other by vote),[53] and the New Jersey Plan, patterned on the Articles of Confederation, which had a Congress with a single house where all states had an equal vote.[54] The upshot was the Connecticut Compromise,[55] which introduced the current set-up in which Senate representation is by state[56] and House representation by population,[57] with representation in the Electoral College equal to the sum of both.[58] There is no veil of ignorance here because the delegates from each state knew their own interest and acted accordingly. But the compromise was in fact a victory for the small states, whose equal power in the Senate on average means that specific appropriations tend to redistribute wealth generated in populous states to programs benefiting smaller states.[59] The result here is consistent with the general theory of bargaining among coalitions. The smaller units who sign on to the deal can extract a disproportionate fraction of the gains.

The remaining structural responses to the demands of government were mentioned in the Introduction. These include the creation of a federal structure, the systematic development of checks and balances, and the protection of individual rights. The structural limitations and the protection of individual rights served a common end: to slow down the response of government where the errors of moving too fast seem to dominate those of moving too slowly.

2

———◆———

The Progressive Response

THE CLASSICAL LIBERAL CONCEPTION of the Constitution had a long historical run of about 150 years, but in the end it was vanquished by the progressive counterrevolution that culminated in critical Supreme Court decisions, on issues of both federalism and individual rights, during the tumultuous 1930s. It should not be supposed, however, that the progressive mindset in constitutional law has vanished from the current intellectual scene simply because many New Deal Depression-era short-term public works and relief programs no longer form a part of the modern American political fabric. The progressive constitutional mindset continues to thrive today with increased urgency. It undergirds both old and new legislative initiatives at the state and federal level, including the post–New Deal expansion of progressive programs during the 1960s, which included not only the civil rights explosion, but also the rise of Medicare and Medicaid, and the full range of expansive new federal enactments during the Nixon years: the Endangered Species Act,[1] the Environmental Protection Agency,[2] the Occupational Safety and Health Act,[3] pension reform,[4] and many more. The term "progressive" has also made a conspicuous comeback since 2000 in the face of the challenges posed by slow growth and economic inequality, which have engendered support for contemporary versions of earlier New Deal programs, dealing with such critical issues as labor, energy, and the environment.

Over this full range of issues, the progressives and their contemporary defenders reject the classical liberal position on two key premises. First, the progressives accept the intrinsic virtues of deliberative democracy and the administrative state, unchecked by strong protections of property and contract. Second, they offer a pessimistic assessment of the performance and even the possibility of unregulated markets in post-industrial society.

Popular Democracy

The first point is well captured in Justice Stephen Breyer's 2005 short book with an instructive title: *Active Liberty: Interpreting Our Democratic Constitution*.[5] That title offers two strong clues as to how Breyer reads the relevance of the progressive revolution to contemporary American constitutional law and practice. The term "active liberty" is used in self-conscious opposition to the classical liberal ideal of negative liberty. Negative liberty is concerned with individuals having freedom *from* various forms of public impositions, including of course all tyrannical demands by the state. Positive liberties necessarily involve specific commitments to a democratic process that allows the state to consciously create what are commonly termed "positive rights"—entitlements (as opposed to mere rights) to housing, health care, education, or jobs, for example. Lest there be any mistake on the matter, *Active Liberty* does not disparage negative liberties, but it necessarily limits their scope by making the claim that "the Constitution [is] centrally focused upon active liberty, upon the right of individuals to participate in democratic self-government."[6] It thus follows, Breyer argues, that "the original Constitution's primary objective" was to "creat[e] a form of government in which all citizens share the government's authority, participating in the creation of public policy."[7] It is therefore no accident that Breyer lays repeated stress on "We the People" in the Constitution's Preamble,[8] precisely because of its hortatory edge.

In similar fashion, Breyer's reference to a "democratic constitution" elides the historical distinction between republican and democratic forms of government. Historically that difference was marked by the danger of a majority vote under a system of universal suffrage without special property protections. Indeed, any expansion in the scope of the franchise strengthens the case for the constitutional entrenchment of individual rights of property and contract. These two elements are of course the key components of any program of negative liberties. Breyer's claim that the Constitution sought to involve "all citizens" in forming public policy is flatly inconsistent with the Constitution's initial preference for restricted franchise and indirect elections. To maintain this position, Breyer is forced to minimize the concern with faction that drove Madison, treating it as a minor obstacle for deliberative democracies. Yet nowhere in his slim volume does Breyer mention, let alone explain away, any of the numerous provisions in the Constitution that limit political participation. Nor does he grapple with any of the endless external commentary, which indicates that the Founders meant what they said and said what they meant when they expressed their uneasiness with popular government.

To make out his expanded case for active liberty, Justice Breyer resorts to an interpretive view that stresses "the likely consequences of the interpretive alternatives, valued in terms of the phrase's purposes."[9] Taken at face value, that approach should not change the balance of interpretation. If any particular phrase of a provision has a classical liberal purpose that tracks the text, then the two approaches should reinforce, not undermine, each other. Yet Breyer's switch in emphasis from text to purpose is meant to exploit a perceived slippage between the two conceptions, so as to let the justices play fast and loose with text. More striking, Breyer's appeal to this supposed interpretive norm does not rest on any overarching normative framework that justifies the endless succession of government interventions in ordinary private transactions. Specifically, at no point does Breyer cash out the fundamental difference in attitude between the classical liberals and the modern progressives toward state-created monopoly. The progressive approach was well articulated by Robert Stern, one of the Roosevelt administration's ablest lawyers and constitutional architects, who summarized the state of play at the end of the New Deal period.[10] Stern emphatically asserted that federal power under the Commerce Clause "was now recognized as a grant of authority permitting Congress to allow interstate commerce to take place on whatever terms it may consider in the interest of national well-being, subject only to other limitations, such as the Due Process Clause."[11] The range of schemes that Stern endorsed makes it clear that if he had been pressed he would show no preference for competition over monopoly, which reflected a principle consistently embodied in New Deal policies.[12] And his caveat about the importance of the Due Process Clause was not meant to revive the substantive protections of liberty and property that had likewise been whittled away in the decade following the 1937 constitutional revolution. Instead, his legitimate concern was with a nascent constitutional revolution that brought increased scrutiny to laws that discriminated against racial and other "discrete and insular minorities," to use Justice Harlan Fiske Stone's phrase from his famous footnote 4 in *United States v. Carolene Products*.[13]

Progressive Economics

This pervasive skepticism on matters of market structure dovetails with the entire substantive progressive program, which often found itself on both sides of the question of how to best respond to the challenge of monopoly power. On the one hand, many progressives were strong defenders of the antitrust laws, which were all to the good when they restricted various territorial and price-fixing arrangements. But the anti-trust program had decidedly different results when invoked in service of a populist tradition that equated bigness with badness. Of greater importance, perhaps, the progressives championed wholesale exemption from the antitrust laws for labor and agricultural cartels, as well as a raft of other restrictive practices that tended to block competition.[14] Zoning[15] and rent control statutes[16] are paradigmatic examples for local real estate markets. But the impulse covered a wide range of dubious trade practices, including, for example, a provision of the National Industrial Recovery Act (NIRA), struck down by the Supreme Court in *A.L.A. Schechter Poultry Corp. v. United States*, that required butchers to purchase entire runs of poultry, including sick chickens.[17]

It is therefore easy to identify a strange but persistent cleavage in the progressive worldview, the great constitutional victories which almost without exception offered protection for its favored, entrenched monopolies, especially in the labor and agricultural markets. For example, the basic structure of the NLRB was intended to force employers to bargain with a single union that represented all workers, including dissenters. Likewise, the Agricultural Adjustment Acts[18] systematically controlled the production of various crops on a comprehensive national basis, thus blocking all efforts of individual farmers to erode its power by intrastate sales or internal consumption of their output on their own farms. These conscious designs received some lofty justifications, often based on notions of democratic participation. The progressives clung to their constitutional view because of their passionate belief that Adam Smith's naïve view of competitive markets was hopelessly out of date now that the Industrial Revolution of the late nineteenth century had transformed the means of production. In their view, these irreversible technological changes required equally permanent changes in the constitutional order. Any naïve optimism that unregulated market forces could bring about some desirable social equilibrium was rejected.

The new champions of the modern administrative state were not content with the narrow point that competitive processes did not work well in certain well-defined market niches. The critique of laissez-faire offered by James Landis and other notables, such as Justice Louis D. Brandeis and Justice Felix Frankfurter, was not confined to railroads, telecommunications, and other network industries in which it was widely understood then, as now, that competitive solutions could not carry the day. Rather, the more fundamental critique was that large organizations necessarily took the same hierarchical form in both government and the private sector. Their approach has been rightly described as corporatism, of which the NIRA scheme struck down in *Schechter* was perhaps the most notable example. Michael Wachter has described the phenomenon, which he notes was by no means buried after *Schechter*, as follows:

> Corporatism views free competition as a destructive force that has to be both controlled and channeled through institutions that practice fair— but not free—competition under the watchful, mediating power of the government. In corporatism, fair competition means the "stabilization of business, with prices at levels that support fair union wages, and economic policy responds to institutional actors such as unions and corporations rather than to individuals."[19]

It is no intellectual coincidence that one of the noted academic champions of the NIRA was Adolf Berle, who also championed the view that the corporation should be a bastion of shareholder democracy, subjecting both directors and officers to external popular pressure through means such as proxy fights and annual meetings. Writing with Gardner Means in *The Modern Corporation and Private Property* in 1932, Berle predicted that "the future might see . . . the corporation, not only on an equal plane with the state, but possibly even superseding it as the dominant form of social organization."[20] Elsewhere he hinted darkly: "Unchecked by present legal balances, a social-economic absolutism of corporate administrators, even if benevolent, might be unsafe."[21] Berle and Means thus devoutly believed that the separation of ownership from management in the public corporation necessarily led to deep and abiding conflicts of interest that only government intervention could solve.

Strong medicine, such as that imposed by the securities acts of 1933 and 1934, was the only way to generate sufficient pushback against the dominance of private firms. Yet this move, and others like it, exposed a second deep cleavage in the modern progressive program that is painfully evident in the writing of Justice Breyer. The implementation of any complex administrative system of regulation can be demanded but not executed by public deliberation. What is needed in all cases is a permanent administrative apparatus staffed by elites whose supposed expertise allows them to make complex judgments on industrial policy. The new generation of experts had to paint on a canvas far more extensive than that needed under the earlier classical liberal model, which, truth be told, could never satisfactorily resolve the nettlesome question of how to best regulate natural monopolies, such as railroads and public utilities. That technical expertise operates on a delegated authority that receives only scant guidance from legislators, who have little specific knowledge of the manifold areas of public regulation: drugs, securities, labor relations, the environment, telecommunications, and pensions. Each area has spawned complex legislative schemes with immense amounts of delegated authority under statutes that allow, and indeed require, unelected administrators to make major policy decisions about the reach of federal programs.

Yet ironically, the Constitution itself says absolutely nothing about the existence, let alone the organization and regulation, of these administrative agencies. Their most conspicuous feature is their combined powers to first make and then enforce rules before their own internal tribunals. That organization represents a conscious and complete inversion of the principle of separation of powers, which Woodrow Wilson dismissed as a "grievous mistake" because its halting action blocks the application of technical knowledge as a force for good.[22] James Landis echoed that theme at the height of the New Deal infatuation with the administrative state, when he argued that separation of powers did not work when the government was concerned "with the stability of an industry."[23] But in that statement, Landis reveals his own misunderstanding of the problem by confusing stability in a legal framework of voluntary exchange, which was the concern of the classical liberals, with the price stabilization program of the New Deal, which destroyed the ability of economic actors to communicate information about the relative scarcity of goods through the price system. Yet his view of stability was consistent with the rules of the era, which listed wage stability in labor markets and parity in agricultural markets as legitimate government objectives and not as a looming peril to all forms of successful commercial innovation and exchange. Daryl Levinson and Richard Pildes have carried the theme forward to modern times: "By virtue of its very success, American democracy ran roughshod over the Madisonian design of separation of powers almost from the outset, preempting the political dynamics that were supposed to provide each branch with a 'will of its own' so that departmental 'ambition' could 'be made to counteract ambition.'"[24] And they administer the coup de grace by continuing, "Few aspects of the Founding generation's political theory are now more clearly anachronistic than their vision of legislative-executive separation of powers."[25] But again, it is critical to ask what makes the theory "anachronistic." The common view today is that the system cannot work in modern times. But the more accurate response is that the entrenched administrative state, especially on issues of fair competition and price stability, causes real economic loss and social dislocation precisely because it hobbles the dynamic elements of markets.

The confusion is not accidental. The rise of the administrative state hardly eliminates the problem of factional intrigue. Quite the opposite, it often intensifies factional struggles during the appointment process. Administrative agencies do not staff themselves. Therefore the president and his allies in Congress will seek to convert tenuous political majorities into powerful administrative ones. Notwithstanding protestations to the contrary, value judgments remain critical in all administrative law settings no matter how technical the issues.

In contrast, markets are more immune to factional intrigue than either legislatures or administrative agencies. Traders only prosper when their trading partners also profit. No self-interested trader, supplier, or customer, whether rich or poor, ordinarily enters voluntarily into losing deals. That one condition alone means that voluntary transactions, no matter how numerous, complex, or diverse, produce expected mutual gains for all involved parties. Hence, the higher the velocity of business transactions in goods and services, the higher the level of human satisfaction, for the parties who win in one transaction have greater resources for new transactions that expand opportunities for third persons. The political conflicts of interest in majority rule are normally obviated in markets by the requirement of mutual consent to voluntary exchange. Likewise with the blockades that necessarily arise when administrative agencies are given the (implicit) monopoly power to license: there may be a thousand parties from whom you can buy computer services, but there are not 999 regulators to whom a party can turn if a single regulator denies a permit—a problem that is only intensified when multiple permits are needed to undertake a single project. If the common law lawyers were right to worry about the dominant position of a common carrier, modern scholars, both within and beyond the legal profession, should not be indifferent to the still greater power that lies in the hands of state regulators in the modern administrative state.

Misunderstanding these different institutional environments has real consequences. In working out the effects of administrative control over business activity, writers in the progressive tradition uniformly missed the profound differences between large corporations that operate in competitive environments and administrative institutions that exert monopoly power at all levels of government. In private businesses, shareholders come together selectively and voluntarily for a common venture. They can work quite well without worrying about the element of territorial inclusion that brings unrelated, or even hostile persons together in political bodies. Corporations can make rules that govern shareholders solely for their investments in the business. In so doing, they can—indeed must—address, and control, the key conflicts of interest to which Berle and Means refer. If they fail to counter the risk of misappropriation, they will not be able to persuade others to trust them with their capital. The competitive pressures are everywhere, for invested capital is not tied to any particular line of business. Working in this environment, corporations will adopt rules by charter for selecting directors and officers in order to counteract the vaunted separation between management and control. These rules cannot eliminate the conflicts of interest—nothing could—but they will nonetheless moderate them so that the gains for the venture are worth the residual costs incurred.

Yet no matter what they do, corporations do not have control over the lives and fortunes of either their investors or employees, who can invest or work elsewhere. But individuals do not have this luxury when they are forced to entrust their fortunes to the officials of the modern administrative state. Corporations, both large and small, face sharp competition from other firms, both large and small, that can woo away their customers with a combination of lower prices and superior products. Their size does not limit in any way, shape, or form the choices available to their potential customers, suppliers, or employees, unless these firms obtain monopoly power, for which the antitrust laws, not the laws of corporate governance, supply the proper response. The relationship between the state and citizen is wholly different. Individuals face a monopoly of power in the hands of the state. If they do not like its commands, they cannot just sell their shares and invest elsewhere. In politics, exit means more than the sale of particular assets. Corporations don't control territories; governments do. Exit from government power therefore necessarily requires emigration outside the power of the state. Exercising that exit right comes at the far higher cost of giving up all of the associations with one's home base. Federalism of course facilitates exit rights by allowing firms that do not like how business is regulated in New Jersey to slide over to Delaware. Corporations did just that en masse after 1913, when Governor Woodrow Wilson's onerous and misguided reforms of New Jersey corporate law propelled the mass exodus to Delaware,[26] precisely because Wilson did not understand that the control of market power does not require upsetting the internal relationships within the firm. The progressives thought that government was right to curb business excesses, so they championed the large government movement in order to curb the exit right and force firms to submit to greater reliance on political control through administrative expertise. But their confusion of business size with market power led to the chronic mistake of preferring supposedly intelligent regulation to individual choice.

But what about the changed circumstances from industrialization on which progressives waxed eloquent? Quite simply, writ large these changes *strengthen* the case for classical liberal solutions that allow for state regulation of monopoly and state provision of infrastructure, but otherwise keep public hands off voluntary transactions in labor, capital, goods, or services. The explanation for this critical inversion does not lie in the increased size of firms. It depends on the increased size of the market. In the Founding period, sharp limitations on transportation and communication necessarily limited the number of firms that could participate in any geographical market. Make the goods in Massachusetts and it is hard to sell them in Alabama if they have to be carried by stagecoach or shipped for hundreds of miles. But introduce the railroad, and the telegraph, and the truck, and the telephone, and all of a sudden competition at a distance can overcome all physical obstacles. What remains of course are legal obstacles to foreign trade, which could either be goods and services from outside the United States or goods and services from outside any particular state. Move to regional, national, and global markets, and competition increases because of the number of firms with strong brands that can sell their wares anywhere. In today's market, the ability of states to cut off transportation and communication becomes even more important than it was in earlier times, which means that federal action, typically by courts, is necessary to prevent individual states from severing the arteries of commerce through unilateral actions.

It is one of the great achievements of the Supreme Court, on both its liberal and conservative sides, that it has worked hard, and with much success, to keep these arteries of commerce open[27] by adhering to classical liberal principles in connection with these interstate activities. Competition, which receives such inconsistent, and often shabby, treatment in the hands of the administrative state, now becomes the highest good. And the grounds for its limitation are two that were as well recognized in 1787 as they are today. One is the prevention of serious externalities like pollution and contaminated goods. The second is the need to make outsiders pay their fair share toward maintaining local infrastructure. But all the fancy forms of protectionism that dominate the administrative state are decisively rejected, and cannot be introduced under the frequent pretext that the exclusion of foreign goods is necessary to protect domestic health and safety. No state can impose clever taxes on agricultural goods and dairy products from outside the jurisdiction that are not paid by local producers by, for example, using differential taxes to eliminate the price advantage of out-of-state milk suppliers[28] or, alternatively, by offering rebates to local producers on uniform taxes that are denied to their out-of-state competitors.[29] The bottom line seems to be as follows. Once Congress speaks, it can rig the price of agricultural foodstuffs in domestic markets in whatever way it sees fit. But if it remains silent, then the states cannot rig these markets in favor of their domestic producers. The striking success of the pro-competitive judicial approach to commerce, even at the height of the Depression, shows that the older classical principles survive only insofar as they block state interference with interstate commerce, but they exert little or no influence in restricting the ability of Congress to impose at the federal level economic restrictions on all sectors of the economy. So the die is now cast. The chief attack against the progressive movement is that its uncritical praise of popular democracy leads it to understate the pervasive risks of faction and to throw its lot into an administrative state that does far better in creating needless monopolies than in controlling them. The question that remains is what tools of interpretation, if any, should lead us to prefer the modern to the classical synthesis in the interpretation of our Constitution. We turn now to the classical liberal and modern views of interpretation and judicial review to find answers to that question.

3

Constitutional Interpretation

The Original and the Prescriptive Constitutions

A NY ACCOUNT of the specifics of constitutional law begins with a disarmingly simple question. What rules and techniques of interpretation are necessary and proper to grasp the meaning of any constitutional text? In fact, this inquiry has two parts. Each demands a different approach. The first portion of the inquiry writes on a blank slate, and asks about the proper understanding of the text when presented in its original written form, unadorned by any previous interpretive efforts. Only matters of principle should be invoked to decide this question, which itself is a vast inquiry that requires, as will become evident, the integration of the particular text with the appropriate background norms of interpretation. The second part of the interpretive enterprise then asks: how should a text be interpreted in light of its previous authoritative renderings?

These basic points are stated with a level of abstraction that needs specific content. The purpose of this chapter is to trace through these multiple themes. I start with interpretive questions that arise as a matter of first principle in order to show that these can be achieved only if they are seen through the lens of the same classical liberal theory that animated the drafting of the original text— a position that incorporates but goes beyond in critical ways the most common form of original meaning as explicated by Justice Antonin Scalia. I then contrast this guarded originalist view with that of the "living constitution," which has gained a strong foothold in current constitutional thought. Next I illustrate the dangers of the newer position in connection with two constitutional issues, the proper interpretation of the "cruel and unusual punishments" clause of the Eighth Amendment and the Second Amendment right to keep and bear arms. Finally, I take the analysis one step further to ask a persistent question: how should judges respond to perceived mistakes in the prior decisional law?

Starting from First Principles

The proper way to read a constitutional provision scarcely differs from the proper way to interpret other documents with legal effect: statutes, regulations, and contracts. In each case, there are two necessary tasks. The first is to figure out the meaning of the written text in light of its standard usage at the time of its adoption. On this matter, at least, it is wise to follow Justice Antonin Scalia's famous line that the best first cut—the qualifications will become clear in a moment—at interpreting the Constitution follows "the original meaning of the text, not what the original draftsmen intended."[1] The great advantage of this approach is that the interpreter is far more likely to find a single standard meaning from reading the text than from attempting to reconcile the various separate understandings of draftsmen in the plural. In effect the rule is similar to the objective theory of contract, which relies largely on the public meaning of ordinary contract language as the guide to interpretation for much the same reason.

Performing constitutional interpretation, however, presents different challenges in different contexts. The Constitution gives Congress the power to "grant letters of Marque and Reprisal."[2] But the process of interpretation is futile for anyone who does not know that these letters include orders from Congress to private parties to seize merchant ships from other nations on the high seas. Other constitutional provisions present quite different interpretive problems. When the Constitution speaks of "freedom of speech, or of the press," it is incumbent to give an account of "freedom" as well as "speech, or the press," and the former quickly touches grand abstractions that often do not have a single settled public meaning. The effort to find a single meaning often requires an explicit resort to the dominant political theory, which need not yield a univocal answer. Different constitutional terms require different approaches for their correct explication.

Nor is this inquiry solved simply by looking at a single term or provision in isolation from the remainder. Clearly issues of structure matter as well. These require a close look at how the various constitutional provisions line up with each other, both within and across the Articles of the Constitution. It also requires a strong sense of the underlying normative framework that animates the provisions of particular sections or entire Articles. As with ordinary contracts, there is always the possibility that particular contexts require some deviation from ordinary meaning. Comparing and contrasting each usage of a particular term in a single document is often instructive.

Once the initial inquiry into the meaning of the stated terms is completed, the second interpretive task asks whether the text as written is subject to a set of unspoken qualifications that either supplement or restrict its application. Both possibilities—as we shall see—are strictly necessary, in order to ensure that constitutional interpretation produces workable and sensible results in light of the overall design and purpose of the contested provision. There is no guarantee that this elaborate gloss has to be interposed in all cases; for example, there are few qualifications that would allow someone under the age of 35 to become a President. But many jurisdictional commands, such as those under the Commerce Clause, and many substantive protections, such as those in the Bill of Rights, offer what can only be termed open invitations to courts, and indeed everyone else, to flesh out the meanings of the key terms in the basic constitutional norm. To give but one simple example, the provision that says that no person shall be deprived of property without "due process of law" does not answer the question of what sort of process is due in any individual case.[3] But by the same token it does not leave the inquiry into levels of process protections solely to the unfettered judicial imagination. It would be an indefensible reading of the Due Process Clause to hold that greater levels of procedural protection are needed for petty offenses than for serious ones. But even if we get the gradient in the right direction, that task does not pair off particular levels of protection with particular forms of government action.[4] It is idle to argue that this task can be avoided because of the latent indeterminacy. It is equally idle to argue that serious justices acting in good faith will all agree on the types of protection needed in particular contexts. In cases of this sort, even the strongest commitment to an originalist method of interpretation requires judges to engage in subsequent elaboration. It is as if the original command requires judges to use their best judgment, given the inability to specify any unique set of procedures for all different cases.

The situation is, moreover, not unique to constitutions. Codes of contract law often specify default provisions to govern questions such as whether the buyer or seller bears the risk of loss for goods shipped in transit. But there is no default provision that requires that when the price is left unspecified it shall be $9.99 whether the item purchased is a second-hand radio or a new diamond ring. "Reasonable price" is the standard, which is by design not rigid but flexible, and necessarily requires some empirical inquiry at the very least into the type of good about which there is a dispute on price. And as with key constitutional terms, the range of correct answers is large but not unlimited. Commercial law has learned to live with such ambiguity. Constitutional law must do so as well.

The role of interpretation, however, does not extend solely to cases of purposive ambiguity. Many legal commands, such as "Congress shall make no law . . . abridging the freedom of speech" cry out not to be taken literally. Rather, the basic norm is read subject to implicit exceptions and background social understandings. Unlike the interpretation of the word "due," these qualifications do not alter or clarify the semantic meanings of the written terms, but they do fill the indispensable role of fleshing out the implied qualifications on the basic doctrine. No matter how carefully one parses the words "freedom of speech," they will not answer three fundamental *nontextual* commitments: the anticircumvention principle, police power justifications, and remedial choices, all of which have their precise common law analogs.[5]

The anticircumvention norm expands the basic scope of constitutional protections by preventing Congress or the states from skirting a constitutional norm without violating its literal meaning. The police power cuts in the opposite direction by recognizing that both Congress and the states may rely on substantive justifications to limit basic liberties in exactly the same fashion as the common law.[6] Both these questions were raised in the 1827 case of *Brown v. Maryland*,[7] which asked whether a Maryland tax of $50 on each importer should be regarded as a tax on imports that violated the constitutional prohibition that forbade the states "to lay any imposts or duties on imports or exports." In striking down the tax, Chief Justice Marshall denounced any effort at constitutional circumvention by imposing the tax on importers instead of imports. Rhetorically, he asked whether the Congress could "shield itself from the just censure to which this attempt to evade the prohibitions of the constitution would expose it, by saying, that this was a tax on the person, not on the article, and that the legislature had a right to tax occupations?"[8] His answer was no.

While the anticircumvention principle broadens the reach of the constitutional provision, the police power narrows it. Traditionally, these potential justifications for government action have been examined under the general rubric of the "police power," which, to list the common categories, examines the limitations on liberty and property that "relate to the safety, health, morals, and general welfare of the public."[9] The entire process that starts with the basic text is expanded in timeless fashion by implication that derives from the normative classical liberal theory that underlies the constitutional prohibition. To take but one example, the First Amendment protection of freedom of speech contains no hint of a police power. Yet just those issues arise when the case law is forced to address the permissible limitations that Congress may place on the freedom of speech, whether we speak of libel, assault, fraud, street riots, national security, political protest, and many more.

Ironically, the phrase "police power" was (at least until modern times) the most ubiquitous phrase in the constitutional lexicon, even though it does not appear in the constitutional text. As noted, that phrase first entered federal constitutional discourse in *Brown*. Thereafter, it quickly spread to cover a wide range of other cases, until it became the centerpiece of all the great nineteenth-century treatises on constitutional law, by Thomas Cooley,[10] Christopher Tiedeman,[11] and Ernst Freund.[12] These words are not inserted to evoke in some oblique way modern notions of the living constitution. Rather they are there because whether we deal with constitutional law or private law, the only way that the law can piece together an entire system is with a method of successive approximations that works through a system of alternating presumptions where the parties in turn seek to introduce new information that restores the balance in their favor. For example, if the basic presumption is in favor of freedom of speech, the standard libertarian prohibitions against the use of force (including the threat of force) and fraud are profound limitations on any claim of freedom of speech that have to be respected as much in the public law as in the private law. Yet the document that sets the basic stage for the analysis is silent on the set of permissible justifications, which means that they can only be added in by way of interpretation.

Finally, the First Amendment does not contain a word about remedies in those instances when Congress violates the freedom of speech of any individual or group. But the courts must decide at a minimum whether to award damages or injunctions. If the former, they must decide on the measure of losses. If the latter, they must decide whether the injunction is subject to time limits or conditions. One simple illustration of the problem is that no court will enjoin the publication of a libel.[13] Nor, as in the famous example of the Pentagon Papers, will it enjoin the publication of classified government documents, unless they are closely tied to national security, like plans for troop movements.[14]

This twofold approach toward constitutional interpretation is not unique to legal argumentation. Indeed it draws its strength from ordinary life. Wittgenstein, for example, gives this provocative example in his *Philosophical Investigations*.[15] Someone asks you to teach a game to a child and you teach the child how to play dice. "I didn't mean that sort of game," the original speaker protests. Is that protest legitimate, Wittgenstein asks, only if he had the objection in mind at the time he made the request? The answer to that question is an emphatic no, given the way language works in ordinary life. His objection to your choice of games does not rest on the definitional point that you somehow did not understand the meaning of the term "game." Rather, the argument is that you ignored one implicit limitation on the request, namely that one does not teach young children how to gamble without some specific authorization. The force of Wittgenstein's example cannot be met by refusing to accept any implied conditions on ordinary requests or orders. Thus, if the speaker mentioned gambling games, it would hardly be taken by implication to authorize games like dueling that expose children to serious risk of physical injury, or games that are blasphemous or obscene. These unstated qualifications reflect some widely shared background norms that allow people to economize on scarce linguistic resources in ordinary communication. The risk that the process will be abused does not allow us to dispense with it altogether.

The stakes are far higher in legislative and constitutional interpretation, but the processes used to read statutory or constitutional commands frequently follow the same two-track process. The table stakes only show that the costs of error are higher. They do not suggest or imply that the techniques that minimize communication error in private conversation and contracts do not work as well for public commands.

My favorite example of how this process works out in a serious interpretive culture comes from the Lex Aquila of around 287 B.C., whose central text stated, quite simply, that "whosoever unlawfully kills a slave of either sex or a herd animal"[16] is responsible in damages. Each word in this spare provision has received intensive elaboration. Does killing only cover the case of strangling the animal or killing it with bows and arrows, or does it cover luring it into traps? Is it unlawful to kill in self-defense or with the consent of the victim? Each of these points in turn opens the argument up to further elaboration. Just what limits apply to either self-defense or consent? The full explication of the text covers many points dealing with scope, excuses, and justification, which require a process of implication that is, notwithstanding differences in subject matter, culture, time, and space, an exact replica of the best tradition of constitutional interpretation.[17] But this statute, like so many others, only makes sense in light of its general purpose (the prevention of violence) when it is read against its background interpretive tradition. This necessarily raises many questions to which the words of the text supply no answer. None of this concern with implied qualifications of basic text makes what is written arbitrary and indeterminate. But it does require an extensive apparatus for its elucidation.

This pressing need for systematic elaboration of basic commands does not negate the possibility of the rule of law, but rather shows how imperative it is that the implicit qualifications be developed in conformity with the basic tenor of the underlying statute. In constitutional settings, for example, no one can understand what is covered by freedom of speech in total ignorance of its intellectual setting: are writings comprehended by speech? Is all speech—including assault, fraud, defamation, and invasion of privacy, for starters—fully protected? Once again, the high stakes in constitutional interpretation may force greater care in analysis, but they do not suggest any way to avoid the two-stage inquiry that is used in contextualizing language in all other social settings: once the meaning of the words spoken is established, the two inquiries that remain involve, first, analogical extension and, second, principled exceptions to the basic norm. These are not fashionable literary moves. They are embedded as part and parcel of every sound interpretive strategy, whether originalist or modern.

The next question is: what does the classical liberal perspective say about the process of interpretation, and why should its vision matter?

The first response involves the commitment to the rule of law as a means to control the arbitrary use of state power, which is one of the essential missions of any constitutional system, regardless of its substantive ends. That rule-of-law ideal is unattainable if the promulgation of any constitutional or statutory command leaves political actors with as much discretion after its publication as they had before. The asserted inability to find clear meanings for any constitutional text renders limited government impossible. It is of course easy to claim that someone else's rules suffer from all that ails ordinary language. But no one can maintain that position when it is his or her commands that are subject to that same relentless form of skepticism. Anyone, regardless of political persuasion, who wishes to advance his own substantive claims must perforce use this methodology. Global claims of skepticism thus stop all political discourse in its tracks.

It is, therefore, not only philosophically unwise to insist on the necessity of linguistic uncertainty, but also practically mischievous. If this claim were true, then it becomes impossible for people to know in advance what is expected of them, so that they can alter their conduct to avoid the sting of the criminal and civil law. Any effort to explain a particular text will be infected with the same fatal flaw as the original, so long as painful elaborations, however well intentioned, are inevitably (since the defect here is linguistic) no clearer than the constitutional texts that they purport to explicate. There are of course all sorts of texts or provisions that are badly drafted, on which interpretation is difficult. But it should not be supposed that these flaws are inherent in all texts, regardless of content, but only in those that fail to exhaust the full potential of language.

No one should foolishly claim, of course, that all texts are necessarily free of ambiguity, given that bad drafting is as possible in constitutions as it is in ordinary contexts. But those ambiguities have to be isolated and demonstrated by showing the two (or more) alternative meanings that a particular text may bear, not by a more ambitious claim that all texts are inherently ambiguous. Key provisions in our Constitution were subject to meticulous debate and draftsmanship, but always against the backdrop of this interpretive tradition, which was familiar to the Founders from their study of both Roman and common law. The Constitution contains many cases of studied ambiguity that necessarily give rise to interpretive tangles. But that is far from any universal norm.

We should, therefore, start from the opposite pole and begin with the conviction that interpretive enterprises are capable of success, and then do our level best to make good on that promise by using the process of explication to draw forth fair implications from any given text.

This basic commitment to the integrity of language is only a minimum condition for successful constitutional interpretation in the classical liberal mode. But it is hardly distinctive to it. The administrative state does not rely only on vague general commands, although those are often part of its repertoire. In addition, it often issues rules that specify in minute detail what can and cannot be done. Of the many and sensible objections to zoning ordinances, the lack of detail and specificity in the relevant ordinances is the last point that comes to mind. No conception of the rule of law will work if it only relies on formal commitments of notice and clarity. Of greater importance is an insistence that the constitutional text must be interpreted in light of supplemental norms that arise from within that classical liberal tradition. We should not doubt that it is possible to give some faithful textual interpretation of the Soviet or Iranian constitution, even though they subordinate all individual liberties to the whim of the state. Closer to home, when the rules of interpretation are applied to the National Labor Relations Act of 1935 and to Title VII the Civil Rights Act of 1964, they cannot yield results consistent with the classical liberal tradition. Both statutes reject the essential principle of freedom of association in competitive labor markets in favor of rules that require employers to deal with employees under the terms specified within the statute. The accurate rendition of those statutes depends on making sure that their basic visions are not compromised by artful exceptions that convert them back into classical liberal doctrines. There is no more warrant for using the rules of interpretation to convert a social democratic statute into a classical liberal one than there is for the opposite. Interpretation, properly understood, explains and illustrates the substantive implications of any given worldview. But interpretation can never transform one view into its rival. No amount of ingenuity or exegesis can make Marx's *The Communist Manifesto* into a defense of the institution of private property.

In its enduring provisions, our Constitution is most emphatically a classical liberal document. Its successful interpretation on all points dealing with text and its surrounding norms should be read in sync with the tradition of strong property rights, voluntary association, and limited government. Only because differing worldviews drive particular questions of interpretation at every level are the debates on textual interpretations so intense. In modern discussions of constitutional interpretation, the creation of an initial presumption, say, in favor of freedom of speech, thus invites examination of the cases in which that presumption can be displaced. In the end any substantive constitutional command is no different from any ordinary proposition that people should (prima facie) keep their promises or (prima facie) not use force and fraud against another. The acceptance of that presumption thus necessarily leads to a constant balancing of interests to take into account the justifications that might be offered for an admitted restriction on a constitutional right. What is much less commonly observed is that, originalist or not, at least one of the interests in the balance has no textual foundation, but must be derived from sources that lie outside the doctrine, even though they are consistent with its basic tenor. It is a dangerous mistake to conflate any form of originalism, which asks how texts were understood when written, with strict textualism, which ignores these necessary but implied exceptions.

A Living Constitution?

This classical approach to constitutional interpretation is at odds with the now fashionable and expansive notion of a "living Constitution," which envisions far more fundamental changes in constitutional interpretation. In its most extreme form, Louis Michael Seidman denounces originalism as an approach that gives undue credit to "a group of white propertied men who have been dead for two centuries, [who] knew nothing of our present situation."[18] Jack Balkin's more modest approach of "Living Originalism" views the "Constitution as an initial framework for governance that sets politics in motion, and that Americans must fill out over time through constitutional construction."[19] The common thread in both these approaches is that modern politics, not classical norms of interpretation, drive the contemporary analysis, which leads where it may. That shift in power locus makes it, of course, far easier to change the basic norms of interpretation in ways that are more congenial to modern progressive notions that both Seidman and Balkin champion.

In taking up this controversial theme, Justice Scalia struck just the right note in the title of his well-known William Howard Taft Constitutional Law Lecture: "Originalism: The Lesser Evil."[20] It is indeed the case that any system of interpretation will fall short in some cases, so that the only inquiry worth asking, with perfection unattainable, is which system has fewer flaws. In Scalia's view, the "living Constitution" comes out second best for the simple reason that once the task of interpretation is unmoored from the text and structure of the Constitution, it becomes virtually impossible to offer a principled account of what new substitute should displace the best (even if uneasy) original reading. In consequence, the arbitrariness of the enterprise necessarily undermines the legitimacy of the courts as forming to an institution outside of politics, and it muddies the line between constitutional principle and democratic politics.

Indeed, the stakes are higher than even his brief but elegant account might suggest because battles over the living constitution become the forum in which to carry out the ongoing debates between the classical liberal and modern progressive positions. The resolution of these debates matters a great deal, for they help to select the background understandings used to frame and explicate the written text. Classical liberals always think first of countering force, fraud, and monopoly. The modern progressives have a much larger list of alleged state interests to work into the question, including the provision of minimum standards of wealth or happiness for all citizens, restraints on the distribution of wealth more generally, and often a full array of positive entitlements, some of which may even have constitutional weight.

In dealing with the unwritten elements of our written Constitution, it is important to be aware of how changed circumstances fit into the question. It is one thing to ask how the traditional visions of limited government and strong property rights can survive in changed circumstances. Thus one could ask whether—and, if so, how—commerce among the several states covers transportation by rail or communication on the web. It is quite another thing to argue that the progressive vision of the world requires jettisoning the older worldview in favor of one that expands the power of the federal government at the expense of the states.[21] Hence, it is not proper to say that changed circumstances make it impossible to find any areas of local commerce or manufacture that lie outside the reach of the federal government. The correct approach is to preserve the balance between national and local regulation as applied to these technological changes. The wrong approach is to argue that these changes make the boundary lines unintelligible or unworkable. Stated otherwise, there is nothing inherent in the notion of a living constitution—that is, one whose interpretation responds to changed circumstances—that drives us inexorably toward more extensive government at the national and state level.

Nonetheless, many modern writers of all political persuasions see in the Constitution a kind of Burkean evolution whereby the text itself becomes modified through repeated usage—usually towards big government.[22] This analogy works well for the English constitution, which functions by slow evolution. But it fails with the American Constitution, which contains specific provisions for constitutional amendment that are intended to make sure the proposed changes satisfy supermajorities at every stage of the process, both federal and state, over an extended period of time, and not at a single instant. Requiring sharp changes rather than the incremental evolution of the common law lets people know where they stand at any given moment, so that they will not be left to speculate on the legal position at any one time. In dealing with these issues, it is tempting to say that a living constitution keeps matters in tune with the times. But often the layers of interpretive confusion are so great that much harm is done by the use of this interpretive mode. Throughout much of this book the argument against the living constitution is that it systematically erodes individual liberty and property protections under the original Constitution. But in some contexts, the greatest danger from the living constitution comes from the opposite direction: the insertion of judicial control over matters that have long been regarded as properly falling within the province of the legislatures—such as the control over the criminal sentences that may be meted out in connection with certain offenses. The Constitution imposes some extrinsic limitations on the process, but the key element in dealing with the issue is how much. On this issue, there is no necessary liberal or conservative direction to any sensible originalist critique of recent constitutional decisions. Just as decisions embracing the living constitution can be erroneous, so too can those that explicitly follow an originalist program. The point is made by comparing the readings of the Eighth Amendment prohibition against cruel and unusual punishments with the Second Amendment's protection of the right to keep and bear arms.

Cruel and Unusual Punishment(s)

On this score, it is instructive how badly the living constitution plays out in the Supreme Court case law on the Eighth Amendment, which reads in full:

> Excessive bail shall not be required, nor excessive fines imposed, nor cruel and unusual punishments inflicted.

Like so much in the Constitution, this provision was not invented out of whole cloth. It was obviously lifted from the 1689 English Bill of Rights promulgated by Parliament in order to pave the accession of William of Orange to the English throne. That document first notes that the Lords Spiritual and Temporal and Commons jointly "declare" a list of "illegal actions," including the suspension of the laws of Parliament. Tucked into this list is the declaration:

> That excessive bail ought not to be required, nor excessive fines imposed, nor cruel and unusual punishments inflicted.[23]

It is noteworthy that the statute is "declaratory," which leaves open the question of whether it should be treated in the same fashion as ordinary legislation. Note that the "ought not" does not have the same coercive pop as "shall not," which is closer to the language of a command. Against this backdrop, what is the correct interpretation of this provision, once it is incorporated into the Bill of Rights? One point of contention involves the question of whether the list of cruel and unusual punishments is closed as of the time of the Bill of Rights. That topic is one to which Justice Scalia has uneasily returned on several occasions. In hedging his bets on "faint-hearted originalism," he observes, "I am confident that public flogging and handbranding would not be sustained by our courts, and any espousal of originalism as a practical theory of exegesis must somehow come to terms with that reality."[24] He also knows the prohibition cannot be limited to cruel devices in use at the time of the Founding, for it makes no sense to say that it is permissible for the state to use electroshock therapy or waterboarding, simply because these devices were unknown at the time of the Founding. The Founders had a good sense of what medieval torture could do and it would be pointless to close the general category of punishments to those in use as of the time. But this view does not require an acceptance of a living constitution. It just recognizes that the text itself is phrased in general terms that themselves are not limited to the forms of punishment that were extant at the time of its promulgation. It would indeed be a dereliction of constitutional duty to refuse to ask whether electroshock therapy, unknown during the Founding period, counted as a cruel and unusual punishment.

Two points, however, do not follow from that sensible accommodation of the historical words to changes in social circumstances. The first is that nothing about this evolutionary strategy allows for a living constitutional judgment of the sort that makes capital punishment unconstitutional under some advanced theory of social morality or some recent empirical studies that capital punishment (as may well be the case) does not further deter crime or murder. Various versions of that position were advanced in *Furman v. Georgia*,[25] where one major source of cleavage within the liberal bloc was whether a per se ban on capital punishment was required, as urged by Justices Brennan and Marshall, or whether the Eighth Amendment prohibition rested on the arbitrary administration of justice, as urged by Justices Douglas, Stewart, and White. That tough line did not last after *Gregg v. Georgia*[26] came down in 1976, nor should it have.

The short answer to that question is that the institution of capital punishment is included with the explicit references in the same Bill of Rights to the fact that no person should be put twice in jeopardy of life and limb; that all capital offenses require presentment by a grand jury; and that no person shall be deprived of life, liberty, or property without due process of law, all of which are found in the Fifth Amendment.[27] Those statements make it clear that capital punishment is outside the realm of cruel and unusual punishment, so that its elimination becomes a question of legislative choice, not constitutional imperative.

The second point is, if anything, of greater importance to the debate about the living constitution. Much of the recent Supreme Court case law on the Eighth Amendment has two central premises: As Justice Elena Kagan wrote recently in *Miller v. Alabama*,

> [T]he Eighth Amendment's prohibition of cruel and unusual punishment guarantees individuals the right not to be subjected to excessive sanctions. That right, we have explained, flows from the basic precept of justice that punishment for crime should be graduated and proportioned to both the offender and the offense. And we view that concept less

through a historical prism than according to the evolving standards of decency that mark the progress of a maturing society.[28]

The correlative principle is "the requirement of individualized sentencing for defendants facing the most serious penalties."[29]

Justice Kagan thus governs her inquiry by three principles. The first is that crimes and punishment should be seen in proportion to each other. The second is that this proportionality should be judged not historically, but in light of evolving standards of decency. The third is that individual sentencing is required in cases that call for serious penalties. Unfortunately, the combination of these three principles allows for an extensive reconstruction of the criminal code of both state and federal governments for, at the very least, all cases that call for death or life imprisonment. That is a striking statement, because it presupposes a level of confidence about the operation of the criminal system that is just not available to anyone. Unlike the relative desirability of competition compared to monopoly—which turns out to be the central issue in many questions of government structure and individual rights—setting and administering a set of criminal sanctions becomes the quintessential legislative function precisely because criminal theory has never produced a definitive answer to any of the questions raised in this short quotation. There is little understanding as to how a principle of proportionality works given the difficulties in measuring the severity of offenses, whether by class or by case. Nor is there any credible constitutional peg for having judicial oversight of these functions based on some judicial reading of public morality and the appropriate standards for judging criminal conduct.

Nor does this modest text give any hook on which to conduct so ambitious an inquiry. The difficulty here is the words "cruel and unusual punishments." The "s" is caught once in Justice Kagan's quotation, dropped in a second quote, and ignored without notice in the passage quoted above. That elision is not by accident. It is just much easier to conduct a free-ranging inquiry under a timeless principle against cruel and unusual punishment than it is to work an inquiry with the pesky "s," which points more clearly to an enumeration of the types of punishments that are off-limits, as addressed by Justice Scalia in his academic writing on the topic. And nothing about the English origins of the clause hints that the great settlement that brought William of

Orange to the throne was intended to crimp the ordinary operation of the criminal justice system in defining criminal offenses and setting punishments for them.

Indeed what is so disconcerting about this entire judicial edifice is the number of debatable categorical judgments that come from on high. Thus *Roper v. Simmons*[30] held that the Eighth Amendment imposed a categorical prohibition against the use of capital punishment for persons under eighteen years of age. In *Graham v. Florida,*[31] a divided Supreme Court held that the Cruel and Unusual Punishments Clause forbade the imposition of a mandatory life sentence without parole against juveniles for nonhomicide offenses. *Miller v. Alabama* held that mandatory life sentences without parole also violated the Eighth Amendment for homicide offenses committed by juveniles. The evident tension in these cases is how the Supreme Court is able to use the same clause to fashion per se rules for capital offenses and ad hoc rules for lesser offenses out of the same clauses. It is equally puzzling how confident the Court is in its selective invocation of evolving standards of decency when the morality and efficiency of capital punishment remains a hot button topic and large numbers of states have resisted efforts to repeal their statutes.

The issue gets no easier when the matter turns to rape, where once again categorical determinations have carried the day. Thus in 1977, a divided Supreme Court in *Coker v. Georgia*[32] ruled out the death penalty in all cases of rape that did not involve death, with the clear implication that the imposition of the death penalty was necessarily confined to (a subclass of) murder cases. That inference became inescapable in *Kennedy v. Louisiana,*[33] which applied the rule to child rape. In *Kennedy,* Justice Anthony Kennedy relied on the broad consensus of states that have removed the death penalty in rape cases, without noting that such consensus in fact counts as an argument for legislative control over the process. His affection for evolving standards of decency produced something of a recent uproar when five members of the Supreme Court struck down the death penalty in cases of child rape—before they learned that Congress had called for just that penalty in its 2006 amendments to the Military Code of Justice.[34] All too often those supposed shifts in public morality result in one-way ratchets, such that the death penalty could never be reimposed if popular sentiment changed on the subject. It is difficult enough to figure out how to make sense of a given text in light of its written context and unwritten background norms. It is most unwise to add yet another degree of freedom into the interpretive process, especially one that allows courts to adopt any substantive principle on any issue that they are called upon to decide.

In my view, the line of cases on cruel and unusual punishments represents a complete breakdown in constitutional interpretation for one class of cases. As constituted, there appear to be no serious limitations on what could be done through this clause to alter the content of state law. One of the uneasy features of *Miller* was that the state conviction rested in part on the application of the doctrines of accomplice liability and felony murder, which hold persons who are part of a criminal operation responsible for deaths caused by others in the course of that activity, even if the individual accused did not know of the action or was not in a position to do anything to stop it. There are obvious strict liability elements in this case. Does it follow that the entire doctrine is cruel and unusual punishment under some principle of proportionality, given that there is clear moral daylight between the actual perpetrator and the second-tier defendant? In addition, does the prohibition on cruel and unusual punishments impose serious limitations on the level of punishment that can be imposed in cases of pure financial loss, especially on senior officials and corporations held liable under a vicarious liability doctrine where they did not control or know about the unlawful activities?

There should in fact be no reason to speculate on these issues. The weaknesses in any theory of criminal punishment make it difficult for the Supreme Court to find any hook on which to tie its own ad hoc jurisprudence, especially in interpreting a clause for which a narrower reading, relating to types of offenses, comports better with the text, history, and structure of the clause. In this instance, no strong reliance interest has emerged that justifies keeping the current doctrine in place. This sorry line of cases makes good the originalist critique of willful Supreme Court justices imposing their views on a defenseless text that is incapable of speaking for itself. The point here is not to take any stand on the merits of legislative reform that deals with the levels of responsibility that could attach at all ages, which may well have much to commend them. But the Eighth Amendment is a poor vehicle to achieve that end, and judicial bodies are ill equipped to measure the changes in popular sentiment to which they purport to find allegiance. The public is, for better or worse, more retributivist in its judgments than the justices of the Supreme Court.

The Right to Keep and Bear Arms

The great vice in *Miller v. Alabama*[35] lay in its eagerness to rip the Cruel and Unusual Punishments Clause from its roots by resort to modern principles of criminology inconsistent with both its text and purpose. The excesses in *Miller* point towards a return to a more nuanced originalist view of constitutional interpretation. But any such originalist venture is hardly risk-free. Indeed, it goes astray if it looks at the meaning of particular words and phrases in isolation from the key structural features of the Constitution. This methodological caveat gains special urgency in properly construing the right to keep and bear arms found in the Second Amendment to the Constitution. That amendment was before the Court in *District of Columbia v. Heller*.[36] The perfect plaintiff, Dick Heller, "a D.C. special police officer authorized to carry a handgun while on duty at the Federal Judicial Center," claimed that the D.C. statute[37] denied him his basic Second Amendment right to keep an operable gun for self-defense in his own home. In a five-to-four decision, Justice Scalia held that "the District's ban on handgun possession in the home violates the Second Amendment, as does its prohibition against rendering any lawful firearm in the home operable for the purpose of immediate self-defense."[38] Yet for all its meticulous care and erudition, Scalia's analysis misfires if only for the simplest of reasons: the Second Amendment does not apply to the District of Columbia, which by definition does not, and cannot, have its own state militia.

Start with the Second Amendment to the Constitution, which reads in its entirety:

> A well regulated Militia, being necessary to the security of a free State, the right of the people to keep and bear Arms, shall not be infringed.[39]

The 1939 decision in *United States v. Miller*[40] had previously upheld against a Second Amendment challenge the National Firearms Act of 1934 (NFA),[41] which required written government approval for the transfer of certain classes of firearms across state lines. In upholding the NFA, Justice James McReynolds consciously juxtaposed the Second Amendment to Article I of the Constitution. Article I divides authority over the militia between the national government and the states as follows:

> To provide for calling forth the Militia to execute the Laws of the Union, suppress Insurrections and repel Invasions;

To provide for organizing, arming, and disciplining, the Militia, and for governing such Part of them as may be employed in the Service of the United States, reserving to the States respectively, the Appointment of the Officers, and the Authority of training the Militia according to the discipline prescribed by Congress.[42]

McReynolds offered no systematic analysis of the interrelationships of these three provisions, but leapt straight to his conclusion: "With obvious purpose [these provisions were] to assure the continuation and render possible the effectiveness of such forces the declaration and guarantee of the Second Amendment were made. It must be interpreted and applied with that end in view."[43]

McReynolds's brief account of the structure and role of the Second Amendment is truer to the structure and function of the Second Amendment than Scalia's more expansive reading in *Heller*. The National Firearms Act of 1934 was enacted before the enormous expansion of the federal commerce power in 1937.[44] Consistent with the earlier, and narrower, view of the Commerce Clause, the Act only allowed Congress to regulate the transportation of certain guns in interstate commerce. The legislation had nothing whatsoever to do with the use of these guns within any state, let alone any home, which then lay well outside Congress's power to regulate. Only the two Militia Clauses in Article I touched activities within the state. The simplest way to read the Second Amendment is as an additional assurance that the specified federal powers over the Militia should not be used to allow the federal government to run roughshod of private individuals who were subject to state power.

It follows therefore that the Second Amendment does not apply to the District of Columbia for the simple reason that it is not a state, and thus has no militia of its own. Congress did not exert its powers over the District through the Commerce Clause, but instead through its direct grant "To exercise exclusive Legislation over" the District of Columbia,[45] which gave it all the police powers over the District that were reserved to the states when acting within their boundaries as of 1934. Nothing that the federal government did in its governance of the District could signal the abolition of the state militia or undermine its effectiveness. The Second Amendment thus reads best as a simple declaration that the federal government has no business regulating what happens within state lines. The best way to reach that result is to demystify the passive voice by adding the words "by the United States" after the words "shall not be infringed," which parallels the approach of the Court in *Barron v. Baltimore*,[46] which refused to extend the Takings Clause (also written in the passive voice) to the states. Justice Stevens was more alert to this federalism dimension, but he overstepped the line in claiming that "[n]o new evidence has surfaced since 1980 supporting the view that the Amendment was intended to curtail the power of Congress to regulate civilian use or misuse of weapons."[47] The simpler and more powerful point is that Congress did not have this supposed power to regulate the use of firearms within the states before the 1937 constitutional revolution.

The federalism focus of the Second Amendment also casts doubts on Justice Scalia's other interpretive moves. To be sure, he is correct to insist that "the right of the people" does indeed refer to the right of ordinary citizens, acting individually, to deal with the use of guns.[48] The threat against which they need protection is federal regulation in the states, an issue that has nothing to do with the ordinary people who live in the District of Columbia. It is therefore a mistake to dismiss the prefatory language as mere surplusage when it sharpens the meaning of the Amendment as a whole. In defense of this view, Scalia notes that several states passed constitutional provisions that protected the individual right to keep and bear arms. In particular, "Pennsylvania's Declaration of Rights of 1776 said: 'That the people have a right to bear arms for the defence of themselves, and the state. . . .'"[49] This and similar clauses make no reference to the militia, but for good reason. They are dealing only with the relationship of the states to their citizens, not the relationship of the federal government to the states. The Second Amendment adds in this reference precisely because it is directed to the federalism issues that were introduced in Article I.

For just these reasons, it seems equally clear that the term "Militia" in the opening phrase of the Second Amendment should carry the same meaning that it has in Article I, where the entire set of state and federal functions are directed to the operation of the organized militia and not to unorganized individuals. That is why the Second Amendment refers to a "well regulated" militia in each state that can operate under standard protocols so that they can be integrated into a single fighting force when called into the active service of the United States. It is for just this reason that McReynolds was correct in noting that the Second

Amendment was needed "to assure the continuation and render possible the effectiveness of such forces."[50]

Justice Scalia's inattention to the federalism issues implicit in the Second Amendment is also apparent in his inaccurate claims that "[t]he phrase 'security of a free state' meant 'security of a free polity,'[51] not security of each of the several States as the dissent below argued."[52] He is also wrong to insist that "the phrase 'security of a free state' and close variations seem to have been terms of art in 18th-century political discourse, meaning a 'free country" or free polity."[53] To the contrary, the Second Amendment is not a disquisition on general political theory; nor does it deal with the relationship of the United States to foreign countries. It addresses a concrete problem of great practical importance for the ambitious exercise of conscious cooperative federalism at the time when the militia was a central part of the overall military apparatus of the nation. More specifically, the Second Amendment addresses a particular problem of federalism that was thought to be untouched by the provisions in Article I, namely whether the national government in its guise of regulating the militia could clamp down on the ability of states to allow their own citizens to carry weapons for whatever purpose they saw fit. Once again, the Second Amendment has no application to the District of Columbia.

The Scalia interpretation is subject to one final major difficulty. Once he strips the prefatory clause from the operative clause of the Second Amendment, the Clause sweeps too broadly as an absolute protection of the right to keep and bear arms. But Justice Scalia acknowledges that "the right secured by the Second Amendment is not unlimited."[54] Consistent with his general view, he notes the need for these limitations, while making clear that the level of scrutiny needed is more "a freestanding 'interest-balancing' approach,"[55] which he rightly regards as insufficient for any enumerated right of the Constitution. But the concern here is not the difficult balancing test that has been applied in the many lower court decisions since *Heller* that have sought to figure out what restrictions may be imposed to prevent the improper use of guns. On remand, and consistent with the tenor of Justice Scalia's opinion, the District of Columbia Circuit jettisoned the low-level rational basis review and applied a relatively muscular intermediate scrutiny to gun registration requirements imposed by a D.C. law enacted in the wake of *Heller*.[56] But there is still much disorder in the house. In *United*

States v. Masciandaro,[57] the court feared that gun litigation over the limits of self-defense would be governed by some "sliding scale" that might play out differently "in litigation over schools, airports, parks, public thoroughfares, and various additional government facilities."[58] That prediction has already proved true. In *Kachalsky v. County* of Westchester,[59] the Second Circuit upheld under this standard a New York State law that required all individuals to demonstrate "proper cause"—that is, a need for special protection—in order to carry a concealed handgun in public.[60] In contrast, the Seventh Circuit in *Moore v. Madigan*[61] took issue with *Kachalsky*[62] in what seems to be the more accurate reading of *Heller*, by holding that the right to bear arms under the Second Amendment required the invalidation of Illinois laws[63] that made it illegal to carry in public a loaded gun ready for use on their person, subject to some narrow exceptions.[64]

It is clearly necessary for the Supreme Court to iron out these evident differences. But no amount of attention to the police power standard going forward answers the antecedent question in *Heller*: why in this context do we need to add in a police power exception to the Second Amendment at all? Keep the prefatory clause in place, and the Amendment protects individual rights by keeping the federal government from meddling with the possession and use of guns within the states. There is no need for any police power analysis at all. The federal government is just out of that business altogether.

Once the *Heller* Court decided to create individual rights against the federal government in the District of Columbia, the next question was whether under its new reading, complete with its police power limitation, it should be extended to the states. This topic was raised in connection with the strict Chicago gun ordinance challenged in *McDonald v. City of Chicago*.[65] Justice Samuel Alito, writing for a five member majority, struck down a Chicago gun law that was similar in strictness to the one enacted in Washington, D.C. The question before the Court was whether *Heller* applied to the states by virtue of the Fourteenth Amendment.[66] Doctrinally, that task was complicated because the great decision in the *Slaughter-House Cases*[67] limited the Privileges or Immunities Clause to the protection of a narrow class of distinctly federal rights, such as the ability to use navigable waters and to petition Congress for the redress of grievances. Justice Alito did not wish to upend this narrow reading of *Slaughter-House*.[68] Even if he had, the traditional list of protected privileges did not include the right to bear arms that was listed in the Second Amendment. Undeterred, he routed the argument through the language of the Due Process Clause of the Fourteenth Amendment, where the right to keep and bear arms counted as a protected form of liberty.[69] He noted that the great tide of Supreme Court cases favored the doctrine of "incorporation" whereby most of the specific guarantees in the first eight amendments of the Bill of Rights were carried over to the states. Owing to the fundamental status of the right of self-defense in the home, Justice Alito concluded that the same rationale applied to a right "deeply rooted in this Nation's history and tradition,"[70] which he then carries forward with detailed analysis from the founding period to the ratification of the Fourteenth Amendment in 1868. Some of that history, but not all of it, make explicit the right to use guns in self-defense in the home.[71]

As a matter of legal history, it is hard to dispute the substantive contention that the right to keep and bear arms had a deep historical resonance. But the overall decision in this case only makes sense by following *Heller* insofar as it completely disregards the intrinsic federalism component in the Second Amendment, whose central purpose is to prevent the federal government from dictating gun control laws to the states to limit their capacity to arm and organize militias. That threat simply does not arise when the state decides on its own initiative to limit the use of guns inside its own borders. The passage of the Fourteenth Amendment was, without question, intended to impose greater limits on state power. But that conclusion cannot be reached by incorporation of the Second Amendment. It can only be reached through the direct application of either the Privileges or Immunities Clause or the Due Process Clause of the Fourteenth Amendment. As to the former, the Supreme Court's highly dubious decision in *United States v. Cruikshank*[72] refused incorporation under the *Slaughter-House Cases'* impossibly narrow construction of the Privileges or Immunities Clause. As it explained curtly, "The second amendment declares that it shall not be infringed; but this, as has been seen, means no more than that it shall not be infringed by Congress."[73] But even if that Clause were given a more sensible reading, it is not clear that the right to keep and bear arms would be on the list, given that it was not included on the list of privileges and immunities set out in *Corfield v. Coryell*.[74] Nor does incorporation through the Due Process Clause make sense either. The

Second Amendment speaks of "the right of the people" to keep and bear arms, where these people are not all persons, but only citizens of the United States. Any effort to read this protection against the states through the Fourteenth Amendment makes it broader as against the states than it does against the federal government.

All in all, then, it does not look as though the bodily incorporation of the Second Amendment nor the effort to shoehorn the right to keep and bear arms directly into the Fourteenth Amendment make sense, especially on originalist grounds. This is not, however, to utter a kind word on behalf of either the D.C. or Chicago statutes, or for that matter to criticize them. In both cases there are credible arguments that strict limitations on the ownership and use of guns tilts the balance of advantage to lawless individuals who are happy to flout the law at the expense of honorable people who feel obliged to comply with it. Getting the right resolution of these empirical issues is vital for the implementation of an intelligent gun policy, but wholly irrelevant to the accurate interpretation of the Second Amendment.

The Second Tier: The Prescriptive Constitution

The major difficulty with the living constitution is that its application leads all too easily, as with the issue of cruel and unusual punishments, to the creation of new law out of whole cloth. The rejection of that position, however, does not necessarily mean that any strong originalist conception has to rule the day in the end, for it is also critical to take into account the notion of a *prescriptive* constitution that is not intended to confer, at least with any enthusiasm, additional powers on the present generation of judges to make law in ways that consciously deviate from past precedents. Rather, the term suggests a more limited judicial role recognizing that certain changes, even of systemic importance, were made by previous judges and should not be undone by the present generation of judges precisely because they have become deeply embedded in the political fabric of the nation. The conscious parallel here is to the common law doctrine of prescription, which allows an individual who has made long use of another's land to claim full title in that easement, so long as his use has been open, notorious, and continuous. The doctrine of prescription converts a set of common law trespasses into a vested right that with time is superior to the claim of the original owner. No sitting judge could grant an easement of this sort to someone who started to trespass yesterday. But by the same token, no judge could deny the validity of an easement that started in a series of trespasses that began years ago. This position splits the difference between a view of unacceptable rigidity that is associated with some originalist positions, while also denying judges the power to initiate, as it were, constitutional error in their own time. This problem does not arise whenever there is good reason to believe that judicial precedent is correct; this question of incremental adjustment to past cases is easy. Now the second court is less likely to fall into error because it can follow both precedent and the original constitutional meaning. But deciding that next case is far more difficult where it is widely believed that the initial interpretation of a text has fallen into error. At this point there is no dominant approach. In some instances, it may well make sense to continue on the path given the accumulated reliance on the earlier precedents. In other cases, it could well be that the weaknesses of the dominant approach are so clear that reversion to a more principled approach is indicated. Yet even here, it is unclear whether courts should adopt an incremental approach in order to ease the case law back in line with sound principle, or should take a more decisive step by making more extensive changes up to and including overruling the previous precedent. Worse still, the problem of mistake is often infectious. Let one clause receive a settled interpretation that is too narrow, and a broader interpretation of another provision could easily take up some of the slack. But rarely will that second measure just neutralize the original mistake. It could go too far or not far enough. Either way it can easily introduce new errors, perhaps of greater severity, of its own. Often the interpretive difficulties snowball out of control, for it is all too common for genuine disputes to arise on both halves of the argument: judges frequently disagree on both the pristine meaning of a text and the appropriate response to error, if any exists, in subsequent interpretation. The problem does not necessarily sort itself out easily with time, for subsequent courts may disagree with one another and generate unresolved confusion, not political or intellectual consensus.

This entire process, however, requires a major adjustment to any originalist program, because the ultimate choices depend less on the text and more on the maintenance of a sound constitutional order. Deciding which questionable interpretations ought to be preserved and extended, and which ought to be cut back, does not admit any standard interpretive answer. At the very least, powerful value judgments have to work themselves into the system, to ask whether the rejection of well-established doctrine will advance or harm the position of the nation as a whole. This inquiry differs from that posed by the living constitution. It does not seek to create new conscious deviations from accepted constitutionality in the text. Rather, it most unhappily requires that the justices of the Supreme Court make judgments about the way in which the rules fit into the overall system.

In dealing with this issue, mistaken judgments cover the full range of constitutional topics, both good and bad. Thus on the positive side of the ledger, it is hard to see why anyone would reject the long-established interpretations of judicial review embodied in *Marbury v. Madison*[75] and *Martin v. Hunter's Lessee*,[76] which establish the institution of judicial review with respect to both federal and state laws. By the same token, should the well-established limitations on standing, first articulated in *Frothingham v. Mellon*,[77] be retained, given the threat that they pose to judicial review under both *Marbury* and *Martin*? In the same vein, it would be most unwise to undo the traditional doctrines associated with the dormant Commerce Clause, which help preserve the operation of competitive markets across state lines even in the absence of specific congressional action under its commerce power. Yet on the other end of the scale, it would have been dangerously foolish to let the doctrines of stare decisis protect the "separate but equal doctrine" of *Plessy v. Ferguson*,[78] which gave legal strength to the institutions of the segregated South, or the narrow reading of the Privileges or Immunities Clause of the Fourteenth Amendment in the *Slaughter-House Cases*[79] and *United States v. Cruikshank*,[80] which limited the power of the federal government to protect the newly recognized black citizens against depredations by state governments.

In all too many cases, the art of interpretation must go beyond the originalist program to deal with these issues. The particular judgments are regrettably ad hoc, but unavoidable. The want of a clean theory is no excuse to bury our collective heads in the sand in the face of major difficulties. The chapters that follow illustrate some of these ambiguities. I start with the judicial power because of the distinct position of judicial review within the American system. But the story carries over to countless other issues of constitutional law, in which it is impossible to escape the weight of the past. The great challenge of constitutional interpretation is to marry together two warring conceptions. A sensible form of originalism (which goes far beyond the "original meaning") can and should be matched with a deep appreciation of how difficult it is to deal with systematic errors in interpretation that perforce creep into all interpretive efforts with the passage of time. In my view, the answer often turns on this simple question: does the original version of the Constitution or its subsequent interpretation do a better job in advancing the ideals of a classical liberal constitution? In all the cases where the doctrines should be kept, a credible claim can be made to that effect. In the sorry cases of racial domination, that position becomes utterly indefensible. Ultimately, the inquiry becomes more nuanced than this simple proposition states, but the basic orientation remains largely unchanged. This dual inquiry starts with the question of judicial review, taken up in the next chapter.

PART TWO

CONSTITUTIONAL STRUCTURES

SECTION I

THE JUDICIAL POWER

4

The Origins of Judicial Review

IN ONE SENSE, any study of our structural Constitution should be as easy as counting from one to three. Start with the legislative power, which is set out in Article I, then move on to the executive power set out in Article II, and follow this with an examination of the judicial power that is found in Article III. The logic behind this simple progression is that laws must be made before they can be enforced, and enforced before they can be applied or challenged in court. Yet almost invariably the study of American constitutional law does not proceed in that direction. Rather, judicial power comes first on the list, followed by the Congress and then the president. The explanation for this deviation from the expected order lies in one historical development that was, for its time, distinctive to the United States: the adoption of the doctrine of judicial review. In its modern formulation, judicial review allows the Supreme Court—and, subject to its oversight, all lower federal and state courts—to strike down laws or block executive actions that exceed constitutional powers or offend one of the individual guarantees that the Constitution creates. Justice John Marshall's masterful, if slippery, decision in *Marbury v. Madison*[1] is commonly held to solidify the power of the Court to declare void and of no effect certain actions by the other two branches of government. This defense of judicial supremacy makes the Court the ultimate arbiter of whether laws satisfy the numerous limitations found in the Constitution.

Judicial Parity versus Judicial Supremacy

In principle, and on balance, I believe that *Marbury* represents a clear victory for the theory of limited government, because its doctrine of judicial supremacy places yet another check on the power of the two political branches. The implicit background assumption is that the initial presumption should be set against new legislation, which is more likely to do harm than good. The overall analysis is, of course, deeply complicated by the erratic nature of Supreme Court decisions, which makes it impossible to give a uniform generalization in favor of either aggressive or minimal judicial review. The opponents of judicial review have a list of horror stories to which they can point. That list would include decisions like *Dred Scott v. Sandford*[2] and *Plessy v. Ferguson*[3] on matters of race. In more modern times it would embrace *Korematsu v. United States*,[4] on Japanese internment during World War II, and, depending on one's view, would also include *Wickard v. Filburn*,[5] *Roe v. Wade*,[6] and *Kelo v. City of New London*.[7]

It is of course just here that the difficulties begin. The simplest way to see the problem is that in *Plessy*, *Korematsu*, *Wickard*, and *Kelo*, the great vice was the failure of the Supreme Court to impose limitations on the political branches of government. Quite simply, the broad definition of the "police power" greased the skids in *Plessy*, *Korematsu*, and *Kelo*, all of which represent serious intrusions into individual rights on matters of race, ethnicity, and private property (keeping it away from the urban renewal bulldozer). The vice in these cases is too little judicial intervention, not too much.

The one case that appears to involve too much judicial intervention is *Roe*, but the explanation, as I have long insisted, cuts exactly in the opposite direction. Any use of a classical liberal theory would recognize that the police power exceptions dealing with health and safety, in this instance of (to use what some would regard as a loaded term) the unborn child, make abortion an area in which legal protection is imperative under a classical liberal theory that starts with a narrow definition of harm.[8] It is that reason, rather than for any supposed reason of limited institutional competence, that makes *Roe*'s qualified defense of abortion on demand so suspect. The correct response is, of course, that the state can refuse to enforce its police powers if it finds it too difficult to do so, but even that concession does not justify a total repeal of all legal protection for unborn children. *Dred Scott* is also a complex case because Chief Justice Roger Taney could have created all his institutional mischief even under the narrow version of judicial review by saying that the courts have to determine who counts as a "citizen" for the purposes of diversity jurisdiction.

At this point, therefore, it looks like something of a draw as to whether too much or too little judicial review is appropriate. But that balance is vitally altered in favor of strong judicial review so long as the justices remember that it is a classical liberal constitution, with strong property rights and limited government, that they are asked to construe. The horrific decisions all come from the unwillingness to respect the equal rights of all persons or the limitations on federal powers. In the current situation, where the Supreme Court has all too often lost its way, the overall balance is hard to calibrate. But it becomes easier to make the judgment when it is recalled that the judicial decisions following classical liberal positions on the dormant Commerce Clause[9] and freedom of speech (which does not include the latest generation of limitations on campaign finance expenditures) are great achievements that could never be sustained under a diffident model of judicial review.

These are, ideally, some of the long-term institutional reasons why *Marbury* survives, as Alexander Bickel wrote,[10] more for Marshall's verbal mastery than for its internal logic; more for its responsiveness to the needs of a new nation than for its fidelity to text.[11] But that expansive reading of judicial supremacy is not the only view of the subject. An alternative conception, which Bickel fleetingly examines,[12] is one that starts from the assumption of a rough parity among the three branches of government. This conception allows no branch to nullify the independent sphere of action of the others, but leaves each the arbiter of its own constitutional power, within very broad boundaries. That position has had its powerful supporters. President Jefferson thought that the judiciary would become a "despotic branch" if allowed to determine which laws were constitutional not only for its own operation but also for the legislature and the executive.[13] President Abraham Lincoln, for his part, saw judicial review as a means whereby "the people will have ceased to be their own rulers," if they allowed the outcomes of litigation to chart the course of a nation.[14]

Any assertion of parity among the branches should not, however, be read to replicate the relationship that exists among sovereign nations under international law, where each is required to respect the autonomous actions of the others undertaken within their own territories.[15] Nations can be autonomous and independent, but the three branches of government must cooperate with each other, so at a minimum, each can be subject to some specific and explicit duties with respect to the other two, without necessarily, however, taking the more drastic step of authorizing the federal courts to override all legislative and executive actions. Even these requirements of limited cooperation are a risky adventure because while the Constitution sets out some detailed requirements of what should be done, it offers not even a glimmer of remedial structure to deal with a breakdown in the system of interlocking prerogatives and obligations that it creates. An element of irreducible political risk necessarily remains no matter whether the claim of judicial supremacy is accepted or rejected.

The obvious questions about *Marbury* and its progeny are whether the strong sense of judicial review is sustainable as a matter of constitutional interpretation and desirable as a matter of first principle. It is here that the troubles begin. I have little doubt, as a matter of normative constitutional theory, about the intrinsic worth of the strong doctrine of judicial review. But that conviction does not permit us to escape the manifest tension between the constitutional text and constitutional theory. Start with this simple observation. It is child's play to draft a constitutional provision that states in no uncertain terms: "The judicial power shall confer on the Supreme Court, and all other state and federal courts, subject to the Supreme Court's final and binding review, the power to invalidate any statute, administrative action, or executive decision, federal or state, that contravenes this Constitution." The United States Constitution contains no provision that remotely resembles this one, which means that this unprecedented judicial power has to be derived by inference from those provisions that are found in the Constitution and the political and intellectual history that formed their background. The decision in *Marbury*, while correct on its own facts, does not support an aggressive reading of judicial review that gives the Court pride of place over the political branches. Instead, it only allows the Court to refuse to hear cases that the Constitution states should be decided elsewhere.

The Historical Background

A dispassionate originalist account—one that is indifferent to the merits of the two positions—shows quite conclusively that judicial supremacy comes off second best in light of the two major historical antecedents to the Constitution: political theory and historical practice. The bottom line is this: our Framers contemplated an independent judiciary with strong institutional protections that stood between political branches of government and the ordinary individual. Judicial supremacy, wisely or not, was not part of that scheme.

In order to understand the advances in political statecraft under the United States Constitution, it is important to set the text against the intellectual temper of the times. For starters, the drafting of the United States Constitution did break new ground in the way it entrenched the independence of the judiciary. But far from allowing the Supreme Court the power to negate and oversee the actions of the Congress and the executive, it had the more modest function of making sure that the Congress and the executive could not treat the judicial branch as a pawn subject to their joint or separate machinations. Put otherwise, the distinctive and unambiguous contribution of the Constitution was to assure first, that all cases of individual punishment had to be meted out through the judiciary, and second, that its judges were independent from the political branches.

The Due Process Clause of the Fifth Amendment, binding against the federal government, provides that "no person shall be deprived of life, liberty, or property, without due process of law."[16] Even in its most modest form, this sweeping provision guarantees that all persons shall have individualized adjudication before they can be subject to any penalties that result in the loss of any of the three entitlements (life, liberty, or property), which are understood to set out a comprehensive list of the essential individual interests within a classical liberal theory. And, in a way that is most timely today, access to the courts is guaranteed, at least in part, not in some mystical and indirect way, but through the use of habeas corpus: "The Privilege of the Writ of Habeas Corpus shall not be suspended, unless when in Cases of Rebellion or Invasion the public Safety may require it."[17] Habeas is the means whereby due process is secured, then as now. On this matter at least, the executive must answer to the writ, so within this space the primacy of the judiciary is secure, which is as it should be, given the magnitude of the liberty interests subject to the exercise of political or executive power. And, as Hamilton recognized in *Federalist No. 78*,[18] the executive was duty-bound to enforce such judgments—even if the courts could not compel it to do so.

The independence of the judiciary is likewise protected: "The Judges, both of the supreme and inferior Courts, shall hold their Offices during good Behaviour, and shall, at stated Times, receive for their Services, a Compensation, which shall not be diminished during their Continuance in Office."[19] If anything, the absence of term limits creates a geriatric problem of the first order, but otherwise the provision ensures that the Congress and the executive cannot suck the lifeblood out of the Court by denying the judges their salaries. The clause requires Congress to act affirmatively by making particular appropriations for the operation of the judicial branch, which is the kind of explicit duty of support that never applies as between sovereign nations.

These protections should not be disparaged for, if respected, they help to prevent the emergence of a police state, which is no mean achievement in a world littered with political disasters. But note what they do not do—which is to place any limitations on the content of the substantive offenses that trigger the use of state power against the individual. That point should come as no surprise, for this view is consistent with all the early thinking on separation of powers, which admitted no place for a strong version of judicial review. Judicial review makes no appearance in Locke's magisterial *Second Treatise of Government*, where the remedy for tyrannical government is the right of revolution, to be exercised with restraint and only in instances of extreme provocation.[20] That system requires the people to throw out the baby with the bathwater insofar as the system knocks out all laws from the earlier sovereign. The selective attack on bad laws through judicial review was not part of Locke's equation.

The same picture emerges with Montesquieu's *Spirit of Laws*, which likewise is silent on any question of judicial review, but insistent on the separation of powers and the independence of the judiciary:

> Again, there is no liberty, if the judiciary power be not separated from the legislative and executive. Were it joined with the legislative, the life and liberty of the subject would be exposed to arbitrary control; for the judge would be then the legislator. Were it joined to the executive power, the judge might behave with violence and oppression. . . .
>
> Of the three powers above mentioned, the judiciary is in some measure next to nothing: there remain, therefore, only two; and as these have need of a regulating power to moderate them, the part of the legislative body composed of the nobility is extremely proper for this purpose. . . .

[I]n general, the legislative power cannot try causes: and much less can it try this particular case, where it represents the party aggrieved, which is the people. . . .

Here then is the fundamental constitution of the government we are treating of. The legislative body being composed of two parts, they check one another by the mutual privilege of rejecting. They are both restrained by the executive power, as the executive is by the legislative.[21]

The point here is that the principle of separation of powers *does* allow the judiciary to place a limitation on executive and legislative power. But the key division of power is between the two political branches, without any distinctive role for the courts other than adjudication of individual cases under the laws set down and enforced by the two other branches. To be sure, this situation got cloudier in England where the House of Lords of the time was both part of the legislative system and, through the law lords, the ultimate source of judicial power. Judicial review is redundant if the highest judicial body is embedded, as at that time, in the upper legislative chamber.[22] The check against tyranny thus depended on checks on royal power through the two Houses of Parliament.

For the most part those checks lay within the political realm. Historically, however, one interesting diversion was in *Dr. Bonham's Case*,[23] which asked whether Parliament could authorize the Royal College of Physicians to impose a fine on a doctor for the practice of medicine without a license, when the Royal College was entitled to keep the proceeds thereof. The judgment of Edward Coke echoed some very familiar propositions about the interaction of the criminal and natural law, which could address either or both of two questions: does the Parliament have the legal power to act in certain ways; and if it does not, how should its various enactments be overturned or construed when they appear to violate the principles of natural law? Coke answered the second question by *construing* the statute narrowly when the question was whether conviction for the illegal practice of medicine allowed for the defendant's incarceration. This "principle of lenity" stems from the proposition that the criminal law should be read to favor the subject, owing to the seriousness of the punishment handed down for committing the offense. In its modern incarnation, the principle is associated with a clear statement rule, which indicates that the loss of traditional common law rights should be only cautiously inferred in cases of ambiguity. But an unambiguous statement of the punishments that may be imposed and the procedures that are used to impose them can defeat both of these rules of construction.

The first question raises more momentous considerations, because Coke holds that the Parliament (or Congress) has no power to pass these laws at all. In *Dr. Bonham's Case*, Coke advanced the proposition with these words:

> And it appears in our books, that in many cases, the common law will controul Acts of Parliament, and sometimes adjudge them to be utterly void: for when an Act of Parliament is against common right and reason, or repugnant, or impossible to be performed, the common law will controul it, and adjudge such Act to be void.[24]

These words appear to carry a very broad sweep and could easily make the courts a roving commission to invalidate any law that does not meet the test of "common right and reason." But in fact they ring true in the narrow context of this conflict of interests case, for the prohibition against bias is regarded as an essential component of "natural law" in the English administrative law tradition, which applies in virtually all cases. The decision does not venture to address the underlying substantive issue of whether the Royal College should have the power to license at all. But political constraints often mediate this crisis. Even if the British constitution, unlike our own, offers no protection against biased processes, in stable times the blatant illustrations of this practice will rarely persist, even if protection against the practice is not guaranteed.

Dr. Bonham's Case, however, did not survive in its narrowest sense. The greatest English legal authority before the formation of the United States was William Blackstone, whose views on this subject reflected the dominant position of many of the thorniest issues of his day. Among the many theoretical tensions in Blackstone's work is that which arises between his strong commitment to the common law institutions of private property, resting on a theory of natural law, and his insistence on the total dominance of Parliament, from whose laws there is no escape, even by the exercise of some supposed Lockean right of revolution. Blackstone is candid, almost to a fault, about the proposition that "if the parliament will positively enact a thing to be done which is unreasonable, I know of no power . . . [that] control[s] it;" for "to set the judicial power above that of the legislature . . . would be subversive of all government."[25] And later on when he speaks of the "jurisdiction of parliament" as "transcendent and absolute," he cites Edward Coke, ironically, and Montesquieu to back him up.[26] There is then no evidence in the work of the legal theorists who influenced our Constitution that speaks of judicial supremacy. So, quite simply, what happened?

5

———————◆———————

Marbury *and* Martin

THE PRE-1787 historical materials supply vital clues to the original
constitutional arrangements on judicial review, but they give little
insight to the path of its eventual evolution. Quite simply, the American Constitution entrenches the judicial power against both the legislature and the executive. But that entrenchment only makes sure that
neither the Congress nor the president can contract the Court's jurisdiction. Neither separation of powers nor checks and balances necessarily allows the Court to rule over either the two political branches
of the federal government or over the states. They merely protect the
judiciary's distinctive institutional competence from political incur-
sions. Nor should this be a surprise: separation of powers calls for the
division of power between two or more branches, but does not specify
exactly what that division should be or why. There is, as John Manning
has observed, no "freestanding" principle of separation of powers that
can be read onto the Constitution.[1] There is no Separation of Powers
Clause, nor was there a detailed public understanding of what the concept required at the time of the Founding. It takes a far more specific
examination to determine how the principle has been instantiated in
the Constitution.

To this point it can be added that the principles of separation of powers, on the one hand, and checks and balances on the other, are always
in tension with each other, for each check diminishes how separate each
sphere of action is from another branch. There is no specific balance of
these twin principles that clearly produces some uniquely right result.
The only thing that can be said with confidence is that some mix of the

two principles is better than a monolithic government, or even a government that rejected checks and balances as it embraced separation of powers. The best reading is that the Constitution balanced the two principles, providing for judicial parity, but not for judicial supremacy.

Read in the spirit in which it was written, the scope of judicial power seems easy to delineate, no matter how unwise parts of the basic scheme seem in retrospect. The provisions that establish the Supreme and inferior federal courts are brief and to the point:

> Section 1. The judicial power of the United States, shall be vested in one Supreme Court, and in such inferior courts as the Congress may from time to time ordain and establish. . . .
>
> Section 2. The judicial power shall extend to all cases, in law and equity, arising under this Constitution, the laws of the United States, and treaties made, or which shall be made, under their authority; . . .
>
> In all cases affecting ambassadors, other public ministers and consuls, and those in which a state shall be party, the Supreme Court shall have original jurisdiction. In all the other cases before mentioned, the Supreme Court shall have appellate jurisdiction, both as to law and fact, with such exceptions, and under such regulations as the Congress shall make.[2]

These precise technical provisions raise several points that bear prominent notice. The first is that the creation of the inferior federal courts is subject to the will of Congress, which thus enjoys an obvious check on the power of the judiciary. It can now abolish much of the judiciary on a wholesale basis, without any showing of cause. All the excess work thus moves into state courts, which have plenary jurisdiction to hear any and all types of cases. The second point is that the Constitution expressly imposes a broad and explicit limitation on the appellate jurisdiction of the Supreme Court—that is, the right to hear an appeal from the inferior courts. (The term "District Court" for a court of first instance is not in Article III. It is introduced only in the Judiciary Act of 1789.) The natural meaning of the text is that Congress, if it chooses, may impose any exceptions and regulations to the Court's jurisdiction, whether based on the type of party or the type of cause that is involved. The only portion of the Supreme Court's jurisdiction that is secure is its original jurisdiction over the limited class of disputes that involve sovereign parties and their official representatives. The obvious explanation for that allocation is that the Founders wanted to create a credible forum in which the United States could litigate its international disputes, which is not possible if the Congress could just withdraw that jurisdiction in its desire to avoid its obligations to foreign sovereigns. The basic structure may not make the Supreme Court look puny, but it does suggest that it is on a short congressional leash. The length of that leash was lengthened, however, in the two important cases decided by the Marshall Court mentioned below, *Marbury* and *Martin*.

Marbury v. Madison

Like most great cases, *Marbury* arose out a simple legal dispute, albeit one with great political import at the time.[3] In the tumultuous final days of the administration of John Adams, he appointed William Marbury as a justice of the peace for Washington, D.C. Although Marbury's papers were signed and sealed, they were not delivered. Once the change in administration took place, William Marbury brought suit against James Madison, the new secretary of state, under Section 13 of the Judiciary Act of 1789, demanding delivery of the commission. In order for Marbury to win his case, he had to show that he was entitled to receive the written confirmation of his office, which therefore had to vest when the commission was signed and sealed by the president, even if delivery had not taken place. That conclusion is subject to some controversy because the rule with respect to ordinary sealed writings is that the gift is only effective once the delivery is made, so there is good reason to think that the vesting occurs only when the commission is out of the hands of the president. If so, Marbury should have lost for the most prosaic of reasons: his appointment had not taken effect in time.

For Chief Justice John Marshall's purposes, however, it would have never sufficed to decide the case on such narrow grounds. Instead, the case only gains urgency when the commission is valid, so that the question is whether Marbury may seek to obtain his commission by a suit in the United States Supreme Court. The relevant provision was Section 13 of the Judiciary Act, which reads in part:

> The Supreme Court shall also have appellate jurisdiction from the circuit courts and courts of the several states, in the cases herein after specially provided for; and shall have power to issue writs of prohibition to the district courts, when proceeding as courts of admiralty and maritime jurisdiction, and writs of mandamus, in cases warranted by the principles and usages of law, to any courts appointed, or persons holding office, under the authority of the United States.

Marshall began the discussion by noting the difference between original and appellate jurisdiction, explaining that in its latter capacity the Court "revises and corrects" the proceedings in a cause already instituted. One way to decide the case was to hold that the entire section refers only to appellate jurisdiction so that the statute did not confer original jurisdiction on the Supreme Court at all, thus making the case go away without reaching any constitutional question. The contrary argument is that after the words "provided for," the remainder of the section dealt with a mix of appellate and original jurisdiction, where in some cases the Supreme Court would address other courts ("to any courts") and in others directly to those "persons holding office, under the authority of the United States."

The question of whether Section 13 confers original jurisdiction could go either way. Yet Marshall was spoiling for a fight, so this prosaic statutory ground would not do. For his long-term institutional agenda, it was more important *how* Marbury lost, rather than *whether* he lost. So Marshall went forward on the assumption that the statute allows this valid cause of action to be brought as an original matter in the Supreme Court, only to strike that law down as unconstitutional.

But why? Marshall began with a long disquisition on the relative hierarchy between mere statutory law and constitutional law. He held virtually as a matter of iron logic that in cases of conflict the statute must yield to the Constitution, so that the action had to be dismissed on this ground since Congress could not confer original jurisdiction on the United States Supreme Court in the Judiciary Act. Under the Constitution, that original jurisdiction covered "all cases affecting Ambassadors, other public Ministers and Consuls, and those to which a state shall be a Party."[4] Lowly justices of the peace fall into none of these exalted categories, so that the Supreme Court cannot be forced to hear them any more than it can be forced to take original jurisdiction in cases involving land title in United States territory. The interpretive issues presented in this case are black and white.

This form of limited judicial control was not novel when *Marbury* was decided. As Philip Hamburger shows in detail in *Law and Judicial Duty*,[5] decisions of this sort were well established in the Thirteen Colonies. One example of this pattern is found in the so-called *Ten Pound Cases* from New Hampshire.[6] As in *Marbury*, lower court judges protected their own jurisdiction from the state legislature by refusing to allow the question of release from debtor's prison to be decided without a trial by jury.[7] The underlying New Hampshire statute stipulated that lawsuits asking for less than ten pounds were to be tried without a jury, in contravention of a New Hampshire constitutional guarantee of a jury trial for over forty shillings, or two pounds. As in *Marbury*, this state claim of unconstitutional legislative power involved the courts only in their defensive posture. The legislature could not order them to use statutory procedures to try cases when the state constitution provides otherwise.

Marbury shared key characteristics with that decision. Since the Court refused to take jurisdiction over the case, it did not have to supply any remedy to Marbury and his coplaintiffs, thereby avoiding any political confrontation with the new administration of Thomas Jefferson. This course of action had the delicious irony that Marshall (who had been an official in the Adams administration) ruled against his own former administration. But dismissing the action did not require him to enlist the cooperation of either the legislative or executive branch because there was nothing for them to do once Marbury just lost. The case therefore did not present an explicit clash between the branches to the point of requiring the enforcement of a judgment against the defendant.

But just how did Marshall get there? For openers, he lifted an argument straight out of Hamilton's *Federalist No. 78*, that any actions of Congress inconsistent with the Constitution were "void" and thus of no effect: "[A] law repugnant to the Constitution is void, and that courts, as well as other departments, are bound by that instrument."[8] Shortly before, Marshall uttered the now famous sentence as to why "It is emphatically the province and duty of the judicial department to say what the law is."[9] He did not present himself as an interloper, but merely as a slave to duty. These two bold statements undergird a strong claim to judicial supremacy over the other branches by virtue of the Court's ability to strike down all laws in conflict with the Constitution. But the next sentence is far wimpier, by suggesting that, when all is said and done, the judiciary's power to say what the law is must be confined to the cases directly before it, or to those laws, such as the Judiciary Act, that deal with judicial administration more generally: "Those who apply the rule to particular cases, must of necessity expound and interpret that rule."[10] Marshall's retreat echoes Hamilton's argument in *Federalist*

No. 78, where he first acknowledges that the courts "must ultimately depend upon the aid of the executive arm even for the efficacy of its judgments."[11] And then, citing Montesquieu, Hamilton endorses the view that the inability to control either the purse or the sword "proves incontestably that the judiciary is beyond comparison the weakest of the three departments of power; that it can never attack with success either of the other two; and that all possible care is requisite to enable it to defend itself against their attacks."[12] The reason the judiciary is the weakest of the three branches is that it only possesses the defensive powers that the theory of parity confers upon it.

Marshall's equivocation in *Marbury* consciously replicates Hamilton's, whose passages read as if the executive, except when executing judgments, stands in parity with the judiciary in the interpretation of the laws. Likewise, the Congress has a like duty to determine the constitutionality of its own measures. Marshall's own account of the Court's power does not quite accord it pride of place over the other branches except insofar as it relates to the adjudication and enforcement of individual cases, where judicial independence, a la Montesquieu, is imperative. Nor do Marshall's examples support any proposition that the legislature and executive must in all cases bend to the Court's will. So what if the Constitution provides that conviction for treason requires the testimony of two witnesses, not just one?[13] Or that no court shall convict under a bill of attainder (that singles out a single person) or under an ex post facto law, in the teeth of constitutional prohibitions to the contrary?[14] So what if judges ought not "close their eyes on the constitution" if the states seek to collect prohibited taxes on "articles exported from any state"?[15] These are all situations that deal with the judicial administration of various constitutional provisions that do nothing to make good on a claim of judicial supremacy.

These instructive examples are subject to two implicit limitations. First, the claim of constitutional priority over statutes is stated only in cases where the conflict between laws is too apparent to deny in good faith. Yet it is more difficult to claim a conflict between the Constitution and a particular law when the Court must decide whether a particular regulation, advanced to prevent, say, fraud, constitutes an unconstitutional restriction of the freedom of speech. Now no simple comparison between two texts is able to resolve the conflict. Even more critical is the sneaky way that Marshall, following Hamilton, chose his examples. Like the *Ten Pound Cases*,[16] all of them involve situations where the legislature or the executive seeks to force courts to take cases that are not theirs to decide, or to decide cases under rules that contravene the Constitution. At this point, there is no need to claim the superiority of the Court over its two parallel institutions. All that is needed is an assertion of judicial parity within a system that requires some cooperation between the branches on the judicial control over individual cases in ways that respects the Court's independence.

Indeed there is more. The Exceptions Clause,[17] which allows Congress to strip the Supreme Court of its appellate jurisdiction when it pleases, is jarringly out of place in a regime of judicial supremacy. But it makes perfectly good sense as written if judicial review *only* allows courts to ward off demands that they hear cases beyond their purview. Yet defenders of the modern sense of judicial review turn cartwheels to make this clause mean anything but what it says. Thus Henry Hart, its most influential exponent, claims that the basic proposition here is that Congress cannot "destroy the essential role of the Supreme Court in the constitutional plan," which neatly sidesteps the question of what that plan is.[18] The judicial ability to repel inappropriate cases does not allow courts to reach out and take the appellate cases they want to hear. So whatever the desirability of Hart's vision of a strong system of judicial review, the Constitution looks as though it just updated Locke and Montesquieu to preserve the independence of the judges in a system that features the strong separation of powers.

It is important to keep this in perspective. Measured against past practices, the Court's ability to hunker down against the combined might of the Congress and the president should not be deprecated as a puny achievement. Indeed, it would be a major mistake to assume that *Marbury*'s logic extends only to disputes that go to the original or appellate jurisdiction of the Supreme Court. Rightly read, *Marbury*'s implications are more profound. The decision necessarily preserves for the Supreme Court—and by implication, all lower federal courts and all state courts— the right to determine the constitutionality of any substantive law that is relevant to any case that comes before it. Thus, if the president seeks to imprison someone for subversive libel—remember the Alien and Sedition Acts of 1798[19]—he must bring that case before some court which then has the constitutional duty to see whether the government's action is in conformity with the Constitution. The same result applies in cases of habeas corpus. In similar fashion, any seizures of property must also be routed through an entrenched independent judiciary.

Andrew Jackson therefore overreacted when uttering his famous remark that "John Marshall has made his decision: *now let him enforce it!*"[20] That element of executive cooperation through enforcement of particular judgments is required by the basic structure of the Constitution. But Jackson *was* on firmer ground when, in vetoing the rechartering of the Second Bank of the United States, he said that "the opinion of the judges has no more authority over Congress than the opinion of Congress has over the judges, and on that point the President is independent of both."[21] The entrenched judiciary does not mean that the courts can override a presidential veto that is based on constitutional arguments that the courts rejected. Nor does it allow the courts to enjoin the activities of the president to set up a bank or to conduct wiretaps even when the Court has found these activities unconstitutional. The judicial-centered reading of *Marbury* offers individuals protection only against arbitrary executive action in cases where they have sought and obtained judicial relief. Any broader conception of the judicial role is at odds with the English regime of parliamentary supremacy. However, even the narrow conception of judicial review implements every safeguard for individual liberty that Locke and Montesquieu thought would come from an independent judiciary.

It was for good reason, then, that Hamilton called the courts "the least dangerous" branch, because they possessed neither the power of the purse nor the sword.[22] He was working under the more restrictive tradition in which courts could not stop independent legislative or executive action. Habeas corpus only kicked in after a person was placed in detention; it gave the individual no way to contest the legality of legislation or executive action *before* detention was imposed. So this system was far from ideal even in individual cases. And therein lies Marshall's genius. He played consciously on the ambiguity of the historical record in order to create the impression that, in the words of David Currie, "the courts were intended to enforce constitutional limits on legislative power," a far broader proposition.[23] And in time, but without real argument, that is just what happened. But it took 155 years, for only in *Cooper v. Aaron*[24] did the Supreme Court for the first time clearly articulate that its power let it order the president to call out the National Guard to quell the resistance against its desegregation order.

In *Cooper v. Aaron*, all the nuances about the scope of original juris-diction were forgotten. Instead, the Court relied on two propositions that now carry the day: first, that the Constitution is higher than any state law and second, Marshall's earlier statement, now skillfully wrenched out of its historical context, that "It is emphatically the province and duty of the judicial department to say what the law is."[25] As an origi-nalist matter, at least, all this is clearly wrong. There is no question that President Eisenhower had the power to call out the National Guard to enforce any desegregation order, even if the courts could not require him to do so. What the decision did was to give Eisenhower political cover against southern charges that he intervened on his own accord. But make no mistake that the long-term battle with segregation was not solely a judicial function. Indeed the Fourteenth Amendment's enforce-ment provision is not judge-centered, but in fact Section 5 states quite the opposite: "The Congress shall have the power to enforce, by appro-priate legislation, the provisions of this article." The amendment makes no mention of the independent judicial enforcement that marks the major developments under the Court's Fourteenth Amendment juris-prudence, including, notably, *Brown v. Board of Education*.[26] Any complete transformation cannot, of course, be justified on originalist grounds. But these epochal decisions have now lasted for three generations. With the passage of time, who would ever want to undo their outcome?

Martin v. Hunter's Lessee

The second of the great early constitutional cases on the scope of judi-cial power was *Martin v. Hunter's Lessee*.[27] The dispute revolved around the ownership of extensive Virginia lands (in which John Marshall claimed an interest and thus recused himself). Martin claimed that the anti-confiscation treaties with Great Britain protected his title against Hunter's claim, which derived from the Virginia state legislature. After much wrangling, the Virginia courts favored Hunter's Virginia title. The Supreme Court denied that title by giving full weight to the Treaty of Paris that ended the Revolutionary War and the Jay Treaty of 1794, which protected the property of British sympathizers.[28] Accordingly, it ordered the Virginia courts to transfer the land to Martin. No way, came the Virginia court's response, arguing that the Supreme Court cannot exercise appellate jurisdiction over the state courts, even when a state court denies the validity of a federal claim. In Virginia's view, Section 25 of the Judiciary Act, which purported to give the Supreme Court appellate power over state court judgments, was therefore void. However, Justice Story (writing because Marshall had recused himself) rejected that view and held that appellate jurisdiction existed. And once again, as a textual and originalist matter, it looks as though he was wrong, perhaps even clearly so.

Justice Story's initial sally was that the words of Article III, "the Judicial power of the United States shall extend to all cases in law and equity," not only conferred the right on the Supreme Court to hear cases that implicated federal questions, but under certain circumstances, including the circumstances of this case, imposed on the Court the duty to hear such cases. As an initial matter, any claim that the word "power" connotes "duty" seems clearly erroneous. The commerce power may give the Congress the power to regulate commerce, but it hardly compels Congress to exercise that power to its full extent. And it hardly follows that any articulation of the judicial power means that Congress must provide at least one avenue whereby any federal question can be subject to review by a federal court. Rather, the scope of the judicial power is determined by the cases that Article III brings within the purview of the courts.

Yet Story sought in large measure to combat this conclusion by invoking the Supremacy Clause, which reads as follows:

This Constitution, and the laws of the United States which shall be made in pursuance thereof; and all treaties made, or which shall be made, under the authority of the United States, shall be the supreme law of the land; and the judges in every state shall be bound thereby, anything in the Constitution or laws of any State to the contrary notwithstanding.[29]

There is no doubt that this provision is intended to create a degree of uniformity across the states by holding that the lowliest federal regulation trumps even the highest state law that is in conflict with it. But in this different context, Story repeats Marshall's mistake by confusing the question of hierarchy of legal norms with the question of who gets to make the decision of how that hierarchy is constructed. The Supremacy Clause here does not refer to any federal review of state courts. Rather, consistent with the general principle of constitutional decentralization, it charges the *judges* in every state with the duty to follow the Constitution. Ironically, if all constitutional questions had the clarity of those posed by Marshall in his account of original jurisdiction, this remedy would be perfectly adequate. No honest judge trained in the law could confuse two witnesses with one, enforce a bill of attainder, or collect a tax on exports. But the complexity of the legal issues in *Martin* clearly invited principled disagreement. So long, therefore, as the state court judges discharged their duty, the Supremacy Clause did not offer the necessary path to uniformity that Story demanded. To Story, the persistence of these "jarring and discordant judgments" could not have been contemplated by the "enlightened convention."[30] He conveniently ignores the possibility that the Framers marched to a more cautious drummer when they provided that the interposition of state court judges would supply a useful check on the nationalist ambitions of federal judges like Story.

The Supremacy Clause then offers no support for the omnipresent claims of federal judicial power. The same is true with respect to the language in Article III, quoted above, that sets out the scope of the appellate power of the Supreme Court. Recall that after setting out the cases in which the United States Supreme Court exercises original jurisdiction, the Constitution offers a concise list of cases in which the Court has appellate jurisdiction. And in so doing, it limits appellate jurisdiction to "all the other Cases before mentioned," all of which arise in the lower federal courts, assuming of course that Congress chose to create them. Indeed, there could not be "appeals" from state courts because they operate in a separate legal system. Nor can it be inferred that the Constitution's list of cases is not exhaustive, for it covers every single case of federal jurisdiction. It is only the Supremacy Clause that covers decisions made in state courts.

It looks therefore as though there are some cases in which the Supreme Court cannot hear a constitutional matter. Story is right to say that the Congress could both create lower courts and pass statutes allowing defendants sued in state court to remove their cases to federal courts. More crucially, however, he did not factor into the analysis the simple point that Congress had no obligation to exercise its power under the Exceptions Clause to block an appeal from the lower federal courts to the Supreme Court. By design, these two checks on the federal judicial power were placed solely within the control of Congress. It therefore becomes incongruous to argue that since some cases can run the gauntlet to reach the Supreme Court if Congress lets them, all cases *must* make it to the Court even if Congress explicitly blocks either removal or appeals, or both. Once again, putting all the pieces together, we see a Constitution that is wary of federal judicial power and (all too) solicitous of state judges. This second experiment with federalism gave Congress far more power than it had under the Articles of Confederation. But it did not guarantee that the Supreme Court had the last word on all matters of judicial interpretation.

The Prescriptive Approach to Judicial Power

What then should be made of the situation that strips the Supreme Court of its distinctive powers to invalidate both federal and state legislation? Viewed with the benefit of hindsight, these changes have to be regarded as unassailable under our prescriptive constitution, born of long and successful usage. Now that we have some distance on the issue, we can see these early decisions neutralized some serious errors in the original constitutional design. Historically, the Framers were so intent on compromise that they did not clearly see the transformations that were needed in order to make Montesquieu's vision of separation of powers work in the context of a presidential system within a federal nation. No longer could "the" legislature act as the single arbitrator of all disputes. Now there was competition from self-interested political parties at both the federal and state levels that made it impossible for the system to articulate any uniform conception of law. It was not only that the president could veto the Second National Bank when the Court held it constitutional, but also that the president and Congress could set up a Second National Bank that the Court had held unconstitutional. After all, the business of government goes far beyond litigation, even if the power of judicial review was confined to it.

As a policy matter, it seems clear that once the new nation was put in place, those two gaps in the original structure had to be plugged, and fast. The system could not run without lower federal courts or without some judicial check on the powers of state courts to strike down federal legislation. Clearly that judgment was made by the Congress when it enacted the Judiciary Act of 1789 before the ink had fully dried on the original Constitution. All the equivocations and compromises needed to get the Constitution through the ratification process no longer seemed to make any sense once the national government was up and running. Is it really possible to think that a great nation could ever operate without the existence of lower federal courts, so that all trials would have to take place within the states? Clearly any such notion was gone from day one, never to return. And once those courts are in place, does it make sense to tolerate a stalemate between the Congress and the executive, while leaving the courts powerless to make sure that the president and the Congress stay within their proper spheres? Inconsistent policies could then take hold at the federal level, and the states could stray from the original constitutional plan. In addition, federal actions could encroach on the domain of the states with no common arbiter. Likewise, the states could adopt inconsistent interpretations of key constitutional provisions, with no independent decider to act as tiebreaker. Both Marshall and Story had the right constitutional instinct that the fluid and indeterminate nature of the situation was untenable, even if they did not have, as it were, the right constitutional text to fix the problem.

It is unclear in retrospect whether either or both of these towering figures had some awareness of the extent to which their novel judgments remade the original constitutional plan. But it is equally clear that, as a political matter, they made the *right* call on both questions, which is why the prescriptive strength of both these decisions, resting on long usage, is so unassailable. Under the conventional modern view, it is manifestly better for the nation as a whole that the Supreme Court has the power of judicial review over any and all legislation, whether state or federal, even though that concentration of power has to make anyone nervous. But this judgment is far *more* sound if we reject the modern progressive synthesis that goes out of its way, even after *Marbury* and *Martin*, to ensure that no structural or individual rights claim stands in the way of the ability of the federal government—and failing that, the states—to regulate general economic and social activities under the highly forgiving rational basis standard of review.

To put this matter in perspective, the classical liberal conception of government starts from very different premises. All proposals that deviate from the basic common law protections of life, liberty, and property should reach the legislature under a presumption of error. Accordingly, the appropriate attitude toward government is one that seeks to slow down, not speed up, the pace of new legislation on these matters. In their own deliberations, it would be absurd for either the Congress or the president to adopt the stance of the rational basis test, which allows them the luxury of their own mistakes. There is no coherent way in which a judicial standard that calls out for deference to the political branches can counsel either of those branches to be deferential to the judiciary in exercising its own powers. Rather, their internal deliberations should be conducted on a strict scrutiny standard, where they do their level best to make sure that their own actions conform with the Constitution. And if they take that duty seriously, then the question of judicial review would be of little consequence because the members of Congress would likely refuse to pass and the president would likely refuse to sign any purported legislation that expanded the scope of their powers beyond their constitutional limits. Conscientious behavior in the political branches could easily undermine the need for judicial review.

Unfortunately, political actors are loath to enforce against themselves any limits on their legal power. It is, to take one recent example, inconceivable that anyone could vote with a clear conscience, as did Senator Arlen Specter, in favor of giving detainees at Guantanamo Bay, in lieu of habeas corpus, highly restrictive rights of access that he believed, rightly, to be wholly unconstitutional.[31] But it becomes easier to vote in favor of unconstitutional laws with the courts there to guard against these political lapses at both the federal and state levels. Given this utter want of self-control, it makes perfectly good sense for the courts to ride herd over the political branches. The prescriptive constitution thus has its greatest force on these questions. The imperfections of the original design were ironed out by powerful decisions whose internal logic nonetheless looks attractive within the constitutional design. That transformation, while welcome on balance, comes, of course, at a price. The judiciary is no longer the least dangerous branch, with neither the purse nor the sword, when it has a huge veto power. Now the least dangerous claim rests instead on the view that the power of judicial review only allows the courts to block legislation, not to implement it. And that, in turn, means that uneasy cases arise when courts seek to order legislatures to appropriate funds to prisons, schools, welfare, or health care. This increased license for judicial intervention becomes more problematic when the courts more eagerly accept the progressive mandate to enforce these positive rights, which are alien to our original constitutional plan.[32] Viewed in this light, many of the more recent developments in constitutional law amount to a retreat from the strong version of *Marbury v. Madison*; some of these modern decisions are, in any event, inconsistent with *Marbury*'s court-centered view. The following chapters turn to the modern legacy of *Marbury* through an analysis of the law governing standing, ripeness, and the political question doctrine.

6

Standing

Background and Origins

T HE AGGRESSIVE REACH of judicial review first articulated in *Marbury v. Madison* frequently puts courts at loggerheads with the political branches of government. In some cases, their relationships follow the predictable course, as each branch seeks to expand its own power at the expense of its rivals. But the diverse range of constitutional conflicts, ancient and modern, make it perilous, even in retrospect, to offer any generalizations about these power struggles. Indeed, courts often seek to rid themselves of matters dumped into their lap. *Marbury* itself sounded that cautionary trope. It is therefore appropriate to start with *Marbury* before turning to the historical evolution of standing.

After Marbury

Chief Justice Marshall was willing to wade where courts could find demonstrable standards to resolve concrete questions—such as whether Marbury's commission had to be delivered to take effect—but quickly backed off matters that required an exercise of political discretion—such as whether Marbury should have been appointed in the first place.[1] In making this distinction, Marshall followed the venerable British practice that reserved the writ of mandamus ("we command") for nondiscretionary acts. Marshall well understood that courts had no power to initiate cases. Their province was to decide cases that others initiated, not to be roving commissions that injected themselves into political disputes. That was the province of the legislature. Nor could any court exercise the continuous oversight needed to organize national defense. That was the job of the president. The division of labor undergirds separation of powers. One inherent limitation on the power of judicial review is that the courts cannot perform the work of all three branches on their own.

Explicit textual provisions also cordon off certain actions from judicial review. The Constitution provides for a distinct system of impeachment, which involves the cooperative efforts of the House as prosecutor and the Senate as judge.[2] In presidential impeachments, the chief justice of the Supreme Court presides.[3] But no independent judicial review overrides the final vote of the Senate, for courts cannot interpose their own view of what types of actions constitute high crimes or misdemeanors. Some measure of judicial diffidence is compelled when the Constitution states, "Each House shall be the Judge of the Elections, Returns, and Qualifications of its Own Members."[4] Likewise, limitation on judicial review follows from the constitutional provision providing that "for any Speech or Debate in either House, they [the members] shall not be questioned in any other Place."[5] Similarly, Article IV leaves the Congress to decide whether new states shall be admitted to the union, subject to certain limitations against the forced merger of two states.[6] And Article V on constitutional amendments has been read to let Congress, not the courts, decide whether a state can ratify an amendment that it initially rejected, thirteen years after it was proposed.[7]

These provisions are unexceptionable in a world of narrow judicial review, previously explicated and now discarded, that lets courts superintend their own jurisdiction but does not permit them to oversee the workings of a coordinate branch of government. But asking courts to carve out further exceptions to their power of judicial review is more problematic in the absence of any such strict prohibition on their general powers.

From a limited government perspective, a broad conception of judicial review, as sanctified by long usage, is desirable precisely because it places additional obstacles in the path of new legislation. To be sure, if all branches of government were equally scrupulous, the endless debate over who enjoys the last word would be inconsequential because all public officials would act as one in single-minded devotion to the Constitution. But on this side of heaven that type of institutional self-abnegation is not in the cards. So the extra hurdle of judicial review is one way to vindicate the presumption against unbridled state power, which is one reason why classical liberals speak of its virtues while modern social democrats put (undue) confidence in political deliberation.[8] But what limitations on judicial review are consistent with the expansive reading of *Marbury*? This chapter examines one such limitation on judicial review whose very function is to undermine that broad conception: the doctrine of standing.

Constitutional Pedigree

The power of judicial review under *Marbury* is subject to one key limitation. The Supreme Court has no power to initiate litigation. It can only strike down laws in the context of legal disputes. One clear consequence of this view is that the Supreme Court, unlike, for example, the Massachusetts Supreme Judicial Court, is not in a position to issue advisory opinions. That point became well established as early as 1793 when the then chief justice, John Jay, in correspondence with President George Washington, refused to issue an advisory opinion on United States treaty obligations with Great Britain and France. In this instance, he did not appeal to the doctrine of standing, but instead relied on the notion of separation of powers when he wrote:

> The lines of Separation drawn by the Constitution between the three Departments of Government, their being in certain Respects checks on each other, and our being judges of a court in the last Resort, are Considerations which afford strong arguments against the Propriety of our extrajudicially deciding the questions alluded to; especially as the Power given by the Constitution to the President of calling on the Heads of Departments for opinions, seems to have been purposely as well as expressly limited to executive Departments.[9]

A similar issue arose in *Hayburn's Case*,[10] where congressional legislation sought to charge federal courts with nonjudicial duties in allowing Revolutionary War veterans to apply for pensions. Three circuit courts refused to perform this task, and the case was eventually bucked up to the Supreme Court, which took the position that the Court could not, consistent with Article III, exercise "any power not in its nature judicial, or, if judicial, not provided for upon the terms the Constitution requires."[11] The Congress then avoided a head-to-head confrontation by amending the statute before it went into effect. Yet once again the objection to the statute was that it asked courts to perform legislative tasks. No thought was given to the proposition that the applicants lacked standing to prosecute their cases, which they surely had even under today's rules.

These early exercises of judicial restraint therefore do not represent the kinds of cases and controversies to which the standing requirement is routinely applied. The idea of standing rests on independent grounds that can be captured in plain English, wholly without regard to any distinctive limitation found in Article III. The basic problem is inherent in all litigation. A complains to B about B's shabby treatment of C. The response to A comes back, "You don't have standing to raise that issue. Let C speak for herself if she wants to." The popular response is understood by all not to be a judgment on the merits of the case. It only indicates that the issue was voiced by the wrong person and should thus be ignored until the right person comes forward.

There is, of course, no reason why a refined version of standing cannot have a critical role in a judicial context, wholly apart from any doctrine of judicial review, and indeed wholly apart from any reference to the United States Supreme Court. Indeed, the standing doctrine gives rise to such legal knots precisely because its humble origins are systematically ignored. At the very least, the standing doctrine blunts, often unnecessarily, the application of *Marbury v. Madison*, even in those cases where the Constitution does not assign (as in cases of impeachment) final authority to either the Congress or the president. In addition, it spreads so broadly that it is invoked to resolve questions involving the joinder of proper parties and the choice of remedies that have little to do with the doctrine in the first place. How this odd state of affairs came to pass is an object lesson in the pitfalls of constitutional interpretation.

The explanation must begin with the prosaic observation that the doctrine of standing is one of the most venerable staples of modern constitutional law. The term "standing," however, makes no appearance in the text of Article III, where the opening words of Section 2 contemplate an expansive vision of the judicial power: "The judicial power shall extend to all cases, in Law and Equity, arising under this Constitution, the Laws of the United States, and Treaties made, or which shall be made, under their Authority."[12] Following this is a long list of cases and controversies organized by party (states, citizens, ambassadors) or kind of case (admiralty or marine jurisdiction). How then did the Supreme Court create by implication a doctrine to unceremoniously throw certain parties out of court, not because their cases are deficient on the merits, but because they are not in the proper position to sue at all?

The debate over standing has modest institutional importance so long as other parties are in a position to take up the battle against specific legislative enactments or executive actions. But the doctrine is so pernicious because, in some cases, *no one* counts as a proper party to press the case forward. And those cases arise far more frequently than one supposes. For example, the United States Treasury recently paid out money to Chrysler and General Motors under its Troubled Asset Relief (TARP) program, which in turn was funneled to pension funds controlled by the United Auto Workers union.[13] There was a real statutory question as to whether these payments were made to "financial institutions," as required under the TARP legislation. Yet no citizen or taxpayer was found to have standing to challenge the disbursement under the odd logic that harm to everyone counts as harm to no one at all.[14]

The origins of this potent standing doctrine date from two companion decisions issued in 1923: *Massachusetts v. Mellon* and *Frothingham v. Mellon*.[15] At issue was whether Congress could pay United States funds to the states in order to promote maternal and infant health under the Maternity Act.[16] The two suits sought to enjoin Andrew Mellon, then treasury secretary, from distributing funds pursuant to his mandate. But according to the Court, neither the private nor state party was in a position to protest the illegality. Nor, as it turned out, did anyone else have the concrete and particularized interest that would allow the litigation to go forward. In consequence, a program that required a major transformation of government power under the spending power[17] escaped review under *Marbury*. The implicit shift in power to the political branches needs no further comment.

Standing outside Constitutional Law

Before explaining why this decision makes no sense as a matter of either constitutional law or political theory, it is necessary to take a step back to examine a question posed earlier: does a standing doctrine make sense for *all* courts, not just the federal courts under Article III, which have limited jurisdiction and a peculiar constitutional pedigree? It does, but not in the way that *Frothingham* envisioned.

To see why, start with some history. The English courts have long adopted a standing doctrine, even though they exercise the type of unlimited jurisdiction that Article III denies to federal courts. The result is sensible enough. A runs down B with a truck: who should sue for B's injury? The right answer is surely B, not some stranger who has witnessed the accident from afar. A more delicate question is whether B's spouse or children may sue for any injuries stemming from the disruption of the family relationship. But the countless persons who knew and liked B are normally so numerous and far removed from the accident that it is easier to keep them out of the loop altogether.

So why is standing thought to be an essential part of the constitutional system, as opposed to a practical doctrine? One answer comes from Judge William Fletcher:

> The essence of a true standing question is the following: Does the plaintiff have a legal right to judicial enforcement of an asserted legal duty? This question should be seen as a question of substantive law, answerable by reference to the statutory or constitutional provision whose protection is invoked.[18]

In a similar vein, David Currie writes: "Whether the answer is labeled 'standing' or 'cause of action', the question is whether the statute or Constitution implicitly authorizes the plaintiff to sue."[19]

Neither position is correct. Saying that B has standing does *not* mean that B has a valid claim against A, let alone one based on a statute or the Constitution. B could lose on the facts if she cannot prove the negligence that state tort law requires for recovery, or if A shows that C hit B instead. B could also lose on the law if she tries to rely on a strict liability theory. Standing only determines who gets to complain about the loss in the first place, on grounds that could be either wise or foolish. The merits of the case, both as a matter of fact and law, raise entirely different issues. Accordingly, standing is best understood from a practical perspective: the best candidate for standing is a person who is exposed to a disproportionate fraction of the adverse consequences that allegedly flow from the action of the defendant. In principle that result is so intuitive, so utterly unrelated to the esoteric jurisprudence of Article III, that no one bothers to think about it in routine torts and contracts cases.

A Tripartite Test

The requirement of the disproportionate injury—whereby the individual plaintiff must show that his harm is greater than and different from that of the rest of the population—has worked itself into the fabric of the federal law of standing, which in its canonical form requires an aggrieved party to satisfy a tripartite test to press a claim in federal courts. *Lujan v. Defenders of Wildlife*[20] states the conventional wisdom:

> First, the plaintiff must have suffered an "injury in fact"—an invasion of a legally protected interest which is (a) concrete and particularized; and (b) "actual or imminent, not 'conjectural' or 'hypothetical.'" Second, there must be a causal connection between the injury and the conduct complained of—the injury has to be "fairly trace[able] to the challenged action of the defendant, and not th[e] result [of] the independent action of some third party not before the court." Third, it must be "likely," as opposed to merely "speculative," that the injury will be "redressed by a favorable decision."[21]

A moment's reflection will show that *each* of these three requirements is satisfied in the simple accident case where A drives his car into B. Nor does the Constitution have any special definition of what counts as an injury in fact. The ordinary tort system has to decide whether spouses or other family members suffer disproportionate injuries, which is generally held to be true for spouses, but not for children.[22] In other contexts, it is necessary to ask whether the destruction of a processing plant causes disproportionate harm to its major customers, where in general the law is ambivalent on when to supply a remedy.[23] There is no constitutional magic in dealing with these questions.

And therein lies the rub. A sensible doctrine of standing in cases of discrete injuries has *nothing* to do with the language of Article III or the distinctive role of the federal courts in *Frothingham*. Nor does it depend, as Justice Scalia elaborated in *Lujan*, on the principle of separation of powers that assigns the enactment of legislation to the Congress and its enforcement to the president.[24] All courts, domestic and foreign, federal and state, confer control over claims to the party with the largest stake in them.

Yet the standing doctrine in this form works in only one direction. For serious isolated injuries, it channels litigation so that the right people are the only ones with keys to the courthouse. But endowing this standing rule with a constitutional pedigree is wholly inconsistent with the language and structure of Article III, on the one hand, and the principle of judicial review, so critical for maintaining limited government, under *Marbury*, on the other. It is yet another instance of misguided originalism in the service of a mistaken version of judicial restraint. Article III,

Section 2 starts out with a bang: "The judicial power shall extend to all cases, in Law and Equity."[25] The words "extend" and "all" are not suitable vehicles for smuggling in a standing limitation. The conventional wisdom then locates Article III's supposed limitation on the power of the federal courts in the words "case" and/or "controversy." These words have some real pop in cases where either Congress or the president seek an advisory opinion from the Court (asking whether a certain act is constitutional)[26] or where the Court is asked to adjudicate a case that is "moot" because it is already settled. No conflict, no case, and no controversy.

The Supreme Court has developed a modest body of law on mootness and ripeness that requires some brief comment. The doctrine of mootness means just what it says. At the time of decision the case no longer involves an actual controversy between the two parties because the issue between them has been mooted or rendered irrelevant because of a change in events.[27] Yet that basic rule does not work well in those situations where it is said that the matter is "capable of repetition, yet evading review."[28] Those words were first uttered in connection with a rate regulation proceeding against a railroad, which raised issues that were sure to come up again as the Interstate Commerce Commission exercised its continuing jurisdiction. Thereafter, these words received their most famous articulation in *Roe v. Wade*,[29] where the Supreme Court decided to tackle the constitutionality of abortion even though Roe could not still be carrying a child conceived in 1970. On this point at least *Roe* surely seems correct, because the litigation is unnecessary until there is some prosecution of the operators of an abortion clinic; yet the litigation is sure to outlast the pregnancy. As a partial solution, the Supreme Court held that the correct procedure is to raise the constitutional question as a defense in the criminal case, and not by a declaratory judgment. Accordingly, the Court refused to hear the request for declaratory judgment by Dr. Halford, an intervenor in this case who was subject to criminal prosecution under Texas law.[30]

The ripeness cases typically follow similar lines, as the Supreme Court has held that if a case is not "ripe," there is no standing to bring it. Thus in *United Public Workers v. Mitchell*,[31] the Court refused to hear challenges to the Hatch Act, which forbade key federal employees from participating in political campaigns, that were brought by parties who desired some guidance on the scope of permissible activities long before any criminal case was brought. Once again the decision seems correct, because it would surely undermine the prohibition against advisory opinions to allow the expedient of joining in the present lawsuit a potential defendant in some future litigation as a way to secure a judicial decision. These cases show that the line between advisory opinions and actual controversies gives rise to some intermediate cases. But it does nothing to undermine the simple insight that where there is no actual conflict, there is no case and no controversy, and hence no federal jurisdiction under Article III.

The Conceptual Problem: Standing in Law and Equity

The big-league confrontation in *Frothingham* involved neither an effort to seek an advisory opinion nor a case or controversy that was moot. In light of the intensity of the dispute, there was controversy galore. The real question here is how to construe the phrase "cases in law and equity," which historically covers the dual system of courts in England and the United States. It is to ignore history to claim that the "law" side of the judicial system is the only one that matters. Thus Cass Sunstein wrongly writes:

> In the context of standing, the reluctance to take this step [to expand standing] has been embodied in a *private law* model of standing—that is, in the idea that standing should be reserved principally to people with *common law* interests and denied to people without such interests.[32]

In making this misguided assertion, Sunstein assumes that the common law model only covers tort-like actions, such as suits against public officials who seize property in order to foreclose on a tax lien. But that position confuses one kind of common law action—that for tortious harm—with the universe of common law actions, which for example always allowed actions for breach of contract and restitution as well. On Sunstein's view, the common law gave "statutory beneficiaries seeking judicial relief" short shrift on the ground that their interests were "legal gratuities." Yet that remarkable position was never, and could never have been, the common law. The parity between benefits withheld and harms caused was clearly articulated by Chief Justice Holt in a short opinion that states: "For wherever a statute enacts anything, or prohibits anything, for the advantage of any person, that person shall have a remedy to recover the advantage given him, or to have satisfaction for the injury done him."[33] There is no reason why standing is any more problematic when it is the government that refuses to perform its statutory obligation to a private party, like the payment of a contractual debt or even the payment of a tax refund.

The errors in Sunstein's position of equating the common law actions with tort actions is compounded by his failure (not unique to him) to take into account the profound role of courts of equity in the judicial system in both the United States and England at the time of the Founding. A short historical digression sets the background for understanding the situation.[34] Under the English practice (which carried over to the United States), the law courts (the King's Bench, the Exchequer, and the Court of Common Pleas) shared one feature in common: a sharply restricted set of remedies. Law courts could order the payment of damages or the return of property the defendant had taken from the plaintiff, but virtually nothing else. A complex legal system needs, however, additional remedies in order to operate effectively. Historically, equity courts evolved as the Lord Chancellor (the king's chief legal officer) first gave relief on an ad hoc basis to aggrieved parties by requiring defendants to perform certain acts on pain of being held in contempt— that is, jailed until certain actions were carried out. Later interventions systematized these remedial rules so that new forms of relief beyond damages were granted as a matter of course. One was an order of *specific performance* for a seller to convey land; another was to *foreclose* a mortgage when the underlying debt was unpaid; a third was an *injunction* to prohibit the sale of property to third parties. In many cases, both monetary damages from law courts and equitable relief from the chancellor were available. Indeed, one reason why today's federal and state judicial systems have unified the courts of law and equity is to permit judges to supply both kinds of relief in a single proceeding.[35] That reorganization of judicial business, of course, does nothing to expand or limit the scope of judicial power under Article III, which always covered both.

For our purposes, however, the key innovations of equity jurisprudence did not relate to sales and mortgages, but to the need for flexible remedies involving complex organizations such as partnerships, corporations, and charitable associations. Initially, these organizations were constituted like limited governments. Their charters permitted them to perform activities related to their core business, but prohibited them from performing acts *ultra vires*, or beyond their powers. The key legal challenge was how courts should respond when the officers or boards of directors exceeded their delegated powers under the charter. In response, courts of equity developed a system of derivative actions that allowed partners, shareholders, and members of charitable organizations to block the performance of proposed illegal transactions and undo the effects of completed illegal transactions. Thus, the Supreme Court itself has held that stockholders are entitled to relief in equity against members of a board of directors who refuse to resist the collection of a tax that might be challenged on constitutional grounds.[36]

These equitable lawsuits proceeded on assumptions that were diametrically opposed to the damages actions in collision cases. Standing in cases "at law" required allowing only the aggrieved party in a dispute with concentrated harms to call the shots. But the great innovations by courts of equity involved allowing suits by large numbers of dispersed individuals with identical small stakes—partners of a firm, members of a church, or shareholders in a corporation—none of whom stand out from the others. If the courts of equity followed the common law rules on standing, *no one* could bring the board of directors or the chief executive officer to heel. A wrong to everyone would be a wrong to no person in particular. The old maxim *ubi jus, ibi remedium*—where there is a right, there must be a remedy—would be systematically flouted in any dispute involving a broad class of individuals.

The courts of equity invoked their flexible remedial powers to avoid this absurd result. Any single partner, shareholder, or member could institute a class action on behalf of the others to enjoin future *ultra vires* acts or to undo (by seeking a return of property) completed ones. A second set of rules consolidated suits to prevent wasteful duplicative proceedings that could lead to inconsistent results. To deter frivolous litigation, the compensation for the class representative was contingent upon (and increased because of) successful prosecution of the case. That compensation was collected either from the defendants or from a fund to which all members of the partnership, corporation, or association contributed pro rata. This elegant system countered the serious free riding problems that would arise if the named plaintiff received no reward for initiating litigation from which all class members gained.

The equitable model of litigation has framed the modern development of class action litigation where many diffuse parties have small but common interests. In line with the basic classical liberal position, it is imperative therefore to look to these class arrangements to see how governments, like partnerships, corporations, and associations, can be forced to abide by the limits of their charters. The parallels here are easy enough to state. Partners, members, and shareholders are like citizens or taxpayers—persons who have a stake in the overall operation of a business. The officers of these bodies are like members of the executive branch. The board of directors functions like a legislative body.

So powerful are the analogies that they have been used with great success at the state level in dealing with abuses of power by local governments. The United States Supreme Court, for example, in *Crampton v. Zabriskie*,[37] let a local taxpayer sue to enjoin illegal government expenditures. Justice Stephen Field concluded emphatically that "it would seem eminently proper for courts of equity to interfere upon the application of the tax-payers of a county to prevent the consummation of a wrong, when the officers of those corporations assume, in excess of their powers, to create burdens upon property-holders."[38] Field found copious support for that proposition in John F. Dillon's well-known treatise on municipal corporations.[39] Note that this proposition did not say that anyone in the world had standing. It was limited to taxpayers, and thus did not include persons in the next town who might have opposed the particular expenditure on the ground of the economic inconvenience that it caused them. After all, it is no concern of theirs that another town has misapplied its own funds to an unlawful project. So understood, the broader doctrines of standing did not allow anyone who claimed to be harmed by actions to sue for that reason alone. The transition from public to private law was made without a hitch. The only ambiguous question is whether the right of suit should be limited to taxpayers or extend to all residents of the town. No big deal, for anyone determined to challenge government power can surely find someone who falls into the former category.

The Formative Period: 1920–1940

Taxpayer and Citizen Standing

In light of this history, why does the standing doctrine make suits "at law" off-limits against executive officers who go beyond their powers under the Constitution? The situation has greater urgency given the expanded scope of government activity in the wake of the progressive revolution. Yet on this issue the law headed off in the wrong direction—when a unanimous Supreme Court in *Frothingham* refused, in a decision written by the conservative Justice George Sutherland, to enjoin the Treasury's expenditures under the Maternity Act.

The merits of the dispute turned on the proper reading of the Spending Clause in Article I: "The Congress shall have Power To lay and collect Taxes, Duties, Imposts and Excises, and to pay the Debts and to provide for the common Defence and general Welfare of the United States."[40] The gist of Frothingham's challenge was that Congress should not be able to accomplish through grants under the Spending Clause what it could not accomplish through direct regulation under the Commerce Clause (as it was construed in 1923, before the Supreme Court's 1937 revolution).

The correct reading of "general Welfare of the United States" ensures that the same goal could not be achieved through the use of tax and/or spending policies. Permissible expenditures under the Constitution are tied to the use of public goods, which must be provided to all alike. To push hard on the corporate analogy, no one would ever say that a transfer payment from one shareholder to another would count as an expenditure for the general welfare of the corporation. That label would be properly reserved for expenditures that the corporation made to lift up the position of all shareholders simultaneously. The standard business judgment rule gives the directors much leeway in deciding which programs achieve that role—at least in the absence of their having entered into transactions where they stood on both sides of the deal, at which point the higher "fair value" standard would generally apply. At this point, the payments under the Maternity Act could not fall within the business judgment rule for government officials because their explicit purpose was to authorize transfer payments to discrete citizens.

The Maternity Act is thus doubly infirm under the Spending Clause. The first constraint is that actions that could not be done by direct regulation under the commerce power cannot be done through taxation and spending policies. The second constraint, wholly apart from the Commerce Clause, is that the internal logic of the Spending Clause blocks these transfer payments. A correct perception of the interconnection between regulation and taxation carried the day in another 1923 decision, the *Child Labor Tax Case*,[41] which held that Congress could not tax firms using child labor before they were allowed to send goods (whether or not made with child labor) into interstate commerce.

The only difference between *Frothingham* and the *Child Labor Tax Case* was that in the latter, the tax was challenged by the party whose operations were undermined, while in *Frothingham* the tax was challenged by a party who protested the way the money would be spent. That difference in procedural posture became decisive, because Frothingham did not have the same distinct pocketbook interest as the firms in the *Child Labor Tax Case*. But why should this procedural fine point matter to the larger question of constitutional structure? Sutherland raised the separation of powers issue—a total nonstarter—that has been repeatedly invoked to explain the doctrine. But the courts here are not asked to administer the Maternity Act; they are asked only to decide whether Congress can make those payments, which it cannot do if the expenditures are not authorized by the Constitution.

Why, it might be asked, should either Frothingham or Massachusetts care if any state can always take the high road and refuse to accept any tainted federal money? Note the shortcomings of that alternative. The revenues that the federal government spends are collected from the citizens of all states, Massachusetts included. Refusing to take the money does not put those tax dollars back into the hands of Massachusetts taxpayers. It only allows the Congress to increase the program expenditures to other states. And at this point, the principle of proportionality between income and expenditures is violated, as Massachusetts citizens are forced to subsidize citizens in states that will take the money. Unless, therefore, the state or its citizens can enjoin the program, they will find themselves on the horns of a prisoner's dilemma. To stay out of the program is to lose out financially. To participate is to abandon their constitutional principles.

Letting both citizens and states sue offers a much-needed escape from that dilemma. Absent standing to enjoin the program, every citizen and every state will prefer to sup at the federal trough instead of doing without the benefits once the tax has been imposed. Given the standing barrier, a program that could (and indeed does) fail on constitutional grounds now succeeds because neither state nor citizen can stop it in its tracks.

What about the precedents that let citizens and taxpayers enjoin local programs that are beyond the power of the municipal government?

Sutherland deflected that challenge by concluding that Massachusetts did not raise a "justiciable controversy, either in its own behalf or as the representative of its citizens."[42] In ordinary English, he thought that there was nothing to litigate. Thereafter, he brushed aside *Crampton v. Zabriskie* and the view articulated in Dillon's treatise:

> But the relation of a taxpayer of the United States to the Federal Government is very different [from a local taxpayer to the municipal government]. His interest in the moneys of the treasury—partly realized from taxation and partly from other sources—is shared with millions of others, is comparatively minute and indeterminable, and the effect upon future taxation, of any payment out of the funds, so remote, fluctuating and uncertain, that no basis is afforded for an appeal to the preventive powers of a court of equity.[43]

Sutherland blithely ignores the entire theory of equitable jurisdiction, where citizen or taxpayer standing becomes ever more imperative precisely because of the increase in the number of affected parties. So we have an unusual double. The so-called originalist position ignores the key words "in equity" to develop an erroneous theory of standing that lets no one attack a program violating the key structural provision of limited government.

That misunderstanding of the two heads of federal law had profound political consequences by narrowing the reach of the federal courts in dealing with constitutional challenges at the dawn of the administrative state. Sunstein takes the odd position that these early decisions all count as part of a conservative plot hatched by judges who were so enamored of the common law rights protected in *Lochner v. New York*[44] and so invested in the common law system of private rights (which Sunstein mischaracterizes), that they sought to thwart the expansion of the administrative state. Thus, Sunstein writes: "The interests of regulated industries could be protected through the courts, whereas the interests of regulatory beneficiaries were to be vindicated through politics or not at all."[45] His statement, as noted, was wrong with respect to regulatory beneficiaries so long as that class is confined to the individuals who were the recipients of statutory rights. But even if that error is put aside, it is hard to see any conservative drift in the early standing cases. These cases were decided by unanimous opinions and gave a chilly reception to novel claims brought by those individuals, like the plaintiffs in *Frothingham* and *Massachusetts*, who sought to stop the march of the welfare state. By conventional understanding, Sutherland was a judicial conservative from whom the decision read like a technical exercise in procedural law, not a covert political statement. Today many conservatives preach the gospel of judicial restraint even with respect to laws that they oppose on substantive grounds. Just that result may explain the unanimity in *Frothingham.*

Competitor Standing

The desire to challenge legislation on constitutional grounds did not suddenly disappear when the most obvious class of parties was denied access to the courts. If the taxpayers cannot protest a grant, how about a competitor to a firm that receives payments from the public treasury? Here the competitive injury is substantial, and the number of potential payments is small. By allowing these suits, the number of challenges to federal programs could be increased, thus closing the standing gap on judicial review. Yet that avenue was also foreclosed when Justice Sutherland held in *Alabama Power Co. v. Ickes*[46] that the Alabama Power Company had no standing to challenge decisions by local governments to enter into competition with it, even when they were backed by federal financial support that was beyond the power of the United States to grant. The payment of state subsidies to private businesses is a key danger under classical liberal theory. The fear is that public subsidies will distort competition by driving out private firms, which will in time lead to a government monopoly—think of the regulation of private health care. But the rival firm cannot mount a valid constitutional challenge that these subsidies are beyond the power of Congress to give. Justice Sutherland invoked the venerable private law principle of *damnum absque iniuria* (harm without legal injury) to deny standing.

Unfortunately, that decision was not a fluke. The next year, in *Tennessee Electric Power Co. v. Tennessee Valley Authority*, eighteen power companies that supplied hydroelectric power in nine southeastern states sought to intervene in public utility hearings at which the Tennessee Valley Authority (TVA) sought to attack the constitutionality of the elaborate government-created regional network for the distribution of electrical power.[47] Once again, that challenge was rebuffed on the grounds of *damnum absque iniuria.*[48] Similarly, in *Ashwander v. Tennessee Valley Authority*,[49] Justice Brandeis invoked equitable principles to allow standing to challenge a particular contract that a given corporation made with the TVA, but did not allow the corporation standing to challenge the constitutionality of the act as a whole. So the attacks are sealed off from both ends. If citizens and taxpayers cannot protest, and competitors are left silent, a large class of controversial legislation escapes judicial review under *Marbury*.

Administrative Standing

The overall legal situation becomes clearer, moreover, by noting the way in which the principle of standing is transformed once the constitutionality of the administrative state is accepted. At this point, the only viable challenges are to particular decisions that government agencies have made within the new constitutional order. These challenges are not meant to upset the apple cart, but to change the owners of particular apples. As such, each decision, no matter how it comes out, adds additional legitimacy to the overall framework. In this regard, it is useful to contrast *Alabama Power* with *FCC v. Sanders Brothers Radio Station*,[50] which arose under the Federal Communications Act of 1934.[51] That statute detailed a procedure that called for comparative hearings to decide whether a particular applicant was entitled to a license to broadcast over a particular frequency.[52] The question in *Sanders* was whether to grant standing to an incumbent broadcaster who claimed that he would be harmed because his broadcast area could not support a second frequency. So stated, this claim for competitive harm is precisely the sort that did not give the plaintiff standing in *Alabama Power*. Nonetheless, the court held that under the FCA, the incumbent counted as a "person aggrieved" whose interests were "adversely affected" by the grant of the license.

The main purpose for allowing competitive standing was to curb administrative abuse. But note the political dynamics of that situation. Challenging a license within the administrative framework explicitly accepts the constitutionality of the basic scheme. So Congress has no problem authorizing a suit to ensure that the administrative agency plays by the rules of the congressional game. Indeed, the Administrative Procedure Act of 1946,[53] which consolidated the work of the New Deal, explicitly stated that any person "adversely affected or aggrieved by agency action" had standing to seek judicial review.[54] Yet at the same time, Congress *never* authorizes standing on this ground to parties that seek to challenge the constitutionality of the underlying statute. The rationale is clear: standing works within the administrative state, but Congress will never go out of its way to let anyone challenge a statute's overall validity.

7

Modern Standing Law

THE ORIGINAL CONTOURS of the standing doctrine were articulated in an environment in which the Supreme Court thought that its main function was to insulate the large administrative state from constitutional challenge, while subjecting decisions made within that framework to judicial review. After the passage of the Administrative Procedure Act of 1946 (APA), however, the constitutional landscape changed radically, for the key constitutional challenges were no longer based on classical liberal claims for economic liberty (typically dead losers on the merits in any case after the New Deal and the corresponding shift in the Court's approach to these claims beginning in 1937). Instead, a wider range of novel claims upset the initial sharp contrast between classical liberalism and its modern progressive alternative.[1] In consequence, the relative unanimity of decision found in the formative period gave way to higher levels of confusion across a wide range of disparate substantive areas.

Citizen Standing

Frothingham's restrictive view of standing continues to insulate questionable government practices from judicial review. In *United States v. Richardson*,[2] the question was whether a law that required CIA expenditures not be made public violated Article I, Section 9, clause 7 of the Constitution, which provides that "a regular Statement and Account of the Receipts and Expenditures of all public Money shall be published from time to time." On the merits, it is hard to determine, first, what level of disclosure is required generally under this provision and, second, whether exceptions to any such general rule might be applicable for covert operations. But the fact that the suit is classified as merely a "generalized citizen grievance" cuts off review of these issues on their merits by making it impossible to bring them into court—which necessarily undercuts *Marbury*'s punch on critical matters of judicial review.

The same wrong analysis (without the secrecy overlay) dominated *Schlesinger v. Reservists Committee to Stop the War*,[3] where the plaintiffs could not challenge the membership of several members of Congress in the military reserves under the incompatibility clause of Article I, Section 6, clause 2, which states that "no Person holding any Office under the United States shall be a Member of either House during his Continuance in Office." Once again, the observation that a "generalized citizen interest" is not sufficient to guarantee standing misses the simple point that if these parties are not allowed to challenge the government action, then no one can ask whether key practices of government comport with the Constitution.

Competitive Harm Again

A similar form of the bifurcated treatment of the standing requirement remains in constitutional cases. To be sure, there are virtually no constitutional challenges to modern economic and social legislation; no one tries to bring suits to attack the minimum wage, which would instantly fall apart on the merits. But the second half of the overall picture—standing in cases of competitive harm—remains an essential part of the administrative state. These monopoly-preserving suits are typically a modest application of the Court's earlier decision in *Sanders Brothers*, now put forward under the banner that asks whether the plaintiff suffered "injury in fact" (which disappointed competitors always do) and whether that injury was "arguably within the zone of protected interests," which also tends to be the case.[4] To be sure, Congress continues to hold the whip hand in cases of this sort insofar as it can, by statute, deny standing to parties that might otherwise meet the injury in fact and zone of danger requirements. Nonetheless, so long as these lawsuits do not challenge the constitutionality of the underlying statutes, there is little reason to block standing in cases where it might improve the administrative process.

Naturally enough, the reversal of the broad standing doctrine in the administrative law context is also intended to protect state-created monopolies, namely congressionally-blessed agricultural cartels that divide monopoly rents between producers and distributors. In *Block v. Community Nutrition Institute*,[5] Justice O'Connor upheld a congressional prohibition on consumer standing on the grounds that the distributors would function as the virtual agents for the consumers, an economic impossibility when distributors share with producers the desire to maintain high prices while only consumers desire low ones. The denial of standing to sue can be used to insulate progressive programs from judicial review, and can do the same for state-run cartels.

Reapportionment

The veritable explosion of new rights since the Warren Court, however, has tended to direct attention away from traditional cases dealing with economic liberties. For example, the question of citizen (or at least voter) standing came to the fore in the reapportionment cases. These cases challenged corrupt districting practices, maintained by small but dominant political factions, which systematically allowed less populous rural districts to have ten or twenty times the political clout of more heavily populated urban ones. This system gave these less populous districts the ability to redistribute local expenditures, such as roads and public works projects, in their direction. The obvious challenge was that the political power of voters in more populous districts had been willfully "debased" or "diluted" by corrupt state districting practices.

In *Baker v. Carr*[6]—a case better known for its treatment of the political question doctrine—the question was whether the plaintiff voters from disadvantaged districts had standing to challenge the system. In any sane system of standing, these diffuse claims should be ripe for judicial review if any impacted party wishes to bring them. But under *Frothingham*, it appears that since all voters in populous districts were aggrieved, none should have had standing. After all, the outcome in *Frothingham* would not have changed if the named plaintiff brought her challenge as a representative of a large class of disaffected Massachusetts citizens.

But in *Baker*, Justice Brennan (with a clear eye to the bottom line) concluded that all citizens have "a plain, direct and adequate interest in maintaining the effectiveness of their votes," which was not "merely a claim of the right possessed by every citizen to require that the government be administered according to law. . . ."[7] *Frothingham* was never mentioned. Why all citizens have standing was left unexplained, except in a general appeal to *Marbury* for the proposition that "the very essence of civil liberty certainly consists in the right of every individual to claim the protection of the laws, whenever he receives an injury."[8] That sentence should have been followed by the question of whether the same difficulties that stood in the way of citizen and taxpayer standing applied here, given that each vote is necessarily only a small part of the larger picture. But all these questions about whether the individual claims had reached a sufficient magnitude were ignored. An opinion that should have overturned *Frothingham* allowed that issue to pass by in silence.

Establishment Clause

The legacy of *Frothingham* has also generated confusion over challenges to government programs under the Establishment Clause of the First Amendment ("Congress shall make no law respecting an establishment of religion. . . ."). Any sensible reading surely contemplates a wide range of diffuse public injuries for which injunctive relief seems appropriate. No one may suffer tangible harm if the Congress designates an official religion for the United States, yet surely someone should be able to challenge that designation. The same must be said of those potential Establishment Clause violations where the federal government gives some improper preference or support to certain religious activities.

The Establishment Clause has been applied against the states, where challenges are not constrained by the Article III standing doctrine. That difference in forum matters. The first of the modern Establishment Clause cases, *Everson v. Board of Education of the Township of Ewing*,[9] arose in state court when a local taxpayer challenged local expenditures used for busing children to parochial school. Freed of the shackles of federal standing, first the New Jersey Supreme Court and then the United States Supreme Court went directly to the merits of the program. Ultimately, the Supreme Court, by a five-to-four vote, found that the expenditures on religious activities were permissible so long as they were part of a comprehensive program also involving nonreligious institutions. The question was interesting and the decision close on the merits, and the noticeable absence of procedural hurdles added clarity to the process, without creating unexpected procedural or doctrinal complications.

Unfortunately, that clarity has not been replicated at the federal level. *Flast v. Cohen*[10] involved a challenge in federal court under the Establishment Clause to federal aid supplied to religious educational institutions under the Elementary and Secondary Education Act of 1965.[11] *Flast* looks like a rerun of *Frothingham*. The plaintiff emerged victorious, but not on any general theory of taxpayer or citizen standing. Instead, Chief Justice Earl Warren crafted an ad hoc exception to *Frothingham* because of a supposed "logical link" or "nexus" between taxpayers and these religion-bound dollars, which rendered their losses more than "incidental."[12] Indeed, the Establishment Clause addressed the fear "that the taxing and spending power would be used to favor one religion over another or to support religion in general."[13] But Warren offered no explanation as to why the Spending Clause did not address a similar transfer of wealth across states under the Maternity Act at issue in *Frothingham*.[14]

Flast now reads like a historical curiosity, as its authority has been eroded, albeit for all the wrong reasons. Two cases mark its erratic decline. First, in *Valley Forge Christian College v. Americans United for separation of Church & State*,[15] the Defense Department gave away excess property to Valley Forge, claiming that this transfer created an indirect public benefit. The plaintiff group sought taxpayer standing to block the transfer under the Establishment Clause. Why, in a word, is the gift of property different from the gift of cash that allows its purchase? Apparently because this action took place pursuant to Congress's power to dispose of excess property under Article IV, Section 3, clause 2, the Property Clause—"The Congress shall have [the] Power to dispose of . . . Property belonging to the United States." But Justice Rehnquist never explained why the Establishment Clause did not apply equally to all exercises of congressional power. Instead, in denying standing to the respondents, he resorted to an empirically dubious claim: that the direct injury requirement of the standing doctrine "tends to assure that the legal questions presented to the court will be resolved, not in the rarefied atmosphere of a debating society, but in a concrete factual context conducive to a realistic appreciation of the consequences of judicial action."[16] Hollow words, for what element of concreteness was missing here, or for that matter in *Frothingham*, where all the facts were of public record? And who better to attack a government giveaway program than an activist institution fully devoted to the separation of church and state, willing to litigate the standing issue clear up to the Supreme Court? Certainly not a disappointed applicant for government property, suffering a loss of only a few dollars as a consequence of not receiving the property.

The next chapter in this unfortunate progression was the Court's 2007 capitulation in *Hein v. Freedom from Religion Foundation*.[17] *Hein* asked whether the *Flast* exception allowed taxpayers to challenge executive branch expenditures in support of faith-based initiatives pursuant to general statutory guidelines. The justices divided into three camps—all of which were mistaken. Justice Samuel Alito, writing for the chief justice and Justice Kennedy, refused to extend *Flast* to these discretionary executive acts, but never explained why they pose a smaller risk of wealth transfer than the legislation pursuant to which these transfers were made. The position is an indefensible form of minimalism that refuses to address first principles. Justices Scalia and Thomas rightly rejected the distinction between legislative and executive action, but wanted to overrule *Flast*, only after belittling serious concerns about constitutional structure by treating them, wrongly, as a form of "mental displeasure."[18] Third, an uneasy coalition led by Justice Souter, speaking for Justices Stevens, Ginsburg, and Breyer, argued that *Flast* governed, but refused to jettison the limitation on taxpayer standing across the board.

More recently, in *Arizona Christian School Tuition Organization v. Winn*,[19] yet another five-to-four decision, the Supreme Court continued the evisceration of what was left of *Flast*. In *Winn*, a group of civil liberties organizations challenged an Arizona statute that supplied tax credits to private individuals who made contributions to school tuition organizations, or STOs, which were worth an estimated $50 million per annum. The plaintiffs argued that *Flast* permitted no meaningful distinction between government expenditures and STOs, even though both are mechanisms by which public funds are funneled to designated secular and religious organizations. The five-member conservative majority distinguished *Flast* and refused to allow the challenge to go forward on embarrassingly thin standing grounds. Justice Kennedy first repeated the common mistake that purports to link standing with separation of powers,[20] even though a sensible standing doctrine has a vital role to play in courts of unlimited jurisdiction. He then backed up that flawed institutional rationale with this novel economic reasoning: "tax credits and governmental expenditures do not both implicate individual tax-payers in sectarian activities. A dissenter whose tax dollars are 'extracted and spent' knows that he has in some small measure been made to con-tribute to an establishment in violation of conscience."[21]

This passage misses the basic point that the plaintiffs' objection is not to the method of transfer but to the fact of transfer. The very fact that these plaintiffs mounted this suit shows that Justice Kagan in dis-sent had to be right in concluding that "[t]axpayers who oppose state aid of religion have equal reason to protest whether that aid flows from the one form of subsidy or the other."[22] On this score the predictable dissent of Justices Scalia and Thomas calling for overruling *Flast* has the virtue of consistency. But it also has the greater vice of blocking the coherent application of judicial review. There is no need to preserve an inexcus-able doctrinal muddle that compares unfavorably with the universal state taxpayer standing rule in *Everson*.

Environmental Harms

Other strands of modern standing doctrine are no tidier. The early envi-ronmental cases quickly applied the "zone of interest" test that originated in the economic harm cases to environmental harms. The only wrinkle in this context was to find the "injury in fact" inflicted on the party who sought to enjoin government officials from approving various projects.

In *Sierra Club v. Morton*,[23] the Sierra Club objected to the decision of the United States Forest Service to allow roads and power lines to be built over Sequoia National Park for the benefit of the Walt Disney Company's Mineral King Ski Resort. The decision did not contest the proposition that anyone who used the national park could object to the project because of its impact on aesthetic or recreational interests. But the Court refused to allow standing to any person who was simply concerned with whether the park was used to enable nearby develop-ment without using the park himself. The entire distinction seems idle because so long as we know that many people will use the park, why should we think that the Sierra Club will not represent their interests given its own enormous institutional stake in environmental issues? The standing decision reached by the Court was pointlessly persnickety.

None of the ostensible standing barriers mentioned in *Sierra Club* place a real dent in the ability of fringe groups to enjoin public projects.

The key difficulty is not with standing per se, but with the set of administrative procedures used to make decisions about the use of public lands. Here, all segments of the public have a legitimate interest, so that no single faction can demand the whip hand as of right. Any sensible legal regime for the development of public property must, accordingly, allow these individuals and interest groups to have some input into the process. Participation dominates ownership entitlements. But it hardly follows from this point that the parties who have a right to appear before the relevant government body should be granted an automatic right to challenge its decision in court when they disagree with the outcome, a topic that I shall address in Chapter 20 in connection with procedural due process. But the political dynamics of unrestricted challenges do require special mention. Broad standing rules necessarily will give a systematic advantage to those outliers who oppose the project. Quite simply, a protected right of appeal gives them a free option of imposing time and money costs on those parties who succeeded in the administrative process.

These crosscurrents are all too evident in litigation under the Endangered Species Act. Thus in *Lujan v. Defenders of Wildlife*,[24] Justice Antonin Scalia was faced with deciding whether individual plaintiffs could challenge a determination by the secretary of the interior holding that Section 7 of the 1973 Endangered Species Act[25] (ESA) was "applicable only to actions within the United States or on the high seas,"[26] but not to projects funded by the United States on foreign soil. The statutory language did not specify the territorial reach of the ESA. The plaintiff environmental groups sought to enforce the broader reading of the statute, under which American agencies doing business in foreign nations or on the high seas had to consult with either the secretary of the interior or the secretary of commerce to address the position of endangered or threatened species. The case raises no substantive constitutional issues, for no one doubts that the legislation could have been drafted either to compel or prohibit the use of this consultation mechanism for overseas ventures.

In principle, then, some person should be able to challenge the refusal of the government to implement the law. Without *Frothingham*, there is no obstacle to standing. With it in place, *Lujan* gave rise to an effort to "find" a private interest that allows for the case to be decided on the merits. To meet the supposed constitutional standard of a protectable interest, the plaintiffs mounted a two-pronged attack. First, one of the named plaintiffs indicated that she had visited Sri Lanka, one of the places where the disputed projects had been undertaken, and that she would be prepared to return there in the future. Second, the plaintiffs insisted that citizen suits were authorized by Congress under an explicit statutory provision that allowed "any person" to bring suit on his own behalf "to enjoin" the activities of the United States.[27]

Justice Scalia then applied this conventional wisdom in ways that drained the requirement of individualized personal injury of all substantive content. He emphatically rejected "as beyond all reason" the view that an individual could claim standing by proving that he habitually goes to the Bronx Zoo to see an endangered species that lives overseas. But surprisingly, Scalia allowed standing for anyone who "observes or works with" a particular endangered species. At this point, the entire exercise becomes a shell game, for an organization need only rummage through its Rolodex to find a suitable plaintiff who has purchased the right airplane ticket. Yet even when that is done, a question remains whether the consultation procedures required are limited only to that species or whether they apply to all others as well. Allow one person to trigger the entire statute, and the requirement of standing is reduced to a pitiable formality. Limit the inquiry to the harms alleged, and the ESA becomes an administrative jumble. So why not make life simple? Just say the following: any citizen has standing to challenge regulations that exceed the permissible scope of statutory authority. If the claim is rejected on the ground that the statute has no extraterritorial reach, the inquiry is at an end. But if it is determined that the ESA has extraterritorial reach, the only remedy that need be granted at the time is a requirement that the regulations be altered to say so. All individual disputes about elephants in Sri Lanka could wait until another day when the matter is ripe for that dispute.

Congress took steps in that sensible direction with Section 7(a)(2) of the ESA, which conferred standing on any citizen to enjoin actions that were inconsistent with the ESA. But in *Lujan*, Justice Scalia took the view that standing was not merely a prudential feature in litigation brought under Article III, but a structural one as well, which meant that Congress could not constitutionally alter the supposed rules governing separation of powers by instructing courts to hear these cases.[28] Scalia's major premise is one correct application of the rule in *Marbury* that the Congress cannot force the courts to assume jurisdiction over types of cases that are outside the scope of Article III. But this rule is applied in the wrong context. Using the correct doctrine of standing, Congress need not authorize actions that already fall within the scope of Article III. The Court's jurisdiction exists unless some independent reason removes these cases from the fold.

It is at just this juncture that issues of redressability enter into the equation, not as part of the doctrine of standing, but as a standard that any court should entertain whenever it considers the provision of equitable relief, where it is always an open question whether the proper relief can be given if certain necessary or indispensable parties are not joined.[29] *Lujan* is of course framed as a request for equitable relief—to require certain government actions. On this issue the same principles of equity apply to all cases regardless of whether they are brought in state or federal court. At this point, the paramount question is whether courts of equity have sufficient remedial powers to undertake the remedial function demanded of them. The problem of continuing oversight of compliance with a potential injunction that was so critical in *Lujan* did not surface in *Frothingham*, where the plaintiffs only sought to shut down a public program once and for all.

These monitoring issues do not go to the issue of standing, but they do shape the exercise of equitable jurisdiction in any court. Traditionally, for example, courts of equity were reluctant to order specific performance of employment contracts on the ground that they did not wish to incur the burdens of constant oversight of private decisions.[30] But in the employment context, actions for damages, and even injunctions against third persons who interfere with existing employment contracts can fill in that enforcement gap by reducing the incentives of any employee to breach his or her contract.[31] No such luxury remains, however, whenever a judicial refusal to resolve the issue of statutory scope leaves the disappointed party with no recourse at all. In addition, since the question here is simply one of law, no court should defer to the supposed expertise of administrative agencies, as is commonly done under today's *Chevron* doctrine.[32] The proper attitude is found in Section 706 of the APA, which rightly reserves interpretive questions of law to the courts.[33]

Accordingly, the "redressability" prong of the general standing test is relevant to the outcome of the case, not because it goes to some supposed constitutional issue of standing, but because it goes to the general question that plagues all courts of equity—can they administer the sort of relief that they think is required? Courts should face this question head-on with sound judicial discretion without converting it into a constitutional issue. Accordingly, in the absence of congressional direction, they can act within their power like any other court of equity, by declining to exercise their jurisdiction if they think that the task of supervision is untenable.

In the end, therefore, *Lujan* would be correct in its outcome only if a court of equity should dismiss the case because all the parties who may be bound or hurt by the decision are not present—a result which makes it proper not to allow, for example, a civil rights organization to question a tax exemption for a racially segregated institution that is not party to the proceedings. Standing should be denied, as it has been, because the targeted institution is not made a party to the case even though its rights are obviously affected.[34] The same is true of citizen suits to remove a hospital's tax exemption for the failure to provide sufficient charitable services.[35] And both of these suits should be tossed out in state courts as well.

An important recent Supreme Court standing decision, *Massachusetts v. Environmental Protection Agency*,[36] evidences a more generous spirit on the question of standing, without any serious recalibration of the basic approach. The Clean Air Act requires the EPA to prescribe standards applicable to emissions of "any air pollutant" from any class of new motor vehicles which—in the EPA administrator's judgment—have caused or contributed to air pollution reasonably anticipated to endanger public health or welfare.[37] The question in the case was whether individual states could force the EPA to conduct rulemaking proceedings with regard to the emission of six "greenhouse gases" on the ground that these were "air pollutants" under the act.

The question whether carbon dioxide counts as a pollutant plays no role in framing the standing question. At first look, *Massachusetts v. Mellon*[38] seems to control on the issues of both citizen and state standing. Nonetheless, Justice Stevens artfully found that Massachusetts suffered a concrete injury from the potential further erosion of its coastal land, much of which was state owned, due to rising sea levels caused by climate change. Putting the claim in this fashion finessed *Massachusetts v. Mellon*, because here the state alleged damage to its property or its "dominion over physical domain," rather than raising just a generalized objection to a federal spending program.[39] On this view, a private owner of coastal land should be in the same position as the state.

Yet ironically, this case is less amenable to judicial resolution than *Frothingham*, even if standing is conceded. The only relief sought in *Frothingham* was an injunction of the expenditures under the Sheppard-Towner Maternity Act of 1921.[40] In *Massachusetts v. EPA*, the form of relief sought was far more complex, because the court order required the EPA to undertake a complex substantive review that (at the time at least) it did not want to do, without any clear sense of what would happen if that review did not meet federal standards. Under the Clean Air Act, this looks like a reach: the EPA's statutory duty is not categorical. Quite the opposite—it kicks in only if "in the [EPA] Administrator's *judgment*,"[41] carbon dioxide emissions pose a significant threat to global warming. Wading into that dispute taxes the institutional capabilities of the Court far more than *Frothingham*'s simple claim that the legislation was *ultra vires*. It is therefore at least reasonable to read the jurisdictional mandate in the Clean Air Act to require at most the administrator's good faith preliminary review of the matter, but not a full-scale hearing. Standing or no, therefore, the plaintiffs should lose on the merits unless they could establish that the EPA was acting in bad faith, which does not seem credible in light of its exhaustive review of the matter.

Justice Stevens was sensitive to those concerns, but held that the *only* grounds to decline to regulate had to relate to the scientific questions surrounding carbon dioxide emissions and global warming. Prudential matters that inform a full consideration of such issues, including the harmonization of the United States with global governance, were not sufficient. Justice Stevens's view cuts the administrator very little slack in an area where Congress seems to have given him a great deal more: nothing seems to prevent the administrator from making a decision on the merits that a further comprehensive investigation is not required on scientific grounds. In the end, therefore, the real objection to *Massachusetts v. EPA* is not over its standing decision. Rather, it goes to the critical question of whether carbon dioxide, when produced in excessive quantities, counts as a pollutant under the Clean Air Act. In my view, the answer is no.[42] The key objection to the extension of the CAA would only go to matters of redressability, which is commonly if mistakenly treated as one of the three prongs of modern standing law. Yet in this context, the point, even if relevant to the exercise of judicial power under Article III, is not difficult because the EPA is only ordered to consider the matter further, not to change the rules. With the shift in political administration, the standing issue was of little consequence. Not so with the decision to label carbon dioxide a pollutant, which has worked a major expansion of the CAA that will doubtless raise many collateral challenges of its own, unconnected to the standing question.

These issues of social control become even more acute where the effort is not to regulate some common feature of the environment, but rather to regulate ordinary development on private lands. This open-ended standing requirement goes hand in hand with the progressive vision that treats broad community veto rights over all new real estate development as essential to sound land planning in both urban and rural settings. The broad definition of standing allows people who cannot stop a new project for its smells and discharges to get a new lease on life in the administrative process. Now a welter of aesthetic interests, dealing with size, mass, color, location, access, and design, are properly before the government. I am uneasy, to say the least, to allow any administrative agency these powers. The proper course of action is for government bodies to condemn a restrictive covenant over property if they are so concerned with these matters. But the liberal standing rules compound the dangers of excessive administrative oversight. No longer is it just the median voter who can veto land use development. Now the most ardent opponent of the project gets the whip hand. The fringes take over.

In sum, the historical evolution of standing from a constitutional doctrine to an administrative law doctrine reveals a deep connection to the choice between classical liberal and modern social democratic theories of government. Within the classical liberal model, any one person should be able to enjoin the operation of an unconstitutional statute, even if everyone else is in favor of it. That proposition follows from the antimajoritarian theory of government and the integrity of structural limitations. Rejecting that position at the dawn of the modern administrative state thus removed one obstacle to the expansion of the overall size of government.

The game changes, however, when the relevant inquiry only concerns *who* gets to determine how to implement a statute that passes constitutional muster. In *Lujan*, environmental groups sought to force the government to expand its activities by challenging its narrow reading on a question of law. In other environmental cases, the power of Congress to expand citizen standing has had, paradoxically, the unfortunate effect of undermining politically responsible institutions even when there is no constitutional defect in their actions. Thus many modern environmental statutes give citizens direct enforcement rights when government administrators choose not to act.[43] These are exactly the sorts of cases where standing ought *not* to be conferred on private groups because of the risk of creating a one-way ratchet. Any system of civil or criminal prosecution involves irreducible elements of discretion. The effect of an unlimited standing rule is to invite parties on the political fringe to displace the judgment of political actors who are likely to be more closely aligned with general public sentiment. How ironic that current law stops private litigation on standing when it is strictly necessary to preserve limited government but allows those suits that tend to undermine the stability of the median voter on matters that are better left to democratic choice.

8

The Political Question Doctrine

S TANDING POSES the initial procedural barrier to all litigants who seek to have their cases heard on the merits. Once it is overcome, the second constitutional obstacle to an adjudication on the merits is the political question doctrine. That doctrine asks whether a court should deem the case "nonjusticiable" (incapable of judicial resolution) on the ground that its resolution properly falls within the province of the Congress or the president.

Origins

The political question doctrine made an early debut in American constitutional law even under the restrictive version of the federal judicial role articulated in *Marbury v. Madison*, which only allows the Supreme Court to protect itself from having to take on cases that do not fall within its appellate or original jurisdiction.[1] Thus even though many cases meet all of the jurisdictional elements of Article III, the Court is not obligated to decide them. As Chief Justice Marshall concluded, these particular controversies are not amenable to judicial resolution because "the President is invested with certain important political powers, in the exercise of which he is to use his own discretion, and is accountable only to his country in his political character, and to his own conscience."[2] Powers are treated as "political" when "[t]hey respect the nation, not individual rights, and being entrusted to the executive, the decision of the executive is conclusive."[3] It turns out that this line between collective goods (with respect to the nation) and individual rights is an excellent first cut at the larger question of which questions are amenable to resolution in the judicial forum.

One obvious political question was whether to nominate Marbury or anyone else to a judicial position; a weightier political power is the authority to negotiate treaties on matters of war and peace, where it is for the executive to make decisions that bind the entire nation, including its passionate dissenters. Another such political question is how and when to declare and wage war, where the responsibilities are divided between the president and the Congress. In one sense, these political actions supply the classic public goods of economic theory, which—like military defense—if provided to one are necessarily provided to all. But they are also the classical political mixed goods (which people want) and bads (which they would rather not have) because dissenters are required to pay tax dollars for collective endeavors that they oppose. In politics, losers abound no matter the outcome: no decision of any court can ease the pain of this visible downside of public deliberation. Nonetheless, given the collective nature of the decision, the correct solution does not give the minority a veto power, but only the right to participate in public deliberations in Congress and elsewhere before the decision is made.

That situation is hardly novel, for it represents the identical solution used in corporate contexts where collective decisions by majority vote follow deliberations under a standard practice that never allows the majority to shut off debate before all points of view have been heard. It is for just this reason that it is mistaken to use a broad definition of public good that covers, for example, private decisions by employers and employees, simply because this relationship is all pervasive. So long as each pair of parties can form its own private understandings in ways that allow others to do the same with respect to their own relationship, those numerous relationships are private, not public, and should be treated as such. The Supreme Court went down the wrong track when it intimated its happiness with a broader definition. As Justice Joseph McKenna once sagely noted, "In some degree, the public interest is concerned in every transaction between men, the sum of the transactions constituting the activities of life."[4]

Given the differences in possible view, the stakes are high in any effort to delineate the boundary line between individual rights and national political affairs. The most comprehensive statement of the appropriate test comes from Justice Brennan's opinion in *Baker v. Carr*—which dealt with malapportionment in districting for state elections. His formulation, which has achieved canonical status, holds that this doctrine applies when there is

> a textually demonstrable constitutional commitment of the issue to a coordinate political department; or a lack of judicially discoverable and manageable standards for resolving it; or the impossibility of deciding without an initial policy determination of a kind clearly for nonjudicial discretion; or the impossibility of a court's undertaking independent resolution without expressing lack of the respect due coordinate branches of government; or an unusual need for unquestioning adherence to a political decision already made; or the potentiality of embarrassment from multifarious pronouncements by various departments on one question.[5]

The reference to "the respect due coordinate branches" shows that the defensive conception of judicial review deriving from *Marbury* remains very much alive. Indeed Brennan's standards bite with special force in the foreign policy arena, where judicial intervention could easily complicate executive branch decisions. Those issues can be so important that it is unwise to have courts render any decision that could compromise general treaty obligations—which can only be negotiated with a keen appreciation of the relevant set of trade-offs. For example, courts have held that domestic antitrust laws do not apply to the OPEC oil cartel because the United States government has to engage constantly with its members on a sovereign-to-sovereign basis.[6] It is just too risky to attack cartels when the international community is so bitterly divided on the issue of their legality.

Yet it hardly follows that the political branches should be afforded the same level of deference regarding domestic issues where both federal and state governments are subject to a single constitution. The constitutional provision that most reveals the delicate relationship between the federal and state governments is the Guarantee Clause, which reads as follows: "The United States shall guarantee to every State in this Union a Republican Form of Government, and shall protect each of them against Invasion; and on Application of the Legislature, or of the Executive (when the Legislature cannot be convened) against domestic Violence."[7] The section contains strong classical liberal themes in its preferred form of government. It also speaks about both foreign invasion and domestic violence as the chief threats to that government. On matters of foreign invasion, it is taken for granted that the United States will intervene militarily, given the common threat. On matters of domestic violence, the response is more nuanced because the state has to apply for assistance, which in some cases it may not want or need. To be sure, the second clause is maddeningly vague as to whether the state's application for protection—through either its legislature or governor—should be addressed to the president or the Congress. But since invasions and violence can erupt at any time, Marshall's instinct in *Marbury* looks right: the application "to suppress insurrections" should be made to the president in his role as commander-in-chief, but—revealing shades of checks and balances—only pursuant to the authority vested in him by Congress.[8] The political branches control at both levels of government, and at first blush it looks as if there is no sensible role for judicial involvement. The political question doctrine thus seems to have a natural home in these cases.

This judgment, however, leaves open the delicate question of how the *first* part of the Guarantee Clause is applied once the risks of violence and invasion have given way to claims for the vindication of individual rights—where Marshall did see a judicial role—that arose out of past conflicts. The issue came to a head in the 1849 case *Luther v. Borden*.[9] That matter arose out of "traitor" Thomas Wilson Dorr's rebellion of 1842, after which he was made governor for a short time before being repulsed, captured, and prosecuted by the prior state government. The plaintiff, a citizen of Massachusetts and a collaborator of Dorr's, brought an action for trespass against the defendants, all citizens of Rhode Island, seeking recovery for property damage caused by breaking and entering. Personal jurisdiction over the case was therefore established on grounds of diversity—those cases that arise between citizens of different states. Standing was established by the evident property damage. The defendants could not credibly deny the charge of deliberate trespass, but they could justify it by claiming that they acted as the lawful sovereign to quell the incipient rebellion, which sought to extend the franchise more broadly than was allowed under the established or "chartered" government—in continuous power since the Charter of 1663. The United States did not intervene with military force, but it did make a public statement favoring the chartered government, which prevailed in the conflict.

Once the conflict was over, neither executive nor legislative action was possible or appropriate. Thus the only issue before the United States Supreme Court, like the lower federal court, was which faction governed in the aftermath of a failed insurrection against an incumbent government. Unfortunately, the failure to sharpen the issue means that *Luther* is commonly read to stand for the proposition that the adjudication of any question pertaining to sovereignty is a political question that should be left to the political branches of government—here, Congress and the president—even though the Court had unquestioned (diversity) jurisdiction over the case. There are passages in the decision that point in this direction,[10] but a more accurate account of the decision is that the federal courts should not decide that question because it was better left to the state tribunals that had already ruled against Dorr and in favor of the charter government.[11]

In such situations, however, there is no reason to assume that the Supreme Court is unable to handle the question of who is in charge if the state courts are silent or have issued conflicting opinions. The concern here is about the untoward consequences of judicial intervention. There was, of course, no special impact of the litigation on the parties to the suit, for the damages requested of the defendant, if granted, could have been collected in the standard way, or by judgment lien if necessary. Administrability was not an issue, as it is with equitable decrees that require continuous judicial supervision. The real issue, therefore, is only with collateral consequences on third parties and public institutions. Yet even these could cut in either direction.

Justice Taney was surely correct to note the huge dislocations that take place whenever the decisions of any legislature (including the brief Dorr interlude) are dismissed as "nullities," for it draws into question the legality of both taxes collected and salaries paid, and thus can precipitate a veritable barrage of litigation over tax refunds and unpaid salaries.[12] Yet those uncertainties persist even if the Court refuses to decide the case, and without an authoritative determination, no one knows the legal rights of the parties. Does the political question doctrine only strike the defense, in which case the damages should be awarded? Or does it lead, as it did in *Luther*, to the dismissal of the entire case, which has the same immediate effect as allowing the judgment?

But why rejoice in this ambiguity? Disagreements over the sharing of power are common in disputes when churches or corporations break up. If the parties cannot resolve their differences among themselves, their only recourse is to a court of general jurisdiction, which has to sort out the claims as best as it can. Rarely is it done perfectly; but it is done. And *Luther* is a factually easy case. The case does not involve two rival claimants who enter an unoccupied territory at the same time. The established government was under attack, and its legislature had received the presidential vote of confidence. The equities would be more delicate if the insurgents had retained power, backed by the support of the president or Congress. The operative principle here is that the courts, in resolving individual disputes over property rights, should not oppose the president, who has primary responsibility for the execution of federal policy. But there is no reason why a judicial decision on the merits should not *rely* on the federal determination to support the incumbent, given the general legal presumption in favor of the legitimate sovereign status of incumbent governments. Certainly there is no reason to support the insurgents because they sought a broader franchise, given that republican principles place powerful limitations on the universal franchise. The central question is not whether the new government is better than the old. Rather it is which government had temporal priority, which is clearly answered in accordance with the familiar principle that prior in time is higher in right.

Accepting that *Luther* should have rejected a political question defense does not resolve all questions about the scope of the Guarantee Clause. After all, the first half of the clause dealing with the republican form of government has some bite even in the absence of invasion or domestic violence. It looks as if the "United States" must ensure that the state, by internal political machinations, does not deprive its citizens of the benefit of republican institutions, as by the formation of a military dictatorship by popular consent.

However, in *Pacific States Telephone & Telegraph Co. v. Oregon*,[13] the Court took the opposite tack and refused to decide that state referenda offended republican principles because they allowed people to make laws while bypassing the legislature. Yet why decline to answer this question, for surely it is no more difficult than countless others that arise under the Constitution? It cannot be for remedial reasons, as the invalidation of a procedure that is the embodiment of direct democracy does not require the kind of continuous supervision needed in other contexts. For this decision to make sense, it must rest on some reasoned argument that referenda, in at least some forms and at some times, are consistent with republican principles. The appropriate line of argument would have to show that the distortions in referenda are smaller than those in legislation, an issue on which no one can speak with confidence—for so much depends on performance levels that can vary from state to state—and one about which views can and do differ sharply.[14] In the end, therefore, the case against judicial intervention rests on the difficulty of coming up with norms for intervention that work across all states.

Modern Applications

The passive decision in *Pacific States* marked the end of an era of judicial passivity. The high costs of that approach, however, became vividly apparent a half century later in the key reapportionment decision of *Baker v. Carr.*[15] Once the Court overcame the standing hurdle, the substantive question was whether Tennessee could be required to reform its unit voting system, which resulted in huge imbalances in electoral power that favored small counties (with a minimum of one representative each) against the large, and growing, metropolitan areas whose populations were systematically and grievously underrepresented. The entrenched power of the small counties resisted any reapportionment in violation of state law for over sixty years, and all previous efforts to resolve the matter through local litigation also ended in utter failure.

In this situation, how could there be any doubt that republican principles were violated? Unlike in *Pacific Telephone States*, direct participation of voters was not an issue. The only question was whether representatives should be allocated by district or under some at-large system. Here again it is useful to resort to the analogy of citizens as shareholders. Ideally each citizen should have one share, or one vote, no matter what decision rule is used to aggregate those shares. Yet it was as if the corporation decided to give additional shares of stock to some individuals, but not to others, so that the minority interest exercised full control to the exclusion of the majority. It is the kind of public choice nightmare that recalls the ancient English system of rotten boroughs, whose abuse fed the fires for the British Reform Act of 1832, which took the first steps toward dismantling that system.[16] It is hard to imagine *any* republican theory of government (including a democratic one) that could mount even a feeble defense of so outrageous a system. Clearly, the United States Congress should be able to do something to deal with this under the Guarantee Clause. After all, by definition, neither Congress nor the president can be bound by a political question doctrine that requires courts to defer to either or to both. In addition, the United States also includes the federal courts. If *Marbury v. Madison* gives the Court the last word on constitutional interpretation, why can the Supreme Court not resolve a constitutional challenge to the legality of the Tennessee system? Indeed, so long as violence and insurrection do not put the matter in the political realm, the Court's views on the constitutionality of the Tennessee system should, if anything, trump those of the Congress.

What is ironic about *Baker v. Carr* is that its entire heated debate over the political question doctrine starts from the premise that *Luther* was rightly decided. Justice Brennan rested that conclusion on two grounds. The first, which does not follow from the Constitution's text, was that the matter was committed to the discretion of the president. The second ground was, incredibly, "the lack of criteria by which a court could determine which form of government was republican."[17] This last point was of course *not* in issue in *Luther*, which only required a decision as to whether the chartered government had been displaced. But forget the factual dispute. The key question is why these twin difficulties of administration and definition magically disappear when the case is decided, as it was, under the Equal Protection Clause. Justice Brennan held that there was no conflict with the executive branch of the government and its need for finality, and that there were discernible principles under the Equal Protection Clause that allowed the Court to use "judicially manageable standards" to decide whether "discrimination [between groups] reflects no policy, but simply arbitrary and capricious action."[18]

Setting aside the question of whether the Equal Protection Clause reaches these structural claims (which, as an originalist matter, it does not), it is evident that neither point makes the slightest bit of sense. Section 5 of the Equal Protection Clause states that Congress shall have the power to enforce the provisions of the amendment by "appropriate legislation."[19] In *Luther*, the president had already spoken so that any conflict could have been easily avoided. In *Baker*, the Congress had not spoken on a long-standing political grievance, which suggests a latent conflict between its attitude and the Court's. Yet on this point, any anxieties over a clash with a "coequal" branch of government do not amount to much, given that the federal political branches had remained silent and could not in any event mount a sensible defense of the state practice.

Likewise, there is nothing to Justice Brennan's point that the Equal Protection Clause offers clear principles that the Guarantee Clause somehow lacks. Ironically, the one justice who clearly saw the problem was Justice Frankfurter, who in his dissent noted both Madison's concern with faction and the British travail with rotten boroughs.[20] He introduced the point to shred Justice Brennan's claim that the institutional issues under the Equal Protection Clause were different from those raised under the Guarantee Clause—which is right as far as it goes. But Frankfurter set the equivalence in the wrong direction by denying the claims under *both* clauses instead of neither. In principle, the correct response in *Baker v. Carr* would have been to overrule *Luther v. Borden.* Any claim that the principles of republican government are unintelligible makes the Constitution itself largely unintelligible and weakens the protections otherwise offered against the dangers of faction and self-interest, dangers that were disturbingly realized by the grisly facts in *Baker.*

Any defense of Justice Brennan's handiwork rests on its correct outcome, not its shabby reasoning. Constitutional law after *Luther* was a question of the second best. Justice Brennan took the path of least resistance to correct an appalling level of political disrepair. In this instance, however, second-best constitutionalism comes at a heavy price. Recall that at the time of the 1787 Founding the term "republican" was used consciously in opposition to democratic government. The institutional arrangements under the republican form of government are eminently compatible with different rules of selection for members of the two houses of state government. Think of the structure of the Senate in the Congress, with its explicit reference to the patrician branch in the Roman Republic. It is therefore very doubtful that any republican theory could endorse the relentless jurisprudence that emerged two years after *Baker* in *Reynolds v. Sims.*[21] There the Court took the hard-line remedial position of "one man, one vote," on the ground that "[l]egislators represent people, not trees or acres."[22] It followed that any effort to inject other matters—at least for the state upper house—on grounds of history, tradition, access, group identity, or the like was systematically excluded from consideration, so that a close numerical equality became a constitutional imperative no matter what Congress might say on the matter.

By contrast, an analysis under the Guarantee Clause should be more receptive to these variations, given that the electoral provisions consciously deviate from any simple "one man, one vote" principle. Yet, ironically, it is unclear just what adjustments that analysis would require relative to the *Reynolds* approach, even if the Court adopted a lower level of scrutiny. The particular scheme in *Reynolds*, for example, allocated seats by county, where a county with fewer than 45,000 persons got one seat, and any county with a population over 600,000, no matter how large, was restricted to twelve seats, greatly disadvantaging city dwellers. I know of no republican theory that would countenance those kinds of differences, which bear no relationship to the special rules for choosing senators at the federal level (originally by, it must be recalled, appointment by the state legislatures). But it does not necessarily follow that a districting system that tracks natural geographical divisions within a state should not tolerate some modest numerical imbalance.

The *Reynolds* standard precluded any such maneuver. Yet the sobering lesson from the reapportionment cases is not how well the judiciary administered its hard numerical standard, but rather the extent of the gerrymandering that local politicians can still get away with under the *Reynolds* standard in the absence of further restrictions on state skullduggery. These stalwart defenders of democracy routinely deploy computers that reflect partisan preference. It only takes irregular districts that let the opposition win handsomely in one or two districts while the dominant party wins the clear majority of districts by far closer, but still predictable margins. No republican theory could countenance this result either. Yet here the Supreme Court has largely washed its hands of these second-order questions. In Justice Byron White's words, the Court has dismissed the entire enterprise as "inevitable" or "unavoidable," which led him to conclude that the case for judicial intervention, given rough proportionality, is now "at its lowest ebb."[23] The erratic case law that follows is further convoluted when the gerrymandering in question is designed to either prop up or reduce the influence of "majority minority districts"—those in which the majority of voters are from racial minorities.[24]

The standard of review lurches from high to low, and the new rules look as though they offend republican and Equal Protection principles after all. The sad conclusion is that the inability to organize the remedial side of the issue can undo much of the good that judicial intervention is supposed to achieve in the first place. Ironically, the best answer might well be a *more* powerful form of judicial intervention, under either the Guarantee or Equal Protection analysis. Let the courts run reapportionment by technical criteria—pretty much any criteria, in fact—that ignore the dominant political ties of voters in the crafting district. There is no good voting theory that tells us how many voters it takes to choose a legislative majority. Uneven distributions of population could on occasion allow a minority party in a districting system to gain control of either or both state houses, or gain a disproportionate membership in the state's delegation to the House of Representatives.

There are two larger lessons here. First, the voting cases are vivid testimony to the pervasive power of individual and group interests, which confirms Madison's original judgment about the corrosive effects of faction. Second, these cases show how difficult it is for courts to fashion remedies to counteract those tendencies. In these circumstances, no one really thinks that the Court should immerse itself in controversies over the conduct of war or on many matters of foreign relations. But it is important to be careful not to push this good insight too far. There are many situations where, perhaps, the wise court will abandon the search for perfection and settle for grabbing the low-hanging fruit—regardless of whether that approach requires more intervention than even the Warren Court could stomach.

THE LEGISLATIVE POWER

THIS NEXT SECTION of the book explores the scope of the legislative power set out in Article I of the Constitution. The central contrast between the classical liberal and progressive visions dominates this area as well. In all relevant cases, the classical liberal view was intent on preserving the key elements of limited government. At the same time, the progressive alternative was dismissive of each of these limitations on federal power, to which it responded in two fashions. First, it tended to soften any of the constitutional limitations on the organization of power at the federal level. Second, it adopted simultaneously a view that the broad reading of federal power necessarily allowed for concurrent federal and state control over virtually all productive activities in which, when the two clashed, federal power took precedence over state power. Yet at the same time, in connection with the so-called dormant Commerce Clause, the progressive worldview moved toward the classical liberal ideal by refusing to let any single state stand in the path of a national market. The differences between these two positions can be briefly summarized as follows: the classical liberal view saw the dangers of both excessive national powers and the fragmentation of the national economy by excessive assertion of state control over a full range of business activities. The progressive view was alert to the dangers of excessive fragmentation but indifferent to those of excessive concentration.

This section thus proceeds as follows. Chapter 9 starts with an account of the theory and early practice of the Commerce Clause from the founding through the Civil War insofar as it authorizes the exercise of federal power. Chapter 10 traces this historical development from the end of the Civil War in 1865 to the pivotal New Deal October Term of 1936. Chapters 11 and 12 deal with the progressive transformation of the early doctrine. Chapter 13 then turns to the complementary issues raised in connection with the congressional powers to tax and spend. Chapter 14 discusses the role of the "necessary and proper clause" as a source of additional federal power. And Chapter 15 rounds out the discussion with an examination of the dormant Commerce Clause. This role of these constitutional limits on legislative power has received ever-greater urgency in light of the divided verdict on the Patient Protection and Affordable Care Act, which dealt extensively with the materials covered in these chapters.

9

The Commerce Power

Theory and Practice, 1787–1865

THE HISTORY of the legislative power under the Constitution is intimately tied to the Commerce Clause, which states simply: "The
Congress shall have power . . . to regulate commerce with foreign
nations, and among the several states, and with the Indian Tribes."[1] As
will become evident, there is an enormous tension between the classical
liberal and progressive views on how this clause should be interpreted.
The determined progressive efforts to expand the reach of federal power
were funneled through the Commerce Clause for one simple reason.
It was strictly required to allow progressive principles to deal with the
massive dislocations of the Great Depression during a time when it was
assumed without argument that national problems required national
solutions that only a robust federal government could provide.

Background and Theory

It is, however, possible, indeed imperative, to reject this expansionist
view by giving a sensible meaning to this clause that comports with a
sound federalist system. "Commerce" should take the meaning that it
has in ordinary language. As with zoning law, the term "commerce"
is used in opposition to the term "manufacturing." As with commercial law, it covers the sale, lease, hire, transportation, and payment
for goods and services. It also covers all aspects of the transportation
of people and goods and services. The Constitution does not allocate
power over all commercial transactions to the national government.

Local commercial transactions—a grocery store sale, a cab ride across town—do not fall within the scope of the Commerce Clause because they are not conducted with foreign nations, among the several states, or with the Indian tribes. Nor does the Commerce Clause cover the common activities that are internal to a state, including agriculture, manufacture, and mining, each of which can be regulated by the state where the activity is located. This interpretation is far too narrow to support most of the modern regulatory efforts of the federal government. But that classical view should not be rejected solely because it is at striking variance with the current constitutional structure. The defense of this earlier, narrower view rests on the relationship between the text of Article I, dealing with the legislative power, and the key structural elements of our original constitutional plan. That article's opening salvo states that the legislative power "herein granted" shall be vested in Congress, which suggests that at least some powers had been retained by the states. Article I then outlines the organization of the two houses of Congress, before defining Congress's *enumerated* powers under Article I, Section 8. The common public understanding of the term "enumerated" suggests that some activities must necessarily lie outside the enumeration, organized in a way to enable a national government to run without undermining the position of the states. The power to borrow money, to set uniform rules for naturalization and bankruptcy, to coin money, to establish post roads, and to regulate patents and copyrights are all key powers whose allocation to the national government could be sensibly justified on particularistic grounds. No one wants fifty separate patent systems. But none of these powers contains the latent capability for expansion found in the simple text of the Commerce Clause. Yet it was not so at the beginning. In describing this enumeration, James Madison wrote as follows in *Federalist No. 45*:

> The powers delegated by the proposed Constitution to the federal government, are few and defined. Those which are to remain in the State governments are numerous and indefinite. The former will be exercised principally on external objects, as war, peace, negotiation, and foreign commerce; with which last the power of taxation will, for the most part, be connected. The powers reserved to the several States will extend to all the objects which, in the ordinary course of affairs, concern the lives, liberties, and properties of the people, and the internal order, improvement, and prosperity of the State.[2]

Two points are worth noticing. First, his description of the federal power refers only to *foreign* commerce, without reference to either commerce among the states or with the Indian tribes. At the very least that rendering is inconsistent with any massive expansion of federal power over interstate commerce. Second, his use of the phrase "lives, liberties, and properties" of the people was no casual reference. It clearly referred back to the parallel phrase in John Locke's *Second Treatise of Government*, which explained that individuals form governments "for the mutual preservation of their lives, liberties and estates, which I call by the general name, property."[3] Madison chose his words wisely when he suggested that the states' authority would *continue to cover* all the legitimate ends of government along Lockean lines under what would become known as their general police power. It is not a credible construction of the basic text to assume that the powers "reserved to the several States" were concurrently granted to the federal government on the ground that commerce among the several states included all productive activities like manufacture, mining, and agriculture within each of the separate states.

This enumeration of federal congressional powers has to be read in conjunction with Section 9 of Article I, which lists the prohibitions on congressional action, two of which bear special note: a prohibition on capitation or direct taxes and a prohibition against imposing a tax or duty on articles exported from any state. Thereafter, Article I, Section 10 lists the prohibitions on the states. Some of these, like the prohibition on coining money, are absolute, but others, like laying duties on imports and exports, are prohibited only when done without the consent of Congress.

The key task of a theory of federalism is to integrate these three types of provisions—limited grants of power to Congress, coupled with limitations on both Congress and the states—into one coherent whole. That integration in turn depends on developing an ideal vision of a federal system against which to compare the original constitutional design and its subsequent transformation. The place to start is the sovereign (that is, irreducibly political) risk of excessive regulation of economic activity inherent in governments at all levels. Governments have monopoly power within their territories that changes in technology do not erode over time. A federalist system counters that risk by creating competition between state governments, which in turn requires open borders between the states that allow for the movement of people and resources. Accordingly, it is critical to create and maintain the national (and international) market for the sales of goods and services. In line with Adam Smith's theory of the division of labor,[4] the efficiency of any market increases with its geographic scope. Larger markets permit greater degrees of specialization, which in turn generates higher levels of social output from any set of initial resource endowments. An adequate federal system therefore must aggressively combat state balkanization of the national market by ensuring the free movement of goods and services across state lines. The desired mobility must also include the ability of individuals and firms to relocate freely across state lines.

In this case, text and function are in perfect alignment, for the sensible functional interpretation of the clause gives power to Congress to regulate the various *cross-border* transactions of this sort so as to prevent their disruption by state actors. In effect, the commerce power creates a national trade zone. It is *not* a national free trade zone, but rather a zone whose characteristics are subject to congressional determination. On the other side of this boundary lie all other forms of productive economic activity within the states, including manufacture, agriculture, and mining. Each of these is local, and each is subject only to state regulation until the goods in question are prepared for shipment into commerce destined for foreign nations, other states, or the Indian tribes. Once they reach their final destination, these goods are no longer subject to federal regulation, but become subject to regulation by the nation, state, or tribe into whose territory they have been sent. The channels of commerce may be kept open and uniform by congressional activity. The individual states, acting in competition with each other, are responsible for all activities that antedate or follow on these interstate transactions. So long as the basic framework holds firm, the commerce power can remain in peaceful coexistence with the other enumerated powers, which are today rendered largely superfluous because the commerce power has been interpreted so expansively.

Jack Balkin (who ignores the above passage from Madison) has recently challenged this narrow rendering of the Commerce Clause by claiming that it is somehow inconsistent with earlier understandings. Balkin insists that it is a mistake to think of commerce as embracing only trade, and argues that the definition of the term should also "focus on the ideas of interaction, exchange, sociability, and the movement of persons that business (in its older sense of being busy or engaged in affairs) exemplifies."[5] There is no doubt that the Commerce Clause was intended to promote these interests of general sociability, but it did so solely by indirection. The opening of borders to trade always results in a liberalization of local markets, even in the absence of any ability to regulate what goes on in those markets.

The basic analysis of our federal system, therefore, should start from the proposition that the simplest and most reliable protection against excessive state regulation is the power of persons to *exit* one state in order to find a more congenial home elsewhere.[6] Exercising an exit right is always costly, even in the absence of legal prohibition or regulation, because it is not easy to simply pick up and leave a long-time home or established business, thereby sacrificing all favorable connections already in place. To be sure, developers can escape excessive regulation by moving elsewhere or threatening to do so by playing off one state or local government against another. But that exit option is of little help to landowners whose wealth is tied up in immobile assets. Nonetheless, a limited but imperfect remedy is better than no remedy at all. Any constitutional scheme that gives local government free rein in regulation is subject to needed discipline through this one method of indirect control. Without exit control, astute state and local governments can tax and regulate only up to the point that individual firms are unwilling to give up their state and local advantages—a constraint that bites more severely on smaller state subunits. At some point the balance shifts to make the exit threat credible. This system of individual self-help thus offers a powerful first line of defense against arbitrary state rule. It is no accident that totalitarian governments work overtime to snuff out exit rights; think of the Berlin Wall. Constitutional government helps counter that form of repression by breaking the monopoly of force that state governments can exercise over individuals.

The concern with government monopoly also has profound implications for the structure of federal power. Exit rights are more difficult to exercise between nations than between states. It is easier to pick up shop in New York and relocate to New Jersey than it is to relocate to Canada or the West Indies. Nor is there any need for any national government to take on the routine tasks of day-to-day governance that state and local governments can already do. Dual sovereignty makes the distribution of power more ticklish, not easier. In light of these common-sense observations, a system of enumerated powers draws its inspiration from the observation that the increased geographical reach of a national government has modest gains for the effective protection of liberty and property, but it sharply increases the risk of the excessive use of federal power. The burden of justification for the expansion of federal regulatory reach thus lies on those who think that the federal government should duplicate the functions already discharged by the states.

But why have *any* federal power at all over economic matters? The theoretical answer lies in the structure of "network industries," such as transportation and communication. Start with some simple geometrical observations. Manufacture, agriculture, and mining by and large take place on squarish-type plots—that is, those with a high area to perimeter ratio. Production does not work well on skinny slivers of land. By the same token, no one can organize transportation and communications networks in squares. The necessary roads, rails, and wires, which are long and slender, invariably have huge perimeter to area ratios as they snake their way across state boundaries. Accordingly, state regulation of network industries poses a real risk of snipping the system into multiple useless segments, thereby gutting its value or shutting it down altogether. On any interstate route—be it for stagecoach, railcar, automobile, or jet plane—it was evident from the outset that, in principle, exit rights could not offer any counterweight against the ability of multiple states to sever these vital networks and create gridlock.[7] The network could only survive if carriers from any state could reach any other state at any time, without interference by any of the states that lay in between. The modern terminology of network industries was not known to the Framers, but the gravity of the problem was. One of the great achievements of the 1648 Peace Treaty of Westphalia[8] was to open up traffic along the Rhine River by prohibiting each small principality from imposing tolls on ships that passed through its waters. State governments acting unilaterally impose the same risk.

This fundamental difference between production and communication has profound implications for the ideal federalist structure. Network industries often, but not inevitably, exhibit monopoly traits, against which some form of rate and access regulation has been regarded as an appropriate antidote since long before the adoption of the Constitution.[9] It is therefore unwise to devise any system that contains a regulatory void such that neither the federal government nor the states are in a position to regulate. Where the risk of regulation at the level of the states is pronounced, moreover, regulation must take place at the national level. For network industries, the risks of federal monopoly exaction are very large, but they are far smaller than the grim possibility of multiple state regulators dismembering what should be operated as a single system. So at the very least, Congress needs to have the power to exclude all forms of state regulation, such that a single hand lies at the tiller. The judgment is that a single federal monopoly poses a smaller risk than multiple state monopolies, which can easily create deadlock by acting at cross purposes with each other. The optimal strategy to offset the risk of federal monopoly that follows from the suppression of state power will require imposing substantive limitations on how the federal government exercises its power. Consider, for example, the constitutional limitations on ratemaking, which asserted themselves in the last third of the nineteenth century as the railroads surged toward economic dominance.[10] Some exercise of federal power is an indispensable element of a sound federal system, but unlimited federal power is not.

These preliminaries allow us to identify the essentials of a sound federal system of regulation: local regulation of productive industries, coupled with prohibitions on the ability of either the states or the national government to inhibit the movement of either people or goods across state lines. Federal regulation is needed to make sure that no states can disrupt the operation of a national network for parochial reasons. These essential features are, moreover, technology *independent*. We do not have to embrace Balkin's expansive notion of "living originalism" to explain how the structure is put together. The basic structure works as well for a world of handicrafts transported by stagecoach and ships as for a world of high-tech manufacturing with high-speed modes of transportation by cars, trucks, railroads, steamships, and airplanes, and high-speed communications by radio, telephone, and the Internet. Indeed, the more efficient the modes of transportation and communication, the *lower* the costs of linking disparate locations together. The expanded scope of the market in goods and services reduces the risk that any local businesses can exercise monopoly power, given the ability to import goods and services from elsewhere. Put otherwise, modern conditions require *less* regulation than earlier ones so long as entry and exit rights are kept in working order. There is no depreciation in the soundness of the basic model over time that justifies a claim for a fundamental reordering of the basic system simply because of the inexorable march of technology.

The Initial Foray: 1797–1865

The early decisions dealing with the Commerce Clause concentrated on policing the border between the national power on the one hand and the reserved power of the states on the other. There was little judicial activity on the scope of the Commerce Clause until the key decision of Chief Justice Marshall in *Gibbons v. Ogden*,[11] which has set the terms of debate until the present day. *Gibbons* asked whether the commerce power allowed the United States to regulate a single continuous journey by boat from Elizabethtown, New Jersey to New York City. The narrower view of the Commerce Clause, as articulated in 1812 by the New York state court in *Livingston v. Van Ingen*,[12] took the position that the clause itself only allowed for a federal presence at the border between two states, thereby denying that interstate commerce extended to navigation after the vessel reached the interior of the state. In rejecting that contention, Chief Justice Marshall insisted that the great clauses of the Constitution had to receive a capacious construction in order to meet the exigencies of the day. It therefore followed from his view that commerce comprehended navigation from one end of the journey to the other, even within the "interior" of a state,[13] or was "confined to prescribing rules for the conduct of individuals in the actual employment of buying and selling or of barter."[14]

But it is simply historical mythmaking to think that *his* broad conception of the Commerce Clause bears even a faint resemblance to the modern interpretation of the clause that leaves virtually no domain of exclusive jurisdiction of the states.

In one famous passage, he wrote: "Comprehensive as the word 'among' is, it may very properly be restricted to that commerce which concerns more States than one."[15] The restrictions here matter. Thus Marshall emphatically stated that inspection laws for goods coming into a state were not part of interstate commerce, for, in line with the tripartite division set out above, they "act upon the subject before it becomes an article of foreign commerce or of commerce among the States, and prepare it for that purpose." Accordingly, "they form a portion of that immense mass of legislation" that is "advantageously exercised by the States themselves. Inspection laws, quarantine laws, health laws of every description, as well as laws for regulating the internal commerce of a State, and those which respect turnpike roads, ferries, &c.,

are component parts of this mass."[16] There is not so much as a verbal hint that agriculture, manufacture, or mining could be subject to federal power given the long list of activities that are excluded from it. To forestall just that conclusion, Marshall was careful to stress that all three heads of the Commerce Clause had to be read in unison, which can easily be done if commerce means, as he insisted, trade or intercourse between two places.[17] The term "commerce," however, becomes totally otiose if the words "manufacture" and "agriculture" are subsumed in the phrase "Congress shall have power . . . to regulate [agriculture, mining, and manufacture] with foreign nations, among the several states, and with the Indian tribes." Such a construction is a grammatical absurdity. Indeed, even the stalwart defendants of the power of Congress to regulate activities within the several states do not make the same claim with respect to either the Foreign Commerce or Indian Commerce Clauses. They recognize that any congressional effort to regulate grain production in the European Union because it influences the price of grain in the United States or on the world market would precipitate huge international repercussions. Furthermore, any effort to regulate each and every aspect of Indian tribal life would wreck any notion of tribal sovereignty, which is fully preserved under the accurate reading that Marshall gave of the Commerce Clause, which he rightly reads as one unified clause, not as three separate ones.

Marshall had powerful political motivations not to run hog wild in his reading of the Commerce Clause. In particular, he was obviously unwilling in the antebellum period to precipitate a constitutional war by intimating that Congress could regulate slavery within the states, even though it was abundantly clear that it could regulate the movement of slaves across state lines and national boundaries. Yet at the same time it was equally well understood that the Congress could not use its power over interstate commerce to regulate the operation of slavery within the several states. As Hamilton wrote: "An unrestrained intercourse between the States themselves will advance the trade of each by an interchange of their respective productions, not only for the supply of reciprocal wants at home, but for exportation to foreign markets."[18] Justice Joseph Story echoed the same sentiment in his *Commentaries on the Constitution of the United States*, when he answered in the negative the questions "whether, under the pretense of an exercise of the power to regulate commerce, congress may in fact impose duties for objects wholly distinct from commerce." And further, "whether a power, exclusively for the regulation of commerce, is a power for the regulation of manufactures?"[19] The interaction between what was then termed the residual state police power and the narrow federal power was bound to generate some difficult conflicts, but these were resolved in a way consistent with Marshall's general approach in *Gibbons*. That conclusion is evident in the 1823 decision in *Corfield v. Coryell*,[20] which summarizes the principle: "Commerce with foreign nations, and among the several states, can mean nothing more than intercourse with those nations, and among those states, for purposes of trade, be the object of the trade what it may; . . ."[21] Everything else was left to state control. The words "nothing more" were taken literally; under this formulation, Justice Bushrod Washington held that Congress did not have the power under the Commerce Clause to regulate the dredging of oysters in Maurice River Cove, New Jersey, unless one of two conditions were satisfied: either the removal of oysters from the shore interfered with the movement of ships in interstate commerce, which it did not, or the oysters themselves became objects of interstate trade after they were harvested.

To be sure, Marshall's conception of the commerce power in *Gibbons* raised its own difficulties. The first concerns the extent to which his interpretation advances or retards the creation of a national competitive market. In practice it clearly does both. The short-term result of *Gibbons* looks procompetitive, for it allowed steam engine competition to take place on interstate runs, even though New York had granted an exclusive franchise for using steam power in New York waters to Robert Fulton, who had in turn assigned it to Ogden. Yet even this conclusion is debatable because Marshall could easily have said, in line with modern cases under the dormant Commerce Clause,[22] that even though Gibbons could not be kept out of New York, he had no right to go there free of charge, and so he could be required to pay the same fees that local shippers had to pay for the use of Fulton's invention in New York waters. That proposition was not discussed, however, and the clear implication of *Gibbons* was that the federal Constitution could trump local monopolies with respect to interstate transactions. However, nothing requires that federal power be exercised in a procompetitive fashion. Indeed, one illustration that Marshall gave of an admittedly valid application of the commerce power was the ability to require that boats in United States waters have American crews, which is of course a quintessential protectionist policy.[23] No state could counter federal anticompetitive efforts. Any effort to restore the competitive ideal did not come from the Commerce Clause itself, but necessarily relied on independent substantive rights found elsewhere in the Constitution.

Yet by the same token, the well-defined scope of the commerce power made it feasible for the Supreme Court in the 1849 *Passenger Cases*[24] to assert that the commerce power was "exclusively vested in Congress"[25] and that it included, as Marshall had intimated earlier, the power to regulate passenger traffic in all its aspects. Accordingly, the Court struck down state taxes that were imposed on all passengers, including aliens, who arrived at a state port by vessel from some foreign port. The movement of persons into the United States was exclusively governed by the federal Constitution. The question of whether commerce was restricted to goods was clearly and correctly answered in the negative. To be sure, there remains some necessary tension between state and federal power, for it seems to follow from the logic of the *Passenger Cases* that state inspection laws for persons could not be used to block the entry of aliens into the United States. Indeed the constant use of the term "concurrent" in both the counsel argument and opinions shows that a watertight division between the two areas is not possible. It is equally clear that the decision is instructive in yet another way, for it indicates the ability of the United States to control immigration (in opposition to naturalization) rests in the federal government under the foreign commerce power, in part because the specific prohibition against "[t]he Migration or Importation of such Persons as any of the States now existing shall think proper to admit" (e.g., slaves) was carved out from the general scope of the Commerce Clause until 1808,[26] from which it is a fair inference that they are subject to the foreign commerce power after that date, as was concluded in the *Passenger Cases*. But for our purposes, the ambiguities over the scope of the Commerce Clause have nothing to do with the conspicuous expansions of the New Deal period.

10

The Commerce Clause in Transition

1865–1937

T HE EXPANSION of the commerce power after the Civil War came about through a set of incremental adjustments, some of which respected the approach of *Gibbons* and others which did not. To see how the law progressed, it is useful to divide the cases into two periods. The first deals with the extent to which the definition of commerce can be expanded to deal with agriculture, manufacture, or mining, where the original line in *Gibbons* largely held firm. The second deals with the complex question of whether the direct regulation or, in some cases, prohibition of people and goods in interstate commerce could be leveraged to limit or override the power of states to exercise their exclusive police power jurisdiction. Let us take these problems up in order.

Commerce versus Manufacture

The basic message that is derived from reading the key cases in this period is how faithfully they adhered to the general outlines of Marshall's approach until the progressive constitutional revolution of 1937. In an unbroken line of cases the tripartite division between activities prior to, during, and after the movement of goods in interstate commerce was uniformly observed, without any apparent worries over difficulties of drawing the line between "direct" and "indirect" effects on interstate commerce. It is of course easy to deride the use of terms like "direct" and "indirect" in this context, by endowing them with a level of ambiguity that they in fact do not contain. To see how this works, read in tandem two passages from the 1888 decision *Kidd v. Pearson*,[1] in which the Court unanimously upheld an Iowa statute that prohibited the manufacture of intoxicating liquors within its borders. The statute was challenged on the ground that it was barred by the Commerce Clause given that the banned products were intended for sale in the interstate market. A unanimous Supreme Court rejected this challenge on the simple ground that Congress had no power over local manufacturing. In the most general form, the Court wrote:

> As has been often said, legislation [by a State] may in a great variety of ways affect commerce and persons engaged in it, without constituting a regulation of it within the meaning of the Constitution, unless, under the guise of police regulations, it imposes a direct burden upon interstate commerce, or interferes directly with its freedom.[2]

But the Court in *Kidd* made it crystal clear how this distinction between direct and indirect regulation applied to the context at hand:

> If it be held that the term [commerce] includes the regulation of all such manufactures as are intended to be the subject of commercial transactions in the future, it is impossible to deny that it would also include all productive industries that contemplate the same thing. The result would be that Congress would be invested, to the exclusion of the States, with the power to regulate, not only manufactures, but also agriculture, horticulture, stock raising, domestic fisheries, mining—in short, every branch of human industry. For is there one of them that does not contemplate, more or less clearly, an interstate or foreign market?[3]

This passage was quoted in full in the more famous decision of *United States v. E. C. Knight*, which held that the antitrust laws did not apply to manufacture within the states. In so doing it urged this general proposition that comes straight out of Marshall's playbook in *Gibbons*: "Commerce succeeds to manufacture and is not a part of it."[4] The Court in *E. C. Knight* went on to note:

> It is vital that the independence of the commercial power and of the police power, and the delimitation between them, however sometimes perplexing, should always be recognized and observed, for while the one furnishes the strongest bond of union, the other is essential to the preservation of the autonomy of the States as required by our dual form of government. . . .[5]

In one sense, the *E. C. Knight* decision was dubious because the antitrust claim there involved the creation of the sugar trust through a merger of firms located in different states, an issue that does not fall obviously into the category of local manufacture or interstate business transaction. Yet the doubts about this application of the antitrust law were generally put aside shortly after *E. C. Knight*, in *Addyston Pipe & Steel Co. v. United States*.[6] Yet none of these disputes about borderline transactions had anything to do with the basic understanding of the reach of the Commerce Clause. One telling piece of evidence on this point comes from the passage of the Pure Food and Drug Act of 1906,[7] a reformist statute if there were ever one. That law forbade the shipment of certain drugs in interstate commerce and allowed Congress to regulate their manufacture in the territories, but *not* in the states. That restriction was promptly removed in 1938 after the transformation in Commerce Clause jurisprudence in the October 1936 term.

The same understanding is reflected in the text of the Twenty-First Amendment, which was drafted in the shadow of cases like *Kidd* and *Knight*. Its key provision reads:

> Section 2. The transportation or importation into any State, Territory, or possession of the United States for delivery or use therein of intoxicating liquors, in violation of the laws thereof, is hereby prohibited.

This provision sought to return to the status quo ante embodied in such cases as *Kidd* before the passage of the Eighteenth Amendment introducing prohibition into the United States. Its repeal by the Twenty-First Amendment sought to return the position to the status quo ante, and toward that end was directed to the transportation or importation of intoxicating liquors by making it clear that, as in the pre-prohibition era, Congress had no power to regulate either the production or consumption of intoxicating liquors in the several states. That provision would never have been drafted in this fashion if manufacture of all commodities were subject to federal power. To be sure, there were cases in which the direct/indirect line was challenged, of which perhaps the most notable instance is the highly controversial application of antitrust law to the activities of labor unions. Thus *United Mine Workers v. Coronado Coal*[8] involved an antitrust action brought by an open shop miner whose property was destroyed by the district union that exercised its jurisdiction over the relevant territory. In dealing with this decision, Chief Justice Taft added a refinement to the direct and indirect test, which ran as follows:

The mere reduction in the supply of an article to be shipped in interstate commerce by the illegal or tortious prevention of its manufacture or production is ordinarily an indirect and remote obstruction to that commerce. But when the intent of those unlawfully preventing the manufacture or production is shown to be to restrain or control the supply entering and moving in interstate commerce, or the price of it in interstate markets, their action is a direct violation of the Anti-Trust Act.[9]

Taft had no intention of upsetting the basic distinction between direct and indirect. But it is an open question whether his qualification to the basic doctrine is correct. The unlawful actions of the miners were manifestly actionable under state law, and it is odd to think that the antitrust laws that normally deal with pricing and other business practices should be pressed into service as a substitute for the state law concerning the willful destruction of property, even if done by parties intent on making sure that nonunion coal did not reach the marketplace. Indeed, after the 1937 constitutional revolution, the Supreme Court adopted just that narrower view in *Apex Hosiery v. Leader*,[10] by refusing to apply the Sherman Act to sit-in strikes. But even if this decision is given its full weight, its specific intent requirement would block its application to virtually all local regulations. In the cases where it mattered most the line between direct and indirect application did not invite practical uncertainty or philosophical speculation. On the ground, the test raised little or no doubt about either its clarity or its good common sense.

Notwithstanding this basic historical pattern, there were some instructive disputes over the reach and scope of the federal power that had this feature. How did one define an "interstate journey," and, more critically, could the federal government use its power over interstate commerce to influence patterns of behavior in manufacturing, agriculture, and mining, which were in theory subject to exclusive regulation by the states?

The first pressure point in an unavoidable line of expansion had to do with the definition of an interstate journey. Just that result was found in *The Daniel Ball*,[11] concerning either goods or people moved on a single journey across state lines, subject to this caveat: "of course that commerce which is carried on entirely within the limits of a state and does not extend to or affect other states."[12] As the context makes clear, all journeys that start in one state do not necessarily "affect" what goes on in another, for the term received here the same narrow reading that it had in *Gibbons*, *Kidd*, and *Coronado Coal*. But other interpretive questions turned out to be more elusive. In dealing with the Federal Employer's Liability Act, for example, the Court struggled before it concluded that Congress had the power to regulate the movement of trains, whose cars sometimes moved in interstate commerce and sometimes did not.[13] The point here was that the safety issues in question arose when and because the trains moved in interstate commerce. A decade later in *Stafford v. Wallace*,[14] the Court held that Congress had the power under the Commerce Clause to regulate rates and safety conditions for stockyards housing livestock that were held for sale or shipment in interstate commerce, on the shaky ground that these pens "are but a throat through which the current flows" and thus "incident" to an interstate journey. The equivocation shows how tricky these judgments can become, for should a different result apply to livestock stored in those same stockyards that had yet to enter interstate commerce? Or if some of the livestock remained in-state while others were sent to different states?

Yet larger issues were waiting in the wings. The first set of maneuvers led to the conclusion that all transportation, whether local or interstate, was subject to federal regulation. The stage was set in *Wabash, St. Louis & Pacific Railway Co. v. Illinois*,[15] where the Supreme Court held that Illinois could not set rates for railroads that were shipping goods into Illinois from other states or out of Illinois into other states. Of course, setting interstate rates falls within the core of the federal commerce power, which Congress had not exercised at all. No matter. *Wabash* soundly guaranteed that no one state could balkanize the transportation grid. Yet at the same time, *Wabash* necessarily created a regulatory void that the Interstate Commerce Act of 1887 (ICA) filled the next year. The ICA covered all routes except those that began and ended within the same state.[16] The ICA cleverly attacked the long-haul/short-haul inversion, whereby the rates in the competitive Chicago to San Francisco market were far lower than the rates on any monopoly segment of that market, such as Kansas City to Omaha. The reason for the inversion is that there were four railroad companies competing for business on the long-haul and only one on most short-haul segments of long-haul lines. The rates were thus adjusted to force those parties who could not find substitute transportation arrangements to bear most of the fixed costs of running the trains, to the immense frustration of the short-haul customers who could not understand why they had to pay more than the long-haul customers who were more costly to serve. Of course, in the absence of regulation it is only by raising prices on the inelastic portion of the demand curve (i.e., price-insensitive customers) that the railroads can recover the fixed costs of their investments. To counteract this price inversion, the 1887 ICA treated the long-haul rates as an upper bound on any short-haul rates. Its effect was to raise long-haul rates and lower short-haul ones in ways that more sensibly distributed the burden across different trips.

It was only a matter of time, however, before all local transportation was swallowed up under the commerce power. That outcome stemmed from two other developments, both of which marked the erosion of classical liberal principles in the definition of federal power, in areas where no one would have expected that substantive concerns with the distinction between force and competition could play a large role in explicating the structural provisions of the Constitution. The first pivotal move occurred in the *Shreveport Rate Cases*,[17] in which Justice Charles Evans Hughes expanded the conception of interstate commerce to allow the federal government to regulate the rates on *intra*state carriers in direct competition with interstate carriers, even though local carriers never ventured into interstate commerce. Justice Hughes insisted that Congress had the right to "protect" interstate commerce so that it "may be conducted upon fair terms and without molestation or hindrance."[18]

These evocative terms were not chosen by accident. They consciously evoked powerful images of protecting interstate commerce from force and fraud. Just that result had been achieved long ago in the 1838 decision of *United States v. Coombs*,[19] which recognized the power of the federal government to protect maritime commerce from criminal attacks launched from within a state, in that case for the theft of merchandise from a ship ground off the coast of New York. Congress could make sure that the use of force did not imperil interstate commerce. But no such risk was involved in *Shreveport*, where the "protective" principle was extended to cover competition from local lines, thereby creating, at least in transportation, false equivalence between force (a negative sum game) and competition (a positive sum game) in contravention of classical liberal theory, which condemns the former and blesses the latter. The ability to subject different networks to different regulators represents a useful division of power, not an inconvenient obstacle to sound economic development. A decade later, the Court held that Congress could also regulate intrastate routes that were *not* in competition with interstate lines, allowing the ICA to create a comprehensive rate base for general railroad regulation.[20] Note the transformation. The initial system of rate regulation sought, however imperfectly, to curb the evils of monopoly. Comprehensive rate regulation inverted the process by setting minimum rates to protect railroads against competition.

Leveraging Legislation over Interstate Commerce

The second assault on the original federalist design took a different tack, which did not bear fruit until the rise of the New Deal. Before 1900 or so, the federal power over interstate commerce was intended to regulate interstate commerce. But even before the rise of the New Deal, Congress imposed regulation on interstate commerce for a different reason: to get at local activities within states that were beyond the direct control of Congress. The first foray in this direction was in 1903 in *Champion v. Ames*, where the Court upheld by a five-to-four vote the power of Congress to prohibit the shipment of lottery tickets in interstate commerce, even if their sale—a subject of intense dispute during the late nineteenth century—was legal in the states from which, and to which, the tickets were shipped.[21] Historically this decision could have come only after the Civil War, for if *Champion* was correct then Congress could have launched (which no one believed at the time) a direct assault on slavery in 1840 by, say, refusing to let cotton made by slave labor into interstate or international markets.

The reason for this result rests on the (former) truism of American constitutional law that the federal government did *not* have under such cases as *Kidd* and *E. C. Knight* a general police power over local activities that were contrary to health and morals. That was part of the "immense mass" of legislation Marshall reserved to the states. The shipment of these lottery tickets in interstate commerce did not pose any threat to interstate commerce, as, for example, arises from the shipment of toxic substances, the kidnapping of innocent persons, or the transportation of prostitutes. Rather, the federal effort was meant to stamp out the lotteries themselves under a broad account of the police power that allowed the government to prevent immorality, dishonesty, or the spread of any evil or harm.[22] Of course, the local lotteries could still operate within the confines of their own states, but shrunken markets could easily lead to their economic demise. It was a genuinely puzzling question as to whether the power of the federal government should be used to alter private conduct that was subject to the police power of the states.

In my view, the answer to that question should be no. As noted earlier, classical liberal theory allows the government to impose limitations on those common carriers that enjoy monopoly positions. They must take all comers on reasonable and nondiscriminatory terms. However, in this context, the monopolist is the federal government, with its exclusive control over the interstate network. The United States in this capacity should be subject to the same scrutiny given to private monopolists and thus denied the ability, as antitrust lawyers like to say, to "leverage" its position over the interstate aspects of transactions to dictate the course of intrastate conduct that lies outside the sphere of its direct control.[23] Quite simply, the loss of access to national markets dwarfs any increase in the costs of production across an entire group of firms. The exercise of federal monopoly power over the transportation grid should thus be restricted to activities that do not alter the initial structural balance that the Constitution set out between the federal government and the states. Preventing or regulating the shipment of toxic materials in interstate commerce poses no threat to areas of exclusive state control.

Prohibiting sales of lottery tickets is a different matter. Indeed, if *Champion* had been decided the other way, it is likely that the Food and Drug Act of 1906 would have fallen as well, given that the shipment of drugs through interstate commerce posed no threat to the instrumentalities of interstate commerce. Intermediate cases, like the shipment of spoiled food[24] or the transportation of prostitutes across state lines for immoral purposes,[25] are closer cases, where the federal power should be sustained, because federal actions are meant to bolster, not countermand, state policies, which have never supported either activity. The risk of federal overreaching, however, is far greater when the federal policy is inconsistent with the policies of the state. On this view, the federal government can only restrict the shipment into interstate commerce of people and goods that pose a threat to the safety and health of people engaged in that commerce. It would not be permissible for Congress to use its power of regulation, for example, to pass a statute that says, "The shipment of all goods and the transportation of all persons in interstate commerce is strictly prohibited." The same condemnation would seem therefore to attach to a statute that provided that no person could ship dairy products, meat, or grain in interstate commerce, even if the federal government was not exercising that power as a way to control internal production within the state. Nor could it use that power to set quotas on the quantity of goods or the number of people shipped in interstate commerce. The Constitution sought to make the United States into one national trade zone, not a no-trade zone. The kinds of police power protections at issue here are those that are standardly incorporated in the international free trade agreements under the aegis of the World Trade Organization, which is equally insistent that public safety and health measures should not be used as a disguise for protectionist legislation.[26] There is no reason to impute a different, hidden agenda here. The clear lesson is that regulation, in the form of "making regular," gives Congress far more scope than prohibitions, for which the federal government faces a far greater burden. The regulation of commerce does allow for the prohibition of some goods from interstate commerce by congressional fiat, but only for cause.

The question was how far Congress could be allowed to put pressure on the arteries of interstate commerce in order to clamp down on production or consumption. The issue came to a boil of in the 1918 decision in *Hammer v. Dagenhart*,[27] where the articles shipped in interstate commerce were standard goods, made by firms that employed child labor. The firms had complied with the North Carolina twelve-year-old minimum child-labor law, but violated the United States' fourteen-year minimum employment age. The controversy over child-labor statutes marked one of the bitterest chapters in nineteenth-century politics, but general economic improvement meant that the use of child labor was on the wane in the first decades of the twentieth century. Indeed there is all too much economic evidence to the effect that, far from protecting children from industrial abuse, child-labor laws drive them into prostitution, begging, and worse.[28] That said, no one doubted that either the federal or state government could impose *some* child-labor law as a health or safety regulation under the police power. The key question is which should prevail when their policies conflict. On this score it was settled that the United States could not regulate child labor directly. But could Congress achieve that result indirectly—by putting restrictions on goods that were shipped into interstate commerce? A great lawyer, John W. Davis (who later was a founding partner of the distinguished firm Davis Polk & Wardwell), argued for the United States that the federal standard was needed in order to prevent state competition from creating a race to the bottom. In effect he held that there was a prisoner's dilemma that no state could beat of its own accord, for no state would dare raise the minimum age for child labor so long as other states kept some lower age. But his position seems overwrought because it requires, contrary to fact, that no state will enact one of these statutes at any age unless all other states go along. In addition, his position mistakenly presupposes that the higher federal standard better balanced the relevant interests, which was far from self-evident, given that in many instances work by younger children could, on average, improve overall family welfare in light of the greater perils to which children could be exposed in the black market. In any case, if allowed, the regulatory tactic could be used to support just about any federal regulation of state labor markets, including minimum wage and maximum hours requirements—areas within the exclusive province of the states at the time.

At this point a bit of economic realism is in order. The ability to sell in national markets will surely exceed whatever cost savings come from using child labor. The five-member majority in *Hammer* was therefore correct to strike down this effort to regulate local matters in order to preserve the original structural division of responsibility between the federal and state governments against unilateral federal regulation intent on undermining it. Indeed, at a time when taxation and regulation were close substitutes, the Court was correct five years later in the *Child Labor Tax Case* to strike down a tax on goods shipped in interstate commerce by firms that had used child labor.[29] As will become clear in the discussion of the taxing power, the key element of sound constitutional construction requires that the taxing power be exercised in parallel with the commerce power, as these cases demanded. For the moment, however, with the approach of the October 1936 Term most of the original constitutional structure is intact, where it fueled the rise of the mightiest nation on the globe. What became of that structure is the topic of the next chapter.

11

***

The Commerce Clause

Transformation to Consolidation, 1937–1995

THE PROGRESSIVE political ideals that had commanded so much attention in the first third of the twentieth century were finally put into
action during the first two terms of Franklin Roosevelt's New Deal pres-
idency, and have been elaborated and expanded ever since. This chapter takes up the consolidation of the progressive worldview from the
tumultuous New Deal period up until 1995, when the counteraction set
in. Chapter 12 picks up the narrative with *United States v. Lopez*, which
it then carries through to the contentious debates over the individual
mandate under the Patient Protection and Affordable Care Act. The purpose of these chapters is to show that the modern attack against the
earlier synthesis fails in two ways. It is not faithful to the constitutional
text or constitutional history, and it is disastrous in its relentless efforts
to cartelize industry after industry through a set of legal devices that
have only served to stymie the economic prosperity and social stability
of the United States.

The Progressive Onslaught

When the progressives were swept into power during the New Deal,
they brought all of their prior beliefs with them. The basic intellectual framework is clear. The progressives remained suspicious of state
solutions and thus insisted on national programs. They remained hostile to free markets and thus favored direct regulation in a wide range
of areas. Historically, the transition was less dramatic than these stark

statements make it appear. No one could claim that the first major planning schemes originated in the Roosevelt administration. There was, for example, the creation of the Federal Trade Commission[1] during the Wilson administration and the major overhaul of the Federal Radio Act[2] during the Coolidge administration. In addition, during the 1920s there were also major progressive initiatives in real estate markets, including the Washington, D.C., rent control laws upheld in 1921 in *Block v. Hirsh*[3] and the Ohio zoning ordinance sustained in 1926 in *Village of Euclid v. Ambler Realty Co.*[4] That same year, the then-noted progressive, Secretary of Commerce Herbert Hoover, issued a revised edition of the Standard State Zoning Enabling Act,[5] which was based on New York City's pioneering zoning ordinance of 1916.[6]

But none of these initiatives put the same type of pressure on the Commerce Clause as the Roosevelt legislation. The National Industrial Relations Act (NIRA)[7] was the first major foray in this direction, and in 1935 it was soundly and unanimously rebuffed by the Supreme Court in *A.L.A. Schechter Poultry Corp. v. United States.*[8] The codes of "fair competition" rules under the act required butchers to purchase entire runs of poultry, including sick chickens. Chief Justice Hughes first noted that NIRA's "codes of fair competition" went far beyond the common law rules and thus created space for an unconstitutional delegation of power.[9] On the commerce power question, the decision echoed *Gibbons*, as Chief Justice Hughes wrote: "In determining how far the federal government may go in controlling intrastate transactions upon the ground that they 'affect' interstate commerce, there is a necessary and well established distinction between direct and indirect effects."[10] *Kidd*[11] was duly cited, and the *Shreveport Rate Case*[12] and *Coronado Coal*[13] were duly distinguished. "[P]ersons employed in slaughtering and selling in local trade are not employed in interstate commerce."[14] End of case.

Nonetheless, *Schechter* proved to be only the opening battle in a longer war.[15] The subsequent battles took place over the National Labor Relations Act passed in 1935,[16] which was upheld in *NLRB v. Jones & Laughlin Steel* (*J&L*),[17] the various Agricultural Adjustment Acts passed between 1933 and 1938,[18] which were upheld in *Wickard v. Filburn*,[19] and the Fair Labor Standard Act of 1938 (FLSA),[20] which was in turn upheld in *United States v. Darby.*[21] Each of these cases generated significant constitutional challenges that resulted in a victory for the United States government—and a radical reorientation of Commerce Clause jurisprudence.

Starting with *J&L*, the major function of the National Labor Relations Act (NLRA)[22] was to prop up union monopolies in labor relations. Its basic structure allowed a union to organize an employer's labor force by majority vote in a secret ballot representation election, after which a victorious union spoke with a single voice for all its members. The statute created labor cartels that contain some involuntary members. In so doing, its overall characteristics are less efficient than those of a single monopolist because for the cartel to survive, each of its members must receive some share of the gains, which means that (as with OPEC and its oil quotas) some portion of the overall output must be transferred from more efficient to less efficient workers. To make the management system work, the NLRA, by design, has to limit the power of internal dissenters in order to allow for the creation of a unified front that shifts the bargaining advantage to the union side. New entry was barred because the union that received the majority position of control was to be the *exclusive* representative of the workers. Competitive labor markets were therefore put on hold. In their place was introduced a bilateral monopoly where the consequences of bargaining breakdown were lockouts and strikes. The deviations that the NLRA works from competitive markets are large and enduring.

But how did Congress make this scheme work within the framework of enumerated powers? The key doctrinal move at this stage was to note that *J&L* was a complex business entity with operations throughout the nation. Of course, that position is consistent with state regulation of local facilities and national regulation with respect to their cross-border transactions. But note the switch. The NLRA states: "The Board is empowered . . . to prevent any person from engaging in any unfair labor practice . . . affecting commerce,"[23] which Chief Justice Hughes promptly recast to say that the act "purports to reach only what may be deemed to burden or obstruct that commerce."[24] The language evokes the ghost of the former classical liberal view that allowed Congress to intervene to prevent the forcible blocking or obstruction of access to interstate commerce. But in practice, *J&L* was no simple rerun of a situation similar to the theft of goods covered by 1838 Supreme Court decision in *United States v. Coombs*,[25] for the NLRA was not directed to cases where either the union or management uses force to block trains from moving in interstate commerce. From day one, the act was construed to cover all actions that "affect" the levels of goods that are manufactured, up or down, within the states, which includes of course any regulation of any workplace behavior. Hughes's earlier expansive, albeit misguided logic in the *Shreveport Rate Case* was carried over from transportation to manufacturing without missing a beat—act one of the New Deal gambit was over.

The second key case was *Darby*, in which a unanimous Supreme Court overruled[26] the earlier decision in *Hammer v. Dagenhart*.[27] *Darby* rested on two erroneous pillars. It assumed that the Congress could. under the FLSA. impose hour and wage restrictions on local firms whether or not they were engaged in interstate transactions. Second, for good measure, in overruling *Hammer* it further explicitly held that the Congress "is free to exclude from the commerce articles whose use in the states for which they are destined it may conceive to be injurious to the public health, morals or welfare, even though the state has not sought to regulate their use."[28] The anticompetitive impact of this account of federal power is not avoided, but celebrated on the grounds that there is a "suppression of nationwide competition in interstate commerce by goods produced under substandard labor conditions,"[29] without first establishing that the federal standards are in any way superior to those of the states. The thought that this new federal initiative might deviate from the original constitutional design was similarly dismissed. Justice Stone acknowledged that the Bill of Rights does contain a Tenth Amendment, which reads: "The powers not delegated to the United States by the Constitution, nor prohibited by it to the States, are reserved to the States respectively, or to the people." But he concludes that this major structural provision is a "truism that all is retained which has not been surrendered,"[30] without ever asking how this formulation makes sense in this context. Under his logic, all economic control has effectively been surrendered. His reasoning is backwards. Given that there is a Tenth Amendment, some area of activity must be reserved to the states. Under Justice Stone's account, that class of activities is an empty set.

The same fast and loose arguments made in connection with labor regulation carry over to agricultural production. Once again, the motivation for regulation is the stabilization of prices through cartel formation. But how can this be done? The answer is through a comprehensive administrative scheme that, of necessity, has to be all-inclusive throughout the United States. More specifically, the cartelization of the agricultural business presents special challenges because of the need to organize large numbers of relatively small farmers into a single cohesive whole that is capable of keeping prices above the competitive level. That task therefore requires the system to solve two tasks simultaneously in ways that are well described in *Wickard v. Filburn*.[31] The first is to determine an overall level of output for each particular crop. This outcome was in fact achieved by having the Department of Agriculture conduct national referenda elections that helped it to determine total nationwide output. The second step is to allocate the total production down to the farm level, which required successive allocations from states to counties to individual farms. Roscoe Filburn ran afoul of this system when he exceeded his allotment of 11.1 acres for wheat, for which he was duly fined $117.11, or 49 cents per bushel for that excess production, which Filburn used to feed his own farm animals.

It should be quite clear that this allocation system was big business and that the regulation of channels of interstate and foreign commerce could not effectively restrict output so long as parties were free to sell their produce within their home states. To redirect produce was thereby to expand total supply at some modest loss of overall efficiency, especially since much of the grain was used for animals that lived in the same states. Closing that avenue of escape from cartel restrictions received its approval in *United States v. Wrightwood Dairy Co.*[32] There, the Supreme Court invoked the protective principle to hold that the United States could regulate the intrastate sale of dairy products in order to preserve the price control system that it wanted to create for interstate sales.

Once Congress plugged the hole of intrastate sales, it had to deal with the next effort by individual farmers to outwit the cartel. It is here that *Wickard* comes into play. If farmers could not sell their wheat to local cattle ranchers, the two firms could still vertically integrate their business in order to evade the federal regulation. By merging wheat and cattle farms, their owners could feed wheat grown on their own farms to their own cattle without engaging in any sale at all. The actions of any one farmer might not amount to much, but the device could easily spread, marking the demise of the cartel. But since the Supreme Court wanted the allocation scheme to work, it allowed for the "aggregation" of individual sales in order to show that the activities in question had a substantial effect on interstate commerce, which it surely did on the price and quantities of goods shipped across borders. Indeed, Justice Jackson put the "consumption of home-grown wheat" at over

20 percent of total output, which meets the substantial effect standard in anyone's book.[33] The sole reason to expand the commerce power, however, was not to stabilize the rules for organizing interstate transactions, which would have been consistent with classical liberal ends. Rather, it was to stabilize the prices of commodities sold throughout the United States, which decidedly runs up against those principles. Yet in *Wickard*, as in *Wrightwood*, the Supreme Court was benignly indifferent to whether the legislation sought, like the Sherman Act,[34] to encourage competition or, like the Agricultural Adjustment Acts,[35] to throttle it.

To make the appropriate doctrinal transition, it was key to show that both *Gibbons* and the *Shreveport Rate Cases* supported the extension of federal power so that neither *Darby*, *Wrightwood*, nor *Wickard* would read like they were conscious departures from earlier precedent. This meant rejecting the earlier views on the appropriateness and workability of the distinction between "direct" and "indirect" effects on interstate commerce.

Here is how it worked. Key sentences were quoted in a fashion that made them seem as if they supported a proposition that was the opposite of that for which they stood. First, in *Darby*, Justice Stone wrote that *Gibbons* stands for the proposition that "[t]he power of Congress over interstate commerce 'is complete in itself, may be exercised to its utmost extent, and acknowledges no limitations other than are prescribed in the Constitution.'" But his quotation omits the prior sentence, which says that the federal power "is the power to regulate, that is, to prescribe the rule by which commerce is to be governed."[36] The domain of commerce for Marshall was limited to cross-border transactions and explicitly excluded the local transactions that Stone subjects to its control.

A similar tactic was used in *Wrightwood Dairy*. In *Gibbons*, Chief Justice Marshall wrote: "Comprehensive as the word 'among' is, it may very properly be *restricted* to that commerce which concerns more States than one."[37] That sentiment was magically transformed in *Wrightwood Dairy* so that the applicable test now read that commerce "*extends* to those activities intrastate which so affect interstate commerce,"[38] or a version that says, "Congress could legislate with respect to all 'commerce which concerns more states than one.'"[39] "Restrict" and "extend" are opposites. "With respect to" conceals the obvious limitations on federal power. Yet such gross mischaracterizations were a key element of the New Deal evolution.

Not to be outdone, in *Wickard v. Filburn*, Justice Jackson wrote as if the law were emerging from a dark intellectual age that inexplicably followed the death of Chief Justice Marshall. "At the beginning, Chief Justice Marshall described the Federal commerce power with a breadth never yet exceeded," he said,[40] citing Marshall's decision in *Gibbons v. Ogden.*[41] Later on he added that it was now necessary "to bring about a *return* to the principles first enunciated by Chief Justice Marshall in *Gibbons v. Ogden. . . .*"[42]

To do so, Justice Jackson found it expedient to rely on a truncated version of the *Shreveport Rate Cases*. Lest there be any doubt on the issue, look closely at the textual makeover. The key quotation from the Hughes opinion in the *Shreveport Rate Cases* is the following:

> [*Congress's*] *authority, extending to these interstate carriers as instruments of interstate commerce, necessarily embraces the right to control their operations in all* matters having such a close and substantial relation to interstate traffic that the control is essential or appropriate to the security of that traffic, to the efficiency of the interstate service, and to the maintenance of conditions under which interstate commerce may be conducted upon fair terms and without molestation or hindrance.[43]

The italicized words were removed from the quotation in *Wickard*. In their place was an introductory sentence penned by Justice Jackson that began, "The opinion of Mr. Justice Hughes found federal intervention constitutionally authorized because of. . . ." He then sets off the rest of the quotation beginning with "matters." If that truncated rendition were correct, no one could explain what the shouting was about. But the blunt truth is that Jackson consciously excluded the italicized words "extending to these interstate carriers as instruments of interstate commerce," which had been inserted by Justice Hughes for the sole purpose of explaining how the *Shreveport Rate Cases* coexisted with *E. C. Knight* (an unquestioned authority at the time). "Naughty" is the kindest word that comes to mind for these self-conscious elisions.

The implications of these cases cannot be understated, given their importance to arguments about the size of government. In dealing with this issue, it is striking that both on and off the Court, the defenders of the broader views of the commerce power take a strongly originalist approach by belittling the opposite conception. For example, in his standard treatise on the matter, Laurence Tribe heaps scorn on the traditional categories, which he dismisses as a "formal and wooden segmentation of economic activity" and a "narrow, and quite abstract, construction."[44]

Tribe not only ignores the economics but also rests his misconceived objection on the improper equation of formal structures with aridity and sterility, when in many legal contexts the reality is anything but that. The key task of any federalist system is to draw workable boundaries of authority between national and state governments. Boundary lines between neighboring states are sharp and clear, so that we know where one begins and the other ends. No jurisdictional lines can be that clear when two sovereigns exert separate domains of control over the same territory. Nonetheless, to make sure that their respective spheres of authority are well understood and respected, the effort should be to achieve the same hard-edged texture of boundaries between different levels of government as exists between neighboring states.

This position is, moreover, fully defensible on modern functionalist grounds. In modern economic theory, it is understood that there can be no competitive equilibrium in a network industry, which is why the passage of the Interstate Commerce Act was such a big deal. But a competitive equilibrium is possible with agriculture, manufacture, and mining, which is why local regulation is preferred, precisely because it is less likely to tend toward monopoly. Indeed, the larger the transportation and communication grid, the stronger the case in modern economic terms for the Founders' original scheme.

It is, therefore, critical to understand the intellectual knots that any so-called economic, practical, or empirical approach can generate. Indeed, what is both notable and regrettable is the extent to which modern scholars turn cartwheels to defend the indefensible proposition that ties *J&L*, *Darby*, and *Wickard* to some updated, or living, version of the original constitutional design. Exhibit A is a short passage from the normally tough-minded Michael Greve, which argues that the Commerce Clause, at least when read in connection with the Necessary and Proper Clause, affords some justification for the New Deal results—much as he recoils from the intellectual banality of the legislative schemes under scrutiny. Thus at one point, he rightly notes: "Far from attempting to govern the world as a global commons, the New Deal attempted to manage it as a collection of cartels; and it was *that* purpose that drove the New Deal's take on the Commerce Clause."[45] Later on, Greve unwisely acquiesces in the inevitable when he writes:

> [T]he New Deal cases prove to be rightly decided or at least well within the constitutional ball park. *Jones & Laughlin* is surely right, so long as one grants its premise that unionization helps to prevent industrial strife. *Wickard*, despite its preposterous analysis, was rightly decided: grant Congress the power to limit the interstate supply of wheat and other commodities, and the power to suppress local evasion follows directly.[46]

Both parts of his analysis are wrong. Empirically, there is no reason to believe that the passage of the Wagner Act[47] did anything to curb industrial strife—quite the opposite. The level of industrial unrest, riveted with costly strikes, reached record heights after the enforced peace (through compulsory arbitration) ended in the aftermath of World War II.[48] It could hardly have been otherwise, because the balky institution of collective bargaining cannot make the same kinds of incremental adjustments to changes in external conditions that firms operating in competitive markets routinely do. So it is not possible to grant any premise about how unions prevent industrial strife. Nor is the point relevant because a determination of a statute's constitutionality has to be made long before it is possible to collect or assess the empirical data as to its purported, and often disputed, economic consequences. That point itself explains yet another of the many hidden advantages of the formal approach. The line between manufacture and interstate sales is clear on the day the statute is passed, so that these contentious empirical issues need not play any part in the overall analysis.

Greve is even more off base on *Wickard*, for the simple reason, explained above,[49] that Congress could not in 1787 or anytime thereafter pass a statute that says no grain shall be shipped in interstate commerce. The power to regulate, as governed by classical liberal principles, requires a showing of cause to keep those goods out of commerce. A feared glut of wheat does not count as one of those reasons, given that it is unrelated to the traditional police power objectives of health and safety. And even if suppressing the sale of wheat across borders were to count as a reason, home consumption would *reduce* the level of cross-border traffic, and is thus consistent with this supposed constitutional objective. In the end, therefore, Greve's novel arguments are more nuanced but no better than the "preposterous" reasoning that he rejects.

If Greve surrenders to the cynicism that drives *Wickard*, Jack Balkin is guilty of excessive optimism in offering, as a living originalist, an unapologetic defense of *Wickard* as "a fairly easy case," which requires some federal solution.[50] In dealing with these issues, Balkin does not begin with (or even mention) Madison's observation in *Federalist No. 45* that "[t]he powers delegated by the proposed Constitution to the federal government, are few and defined."[51] Instead he prefers to start with a well-known passage from James Wilson delivered to the Pennsylvania ratifying convention in November 1787, which reads:

> Whatever object of government is confined, in its operation and effects, within the bounds of a particular state, should be considered as belonging to the government of that state; whatever object of government extends, in its operations or effects, beyond the bounds of a particular state, should be considered as belonging to the government of the United States.[52]

Standing alone, his claim rings false because it states that these matters fall to either the states or the federal government. *Wickard*, for its part, is written on the premise that there is concurrent power at both levels of government. That perception is strikingly confirmed by the next passage that Balkin quotes, which shows that Wilson sensed that this broad formulation could be difficult to apply, so he then states how the Framers resolved that problem:

> In order to lessen or remove the difficulty arising from discretionary construction on this subject, an enumeration of particular instances, in which the application of the principle ought to take place, has been attempted with much industry and care.[53]

Balkin reads the second passage as supporting *Wickard* on the ground that "the purpose of the enumeration was not to *displace* the principle but to *enact* it."[54] And so it was. But the stress on "particular instances" shows that its enactment did not embrace any of the major concerns that led to *Wickard*, all of which were rejected prior to the New Deal period. It is therefore not possible to draw any broad inference that renders the entire system of enumerated powers nugatory as a fair implication of the original position. Note too that in making this general observation, Wilson puts forward a general approach without mentioning the Commerce Clause specifically, let alone endowing it with super-human powers. Indeed, later on, Wilson (who ran on interminably) explicitly rejected the argument that the Necessary and Proper Clause "gives to Congress a power of legislating generally."[55] Read in context, Wilson sounds more like Madison in *Federalist No. 45* than the Justice Jackson of *Wickard*.

Balkin's expansive reading, then, is inconsistent with Wilson's own words. But even if it were not, how could this one passage, quoted in isolation, be leveraged to defend the outcome in *Wickard*? For Balkin, the key functional point starts with the correct observation that farmers face two problems. The first is dealing with the uncertainties in natural conditions that make it difficult to project the supply of agricultural produce, and hence the price of any given commodity. That variability is the reason why agricultural commodities are routinely exempt from price control statutes. The second problem is that the large number of small farmers makes it very difficult for farmers to coordinate their output to reach what Balkin candidly acknowledges to be a cartel price. Accordingly, he notes correctly that "states are separately incompetent to limit agricultural production"[56]—a misleading phrase that I shall examine later in more detail[57]—which of course means that only something like the Agricultural Adjustment Acts could facilitate those output restrictions.

His argument fails under any classical liberal constitution because the state-run cartel is the problem, not the solution, to the general question of agricultural production, which suggests that a better outcome is achieved by leaving the issue to the states. Yet at the same time, individual farmers can handle the vagaries of future production without federal intervention, for an active competitive market does exist, which allows farmers to control these risks through forward sales or a variety of financial hedges. It is important to recognize that Balkin's incantation of "spillover effects and collective action problems"[58] is vice's homage to virtue.

Here's why. In the standard economic literature, each of these terms addresses private actions that drive an economy further from a competitive solution. Regulation is thus needed to protect against the pollution that arises from agricultural production. A collective action problem arises when a necessary public good cannot be provided for voluntarily, so that some coercion is needed to make the social system more efficient than before. But it remains a good thing for competition to undermine cartels, not a bad one. The commerce power should never be extended beyond its original meaning to give voice to such antisocial programs as crop supports. Nor does that same incantation of spillover effects and collective action problems support the FLSA, whose minimum wage and overtime provisions threw huge distortions into all labor markets.

Leaving these issues to the state always improves social welfare because the exit right can then operate as a powerful constraint against abusive government behavior. The deification of government monopolies, without any awareness of their dislocations, is thus complete.

The Post–New Deal Period: 1942–1995

The Supreme Court decisions between *Wickard* and *Lopez* followed a predictable course, yielding many outcomes—some of which were mundane, and others of which were momentous in their social importance. Doctrinally, these extensions of federal power have often relied on the "cumulative effect" principle, which indicates that the operative question is never whether a single act of a given class has an effect on interstate commerce, but whether all the acts within that class will. Less than momentous was *Perez v. United States*,[59] which allowed for the successful criminal prosecution of small-time credit extortion. However, the same principle was used with far greater effect in *Heart of Atlanta Motel, Inc. v. United States*,[60] which upheld the application of the Civil Rights Act of 1964 to hotels and motels whose customers often came from across state lines, and in *Katzenbach v. McClung*,[61] in which the sole interstate connection was that the food served at some restaurants came from sources outside the state. The former of these decisions is surely closer to the line if one perceives hotels and motels as part of the transportation grid that was comfortably subject to federal power under *Gibbons*. But it tracks very poorly with efforts to apply that logic to destination hotels and luxury resorts, which are hardly midpoints in continuous journeys. *Katzenbach*, meanwhile, does not make any pretense that the services supplied in local restaurants are in interstate commerce, but only that the food served is acquired through interstate commerce, which applies to hotels and motels as well. For those who think that an antidiscrimination law dealing with private businesses is a good thing, these decisions will not raise a ripple of concern, given how they necessarily follow from the earlier cases dealing with labor relations and agriculture. And there is no doubt that the federal intervention was welcome insofar as it broke the ghastly state monopoly under Jim Crow, which resulted in a breakdown of the protection of basic political and civil rights, which themselves had collapsed dramatically after the Civil War.[62] But make no mistake about it: in the long run, the 1964 Civil Rights Act, especially in the area of employment, did little or nothing to open markets. To the contrary, it stifled innovation by new competitors who did not meet some preconceived government conception of fair labor markets. The 1964 act, however, did wonders in sweeping away the residue of state-enforced segregation in the late 1960s. But after that time, it is hard to detect any net benefit for its aggressive application of disparate impact tests and other devices.[63] Government powers are rigid. They do not allow people who dissent from the social consensus to express their own preferences in private activities. Ironically, the 1964 statute adopted a color-blind principle that slowed down the rise of affirmative action programs that were much in demand after the massive racial unrest in the late 1960s.

The civil rights cases did not, however, mark any major change in principle from earlier decisions. The one major doctrinal development in this area arose from the extension of the Fair Labor Standards Act of 1938[64] whose constitutionality was upheld in *Darby*[65] as applied to state and local employees. Such employees were exempted from the original statute, but the political forces in favor of expanded federal power slowly chipped away at these exemptions. In 1961, the exemption from the FLSA was lifted for the activities of state and local governments for "enterprises" that engaged in commerce or the production of goods for commerce.[66] In 1966, employees at state hospitals, schools, and other institutions were brought under the umbrella of the act.[67] Finally, in 1974, the FLSA was amended to cover essentially all state and local employees.[68] The Supreme Court happily ratified the initial extensions of the statute in its 1968 decision in *Maryland v. Wirtz*,[69] over the dissent of Justices William O. Douglas and Potter Stewart, who did not pitch their opposition to these developments under the Commerce Clause. Instead, they saw, rightly in my view, a major interference with coequal state sovereignty that was inconsistent with the Tenth Amendment's reservation of powers to the states, which *Darby* had effectively gutted. That objection picked up steam in *National League of Cities v. Usery*,[70] which struck down the extension of the FLSA to the activities of state and local governments that fell within "areas of traditional government function."

A host of lower court decisions followed, with determinations that licensing drivers and operating ambulances, waste disposal activities, and municipal airports were traditional government functions, while issuing industrial development bonds, making rules for intrastate natural gas sales, and regulating air and traffic were not. Nine years later,

Justice Blackmun, who originally had gone along with the majority in *National League of Cities*, found these classification problems intractable in *Garcia v. San Antonio Metropolitan Transit Authority*,[71] where the question was whether the minimum wage and overtime provisions of the FLSA applied to a public mass transit authority, thus permitting the federal government to set hours and wages for all municipal employees. The concern with independent state sovereignty was regarded as a relevant issue, but one which was taken care of through the political and not the constitutional process.

The entire debate has a surreal air, owing to the original wrong turn on the Commerce Clause itself. At no point in this line of cases did anyone cast any doubt on the soundness of the *Darby* decision. The simple view that most of these activities of local governments fell outside the scope of the Commerce Clause was thus never applied. Taken seriously, that would allow the federal government to regulate local and state governments only in those cases in which they operated municipal airports that served interstate runs, and little else. At that point, the question of whether hospital workers could be distinguished from police officers disappears from view.

The decision in *Garcia*, moreover, draws sharply into question the modern extension of constitutional federalism insofar as it assumes that political checks will save the states from federal regulation that they do not want, as has been elegantly urged, first by Herbert Wechsler and later by Jesse Choper.[72] Obviously, these forces did not work to protect state and local governments from the major extensions of the FLSA. The major check that the states once had over the Congress—their power to appoint senators—had been stripped away by the Seventeenth Amendment in 1913, and the powerful forces arrayed in favor of minimum wage coverage had achieved their ends. It was incomprehensible in 1787 that the national government could override the judgment of the individual states in how they organized their internal administrative operations. The list of prohibitions on state conduct that were set out in Article I, Section 8, clause 10 referred to the capacity of the states to enact certain kinds of laws. None so much as hinted that this ability to force changes in labor laws would necessarily influence how state and local governments allocated work within their respective bureaucracies. Nor did they discuss how this would necessarily impose on them the hard choices about whether to borrow funds, raise taxes, or curtail services. It was almost as if the adoption of the minimum wage and overtime rules could work a simple cash transfer from taxpayers to employees, without any collateral consequences on how the state hired and assigned these workers their duties. The ability of one sovereign to shape the operational decisions of others constitutes a huge infringement on state sovereignty that is apparent to anyone who is not committed to the New Deal dogma of comprehensive federal regulation.

Moreover, the decision here is not saved by the view that the requirements imposed on the states are no more onerous than those that are imposed on other actors. That argument was made in *Fry v. United States*,[73] which held, in good *Wickard* fashion, that a wage and price control system could be imposed on state governments in order to prevent the erosion of a regulatory scheme that was yet another disaster—constitutionally and economically—from the outset.

The lessons that are learned from the sorry episode of endless federal regulation is that one bad turn begets another. Start down the road where enumerated powers look like an archaic principle, and quickly, the entire system of federalism is stood on its head. That result is not a necessary consequence of modernity. It stems from a deep commitment in the progressive approach that finds all legislative interferences in labor and product markets to fall within the purview of Congress. Under that view of the world, nothing stands in the path of federal regulation. What is most amazing about the story is that it did not replicate itself in connection with the state powers of regulation and taxation that are subject to a far stricter regime under the dormant Commerce Clause, which is the subject of Chapter 15.

12

Constitutional Pushback

1995 to Present, from *Lopez* to *NFIB*

T HE LAST STAGE of constitutional development started in 1995 with *United States v. Lopez*,[1] where Chief Justice Rehnquist, writing for a narrow five-to-four majority, struck down the Gun-Free School Zones Act, which forbade carrying a gun within 1,000 feet of a school.[2] In one sense, the opinion reads as a sea change insofar as it indicated that there was at least some outer limit on the scope of federal power, if only because a federal statute was actually struck down for exceeding the bounds of the Commerce Clause. But at root, the opinions in *Lopez* do nothing to unpack the deep contradictions in Commerce Clause interpretation. Chief Justice Rehnquist uneasily embraced both James Madison and *Wickard* simultaneously in his highly influential account of the three strands of the commerce power.[3] Thus, after a quick review of all the familiar precedents from *Gibbons* through *Perez*, he writes as if these cases rest on a single harmonious vision of the commerce power:

> Consistent with this structure, we have identified three broad categories of activity that Congress may regulate under its commerce power. First, Congress may regulate the use of the channels of interstate commerce [*Darby*]. Second, Congress is empowered to regulate and protect the instrumentalities of interstate commerce, or persons or things in interstate commerce, even though the threat may come only from intrastate activities [*Shreveport*]. Finally, Congress' commerce authority includes the power to regulate those activities having a substantial relation to interstate commerce [*Jones & Laughlin*].[4]

At no point does he trouble himself with the deep ironies in his position. Thus his brief account of the first category does not explain why

Darby was right to overrule *Hammer v. Dagenhart*. The simple reference to the power to regulate the channels of interstate commerce, which stems from *Gibbons*, is therefore restated in a conceptual void. Likewise, Rehnquist writes as if he is blissfully unaware of either the internal difficulties of that case or the way in which Justice Jackson in *Wickard* expanded it from transportation and communication to agriculture and manufacturing. Thus, his matter-of-fact acceptance of *Wickard* meant that his view ratified from the conservative side of the Court the enormous expansion of federal power.[5] The overall situation was not improved by the concurrence of Justice Anthony Kennedy, whose linguistic skepticism led to the dubious conclusion that "semantic or formalistic categories" can't be used to define commerce.[6] But his philosophical point gets it exactly backwards for, as noted, jurisdictional questions should be settled by the kind of clear boundaries used to separate landowners, delineate lanes on public roads, or define the basic rules of virtually all sports.

A Constitutional Sea Change?

At this point, the only question is just what did the chief justice see as his mission. The answer is more doctrinal than institutional. What he did was decide to show that the principle of enumerated powers was alive even within the *Wickard* framework, because he could be clever enough to beat Justice Jackson at his own game, by demonstrating that federal enforcement of the gun law did not substantially influence either the quantity of goods shipped in interstate commerce or the price at which they were shipped. So there are limits on the commerce power after all. But the cleverness that drove this rationale ensured that his exceptions would look like parched fruit on the vine—incapable of any further growth. To be sure, the usual five-to-four split in *United States v. Morrison*[7] struck down that portion of the Violence against Women Act of 1994[8] that purported to make a dormitory rape a federal offense on the ground that its indirect economic consequences were not sufficient to support federal power. But that decision had little practical effect, for here, as in *Lopez*, the challenged conduct was long held criminal under state law.

What really matters is how the *Lopez* synthesis plays out when there is a serious policy conflict between the federal government and the states. That issue came to the fore with *Gonzales v. Raich*,[9] in which the clash between the California Compassionate Use Act,[10] which legalized the use of marijuana for medical purposes, and the federal Controlled Substances Act,[11] which rendered illegal the private possession and use of marijuana, is too plain to dispute. The private parties structured their transactions so as to eliminate all possible interstate economic transactions. Respondent Monson grew her own marijuana; respondent Raich received hers as a gift from two friends. Both used it under medical supervision. Neither could find any other substitute. But for a six-member Supreme Court majority, all this fine-tuning was to no avail. The one-two punch of *Wickard* and *Perez* allowed for the needed aggregation that allowed the federal policy to prevail. The uniform national response squashed out this program of state experiment. And thus the *Lopez* boomlet came to an end.

The Conservative Attack on Health Care Legislation

It is an open question whether this boomlet was revived by the Supreme Court's recent decision on the Patient Protection and Affordable Care Act (ACA), known everywhere as "ObamaCare." It is impossible in a short compass to describe fully all of the complex provisions of this statute.[12] Nor would it be necessary to do so, as the ACA would be dead-on-arrival, if the pre–New Deal understandings of the Commerce Clause held. But in this new environment, it is critical to lay out a few key provisions to set the context for the now-famous debate over the individual mandate. The crux of this discussion begins with the key difference between market insurance and social insurance. Under the former, the market operates because each individual pays a premium that is in subjective terms less costly than the set of health care benefits that he or she gets from the private insurer. Under this system, no particular individual worries about who else is in his or her pool because the pressure of market forces eliminates any cross-subsidization among parties. The good news is that these insurance pools will prove stable over time because rational insurers have no incentive to incur large losses by undercharging their unprofitable customers who will happily stay. Nor do they have an incentive to overcharge their profitable customers, lest they will drive them into the arms of rival insurers offering lower rates. That pressure also gives an incentive for maintaining good health to individual insureds, who can then cash out in the form of lower health insurance premiums. The downside to this market solution is that in a voluntary market, individuals who are known to be high risk will only be able to get insurance at high rates that reflect their risk—rates that may be beyond their capacity to pay. This problem has been acknowledged on all sides of the political spectrum for years, because no one wants to take the position that it is just fine to let a baby die on the doorsteps of a hospital because of the inability to pay.[13] The question becomes what is the best institutional response to the problem, which before the rise of government included all sorts of extensive private and charitable activities in that direction, and, of course, public funding of hospitals and wards for the indigent. There have been occasional charges of neglect and abandonment, but in practice these turned out to be few and far between, and were often overstated for political advantage.[14]

The explicit assumption behind the ACA is that these lesser means all fail. The key evidence for this proposition has been said to be the inexorable increase in the numbers of uninsured individuals. The defenders of ACA do not have a clear explanation as to why with greater prosperity the number of individuals who need insurance should be on the increase, and they certainly do not accept the proposition that it could be attributable to current regulations on the books that require employers to meet certain health care minimum mandates if they wish to cover their employees. These mandates are costly, and their cumulative impact could easily make employer-based insurance an unappetizing proposition for employers and employees alike. A catalogue of mandates produced by the Council for Affordable Health Insurance (CAHI) listed some 2,262 separate state mandates as of 2011, an increase of more than 300 since 2009.[15] The percentage of persons with employer-based insurance dropped from about 65 to 45 percent between 2007 and 2012.[16] This is not a small problem.

The solution reached under the ACA was to double down on coercion. Instead of removing licensing and other barriers to entry, Congress decided to impose a set of extensive requirements that all insurance firms had to meet in order to remain in the health insurance business. Among these were guaranteed issue rules that prevented firms from picking their own clients or setting prices based on preexisting conditions. These in turn were matched with rules that allowed individuals to opt out of any insurance coverage at any time. The obvious risk here is one of customer opportunism, whereby coverage is purchased by individuals who know that they need surgery or other treatment. That coverage is promptly dropped when the treatment runs its course. Ordinary insurance policies have dealt with this risk by requiring waiting periods before receiving coverage on preexisting conditions. They have also required that policies be taken for fixed terms, both of which do much to stop opportunism, but little to deter coverage. Other provisions of the ACA require a system of community rating whereby young people with low risks are charged premiums in excess of the amount needed to supply coverage, with the explicit purpose of cross-subsidizing older individuals with higher risk profiles. Again the risk is clear. Young people will flee from policies that charge them prices in excess of value.

The system that demands cross-subsidization is thus unstable. In order to counter that instability, the ACA added a requirement under which many persons who do not have private insurance have to pay a fee to the Internal Revenue Service. The stated purpose of the fee is that it is part of the system to block private abuse. In one sense, its greatest defect is that the number in question could prove too low to achieve its stated end. But in the constitutional setting, the question was whether the mandate gave an opening to challenge this portion of the ACA on constitutional grounds, even with the *Wickard* line of cases on the books. In one sense, defending the statute against a Commerce Clause challenge could be easy given the huge size of the integrated health care market. The point was not lost on Justice Ginsburg in her concurring opinion, which insisted that *Wickard* controlled: "Collectively, Americans spent $2.5 trillion on health care in 2009, accounting for 17.6% of our Nation's economy."[17] Other commentators have had the same impatience with what they see as the entire Commerce Clause fiasco. Harvard professor Charles Fried, a former solicitor general in the Reagan administration, thinks that the entire issue can be made in staccato like fashion. "Health care is interstate commerce. Is this a regulation of it? Yes. End of story."[18]

Unfortunately, it is not. There are counterarguments. Heath care is not a form of commerce. There are firms that supply health care services whose local activities are in interstate commerce under the modern definition of that term. The regulation of their practices was extensive long before *Wickard*, but only at the state level under the 1869 decision in *Paul v. Virginia*,[19] which survived until it was overruled by the 1944 decision in *United States v. South-Eastern Underwriting*.[20] But the regulation of customers takes a different arc from the regulation of firms. Surely, they can be prevented from submitting fraudulent applications. But for people who are neither customers nor prospective customers, I know of no precedent seeking to require coverage unless they wish to participate in some activity like driving on public highways. It follows therefore that under the current regime, Justice Kennedy's pointed question in oral argument—"Can you create commerce in order to regulate it?"—at the very least requires an answer.

That question quickly gives rise to an immense debate over whether it is possible to regulate "pure inactivity," where it poses at least these puzzles: At any given time, I am not engaged in millions of activities; can I be taxed or penalized for not cutting wood, not cycling, not eating pancakes, or not playing croquet? It was just this line of argument that led the swing vote in this case, Chief Justice Roberts, to conclude, not unreasonably, that even under *Wickard* and its progeny, the individual mandate fell outside the scope of congressional power. "The power to *regulate* commerce presupposes the existence of commercial activity to be regulated. If the power to 'regulate' included the power to create it, many of the provisions in the Constitution [relating to other enumerated powers] would be superfluous."[21] This position is defensible in the second-best world that takes *Wickard* as its baseline, for it is doubtful that any of its New Deal defenders would have put any stock in the action/inaction line that came to dominate the constitutional debate. But at this point the case rests on the prescriptive claim that it is not possible seventy years after *Wickard* to undo the huge network of federal regulations whose constitutionality rests on its soundness. But precisely because the defense of *Wickard* rests only on prescriptive grounds, it supplies no justification for the *extension* of federal power into new areas. I would therefore vote to strike the individual mandate down on just this limited ground.[22] There is no reliance interest based on long usage that constitutionally justifies a program that has yet to go into effect.

The Liberal Response

On this point, of course, others might wish to differ. But what is so distressing about the current defenses of the individual mandate is that its supporters shun the modest proposition that it is too late in the day to challenge *Wickard*'s pedigree. Instead the defense of the individual mandate is placed on originalist grounds, namely rationales that track Balkin's flawed reading of earlier texts, in which the cut-and-paste method turns both the historical record and economic logic upside down. Here is one critical analysis of how Justice Ginsburg's opinion does precisely that.

Her argument starts with the view that "States cannot resolve the problem of the uninsured on their own."[23] That statement is made without the slightest recognition of the many unwise state and federal regulatory initiatives that have made matters worse. She posits a collective action problem that requires the federal government to step in where the states have failed to act in order to avoid the race to the bottom when generous states find themselves at a competitive disadvantage with their neighbors.[24] There is not the slightest recognition of the virtues of competitive federalism, whose central tenet stems from Justice Brandeis's famous observation that states act as laboratories, offering room for experimentation that can avoid many of the huge structural mistakes that are built into the warp and woof of the ACA. She then compounds this mistake by positing a market failure because markets do not tolerate, let alone generate, the kind of cross-subsidies that she thinks a sound health care system should put in place. And she furthers the confusion by making it appear as though there is some market failure because some people are unwilling to purchase health insurance in, we must not forget, a market that is rigged against their interests.

She then segues from her threadbare economic account of the health insurance market to the constitutional challenges under the Commerce Clause:

> *The Framers' solution was the Commerce Clause, which, as they perceived it, granted Congress the authority to enact economic legislation* "in all Cases for the general Interests of the Union, and also in those Cases to which the States are separately incompetent." 2 *Records of the Federal Convention of 1787*, pp. 131–132, ¶8 (M. Farrand rev. 1966).[25]

These records say no such thing. The italicized words are a judicial invention. The full text of the original reads as follows:

> *That the Legislature* of the United States ought to possess the legislative Rights vested in Congress by the Confederation; and moreover to legislate in all Cases for the general Interests of the Union, and also in those Cases to which the States are separately incompetent, or in which the Harmony of the United States may be interrupted.

Compare the italicized words in the two texts to see how the history is twisted. The original text does not refer to the Commerce Clause at all. Indeed there is nothing in the passages surrounding this text that make any reference to the Commerce Clause either. The original textual reference is to "the Legislature," which has all sorts of enumerated powers to which the rest of the paragraph could apply: the power to tax and spend, the power to establish post roads, the power to raise an army and navy, and to organize the militia—all fit the general description of the "general Interests of the Union." But adding the gloss that the Constitution "granted Congress the authority to enact economic legislation" lends a misleading specificity to this provision that is utterly inconsistent with the original context, which is in search of much larger themes. Indeed the sentence before the passage quoted above reads: "Resolved That in the second Branch of the Legislature of the United States each State shall have an equal Vote."

The most that can be said is that the Commerce Clause is one position among many that helps this issue. But it gives no reason to think that Justice Ginsburg's vision had any traction with a group of Federalists and Anti-Federalists, all of whom were champions of limited government in a world that had no place whatsoever for positive rights and forced transfer payments instituted by a dominant national government. It is perfectly sensible to say that the commerce power allowed Congress to counteract the threat of local regulations to interstate trade, defined as Chief Justice Marshall stated in *Gibbons*. Nor can Justice Ginsburg displace these considerations by invoking the words "general Interests of the Union," which refer to those matters that concern the United States as a whole, not the welfare of individual citizens within it. That concern is evident in the account of the power of Congress under the Spending Clause, which is related to "the general welfare of the United States," not the health care of any individual.[26]

Likewise, the question of where states are "separately incompetent" does raise important issues that the Commerce Clause was supposed to solve. On the one hand, it allowed for Congress to specify rules of interstate trade to expand the scope of the market. Regrettably, it also, in connection with foreign commerce, allowed the use of protective tariffs to reduce trade. But at no point in the early accounts of the Commerce Clause is there any embrace of a positive right to health care guaranteed by government; the states are not "separately incompetent" to provide these services if they so choose.

Finally, Justice Ginsburg's effort to bring in collective action and prisoner's dilemma games misunderstands how those operations work.[27] The standard prisoner's dilemma game presupposes two prisoners who have

identical preference functions: each would rather go free than be convicted of a crime. Both know if each remains silent they will achieve their
common end. But so long as they cannot communicate each will pursue
his "dominant strategy," which is to speak, such that no matter what the
other does he is better off speaking. But that does not begin to remotely
describe the situation here, where there are profound policy disagreements about which collective solutions work, including fierce opposition
on the substance to the ACA's basic policy choices. Nor is there any reason
to think that state plans will fail unless all other states fall into line. The
Massachusetts universal health care program, which faces acute health
care pressures of its own, is not the only exemplar. The Healthy Indiana
Plan[28] is a more successful approach to dealing with the uninsured that
does not look like a Rube Goldberg contraption; yet the Ginsburg decision makes no mention of this counterexample to the supposed prisoner's
dilemma. More generally, it would be wrong to think that the Framers,
or anyone else, think that the greatest risk to sound policy decisions is
decentralized control. The greater risk in the rough and tumble environment of national politics is that a willful majority will impose its preferences on a vulnerable minority that vehemently resists all proposals for
centralization. Federal legislation allows states like Texas and Indiana to
join in the federal plan without fear of competition, if only they thought
it did any good. But of course they do not. The opposition of twenty-six
Republican governors to the Medicaid extension highlights the deep
ideological divide. There is no reason to think that they are wrong, any
more than there is good reason to think that the strict federal child labor
law struck down in *Hammer* was superior socially to North Carolina's own
child labor law. To a classical liberal, centralization poses far greater risks
than decentralized decisions that place states in competition with each
other. It is only the progressive love affair with national monopolies that
treats competitive federalism as a destructive prisoner's dilemma game.

The weaknesses in Justice Ginsburg's opinion are not cured by
the academic defense of her position. I cannot recall a single pro-ACA
account of *Gibbons* that ever bothered to state its facts or to distinguish
away the restrictive language that Chief Justice Marshall inserted to
limit its language. Instead, Einer Elhauge excitedly questions, "If Health
Insurance Mandates Are Unconstitutional, Why Did the Founding
Fathers Back Them?"[29] The clincher was that "[Congress] enacted a
federal law requiring the seamen to buy hospital insurance for themselves. That's right, Congress enacted an individual mandate requiring

the purchase of health insurance."[30] All that is missing is a more precise account of the circumstances. The 1798 statute was entitled "An Act for the relief of sick and disabled Seamen."[31] Its core provision required the master or owner of every foreign vessel coming into United States ports to take (out of seamen's wages no less) a fixed sum which was to be spent "to provide for the temporary relief and maintenance of sick or disabled seamen, in the hospitals or other proper institutions now established in the several ports of the United States," where the president had the discretion "to cause buildings, when necessary, to be erected as hospitals for the accommodation of sick and disabled seamen."

There is no doubt that this statute imposes duties on foreign vessels, but the circumstances are wholly different from the ones at hand. The mandate was not imposed on persons who were not engaged in any form of commerce. Instead, it was imposed on foreign ships entering into the United States, which lies of course at the core of the foreign commerce power. The conditions in question were not imposed on some mysterious form of inactivity, but rather they were designed to make sure that the seamen who came into the United States did not impose a burden on the rest of the population. These conditions were thus intended to prevent, not to create, cross-subsidies between different groups of persons. Indeed the use of excess funds to construct hospitals for the care of these seamen explains why this statute is utterly unproblematic even under the narrowest reading of the Commerce Clause, which is why it was passed by in silence for so many years.

Elhauge is on no stronger ground when he cites to the Militia Acts of 1792.[32] The respective titles of these two acts were "An Act to provide for calling forth the Militia to execute the laws of the Union, suppress insurrections and repel invasions" and "An Act more effectually to provide for the National Defence by establishing an Uniform Militia throughout the United States." One requirement of these laws was that every able-bodied white male between the ages of eighteen and forty-five "provide himself with a good musket or firelock" and other forms of equipment. But as is evident from the titles of the two statutes, this action proceeded under the Militia Clauses, which envisioned explicit cooperation between state and federal government under a provision that gave Congress the power

> [t]o provide for organizing, arming, and disciplining, the Militia, and for
> governing such Part of them as may be employed in the Service of the

United States, reserving to the States respectively, the Appointment of the Officers, and the Authority of training the Militia according to the discipline prescribed by Congress.[33]

What this provision has to do with the Commerce Clause Elhauge never explains.

In addition to these highly specific attacks, there are endless broadsides that vilify the critics of the individual mandate in harsh but uninformed terms. Andrew Koppelman thinks that any criticism of the ACA must necessarily rest on "tough luck" libertarianism, undergirded by a system of "absolute" property rights, by which people have not only the right, but also the duty, to let other individuals suffer.[34] But the framers of the current challenge (of which I am not one) crafted their view so that it would leave the existing versions of Medicare and Medicaid intact. Nor at any point would it be credible to base an attack on any government program on this hard-line libertarian view, for the simple reason that the Constitution is not a libertarian document. Most emphatically, it is a classical liberal document that allows for both taxation and eminent domain. Nor is the issue of wealth distribution at the core of this debate, which is only over whether the federal government can regulate this activity. What the attack surely does is call into question the growth of government power, which thus far has been subject to no intellectual opposition among the fashionable political elites. On this score, it is notable that most judicial conservatives are not willing to take up the cudgels themselves. Indeed the current political reality is such that in the lower courts prominent judges like Jeffrey Sutton on the Sixth Circuit and Laurence Silberman on the District of Columbia Circuit both voted to sustain the individual mandate. As Silberman put the point in *Seven-Sky v. Holder*,[35] "The right to be free from federal regulation is not absolute, and yields to the imperative that Congress be free to forge national solutions to national problems, no matter how local—or seemingly passive—their individual origins." No one has ever disputed the first half of that sentence. But the second half encapsulates the fundamental mistake of the modern progressive mindset. In this instance the "national problem" is Congress, for which there is only a constitutional, not a political, solution. That insight has been lost not only with respect to the commerce power, but also with respect to the congressional power to tax and spend, which the next chapter addresses.

13

Enumerated Powers

Taxing and Spending

THE COMPREHENSIVE DISCUSSION of the Commerce Clause addresses the question of when and how Congress may regulate. But that clause cannot be read in isolation from other key powers afforded to the federal government, which may be exercised in tandem with it. The most important of these for general purposes is the spending power, whose history has followed a path parallel to that of the commerce power. At the beginning, the restrictions found in the clause were respected at the legislative and presidential levels, so that the functions exercised by the federal government, consistent with the theory of limited government, were tightly restrained to those expenditures which, to the extent that was institutionally feasible, benefited the United States as a whole, and not just one particular segment of it. But as the constitutional constraints on congressional power were eroded, the same pattern took place with the Spending Clause. Thus the same progressive desire for a large administrative state and extensive transfer programs reshaped the Spending Clause to what it is today: only a modest restraint on the power of Congress to regulate ordinary individuals. Yet at the same time, restrictions contained in the Spending Clause have been subject to an uncertain revival in *National Federation of Independent Business v. Sebelius (NFIB)*[1] with respect to the exercise of federal power against the states.

The Original Plan

In order to set the stage, it is necessary to set out the full text of the Spending Clause:

The Congress shall have Power To lay and collect Taxes, Duties, Imposts and Excises, to pay the Debts and provide for the common Defence and general Welfare of the United States; but all Duties, Imposts and Excises shall be uniform throughout the United States.[2]

Most critically, this provision allows the national government by its own actions to raise all revenues needed to discharge its own obligations. With one stroke, the Constitution eliminates the need for the United States to beg for funds from the states, as it had to do under the Articles of Confederation. But any system of limited government must impose some limits on the proper objects of taxation, just as it must place restrictions on its close substitute, the power to regulate.[3] Accordingly, Article I, Section 8 covers both domestic transactions, for which the excise tax is relevant, and international transactions subject to duties and imposts.

The inquiry thus becomes: to what ends may these taxing powers be exercised? The key phrases are "to pay the Debts and provide for the common Defence and general Welfare of the United States," where it should be understood that references to both the common defense and the general welfare are "of the United States." In most discussions of the clause, those last four words are left out, so that the power now relates to the "general Welfare," which leads to such incautious statements by Supreme Court justices who ordinarily take opposite positions in particular cases. Both sides of this misconceived debate are evident in the *NFIB* decision, which upheld the individual health insurance mandate under this clause. Justice Ginsburg, speaking for that expansive reading, wrote, "Congress has broad authority to construct or adjust spending programs to meet its contemporary understanding of 'the general Welfare.'"[4] The four conservative dissenting justices essentially conceded the point when they wrote "[t]he power to make any expenditure that furthers 'the general welfare' is obviously very broad."[5]

Both sides are clearly wrong. As was mentioned in connection with *Frothingham v. Mellon*,[6] the Spending Clause should be read to refer only to public goods—benefits that can be supplied to one person only if they are similarly extended to others.[7] That inference is supportable even without the words "of the United States," for all three elements in the sequence refer to collective actions. The debts in question are those of the United States, not of random citizens. National defense is a classic public good. The correct stress on the word "general" is in opposition to particularized or local. The addition of the four words "of the United States" only fortifies the inference by showing that the expenditures must be for the overall benefit of the United States as a whole. A provision of this sort is absolutely essential to combat the well-understood risks of faction, which can thrive when transfers between parties are possible through the combined operation of the taxing and spending powers. The point here can be made by thinking about the United States as a public corporation, where it is hornbook law that corporate expenditures by the directors and officers should be for the benefit of the corporation, which is the antithesis of coerced transfer payments from one class of shareholders to another.

This accurate textual reading serves two essential functions. First, it imposes an effective limit on the ability of the United States to use taxation as a disguised system of wealth transfer—with its usual negative social consequences—either between individuals or between states. Yet just that result happens once "general Welfare" has been read to encompass transfer programs on an unimagined scale, all on the dubious ground that everyone indirectly benefits when wealth is taken from A and given to B. Second, this reading makes the spending power congruent with the other limitations on the power to tax that are found in Article I, including the requirement in Section 9, Clause 4, which provides:

> No Capitation, or other direct, Tax shall be laid, unless in Proportion to the Census or Enumeration herein before directed to be taken.

That provision, which covers not only head taxes but also taxes levied on the ownership of land, was introduced to prevent a redistribution of wealth from rich to poor states because apportionment by population imposes high effective rates of taxation on the poorer states for the maintenance of national collective ends.[8] The same general observation can be made about the uniformity requirement, which likewise was designed to prevent redistribution of wealth among states. Story put the point as follows:

> It [the requirement of uniform taxes] was to cut off all undue preferences of one state over another in the regulation of subjects affecting their common interests. Unless duties, imposts, and excises were uniform, the grossest and most oppressive inequalities, vitally affecting the pursuits and employments of the people of different states, might exist.[9]

Story's objection is not to a general prohibition against systems of wealth transfer from rich to poor individuals, for those could be done by the states individually, each in accordance with its own policies.

Finally, any broad reading of the spending power makes the scope of taxation no broader than the power of direct regulation, such that Congress does not have any strong institutional incentive to funnel its government programs through one channel or the other. It would be passing strange that the Founders would have attached no substantive limitations to the powers to tax and spend, when all the other enumerated powers are carefully delimited. Allowing those powers at the center to go beyond what the Articles of Confederation conferred on Congress was bold enough. To throw caution to the wind by making the powers to tax and spend unlimited would have been inconceivably reckless for individuals with such cautious attitudes toward government. The "broad" reading of the Spending Clause is antithetical to its text, structure, and history. It suffers from the same defects as efforts to expand the meaning of the Commerce Clause by giving a broad reading to the phrase "national interest"[10] in connection with treatment of the individual mandate.

The early interpretations of the Spending Clause bear out this narrow interpretation. James Madison understood the close substitutability of taxation and regulation and thus argued that the proper objects of taxation under Article I, Section 1 were limited to the activities that Congress could regulate elsewhere under Article I, Section 8.[11] Alexander Hamilton, by contrast, took pains to insist that the term "general Welfare" should be given a "comprehensive" reading such that "there seems to be no room for doubt that whatever concerns the general interests of learning of agriculture of manufactures and of commerce is within the sphere of the national councils, as far as regards an application of money."[12] For Hamilton, the only limitation on the power was that revenues be spent for national, not local, purposes. The political branches of government followed this rendition more or less faithfully for well over a century.[13] Madison himself vetoed an internal improvements bill devoted to the construction of roads and canals on the ground that it invoked a broad reading that would render the list of enumerated powers "nugatory and improper."[14] James Buchanan took the same position when he vetoed a college land grant bill on similar grounds.[15] Michael Greve expresses some caution about this view by noting the ambitious scale of public works, which included "lighthouses, harbors and sundry other local projects, with nary a peep of opposition from presidents."[16] It is indeed the case that no public good, from streetlights to defense, provides uniform benefits to all persons. Indeed many people have long protested the completion of particular roads and government structures. But that test for uniform benefits is too restrictive for dealing with public goods. One key feature with lighthouses and harbors is that they are widely distributed across the country so that taken as a package, their benefits are likely to be diffuse as well. In addition, each local project is itself a public good, which, if available to one person, must be open to all others. To be sure, the rate of utilization among individuals is likely to differ, but that objection will be true in every case, and thus should be given weight in none. The only requirement for a public good is open access at the general, or national level. These early historical practices of allowing some public improvements and not others to be subject to federal financing therefore lend no support for thinking that transfer payments between parties are consonant with the general welfare.

The New Deal Response

These interpretive questions did not reach the courts until the tumultuous days of the New Deal, which brought the issue to a head in *United States v. Butler*.[17] *Butler* purported to adopt Hamilton's broader reading of the clause for programs that bore no relationship to the various public works programs just considered. The case arose out of Congress's ill-conceived efforts under the Agricultural Adjustment Act of 1933[18] (AAA) to "stabilize" agricultural payments by paying farmers money *not* to grow certain types of crops. The scheme was classic cartel-like behavior to restrict output in order to raise prices. Cheating by cartel members always threatens their cohesion, such that legislators who want to utilize cartels have to devise ways to secure compliance. Under the AAA scheme, this was done by imposing processing fees on farmers as their crops moved toward consumer markets. Individual farmers could not escape the tax on the produce sold by turning down the programmatic benefits. So each rational farmer had an unshakeable incentive to comply with the output restrictions. The question in *Butler*, which relied on the extended principles dealing with courts of equity developed in Chapter 7, was whether a corporation in receivership could resist the tax on the ground that it did not advance the general welfare.

The case resulted in a split decision. As a formal matter, the Court in *Butler* rejected the Madisonian conception that tethered general welfare to the other regulatory powers of Congress. On the alternative view, which Hamilton articulated, only the inherent limitations found in the clause itself mattered, all of which Hamilton wrongly ignored. So it looked as if the tax should be sustained given Hamilton's framework that treated control of agriculture as a permissible government end. But in a sharp reversal at the eleventh hour, Justice Owen Roberts found that since Congress did not have the direct power to regulate agriculture, it did not have the power to do so indirectly by its combined taxing and spending program. Roberts thus honored the original constitutional scheme by precluding taxation where direct regulation was forbidden. The issue quickly became moot, however, after the inexorable New Deal expansion of Congress's commerce power to cover all economic transactions, however located and situated. At that point, the argument about substitution flips over. The intrinsic limitations in the three stated ends of the Spending Clause may now receive a broad reading. With a newly bulked up Commerce Clause, everything is allowed by direct regulation. And it becomes impossible to resist any taxation scheme toward the same end. One part of the original bulwark against large government was thus overrun.

The ambiguities found in *Butler* were elaborated in the next of the great Spending Clause cases, *Steward Machine Co. v. Davis*,[19] which involved a very different form of integration between the federal government and the state. Title IX of the Social Security Act of 1935[20] imposed a federal payroll tax on employers, with this caveat: if the employer chose to pay funds into a qualified state plan that met certain minimum federal standards, the federal government would credit it with 90 percent of the funds otherwise owing to the federal government. The structure of this program bears a close relationship to that of *Butler*, in that in both cases Congress sought to use its taxation powers in order to overcome the then-regnant limitations of the Commerce Clause. The key difference, however, was that the decision in *Steward Machine* came down just weeks after *Jones & Laughlin Steel*[21] had unshackled the Commerce Clause from 150 years of precedent. Under that brave new world order, Title IX should be regarded as unquestionably constitutional. Now, if not in 1935, the federal government is in a position to take over the operation of the unemployment program; the tax and return strategy no longer counts as an evasion of the constitutional limits found under the commerce power.

None of this was apparent to any of the justices in *Steward Machine*, which does not mention the Commerce Clause at all. Instead, the exercise under the Spending Clause was treated as if the constitutional landscape remained unchanged since 1935. Starting from that premise, the legislation was sustained by a five-to-four vote. Justice James McReynolds, writing for the conservative minority, would have struck the law down for flouting a doctrine once "firmly established" that "the States remained really free to exercise governmental powers, not delegated or prohibited, without interference by the Federal Government through threats of punitive measures or offers of seductive favors."[22] His manifest fear was that through these conditional grants, the United States could thus "assume all that duty of either public philanthropy or public necessity to the dependent, the orphan, the sick, or the needy which is now discharged by the States themselves or by corporate institutions or private endowments existing under the legislation of the States."[23] Under the old order, his position is correct because this combination of sticks (taxes) and carrots (rebates) necessarily alters the balance of power between the federal government and the states. Put the federal program in place, and states have the option as to whether to run this program, but they no longer have the option to run no program at all, or to run a program different from the one that meets federal standards. The circumvention risk is the same as it was in *Butler*. The purpose of this scheme is to foreclose even sensible types of local experimentation of the kind Justice Brandeis lauded in *New State Ice Co. v. Liebmann*: "It is one of the happy incidents of the federal system that a single courageous State may, if its citizens choose, serve as a laboratory; and try novel social and economic experiments without risk to the rest of the country."[24] *Steward Machine* shut those laboratories down.

Seeing the world through a pre-1937 lens, Justice Cardozo, writing for the five-member progressive majority, adopted a different strategy that preserved some, but not all, limits on the scope of federal power. Cardozo did not seek to overturn *Butler*, but he scrupulously sought to distinguish it, chiefly on the ground that money taken from state citizens was returned in large measure to those same states, so that there was little risk that the program would massively redistribute wealth across states. The loss in state sovereignty was measured by the (presumed) modest gap between the state's own preferred unemployment program and that of the federal government. Having taken that position, Cardozo was then forced to treat the line between coercion and temptation ultimately as a matter of degree. With one eye on the McReynolds dissent, he wrote as follows:

> In like manner, every rebate from a tax when conditioned upon conduct is in some measure a temptation. But to hold that motive or temptation is equivalent to coercion is to plunge the law in endless difficulties. The outcome of such a doctrine is the acceptance of a philosophical determinism by which choice becomes impossible. Till now, the law has been guided by a robust common sense which assumes the freedom of the will as a working hypothesis in the solution of its problems. The wisdom of the hypothesis has illustration in this case. Nothing in the case suggests the exertion of a power akin to undue influence, if we assume that such a concept can ever be applied with fitness to the relations between state and nation. Even on that assumption, the location of the point at which pressure turns into compulsion, and ceases to be inducement, would be a question of degree—at times, perhaps, of fact.[25]

This extended passage "plunges" the law into the very conceptual difficulties that Cardozo sought to avoid. First of all, it is clear that the notion of coercion can apply to entities as well as persons, to corporations as well as governments. In this case, the complication arises because the tax is imposed on individuals within the state, and the money is then returned to the state government. But the only sensible way to see this relationship is to treat each state as if it were linked to its citizens. After all, the system would break if the revenues collected from the citizens of state A were paid into the coffers of state B.

With that settled, Cardozo well understood that if the distinction between coercion and temptation is a matter of degree, no one will know exactly where to draw the line. The want of strong conceptual tools will then by default place that decision in the hands of the Congress, whose discretion will be challenged rarely, if at all. But Cardozo's "robust common sense" does reduce fundamental distinctions to squishy questions of degree. The consequences of coercion and temptation differ dramatically. We use boundary lines to determine fair and foul balls. The same is true here. Accordingly, the correct analysis draws a *hard-edged* line between the two whenever (which is most always) the property rights involved in any dispute are well defined. Put an individual to a choice between his money and his life, and he has been coerced even though the element of choice remains. This threat works because the victim prefers his life and the assailant prefers the money, so that the resulting deal works to the benefit of both. But step back from the antecedent threat and the coercion becomes clear, because each person is entitled to both his money *and* his life, and thus should not be forced to choose between them. Yet the landscape changes completely with the ordinary bargain in those cases where one person refuses to sell his goods or render his services to another unless she agrees to meet his price. It is in general permissible to put people to a choice between *your* property and *mine.*

By way of example, suppose one person goes up to a stranger and puts a gun to his head in order to get $10 to buy a train ticket. He refuses to take any additional money. The act is still one of coercion whether the person subjected to the threat has $10 or $1,000 in his pocket. It is the kind of choice that is offered, not the amount taken, that matters to the offer/threat distinction. The question of the degree only goes to the extent, not the fact of coercion. Title IX is thus coercive and survives post-1937 only because the weak constitutional protection of property rights places a huge wedge between the public law and its private analogies.

This omnipresent problem of coercion is subject to yet another complication in its relationship to monopoly power of the sort possessed by a common carrier that runs, by assumption, the only train or inn to which travelers may turn. These carriers have long been required to deal with everyone on reasonable and nondiscriminatory (or RAND) terms. The libertarian account of coercion as the use or threat of force is not implicated by this refusal to deal, which is the only position that allows competitive markets to operate. But in the monopoly setting, the consequences of refusal are no longer service by someone else at roughly the same price and terms, but no service at all. From the earliest times, therefore, the common carrier has the correlative duty to serve. Most notably, Sir Matthew Hale first announced the principle that some services were "affected with the public interest" in the late seventeenth century in his treatise *De Portis Maribus* (Concerning the Gates to the Sea).[26] His account was then turned into law in the great English case of *Allnutt v. Inglis,*[27] which held that any party that holds either a legal or natural monopoly must deal with all comers on reasonable and nondiscriminatory terms. Lord Ellenborough thus put the point as follows:

There is no doubt that the general principle is favored, both in law and justice, that every man may fix what price he pleases upon his own property, or the use of it; but if for a particular purpose the public have a right to resort to his premises and make use of them, and he have a monopoly in them for that purpose, if he will take the benefit of that monopoly, he must, as an equivalent, perform the duty attached to it on reasonable terms.[28]

Allnutt v. Inglis made its way firmly into the American constitutional law of rate regulation in *Munn v. Illinois*,[29] where this passage was quoted in full. Its basic point is that no one who enjoys a monopoly position is allowed to give prospective customers take-it-or-leave-it offers that deviate from the competitive equilibrium, but must instead supply the relevant goods on reasonable and nondiscriminatory terms. The term "coercion" is often used, somewhat uncritically to cover this effort to remove the specter of monopoly profits. But the existence of this duty, which gives rise to an immense literature of its own on matters of rate regulation, is a necessary component of any analysis of coercion.

Modern Developments

These interlocking themes surfaced some fifty years after *Butler* and *Steward Machine* when the Court revisited the limits on Congress's powers to tax and spend in *South Dakota v. Dole*.[30] The question before the Court in *Dole* had to do with the interaction between the Commerce Clause and the Twenty-First Amendment repealing prohibition, which was adopted in 1933, before the 1937 expansion of the commerce power. Specifically at issue was a 1984 federal statute[31] that authorized the secretary of transportation, then Elizabeth Dole, to withhold 5 percent of federal highway funds otherwise payable to states "in which the purchase or public possession . . . of any alcoholic beverage by a person who is less than twenty-one years of age is lawful." The moneys were withheld from South Dakota because it permitted persons nineteen years or older to purchase beer containing 3.2 percent alcohol. Section 2 of the Twenty-First Amendment provides:

The transportation or importation into any State, Territory, or possession of the United States for delivery or use therein of intoxicating liquors, in violation of the laws thereof, is hereby prohibited.

The purpose of this amendment was to turn the constitutional clock back to the situation that existed prior to the adoption of the Eighteenth Amendment imposing prohibition, when cases like *Kidd v. Pearson*[32] allocated the regulation of the consumption and production of alcohol to the states. An earlier Supreme Court decision reached just that conclusion by holding that the "Twenty-first Amendment grants the States virtually complete control over whether to permit importation or sale of liquor and how to structure the liquor distribution system."[33] The key question therefore was whether the power to condition federal spending allowed the federal government to work around that limitation by imposing this threat. The two dissenters in the decision, Justices Brennan and O'Connor, applied the basic anticircumvention rule in voting to strike down this scheme. Justice Brennan's brief opinion held that "Congress cannot condition a federal grant in a fashion that abridges this right,"[34] i.e., those powers reserved to the states under the Twenty-First Amendment. Justice O'Connor wrote a more extended version of the argument that tracked the position set out above. Without mentioning *Hammer v. Dagenhart*[35] or the *Child Labor Tax Case*[36] (doubtless because of their bad constitutional odor), she concluded that the powers to tax and spend had to be read in parallel with the scope of the commerce power. Since the 1937 general transformation did not displace the Twenty-First Amendment, the effort to use the spending power to alter the distribution of federal-state relationships failed.

Implicit in this argument is an acceptance that the doctrine of unconstitutional conditions attaches to each and every exercise of federal power. Chief Justice Rehnquist rejected the proposition that any condition could be attached to the federal spending power, but declined to take the categorical approach of Justices Brennan and O'Connor. Instead, he consciously built on Cardozo's earlier decision in *Steward Machine* in ways that softened the general application of the doctrine. His four conditions were as follows:

> The first of these limitations is derived from the language of the Constitution itself: the exercise of the spending power must be in pursuit of "the general Welfare." In considering whether a particular expenditure is intended to serve general public purposes, courts should defer substantially to the judgment of Congress. Second, we have required that, if Congress desires to condition the States' receipt of federal funds, it "must do so unambiguously . . . enabl[ing] the States to exercise their choice knowingly, cognizant of the consequences of their participation." Third,

our cases have suggested (without significant elaboration) that conditions on federal grants might be illegitimate if they are unrelated "to the federal interest in particular national projects or programs." Finally, we have noted that other constitutional provisions may provide an independent bar to the conditional grant of federal funds.[37]

There are serious difficulties with each of these components. The first condition overreads the extent of the term "general Welfare" and thus confers unwarranted discretion on Congress. The second limitation, dealing with clear notice, imposes at most a weak drafting constraint on Congress that was easily satisfied in *Dole*. The third requirement, on relatedness, imposes a "germaneness" requirement,[38] demanding some connection between the grant and a legitimate public purpose. On this score, the outcome is sketchy because the federal prohibition against drinking is in no way tethered to driving on public highways, but covers all activities. The fourth condition is clearly sensible, but comes into play only in a few cases.

The frailness of these constraints becomes evident when Rehnquist turns to his analysis of the recurrent coercion question. Placing heavy reliance on *Steward Machine*, Rehnquist writes:

> Our decisions have recognized that, in some circumstances, the financial inducement offered by Congress might be so coercive as to pass the point at which "pressure turns into compulsion." *Steward Machine Co. v. Davis* . . . Here, however, Congress has directed only that a State desiring to establish a minimum drinking age lower than 21 lose a relatively small percentage of certain federal highway funds. Petitioner contends that the coercive nature of this program is evident from the degree of success it has achieved. We cannot conclude, however, that a conditional grant of federal money of this sort is unconstitutional simply by reason of its success in achieving the congressional objective.
>
> When we consider, for a moment, that all South Dakota would lose if she adheres to her chosen course as to a suitable minimum drinking age is 5% of the funds otherwise obtainable under specified highway grant programs, the argument as to coercion is shown to be more rhetoric than fact. . . .
>
> Here Congress has offered relatively mild encouragement to the States to enact higher minimum drinking ages than they would otherwise choose. But the enactment of such laws remains the prerogative of the States not merely in theory, but in fact.[39]

Rehnquist has swallowed whole every intellectual confusion found in *Steward Machine*. The analytic question that remains is to find, under his formulation, the point where pressure turns into compulsion. There is of course no such point, so all the subsequent cases fell short of coercion, even when withholding as much as 95 percent of the expenditures.[40]

Thus stands the unsatisfactory state of play until the recent decision in *NFIB*, where the use of the power to tax and spend came up both in connection with the individual mandate and the so-called Medicaid extension program. Dealing with the former, the decisive vote in this case belonged to Chief Justice Roberts, who held that the ACA could not be sustained under the Commerce Clause because the government could not force individuals to engage in conduct that it could then regulate. But there is a correlative inference that Roberts refuses to draw. Just as Congress cannot regulate inactivity, there is no general theory of taxation that taxes economic inactivity. Taxes are imposed on earned and investment income; on engaging in specific transactions, like sales and leases; and on the ownership of real property and other assets. No tax has ever been imposed for not dancing, eating, or thinking. That point alone should have cautioned him against sustaining this mandate, but to no avail. After his torturous explanation of why what Congress called a penalty should now be viewed as a tax, he compounds the difficulty by refusing to read the taxing power in harmony with the commerce power. To be sure, he dutifully cites both the *Child Labor Tax Case*[41] and *Butler*,[42] even though these cut the opposite way. Both cases stand for parity between powers to regulate commerce and to tax and spend. Once the inactivity limitation precludes federal power under the Commerce Clause, the infirmity under the Spending Clause should follow as a matter of course. The mandate should fall. The argument rejected by every court below sprouted wings in the Supreme Court.

The received wisdom on these issues does not rest on this discussion of parity but on the ground that the rational basis test imposes no serious limitations on the way in which Congress decides to use the tax code. It is thus commonplace today to speak of the tax expenditure budget, which counts as a departure from the normal tax budget that is intended to provide particular benefits in order to favor some particular industry, activity, or class of persons.[43] These benefits could cover everything from benefits to married couples that file joint returns to benefits to individuals who install extra insulation in their windows. Under current law, the great challenge is to explain why the individual mandate should suffer a different fate from all these provisions, when it could be recast as a forgiveness of a tax liability for those who procure the required level of health care insurance. There is no neat answer to this question under the rational basis test of the modern law. But this contention is easily rejected on the originalist view that the Spending Clause prohibits all transfer payments between ordinary individuals. At this point, the anticircumvention principle comes into play, so that the test bans the use of tax expenditures where direct payments to a given person with respect to a given activity would run afoul of the limitations built into the clause. It is precisely because the strong view of the taxing and spending power is rejected that it becomes difficult to use Roberts's inconclusive discussion of the tax-versus-penalty debate to strike down this new use of the taxing power.[44]

Chief Justice Roberts thus may well be right after all on the taxing power. But if so, what was so odd about this performance was Roberts's profound shift in gears in striking down portions of Title II of the ACA, whose Medicaid extension provision required states to forfeit all their Medicaid revenues if they refused to supply Medicaid benefits to all individuals who earned less than 133 percent of poverty-level income and to freeze their Medicaid benefits at current levels to existing recipients.[45] In exchange for compliance, the government offered to cover the full costs of the extra payments up to 2016, and no less than 90 percent thereafter.[46] The program also required the states to pick up the administrative expenditures for a program that could add about seventeen million people to the rolls.[47]

Many states with Democratic governors and legislatures liked the terms of the deal, which they accepted without complaint. But twenty-six states with Republican governors, headed by Florida and Texas, did not wish to accept the deal, and thus sought to invalidate either the condition, or indeed all of Title II, on the grounds that the rest of the title could not be severed from this condition. Following the analysis in *South Dakota v. Dole*, the case looks like a loser. Indeed no federal court that reviewed the issue was prepared to strike down the Medicaid extension, which only made it to the Supreme Court because it ordered the issue to be briefed on both sides.[48] Once there, the coercion arguments made a comeback sufficient to attract not only the four conservative justices, but Justices Breyer and Kagan as well.

The chief justice starts by noting that the conditions attached were like "a gun to the head" of the states.[49] That rather misplaced use of the force language turns attention away from the only issue in the case, which is whether it is permissible for the federal government to attach this condition to its monopoly power of taxing and spending. On that point, Chief Justice Roberts begins by noting that Spending Clause legislation is "much in the nature of a *contract*,"[50] and thus carries with it the standard limitations that attach to freedom of contract. Such limitations should in principle include the familiar restrictions of reasonable and nondiscriminatory service. Chief Justice Roberts of course does not utter the word "monopoly" in his opinion. Yet just as with the law of antitrust and common carriers he is, perforce, in the constitutional business of trying to sort out the difference between illicit conditions that leverage monopoly power and efficient conditions that rationalize the way in which the grants should be spent, which include conditions that let the federal government insist that Medicaid funds be spent on Medicaid purposes. Yet on the opposite side of the line are those conditions that are likely to run afoul of common carrier and antitrust restrictions on exclusive dealing or tying arrangements.[51] At this point, the Medicaid restrictions fall on the opposite side of the line. "Conditions that do not here govern the use of the funds, however, cannot be justified on that basis. When, for example, such conditions take the form of threats to terminate other significant independent grants, the conditions are properly viewed as a means of pressuring the States to accept policy changes."[52] The logic behind this position is this: the citizens of each of the states have to be considered, as noted earlier, as being equivalent to the state itself. The threat in question therefore is not one that just says, "Don't like our conditions? Don't play." It is one that says that if you don't like our conditions, you can avoid them only if you forfeit all the taxes paid to the federal government, where they can then be spent to help other states.

To be sure, this case is in a sense *weaker* than both *Butler* and *Steward Machinery* because the federal government today has unquestioned power to create and administer a Medicaid program. But at the same time, the explicit linkage means that dropping out of the program comes only at prohibitive costs. No common carrier could say, by way of comparison, that it will only carry people who agree to give them all their business whenever possible, or have an exclusive dealing provision that says if you want to advertise in my dominant newspaper, you cannot advertise on local radio stations as well.[53] In none of these cases would it be a defense for the aggrieved party to have consented to the transaction in question. That principle, which was not mentioned in the Roberts decision, lends strength to his view that the power "to alter, amend, or repeal" the statute did not exempt the government from the general strictures associated with judicial review.[54]

At this point, all that remains is for the chief justice to finesse the language from *Steward Machine*, which asked whether pressure had turned to compulsion. Without mentioning the four *Dole* factors, he distinguishes the case both on the size of the sacrifice required and on its discontinuous nature, which made it a new program instead of an old one. Descriptively, no one ever contested that the Medicaid extension was such a new program. But it was also possible, at least in theory, for Congress to repeal the whole statute, lock, stock, and barrel, and put a new one in its place. That course of action could not be done in practice. Any effort to repeal and repass the legislation in the same bill looks like a sham intended to evade the application of the doctrine of unconstitutional conditions. Worse still, that huge sea change could disrupt all sorts of private arrangements whose validity was predicated on the continued operation of the older statute. Once it is recognized that freedom of contract cannot be the operative principle in dealing with conditional spending cases, the inability to find a strong efficiency justification for the extension makes the decision to strike down this option acceptable. The federal government could not have said that if you turn down the Medicaid extension, you lose all federal aid to education. This case is close enough to that to require the same result. Ironically, the chief justice's opinion leaves uncertain whether the *Dole* line between coercion and encouragement is still viable at all. Correctly understood, *Dole* is an easy case in which the condition was wrongly allowed to stand, while *NFIB* is a more difficult case in which the offending principle was struck down. The one point that does shine through is this: the outcome in Spending Clause cases, as everywhere else, turns on the willingness to accept the rational basis test. In *NFIB*, Justice Roberts stiffened his spine with respect to the Medicaid extension, but not the individual mandate, which explains the discordant results for the two provisions. The ultimate direction of this saga has yet to play itself out.

14

The Necessary and Proper Clause

No discussion of the legislative power is complete without some examination of the Necessary and Proper Clause, the final clause in Article I, Section 8, which gives Congress the following power:

> To make all Laws which shall be necessary and proper for carrying into Execution the foregoing Powers, and all other Powers vested by this Constitution in the Government of the United States, or in any Department or Officer thereof.[1]

Stated in this form, the clause not only gives an added boost to the specific powers conferred upon Congress, but it also allows Congress to augment the powers of any government actor, including those in the executive and judicial branches. In one sense, it is an open question whether the inclusion of this clause in the Constitution was necessary or proper, given that the types of ancillary powers it addresses, under orthodox interpretive principles, would likely be read into the document anyway. It was just that view that prompted both Madison and Hamilton to treat the clause as largely redundant—which, whatever that means, does not mean transformative.[2] Their opinion may be too restrictive, for the clause does introduce some play in the joints, so as to allow each branch of government to carry into execution its enumerated powers. One common way of putting the point is that the clause allows for the use of "incidental" powers needed to effectuate the enumerated powers, but does not allow Congress to set out for itself new substantive powers that were not set out in the earlier enumeration.[3] Ample means are made available to achieve stated ends. But, as John Marshall recognized—first in *McCulloch v. Maryland*[4] and then in *Gibbons v. Ogden*[5]—the clause does not expand the permissible set of powers that the Constitution confers on Congress.

The Final Piece of the Legislative Puzzle

Within this general functional approach, just what do the terms "necessary" and "proper" mean? The secret of sound constitutional interpretation is to take it one word at a time, by asking first what is "necessary" and then what is "proper."[6] In dealing with this issue, the first of these terms expresses some close means/ends connection, which is impossible to specify exactly, but which lies somewhere between "appropriate" and "indispensable," both of which appear elsewhere in the Constitution. The term "proper" implies that the action in addition meet some normative standard of propriety, which is also difficult to pin down with great exactitude.

Nonetheless, recent research by Gary Lawson, Geoffrey Miller, Robert Natalson, and Guy Seidman has shown that by 1787 there were enough well-developed private law analogies to the use of these terms that no court needed to fly blind in interpreting them. Thus phrases of this import appear commonly enough in corporate charters, real estate deeds, and trust instruments to give some sense as to their purpose. They are to make sure that parties entrusted with the care of other individuals have sufficient power to discharge their duties, but not so much as to abuse that relationship. Indeed, it is worth noting that the Necessary and Proper Clause of 1787 antedates the adoption of the Bill of Rights in 1791. But it is not too great a leap to indicate that it seeks to capture in three words many of those key concepts. It is hard to think that any actions of a judiciary could be regarded as proper if they showed partiality to one side or failed to allow for a hearing, or that any government official given power to discharge public funds could systematically favor those allied with him. Put otherwise, as with all the other provisions in a charter dedicated to limited government, the selfsame clause both gives and restrains the use of power by, as the clause itself makes evident, all branches or departments of government. It is for just this reason that the clause "required delegated power to be exercised with impartiality, efficacy, proportionality, and regard for people's rights."[7]

In addition, there is good reason to believe on the strength of recent research by William Baude that the clause contained an important federalism dimension.[8] Baude has shown by an exhaustive analysis of the early evidence that the Necessary and Proper Clause did not, at least in accordance with established practice, allow the federal government to exercise the power of eminent domain within the states, even though it could exercise that power in the territories. Indeed, he notes that the first federal acceptance of this general power within the states dates to the case of *Kohl v. United States* in 1875, which treated that power as "essential to its independent existence and perpetuity"[9]—as it surely is. There is no linguistic permutation of the phrase "necessary and proper" that appears to prevent Congress from condemning land to build a post office or to extend a post road if it so chose, in connection with its power "To establish Post Offices and post Roads."[10]

To see why, it is clear that the voluntary acquisition of land for these purposes is surely covered by any account of the clause. Given the risk that private landowners could hold out for exorbitant sums if the federal government could not condemn their land for roads, how could it not be "necessary" for the United States to have the power of condemnation for this evident "public use"? For such condemnation to be made "proper," one might simply add that "just compensation" be provided; with only a small dollop of imagination, "proper" here reads like a full-blown Takings Clause.

This textual appearance is deceptive, however, when placed in historical context. Baude's core observation is that "proper" in this context requires a respect for the system of dual sovereignty that the Constitution creates.[11] Eminent domain is an extraordinary power of the sovereign to take property that is denied to ordinary people acting on their own initiative. There can therefore be only one sovereign in any territory capable of exercising that supreme power. It would be unthinkable to strip the states of that power, so it was a federal government of enumerated and limited power that was deprived of the eminent domain power. Eminent domain is not on the list of distinct enumerated powers that the Constitution gives to the federal government over the states, so the federal government may exercise this power only in the District of Columbia and the territories (which was a much bigger issue then than it is now).[12] Of course, the federal government did require land located within the states, which it obtained, apparently without difficulty, through cooperative arrangements with the states, who condemned land on behalf of the federal government. Baude points out several examples, involving, for example, New York and New Jersey statutes that authorized the taking of property to outfit a federal lighthouse at Sandy Hook.[13]

Indeed it is only this federalist construction that explains other key provisions of the Constitution. Article I, Section 8, clause 17 provides that the Congress may "exercise like Authority over all Places purchased by the Consent of the Legislature of the State in which the Same shall be, for the Erection of Forts, Magazines, Arsenals, dock-Yards and other needful Buildings." This clause appears just before the Necessary and Proper Clause, and this narrow list of public projects is repeated seriatim in a Massachusetts statute that authorized the United States to take land on Governor's Island in Boston Harbor.[14] The word "needful," moreover, is found only in one other place in the Constitution, namely in Article IV, Section 3, clause 2, which most instructively states that "The Congress shall have Power to dispose of and make all needful Rules and Regulations respecting the Territory or other Property belonging to the United States; . . ." The word "needful" in this provision covers not only the power to dispose of property but also the power to condemn it for the very same type of facilities for which cooperative arrangements are introduced in Article I, Section 8, clause 17. In addition, the instructive words "like authority" confer the same powers over this very restricted class of what today are called "essential facilities" that the Congress has over the District of Columbia, whose creation is also authorized in clause 17. The need to obtain the consent of the state to acquire these facilities tends strongly to confirm the Baude hypothesis, and to explain the restrictive interpretation that should be given to the Necessary and Proper Clause as it deals both with individual rights and federalism issues.

Both these dimensions are important to tracing the history of the Necessary and Proper Clause after its adoption, where it becomes evident that nothing insulated the clause from the continuous pressure to expand the scope of federal powers beyond their original confines. It is instructive to follow its course over the same historical arc that has been traversed already, chiefly in connection with the spending and commerce powers, taking special note of how these have evolved both before and after the constitutional watershed of the Court's 1936–1937 term. Accordingly, I shall cover the creation of the national banks, the use of greenbacks as legal tender, and the rise of the modern administrative state. In this instance, the great expansion of the clause occurred *prior to* the Progressive Era. Indeed, in modern times, with the expansion of Congress's powers over commerce, taxing, and spending, the Necessary and Proper Clause has, if anything, retreated in its scope and influence.

The Saga of the Two National Banks

The Supreme Court's initial foray into the Necessary and Proper Clause came in the famous 1819 case of *McCulloch v. Maryland*,[15] where Chief Justice Marshall concluded that the clause had enough running room to confer on Congress the power to establish a national bank, a private corporation in which the United States had a 20 percent equity stake. The enumerated powers in Article I, Section 8 allow Congress to borrow money on the credit of the United States, to coin money, and to punish counterfeiting. Surely the Necessary and Proper Clause allows Congress to establish a mint to do the coinage, just as the power to tax allows Congress to move revenues it collects from place to place. From the earliest times, howls of protest were raised against the thought that legislation had to bog itself down on these small matters of managerial detail that were not proper objects of legislation. Congress's power to establish post roads did not require it to map out the details of each route.[16] Or as Justice Strong stated in the *Legal Tender Cases:* "Under the power to establish post-offices and post-roads Congress has provided for carrying the mails, punishing theft of letters and mail robberies, and even for transporting the mails to foreign countries."[17] Condemnation of land is, however, not mentioned.

All these cases have a goodness of fit—neither too broad nor too narrow—that makes the inference irresistible no matter how rigorous the judicial scrutiny. The chosen activities only cover areas where Congress is authorized to act, without trenching on areas off-limits to it. But a national bank enters into many types of transactions, such as private loans that are unrelated to any enumerated governmental function. The classical liberal presumption in favor of limited government militates against extending Congress's power to charter a bank.

Nonetheless, Chief Justice Marshall upheld the charter for a unanimous Court. In reaching his conclusion, he had the weight of history on his side, given that Congress had chartered a First National Bank in 1791, which lasted for twenty years. The initial authorization of the bank was itself contested between Hamilton and Madison (who had also differed on the scope of the spending power),[18] when Madison, joined by Jefferson, took the position that all of the enumerated powers of the federal government, including the power to borrow money or to regulate commerce, "can all be carried into execution without a bank. A bank therefore is not *necessary*, and consequently not authorized by this phrase."[19] But at that time, at least, Hamilton prevailed by insisting that by both the "grammatical and popular" senses of the term, "*necessary* often means no more than *needful, requisite, incidental, useful,* or *conductive to.*"[20]

As a legal matter, the question of constitutional power to establish a national bank must be resolved independent of any view of the success of the bank in its commercial operations, which in this instance were substantial. Nonetheless, the relative success of the First National Bank made it easier for Marshall to follow Hamilton and sustain the creation of the Second National Bank under the Necessary and Proper Clause.[21] He opened that defense of the bank by noting the "embarrassments" under the Articles of Confederation,[22] and with the emotively powerful observation that "we must never forget, that it is a *constitution* we are expounding."[23] But which way does this nostrum cut? The classical liberal reads that stirring proposition as a two-sided warning: it is necessary to be sure that Congress has the powers it needs; it is equally necessary to make sure that Congress does not overstep the limits on its power. Marshall, however, paid heed only to the first when he read the clause also to confer large "discretion" on Congress to adapt means to ends, concluding with this oft-quoted flourish:

> We admit, as all must admit, that the powers of the government are limited, and that its limits are not to be transcended. But we think the sound construction of the constitution must allow to the national legislature that discretion, with respect to the means by which the powers it confers are to be carried into execution, which will enable that body to perform the high duties assigned to it, in the manner most beneficial to the people. Let the end be legitimate, let it be within the scope of the constitution, and all means which are appropriate, which are plainly adapted to that end, which are not prohibited, but consist with the letter and spirit of the constitution, are constitutional.[24]

Any fears of abusive faction get short shrift in *McCulloch* by the undefended assertion that Congress, on this or any other matter, will act "in the manner most beneficial to the people." More critically, note

Marshall's conscious and crafty transformation of the textual question: if the means chosen are "necessary" and "proper" for the task at hand, actions that are unnecessary or improper should not cut it. But Marshall bundled these two separate requirements into a single pallid word: "appropriate." Introducing a word that is *not* in the constitutional text necessarily expanded the scope of government power. It is more difficult to sustain the bank as "necessary" if government operations could well run without it. On this matter, it has been pointed out that the First Bank of the United States had helped raise credit for the United States, which was lacking during the War of 1812 after the First Bank's charter had not been renewed.[25] But there remains the question of whether, in the absence of a national bank, more state-chartered banks would have been available to fill that gap—given that their number doubled between 1811 and 1816.[26] And other institutions handled financial matters once the Second National Bank went out of business in 1836. So it is fair to ask why the United States must do its business through a bank in which it has a minority stake when so many state-chartered banks are already in business. Unfortunately, Marshall did not outline any specific inconveniences of not having the national bank, which might have made out his case under a narrower reading of the Necessary and Proper Clause. Indeed he chose this abstract path precisely because he was intent on defending Hamilton's broader view. It is also worth noting that a decision that keeps the United States from engaging in ordinary banking functions does not necessarily doom the specialized Federal Reserve Bank, which operates as the bank of banks, with obvious regulatory functions.

But what about the term "proper," which disappears under Marshall's deft reinterpretation? Try this: means are proper if they do not trench unduly into areas that are off-limits to the federal government, including participation in ordinary banking activities. Taking both halves of the clause seriously does not yield any simple mechanical test. But it does rule out Marshall's expansive reading in favor of a more circumspect view that compares two types of error: blocking the bank and denying Congress some legitimate powers, relative to allowing the bank and granting Congress unauthorized powers. That choice seems quite easy: the bank should not be allowed. Although the First Bank had performed well, the administration of the Second Bank was marred with corruption and incompetence before Andrew Jackson let it die, which it did without any visible inconvenience to the public whose interests it was said to serve.[27]

One additional textualist argument Chief Justice Marshall used to justify his more capacious reading of the Necessary and Proper Clause was to compare the word "necessary" with the words "absolutely necessary" in Article I, Section 10, clause 2:

> No State shall, without the Consent of Congress, lay any Imposts or Duties on Imports or Exports, except what may be absolutely necessary for executing its inspection Laws: and the net Produce of all Duties and Imposts, laid by any State on Imports or Exports, shall be for the Use of the Treasury of the United States; and all such Laws shall be subject to the Revision and Controul of the Congress.

This carefully wrought structure provides inspired defense of free trade in multiple layers: first Congress must consent to the imposition; then it must be absolutely necessary; then the net proceeds over the cost of collection are remitted to Congress. Finally, once the process is in place, the entire scheme is subject to a second round of congressional control. If one thing is clear from this series of obstacles, it is that the Constitution took strong measures to create an internal free trade zone consistent with classical liberal principles in a way in which the evident willingness to tolerate external tariffs was not.

But focus solely on the use of the words "absolutely necessary." Do they support the transformation of "necessary and proper" into "appropriate"? Not really, because the two clauses are distinguishable even if the narrower reading of "necessary and proper," urged above, is accepted. Any effort to create a free trade zone among states has to combat the risks of contagion and infection that count as obvious harms. Every free trade regime has to allow for that protective exercise of domestic sovereign power. But by the same token, the Constitution, alert to the risk of circumvention, did not permit states to transform these inspection laws into disguised tariff or trade barriers, which explains the use of the words "absolutely necessary" and the transfer of net proceeds to the U.S. Treasury. Hence, applying two kinds of error analysis in dealing with the Import/Export Clause has a very different valence than it does for the Necessary and Proper Clause. The Constitution guards against the risks of over-inspection, not under-inspection. But with necessary *and* proper, both over- and under-regulation are risks to be reckoned on.

It is therefore a mistake to assume that there is no middle ground between strict scrutiny of imposts on imports and exports and broad discretion for Congress to create a bank. Stated in the now-canonical terms of modern constitutional theory, the law offers three, not two, standards of judicial scrutiny for any piece of legislation. The first of these, exemplified in the Import/Export Clause, is strict scrutiny. At the opposite end lies what is termed, misleadingly, a "rational basis" approach, which sustains legislation so long as any barely respectable reason can be given in its favor, no matter how strong the arguments against it. Marshall adopted this approach in *McCulloch*. In so doing he skipped over all forms of intermediate scrutiny that weigh equally the risk of too much and too little government. By gravitating to the rational basis test, Marshall set the groundwork for the latest progressive movement, which is why the two major architects of limited judicial review—James Bradley Thayer and Felix Frankfurter—adored Marshall's tour-de-force in *McCulloch*.[28]

The Legal Tender Cases

Marshall's choice of language shaped the judicial debates in the *Legal Tender Cases*, now largely neglected, which arose after the turmoil of the Civil War. The simple question was whether the Congress had the power to substitute greenbacks for gold and silver coin in the payment of debts. On this matter, the Supreme Court did one of its famous flip-flops, so that it first struck down the law, and then upheld it shortly thereafter. The issue first arose in the most prosaic of circumstances. In *Hepburn v. Griswold*,[29] Hepburn gave Griswold in 1860 a note for 11,250 "dollars," which Hepburn sought to repay in greenbacks. He relied on an 1862 federal statute, passed at the height of the Civil War, authorizing the issuance of paper money, which it then declared should be "a legal tender in payment of all debts, public or private." Justice Chase held that the Necessary and Proper Clause did not give Congress either power. His decision was promptly overruled the next year in the *Legal Tender Cases*,[30] which is why paper money is still with us.

Notwithstanding his historical defeat, Chase's view is closer to the constitutional text and understandable, if not entirely defensible, on classical liberal principles. First, the statute retroactively altered the terms of many contracts to shift wealth from the creditor to the debtor by allowing payment of the debt with cheaper dollars. How does this differ from allowing a party who borrowed a gold chalice to return a brass chalice of the same type? In both cases there are forced exchanges on unequal terms, which is yet another form of taking that should be caught by the anticircumvention principle. On this point at least, the condemnation should be unequivocal. No system of limited government looks with favor on *retroactive* legislation. And the Constitution provides that "No State shall . . . make any Thing but gold and silver Coin a Tender in the Payment of Debts; pass any . . . ex post facto Law, or Law impairing the Obligation of Contracts."[31] But these provisions only bind the states, and not the federal government.

How to fill the void? Start with matters of federal power and then move on to individual rights. Congress has no general powers, so there is no need to include a prohibition against paper money parallel to that found against the states, which otherwise have plenary jurisdiction. So the inquiry must ask: pursuant to which enumerated power did Congress pass the Legal Tender Act? The Necessary and Proper Clause offers its ancillary boost only if we can identify the enumerated power to which it attaches. Note that Congress has power "to coin money, regulate the value thereof, and of foreign coin. . . ."[32] But a clause that authorizes coining money seems to prohibit printing greenbacks, which cannot be circumvented by making $100 coins out of worthless metal. The words "coin money" must be read to mean "coin money out of gold and silver" so as to put it in harmony with the provisions of Article I, Section 10. That power to coin money, of course, does not prevent the circulation of paper receipts that can be redeemed no questions asked for gold or silver: here the mandatory redemption feature prevents any debasing of the currency. So read, the "coin money" clause complements the inability of the state to make anything other than gold or silver legal tender. Therefore, the Necessary and Proper Clause does not advance the federal government's case. Paper money backed by no fixed assets (so-called fiat money) is not needed to coin gold and silver. Nor is it proper for Congress to adopt any strategy that subverts a stated limitation on its own powers. So far, it's a no go.

Perhaps, however, Congress may issue greenbacks under its power to regulate commerce among the states, with foreign nations, and the Indian tribes.[33] But moving in this direction makes it unnecessary to give Congress the more limited power to coin money. So "commerce" must be read narrowly enough so that it does not render superfluous every other congressional power—a lesson long forgotten today. If commerce is confined to interstate transactions, why is it necessary to print fiat currency? Commerce has long operated on negotiable instruments and bills of exchange with little need for greenbacks. Any action that subverts the basic structure of the fiscal Constitution is hardly necessary. Nor is it proper to upset the balance between the federal and state governments by allowing Congress to regulate purely internal debt transactions within the states, including many that have little or nothing to do with commerce (as understood in its pre-1937 sense). As a matter of constitutional principle, therefore, the Legal Tender laws should fall by the wayside, thereby preserving both the rule of law and the stability of private expectations.

Historically, these arguments against greenbacks came out second best because intermediate scrutiny under the Necessary and Proper Clause gave way to a far more lax standard. Justice Strong trumped *McCulloch* by holding that the weight of historical tradition conferred "a very wide discretion . . . in the selection of the necessary and proper means to carry into effect the great objects for which the government was framed, and this discretion has generally been unquestioned, or, if questioned, sanctioned by this court."[34] The rational basis standard gutted the Necessary and Proper Clause. The 1871 *Legal Tender Cases* thus gave to Congress the power to issue paper currency on the ground that it was held by virtually all other sovereigns—none of which operated under constitutional restrictions remotely similar to our own.

But suppose the power to coin money did carry with it the ability to issue greenbacks. The Legal Tender Act is still invalid. Classical liberal theory is rightly suspicious of state monopolies over all sorts of goods and services, including the supply of money. That suspicion, so evident in *The Federalist Papers* with its denunciation of "the pestilent effects of paper money on the necessary confidence between man and man,"[35] rightly carries over to the state control of currency, given the arbitrary power to either inflate or deflate the currency. One way to counteract this risk is to let the government print whatever (cheap) currency it will, but to discipline its behavior by allowing other banks to issue their own currency (whether or not backed by gold) in competition with the federal government. It seems neither necessary nor proper to confer a monopoly on the printing press in the federal government.

The Federal Reserve Bank

The broad construction of the Necessary and Proper Clause in the *Legal Tender Cases* was instrumental in allowing Congress to create the Federal Reserve Bank System of 1913.[36] Indeed, when the constitutionality of that bank was challenged in *Raichle v. Federal Reserve Bank*, the Second Circuit swatted down the objectors.[37] Bad timing. *Raichle* was decided in July of 1929. With erring prescience, Judge Augustus N. Hand praised the Federal Reserve System as a "great improvement over what went before"—two months before the October 1929 crash. Indeed, the present Federal Reserve differs in both structure and function from Marshall's Second Bank of the United States because it is limited to organizing transactions among its member banks, without making loans to the general public in competition with those banks. The Fed uses many devices to keep the currency on an even keel. These include the setting of reserve requirements for member banks and engaging in open market transactions, whereby its decision to buy or sell money and treasury notes influences the market rate of interest for loans that private depository institutions make to other member banks. The Federal Reserve is also allowed to issue legal tender, called Federal Reserve notes.

There is, however, no safe haven from the risks of state monopoly power, because when the Fed makes an error, it can easily have vast repercussions. During the Great Depression, the Fed's contraction of the money supply led to a major deflation—fewer dollars chasing the same amount of goods—that denied the market much-needed liquidity. The steep deflation of the 1930s fueled mass foreclosures, as farmers were unable to pay back loans denominated in dollars that rose in value, so that what appeared to be a $100 debt was in real terms, say, $150. The disruption on one side of the loan cycle impacted the other, for with mortgage loans in default the banks, in their role as middleman, could not honor their deposits. And the runs on banks led to bank holidays. Futile efforts to break the spiral of mortgage foreclosure only shifted the losses back and forth between innocent parties, but did nothing to undo the damage of the rapid deflation, which altered in dramatic and unforeseen ways the financial terms of every private and public transaction in the United States. In modern times, the relentless Federal Reserve cheap money policy also contributed to the real estate bubble that burst in 2007 and has yet to heal.[38]

Private currencies could fall prey to these risks as well. But do not underestimate the virtues of diversification, even in currency markets. Let one currency depreciate, and individuals can switch to other currencies that hold their value, substituting competitive discipline for a rigid government regime. It is therefore tempting to ask whether today's mass of foreclosures would have occurred if the government did not subsidize the mischievous activities of its two mortgage banks, Fannie Mae and Freddie Mac. I sympathize with Ron Paul's position that the Federal Reserve is unconstitutional because the Congress lacks the power to create any bank: "The United States Constitution grants to Congress the authority to coin money and regulate the value of the currency. The Constitution does not give Congress the authority to delegate control over monetary policy to a central bank."[39]

But how sound is this constitutional structure, which implicitly imposes a gold standard? It does have the advantage of preventing actions that debase the currency. But it also ties the money supply to the amount of certain scarce commodities, which can fluctuate with new discoveries that expand supply or new industrial uses that reduce it. For all its apparent virtue to Madison, the gold standard offers no insulation from the vicissitudes of economic activity. In principle, the monetarist approach of Milton Friedman that ties the money supply to the amount of goods and services in the economy represents a coherent effort to keep the discipline that the gold standard supplies without tying the fortunes of the economic system to the unpredictable price movements of a single commodity.[40] The constitutional implications of that shift, however, are profound. Under the original constitutional scheme, the ban on the use of fiat currency at both the state and federal levels is a discrete command that is enforceable under the traditional doctrines of judicial review. There are discrete acts that violate the standard, and others that comply with it. But once monetarism becomes entrenched as the dominant policy, no coherent form of judicial oversight is possible, so that the entire fiscal constitution now becomes at best aspirational, and the real work becomes political. In this instance, the shift has to be viewed with mixed emotion. The monetarist policies did much to supply a stable currency and curb inflation from the early Reagan years to the present time. But only time will tell whether the system can withstand the twists and turns of the current cheap money policy that will eventually stoke up inflation. But for our purposes, the constitutional transformation of the Necessary and Proper Clause has ushered in a revolution that no one can reverse today, even if one wanted to. The prescriptive constitution has taken over on these monetary matters. The originalist solution has been put to one side. Given its infirmities, no one should seek to revive it.

The Necessary and Proper Clause in the Progressive Era

As the earlier chapters have documented, the chief transformation of the progressives has been the expansion of federal powers chiefly under broad renderings of the spending, taxing, and commerce powers. At root, both of these transformations have expanded the mission of the federal government far beyond the creation of public goods on the one hand or creating an internal free trade zone on the other. Instead, with the use of the rational basis test, the class of permissible government ends has increased. Necessarily, the set of means to meet those ends has to expand as well under any reading of the Necessary and Proper Clause. At this point a paradox arises. The clause can be read broadly to expand the use of federal power. Yet at the same time, its role could easily be *reduced* because the vast expansion of the explicit enumerated powers leaves less for that clause to do. On balance, the second option seems more plausible.

Much of the use of the Necessary and Proper Clause relates to the expansion of the commerce power. Even before 1937, the pivotal case of *Champion v. Ames*[41] invoked the Necessary and Proper Clause to give Congress the power to regulate the shipment of lottery tickets in interstate commerce, despite their legality both in the producing and the receiving states, because their use "has grown into disrepute and has become offensive to the entire people of the nation."[42] Yet there was no showing that the states wanting to prevent their manufacture or use were unable to do so. Justice Harlan's reference to "an entire people" is thus a conscious exaggeration that took a hotly contested issue at the state level and granted one point of view national approval, thereby undermining all the virtues of competitive federalism on matters of morals. But with the rise of the 1937 revolution, the Necessary and Proper Clause lost its critical role, as the production and use of lottery tickets within the states thereafter fell under Congress's commerce power.

In the post-1937 period, moreover, the Necessary and Proper Clause itself did not drive the huge transformation of the commerce power. But it was instrumental in shaping the textual arguments.[43] Thus in *NLRB v. Jones & Laughlin Steel*,[44] the government defended the NLRA on its statutory findings that the control of production prior to the entry of goods into interstate commerce was needed to prevent "strikes and other forms of industrial strife or unrest, which have the intent or the necessary effect of burdening or obstructing commerce."[45] In *Jones & Laughlin*, Chief Justice Hughes endorsed just this view by insisting that Congress could find that collective bargaining is "necessary to protect interstate commerce from the paralyzing consequences of industrial war. . . . Experience has abundantly demonstrated that the recognition of the right of employees to self-organization and to have representatives of their own choosing for the purpose of collective bargaining is often an essential condition of industrial peace."[46] But at that point he did not invoke the clause itself to carry the day.

The subsequent history taught the opposite lesson about the impact of the NLRA on industrial peace. To be sure, with this huge statutory assist, union membership surged from about three million to fifteen million workers in little over a decade. Within months after the adoption of the NLRA, the Committee for Industrial Organization (which morphed into the Congress of Industrial Organizations in 1938) was formed, and some of its member unions were involved in sit-down strikes, which arose out of poisoned management-labor relationships that the NLRA did little to ease.[47] Indeed, the instability of labor relations turned sour after the temporary truce during World War II, as the nation experienced a succession of long and crippling strikes "which involved over three million workers in 1945 and which affected many important industries including coal electrical manufacturing, oil refining, longshoring, railroads and steel."[48] One response was the passage of the Taft-Hartley Act of 1947,[49] which congressional Republicans enacted over President Harry Truman's veto. It is only by the grace of the rational basis test that the NLRA passed constitutional muster, for, whatever its lofty aspirations, the collective bargaining process replaced competitive markets with a bilateral monopoly scheme that was in the 1940s especially prone to catastrophic breakdowns, often leading to strikes, lockouts, and violence. The correct way to ensure industrial peace involves the determination to punish and enjoin violence by either side, wherever and whenever it occurs, which involves only the straightforward application of classical liberal principles. By any objective standard, the

NLRA was neither necessary nor proper. But historically, the driver that secured its constitutionality was the transformed understanding of the Commerce Clause, not any supposed add-on through the Necessary and Proper Clause.

The same overall conclusion applies to subsequent invocations of the Necessary and Proper Clause as an adjunct to the Commerce Clause. One notable example of that power is *Gonzalez v. Raich*,[50] in which Justice Stevens squarely invoked the Necessary and Proper Clause to allow Congress to prohibit the cultivation and use of marijuana in California for medical purposes in two carefully constructed test cases where none of the marijuana in question was either transported in interstate commerce or sold in local commerce. But the Necessary and Proper Clause functioned largely as filler, as all the heavy emphasis was on *Wickard*'s insistence that any change in local production or consumption necessarily influenced the flow of traffic in interstate commerce. Allowing its use even in these few cases would leave a "gaping hole," or so Justice Stevens concluded, in the Controlled Substances Act, which itself makes no exception for medical uses of marijuana.[51] The Necessary and Proper Clause again looks like a decidedly second-tier player.

Just that same attitude carried over to *NFIB v. Sebelius*,[52] where Chief Justice Roberts refused to use that clause to fill in the gaps left by the Commerce Clause, which on his view did not give Congress the power to force people to enter into business transactions. Refusing to let "deference in matters of policy . . . become abdication in matters of law,"[53] he concluded that the Necessary and Proper Clause was only "derivative of, and in service to, a granted power."[54]

That carefully limited phrase does not return the law to an original view that the Necessary and Proper Clause applies only to means, and does not expand the legitimate ends of federal power. But it represents a sharp move in that direction. Indeed the three cases that the chief justice cites confirm that narrowish reading of the clause. Thus he noted that in *United States v. Comstock*,[55] the Court had "upheld provisions permitting continued confinement of those *already in federal custody* when they could not be safely released."[56] That determination, moreover, was hedged in by the key limitation that the statute was "narrow in scope"[57] and did not confer on Congress a general police power, which is reserved to the states. Similarly, it seems hardly a stretch to allow federal legislation to toll the operation of state statutes of limitations while, as he noted, "cases are *pending in federal court*,"[58] which is just the kind of house-keeping arrangement that is always needed to coordinate overlapping litigation in federal and state courts. Finally, in *Sabri v. United States*, the Court unanimously sustained under the Necessary and Proper Clause legislation "criminalizing bribes involving organizations *receiving federal funds*."[59] Once again the broad jurisprudence of the Spending Clause did all the heavy work, by expanding the class of permissible expenditures. It makes no sense to say that the United States does not have power under the Necessary and Proper Clause to prevent these funds from being misspent, and there is no doubt that this statute would have been easily sustained if it had been passed in 1790. It is equally telling that when Chief Justice Roberts addressed the power of Congress to justify the individual mandate as a tax, the Necessary and Proper Clause played no part in his analysis, which in his view turned entirely on the distinction between taxes and penalties.

The overall message on this point is clear. The true damage to the classical liberal Constitution came with the huge expansions of the Commerce Clause and the taxing and spending power. With these achieved, the Necessary and Proper Clause recedes in importance. The italicized passages in Justice Roberts's *NFIB* opinion tell the whole story. In modern times, the Necessary and Proper Clause in and of itself has not proved to be the driving force in the progressive reinterpretation of the Constitution.

15

—◆—

The Dormant Commerce Clause

O UR EXAMINATION of the commerce power has thus far been limited
to cases where Congress has explicitly exercised its regulatory
power over certain activities. The question left untouched is whether
Congress's simple power to regulate interstate commerce in and of
itself blocks state legislation over those same areas. That is the question of the dormant Commerce Clause. Before 1937, the scope of this
problem was necessarily limited by the then-recognized limitations on
the scope of the commerce power. Thus the issue could arise in connection with transportation and communication across state lines, but
it could not normally emerge in connection with agriculture, manufacture, and mining, which were understood to fall outside the sphere
of Congress's authority. But once the scope of the commerce power
was expanded to cover all productive activities, the potential scope
of the dormant Commerce Clause could have expanded to subject all
traditional forms of state regulation to an implicit federal constitutional override, even in the face of federal inaction. Yet movements
in that direction have been halting because any aggressive reading
of the dormant Commerce Clause could pose sharp limitations on
states' exercise of their normal police powers, whose preservation was
an essential part of the progressive's constitutional plan. The dormant
Commerce Clause thus operates with considerable power on matters
of interstate trade, or issues closely related to it, but with far less power
in the newer regions of federal power.

The Origins of the Dormant Commerce Power

Yet where does this dormant power come from in the first place? In one sense, there is clearly some textual effort in the Constitution to delineate certain areas that are prohibited to the states. Thus just as Article I, Section 8 delineates the federal powers, Article I, Section 10 contains a complex list of prohibitions on the activities that states can undertake. Article I, Section 10, clause 1 has a categorical prohibition on the ability of states to grant Letters of Marque and Reprisal or coin money, which means that both these powers are within the exclusive power of the federal government. It also contains a critical provision that says "No State . . . shall . . . pass . . . any . . . Law impairing the Obligation of Contracts." One possible way to read this is to say that the federal government has exclusive control over all contracts, perhaps through the Commerce Clause. Yet that expansive reading seems implausible, if only because the Commerce Clause as then understood only regulated interstate transactions, and not those local contracts dealing with the full range of activities that had nothing to do with commerce at all. At this point, the two pieces do not fit together like hand and glove, a point that was explicitly acknowledged by Justice Bushrod Washington in *Ogden v. Saunders*,[1] in a decision that held that the Contracts Clause offered no protection from discharge in bankruptcy to contracts as yet not made.

This inconclusive textual discussion helps explain the constant debates over whether the extent to which any power vested in Congress is exclusive or concurrent. There is in general a clear preference in the original design to clearly demarcate federal and state spheres. Nonetheless, as a matter of textual interpretation, this pedigree of the dormant Commerce Clause is shaky at best. Unlike the provisions in Article I, Section 10, clause 1, there is no clause that provides: "No state shall regulate commerce with foreign nations, among the several states, or with the Indian tribes." The Commerce Clause, which is found in Article I, Section 8, does not read as though it should be treated as a limitation on the power of the states. The sensible textual interpretation postpones consideration of any clash between federal and state powers until Congress has passed a particular law, to which states must give way under the Supremacy Clause[2] in the event of conflict. State governments are free in the zone of overlap to exercise their traditional police powers so long as Congress has not spoken.

Chief Justice Marshall implicitly accepted that textual position in *Gibbons v. Ogden* when he ruled, dubiously, that a federal licensing statute displaced the state franchise law governing navigation rights between Elizabethtown, New Jersey, and New York City.[3] Justice Johnson, however, launched the dormant Commerce Clause jurisprudence by holding that the state law had to be displaced even if no federal law had been on the books.[4] In his view, only that tough posture could keep state waters open to interstate commerce. The obvious objection to his position is that Congress could displace state law by passing a law that explicitly allowed the use of steam power on all interstate journeys. But under the Johnson formulation the default position is flipped over in good classical liberal fashion to support a presumption of free trade unless and until Congress declares otherwise. Since federal legislation of that sort is never easy to pass, the dormant commerce power tends to be a formidable obstacle to many actual or potential barriers to interstate trade. The assertion of the dormant commerce power in this context is all the more striking because there need not be any obvious discrimination against interstate commerce, given that all local voyages by New Yorkers were governed by the franchise that Ogden exercised in New York waters. *Gibbons* just represents the odd conclusion that ships engaged in interstate journeys need not pay the same licensee fees that Ogden could charge for intrastate journeys, which under *Gibbons* were "purely interior" journeys that Congress could not regulate.

Despite its confused beginnings, make no mistake about it: free competition and the free movement of goods and services across state lines are the driving forces behind the Supreme Court's take on the dormant Commerce Clause. It is a judicial invention that is not easily defensible on narrow originalist grounds. But under the prescriptive constitution, the dormant Commerce Clause should nonetheless be incorporated into modern constitutional law, given that the enormous boost it supplies to free trade is eminently consistent with classical liberal principles. Moreover, the recognition of the dormant Commerce Clause is further strengthened by the presence of the Privileges and Immunities Clause of Article IV, Section 2, clause 1: "The Citizens of each State shall be entitled to all Privileges and Immunities of Citizens in the several States." That clause also embodies an antidiscrimination norm, with freedom of cross-border trade for citizens as one of its core commitments. The clause thus covers much, but by no means all the territory associated with the dormant Commerce Clause doctrine.

The split between the two clauses derives from the Court's 1869 decision in *Paul v. Virginia*,[5] which held that corporations did not count as citizens, so that only individuals received the protections of the Privileges and Immunities Clause. However, that view is not immune from challenge. A partnership consisting solely of citizens should be protected. Why then deny those individuals that same protection when their home state endows them with limited liability in the corporate form? It is easy enough to require them to register for service of process in all states in which they do business, just like home-grown corporations. Furthermore, corporations are already treated as citizens for the purposes of diversity jurisdiction—that is, in disputes between citizens of different states, which can be litigated in federal court—even in the absence of a federal constitutional or statutory claim.[6] So why not adopt that same concept for privileges and immunities when that reading so clearly serves the constitutional end of creating a national free trade zone?

The benefits of this free trade doctrine were well articulated in *H. P. Hood & Sons, Inc. v. Du Mond*,[7] where Justice Jackson took a 180-degree turn from his statist decision in *Wickard v. Filburn*.[8] In *Wickard* he read the affirmative commerce power broadly enough to allow Congress to organize nationwide agricultural cartels. In *Hood*, he championed the exact opposite response to state efforts to cartelize by striking down a decision of New York State's commissioner of agriculture and markets to block construction of a new plant in New York for a Massachusetts milk company serving the Boston market. The commissioner reasoned that to build the plant would be the source of "destructive competition" to incumbent local businesses that he believed were already adequate to serve the market. Speaking for a bare five-member majority, Jackson responded:

> Our system, fostered by the Commerce Clause, is that every farmer and every craftsman shall be encouraged to produce by the certainty that he will have free access to every market in the Nation, that no home embargoes will withhold his export, and no foreign state will by customs duties or regulations exclude them. Likewise, every consumer may look to the free competition from every producing area in the Nation to protect him from exploitation by any. Such was the vision of the Founders; such has been the doctrine of this Court which has given it reality.[9]

There is little to quarrel with in this vision. What remains is the issue of its implementation. One key component is simply a question of whether the restrictions imposed on the free flow of interstate commerce are justified by the local benefits that it supplies, even in the absence of discrimination against interstate commerce. The standard articulation of that view is that an evenhanded regulation of local activities will normally escape constitutional challenge unless the burden it imposes on interstate commerce "is clearly excessive in relation to the putative local benefits."[10] This standard in turn requires some inquiry into whether a less restrictive regulation could achieve the same legitimate local end. Just that test was used to strike down an agricultural statute that required an Arizona grower of cantaloupes to build an expensive in-state plant to package them instead of shipping them for crating to a nearby California facility that could do the job more cheaply.[11]

A second component of the overall strategy avoids the need to make this kind of balance by invoking an ingenious compromise—a nondiscrimination rule—for both international and domestic trade. That rule in clever fashion both respects and limits the power of any governments to regulate outsiders. In one sense, the level of judicial oversight in applying the nondiscrimination principle is less than it is in the balancing cases, in which the state law may be struck down even if it treats local and foreign commerce evenhandedly. However, the nondiscrimination rule works well precisely for that reason: the Court does not have to make a direct assessment of the relationship between the federal interest in the free flow of commerce and the state police power interest in the protection of the health and safety of persons and property. Rather than attack the state's pursuit of its own objectives, the Court just tells each state that it cannot discriminate against commerce from outside the state in the exercise of its customary legal powers.

This antidiscrimination norm works best in those cases where no strong political theory points to a unique answer about what norm counts as the proper exercise of state power in the context of the case's particularized facts. For example, no one can be sure that the ideal sales tax is 1 percent or 5 percent, but it is clear that the taxes in question should be the same for in-state and out-of-state parties if competitive balance is to be maintained. Furthermore, the anticircumvention norm means that this prohibition cannot be evaded by collecting equal taxes from local and out-of-state producers, only to provide a subsidy for the former out of the revenues collected from the latter.[12] That same approach also covers tax deductions, rendering unconstitutional a Maine statute that offered a charitable exemption on local property used primarily by in-state residents but denied the same privilege for a camp that primarily benefited out-of-state children.[13] On matters of regulation, we could debate endlessly whether the minimum age for driving a taxicab should be twenty-one or twenty-five. However, what is flatly unacceptable without powerful explanation is a statute that imposes an age limit of twenty-five on the outsider while allowing insiders to drive cabs at age twenty-one. The use of the antidiscrimination rule is a powerful tool that ordinarily forces dominant in-state political forces to recognize that their efforts to cripple their out-of-state competitors comes at the price of imposing like limitations on domestic firms that engage in parallel activities. This norm thus tends to drive parties toward sensible political accommodations without injecting the Supreme Court into the middle of struggles over the substantive merits of particular taxes and regulations. At the same time, the antidiscrimination norm prevents abuse in the opposite direction: no outsider may demand to be freed from regulations that bind its domestic competitors. To return to *Gibbons*, New Jersey steamboats on the interstate route cannot ask to be freed of a local license fee that is charged to New York steamboats making the same interstate runs.

It is now necessary to look at these two classes of cases—those applying a balancing test and those applying an antidiscrimination norm—in some greater detail.

The Balance of National and State Interests

The origin of the balancing test dates back to early cases that examined the trade-off between the free flow of navigation and a state's need to exercise its police power control over health and safety issues. In the earliest case on this conflict, *Willson v. Black Bird Creek Marsh Co.*,[14] the Court refused to find a dormant Commerce Clause violation when Delaware authorized a dam blocking a navigable interstate creek, given the local improvements that the dam created for nearby land. The case differs from *Corfield*, where the prohibition on collecting oysters did not interfere with interstate navigation at all.[15] But the trade-offs involved with this added interference to both local and interstate navigation seems close enough that some explicit exercise of federal commerce power should be required to stop its construction. The situation worked out quite differently in *Cooley v. Board of Wardens*,[16] which wrongly upheld on safety grounds a statute that appeared to require all ships entering the Philadelphia port to use a local pilot in aid of navigation. This law looks like a safety statute until one detail is added: The requirement of a local pilot did not apply for ships that paid a penalty equal to half the pilot's fee, which funds were transferred into the local pilots' pension fund. Compliance with a safety provision is usually not made optional for the regulated party. In contrast, protectionist statutes are quite content to extract either the work or the profit that would have been obtained had the work been done.

Later cases are built of sterner stuff. Safety justifications carried the day in *South Carolina State Highway Department v. Barnwell Bros.*,[17] where the curvy in-state roads were held to justify a rule requiring that all trucks, both local and out-of-state, comply with length and weight restrictions that were lower than those recommended by national standards. In an evenly balanced case, Justice Stone held that the state proprietary claim over the roads coupled with the evenhanded nature of the restriction saved the regulation. But seven years later, he promptly and properly distinguished *Barnwell* in *Southern Pacific Ry. v. Arizona*,[18] where the state requirement that all trains be of shorter length in Arizona than elsewhere imposed real inconvenience on interstate traffic. Here, again, local and interstate traffic were both subject to identical rules. Nonetheless Arizona's justification for the burden on interstate commerce could not carry the day because of the utter absence of any distinctive topological feature of its railroad tracks that required Arizona to deviate unilaterally from the national standard, when in fact the extra hooking and unhooking of cars could only increase the risk of accidents. In effect, the Court adopted a focal-point solution that worked for the benefit of all states even when they could not coordinate their behavior. These conflicts between state policies could easily give rise to many difficult issues where the terrain is irregular, but should not do so for modern interstate highways that are engineered to uniform standards.[19] That is not the kind of issue that should routinely make it up to the Supreme Court. It is therefore not surprising that by the early 1980s Congress empowered the Department of Transportation (DOT), through the Tandem Truck Safety Act, to make the same trade-offs administratively that were previously required under the case law, which displaced the *Kassel* line of cases by allowing states to petition the Department of Transportation to block the use of larger trucks and tandem trailers on select portions of the interstate highway system that they considered unsafe for such vehicles.[20] In effect, that statute facilitated the resolution of these claims by taking into account the same issues that arose in the litigated cases, a strong indication that the Supreme Court's judicial rules had accurately identified the relevant conflicts.

The Nondiscrimination Rule

The nondiscrimination rule has also given rise to difficult interpretive questions that are best explicable within the classical liberal framework. The first critical question is whether discrimination is measured by the words of the statute or by the intended or probable effect of its policy. The trade-offs here are familiar. The rule that requires explicit discrimination is applied easily: the cases that are struck down are relatively clear, and there are few cases in which the court will unduly invade the province of the state legislature. However, the limitations of that approach are of greater weight, for the state governments that are aware of the limitations of federal intervention will work overtime to craft formally neutral rules with devastating anticompetitive effects. The key question is how difficult it is for courts to peel away the pretext to get to the pith. In many cases, this can be done with relative aplomb.

One early case that pierced purported police power regulations arose in the dairy industry, which has long been a hotbed of protectionist regulation. In *Dean Milk Co. v. Madison*,[21] the City of Madison passed an ordinance that required all milk sold within the city to be processed at plants located within five miles of the city limits. The ostensible justification was to facilitate its inspection of milk meant for local consumption. Its obvious economic effect, however, was to create a huge local monopoly for the fortunate local pasteurizers. Madison defended the bill against the charge of discrimination on the ground that it hit just as hard at Wisconsin processors outside the protected zone, so that the ordinance could not be condemned for being directed solely at out-of-state firms. Yet this riff on the nondiscrimination argument misses the central point of the principle, which is that courts should look with greater favor on legislation that hits its proponents as hard as its targets. That is just not the case when firms elsewhere in Wisconsin have no say in the passage of the local ordinance, so that discrimination against them compounds, rather than diminishes, the flaws in the legislation. So the issue boils down to the protection of health, and on that score Madison failed to show that the standards adopted elsewhere were slack relative to those imposed locally. So long as the citizens of other states and locales had no difficulties with the safety of their processing plants, the correct application of the nondiscrimination principle did not leave people in Madison unprotected against health hazards. The Court rightly dismissed the entire statute as a protectionist law masquerading as a police power measure. State discrimination against out-of-state commerce cannot survive when nondiscriminatory alternatives are available.[22]

Health is, of course, not the only legitimate objective of a sensible police power. The prevention of fraud regarding the quality of products and confusion with respect to proper branding are also within the police powers. But once again, courts have to examine whether the purported regulation of fraud or confusion is just a pretext for anticompetitive regulation. *Hunt v. Washington State Apple Advertising Commission*[23] illustrates the danger. North Carolina required all in- and out-of-state apple producers to ship apples only in closed containers that bore "no grade other than the applicable U.S. grade or standard." The statute is neutral on its face. But its disparate impact is evident from the institutional background. Washington State, which produces superior apples, developed a grading system more precise, and thus more informative, than the federal standard. To require Washington growers to use only standard USDA labels puts its sellers to the unacceptable choice of having to devise special labels for apples destined for North Carolina, to reduce the average quality of the produce sent into North Carolina, or to abandon that market altogether. Within any competitive framework, the last thing that government ought to do is *reduce* the amount of true information available to consumers. So the Court rightly put to North Carolina the task of finding some normative justification for its objections. The state weakly suggested its statute was intended to guard against confusion and fraud. Those ends are surely legitimate, but the means chosen had the precise opposite effect. The Court's decision to strike down the statute in *Hunt* shows in picture-perfect fashion how a classical liberal theory infuses the understanding of the dormant Commerce Clause.

In other cases, however, the justification for state intervention has more clout. Thus in *Maine v. Taylor*,[24] the question was whether to sustain a criminal conviction for importing baitfish from outside the state. The discrimination against foreign commerce was explicit, and any justification was subject to "the strictest scrutiny."[25] The dormant Commerce Clause thus rejects the rational basis mentality that allows any state action so long as there is some conceivable public justification that the statutory scheme advances. Nonetheless, that burden was met by justifications that track precisely classical liberal principles. The importation of baitfish carried with it the risk of parasites to local marine life and the danger of driving native species from their habitat. The total ban was in some sense excessive, but no technology existed for separating dangerous from benign baitfish, and the Supreme Court upheld the statute as it should have.

Trade Regulation and Taxation

The application of the dormant Commerce Clause to many systems of trade regulation and taxation has been far more cautious. In these cases the tax is imposed not only on cross-border transactions, but also on the domestic activities that take place solely within one state. The statutes themselves are usually facially neutral, but they are also statutes passed with an explicit redistributive agenda that is usually apparent from facts in the public domain at the time of passage. To get at the anticompetitive consequences of these statutes requires a little digging, which, on balance, the Supreme Court has not been prepared to do, at a real social cost. Here are a few representative cases.

In *Exxon Corp. v. Maryland*,[26] Maryland banned all gasoline producers and refiners from operating retail outlets within the state. To its knowledge, Exxon was the only producer caught by the prohibition. Several other refiners were also caught, but there were no Maryland producers or refiners. Clearly, the statute would meet a constitutional standard that requires proof of formal discrimination to strike down state economic regulations. But the test for disparate impact runs up against this puzzle: How effective can the antidiscrimination law be when only outsiders are caught by the prohibition? At this point warning bells should go off because of the known certainty in the Maryland legislature that the statute would only hit a feared outsider.

The proper theory thus would strike down this prohibition unless and until it were shown that blocking the mode of distribution of Exxon and the out-of-state refiners had some legitimate justification. Maryland claimed that it was acting in response to the shortage of supply owing to the 1973 decrease in petroleum after the Arab boycott of the United States. But a change in economic conditions is hardly a reason to ditch a competitive model unless the business practices violate some principle of antitrust law, which was not the case here. The statute thus looks like straightforward protectionism in favor of its local retail outlets that should be caught by the statute, but Justice Stevens held, wrongly, that objections to the statute related only "to the wisdom of the statute, not to its burdens on commerce."[27] That line of argument could work in areas where the level of constitutional scrutiny is low, but the entire thrust of Justice Jackson's remarks in *H. P. Hood* show that this distinction is not maintainable in the face of the strong substantive commitment to open competition under the dormant Commerce Clause.

The same difficulties arise with respect to taxes that are neutral in form but disparate in impact. In *Commonwealth Edison Co. v. Montana*,[28] Montana imposed an excise tax on low-sulfur coal mined within the state, over 90 percent of which was destined for sale in other states. The passage of this tax was accompanied by a reduction in the income tax and property taxes that fell exclusively on Montana residents. Owing to the huge concentrations of low-sulfur coal in the state, huge chunks of the tax were passed on to out-of-state parties who did not, of course, share in the reductions on property and income taxes within the state. As a formal matter, the tax applied before the coal entered into commerce. But the Supreme Court rightly held that this fact alone did not insulate the tax from scrutiny under the dormant Commerce Clause. The issue then turned to whether, in sorting out the effects of the tax, it met the following four-part test, which upholds the tax if it "is applied to an activity with a substantial nexus with the taxing State, is fairly apportioned, does not discriminate against interstate commerce, and is fairly related to the services provided by the State."[29] One way to read this test is to insist that it blocks any tax, which when taken in context, results in a redistribution of wealth from out-of-state to in-state individuals, which this tax surely does. But, as ever, the level of scrutiny is decisive, and here Justice Thurgood Marshall took the position that this test only required that there be some nexus between the property and the state that taxes it, but there need be no showing that the amount of tax bore any relationship to the services received. Put otherwise, the traditional Lockean justification for taxation—to increase government services that increase to each person the value of the liberty and property that he retains—formed no part of his analysis.

The tension between this case and the subsequent decision in *West Lynn Creamery, Inc. v. Healy*[30] should be evident. In that case, a tax on sales to Massachusetts dairy retailers was directly linked to a rebate for Massachusetts dairy farmers, thus exposing only out-of-state farmers to the tax. In this case, the tax in question was linked to the overall reduction in exclusive in-state taxes. Justice Stevens struck down the dual combination because of its obvious differential impact on in-state and out-of-state producers. The subsidy provided by the state could not be looked at in isolation from the tax, when both were executed as part of a single scheme. The anticircumvention principle was thus deployed to backstop the antiredistributive attitude of the classical liberal approach that had been rejected in *Commonwealth Edison*.[31] This is in sharp contrast to the general New Deal acceptance of a rational basis test that shields all government taxation schemes from constitutional challenge so long as peace and good order is retained.[32]

Unfortunately, however, the Court has been unable to develop a consistent view on the question of competition between local and interstate businesses. In *General Motors Corp. v. Tracy*[33] the general tax regime subjected sales of natural gas to a 5 percent tax if purchased from an in-state supplier and a 5 percent compensating use tax if purchased from an out-of-state supplier. Ohio law also exempted from the 5 percent local sales tax any sales by an in-state "local distribution company" or LDC operated by a local regulated public utility. GM purchased all of its needs for the tax years in question from an out-of-state supplier subject to the tax, and Tracy, the Ohio tax commissioner, rebuffed its demand for a tax refund.

In the Supreme Court, Justice Souter held that GM was not entitled to the refund on the ground that the natural gas that GM had purchased was not "substantially similar" to that which was locally supplied. In his view, the source of the difference was that GM purchased natural gas in an unregulated market without any special protections, while the LDCs were required to sell the gas "bundled" with a variety of protections, including the need to sell their natural gas at just and reasonable and nondiscriminatory rates, and to meet a variety of disclosure and record-ing requirements.[34] At that point, Justice Souter concluded that "con-ceptually" the nondiscrimination obligation could not apply because "the difference in products may mean that the different entities serve different markets, and would continue to do so even if the supposedly discriminatory burden were removed."[35]

Unfortunately, this argument that what "may" happen need not happen misses the point. There is no question that if the LDCs and the interstate suppliers chose to collude on prices, they would run afoul of the antitrust laws precisely because their products are close enough sub-stitutes that they count as part of the same market. It is surely not the case that all buyers from the LDC are completely unresponsive to the relative tax rates between the two kinds of natural gas in the market. Narrow the price differential by the elimination of the tax, and some buyers would surely shift suppliers. It is not as though the two markets were separated by any explicit legal barrier. At this point, the same tax rate eliminates one key distortion in the market, such that consumers can then decide with accurate pricing information whether they prefer to take the bundled or unbundled product.

The danger in the Court's decision is that there are countless situ-ations in which different competitors offer a different mix of goods and services, and the artificially narrow definition of the relevant market in *Tracy* thus invites all forms of local protection. One recent illustration of this problem arose in *National Association of Optometrists & Opticians v. Har-ris*[36] where the California Business and Professions Code prevents opti-cians and optical companies from offering for sale prescription eyeglasses at any location that performs eye examinations. These companies cannot co-locate by renting space on their premises with licensed optometrists and ophthalmologists. But those same optometrists and ophthalmolo-gists who conduct these eye examinations may offer one-stop shopping by selling eyeglasses to their customers. In principle it might be possible to distinguish this case from *Tracy*, but the Ninth Circuit declined that invitation. But there is no reason to require that determination at all. Here the differential treatment cuts far more deeply than the 5 percent tax rate. Rather than getting into these esoteric distinctions, the correct response is to apply the nondiscrimination rule to any situation where there is some respectable overlap between customers, and then let the market adjust by setting prices and the terms of sale and services in an efficient way. The artificially narrow definition of what counts as the relevant market in *Tracy* can only work to undermine the good work that is otherwise done through the dormant Commerce Clause.

Market Participant

Thus far I have considered the dormant Commerce Clause as it relates to state regulation of private activities. But once property is under state control, does its ownership position give a state additional power to discriminate in favor of its citizens in disposing and using those resources? That favoritism is allowed for governments under the "market participation" exception to the dormant Commerce Clause, wherein the ownership claim adds to state powers. Just that position was taken as early as *Corfield v. Coryell*,[37] which in addition to its discussion of the commerce power, also held that the state, as owner of the oysters in the riverbeds, could exclude out-of-state parties from their capture. The question then arises as to why the state should be allowed to act as if that wildlife were its own. The strongest explanation deals with the dangers of overhunting and overfishing common pool assets to their extinction. Controlling those risks obviously raises extra difficulties for wildlife that can cross state borders, unlike public lands and mineral deposits. However, the question still arises whether the state in this quasi-ownership position should be able to so restrict the capture and sale of wildlife, to which the answer appears to be no. The duty of the state as a public owner is to maximize the value of resources under its command for the citizens of the state. The best mechanism to achieve that end is to auction the rights to the highest bidder. Those bids will in turn be higher if outsiders are entitled to bid. In this context, the case against protectionism applies with equal force to goods that are held in state hands and to those which are not.

The modern cases tend to give too much leeway to the states under the so-called market participant doctrine. For example, *Hughes v. Alexandria Scrap Corp.*[38] wrongly allowed Maryland to conduct a program wherein it purchased scrapped automobiles from both in-state and out-of-state processors, but required less extensive documentation from in-state companies than from out-of-state firms. What possible advantage accrues to the citizens of the state as a whole from subsidizing inefficient local companies? The situation was no better in *Reeves, Inc. v.*

Stake,[39] which allowed a state-owned cement plant in South Dakota to restrict sales of its entire output to preferentially supply local firms first. Once again, why should out-of-state citizens incur the loss in revenue in order to favor a few firms?

The bad decision in *Reeves* forced the Court to use fancy footwork in *South-Central Timber Development, Inc. v. Wunnicke*[40] to invalidate an Alaska law that required purchasers of state-owned timber to process it in local sawmills. The obvious objection to this rule is that the price that Alaska generates for the timber will be reduced by the increase in the cost of the complementary service it imposes. That favoritism hurts the public at large in order to give a benefit for the sheltered buyers. The Court struck down the scheme by invoking a rule that the seller of goods could not impose restraints on the way in which its purchaser utilizes or deals that property to others. Yet nowhere does it explain why only local persons should be allowed to bid in the first place. This decision would have been far easier if it had never gone down the wrong "market participant" path of *Alexandria Scrap* in the first place. It is vain to argue, as some have, that the market participant doctrine is less "coercive" than the direct regulation of private affairs.[41] The invocation of coercion in this case diverts us from the central task of sound government, namely the maximization of social welfare, which requires expunging all protectionist doctrines. In a real sense, the rules here are only a replay of the analytical considerations that govern the use of the doctrine of unconstitutional conditions: in all cases the state's powers as an *owner* are limited to the pursuit of the same limited objectives that the state may properly pursue as a *regulator*.[42]

The last issue that requires special attention under the dormant Commerce Clause deals with the recurrent question of whether any state or local government can give preference to local waste at local waste disposal facilities. The orthodox response in American constitutional law is that the disposal of bads—waste products with negative value—is subject to the same nondiscrimination rules as the disposal of goods—ordinary products with positive value. If the two types of things are the same, no explicit discrimination between in- and out-of-state commerce is allowed. In *City of Philadelphia v. New Jersey*,[43] the question was whether a New Jersey law that prohibited the importation of most "solid or liquid waste which originated or was collected outside the territorial limits of the State" could survive challenge under the dormant

Commerce Clause. Justice Stewart recited the usual evils of protectionism to which the clause was directed and concluded that the state had failed to make out a legitimate claim that the statute was required to prevent environmental deterioration within state boundaries, be it to reduce the cost of waste disposal or to preserve open lands. In the Court's view, New Jersey failed because it could not show "some reason apart from their origin, to treat [the articles of commerce] differently."[44]

This line of argument takes too narrow a view of the issue, because the key question deals not only with the allocation of space in existing waste dumps, but with the willingness of the state to create these dumpsites in the first place. If the restriction to in-state waste is allowed, the state will have an incentive to expand its local capacity to meet the local demand. The state gains as its locally situated waste moves from less to more secure sites within the state. The state in effect swaps out a larger externality of uncontained waste for the smaller one of contained waste. Under the equal access rule, however, states will have an incentive to limit the opening of new local dumpsites, since the acceptance of waste from elsewhere creates an additional small risk, without offsetting the larger one of uncontained waste. Ironically, therefore, the more restrictive policy of reserving local dumpsites for local waste should expand the nationwide capacity for storing waste.

We have some real evidence of this phenomenon from the well-known decision in *New York v. United States*,[45] which dealt with a statutory scheme for nuclear waste. Consistent with the argument made above, the number of waste sites in the United States had been dwindling in the 1970s, as states reduced capacity across the board on a nondiscriminatory basis. The Low-Level Radioactive Waste Policy Amendments Act of 1985[46] took note of this stubborn fact and deliberately ousted the non-discrimination rule adopted in *Philadelphia* by authorizing state governments to impose surtaxes on waste from out-of-state sources. The state keeps a fraction of the revenue for itself and turns another fraction over to the Department of Energy, which uses it to reward states that have achieved certain set milestones in the distribution of the waste in question. In addition, the statute authorized states and regional compacts to increase gradually the charges that they place on noncooperating states that don't expand their local capacity. And finally (in a provision that was struck down as "commandeering" state governments), the statute sought to require states to take title to orphan nuclear waste.

This elaborate framework is not needed to encourage states to accept goods from outside their borders. But even with the program in place the disposal of nuclear waste suffers from a huge "Not in My Backyard" (NIMBY) problem. For some time it appeared as though Yucca Mountain in Nevada would be the disposal site of choice, but that was stoutly rebuffed by Senator Harry Reid and, after years of fruitless struggle, was finally abandoned by executive order on January 30, 2010.[47] Naturally, no new site has yet been selected, so that dicey temporary sites now look to be permanent, until a special blue ribbon panel recommends yet another site, which in turn will be subject to a new set of local reactions. Waste presents distinct problems of its own.

In contrast to *Philadelphia*, the shoe was on the other foot in *C & A Carbone, Inc. v. Town of Clarkstown*,[48] where the question was whether the township could require local producers of waste to obey a local "flow control" ordinance. The ordinance required all firms within Clarkstown to dispose of their waste through its subsidized station that separated recyclable from nonrecyclable items. Carbone was required to use that facility even after it did its own sorting, which meant that it had to forgo the cheaper option of processing its own waste and disposing it in out-of-state landfills. The Supreme Court held that *Dean Milk* controlled and struck down the ordinance. That result is, moreover, correct even if *Philadelphia* was wrong. The downward cycle in disposing of waste plays no role in a case where the local government wishes to monopolize a business. At this point the case deals with competition in services, not with negative externalities, so the usual presumption against preferential treatment holds.

To sum up, the dormant Commerce Clause represents a welcome departure from the rules of strict constitutional construction. There are mistakes in this area, but they do not stem from any excessive form of judicial intervention. Rather, these errors stem from a willingness to take antiprotectionist rationales to their logical conclusion in all realms of taxation and regulation. These cases, moreover, present a larger conceptual puzzle. Why is it that justices, like Robert Jackson, who champion aggressive federal regulation that stifles competition are so alert, with less textual justification, to pounce on state laws that have exactly those undesirable effects? The answer appears to be that these justices fear balkanization by the states more than they fear monopolization by the federal government. In a sense, their position makes some crude sense because the adverse consequences of balkanization result in a cycle of commercial disruption too evident to ignore. In contrast, the evils of monopolization and cartelization are harder to detect because they do not involve overt disruption in the marketplace, but subtler changes in the quantity and price of goods sold in interstate commerce. And there is a naïve sense that Congress as a national body can transcend the petty localisms that drive the dormant Commerce Clause analysis.

Unfortunately, there is a good deal of conceptual blindness in these purported distinctions. The antitrust laws have no difficulty in dealing with the problems of monopolization and cartelization, and indeed recognize cases—like check-clearing services and telecommunications—where cooperation between competitors on certain business issues does not give carte blanche to fix prices. The various justifications that do allow some local regulations to survive antitrust scrutiny could be transported over to the congressional exercise of power if only the justices were willing to engage in the same sensible presumption of distrust for federal regulation that they do for state regulation. States may well be provincial in their motivations. However, it hardly follows that Congress looks at these issues from a perch that immunizes it from the same kind of preferential failings that are so evident in much state regulation, as its sorry record in labor and agriculture so clearly shows. In the end, the classical liberal accounts of government that have done tolerably well in controlling the states should be brought once again to bear on the federal government.

THE EXECUTIVE POWER

16

Basic Principles and Domestic Powers

THE LAST KEY PIECE of our constitutional architecture is the executive
branch. As a matter of institutional design, the Founders chose a
unitary executive, with a single president perched on top of a complex
pyramid of lesser officials in the executive branch (or, as they called it,
"department"). The central challenge in understanding how the president fits into the overall constitutional structure is found in the tension
between two key clauses, which highlight the tension in any system
of limited government. Section 1 leads off with a pop: "The executive
power shall be vested in a President of the United States of America."
The verb "vest" conveys a powerful image, for the term "vested," as in
fully clothed, has long been used to indicate a fully protected right, not
one that is either contingent or inchoate. The president thus has the
whip hand.

Any such power, if left untrammeled, carries with it the danger
of abuse, if not tyranny. No trustee who is put in charge of an operation can treat his trust as though it were a fiefdom that he and he
alone owns. All trustees of private wealth, all guardians of children and
incompetent individuals are subject to correlative duties to their beneficiaries precisely to negate the inference that vested powers are akin
to strong ownership of trust assets. The president is not the owner of a
nation, but a fiduciary, who is subject to the same type of constraints.
The counterweight to the vesting clause in Article II therefore comes
in the critical clause in Article II, Section 3, which simply says that "he
shall take care that the laws be faithfully executed." The use of the verb
"be" is no accident. His duties extend not only to the duties that fall

upon him personally in his official capacity, but also impose on him a duty of oversight to see that all lesser officials within the executive branch respect the same set of fiduciary duties that are imposed on the president. In addition to these two benchmarks, Article II also contains specific provisions that deal with such critical issues as his position as commander-in-chief, his responsibility to appoint inferior officers who will be accountable to him, his power to issue pardons, and his right to receive ambassadors and other public ministers. These are extensive powers, and the central structural question is whether Article II sets the right balance between the powers conferred on him and the restraints to which he is subject.

A Delicate Balance

In thinking about this issue, it is critical to note that the Framers could have opted for other institutional designs. Many state governments "unbundle" the executive power[1] so that, for example, the attorney general is elected independently of the governor. Global judgments on these matters are always hard to make. Nonetheless, the split between offices has some pluses and minuses: the efficiency of the office is likely to be reduced by divided authority, but the check against executive aggrandizement is strengthened. The attorney general could investigate the president and other officers in the executive branch for misconduct, but could also do so for political reasons, especially if the two political leaders are from different parties. Wholly apart from any risk of abuse, the creation of the separate office could result in a greater fragmentation of executive power, which could easily hamper law enforcement efforts.

A brief experiment with this divided power was tried at the federal level by the statutory creation of "special prosecutors" under the Independent Counsel Act,[2] passed in 1978 in the aftermath of the Nixon Watergate scandal. The law was intended to better control the risk of misconduct by high officials in the executive branch. The theory behind the statute was that conflicts of interest made it unlikely that anyone in the attorney general's office would take a hard look at presidential misconduct after what came to be called "the Saturday Night Massacre" in which Robert H. Bork, as the acting attorney general, fired Archibald Cox, the special prosecutor assigned to the case, under orders from President Nixon.[3] No one quarrels with the fact that massive abuses then led less than a year later to Richard Nixon's resignation under threat of impeachment. But the great vice of the Independent Counsel Act is that in the aftermath of Watergate it refought the last war, when in subsequent cases the lack of institutional control over the special prosecutor led to overzealous prosecutors unchecked by any institution. The Supreme Court sustained this statutory scheme over the passionate and prescient dissent of Justice Scalia in *Morrison v. Olson*.[4] Yet, ironically, the consistent overreaching by these independent "special prosecutors" meant that this legislation was allowed to lapse in 1999.[5] The simple point is that it is exceedingly difficult to get the right institutional balances even when views on the relevant trade-offs are widely shared across the political spectrum.

Our current constitutional position thus embodies a "unitary" executive power, vested in a single person, with the necessary risks that entails. The details of that unitary system are complicated by the existence of heads of departments who have a power base that is not fully dependent on the president. The exact determination of these powers, as well as other details of the executive branch, has left many issues for disputation. That said, however, the basic constitutional structure remains tolerably clear. Unlike the prime minister in a parliamentary system, the president is chosen for a term of four years[6] and he may be removed from office earlier only by impeachment by the House and conviction by the Senate for some high crime or misdemeanor.[7] In order to further protect his independence in office, the president's compensation shall be neither increased nor decreased during his term in office,[8] but that constitutional provision does not protect him from the ravages of inflation that strike all persons, public or private. Nor can the president receive any other "Emolument" while in office.[9] Entrenching the president is thus the opening gambit in an elaborate system replete with separate powers for the executive branch and checks and balances among the several branches.

Regardless of the configuration of executive power, one nagging question remains. What is there that keeps the president, be his powers large or small, acting in ways that conform to the basic constitutional dictates? One answer is that there is really nothing in the Constitution or laws that achieves that particular result, such that compliance relies on an uneasy combination of political pushback from other branches of government and some diffuse sense of public opinion. Just that realist view has been advanced with much force and confidence in a recent book, *The Executive Unbound: After the Madisonian Republic*,[10] by Eric Posner and Adrian Vermeule, who write, more or less categorically, that "law does little to constrain the modern executive."[11] There is of course much historical evidence of constitutions that have failed to hold nations together. Their breakdown is always attributable to some ill-fated mix of institutional design and the people who run them. But, by the same token, it is important to ask why some constitutional forms have on balance succeeded. On this point, it is critical to note that the Posner/Vermeule thesis overstates two grounds for skepticism: linguistic and moral. There are of course gaps in any system of rules, but it is a serious mistake to assume that all language is so plastic that any willful person can defend any interpretation against all comers. That is certainly true even for the modern executive: his term of office lasts four years; he needs Senate confirmation of senior appointments; he is vested with the power of commander-in-chief; and he has the absolute power to grant or deny pardons[12] and to make recess appointments.[13]

Since so few cases result in litigation, moreover, it is hard to explain why the president seems to stay within appropriate bounds even when clear boundaries are not evident: is it that the social sanctions of which Posner and Vermeule speak are exceedingly potent, or that the internalized sense of legal obligation on key officials is so great? The president has lots of lawyers at his disposal, but their sole job is not to find clever ways for him to beat the system. Often it is to instruct him on what the norm is so that he can do the right thing unilaterally, without compulsion. The entire pardon office is set up to encourage some cohesive law-like consistency on an issue where the president's power is concededly absolute, so strong is the impulse to create rule of law practices even when they are not required.

This set of practices gives rise to the following methodological puzzle. Since legal, political, and social forces are always present, and usually cut in the same way, it becomes hard in practice to tease out their separate influences. The basic ambiguity in all these cases is captured in the phrase "virtue is its own reward," which has two meanings. It can refer to the sensation of self-respect that one gets from compliance with legal norms. Or it can refer to the prudential wisdom of complying with legal norms as the best way to keep out of trouble. As Richard Pildes writes in his review of *The Executive Unbound*, the matter is to some extent overdetermined in "that the single *most powerful* signal of that willingness to be constrained, particularly in American political culture, is probably the President's willingness to comply with law."[14] Unless that attitude of willingness to work within the law is on constant public display, the president will drive away other political actors whose cooperation is necessary for his success.

By way of comparison, it is clear that the CEO of a business firm or charitable institution cannot just rule by decree but must consider how to coordinate his activities with other players in the organization, on whose long-term cooperation his own success depends. Presidents are really no different from business types in their need to worry about what everyone else worries about, namely, to follow Daryl Levinson's list, "coordination, reputation, repeat-play, reciprocity, asset-specific investment, and positive political feedback mechanisms."[15] Indeed, these issues are endemic to all forms of social cooperation, so it is likely that psychological dispositions will evolve to make people comfortable most of the time with discharging their fiduciary duties, without looking over their shoulders at the law. They do very well by trying to do the right thing. That want of introspection and calculation turns out to be a powerful way to secure compliance, and the dangerous implication of the Posner/Vermeule position is that their descriptive account will be taken by some as a reason to weaken the complex, albeit fragile, set of legal and social constraints that attach to people in high office. Surely sanctions, like impeachment, are needed to deal with major deviations from rules, but in most cases the mix of internal obligation and external enforcement mechanisms seems to work tolerably well.

At this point, therefore, the inquiry turns from the existential matters of compliance to the key design choices of how the United States Constitution puts these pieces together. The topics here form a heterogeneous mass, whose contours are determined in part by the particular provisions of Article II of the Constitution and in part by some underlying notion of executive power. Historically, our constitutional structure starts off with a reflection of the Lockean concerns with limited government. Locke himself derived the separation of the executive from the legislative by an appeal to their different functions:

> But because the laws, that are at once, and in a short time made, have a constant and lasting force, and need a perpetual execution, or an attendance thereunto; therefore it is necessary there should be a power

always in being, which should see to the execution of the laws that are made, and remain in force. And thus the legislative and executive power come often to be separated.[16]

That separation has, like all institutional arrangements, its positives and negatives. On the negative side, strict separation allows, as noted, for the improper concentration of executive power in the hands of a single individual. Yet simultaneously, the Founders feared that dividing power within the executive branch—think of the Roman system of two consuls—could lead to paralysis, with devastating consequences, especially when facing foreign threats or domestic unrest, where the latter was a far greater concern in the Founding Era than it is today. The basic design thus walks the fine line between these two extremes, by ensuring that the president has the sufficient "energy" that Hamilton regarded as "essential" for responding to foreign attacks, for setting out the "steady administration of the laws," and for guarding against legislative combinations and factions.[17] Hamilton also thought that the four-year term was needed to give the president a permanent stake in the performance of his office,[18] without creating the risk of a de facto monarchy. Without that term length protection, the president could be subject to being "at the absolute devotion of the legislative" branch.[19] By way of offset, the Constitution imposes on the president the obligation to "take Care that the Laws be faithfully executed"[20] and subjects his senior appointments to senatorial confirmation.[21]

In the section preceding the Take Care Clause, the president was given the absolute power to grant reprieves and pardons for offenses against the United States.[22] He also enjoys other prerogatives, including the right to receive ambassadors.[23] Most critically, the president is also the commander-in-chief of our military forces,[24] which raises a key question regarding his "inherent" power to deal with foreign nations and with individuals charged with being enemy combatants.

In order to see how this system works, I shall attack all of these issues regarding executive power in the following order. This chapter deals with domestic matters. The first section addresses the thorny issue of who has the power to make appointments to and removals from various offices both within and outside of the executive branch. The second section of this chapter deals with delegation of power to the president by Congress.

Chapter 17 will examine the interactions between the rise and fall of the delegation doctrine, both as it applies to traditional functions lodged in the executive branch, and those that take advantage of the peculiar status of independent agencies under the Constitution. Chapter 18 will then deal with the role of the president in foreign affairs generally. That inquiry has two separate parts. The first examines the interaction between the president and Congress with respect to Congress's legislative powers, to legislation that must be approved by both houses of Congress, and also to the Senate in relation to treaties (which must be approved by two-thirds of the senators present).[25] The second part analyzes the position of the president in his role as "Commander in Chief of the Army and Navy of the United States, and the Militia of the several States, when called into the actual Service of the United States."[26] Each of these topics has profound implications for both the structural success of the American Constitution and its ability to balance the vexed trade-offs between individual claims of liberty and collective claims of national security. It is therefore necessary to consider the scope of the writ of habeas corpus insofar as it relates to the conduct of foreign affairs.

The Appointment and Removal of Federal Officials

No chief executive can discharge all of the obligations of any major office without the assistance of agents who are subordinate to his will. With respect to the office of the president, the question of who these agents are and how they might operate is reflected in the Appointments Clause and its complex structure, which reflects the Framers' deep commitment to both the separation of powers and checks and balances. The relevant portions of that clause read:

> He . . . shall nominate, and by and with the Advice and Consent of the Senate, shall appoint Ambassadors, other public Ministers and Consuls, Judges of the supreme Court, and all other Officers of the United States, whose Appointments are not herein otherwise provided for, and which shall be established by Law: but the Congress may by Law vest the Appointment of such inferior Officers, as they think proper, in the President alone, in the Courts of Law, or in the Heads of Departments.[27]

The initial question is why does the president not have the sole power to appoint senior government officials without having to first obtain a majority of votes in the United States Senate? This puzzle arises because both corporate and parliamentary systems typically give the head officer exclusive power to appoint his team. The key difference, however, is that in both corporate and parliamentary systems, that head serves at the pleasure of a board of directors who can dismiss the executive officials at will. The political equivalent in a parliamentary system is a vote of no confidence, after which the government falls and a new election must be held. Given that reserved power, little is gained by the executive with respect to his appointive powers. Note that the power of Congress to dismiss the executive at will would signal the end of separation of powers, which the president's four-year term preserves. Having another body pass on his key appointments is thus a substitute safeguard given the unqualified power of dismissal that he retains.

The desire to curb executive power over appointments is even stronger for persons, like judges, who are not part of the executive branch. Left unchecked, the president could stack the judicial branch with his own lackeys. Since federal judicial offices are held "during good Behaviour,"[28] which typically means for life, the president's nominees will outlast his term of office, which supplies an additional incentive for denying the president any plenary appointment power. Life tenure for judges has turned out to be one of the great structural mistakes of the Constitution,[29] with profound implications for the durability of the original tripartite structure. A long term of years, say eighteen for the Supreme Court, would preserve judicial independence, reduce the stakes on each new appointment, and secure the orderly rotation in office that could prevent the formation of a Supreme Court gerontocracy. But that mistaken choice to grant life tenure makes the senatorial constraints even more important.

It is significant to note that this power to turn down presidential judicial nominees or other executive appointments is vested not in the House of Representatives or even in both houses in combination. Requiring approval in both houses surely would be too cumbersome to enable appointments to take effect within a sensible time frame. The creative tension between the Senate and the House makes good sense in slowing down legislation, but not appointments, especially since delays would surely be routine, as many qualified candidates may not meet the approval of both houses of Congress, given that they are selected on different time cycles and for different reasons. So the need for expedition leaves the choice of either the House or the Senate, acting alone. The implicit elitism of the Founders' republican model probably explains why they lodged this power with the smaller of the two houses, the Senate, whose members were all appointed by state legislatures at the time.

The structure of the Appointments Clause makes it clear that the initial nomination is the president's alone to make; the reference to "by and with the Advice and Consent of the Senate"[30] is triggered only after the nomination is made. Unfortunately, no one can offer a coherent account of the "advice" portion of this provision. What matters therefore is consent to key nominations and the complex politics that it generates. Doubtful senators can always threaten to vote against an appointment unless the president makes some suitable concession, including perhaps a "package deal" that includes some nominees desired by those senators as the price for getting presidential nominations through. That ability to bargain, however, necessarily depends on the creation of a blocking Senate coalition, which is never easy to form. The opponents know that only a bare majority is needed for Senate confirmation, and there are strong political pressures against leaving major positions open indefinitely. Maneuvers to block cloture may be effective in some situations, but so long as the president is prepared to move toward the center some nominee is likely to get through. The vociferous opposition of a few cannot block the decision of a solid majority.

Most importantly, the Senate must exercise its power of consent on an up-or-down, all-or-nothing basis only; either the nominee gets the job or he does not. The nomination cannot be approved subject to any ad hoc restrictions or limitations on powers of the nominee in public office, all of which will necessarily alter the system of constitutional balance. Thus the attorney general cannot be approved so long as he agrees to recuse himself from all antitrust or civil rights cases. At no point, moreover, does the Senate have to give public reasons for its decision, although individual senators are surely entitled to have their public say. Quite simply, any "for cause" standard is no more administrable in this context than for the College of Cardinals in Rome. Any other alternative would have horrible institutional consequences. Imagine, for example, how the judiciary would look if judges, particularly on the Supreme Court, could decide in advance to recuse themselves from, say, constitutional cases or antitrust matters, or if they were forced to do so by limitations imposed on their nomination approval by the Senate. If we let different judges cut unique deals, no one would be able to figure out what the term "one" Supreme Court means.[31] Imagine, too, how awkward it would be to assemble a cabinet whose appointments were hedged about by different substantive limitations on the matters they could deal with. Of course, many departments set out duties for their occupants pursuant to some statutory scheme. But that is a far cry from telling a department head that he cannot speak to others about his work or that he must take his office without having the same set of powers as his predecessor. Up-or-down and all-or-nothing rules of decision-making are best understood as *structural* constraints, which cannot be waived even with the blessing of the president and a unanimous Senate.

Recess Appointments

The basic structure of the Appointments Clause for those officers who need Senate approval gives guidance as to the appropriate interpretation of the president's power to issue recess appointments:[32]

> The President shall have Power to fill up all Vacancies that may happen during the Recess of the Senate, by granting Commissions which shall expire at the End of their next Session.[33]

Wholly apart from any historical practice, one key phrase in this clause refers to vacancies that "may happen" when the Senate is not in session. The clear cases to which this applies are those where the office falls vacant when the Senate is not in a position to confirm the substitute and the president needs to perform his executive function. To allow the appointment to last only until the Senate comes back into session could create a tenure of office in which no useful work could be done. To allow the appointment to last indefinitely or for a long term is in effect to undercut the role of the Senate confirmation process. The compromise position allows the appointment to go for the remainder of a session, which in no case is more than two years. The original interpretation of this document in 1792 by the first attorney general, Edmund Randolph, gave a narrow scope to recess appointments,[34] given that they were an exception to the basic power of the Senate in the overall constitutional scheme.

Two other textualist arguments bolster the position that the president's power to make recess appointments should be narrowly construed. First, the term "vacancy" is best read as requiring that the office be up and running before any recess appointment can be made. Accordingly, the historical evidence suggests that the president cannot use his power to make recess appointments that are in fact initial appointments to fill a newly created position,[35] because it would have "deprived the Senate of its ability to influence the direction of a newly created agency at a critical time."[36] Second, in *Noel Canning v. NLRB*,[37] the Circuit Court for the District of Columbia held that the term "the Recess" only "refers to the intersession recess of the Senate"[38] when the Senate is not available to consider the matter. That does not include, as the NLRB had argued, the shorter periods of adjournment when the Senate is open for business, including on August 5, 2011, for such legislation as the Airport and Airway Extension Act of 2011[39] or, more significantly, on December 23, 2011, when the Senate passed the Temporary Payroll Tax Cut Continuation Act of 2011,[40] which was during the same adjournment order that was in place when the President made his disputed "recess" appointments. Both laws were signed by the president in the ordinary course of business. The case is not destined for review to the Supreme Court.[41]

What is striking about the modern process is that the use of recess appointments has become so far more extensive today that they have come to serve a very different function, chiefly to allow the president to appoint controversial nominees to key administrative positions, such as John Bolton as ambassador to the United Nations,[42] Craig Becker to the National Labor Relations Board,[43] and Richard Cordray as the head of the newly created Consumer Financial Protection Bureau created under the Dodd-Frank financial reform statute.[44] Under these circumstances, both the spirit and letter of the constitutional text dealing with recess appointments are manifestly violated. Textually, the president is not even allowed to fill up offices that *remain open* during vacancies because they did not happen during the recess, which was Randolph's view of the matter. Nor does the text of the Constitution allow the president to make recess appointments for newly created offices, even if these vacancies emerged when the Senate was in recess. The Framers' decisions on these key points to deny the president any power to fill up the office and amount to an invitation to the Senate, especially when in the control of the opposite party, to stonewall nominations. In and of itself, this might well be a good thing because it would force the president to nominate candidates who would not inspire that level of opposition, there is much to be said for giving the word "happen" its literal interpretation. The balance of convenience is so close that there is no case for deviating from a clear textual command. But if the broader version of the president's power to make recess appointments is accepted, as an awkward constitutional compromise, the *only* person who should *never* be considered for the position is the nominee who could not gain approval through the regular process. It is always an open question whether a fresh nominee would have inspired Senate ire. But there is no doubt on that score about the nominee whose nomination has been stalled, or even rejected, by the Senate.

The historical practice has long been the opposite direction, so the question is whether that practice should be incorporated as part of the prescriptive constitution. The correct answer in this context is in the negative. The textual violation is clear; the new practice introduces serious institutional dangers; and no reliance interest protects the old practice so long as sitting appointments are not upended before the end of the current session. It is far better to accept the original design. Of equal importance, moreover, the respect for separation of powers should condemn yet another novel practice in the recent disputes, where President Obama refused to respect the Senate practice of avoiding a recess by keeping itself in pro forma session for three-day periods in order to forestall the application of these recess appointments. The Senate should be regarded as the controller of its own actions. Even so stout a defender of presidential power as John Yoo has taken the position that "[i]t is up to the Senate to decide when it is in session or not," such that "[t]he President cannot decide the legitimacy of the activities of the Senate any more than he could for the other branches, and vice versa."[45] It is hard to quarrel with this position, which raises the unhappy point that many actions of the NLRB and the Consumer Financial Protection Bureau may themselves be thrown into unnecessary doubt.

Who Appoints Whom and to What?

The next set of appointment issues concerns the extent to which Congress can alter the basic process of presidential appointments with Senate confirmation. With respect to "Ambassadors, other public Ministers and Consuls, Judges of the supreme Court, and all other Officers of the United States" who are not inferior officers, the process is etched in stone.[46] Only the president may make these appointments. It was therefore an easy and correct decision for the unanimous Supreme Court in *Buckley v. Valeo*[47] to strike down provisions of the Federal Election

Campaign Act of 1971[48] on the ground that neither the House nor Senate could have any role in appointing four of the six voting members of the Federal Election Commission (FEC), given its vast regulatory, investigative, and enforcement powers. In this instance, there was no need to decide whether the members of the board were merely inferior officers who could be appointed by the president alone, the courts of law, or the heads of departments, for none of those categories include Congress. Nor was it possible to justify a departure from strict text in order to stop the president from loading the FEC with people who would work overtime to ensure his reelection. In this instance, FEC members with their extensive powers do not by any stretch of the imagination look to be inferior.

The relative fixity in dealing with officers generally contrasts with the legal thicket that surrounds the nomination and appointment of "inferior" officers,[49] who presumably work for some "principal" or at least "superior" officer. It is a sign of serious textual difficulties that the Constitution does not use either term. The common term today is "principal" officer, which suggests an individual at the top of the hierarchy. But the more accurate term is "superior" officer, which suggests a chain of command from top to bottom. The use of that term invites a constitutional stalemate, however, because there are often three or more officers in the chain of command. Yet the Constitution only has places for two classes, not three or more. Some persons located in the middle of complex hierarchies have to be assigned to one side of the line or the other, without the slightest guidance as to how this is to be done.

The point has profound implications for all constitutional governance issues. In any organizational pyramid, that cluster of intermediate officers—to coin a phrase—will necessarily grow with time, for by definition both the number and fraction of positions in the middle of the pyramid will necessarily increase as more tiers are added to the basic structure. At this point, the Constitution does open up some strategic choices for Congress, which may be tempted to enact legislation—if need be over a presidential veto—that bypasses the president by vesting the power of appointment of key inferior officials in the head of some executive department in order to undercut the power of the president. And since Congress may, as they (a "they" that is consistent with British but not standard American usage) think proper, these choices remain largely in the political domain.[50] In most instances, this compromise would be modest because, by definition, inferior officers are those who must defer to superior officers, including the president, who retain most of the authority over policy choices. But the wavy line between principal and inferior officers is not defined in the Constitution, and Congress surely has at least some incentive to push the envelope by entrenching key persons outside of presidential control. To make matters yet more complex, there are, of necessity, many government employees who, like enlisted service members, are neither kind of officer. Yet the Appointments Clause makes no reference to this third class of individuals, and thus assigns no way in which they are to be appointed.

All in all, this is no pretty situation. No matter how well one thinks of the Framers, it is clear that the clunky processes specified under the Appointments Clause are not easily scalable even in a world where the activities of Congress are limited by the doctrine of enumerated powers.[51] They are even less so in the current legal environment, with its far more ambitious government interventions, which requires a far more complex apparatus than any that could have been envisioned by the Framers. It should therefore come as no surprise that there has been a sharp rise in litigation over the scope of this clause driven by the need to staff these critical positions. To treat all these appointments as dealing with principal officers requires extensive confirmation hearings before a Senate not of thirty members but of one hundred members, who are all distracted by a range of committees and tasks not imaginable in 1787. In most instances the threat of an inundation of time-consuming appointments will therefore move both the president and the Congress in the direction of turning principal officers into inferior ones in order to vest their appointment in, as the case may be, "the President, the Courts of Law, or in the Heads of Departments." Similarly, there will be equal pressures to convert some inferior officers into ordinary employees in order to allow for their appointment by persons who are themselves inferior officers and therefore unable under the current constitutional scheme to appoint any inferior officers.

Theoretically, the rigid structure of the Appointments Clause is surely informed by the theory of limited government with its stress on the twin principles of separation of powers and checks and balances. But I can think of no devotee of limited government who would treat the current constitutional structure as ideal. Indeed, on these structural issues, devotees of limited government are likely to have spirited disagreements among themselves as to the preferred structure. Indeed, on this issue thinkers on all sides of the political spectrum are likely to have a high degree of tolerance for the new schemes of appointment introduced for dealing with the large cast of intermediate officers that lies between principal officers and low-level employees. But that unanimity is likely to diminish with certain high-level appointments of key officers or commissions who bear scant resemblance to the mass of deputy undersecretaries, assistant secretaries, and deputy assistant secretaries who are commonly found in every government department today. It is important to take these two different types of cases up in sequence.

The first notable controversy over a government official with unique powers was *Morrison v. Olson*,[52] a dispute over whether the "independent counsel" under the 1978 Ethics in Government Act[53] could be treated as an inferior officer subject to appointment by the attorney general without Senate confirmation. Chief Justice Rehnquist wrote a long and unpersuasive opinion that he was an inferior officer under a three-part test: subject to removal by a superior officer, with limited duties, and in a limited jurisdiction. The first point is something of a sham because removal is possible only under a narrow definition of cause, which imposes few operational limits on the office. The latter two points taken together would make, as Justice Scalia acidly noted in his dissent, the ambassador to Luxembourg an inferior officer "simply because Luxembourg is small." Indeed the real tip-off in this case is that the label "independent counsel" carries with it no badge of inferiority. Requiring Senate confirmation on this singular occasion would hardly slow the confirmation process to a crawl and would impose a needed institutional check on what has always been litigation with profound political implications.

The landscape changes once the question concerns the appointments process put into place for members of the Coast Guard Court of Criminal Appeals, a specialized body with multiple members. At this point, the balance of convenience runs the other way, for there seems to be little functional reason to require the Senate to pass on multiple appointments for courts of limited jurisdiction that look to be entirely insulated from politics. It is therefore no surprise that Justice Scalia, writing in *Edmond v. United States*,[54] found these judges to be inferior officers by invoking with complete comfort the same three factors that he railed against in *Morrison*, because their work is "directed and supervised at some level by others who were appointed by presidential nomination with advice and consent of the Senate."[55] To be sure, these judges pass on death sentences, dishonorable discharges, and prison sentences of more than one year. Their overall work is subject to supervision by both the judge advocate general and the secretary of transportation, neither of whom can intervene in individual cases. Justice Scalia did think that these variables mattered, but only to establish their status as inferior officers, not mere employees outside the Appointments Clause altogether.

In principle, the case should come out the other way on the ground that any appellate judge is no more inferior within her own domain than the appellate judges on the various circuit courts of appeal. But at this point, pragmatic impulses trump formal considerations. That sense was evident in *Freytag v. Commissioner,*[56] which took the same general approach in finding the special trial court judges assisting Tax Court judges (who are subject to Senate confirmation) to be inferior officers who could therefore be appointed by the chief judge of the Tax Court, an eminently sensible determination given their numbers and their general place in the institutional hierarchy, even if the Court divided on the question of whether the chief of the Tax Court (which itself is an Article I court whose members serve only for a limited term) should be considered as the leader of a court of law or the head of a department, given that it was surely one or the other. *Freytag* in turn set the stage for a dispute over the status of the administrative law judges (ALJs) who hear cases brought by the Federal Deposit Insurance Corporation (FDIC) to remove senior bank officials from their posts because of misconduct.

In *Landry v. FDIC*[57] Judge Steven Williams concluded that these judges are only employees of the United States who can therefore be appointed by the FDIC from its own pool of administrative judges. Their decisions are not final, but have to be approved by the FDIC's board of directors, whom *Landry* did not consider to be heads of departments under the Appointments Clause. Judge Williams relied on the fact that the ALJs do not have final authority over cases, which seems odd since the decisions of all inferior officers are routinely subject to review by superior officers. ALJs also have powers that are not vested in the FDIC board, including, as the dissent of Judge Randolph observed, the ability to "issue subpoenas, rule on proffers of evidence, regulate the course of a hearing, and make or recommend decisions."[58] In *Landry*, Senate confirmation was not at issue, such that there would seem to be no reason to shrink the definition of an inferior officer so that it excludes those persons with genuine discretion in office who were appointed by departmental heads.

Removal of Federal Officers

The Appointments Clause also contains another gaping hole: the detailed provisions on presidential appointments are not matched with a single word that deals with the question of the president's power to remove subordinate officials from office. The question thus arises as to how that issue should be treated. One possibility is that the Senate's initial approval could specify that its consent is required for removal from office. Another is that the Constitution should be read as imposing a like requirement of the Senate's consent for removal to bookend its consent for appointment. By and large, however, these proposals have been solidly rejected by consistent presidential practice, across all major political parties, of having all senior appointees in the executive branch serve at the pleasure of the president and thus be removable at will.[59] The (weak) textual basis for this policy is that any other system would be inconsistent with the president's obligation "to take Care that the Laws be faithfully executed,"[60] which he could hardly do with individuals in office who would not do his bidding. That argument, standing alone, is less than persuasive, especially in light of the counterargument that appointing strong, independent subordinates serves as a safeguard against presidential misconduct.

Nonetheless, on balance, this position seems correct for functional reasons that are not inconsistent with the text. In a world in which the secretary of state or defense could not be removed from office by the president, there would be no way for anyone to know whether they speak authoritatively for the president. It is not feasible for a president to countermand each and every order by the head of a department. And it surely leaves everyone in a lurch to have the president issue a blanket statement that any and all orders of the secretary of state, for example, should be ignored when the secretary of state is free to ignore the president's wishes. The result is not divided authority as with the unbundled executive, where at least the roles are clear. It is warring factions within the executive, which, if occurring on multiple occasions, could threaten to reduce the president to a bit player in his own administration. In the end, therefore, the effective operation of the system depends on the ability of the president to place in key offices those loyal to his vision of the job. His decision to fire any official for insubordination is, moreover, subject to a strong indirect check because the Senate still has to consent to the appointment of a replacement, which will not be easily accomplished if the previous dismissal raises senatorial ire. It has therefore been settled since Chief Justice William Taft, himself a former president, wrote in *Myers v. United States*[61] that, for executive branch employees, even as low as a postmaster of the first class in Portland, Oregon, it would be intolerable to saddle the president with subordinate executive officers "who by their inefficient service under him, by their lack of loyalty to the service, or by their different views of policy might make his taking care that the laws be faithfully executed most difficult or impossible."[62]

The *Myers* decision had some real heft, for it overturned the 1867 Tenure of Office Act,[63] which provided that the president could not remove from office anyone whose appointment had been subject to Senate approval until the Senate had confirmed the nomination of his successor. In effect, that statute deprived the president of the power of removal without the consent of the Senate. The act was a big deal. In fact, it was for a violation of this provision that President Andrew Johnson was impeached and almost removed from office in 1868.[64]

Myers did not, however, seek to upset two earlier rules that did limit presidential removal power. First, Chief Justice Taft went out of his way to distinguish the Pendleton Civil Service Act,[65] which replaced the spoils system with a merit system under which covered inferior civil servants could not be removed at the whim of the president.[66] The textual foundation for the position taken in that act was tenuous, to say the least. The Congress may "vest" inferior appointments in either the president, the courts, or the heads of departments.[67] But the use of the term "vest" suggests that Congress has authority over assigning control of the appointment decision, not that these appointment decisions could then be subject to oversight and nullification by a Civil Service Commission that is not answerable to the president, as set out in that statute. But rather than presupposing that low-level functionaries count as inferior officers covered by the Appointments Clause, perhaps the better reading is that they are just simple employees who are not covered in any way, shape, or form by anything in Article II. At this point, it looks as though the Necessary and Proper Clause ought to kick in to allow Congress to *augment* the power of the heads of department to make these hires for "carrying into Execution the foregoing Powers, and all other Powers vested by this Constitution in the Government of the United States, or in any Department or Officer thereof."[68]

It would be very odd, however, if Congress could prohibit the president or heads of departments from making any such appointments because they were not covered by the Appointments Clause. Rather than wade into this thicket, Taft wisely did not seek to ground his conclusion in text, but rather appealed to the prescriptive constitution when he wrote that "a contemporaneous legislative exposition of the Constitution when the founders of our Government and framers of our Constitution were actively participating in public affairs, acquiesced in for a long term of years, fixes the construction to be given its provisions."[69]

The second precedent was judicial. Taft's views on the Civil Service Act, however, are in evident tension with the earlier questionable Supreme Court decision in *United States v. Perkins*,[70] which held that when Congress vests the appointment of inferior officers in the heads of departments, "it may limit and restrict the power of removal as it deems best for the public interest."[71] Putting any limitations into that broad phrase was not possible within the context of the case. There a naval cadet-engineer was honorably discharged against his will by the secretary of the navy. The applicable statutes only allowed for dismissal for cause. In this action for back pay, the navel cadet was treated as an inferior officer of the United States who did not therefore serve at the pleasure of the president or of any of his senior officers, of whom the secretary of the navy was presumably one. Left unsettled by this decision, however, are three key issues.

The first is whether the *Congress* may give itself some say in the *dismissal* of inferior officers, given that the Appointments Clause speaks only to the distribution of the appointments power among "the President alone, in the Courts of Law, or in the heads of Departments." The Congress is not on this list, because of genuine separation of powers concerns. The second is whether the naval cadet was also entitled to reinstatement in the face of a general rule that normally refuses to allow any court to award specific performance of an employment contract. Given the silence on removal of inferior officers and the use of the judicial rule applicable in the courts of equity, the answer should be no. The third is whether the "public interest" allows the Congress to go one step further by requiring the consent of either the Senate, the House of Representatives, both houses together, or even the courts of law, to secure a dismissal of an inferior officer. Again the answer should be no, on the same separation of powers concerns that keep the Congress out of making appointments altogether.

Read in context of the larger question of removal, *Perkins* flips the term "vests" on its head by stripping away most of the power from the president or department head and taking the odd position that a cadre of lower-level functionaries could block the president from the orderly discharge of his duties. The suggestion that a removal could be blocked by a branch of government in which the officer did not work seems equally absurd because the blocking power here could easily let one branch of government frustrate the routine operations of another. The sensible way to fill this gap is to give the responsible persons in each branch of government authority over their own staffs. Indeed, the entire question is whether that form of job protection should be given to inferior personnel who do not exercise real control over policy. The tangle that emerges on this simple issue suggests looming complications in the supposed inability of the president to dismiss, at will, members of independent agencies, which can only be addressed (and will be in Chapter 17) once the general doctrine of delegation is understood.

17

Delegation and the Rise of
Independent Agencies

T HE ANALYSIS of executive power has thus far been conducted in connection with issues of structure that long predated the New Deal.
The implicit assumption in that model is a tripartite division of functions
that denies any overlap between legislative and executive powers. The
Congress first does its job in creating law and then turns the matter over
to the executive for implementation and enforcement. But this com-
partmentalization can never be made airtight. Accordingly, this chapter
starts with a theoretical explanation of the administrative inevitability of
delegation and then discusses the patterns of what I call "trusted delegations," followed by an analysis of recurrent issues on delegation including the legislative veto, the balanced budget amendment, and, finally,
delegation to independent agencies, which is one of the cardinal features of the New Deal transformation.

The Inevitability of Delegation

Virtually all laws require some degree of discretion and intelligence in
their execution, especially if they are to be faithfully executed. Often,
Congress, in the passage of legislation, quite explicitly delegates power
to the president for making future decisions that are better made quickly
in light of circumstances that cannot be known at the time of the initial
delegation. That effort to allow the president to make sensible decisions
based on updated information should not create any institutional angst.
These arrangements parallel the division of responsibility between a

board of directors and the chief executive officer in the standard large corporation whose ultimate "citizens" are its shareholders. As Locke noted, the executive is always on call even if the legislature is not in session or the corporation is not open for business.[1] Decisions that require this form of discretion should be regarded as an indispensable part of the overall job of an executive officer. Thus, Congress's exercise of its power to delegate in these circumstances is not inconsistent with either the rule of law or the particular strictures of the United States Constitution.

Accordingly, the background norm of interpretation must guard against excessive literalism. As with corporate situations, legislation contains both implied powers and implied prohibitions. Actions of uncertain legality are often subject to retroactive approval or retroactive condemnation. When truly unanticipated circumstances arise, it is always a fair question whether the claimed necessity should activate the "inherent" powers of the president or require that he seek congressional approval lest he stray unilaterally from the chosen line. Thus, the broad strictures of the Constitution create a "relational contract" between the president and the Congress, the precise contours of which cannot be set out exhaustively in advance. Where Congress wishes to put tighter binds on the president, it can often to do so by legislation, but even here there must be some outer, if undefined, limit beyond which further action by the Congress would unconstitutionally strip the president of his power to see that the laws be faithfully executed. Any president who is placed into a congressional straitjacket cannot exercise that duty.

Just this approach explains the early disputes over how to choose the locations of post offices and post roads.[2] One important, if neglected, power given to Congress in the Constitution is the power to "establish Post Offices and post Roads,"[3] which appears in the same list in Article I of congressional enumerated powers as the Commerce Clause.[4] Congress has done its work if it identifies the cities that need post offices and post roads, leaving it to the president and his postmaster general (initially a much bigger job in the administrative hierarchy than it is today) to determine their precise locations and to negotiate leases or construction. However, designating sites for these offices and roads offered handsome advantages for nearby businesses, which Congress sought to claw back for itself by preparing a specific list of structures and locations for the president to establish.[5] But that level of detail is not usually sustainable once the scope of a business has expanded, as the United States

Postal Service has, especially since Congress is preoccupied with many other tasks. So, sooner or later, Congress must delegate to the president the power to select and implement particular projects that fit the overall business plan set out in the enabling legislation.

Trusted Delegations

Nonetheless, eventually there has to be some line that cannot be crossed if the separation of powers is to be maintained. Congress, for example, could not simply tell the president to just design a post office system, a securities and exchange act, a tax code, or a military. Some respect has to be paid to the old maxim, *delegatus non potest delegare:* the one to whom power is delegated cannot himself further delegate that power. In this instance, Congress itself should be treated as a legislative body that receives delegated authority from either the states or the people: the artful use of the passive voice in Article I speaks only of "all legislative Powers herein granted,"[6] without saying by whom. But either way, the obvious risk of delegation is that the new delegatee may hold preferences at odds with those of Congress.

The political question, however, is how often this breakdown in relations is likely to happen. The answer is, less often than might be expected. Any full appreciation of the fault lines in the United States Constitution must recognize that the two dominant considerations run in opposite directions. The first is the long-term institutional differences among the branches, which lead each to defend its prerogatives against the others. The second is that political alliances can cross the departmental divide. While some analysts think that the branch differences always yield to party differences,[7] on some issues, institutional arrangements actually matter more. For example, with executive privilege before congressional committees, the clashing institutional prerogatives of the two branches could easily take precedence over political alliances. In most instances, moreover, give the devil his due: congressionally delegated power to the executive branch will usually take into account any future differences in their political views. The dangers of a runaway executive are something that the Congress could easily anticipate and guard against if it chooses to do so.

To all appearances, permanent, or life tenure delegations raise a tricky veil of ignorance problem. The dominant political party today may lose its power in years to come. The real danger with those delegations is thus the opposite of what is commonly expected. Most commonly, the delegation will initially take place between a president and Congress who share a common end. They seal the deal by limiting the delegation to the short time periods during which both the president and the present Congress remain in power. Those cooperative actions across the branches thus work to *increase* the size of government, which in turn allows it to complete novel tasks that the principle of separation of powers, if it were stronger, could block.

This approach helps to explain the political forces at work in the two well-known 1935 nondelegation decisions of *Panama Refining Co. v. Ryan*[8] and *A.L.A. Schechter Poultry Corp. v. United States*.[9] Both of these decisions rejected President Roosevelt's actions pursuant to the National Industrial Recovery Act of 1933 (NIRA)[10] on grounds that the actions were a result of excessive delegation to the executive branch. At issue in *Panama Refining* was a provision of the NIRA that authorized the president to prohibit the flow of "hot oil"—i.e., oil produced in excess of quantities allowed under applicable state law—in interstate commerce. Oversupply and market destabilization were the fears of the moment.[11] The purpose of the prohibition was to constrain output in an effort to prop up prices. The actual economics of the transaction are quite complicated because the case involved the interaction of an ordinary cartel and a conservation-based need to keep wells open that would otherwise have lost productive capacity if shut down prematurely. None of this mattered to the Court, however, which found an ostensible abuse of delegation because the NIRA did not specify the circumstances or grounds that triggered the president's exercise of his statutory power.[12]

For its part, *Schechter Poultry* had a far broader significance because it struck down the large number of codes of fair competition that the president used to organize cartels in various industries. This was no small operation. In the eighteen months between August 1933 and February 1935, the frenzied activities of the Roosevelt administration generated some 546 codes, 185 supplemental codes, 685 amendments, and over 11,000 administrative orders.[13] The congressional marching orders specified "that such code or codes are not designed to promote monopolies or to eliminate or oppress small enterprises and will not operate to discriminate against them. . . ."[14] This noble sentiment sounds great until one realizes that the opposition to monopoly is not meant to promote competition. Instead, federal power is used to create and protect multi-member cartels, with their larger voting bases, even though these cartels, which have to set aside production quotas for inefficient members, perform less well on average than the monopolies they displace.

Given their objectives, it should come as no surprise that no one in the heavily Democratic Congress in 1933 had ever expressed any qualms about the president's performance under either program. The challenges in both *Schechter Poultry* and *Panama Refining* were mounted by regulated firms that chafed under the various NIRA regulations. It was therefore misplaced, in *Schechter Poultry*, for a politically clueless Justice Cardozo to attack these schemes as a form of "delegation running riot,"[15] in the absence of any evidence of even the slightest discrepancy between the grand congressional plan and its administrative implementation, at a time when both the president and Congress shared the same aspirations. Both cases went off the rails because they ignored the one key feature of these delegations: that their structural features kept the president in line with Congress. The NIRA had a *two-year* statutory window that ran from June 1933 to June 1935. The Democratic majorities in Congress knew that during this short period of time, a Democratic president would remain in office. The expansive grant of delegation therefore was to friend, not foe. Congress solved its delegation doctrine problem by a simple technique that minimized political risk by keeping the president on a short two-year leash. The key vice of this delegation was exactly what proponents of separation of powers should fear. This effective interbranch cooperation led to the illicit creation of cartels, with only a momentary disruption in the wake of the Court's decisions.[16]

Once the New Deal mindset was firmly in place, however, it was just a matter of time before all teeth were taken out of the delegation doctrine. At the same time, the Supreme Court undercut the constitutional protection of economic liberties and rejected well-established limits on Congress's commerce power as useless artifacts of an earlier age of limited government. By 1944, it was clear, especially in wartime, that the president had free rein over the economy. More concretely, the Court sustained the Emergency Price Control Act of 1942,[17] which set up the Office of Price Administration, whose administrator was appointed by President Franklin Roosevelt. The standard of delegation under the statute called for the prices to be "fair and equitable,"[18] which in some sense is equivalent to "reasonable under the circumstances." That phrase has been used in rate regulation where its office is to find ways to reduce monopoly profits to competitive levels at reasonable cost. But a general price control statute applies with equal force to competitive and monopolistic industries, and thus cannot perform that task. The delegation therefore invites a problematic effort to rely on historical prices to deal with shortages, while historical prices become more and more irrelevant as months go by and conditions change. Post-1937, this particular economic scheme no longer offended constitutional values. And at that point, the decision to sustain the delegation looked well-nigh inexorable because no one could conjure up legislative language that was more specific, yet also broad enough to enable the executive to administer such a vast economic program.

As such, the judicial decision in *Schechter Poultry* rescued a short-term, wartime emergency statute. The same result, alas, was true for the ill-fated Nixon price controls, which could not hide behind the fig leaf of wartime necessity. But Congress only authorized that scheme for ninety days, after which it expired.[19] And so the delegation doctrine survives when Congress and the president speak with one voice in rejecting the classical liberal vision that prefers competition to regulation. But in all these cases, the damage is self-limiting as long as Congress can keep the relevant time period short. Trust matters, but it is only doled out in small quantities.

The Legislative Veto

The political landscape between the executive branch and Congress changes when the latter distrusts the actions taken by the former. In such cases, Congress takes a far more active role. The issue, for example, of the routine administration of our byzantine former Immigration and Naturalization Service (INS) posed this dilemma. There was no way that Congress could limit the executive branch to a short time period, analogous to the two-year time window for the NIRA. So, in its effort to control executive discretion, Congress moved to the opposite extreme and micromanaged the executive branch in ways that cut out the president to the greatest extent possible. Just these calculations accounted for the rise in one- or two-house legislative vetoes to countermand executive decisions that set off warning bells. As a formal matter, this practice was negated by the Supreme Court in *Immigration & Naturalization Service v. Chadha*,[20] which arose from a one-house veto of the attorney general's decision to *suspend* Chadha's deportation. Under the statute, only suspensions of deportation, and *not* an attorney general decision to deport, were subject to reversal by either house. Most people would surmise that if Congress intervened, it would be to protect the liberty of the individual and prevent deportation, but it was just the opposite.

At first look, this odd (but common) scheme does not look like legislation at all. The case looks like a one-sided form of adjudication that should not come before Congress, which was the sensible position of Justice Lewis Powell.[21] And yet Chief Justice Warren Burger regarded this peculiar exercise of government power as purported legislation that failed to meet the formal requirements of legislation, namely that it first be approved by both houses ("Bicameralism")[22] and then by the president ("Presentment").[23] Invoking *fait iustitia, ruat coelum*—"let justice reign, even if the heavens fall"—the chief justice wrote that "the fact that a given law or procedure is efficient, convenient, and useful in facilitating functions of government, standing alone, will not save it if it is contrary to the Constitution. Convenience and efficiency are not the primary objectives—or the hallmarks—of democratic government. . . ."[24] Justice Byron White in dissent saw in this an attack on the sensible distribution of powers in Congress, given that this particular mode of doing business was authorized by prior overarching legislation that fully met those two requirements.[25]

These formal issues, however, miss the key point of this debate. Immigration was a hot button issue then, just as it is now. Congress saw no reason to interfere when deportation was ordered because the immigrant himself had every incentive to fight those charges through the courts. But Congress, driven by anti-immigrant sentiment, feared that the attorney general would enter into a collusive settlement with the immigrant that would take the case out of the courts, hence justifying congressional intervention. As Justice White pointed out in dissent, these one- and two-house vetoes dominate in an age of distrust—and these provisions have continued to be inserted into new legislation in the quarter-century since *Chadha*.[26] The episode points out one key advantage that Congress enjoys in its ongoing battle with the Court: Congress has continuous power of action, while the Court can only intervene episodically.

As a matter of first principle, however, it is hard to get too agitated about *Chadha's* deviation from the original constitutional plan. In practice, the doctrine of separation of powers is conceptually underpowered. It only requires some division of authority to slow down the pace of regulation. Other schemes with very different properties could also work in the same direction, even if they do not meet current constitutional standards. It is therefore difficult to see the structural risks in incorporating the one-house veto into the separation of powers system. However, as is so often the case, textualism and functionalism lead to somewhat different outcomes. This is also true with respect to executive power. And matters get no easier with the introduction of independent administrative agencies, discussed later in this chapter.

Balanced Budget Amendment

The theme of congressional distrust of executive power also explains the passage of the Balanced Budget and Emergency Deficit Control Act of 1985[27] (Gramm-Rudman-Hollings), by which Congress sought to enlist the services of the comptroller general to rein in public spending. Far from indicating distaste for the separation of powers, the act sought to create a complex divided structure that fit in with the general philosophy. The president was to appoint a comptroller general from a list prepared by the Speaker of the House and the Senate president pro tem.[28] Once selected, that individual had to be confirmed by the Senate, after which he could be removed from office "at any time" by the way in which legislation is usually passed: approval in both houses and acceptance by the president or by two-thirds of each house overriding a presidential veto.[29] This convoluted procedure was animated by the same suspicion of government that drives the basic doctrine of separation of powers. Nonetheless, its variance from the constitutional scheme proved fatal because the "Constitution does not contemplate an active role for Congress in the supervision of officers charged with the execution of the laws it enacts."[30] In this instance, Chief Justice Burger referred back to the formalist view of matters, holding that the efficiency or convenience of a given procedure will not spare it from constitutional scrutiny. This objection has greater force here than it does with *Chadha* precisely because no one could dispute the simple fact that this comprehensive reorganization realigned government powers for the long-term basis in a way in which *Chadha*'s veto override did not.

At that point, the case for making out some supposed efficiency was sufficiently speculative that it would have been unwise to take the same hands-off attitude that the Court has adopted, for example, in dealing with the appointment of inferior officers. The original constitutional structure should stand against this new challenge, which cannot of course be counted from birth as part of the prescriptive constitution, as developed in Chapter 3.

Delegation to Independent Agencies

The analysis thus far has looked at removal and nondelegation as separate constraints on executive power. The full effect of these doctrines, however, comes from their combined effect as manifested in the creation of independent agencies that receive extensive powers delegated to them by Congress. These agencies, which include the Federal Trade Commission (FTC), the Federal Communications Commission (FCC), the Securities and Exchange Commission (SEC), and the National Labor Relations Board (NLRB), all share two characteristics. First, they are classified as "independent" of the president because he does not have the power to remove their members at will, but can do so only for the reasons set out by Congress in the statute creating the relevant agency, usually requiring a showing of "cause."[31] These administrators typically have terms, also set out by statute, that are longer than a presidential four-year term: FTC commissioners are appointed for seven-year terms;[32] FCC commissioners,[33] SEC commissioners,[34] and NLRB members[35] are all appointed for five-year terms. Second, these agencies often exercise extensive congressionally delegated powers. Thus, for example, the FCC may make rules and decisions that serve the "public convenience, interest, or necessity" in allocating rights along the radio spectrum.[36]

There is little dispute that the growth of independent agencies depended on gutting the president's inherent removal power and the nondelegation doctrine, which accordingly was done during the Progressive and New Deal eras. The first independent agency to be created was the Interstate Commerce Commission, which went into operation in 1887 to regulate railroad rates. It was run by an expert board whose first chairman was the great judge Thomas M. Cooley, who resigned his position as chief justice of the Michigan Supreme Court to head this bold new venture.[37] But the precise legal status of the members of these various commissions was only settled forty-seven years later, when the Supreme Court in *Humphrey's Executor v. United States*[38] held that the president did not possess the power to dismiss commission members because of policy differences.[39] The Court's explanation, however, can inspire no confidence: FTC members were executive branch members beyond the scope of the president's removal power, the Court said, because the Commission "acts in part quasi-legislatively and in part quasi-judicially."[40]

Oh. The Constitution does not contain any mention of one, let alone two, quasi branches. Where, then, is the textual warrant for creating these distinct commissions that have no legislative, executive, or judicial pedigree, but in fact contain a complex amalgam of all three powers, including the ability to adjudicate disputes that the agency's own prosecutors bring before that agency? The purported justification for this odd institutional arrangement rests on an aggressive reading of the Necessary and Proper Clause already considered in Chapter 14.[41] Recall that the normative key for interpreting this clause is faithful adherence to an intelligent literalism: stress its two key terms, "necessary" and "proper," in order to decide whether any proposed structural innovation meets constitutional standards. After much learned academic debate,[42] the textual answer is in the negative. In this context, "necessary" means much needed to effectuate a particular program. There is no requirement under the clause that the actions must be indispensable. "Proper" still covers actions done consistently with all other binding legal constraints. In this context, it is not necessary to create complex independent entities when the powers of the president and the heads of departments can be supplemented by additional powers as needed. Nor is it proper to introduce a new system of governance that undermines both the safeguards of separation of powers and of checks and balances found in the Constitution. The president still enjoys his power of removal over heads of departments even if he cannot give them a direct order to perform a certain action. Hence, it is neither necessary nor proper to create a new set of institutions for which there is no explicit constitutional roadmap.

Thus we now come face to face with the role of the prescriptive constitution, in which the creation of independent agencies has become well entrenched over time. Is there any reason to undo this *fait accompli*, in whole or in part, in the light of hindsight? The ardent defenders of the modern administrative state frequently laud the creation of this "fourth branch of government."[43] And to an extent they have a point, given the erosion of the nondelegation doctrine. Independent agencies became necessary when Congress could not develop a detailed statutory rule to implement regulation that the progressives thought was an indispensable response to the new industrial age. Ratemaking and industrial accidents were at the top of that agenda. Rates had to be set to prevent monopoly railroads from gaining excessive profits,[44] and industrial accidents required displacing the older common law rules of negligence and contributory negligence with a statutory workers' compensation system that provided limited damage awards for accidents that arise out of and in the course of employment, unless brought about by the willful neglect of the injured worker.[45] The states entrusted both jobs to specialized commissions that operated outside of the judicial system. The complex calculations for ratemaking were assigned to public utility commissions, not courts;[46] workers' compensation commissions heard the huge run of industrial accident cases.[47] The challenge for the progressives was, quite simply, to ensure that these good practices in the states were not stymied by bad constitutional law when carried over to the federal system, notwithstanding the textual commitment to a separation of powers.

The difficulty at the federal level was still more acute because all federal judges served during good behavior, i.e., with de facto life tenure. That level of protection, however, did not seem appropriate for judges working in specialized tribunals, including the bankruptcy and tax courts. Over time, these specialized bodies evolved such that "referees" in bankruptcy and "members" of the tax court became Article I "judges" who, while subject to Senate confirmation, serve for terms of fourteen and fifteen years, respectively.[48] On this occasion, at least, prudent Supreme Court decisions overcame the excessive rigidities of original constitutional structure that were ill adapted even to a modest expansion of the administrative state. The Court eventually allowed the Article I bankruptcy courts to continue operating,[49] the EPA to resolve contract disputes regarding compensation that one pesticide company had to pay another for the use of the latter's trade secrets,[50] and the Commodities Futures Trading Commission to adjudicate ordinary state law contract disputes that arose as counterclaims in disputes that unquestionably fell within the CFTC's jurisdiction.[51]

In critiquing this development, recall that the original constitutional decision to afford federal judges life tenure rested on the mistaken belief that only this extreme measure could preserve judicial independence.[52] In everyday practice, however, the long terms of office granted to Article I judges mark a major improvement over the original constitutional design. The finite term still guards against arbitrary removal from office. Plus, any orderly rotation in office has the additional advantage of making it more difficult for a few judges to wield an extraordinary degree of power, as too often occurs on the Supreme Court. In many cases, term limits obviate the need for painful efforts to remove for cause any judges who have grown lazy or even senile while in office. The classical liberal belief in both a separation of powers and checks and balances is in no way compromised by this welcome switch in orientation. Only the purist could protest the verbal gymnastics of the Supreme Court that brought about the legitimation of Article I courts in *Humphrey's Executor*. The restrained functionalist happily looks the other way on these doctrinal maneuvers and wishes the same limits could be imposed on Supreme Court justices. Now that Article I judges have been in office for seventy-five years, we should not try to turn back the clock on a modest reform that makes good institutional sense.

The same, however, cannot be said of much of the work that is done by the independent agencies that do not set rates, administer the bankruptcy code, decide tax cases, or resolve accident claims. Independent agencies with broader authorities set, either by rulemaking or decision, the long-term policies of the United States on deeply divisive issues. Indeed, it was in just these hot button areas, such as transportation, labor, and telecommunications, that the progressives abandoned their own ostensible conviction that neutral experts, left to their own devices, could transcend partisan politics. The following examples demonstrate how these agencies have played out in practice.

When Congress delegated extensive powers to the president to form cartels under the NIRA, the short duration of the program allowed Congress to prevent these delegated powers from falling into enemy hands, i.e., a president in the opposite party.[53] However, implementing a progressive labor or telecommunications policy can never be done in a short compass of time. Congress, therefore, had to find other techniques to control the risk of presidential capture of the agencies implementing these policies. This particular task could not be done by using precise terms of delegation. The number and nature of the unknowns were sufficiently large that tight mandates would cripple an agency's efforts to create any ambitious progressive vision. The broad mandates needed, however, would only make sense if the president could not stack the deck, which explains why the independence of agency members becomes the key. Establishing independent agencies allows for legislative deals that remain stable over time. That power is not needed, however, to enforce common law rules, which becomes evident from a brief account of the evolution of three important agencies: the FCC, the NLRB, and the Public Corporation Accounting Oversight Board (PCAOB).

FCC

Let us turn first to the FCC, which is charged under statute with the allocation of spectrum for broadcast use. In principle it is possible to take two alternative approaches to the question of how frequencies are assigned. The first rests on the standard common law property rule that allocates a portion of the spectrum to the party who makes first use of it.[54] This system gained some traction in the early 1920s, most notably in the *Oak Leaves* case,[55] when commercial radio first became viable and a system of property rights was adopted to take into account the peculiar features of the spectrum. The key element in this system is to create an exclusive band of rights, some frequency over a certain geographical territory that can be turned over in perpetuity to a single person having all the attributes of a common law owner. That person could exclude all other persons from broadcasting on that frequency and from interfering with his use of the frequency. So long as broadcast stations were few and far between, new entrants situated themselves along the spectrum in ways that avoided serious signal interference. Technical advances allowed the first commercial station, KDKA, to go on the air in Pittsburgh in 1920. By 1923, the strains of this first possession system became evident when several hundred stations were in operation throughout the country on a narrow slice of spectrum that commerce reserved for that purpose. The situation became "chaotic" in 1926 when several key lower court decisions denied Secretary of Commerce Herbert Hoover the power to exclude individual applicants from frequencies allocated to civilian use.[56] Matters got even worse on April 16, 1926, when an Illinois federal district court held that the secretary of commerce was wholly without power to restrict the power, frequency, or hours of operation of any given station.[57]

Side by side with this common law system lay the demands of the administrative state.[58] In 1912, federal legislation gave the United States control over the spectrum, much of which was turned over to the navy for maritime operations.[59] With one stroke, the federal government bypassed the traditional common law rules of first possession. At the time of the passage of the Radio Act of 1927,[60] the government could have defined a system of property rights both in terms of frequency and territory and sold the frequencies to the highest bidder at an auction. Once those initial rights were defined, the new owner could use, sell, lease, or mortgage that spectrum interest as he saw fit. Owners could even leave part of their spectrum unused for a time, without fear that a new user would slip in to claim ownership. Private decisions would thus respond to prices and market incentives in deciding who owned what portion of the spectrum and how it was used. Common law rules, as administered in either federal or state court, could have easily handled all of the issues of implementation that might have occurred without having to create the FCC. Only three things would be required: first, a system to record spectrum rights; second, a set of actions to enjoin interference across spectrum bands; and third, a system to allow for the sale and licensing of these frequencies on whatever terms and conditions its owner chose to adopt.

The last thing, however, that any progressive wanted was private ownership of the spectrum free from political control. The progressives' main mission was to displace "barbaric" common law rules with "sensible" legislation.[61] Delegation under the banner of public interest, convenience, and necessity played into the grander aspirations of those like progressive Justice Felix Frankfurter, who wrote:

> The Act itself establishes that the Commission's powers are not limited to the engineering and technical aspects of regulation of radio communication. Yet we are asked to regard the Commission as a kind of traffic officer, policing the wave lengths to prevent stations from interfering with each other. But the Act does not restrict the Commission merely to supervision of the traffic. It puts upon the Commission the burden of determining the composition of that traffic. The facilities of radio are not large enough to accommodate all who wish to use them. Methods must be devised for choosing from among the many who apply. And since Congress itself could not do this, it committed the task to the Commission.[62]

Unfortunately, this ambitious goal has proved resistant to orderly application after decades of futile regulatory initiatives. The control of interference is of course a valid government function, but that could be done by allowing private rights of action against those who interfere. Why must the government determine the composition of the traffic when a bidding system could put that function in private hands? Would anyone say the same with respect to the use of a public highway? Scarcity is hardly the explanation, for that is the reason that prices are used in any market—to isolate high-value users. And the methods to be used by government regulators were, and are, largely unknown. Quite simply, the FCC, in its almost seventy years, has yet to develop any consistent methodology to determine what makes a good applicant for broadcast ownership. It develops odd tests that deal with composition of ownership, local connections, and past experience, which give no insight into whether the prospective owners actually know how to run a radio station that satisfies consumers. The FCC makes the curious assumption that targeting broad audiences is preferable to niche programming. In its misguided moment of glory, it removed the license of the Cosmopolitan Broadcasting Company when the CBC had the sensible idea of leasing out blocks of time to customers so as to allow market forces to permit minority voices to speak on the airwaves even though they are not large enough to own a station of their own.[63] This system is expensive and unresponsive. Granting perpetual and alienable licenses would have eased much of the pain in this area.

NLRB

The NLRB, our second example, operates in a different fashion. It makes few rules, but decides many cases. The division in board membership along party lines shows no signs of disinterested expertise based on scientific principles. The Democratic members tend to favor unions on all key issues. The Republicans tend to favor management. The courts would be hard pressed to discharge the NLRB's statutory responsibilities to supervise bitter union elections in which employers and unions inveigh at each other under complex rules that require NLRB enforcement. The passage of the NLRA extended the earlier exemption of unions from the antitrust laws by denying an employer the right to refuse to bargain with a union. This system of forced interactions requires constant government oversight because employers have a strong incentive to try to get out from under union dominion, while union leaders simultaneously work to preserve their dominant position. The system, however, is clearly failing in the private sector, as the latest numbers indicate that only about 6.9 percent of private employees are union members.[64] It can only survive if protected by an administrative body with constant oversight.

Ironically, the NLRA statutory scheme too is now in danger of failing. For several years, the NLRB tried to operate with only two of its five positions filled, a maneuver that was rightly slapped down by the United States Supreme Court in *New Process Steel, L.P. v. National Labor Relations Board*, albeit by only a five-to-four majority.[65] More recently, in *Noel Canning v. NLRB*, the Circuit Court for the District of Columbia rightly struck down President Obama's effort to fill the vacant seats by recess appointment.[66]

An important lesson about administrative law emerges from the recent travails of the NLRB. Whatever one might think about the ambiguous status of Article I judges, there should be unified and firm opposition to any system that vests any judicial power whatsoever in a board that builds in on the ground floor sharp political division and deep mutual distrust. Adjudication of individual disputes, including all trial and appellate work, should be done within the judicial system, period. As to the independent agencies themselves, reconstituting them in the executive branch would probably not make all that much difference in their day-to-day operations. So on this issue, the correct response, which is so urgent in the context of labor relations, is to return to the substantive common law rules on property, contract, and tort. The rejection of these common law rules was the major, if regrettable, development of the Progressive Era. Returning to them would reduce the level of discretion placed in political hands.[67]

PCAOB

The rise of the administrative state also brings back to the fore many of the Appointments Clause issues already considered in connection with traditional government officers. Political jousting between the president and the Congress gave rise to important issues about the structure of independent administrative agencies that were inconclusively resolved in *Free Enterprise Fund (FEF) v. Public Corporation Accounting Oversight Board (PCAOB)*.[68] In that case, the FEF challenged the constitutionality of the portion of the Sarbanes-Oxley Act (Sarbox)[69] that created the PCAOB to oversee the implementation of a wide range of accounting reforms for publicly held corporations. The members of the PCAOB were appointed by the Securities and Exchange Commission (SEC) commissioners and, under Sarbox, were removable by the SEC commissioners only for cause, narrowly defined. The SEC commissioners in turn could be removed from office by the president, but again, only for cause, narrowly defined as covering "inefficiency, neglect of duty, or malfeasance in office," all rare events. The final decisions of the PCAOB were subject to review by the SEC, but the PCAOB could use its extensive powers to investigate cases and initiate proceedings against individual firms without receiving prior approval from the SEC.

As might be expected, the four liberal members of the Supreme Court were comfortable with the procedures as they stood, but the five conservative members of the Court were troubled by the use of a complex dual system of appointments that interposed the SEC between the president and the PCAOB, when the SEC is itself an independent agency. Chief Justice Roberts found the case troublesome because the dual level of insulation that Sarbox afforded the members of the PCAOB was inconsistent with the constitutional requirement that all the executive power be "vested" in the president. But his remedy for the problem can best be described as cosmetic. He first severed from the statute all the for-cause requirements that limited the ability of the SEC commissioners to fire members of the PCAOB, which was probably incorrect given that the decision materially changes an integral portion of the law that Congress passed.[70] That maneuver meant that there was only one layer of "for-cause" insulation between the PCAOB and the president. But the difference is surely cosmetic, for one layer of for-cause protection is quite sufficient to keep the president from having any role in the decision. Thus the odds are less than one in a thousand that any SEC commissioner could be removed for cause, even assuming that this removal would alter the balance of power in the commission. The addition of the second layer increases the level of insulation from about 99.9 percent to about 99.999 percent. Many new digits added to the calculation, but they are all on the wrong side of the decimal point. The battle with respect to independent agencies is over, but the battle over the rights of individuals before these agencies has just begun. The true danger in *PCAOB* lies in the power of the board to initiate investigations of firms in the securities industry, where the whiff of scandal is enough to lead state agencies to pull their licenses and cause customers to flee—as evidenced by the rapid, and unjustified, downfall of Arthur Andersen, the alleged indiscretions of which were the impetus for the drafting of Sarbox.[71] It is the want of that form of protection that matters, as I shall argue in connection with the discussion of procedural and substantive due process in Chapter 20.

18

Foreign and Military Affairs

T HE PREVIOUS CHAPTERS played out the connections between executive, legislative, and judicial affairs in domestic situations, where it is difficult to make any global assessment over their relative strengths. The balance of power plays out quite differently in the area of foreign affairs, where presidential expedition in the face of crisis becomes the focal point of the constitutional design. The role of the Congress remains important, but it has unmistakably yielded ground to the president relative to the original constitutional structure since the earliest days of the nation. The judicial branch beats a hasty retreat from these issues except in those matters that involve the individual rights of those in government custody. The role of independent administrative agencies, which are never built for speed, comes up, at most, in peripheral ways.

Foreign Affairs and Congressional–Executive Interaction

The most obvious source of difference found in foreign affairs is that Congress, like all lumbering, deliberative bodies, is not suitable for discharging two key functions of government. First, Congress necessarily lacks internal cohesion that would allow it to negotiate with foreign nations in an effective fashion. This is why the Constitution vests in the president the power to make treaties with foreign nations, with the advice and consent of two-thirds of the senators present.[1] Note that here, as with key presidential nominations of executive branch officials, the House of Representatives is completely cut out of the process, doubtless because of the added difficulty and delay of securing approval from a second house of Congress. Another problem is Congress's inability to move nimbly and quickly in response to changes in conditions that could influence the use of force or diplomatic suasion. The lion's share of these tasks therefore necessarily falls to the president.

It hardly follows from these considerations, however, that Congress should have no role to play in foreign affairs. There are many matters on which it is possible to both form and implement coherent long-term legislative policies of the type entrusted to Congress. Indeed, a good fraction of the enumerated powers contained in Article I, Section 8 relate to some cross between foreign and military affairs. Exhibit A is the power that Congress has to regulate commerce with foreign nations.[2] The direct regulation of tariffs and trade forms a key portion of foreign policy, both inside the World Trade Organization and independently of it. For example, the Webb-Pomerene Act of 1918[3]—itself a testament to trade folly—exempts from the sanctions of antitrust laws American cartels that sell goods for the export market. The Foreign Commerce Clause[4] also impacts national security by allowing the United States Congress to prohibit the sales of sensitive technologies overseas. Both issues are amenable to long-term legislative solutions that should, and do, bind the president in the execution of his official duties.

In addition, many of the explicit powers afforded Congress under Article I necessarily deal with war and thus with foreign affairs. For example, the power to establish tribunals inferior to the Supreme Court[5] surely encompasses not only the creation of permanent Article III courts, but also of military and other tribunals of a shorter duration.[6] The congressional power "to define and punish Piracies and Felonies committed on the high Seas, and Offenses against the Law of Nations"[7] has obvious international implications, as does the power "To declare War, grant Letters of Marque and Reprisal,"[8] the power to "raise and support Armies,"[9] to "provide and maintain a Navy,"[10] to "make Rules for the Government and Regulation of the land and naval Forces,"[11] and, as will become clear, to govern and organize the militia.[12]

The hard issue across the board is how to organize the distribution of powers in foreign and military affairs in a way that respects the division between the legislative and executive branches. This inquiry is not made any easier by the sensible decision of the judiciary to stay out of the disputes resulting from those two branches' internecine quarrels, by deciding cases on the grounds that the claimants lack standing[13] or because these cases necessarily raise nonjusticiable political questions.[14] On this issue, the level of success depends on many of the same ingredients as in the domestic context, such that it is critical to know whether any particular assertion of executive authority arises out of a trust relationship between the two branches or, alternatively, in an atmosphere of abiding distrust. Unlike many of the questions that deal with the scope of legislative and judicial powers, the object here is to expect as much disagreement as one finds in corporate disputes between a board of directors and the CEO. The basic approach to American constitutionalism talks endlessly about the need for checks and balances between separate branches of government. But in this area, as in others, the constitutional strictures do not dictate exactly what these boundary lines should be.

In addressing these issues, the Supreme Court got off on the wrong foot in its key 1936 decision in *United States v. Curtiss-Wright Export Corp.*[15] That case arose out of a criminal prosecution of a defendant for the sale of fifteen machine guns to Bolivia, which was then engaged in the bloody Chaco War with Paraguay. This sale was in violation of an arms embargo proclaimed by President Franklin Roosevelt on the same day that Congress had authorized him to act if he thought that the situation merited United States intervention.[16] Congress had also allowed him the power to rescind that proclamation unilaterally,[17] which in fact he did some six months later. The defense to the prosecution rested on the claim of excessive congressional delegation to the president, under which a proclamation was to be made only "if" the president found that imposing the embargo would contribute to peace in the region.[18] As with the delegations under the NIRA, Congress was not squawking about the president's actions, for there was no slippage between its joint resolution and his proclamation.

Justice Sutherland's majority opinion in *Curtiss-Wright* could have stressed the continuity of purpose between the two branches of government, without venturing into the more turbulent waters of defining the respective spheres of presidential and congressional influence in the absence of conflict between the two branches. Nonetheless, he rose to the bait in an opinion that surely overstated the dominance of the president in foreign relations. Sutherland insisted that the authority of the federal government in domestic issues derived from the enumerated grants in the Constitution[19]—note this opinion was penned before the huge 1937 transformation in the scope of the Commerce Clause from which Sutherland dissented.[20] In contrast, the powers of the federal government in foreign affairs, he said, were not derived from the Constitution itself, but were directly passed from the English Crown to the United States, qua nation, prior to the adoption of the Constitution and independently of its ratification.[21] That huge chunk of implied or inherent powers within the federal government, in his view, existed because "[t]he powers to declare and wage war, to conclude peace, to make treaties, to maintain diplomatic relations with other sovereignties, if they had never been mentioned in the Constitution, would have vested in the federal government as necessary concomitants of nationality."[22] That proposition, which flies in the face of the ratification process, does not actually determine the distribution of powers between the two branches of the federal government. But Sutherland went further to make just that leap when he concluded: "In this vast external realm, with its important, complicated, delicate and manifold problems, the President alone has the power to speak or listen as a representative of the nation."[23] But why allow such potential lawlessness? There is a perfectly respectable model already in place that gives the president the power to act, but only within the limitations that Congress imposes on him. The inability to have perfect sanctions against presidential misconduct hardly seems to be a reason to celebrate its occurrence. It would have been far better to say that the tight connection between the authorization by Congress and its implementation by the president in this situation simply went as both bodies had wished. Sutherland did not have to speak on a question of executive power that was not before him.

The President as Commander-in-Chief

In addition to his general powers to regulate foreign affairs, the president also "shall be Commander in Chief of the Army and Navy of the United States, and of the Militia of the several States, when called into the actual Service of the United States."[24] The basic structure of this provision is made evident from *Federalist No. 69*, which is the key primary source that deals with this question. That paper states that the president's powers in this regard are "inferior to that of either the monarch or the governor,"[25] referring to the king of England and the governor of New York. That conclusion is confirmed by the text of Articles I and II, which make the president the commander-in-chief of the militia when called—note the passive voice—into the active service of the United States, which the president can do only pursuant to an explicit delegation of power from Congress.[26] These structural provisions alone offer additional confirmation that the president ordinarily cannot do just what he wants, even on foreign affairs issues.

Nor is this conclusion disrupted by a wholly wrongheaded appeal to *Federalist No. 64,* which contains the selective tidbit that says the president "will be able to manage the business of intelligence in such manner as prudence may suggest."[27] This quotation, which arose concerning the relationship between the president and the Senate in connection with treaty ratification, only specified that "intelligence," in the sense of advice that the president receives about the treaty, did not have to be revealed to the Senate unless the president chose to do so.

The obvious purpose of this provision is to ensure that there is civilian control over the military. But its exact contours in relation to the president's control over foreign affairs are somewhat indefinite. That fuzziness came to the fore in the *Steel Seizure Case,*[28] in which the Supreme Court held that President Truman had acted outside of his exclusive executive powers when he ordered, without congressional authorization, the seizure of steel mills in order to avert a strike that he feared would paralyze the wartime production of munitions. The first point is that the *Steel Seizure Case* embarrasses the hard-and-fast distinction between domestic and foreign affairs that lay at the root of *Curtiss-Wright.* It is equally clear that the action itself did not relate to the day-to-day conduct of the war. The *Steel Seizure Case* generated a great diversity of views on second-tier issues dealing with the fine points of executive power, but on its facts, the case was not close: the president had clearly exceeded his constitutional powers, including those as commander-in-chief. Utterly missing was anything like the congressional resolution that supported Roosevelt's actions in *Curtiss-Wright.* The president was, at best, acting on his own authority, with no law to execute faithfully and no instantaneous threat to respond to. There was a strong argument that his actions were precluded by the various provisions of labor law, dating from 1947, that were intended to deal with strikes disruptive to the economy.[29]

In this case, it hardly matters whether we think of constitutional powers as rigid and formal or as fluid and functional. Justice Jackson developed a three-part test of presidential powers. The president is at his zenith when he acts pursuant to authorization from Congress; in uncertain territory when he acts on his own initiative; and "at his lowest ebb" when he acts, as in this case, on his own authority as commander-in-chief in the face of contrary legislation.[30] Put simply, there were no laws for Truman as executive to faithfully execute and no army or naval forces to supervise in his role as commander-in-chief.

The *Steel Seizure Case* set up a level of distrust about the scope of presidential power that has influenced subsequent events. For example, the 1964 Gulf of Tonkin Resolution made it clear that Congress was "prepared" to follow the president's decision on whether to commit troops to Southeast Asia, without insisting on further actions on their part before hostilities commenced.[31] The obvious and unresolved question is whether this action constitutes an impermissible delegation of Congress's power to declare war when no imminent necessity required its abnegation of authority.[32] The rocky course of the Vietnam War in turn produced the War Powers Act of 1973,[33] which passed over President Nixon's veto. Although the procedures addressed in this act cannot easily be crammed into a nutshell, everyone nevertheless concedes that the president has to act with defensive force to repel an attack against the United States, and may do so in his capacity as commander-in-chief without explicit congressional command.[34] What starts as a defensive effort, however, could easily expand to embrace other objectives. So the War Powers Act sought to claw back for Congress some of its power by requiring the issuance of a set of presidential reports on the status of a conflict. The first of these reports would be due forty-eight hours after a conflict begins and requires some explanation for the circumstances leading to the use of force, the constitutional justification for its use, and the prospects of any greater war.[35] By day sixty—sooner if Congress so decides—the president's power to act unilaterally is said to come to an end, so that he must either receive a declaration of war from Congress or further authorization for the continued use of force.[36]

What happens, however, if the president does not comply is never made quite clear, for the status of defensive wars receives no satisfactory textual answer. Indeed, whether the War Powers Act covers the initiation of some kind of hostilities is itself a subject on which no consensus exists.[37] The indeterminacy of this delicate process should come as no surprise.

The question of what counts as a declaration of war is itself far from clear once formal declarations of war are put to one side. John Yoo, former Department of Justice, Office of Legal Counsel attorney and author of the highly controversial (to say the least) Torture Memorandum,[38] has taken what I regard as an implausible position that the president may wage an offensive war even if the Congress has not declared war, or even if it explicitly refuses to declare one.[39] This position reduces the congressional power to declare war to a bookkeeping operation that may trigger certain domestic obligations, but it shreds the system of divided powers on which the Constitution necessarily rests. Letting Congress declare and the president wage (as he must) the war seems to be the far better reading of the basic text, and it avoids even the appearance of open confusion on matters of primary importance to the nation.

Even this emphatic rejection of Yoo's position does not resolve all open questions on this matter. It appears that the declaration of war need not be only in formal terms, but could easily involve those actions, such as the authorization of funds for particular struggles, that are incoherent unless some state of war exists.[40] Avoiding formal declarations of war could easily allow the United States to escape getting boxed in by various statutory or treaty obligations that could be triggered by a formal declaration. As this ever-increasing level of friction between Congress and the president shows, the Constitution does not have the requisite level of precision to resolve the huge range of day-to-day disputes. All that can be said with some degree of confidence is that the president's power to act unilaterally gives him a persistent tactical advantage over the disorganized coalitions that occupy the halls of Congress. As a normative matter, the classical liberal approach praises the effort to divide powers, but it has little to say (which is no different from any rival theory) as to how these powers are to be divided. Once the aura of distrust arises, the complications are sure to follow.

The level of distrust that drove the adoption of the War Powers Act is evident in the subsequent skirmishes between Congress and the president. One of the most recent of these disputes involved the power of President George W. Bush to order domestic wiretaps of foreign nations for the purposes of gathering intelligence that he (and many others) thought necessary to fight the War on Terror. The key obstacle to the Bush Administration's decision was that the Foreign Intelligence Surveillance Act (FISA),[41] which had been passed after major intelligence abuses during the 1970s came to light, limited the power of President Bush to gather information on his own. The issue was further clouded by the passage, in the wake of the tragic events of 9/11/2001, of the Authorization of the Use of Military Force Act (AUMF),[42] which gave the president the authority

> to use all necessary and appropriate force against those nations, orga-
> nizations, or persons he determines planned, authorized, committed,
> or aided the terrorist attacks that occurred on September 11, 2001, or
> harbored such organizations or persons, in order to prevent any future
> acts of international terrorism against the United States by such nations,
> organizations or persons.[43]

On the question of statutory authority, it would be strange if the AUMF either suspended or repealed the detailed structures set out under FISA. Repeals by implication are rightly disfavored, especially when there is no plausible conflict between the two statutes. It is doubt-less the case that the FISA procedures are pokey and inadequate, but if so, that is a matter for Congress to change, not for the president to alter unilaterally. The risks of excessive concentrations of power are every-where to be found.

Nor is there anything to the claim that some "inherent powers" of the president as commander-in-chief alter the balance set out in the Constitution. It is instructive that the word "power," which is used in Article II, Section 2, does not appear in the clause that defines the pres-ident's role as commander-in-chief, even though it is used to define the president's power to grant reprieves and pardons.[44] It is thus not appro-priate to pit the president's powers in this context against the explicit powers that Congress has "[t]o make Rules for the Government and Regulation of the land and naval Forces,"[45] which are in no way thought to be incompatible with the president's job as commander-in-chief. The key point of this designation is to give the president control over the mil-itary, which poses less of a threat to the nation when it operates under civilian control. But, in and of itself, that key institutional arrangement does nothing to expand the powers of the president vis-à-vis Congress. The key challenge is to determine the sphere of presidential discretion when Congress has been silent. Clearly, some action has to be taken, and it is right to assume that the Necessary and Proper Clause gives the president discretion on these matters when Congress is silent.[46]

As might be expected, John Yoo is again the leading defender of an absolutist account of presidential power here. In his well-known Tor-ture Memorandum, Yoo claims without any textual evidence that "The

Framers understood the Commander-in-Chief Clause to grant the President the fullest range of power recognized at the time of the ratification as belonging to the military commander."[47] That statement, standing alone, does not indicate what should happen when Congress passes a law that seeks to restrain presidential authority. But later passages in this same memo make clear Yoo's views on that, as well: "Congress cannot interfere with the President's exercise of his authority as Commander in Chief to control the conduct of operations during a war."[48] At no point, however, does Yoo explain what, if anything, is left for Congress after this provision is carved out, nor does he discuss the account of the commander-in-chief found in *Federalist No. 69*, or give so much as a single word of attention to the extensive discussion of the commander-in-chief "power" found in the *Steel Seizure Case*.[49] As for the ability to set rules to regulate the operations of the military forces, his memo baldly concludes, again without authority: "Our Office has determined that Congress cannot exercise its authority to make rules for the Armed Forces to regulate military commissions."[50] Again, no independent authority is provided for these conclusions.

There are real costs to this overclaiming of power for the president, for the question of inherent power needs a sensitive treatment on a number of hard borderline questions dealing with the relationship between the president and Congress. These questions include, for example, the extent to which Congress can limit or direct operations in the field with its declaration of war. For instance, could Congress have insisted that the president not conduct land or air operations against North Vietnam in its own territory? Or that the president not use nuclear weapons in Iraq? At some level, these issues cannot be resolved effectively either by textual or functional analysis. In the end, a political accommodation has to be reached, informed by the relative spheres of authority. On operational matters, the nod would go to the president, at least as to matters of tactics within a given theater of war, but not, at a guess, on the expansion of war to a new theater.[51] On the use of nuclear arms in the Middle East, the betting here is that the president would, in the end, yield to a congressional prohibition. It is a sad but true commentary that the harder one pushes on these constitutional provisions, the less they reveal about the difficult cases at the margin. This part of the Constitution is therefore best understood more as a framework for future elaborations than as a perfect contingent state contract. Classical liberal theory cannot pull rabbits out of hats. The choice of structural divisions of power is always harder to articulate than the theory of rights that these constitutional structures are intended to correct.

Habeas Corpus

The assertion of presidential power also has an intimate connection with the venerable Great Writ of Habeas Corpus. Of English origin, this writ—meaning "may you present the body"—required those holding a prisoner in custody to bring that person before a court so that it could determine the legality of the prisoner's detention and order release if the conditions justifying continued detention were not found. This writ represents an obvious use of judicial power to limit the forces of either presidential or congressional power, or some combination of both. The writ comes into play in modern times because the bloated assertions of President Bush's commander-in-chief powers led to his unilateral decision to deny the writ of habeas corpus to any person held in detention on an executive determination that the person was an "unlawful enemy combatant."[52]

The constitutional story starts with the Suspension Clause, which in its entirety reads: "The Privilege of the Writ of Habeas Corpus shall not be suspended, unless when in Cases of Rebellion or Invasion the public Safety may require it."[53] Not atypically, this clause begins *in medias res*. Far from offering any succinct statement of when habeas corpus is normally available, it only places strong limitations on any government effort to curtail or suspend its use.

The clause itself is drafted in the passive voice, which leaves unanswered the question as to just who can suspend the writ when these conditions are said to be satisfied—which is itself far from evident. Since the clause is located in Article I, it looks as though Congress, and not the president, should enjoy the power. In fact, while riding circuit,[54] Chief Justice Roger Taney concluded in *Ex parte Merryman*[55] that only Congress, and not President Lincoln, could suspend the writ. This decision seems to take it as settled that any condition for "Rebellion or Invasion" was amply satisfied, whether or not Maryland was about to secede from the Union, so that deciding who could suspend the writ was the only problem. But on reflection, Chief Justice Taney seems wrong to have placed so much weight on the location of the clause in determining how it should be triggered. If the authority is divided between Congress and the president, neither Article I nor Article II gives this provision a good home. The best analogy in this case is to the Guaranty Clause located in Article IV, Section 4, which allows states to petition the United States for assistance, first from the legislature, but then from the executive if the legislature cannot be convened.[56] Dividing authority in cases of necessity seems sensible. Ordinarily, Congress should do the work, but in times of necessity, the president can often act first, subject to congressional ratification, which Congress eventually supplied to Lincoln.[57] This division is always messy, but it in no way extended to the days and weeks after 9/11, when order was no longer subject to any imminent threat.

But what about the larger question that lurks just beneath the surface? When is habeas required in the first place? The initial response to this question necessarily requires some historical account of the circumstances under which the writ was available in 1789, difficult as that might be.[58] Perhaps the most fundamental principle, with unquestionable relevance today, is that habeas applies with equal force to citizens and aliens, such that the latter cannot be denied the benefits of the writ solely by virtue of their status.[59] By the same token, the writ does not ordinarily apply to individual members of enemy armed services who are captured on the battlefield, when there is no doubt that their lawful combatant status makes them prisoners of war subject, usually, to the Geneva Conventions. In such cases, there is, as it were, no available writ to suspend. The trouble starts when individuals are taken into custody under circumstances in which their legal status, and thus their eligibility for habeas, is unclear, as with individuals who are turned in by bounty hunters or seized based on tips by informants far away from any battlefield.[60] Should they receive a hearing on the jurisdictional question of whether they are entitled to request the writ in the first place?

Notwithstanding presidential claims of exclusive control, that question does, and should, receive an emphatic yes, especially for persons seized overseas and detained at Guantanamo Bay Naval Base, over which the United States exercises indefinite control by treaty, even though Cuba retains "ultimate sovereignty."[61] In one sense, this conclusion could potentially be undermined by the modern habeas statute, to which Justice Scalia appealed in his dissent in *Rasul v. Bush*.[62] The statute provides: "Writs of habeas corpus may be granted by the Supreme Court, any justice thereof, the district courts and any circuit judge within their respective jurisdictions."[63] But this decidedly puts the jurisdictional cart before the constitutional horse. If the writ is available, then the United States system must find a place to accommodate it. The right to habeas corpus would not have become a dead letter even if Congress had decided in 1789 not to set up any district courts. If the Supreme Court did not have original jurisdiction, some state court would have to step forward and hear the case of foreign detentions. But so long as the federal courts are in session, at least one must step forward to hear the case, for Congress cannot deny a constitutional right by simply refusing to designate a court in which it might be heard.

There is also a larger lesson here: No system of limited government can allow an interested administrator to determine unilaterally the contested status of a person subject to an indefinite incarceration. Indeed, the difficult question with this analysis is why some people believe that a detainee must be located on American territory in order for the writ to apply. It has long been settled that American citizens detained on foreign soil are entitled to the writ,[64] so that necessarily means that no set of logistical or jurisdictional issues should block the availability of the writ for noncitizen persons held outside of the United States. Citizens and aliens are entitled to a parity of treatment within our borders. Why not overseas? The Suspension Clause contains no territorial component, save insofar as it is a domestic invasion or rebellion that allows for its suspension, not activities elsewhere. So the correct solution is to preserve parity between citizens and aliens outside of the United States, just as the clause does for citizens and aliens within the United States.

Doctrinally, alas, it is well settled that aliens detained overseas do not receive constitutional protection against the actions of agents of the United States.[65] For example, the Fourth Amendment prohibition against unreasonable searches and seizures does not reach aliens overseas whose rights are violated by American agents.[66] But, at least in those cases, the American officials are subject to the restrictions that other nations impose for the protection of their citizens. However, detainees under American custody outside of the territorial limits of the United States are kept on military bases to which the protections of local laws do not run.

The adverse consequences of elevating territory over control are evident in a recent decision, *Al-Maqaleh v. Gates*,[67] where the Court of Appeals for the District of Columbia held that detainees shipped from various points across the globe to Bagram Air Force Base in Afghanistan have fewer (if any) procedural rights than they would have had if sent by the United States to Guantanamo Bay. One can concede that the difficulties of confinement under battle conditions postpone the need for habeas, but Chief Judge David Sentelle, along with Judges Harry Edwards and David Tatel, missed the obvious point that District Court Judge John Bates understood: this difficulty of administration was "largely of the Executive's own choosing."[68] It makes a mockery of constitutional law to nullify someone's constitutional protections by simply whisking him or her out of the United States. Furthermore, as will become clear, while there are many issues on which citizenship is and should be a critical issue, detention in facilities without due process and constitutional rights should not be one of them.

PART THREE

INDIVIDUAL RIGHTS

PROPERTY, CONTRACT, AND LIBERTY

19

From Structural Protections
to Individual Rights

THE PREVIOUS PORTIONS of this book have explained the classical liberal approach to critical issues of constitutional structure. At first blush, it seems unlikely that any examination of substantive rights should be related to these structural matters. But historically and analytically, constitutional structure and substantive rights have in fact always been intimately connected. Adopt a restrictive account of standing, and it becomes far easier for Congress to create legal monopolies and cartels. Permit permanent independent administrative agencies, and it becomes far easier for Congress and the executive to displace traditional property rights. Or, develop a sensible version of the dormant Commerce Clause, and it becomes much harder for states to limit free commerce in goods and services through protectionist trade barriers. Every sound structural limitation tracks classical liberal theory by limiting government intervention, either at the federal or state level, to cases of force, fraud, and monopoly. On the other hand, adopt the progressive vision, and an expanded view of government regulation will facilitate the creation of monopoly institutions.

The Police Power

The framework for analyzing structural matters revolves around two issues: scope and justification. Scope defines the breadth of the original constitutional structure. The early constitutional doctrine limited the scope of the Commerce Clause to cross-border transactions, while the modern doctrine goes much further. The expansion of Congress's power to regulate in so many spheres necessarily increases the likelihood that a broader reading of the dormant Commerce Clause could invalidate some additional state regulation. Yet by the same token it would be a mistake to think of the dormant Commerce Clause in absolutist terms. The most ardent free trader still supports restrictions on poisonous goods and foreign spies entering the country. But what is the free trader to do when the authority to impose regulation on various economic activities is not explicitly contained in the Constitution? Judges must search for justifications that allow public authorities to regulate in areas that are presumptively off-limits. The customary head for this second inquiry was the "police power," a phrase that once had the virtue of meaning what it said. The police must use force to enforce the law, so the question is: under what circumstances is it appropriate for them to exercise that power? Traditionally, the power covered matters of safety, health, general welfare, and morals of the community.

It is here the interpretive difficulties begin. The Constitution contains not a single textual reference to this central organizing concept. Obviously then, judges cannot parse the semantic or original meaning (either public or private) of particular words not present in the text of the Constitution. Instead, they necessarily *imply* substantive limitations in the scope of particular constitutional doctrines. But why must some conception of the police power be read into the Constitution, and why associate it only with those four traditional heads mentioned above? Are they all necessary? Should additional ones be added?

The only way to evaluate the proposed heads of police power is to test them against the underlying normative theory that animated the inclusion of the basic guarantees into the constitutional text. That approach meshes perfectly with the classical liberal proposition that all state action should be examined under a presumption of error, which has led in turn to a broad recognition of individual rights that can be limited only by a strong showing of a state interest in regulation. The dominant assumption in progressive thought runs in the opposite direction. It follows two imperatives. One is to narrow or reduce the scope of substantive protections of individual rights. The other is to allow the state the benefit of broad new justifications for regulation that go beyond those found in the original police power quartet. The key exceptions to this rule reflect one important overlap between modern progressive and classical liberal theory. Thus, in areas of speech, religion, and privacy, progressives often, but not uniformly, support a broad reading of the basic protection and a narrow reading of the police power in order to promote a regime that allows for full participation in the political process. Ironically, many nineteenth-century judges were far more statist on matters of morality and religion than on economic and property rights issues, and thus took the opposite position. The correct approach, I believe, is to apply the same small government framework to all individual interests, whether they are classified as economic, expressive, or intimate.[1]

At this juncture we again have to address the theory of individual rights. Across the broad spectrum of cases, the inquiry is: what analytical tool allows us to decide whether to opt for the classical liberal or the progressive agenda? What approach should be adopted in order to harmonize the scope of basic protection of liberty and property with state police power justification? Once again the clashing progressive and classical liberal answers are illustrative of the basic tension. In dealing with the affirmative grant of power to Congress under the Commerce Clause, the progressives saw little danger in expanding federal power, which led to a rational basis test and an all-inclusive account of the commerce power. Under the progressive worldview, the operative terminology asks whether the government could advance some "conceivable" justification for the program that it puts forward. If it can, the Court will not second guess the state either on the soundness of the ends or on the appropriateness of the means, because it does not "sit as a super legislature" on the wisdom of particular statutes and ordinances, all of which are left to the political branches.[2] That same rational basis test has also led to a narrow construction of the permissible limitations on that power, so that state and local governments cannot even invoke the indubitable historical claim of equal sovereignty to block federal labor legislation, which today governs states' relationships with their own employees.[3]

But switch over to the dormant Commerce Clause, and the operative test is now strict scrutiny. The same Court that sees little danger in government-sponsored nationwide cartels sees great danger in the balkanization of the common trade zone. Given that perception, dormant commerce cases attract strict scrutiny, which quickly translates into a broad basic protection coupled with narrow public justifications that must, to use the standard language, reflect some "compelling state interest." Consistent with this general theme, the Court worries first about the stated ends the legislation is meant to serve, which are narrowly defined, usually in ways that reflect the classical liberal concerns about such key questions as force and fraud or the protection of minors. Its second step is to examine closely the "fit" between these legitimate ends and the means chosen to achieve them. "Narrow tailoring" to reduce the risks of over- and under-inclusion is the order of the day.

In the middle lies the appropriately named test of "intermediate scrutiny," which in its typical verbal formulation asks whether a particular piece of legislation advances important government interests by means that are reasonably adapted or substantially related to the ends in question. Some choice in the statement of ends, or slippage in the choice of means, is surely tolerated. Thus, *Craig v. Boren* struck down different minimum drinking ages—twenty-one for men and eighteen for women—for 3.2 percent beer on the ground that "classifications by gender must serve important governmental objectives and must be substantially related to achievement of those objectives."[4] Functionally speaking, as a first approximation, intermediate scrutiny treats the dangers of over- and under-regulation as having equal weight, and thus sets no initial presumption either way. In these cases the usual verbal formulation speaks about requiring the government to show an important social end that it seeks to achieve by appropriate means. There is in effect more give on both parts of the analysis than under strict scrutiny. In most cases, the Court tends to run to either strict scrutiny or rational basis review, with relatively few cases dealing with intermediate scrutiny. Cases involving sex discrimination or the status of illegitimate children often fit into the middle category.[5]

These three standards of review—strict scrutiny, intermediate scrutiny, and rational basis—can be expressed as competing attitudes toward the two forms of error. Here is a way to put numbers to the different verbal formulations. Strict scrutiny weighs over-regulation as, say, ten times more serious than under-regulation. Rational basis goes in the opposite direction, so that under-regulation is rated as ten times more dangerous than over-regulation. That combined ratio is a one hundred to one difference, which neatly explains why strict scrutiny is usually a death sentence while rational basis is invariably toothless. Anyone can quarrel with the choice of numbers, but they cannot dispute either the direction or the power of the coefficients. Thus, let "a" (with a value of 10) be the differential for strict scrutiny against government regulation and "b" (with a value of .1) be the differential for rational basis in favor of regulation, where "a/b" (10/0.1), their ratio, represents the hundred-fold difference in odds as one moves from one standard of review to the other. Intermediate scrutiny could be modeled as a situation where both these coefficients are equal to one, so that there is no initial bias either way. In practice, however, it tends to lie somewhat closer to strict scrutiny than to rational basis. In light of these realities, it is useful to recall the late Gerald Gunther's famous quip about two-tier scrutiny: "Some situations evoked the aggressive 'new' equal protection, with scrutiny that was 'strict' in theory and fatal in fact; in other contexts, the deferential 'old' equal protection reigned, with minimal scrutiny in theory and virtually none in fact."[6] What he says about equal protection applies to all other constitutional provisions as well.

Fundamental Rights and Suspect Classifications

All these tests carry over to treatment of individual rights under the Constitution. The collection of individual rights under the Constitution is impressive and it comes from multiple sources. In this book, I confine myself to an examination of individual rights that have nothing to do with criminal law. Thus, the First Amendment states that Congress shall make no law "respecting an establishment of religion, or prohibiting the free exercise thereof." Moreover, Congress shall make no law "abridging the freedom of speech, or of the press." In similar form, the Second Amendment declares: "A well regulated Militia, being necessary to the security of a free State, the right of the people to keep and bear Arms, shall not be infringed." The Fifth Amendment protection afforded to private property is equally categorical: "[N]or shall private property be taken for public use, without just compensation." That categorical form tracks the Contracts Clause in Article I, stating: "No state shall . . . pass any . . . Law impairing the Obligation of Contracts." The question of individual rights was complicated by the passage in 1868 of the Fourteenth Amendment during the Reconstruction Era. And while Section 1 of the Fourteenth Amendment does not contain individual substantive guarantees, the protections that it affords to privileges and immunities, to due process, and to equal protection of the laws are again stated as invariant rules. It is helpful to set out its first provision in full to organize much of this discussion.

Amendment XIV

Section 1: All persons born or naturalized in the United States, and subject to the jurisdiction thereof, are citizens of the United States and of the State wherein they reside. No State shall make or enforce any law which shall abridge the privileges or immunities of citizens of the United States; nor shall any State deprive any person of life, liberty, or property, without due process of law; nor deny to any person within its jurisdiction the equal protection of the laws.

Quickly summarized, the first sentence of that amendment overturns the decision in *Dred Scott v. Sanford*,[7] by making all former slaves citizens. The payoff to citizenship is found in the Privileges or Immunities Clause, which looks as though it offers a full menu of privileges and immunities, none of which are set out in the Fourteenth Amendment or in the closely related provision in Article IV, Section 2, Clause 1, which states, "The Citizens of each State shall be entitled to all Privileges and Immunities of Citizens in the several States." The one clear inference that can be drawn from the location of the Privileges or Immunities Clause is that it appears to provide more expansive rights to the more limited class of "citizens" than do the Due Process and Equal Protection Clauses, which appear to give a smaller set of rights to a broader class of "person[s]." On its face—and the point is hotly contested—it appears that the Privileges or Immunities Clause offers individual substantive protection of these rights, and not just the protection against improper discrimination between groups, such as racial groups.

None of these provisions is self-explanatory and each of them requires an extensive interpretive apparatus to be put into sensible perspective. One constant theme that arises is whether any of these particular provisions incorporate the various protections, both civil and criminal, for individuals found in the Bill of Rights. The Privileges or Immunities Clause looks to be the most plausible candidate for that task, but it was given so narrow an interpretation in the *Slaughter-House Cases* in 1873[8] that the link between the Bill of Rights (which applied to the federal government) and the states had to be forged, if at all, through the Due Process Clause whose procedural orientation looks ill-suited for that task.

Wholly apart from incorporation, the Fourteenth Amendment poses another set of interpretive challenges. First, what is the appropriate standard of review for applying each of these provisions? Second, how does that standard of review play out in connection with the two central challenges of interpretation? The first of these risks is that of circumvention of basic guarantees by strategic legislative behavior. The second involves the set of permissible justifications for various government actions. These questions were also relevant in understanding the varied treatment of the Commerce Clause—strict scrutiny in some cases and rational basis in others.

Most critically, the Constitution contains not a single word of text that points in any direction on any of these questions. So the explanation has to come from nontextual sources. The most appealing explanation for differential levels of scrutiny on matters of individual rights stems from the famous Footnote 4 in *United States v. Carolene Products Co.*[9]—another of the dreary succession of dairy cases in which the Court turned a blind eye to special interest legislation—which was decided one year after the triumph of the progressives on matters of federalism and economic liberties. Thus the 1937 decision of the Supreme Court in *West Coast Hotel v. Parrish*,[10] overruling its 1923 decision in *Adkins v. Children's Hospital*,[11] sustained a minimum wage law that extended only to women. At this point in time, the attention was shifting sharply from these issues to questions of civil liberties and race, where the corrupt political institutions in the South had gone a long way to entrenching segregationist institutions (with which no classical liberal has the slightest patience).

In his effort to explain why stepped-up scrutiny was needed to counter government failure in the race cases, Justice Stone in his famous Footnote 4 adopted a theory of constitutional interpretation that asked, in the explicit context of race, "whether prejudice against discrete and insular minorities may be a special condition, which tends seriously to curtail the operation of those political processes ordinarily to be relied upon to protect minorities, and which may call for a correspondingly more searching judicial inquiry."[12] The argument, which is extensively elaborated in John Hart Ely's *Democracy and Distrust*,[13] contains strong echoes of the earlier concern with factions that animated James Madison in *The Federalist Papers*.[14] Indeed, rightly understood, the protection of beleaguered minorities is a powerful instantiation of that theory, especially when those so prejudiced are formally excluded from the polls.

Yet if Justice Stone is right to mount the judicial charge in the race cases involving "discrete and insular" minorities, he is surely wrong to retreat from the basic insight everywhere else. It was easy in the race cases to identify the fatal misalignment of power. And it is easy to show the loss of both property rights and economic liberties that followed from excluding particular groups from the political process or marginalizing their influence. But, in line with Madison, it hardly follows that property owners and employers cannot on occasion find themselves in the same vulnerable position. Is a landowner who wants to develop property a member of a discrete and insular minority if all his neighbors don't want him to build? Is an out-of-town landlord a member of a discrete and insular minority when the resident tenants push hard for a rent control statute? Are employers an embattled minority when large numbers of workers demand strong labor unions whose organizational activities are protected by the state?

The answer to these questions differs from the race cases in one important way. In 1938, there was no need to run a detailed inquiry to discover that the political game was shamelessly rigged. In contrast, in fluid modern environments, when voting rights are secure, no one can simply posit that members of any group have been stripped of their ability to participate effectively in the political process. In all cases, we get more information once the political process has run its course in any particular dispute. At that time it should be possible *across the board* to examine the *outcomes* of a particular process to determine whether they bring about major wealth transfers between persons or groups.

As with structural issues, any full analysis of rights manifests itself in two dimensions. The first involves particular protection of some designated activity or institution, such as speech, religion, contract, property, and, most recently, guns. The second involves nondiscrimination rules, often found in free trade contexts, which find explicit expression in the Equal Protection Clause of the Constitution. The interplay between individual rights and nondiscrimination rules often proves elusive, for many complex claims contain both dimensions. The matter is further complicated because procedural rights often require an amalgam of both discrete protections and safeguards against preferential treatment.

Predictably, the analysis of the proffered state justifications for limiting individual constitutional guarantees follows the path that it took on structural matters. The classical liberal position gives narrow weight to purported justifications both as to the ends the state chooses and the means it uses to achieve them. The progressive mindset takes the opposite view on both questions. And as the difference between strict scrutiny and rational basis approaches the one-hundred-to-one ratio mentioned above, the choice of worldview exerts a profound effect on the size of government. As an ardent defender of the classical liberal conception across the board, it is no secret where I come out: there are some cases (e.g., monopoly issues) in which intermediate scrutiny is the correct approach. But there are virtually no cases, except perhaps on some narrow national security questions, where rational basis sets the right standard of review.

This section examines this interplay of basic rights and state justification in the context of explicit constitutional guarantees of individual rights, all of which are articulated in categorical form. All forms of individual protection are broken into two halves. The first of these defines an individual right worthy of government protection. The second justifies the use of police power to enforce the right. That complex interplay between basic rights and state justification determines the shape of our modern institutions. The following section highlights some of the key features.

Negative and Positive Liberties

The initial substantive inquiry thus concerns the content of the discrete constitutional guarantee. Our Constitution phrases all individual entitlements in negative form, reflecting the social objective to prevent government from trenching on vested rights. Nowhere does the text state that either the federal or state government owes anyone a job, a home, a car, health care, a minimum standard of living, or a free trip to the Bahamas. To be sure, negative liberties protect jobs, homes, cars, health care, standards of living, and vacations, but only in a restricted sense. While there is no affirmative duty on the state to supply jobs, there is a requirement that government not block or burden employment—be it by taxes or regulation—except under some narrow police power justification.

The system-wide difference between positive and negative rights is palpable. Positive rights always carry correlative duties to supply some bundle of goods or services, whose content cannot be determined with any generality. Even after the appropriate bundle is identified, it must then be funded by the government, which must raise the needed revenues from some fraction of the population through taxation. Answers to the questions of how much support, what levels of taxation, and against what groups, all depend heavily on resource constraints and particular institutional details that no constitutional regime could hope to anticipate in advance. Those modern constitutions that espouse positive rights to jobs, housing, and health care *never* put strong duties on government to supply particular jobs or houses. Those constitutional norms operate only in the world of aspirations, as precatory norms that the legislature has to deal with in good faith, often under the prodding of the courts. Positive rights thus require a much more complicated institutional system than negative ones.

The rejection of positive rights in the American system rules out the possibility that anyone could exert a strong constitutional entitlement claim against the government. It follows that there is no occasion to address the justifications for denying provision of nonexistent positive rights. Modern American constitutional law, however, virtually invites the legislature at both the federal and state levels to adopt schemes of redistribution that the Constitution itself is powerless to impose. Medicare, Medicaid, and Social Security all have the capacity to bankrupt the nation. Yet the bewildering cross-subsidies embedded into their basic design are not subject to any fundamental constitutional challenges, except at the edges. It is therefore quite unlikely as of this writing that the extensive health care legislation passed during the Obama administration will be constitutionally undermined, notwithstanding the heavy duties of cross-subsidization that it places on individuals and firms alike. The soothing balm of rational basis review will likely allow some court to craft a suitable justification for the massive state intervention, which would not be viable if a higher level of scrutiny were invoked.

The classical liberal worldview does not accept this compromise position whereby the Constitution allows but does not require massive forms of wealth redistribution. Rather, it starts from the assumption that the basic system of negative liberties limits the use of taxes and regulations to overcoming coordination problems for public goods—e.g., infrastructure—that generate across-the-board benefits, *without* requiring huge transfer programs among citizens. That position runs into fierce objection from those who regard the redistribution from rich to poor as a moral imperative in light of the diminishing marginal utility of wealth. Yet even that justification offers no comfort for the countless redistributive programs that often work at cross-purposes with that objective, including the huge number of industry-specific subsidies for agriculture, transportation, or real estate development, which do nothing to alleviate rich/poor differentials.

Attacking these practices without taking down comprehensive and systematic government redistribution is theoretically possible. But a piecemeal approach offers small benefits to the average member of the public, yet poses a huge threat to those who benefit from each particular subsidy. The task of unraveling the complex network of taxes and subsidies is doomed to founder. Virtually all modern judges, both liberal and conservative, will not touch this fundamental problem with a ten-foot pole. So it will have to suffice to register a principled objection. This Part does just that by comparing the classical liberal and progressive views.

The task that remains is to organize the particular topics that are guided by these general principles. In so doing, I take a guarded historical approach. I begin in Chapter 20 with a discussion of the procedural due process issues explicitly set out in the Due Process Clauses of both the Fifth and the Fourteenth Amendments. In Chapter 21, I take up the question of economic liberties and freedom of contract, which was the first of the individual guarantees to come into constitutional prominence, especially after the Civil War. Next I attack the issues relating to the taking and regulation of real property in Chapter 22. Chapter 23 then addresses key issues of personal liberties, including such hot button issues as contraception, abortion, homosexual sodomy, and gay marriage. Once I am done with these traditional issues, I turn next in Chapters 24 to 28 to the complex issues raised in connection with the guarantees of freedom of speech, and in Chapters 29 to 32 to those issues that concern both the establishment of religion and the free exercise thereof. Once that is finished, in Chapters 33 to 35 I examine the various classification issues that are raised in connection with the guarantees of equal protection of the laws, relating to race, sex, alienage, and other potentially suspect classifications.

20

Procedural Due Process
Implementing the Classical Liberal Ideal

I N DEALING WITH the transition from structural protections to individual rights, it is appropriate to begin with an analysis of the one protection that explicitly limits both the national and state governments: the Due Process Clause. As its name suggests, it offers a set of procedural safeguards against the loss of any substantive entitlement. The Fifth Amendment of the Constitution, part of the Bill of Rights, states "nor [shall any person] be deprived of life, liberty, or property, without due process of law"—by the United States. The analogous provision of the Fourteenth Amendment reads "nor shall any state deprive any person of life, liberty, or property, without due process of law." It should go without saying that some provisions of this sort form a necessary component to a classical liberal constitution, for nowhere is the need for limited government stronger than in controlling the potential abuses of government when it exerts its political power. These procedural guarantees come into play whenever the state exercises its monopoly power over the life, liberty, or property of persons subject to its jurisdiction.

A Universal Guarantee

The origins of these clauses go back to the English Magna Carta of 1215 whose key provisions, Clauses 39 and 40, read as follows:

> 39. No freemen shall be taken or imprisoned or disseised or exiled or in any way destroyed, nor will we go upon him nor send upon him, except by the lawful judgment of his peers or by the law of the land.

40. To no one will we sell, to no one will we refuse or delay, right or justice.

A comparison between the Magna Carta and the two Due Process Clauses reveals some instructive textual differences. First, the term "freeman" in the Magna Carta is narrower than the term "person" in the two Due Process Clauses, and it applies only to that limited class of individual persons not tied as serfs to the land. The subsequent generalization to all persons in the Due Process Clauses represents a powerful evolution of the law such that differences in personal status that once mattered are no longer relevant. Indeed, this welcome simplification of the law of persons counts as one of the great advances in the cause of liberty, because on its face (even when slavery was entrenched) it covers all persons regardless of sex, race, religion, ethnicity, or prior condition of servitude. Second, and in similar fashion, the words "taken, imprisoned or disseised [technically, dispossessed from a freehold interest], or exiled or in any way destroyed" offer a broad but specific list of sanctions that could well be narrower than the single word "deprived," which covers not only the above actions, but also sanctions such as fines or loss of license, which do not seem to be covered by the phrase "go upon him nor send upon him." Third, the Magna Carta refers to loss only through adjudication, with its emphasis on the words "lawful judgment." This leaves open the question of whether its protection applies (as it should) to individuals who are subject to individual sanctions by administrative or legislative actions. Bills of attainder were, for example, commonplace in England, but it is doubtful that the Magna Carta imposes restraints on that parliamentary strategy. The United States Constitution closes that gap when it explicitly provides first that "no Bill of Attainder . . . shall be passed"[1] at the federal level, and further that "no state shall . . . pass any Bill of Attainder."[2] Fourth, the peculiar disjunction between "of his peers" and "by the law of the land" suggests a procedural limitation—namely the jury process—in the first phrase that contrasts with the greater universality of the second. The words "by the law of the land" require procedural rules be general and well established, but they fail to specify any independent minimum set of required procedural safeguards. Finally, the basic guarantees under the Magna Carta are strengthened by the general language in Clause 40, which guarantees all persons (not just freemen) access to the basic system of justice. The state cannot employ its monopoly over the use of force to "refuse or delay" the disposition of judgment, but (like all private monopolists) is subject to render reasonable and nondiscriminatory service to the people whom it governs.

The words of the Magna Carta were altered as its guarantees made their way into American law through the Due Process Clauses. The reasons for the terminological switch from "the law of the land" to "due process of law" are not entirely clear. Nonetheless, in 1856, the Supreme Court, in its first foray into the issue in *Murray's Lessee v. Hoboken Land & Improvement Co.*,[3] held that the two phrases "were undoubtedly intended to convey the same meaning"[4]—only to reject, on the strength of a uniform English practice, the claim that the Due Process Clause required the federal government to give its tax collectors a hearing *before* determining what sums they owed to the state. On a recurrent theme, the Court held that a hearing for disputed claims held after collection sufficed, since interest payments could make the tax collectors financially whole. The amalgam of customary practice makes sense in an area where the textual commitments are far from clear. But by the same token, it would be overhasty to ignore the subtle transformation in approach that emerges by replacing the phrase "due process of law" with the phrase "by the law of the land." The words "due process" still require uniformity across like cases, but they also make explicit some guarantee of minimum process, as hard as it is to specify in advance the content of those guarantees. All of this falls far short of the modern developments of substantive due process. But it does make clear that in the antebellum period, the Fifth Amendment's Due Process Clause did touch some forms of regulation that impacted the operation of the judicial system in particular cases. One way of stating the prevailing accommodation is offered by Nathan Chapman and Michael McConnell: "Legislative acts violated due process not because they were unreasonable or in violation of higher law, but because they exercised judicial power or abrogated common law procedural protections."[5] But even this formulation is not quite right because it glosses over the driving forces that generated these common law rules, which, as will become clear, were embodied in the natural law tradition of due process.

This short historical tour helps reject the cynic's protest that the phrase "due process of law" offers no real protection because it has no discernible content.[6] Indeed, the universality of the two Due Process Clauses is ultimately the source of their strength. The cynic's case is disproved not by some knockdown doctrinal argument, but by the simple fact that no known system of law has ever turned its back on the view that some degree of process is necessarily required before the state deprives individuals of their lives, liberties, or property. The essential components of this position long antedate the Magna Carta, for they are captured in the early Roman maxims *audi alteram partem* (hear the other side) and *nemo judex in causa sua* (no person should be a judge in his own cause).

It takes little imagination to tease out some essential components of due process from these bare commands. "Hear the other side" means that no judge should be able to make a decision adverse to a party who has not had his say in court. From that simple requirement, it is a short journey to hold that any hearing will give the needed chance to speak only if the individual has clear notice of the charges that are raised against him, both as to the particulars of the case and their legal basis. That notice requirement in turn will meet minimum standards only if an indictment or other charge is couched in language intelligible to the accused or other defendant, which is not possible if the underlying law is vague, opaque, confused, or internally contradictory. The ability to receive notice of potential public penalty prior to undertaking private action is critically dependent on the simple proposition that all laws be prospective in their application. Hence, by the conventional wisdom no person can be bound retroactively by a rule that is promulgated after particular actions are taken.

For its part, the requirement that no person be a judge in his own cause is in fact a particularized version of a more general requirement, namely that the decider of any particular case cannot have an interest in its outcome, where that interest covers, in addition to himself, all persons and groups with whom he is aligned or is seen to be aligned. The broad position was explicitly adopted in *Dr. Bonham's Case*,[7] which held that the members of the College of Physicians could not pass on Dr. Bonham's license to practice medicine in London when it stood to gain from any fines imposed on him. Edward Coke, C.J., elevated this prohibition against bias into a principle that arguably trumped the commands of Parliament, with his famous statement "the common law will controul acts of parliament, and sometimes adjudge them to be utterly void."[8]

James R. Stoner made a credible argument that Coke did not intend this statement to reject the principle of parliamentary supremacy, but instead thought only that the presumption against bias should hold under principles of "natural justice"—the instructive modern English term for the procedural protections that fall under due process in the American context.[9] But whatever the correct historical view, the projected constitutional status of rules against bias was rejected in England, most decisively on the authority of William Blackstone, who championed an unlimited version of parliamentary supremacy on the ground that "no power" under English law was "with authority to control [an act of Parliament]" on the sole ground that it was "contrary to reason."[10] Nonetheless, just that basic position found constitutional roots in the United States through the Due Process Clause of the Fifth Amendment, which includes a general constitutional prohibition against bias.

Analytically, there is a tight connection between procedural bias and the substantive protection of life, liberty, and property, which is one reason why the ostensible oxymoron "substantive due process"—John Hart Ely famously compared it to "green pastel redness"[11]—has persisted historically. One reason we care about procedure is because we know that it affects substance. For example, suppose that one side wins with a single die if it comes up odd and loses if it comes up even. Loading the die so that the odd numbers are now three times as likely to come up as the even ones switches the odds of winning from 50/50 to 75/25. If there is $100 at stake, the loaded die is tantamount to an illicit wealth transfer of $25 from one side to the other. Procedural devices thus always interact with substance, which is why historically takings and due process are so closely linked. Similar arguments apply to all the other guarantees bundled into due process. Bad procedures generate bad outcomes that necessarily lead to unprincipled deviations from the ideals chosen by the substantive law. These flip-flops not only lead to inconsistent results in parallel cases, but they also create massive uncertainties that can destabilize markets and undermine the rule of law.

From these simple observations, it becomes clear that the due process guarantee has succeeded because its essential ingredients map onto the requirements for the rule of law, precisely because its procedural requirements are not tethered to any particular view of substantive law.[12] In principle at least, the requirements of due process are applied to all substantive regimes, from the small government classical liberal state to the modern progressive state, with its very different objectives. Nonetheless, in practice it turns out that it is easier to adhere to these rule of law guarantees in the smaller classical liberal state with its well-defined conceptions of property, in vogue at the time of the Founding.[13] Quite simply, the vast amounts of discretion conferred in the modern progressive state are in practice in constant tension with the traditional guarantees of procedural due process.

To see how these various issues play out, I shall examine some of the major interpretive problems that appear in connection with the Due Process Clause. First, what government actions trigger the due process guarantees? Second, to whom are the protections of due process extended? Third, what is the scope of life, liberty, and property under the two Due Process Clauses? Fourth, what process is due to various parties in various situations?

The Internal Operation of the Due Process Clause

State Action

The potential scope of both Due Process Clauses depends intimately on the kinds of government action that they cover. Clause 39 of the Magna Carta only applies to lawful judgments, which are always the product of litigation, but applies far less clearly to other forms of government action, including general legislation that prescribes the substantive rules that govern litigation in particular disputes. There is little doubt that the standard trial is in fact a central focus of the protection of any Due Process Clause, given the consequences of an adverse judgment against the defendant, which allows the sheriff to seize any of the defendant's property located within the jurisdiction. That same judgment, moreover, can also form the basis of action to seize property located in another state whose government under our constitutional scheme has to give "full faith and credit" to any judgment of a sister state.[14] It is, of course, only possible to give automatic enforcement to prior judgments from other states if there is some collective confidence that those earlier adjudications were done under proper procedures.

The situation becomes more difficult because courts are not the only bodies whose decisions can deprive any person of life, liberty, or property. Any number of administrative tribunals can, for example, determine whether a person owes taxes, has become a citizen, receives a driver's or broadcast license, or is eligible for the draft. The rise of the administrative state means that governments today must grapple with many different types of disputes, calibrating their procedures to deal with them appropriately. Accordingly, under the American system a party can raise two challenges in any given case. The first asks whether the procedures promised were given; the second uses a constitutional lens to examine the soundness of those procedures.

Under the English practice of parliamentary supremacy, only the first issue is in play. In contrast, under the American system, the Due Process Clause controls all exercises of sovereign power. In *Yick Wo v. Hopkins*,[15] it was held that both the Equal Protection Clause and the two Due Process Clauses are "universal in their application, to all persons within the territorial jurisdiction, without regard to any differences of race, of color, or of nationality."[16] The expansive "universal" suggests that the guarantees in question are comprehensive. In contrast, the phrase "within the territorial jurisdiction" suggests that the due process guarantees (and the writ of habeas corpus which is closely allied with it), do not apply with respect to aliens (not citizens) who are detained outside of the territory of the United States on the simple ground that the United States does not exert sovereign power over them.[17] The borderline case on this view asks whether due process guarantees run to persons held at the naval base in Guantanamo Bay: notwithstanding Cuba's "ultimate sovereignty" over the territory, the United States exercises "complete jurisdiction and control" over the base given our extensive treaty rights with Cuba. In contrast, the United States does not exert such control over places like Landsberg Prison in Germany, where in the aftermath of the Second World War it was held that the standard procedural protections do not apply.[18]

This entire line of Supreme Court cases cuts against any sensible reading of the Due Process Clause by refusing to allow it any extraterritorial application, even though the clause itself contains no territorial limitation. Why then imply one into the text? The key question should not be whether the United States has control over the territory in which the alien is located, but whether it has effective control over the prisoner who claims rights against the United States. Imposing these protections, whether by statute or constitutional mandate, is an internal matter for the United States, to which the Germans, for example, were supremely indifferent at the end of World War II. There are many reasons why ordinary prisoners of war should not receive any special procedural protections, but all of those are related to their status as enemy combatants and not to the place of their incarceration. Where genuine questions arise as to whether a given individual is in fact an enemy combatant, it is no more difficult to give voice to those concerns in Germany than it is in the United States. If we can extend that procedural protection to citizens held outside the United States, we can extend it to aliens outside the United States, even if they are not citizens, so long as they are in the custody of American officials. It is therefore hard to see why this massive deprivation of personal liberty should fall outside the constitutional protections of due process. The simple solution is that the level of protection required should be the same regardless of where the government decides the incarceration takes place, which is a standard that is as easy to administer as any other.

Persons Protected

The basic observation that follows from the above discussion is that the due process protections found in both amendments cover not only citizens, but all persons—without question a more inclusive term. At the very least that broader definition reaches aliens who are natural persons, a point that was clearly accepted in *Yick Wo*, which extended the Due Process Clauses to Chinese subjects residing in the United States. It is a somewhat more difficult question to ask whether these provisions should apply to partnerships, associations, and corporations that are assemblages of persons who often receive the benefit of special protections, such as limited liability, that can only be conferred by operation of law. In one sense, that extension makes no sense because abstract entities cannot lose either their lives to execution or their liberties to imprisonment. Nonetheless these entities are empowered to acquire, hold, and dispose of property, and there is an extensive body of law today that deals with criminal punishment of corporations for the wrongs vicariously charged to them for the acts of their various senior officials and employees. It seems very odd to say that the extensive set of due process protections should apply to the property that individuals hold as common owners, but only so long as that common ownership is not put behind some limited liability corporation. Recall that limited liability allows for businesses to expand by permitting individuals to commit some, but not all of their wealth to a venture that they do not run. These corporations get the procedural protections afforded to other persons, because the property that they hold in corporate solution necessarily redounds to the benefit of the individual shareholders. All other areas of the law have special rules to deal with the status of corporations, including rules that govern the service of process on corporations or, ironically, their status as citizens for the purpose of diversity jurisdiction, which allows them to sue or be sued in federal court.[19] That broader protection seems fully warranted, lest corporate assets be seized with impunity.

Life, Liberty, or Property

The scope of protection under both Due Process Clauses is limited to "life, liberty or property." The obvious rights included under this rubric are those which are protected under classical liberal theories of government. But the scope of the Due Process Clause can also extend to various rights that are created by government as part and parcel of the modern administrative state. I shall take these up in order.

Private Rights. The initial question is how far life, liberty, and property extend, by asking what other interests might prove worthy of legal protection. The phrase itself occupies an honorable niche in political theory as a modernized version of John Locke's famous trio of "lives, liberties, and estates," the preservation of which explains why men quit the state of nature and put themselves under government.[20] The three elements received an early explication in Blackstone, which covers, most critically, those interests that under his natural law theory individuals enjoy prior to and independent of any form of government action. Thus Blackstone famously notes that the right to life, or in his terms the "right of personal security," consists of "a person's legal and uninterrupted enjoyment of his life, his limbs, his body, his health, and his reputation."[21] As a matter of general construction, it would be odd indeed if a person were protected from execution but not from the loss of limb or deliberate exposure to various diseases, so that the protection of the first easily covers all the others by analogical extension. By the same token, including reputation under personal security is terminologically problematic. The law of defamation protects that interest as a way to ensure that individuals do not lose the capacity to enter into gainful relationships, both business and social, with some third person or persons.[22] In some cases, defamation can lead to death, as with false charges of treason to the sovereign. But most cases involve only relational interests. Yet the point is not of ultimate concern in the American context, for despite the failure to treat the protection from defamation as part of life, that judgment does not exclude its protection under both liberty and property.

The notion of liberty in the state of nature included at a minimum "the power of locomotion, of changing one's direction and removing one's person to whatsoever place one's own inclination may direct."[23] As stated, it looks as though this freedom of motion cannot be constrained by the private lands owned by others. But it seems quite clear that Blackstone by this enumeration did not mean to eviscerate the institution of private property, but only to ensure that individuals received protection against false imprisonment and against others blocking their rights of way on public highways, waterways, and beaches. Left out of this statement of individual liberty is the ability of any one person to dispose of either his labor or tangible property to others, that is, an interest in the liberty of contract that later plays so large a role in American history. But the logic for inclusion of this right is compelling if one takes the limiting case and assumes that a government decrees that no individual is entitled as of right to enter into any transactions from a common purchase of food, to an employment contract, to a contract of marriage. And once the larger claim to liberty is extended, it becomes an impossible to insist that partial losses of liberty—e.g., you cannot buy some foods, work for some persons, or marry others—do not fall into the same class of protected liberties. By the same token the protection of property covered, in Blackstone's famous formulation, of "that sole and despotic dominion which one man claims and exercises over the external things of the world, in total exclusion of the right of any other individual in the universe,"[24] at the very least all "the estates" to which Locke made reference in his trio of "lives, liberties, and estates."

This argument from analogy, and the need to prevent government at all levels from overreaching its authority, makes it imperative that the liberty under the Due Process Clause cover all those interests that were mentioned in Blackstone, and many others in addition. And so it has come to pass. In *Meyer v. Nebraska*,[25] the Court struck down a statute that forbade the instruction of foreign language—in that case, specifically German—for students who had not attained an eighth-grade education. The case was decided on substantive due process grounds, but surely the catalogue of interests set out by Justice James McReynolds also is deserving of procedural protections:

Without doubt, [liberty] denotes not merely freedom from bodily restraint, but also the right of the individual to contract, to engage in any of the common occupations of life, to acquire useful knowledge, to marry, establish a home and bring up children, to worship God according to the dictates of his own conscience, and generally to enjoy those privileges long recognized at common law as essential to the orderly pursuit of happiness by free men.[26]

Quite simply, it is the full set of liberties that one has in the state of nature, not just some arbitrarily selected subset, that receive protection under the clause. In addition, a credible case can be made to include reputation on this list in light of the standard definition from Locke, quoted above.[27] It is widely accepted that no person can use force to deter third persons from associating or dealing with the plaintiff.[28] The use of false words has just that effect, which explains why the tort of defamation goes back at least to Roman times: it falls squarely within the libertarian prohibition against the use of force and fraud. In *Joint Anti-Fascist Refugee Committee v. McGrath*[29] the United States listed the Refugee Committee as a Communist organization, which in the heated atmosphere of the 1950s was unquestionably a defamatory communication. The Supreme Court granted the plaintiff's request for delisting on the ground that their inclusion was an arbitrary and unauthorized act that was not entitled to judicial deference.[30] This view of the matter is consistent with the law of defamation, which has long given remedies to plaintiffs who cannot identify the third persons who were driven away from them by the defendant's statements.[31] It is not difficult to conclude that any such official determination should have been made only after the Refugee League had a chance to contest it, precisely because, as Justice Frankfurter urged, a wide range of parties may use the designation "as ground for rejection of applications for commissions in the armed forces or for permits for meetings in the auditoriums of public housing projects,"[32] and lots of private business opportunities as well.

The last element in this list is property. The use of the broader term surely covers private property, so that the deprivation of land, or of any interest in land like a mortgage or a life estate, is protected against deprivation under the Due Process Clauses. The same argument would be made with respect to goods and animals that a person owns, and the same process of analogy surely extends to cover various forms of intellectual property, including patents, copyrights, trade names, and trade secrets already created under the terms of the applicable patent and copyright acts or the rules of state law. Access to and use of public roads and facilities is not a form of private property, but is a form of common property to which parties all have access in the state of nature. These interests too seem to count as a protected form of property, so that the state cannot strip a person of those access and use rights without going through the same procedures applicable in other cases. Likewise, the disparagement of a person's goods, itself a species of defamation, should be subject to constitutional protection as a form of general damages, which should have controlled in *Joint Anti-Fascist Refugee Committee*. The tort of defamation only depends on knowing that third persons have avoided the plaintiff. It does not depend on knowing exactly who they are.

This catalog of interests includes (with the exception of patents and copyrights) all the property interests that one brings into society under a Lockean theory, which makes it clear that property interests are acquired by individual actions—typically occupation of land, chattels, and animals—that are in no way dependent for their validity on the actions of any government.[33] But that pristine view of property cannot survive the creation of the state when it exercises its undeniable powers, which include its power to dispose of property, to enter into contracts, to run prisons, or to issue various kinds of permits and licenses allowing individuals and firms to engage in certain activities, sometimes on their own property and other times on public property. Licenses to practice medicine or law fall into the first category. Licenses to drive on public roads fall into the second category. The power of the state seems greater in those cases where the interests of any individual are shared with others, for the state necessarily must be able to exercise extensive management prerogatives to keep the system going. The obvious question here is how to apply the requirements of due process that emerged in a simple state of nature in a complex society in which government officials perform all sorts of different functions, some of which are distinctive to government and others that are not.

At this point, the older conception of judgments rendered in accordance with the law of the land has nothing to say about the way in which the state structures or restructures entitlements. The only protection that it offers, and it is one of huge importance, is protection against extraordinary procedures of the sort that can lead to Star Chamber proceedings and summary executions. The reason that this requirement has bite is that it formally imposes a nondiscrimination rule of sorts that means for any given class of substantive wrongs, the people who make the laws have to live by the laws they make for others. No one can claim that this impartiality will be routinely observed in practice. But it is clear that any ideal of equal justice under law will fail if those who govern can impose restraints on their rivals that do not apply to themselves. Under any constitutional regime of due process, the nondiscrimination provision must supplement a powerful set of property-like norms in order to provide comprehensive protection against the excesses of government power.

Government Grants, Contracts, and Licenses. The next question is how far the two Due Process Clauses extend to government grants and government licenses. The issue received its most famous academic articulation in Charles A. Reich's *The New Property*,[34] which noted that modern government does more than protect the traditional form of private property insofar as it "pours forth wealth: money benefits, services, contracts, franchises, and licenses."[35] The deprivation of any of these interests must be tested against the requirements, which can differ across different types. In this section, I begin with government conveyances, which can often be tested by traditional property principles, and then move on to examine how these rules play out in dealing with government employment contracts, welfare payments, and social security benefits. In some cases, the point of tension comes in the definition of the property right that is protected under the Due Process Clauses, and others in which the issue relates to the procedures that must be afforded to see that these are protected. Although this distinction between government grants and government employment contracts may blur at the margins, it offers an instructive way to organize the overall analysis.

In tackling this question, the easiest cases are those that deal with the government disposition of publicly owned property, which, once conveyed, has the same status as any other piece of private property. The government may have explicitly reserved a right to reclaim the property, just as other property owners may do. But if the conveyance is outright and unconditional, the property is protected to the same degree, both substantively and procedurally, as any other common law interest. Accordingly, the government can retake it, but only if it provides the same just compensation that is needed in any other case.[36] The situation with respect to government contracts is the same. Contracts for the performance of work are often complex arrangements that contain all sorts of conditions and stipulations that reflect the joint decisions of the parties on how best to conduct their combined venture. Where the government acts within the scope of its stated contract rights, it does not face any due process claims. Thus if a particular grant allows the government to recoup property at will from its donor, there is no due process (or just compensation) claim when the government exercises its reserved rights.

The following examples show a few key elements in the basic structure of the underlying contract and property rights driving the due process analysis. In *United States v. Fuller*,[37] the government condemned ranchland the owners of which had been allowed to access public grazing lands under government licenses terminable at will. The Court, through Justice William Rehnquist, concluded that no compensation was owed for the lost grazing rights when these were revoked before the land was condemned. In *Bailey v. Richardson*,[38] the Court of Appeals in a national security case stated that "[i]t has been held repeatedly and consistently that Government employ is not 'property'" so that the presumption is that "in the absence of statute or ancient custom," the office is "held at will of the appointing authority," just like an ordinary contract in the private sector.[39]

The same logic about the contract at will has been applied in other cases as well. In *Cafeteria and Restaurant Workers, Local 473, AFL-CIO v. McElroy*,[40] a short-order cook on a military base was held to be an employee-at-will who could not protest her dismissal on grounds that she had not satisfied the government's requirements for a security clearance. The case had an odd posture because the commanding officer purported to find cause for her dismissal when under the contract none was needed because "it has become a settled principle that government employment, in the absence of legislation, can be revoked at the will of the appointing officer."[41] From this premise, it appears that any government factual determination was an optional safeguard to the employee that did not harden into a fixed constitutional right, which is probably a good thing lest such dismissals be made without any explanation at all. But if the determination of the appropriate security risk is necessary by statute, a hearing is in fact required to establish that statutory cause for dismissal. Optional procedures that are customarily invoked, but not legally required, generally fall outside the scope of the Due Process Clause.

The procedures in question deal not only with security interests but with other employment contexts, where the distinction between contracts that can be terminated (or not renewed) at will and term contracts can rise to constitutional significance. Thus, in *Board of Regents of State Colleges v. Roth*,[42] the Court denied any property interest to a nontenured professor whose one-year contract was not renewed on its expiration. Tenured professors with binding contracts at public universities can be dismissed only with cause, and in these instances the Due Process Clause applies.[43]

The question then arises whether the existence of some property interest is necessary in all cases to invoke traditional due process protections. On this point, the answer seems to be in the negative, for reasons that relate not to the protection of property as such, but to the ubiquitous doctrine of unconstitutional conditions, which says that even when the government may decide at will whether to grant a benefit or not, it cannot do so for reasons that allow it to distort the political process.[44] Thus, to give a simple example, the government by virtue of its ownership of the public roads cannot exclude Republicans when it admits Democrats, even though it can in many instances exclude both. The use of public power is scrutinized not because individuals have guaranteed rights of access, but because without that constraint the government of all the people can use its power to shift benefits to its favored clientele, with obvious dangers to the integrity and stability of the political process. That same concern applies in employment contexts as well, such that it has been uniformly held that once a government employee[45] or a teacher on a term or at-will contract[46] alleges that his dismissal was based on political speech, a hearing of some sort is required to resolve the dispute. Even though the individual in question "has no 'right' to a valuable governmental benefit, and even though the government may deny him the benefit for any number of reasons, there are some reasons upon which the government may not rely."[47]

The hard question in this area of grants and employment contracts is the degree to which the government can adopt a strategy that first designates that the relationship may be terminated for cause, and then insists that it can specify whatever procedures it chooses to see whether that cause has been made out. As a general matter, private employers are in exactly that position. There is no requirement, for example, that private employers must give the employee a hearing before an independent party prior to invoking their power to dismiss. It is perfectly appropriate for the dismissal to take place at the discretion of a single supervisory employee if the procedures so call for it. At that point, the for-cause determination cannot be challenged on its merits solely because the procedures invoked do not meet some independent standard. In these cases, the level of protection afforded is a function of some combination of market conditions and individual bargaining. The firm that gives little protection will have to offer some extra compensation to employees, especially if they are asked to make front-end investments in their new jobs. In competitive labor markets, the "greater" right to fire at will allows the firm to condition employment rights as it pleases, unless some statutory requirement intervenes.

In the early case of *Arnett v. Kennedy*,[48] Justice Rehnquist applied this general view of the world to a nonprobationary civil service employee in the Office of Economic Opportunity who was dismissed for falsely and recklessly accusing his superior of bribery. The applicable provisions of the Lloyd-La Follette Act[49] gave him a right to reply to the charges against him and to inspect the record on which those charges were based, but it did not afford him a full trial-type hearing before his dismissal from office could be put into effect. The statute also provided Kennedy with the right to a post-dismissal hearing, with back pay in the event that the earlier dismissal was in error. The decision of the three-member district court panel found that the omission of the prior hearing counted as a failure to afford the needed level of due process protection.[50] That decision was reversed in the Supreme Court by a fractured majority that relied on two different approaches. Justice Rehnquist, whose position commanded only two other votes, insisted that the substantive and procedural elements of the employment contract could not be disentangled. The procedures were bound up in the definition of the substantive property right, such that the employee "must take the bitter with the sweet."[51] The more cautious view of Justices Powell and Blackmun was that the full package of benefits passed muster, not on this freedom of contract ground, but for the simple reason that the full mixture of pre- and post-termination protections sufficed "by providing a reasonable accommodation of the competing interests."[52] Justice White dissented on the ground that the Due Process Clause did indeed require a pre-termination hearing. His views came to dominate a decade later in *Cleveland Board of Education v. Loudermill*,[53] which held that the pre-termination process was indeed required for teachers who could only be dismissed for cause, insisting that the substance and procedures had to be kept distinct, for "[w]ere the rule otherwise, the Clause would be reduced to a mere tautology."[54]

In these public employment cases, the disfavored Rehnquist position is in principle correct. The initial point is that the Due Process Clause is not reduced to a tautology in all cases so long as it provides standard protections for preexisting property that the state does not create by its own contracts. In this latter setting, there is ample evidence that the political process already provides some forms of protection, such as the statutory protections made available in *Arnett*, so that the central challenge is to figure out why those fall short. In this regard, one touchstone is the level of protection that is afforded teachers under contracts that they enter into with private employers in competitive markets, where the legal norm typically tolerates arrangements under which employees may be dismissed at will. In those contexts, a well-drafted contract seamlessly covers both substantive and procedural issues. Wholly apart from union contracts, most employers find it in their interest to extend additional protections against arbitrary dismissal in order to attract qualified teachers into their ranks. I see no reason why public bodies should be encumbered by heavy protections against dismissal, when these are capable of imposing major dislocations on the operation of the system as a whole. The teaching market remains competitive, so much is lost by imposing a straitjacket—indeed the wrong straitjacket—on school districts which should presumptively be allowed the same level of discretion on their administrative affairs as private institutions. Neither *Arnett* nor *Loudermill* raised any issue of the abuse of government power that might trigger the application of the unconstitutional conditions doctrine, so the decision should be regarded as an unfortunate ossification of public employment law, and not a wise protection of individual constitutional rights.

What Process Is Due

In light of the previous discussion, there is often a complex relationship between the definition of property rights and the procedural protections that the state should offer against their deprivation. Yet, as the earlier discussion indicates, the level of protection required should vary as a function of whether the rights claims are individual rights in the Lockean tradition versus those which are created by contract with or grant from the state. In dealing with the former category, the most dangerous application of state power lies in the imposition of criminal sanctions that can result in the loss of life, liberty, or property, and at this point the level of protections is at its zenith. Thus in an endless array of cases, the Supreme Court has aggressively applied the Due Process Clause guarantees. Thus due process requires proof beyond a reasonable doubt in juvenile delinquency proceedings in all instances where a juvenile is charged with an act that would be a crime if committed by an adult,[55] and in cases of hate crimes, all aggravating elements are subject to a similar high standard of proof.[56] There is no dispute that the most extensive protections should be conferred on individuals charged with serious crimes that could result in death, imprisonment, or forfeiture of property.

The situation differs once the government seeks to deprive individuals of rights that they receive from the government by way of contract or grant. The arguments above about *Arnett* and *Loudermill* make the case that loss of employment in competitive markets should not be subject to special protections. The question is whether the mix of pre-termination and post-termination protections that a government agency is prepared to give should apply in other contexts. The early decision in *Murray's Lessee* takes the sensible position that ex ante protections can be constitutionally reduced where ex post relief can correct the imbalances in question by the payment of money with interest. Applying this principle to the public context, the question of whether someone is entitled to a pre-termination hearing is tantamount to asking whether the government can be enjoined from taking away those benefits first. That inquiry closely resembles the balancing of equities in the private law. That inquiry is commonly undertaken to determine whether a private party should receive an injunction against either a private or public body by asking this one deceptively simple question of "the requirements of equity practice with a background of several hundred years of history."[57] A court "must balance the competing claims of injury and must consider the effect on each party of the granting or withholding of the requested relief."[58] That choice is often said to reduce to four factors under which the plaintiff who seeks a permanent injunction must demonstrate:

(1) that it has suffered an irreparable injury; (2) that remedies available at law, such as monetary damages, are inadequate to compensate for that injury; (3) that, considering the balance of hardships between the plaintiff and defendant, a remedy in equity is warranted; and (4) that the public interest would not be disserved by a permanent injunction.[59]

In dealing with these factors, the first and second are best understood as mirror images of each other. The third addresses many of the issues relevant here, because it poses directly the question of the costs of two kinds of error, which in *Murray's Lessee* was resolved in favor of the government. The last factor is sufficiently pliable that it often has little influence at all once the other factors have been taken into account. On this score, the logic in favor of the government's position in *Murray's Lessee* is that it minimizes on the sum of error and transaction costs, which is the prime objective of any system that seeks to balance equities between the parties. So long as the government knows that its decisions can be challenged after the fact, it should take steps to reduce the likelihood of costly review. Accordingly, that heightened level of care should reduce the fraction of cases that require more extensive post-termination procedures. The after-the-fact hearing should cut down on the error rate in pre-termination hearings.

That same logic applies, perhaps with greater force, in *North American Cold Storage Co. v. City of Chicago*,[60] where Justice Rufus Peckham (of fame for his defense of liberty of contract in *Lochner v. New York*)[61] took the position that Chicago could seize and destroy food that it found "putrid, decayed, poisonous or infected" on the grounds that a post-seizure hearing at which compensation for goods improperly seized could be supplied, precisely because the city's exercise of its police power responsibilities could easily be compromised by delay. The decision involves, in the case of private right, the correct balancing under the Due Process Clause of two kinds of errors. The harms caused by the distribution of these dangerous products are widespread and irreversible. The harms caused by their incorrect seizure can be corrected by money. The general principles for balancing equities thus offer a roadmap as to what process is "due" in this class of cases. The same rule applies also, albeit with somewhat less urgency, to the summary collection of back taxes sustained in *Phillips v. Commissioner of Internal Revenue*,[62] for here the risk of insolvency of the taxpayer is greater than that of the United States Treasury. Yet ironically, when the issue comes to the question of whether private parties should be entitled to ex parte relief, the Court showed a great hostility to those procedures in *Sniadach v. Family Finance Corp.*,[63] when a majority of the Supreme Court invalidated a Wisconsin garnishment procedure under which the creditor was allowed to attach the assets before giving notice to the garnishee. In a consumer case, Justice Douglas held that even same-day notice did not meet the requirements of due process, a conclusion that seems both overwrought and wrong so long as the debtor has a chance to contest the lien before it is foreclosed. The risk that the moneys will disappear before they are attached is at least as great as it is in the tax cases, and the protections to the debtor far stronger. The balance of error clearly allows, even if it does not compel, the Wisconsin procedure, so that in this case at least Justice Black's protest that the Court acted as if it "had been granted a super-legislative power" has some real traction.[64]

The question of the appropriate balance carries over as well to the issuance by governments of various permits and licenses. Only here the balance shifts because, given the central role of the state, the individual in question no longer has the benefit of multiple options in the competitive market but has to deal with the monopoly power of the state which, as noted earlier, imposes general duties on it to deal with all persons in a reasonable and nondiscriminatory matter, such that on any correct balance of interests the case for a pre-termination hearing becomes stronger than might otherwise prove the case. Thus in *Bell v. Burson*,[65] Georgia law provided that the license of an uninsured driver had to be suspended if he did not have sufficient funds to serve as security against the pending claim. The Supreme Court, speaking through Justice Brennan, held that this determination required a pre-termination hearing for answering that question. Unlike *Loudermill*, the government licensee acted as a monopoly regulator, not as a participant in a competitive market. These proceedings had nothing to do with the potential safety risk that the driver posed to third parties, so the balance of equities seems to favor the pre-termination hearing, especially in the case of a clergyman who needed to drive his car to perform his duties in several rural counties. Suspending the license does not put any cash into the hands of a potential tort victim, but it could easily deprive the driver of his livelihood. Other cases may present a different balance of equities, but a per se rule in favor of the hearings should be adopted for its ease of administration.

The role of monopoly power is evident in *Wisconsin v. Constantineau*,[66] when state law forbade the sale of intoxicating liquors to any person who "by excessive drinking" exposed himself or his family "to want" or to becoming "dangerous to the peace."[67] The case is a rerun of the defamation issues raised in *Joint Anti-Fascist Refugee Committee*, with the following twist. The defamation in question was caused by posted notices in all liquor stores in town, instructing them not to sell to the plaintiffs, which lent a degree of specificity to the government regulation that was not present in the earlier case. But either way, so long as defamation does invade a liberty interest, the hearing is required because of the blanket effect of the regulation. Those governed by it have no other market alternative.

The most difficult cases perhaps are those that involve the distribution of government benefits, of which the two most common types deal with welfare and social security. In neither case is the government the only party that can supply this form of protection. Yet by the same token, the vulnerability of the target population makes the "bitter with the sweet" argument from *Arnett* more difficult to swallow. Fortunately, the cases that challenge various termination schemes have never adopted the position that they may be cut off at will, so that the only question is whether the constitutional concerns with procedural due process are sufficient to overrule state decisions that allow the cancellation of benefits only after an elaborate pre-termination examination of the record. That procedure included notification in writing of the reasons for the determination and allowed the welfare recipient to present in writing objections, alone or with the aid of a lawyer, to a unit supervisor within seven days of that notification. But the procedures did not call for a full-blown pre-termination hearing. In *Goldberg v. Kelly*,[68] Justice Brennan led a six-member majority of the Court to hold that the pre-termination hearing was strictly necessary in this case, in light of the severe dislocation that the loss of welfare benefits can cause. Even if we assume that welfare benefits should be treated as a "right" and not a "privilege," it hardly follows that the extra layer of protection is needed. Not only is there the additional expense of multiple hearings, but there is also the risk that the delay in removing some individuals from the welfare rolls will reduce the rate at which new individuals can be enrolled. Unless therefore there is some reason to think that the error rate of those

pre-termination procedures is high, these measures seem to satisfy all
constitutional standards, especially since it is unclear exactly how the
proposed hearing should take place. Quite simply, the calipers used to
determine the balance of equities does not drive toward this result.

The parallel situation under social security involves the termination
of social security disability payments, where once again the administrative procedures involved had elaborate pre-termination procedures
without benefit of a full pre-termination hearing. It is an open question
whether the loss of benefits counts more for a welfare recipient than a
disabled person, but in *Mathews v. Eldridge*,[69] the Court used a three-part
balancing test which resembles the balancing of equities in private law:

> [F]irst, the private interest that will be affected by the official action; sec-
> ond, the risk of an erroneous deprivation of such interest through the
> procedures used, and the probable value, if any, of additional or substitute
> procedural safeguards; and, finally, the Government's interest, including
> the function involved and the fiscal and administrative burdens that the
> additional or substitute procedural requirement would entail.[70]

In the end, *Mathews* isolated *Goldberg*, by holding that welfare termination proceedings are more draconian than the loss of disability benefits, because the former termination is based on "financial need" while
disability benefits are not. Yet the entire distinction seems fragile beyond
belief given that most people with disabilities have financial needs as
well. Therefore, *Mathews* should be read as a gentle repudiation of *Goldberg*, which itself does not seem deserving of continued support even in
the restricted area of welfare benefits.

Taken as a whole, this brief survey of procedural due process by and
large shows the retention of classical liberal principles throughout an
area in which the dangers of the use of state power are greatest. Consistent with that theory, the procedural protections should be the strongest
when the state seeks to deprive individuals of life, liberty, or property,
which it is the purpose of the government to protect. That protection is
also greatest in those cases, as with the issuance of permits and licenses,
where the state in the exercise of its monopoly power is obliged to treat
all persons in a reasonable and nondiscriminatory fashion. The claims
for constitutional protection are weakest when the government functions in a competitive market or supplies benefits to individuals that it is
not obliged to do, as in cases of welfare and social security benefits. The

correspondence between general theory and legal results holds quite strong in this area, with the notable exception being *Goldberg v. Kelly*, which is one case in which the progressive mindset has influenced for the worse the overall direction of the law. That progressive influence has had far greater effects in many substantive areas that involve traditional concerns with liberty and property, as the next chapter suggests.

21

Freedom of Contract

IN THE DOMAIN of negative rights, the initial constitutional forays had to
do with property rights and economic liberties. Historically, the magnitude of the shift in political and constitutional orientation between the
(largely) classical liberal and the (largely) progressive view is captured
in one critical flip-flop. Roughly speaking, economic liberties, and to
a lesser extent property rights, received strong protection in the pre-
1937 era and far weaker protection thereafter. Personal rights travel the
reverse track from weak protection before the New Deal transformation
to stronger protection thereafter. In both settings, the interplay between
the scope of the basic right and the scope of the justification tells the tale.
It is worth tracing the journeys in broad outline. This chapter looks at
freedom of contract; the next chapter looks at takings of private property.

Freedom of Contract, Then and Now

Classical liberal theory contains no limiting principle that accounts for a
categorical difference between economic and personal rights. The basic
rules speak of strong autonomy and property rights alike, which form
the bases for voluntary transactions initiated for mutual gain. Subjective estimations of value are what drive voluntary exchange. The standard contract theory leaves it for the parties to decide on the goods or
services that constitute part of the exchange, and thereafter the price,
terms, and conditions on which the exchange takes place. That theory
takes the same view toward noneconomic associational matters dealing
with the formation of families, partnerships, churches, and the like. The

subdivisions within the grand theory—sales, mortgages, partnerships, leases, employment—only mark out specialized areas to aid in setting default provisions to fill in the terms of contracts, some of which have been left unstated (e.g., implied warranties on the quality of goods sold).

Freedom of contract in classical liberal theory thus becomes a universal ideal that does not turn on content-based norms. The only limitations that matter deal with two issues, both of which afford police power justifications for regulation: first, fraud and other misconduct in forming the agreement and second, adverse effects on third parties, as with conspiracies to commit crimes, raise prices, or organize cartels. Otherwise, to the classical liberal, the terms of the contract were left for the parties to devise.

Historically, however, matters were never so tidy. Economic liberty was strongly (if imperfectly) protected until the 1937 Supreme Court transformation. Thus, the old Supreme Court cases supported competition over both government and private monopolies, even if they could not formally explain why. Health and safety were construed narrowly to strike down anticompetitive legislation that often bore heaviest on persons with little political power. Under this paradigm, a maximum hours law for bakers was rejected as an infringement of basic liberty in the (in)famous 1905 decision of *Lochner v. New York*.[1]

The old Court was right and the modern critics are wrong. Doctrinally, two moves drove the *Lochner* invalidation of the New York maximum hours law. The first was a broad reading of liberty under the Due Process Clause of the Fourteenth Amendment.[2] That move was first accomplished by Justice Rufus Peckham in the 1897 decision in *Allgeyer v. Louisiana*:

> The liberty mentioned in that [Fourteenth] amendment means not only the right of the citizen to be free from the mere physical restraint of his person, as by incarceration, but the term is deemed to embrace the right of the citizen to be free in the enjoyment of all his faculties; to be free to use them in all lawful ways; to live and work where he will; to earn his livelihood by any lawful calling; to pursue any livelihood or avocation, and for that purpose to enter into all contracts which may be proper, necessary and essential to his carrying out to a successful conclusion the purposes above mentioned.[3]

The second stage of the *Lochner* argument treated the New York law as a "labor" statute intended to disrupt competition outside the legitimate police power interest in safety and health. That conclusion has been strongly attacked, but Justice Peckham surely had the better argument. The hour restrictions in question were limited only to those types of bakers who were directly competing with union bakers, not those in other lines that might be subject to the same health and safety risks. In Lochner, the union bakers worked a night and a morning shift, both of which could meet the ten-hour restrictions. Lochner's bakers worked longer hours, but slept in separate quarters on the premises between their evening and morning shifts, which accounted for their long hours. None of the bakers complained about the arrangement in what was, after all, a criminal prosecution.

This facially neutral statute thus had a disparate impact on two competitive forms of production. The World Trade Organization today is on the lookout for protectionist legislation or administrative actions that masquerade as health statutes.[4] Justice Peckham anticipated that approach when courts had trouble getting hard evidence on the slippery question of legislative motivation. Justice John Marshall Harlan's dissent stressed genuine health issues in bakeries over time and around the world, but did not examine either the structure of this statute or the institutional context that surrounded the legislation. Justice Oliver Wendell Holmes's lone dissent merely asserted that the law could be justified on grounds of health.

The rival progressive view attacked both halves of the classical liberal synthesis. Under the progressive view, "liberty" in the Fourteenth Amendment only applied to incarceration and other restrictions on an individual's physical movement.[5] That view also gave a broad reading to the police power by rejecting Justice Peckham's four-part test in favor of a position that allowed the state to interfere with market forces to equalize the vast disparities of wealth between corporate employers and their individual employees. Within the classical legal tradition, the subsequent decisions in *Adair v. United States*[6] and *Coppage v. Kansas*,[7] which both involved striking down statutes that required employers to bargain collectively with workers, were easy results, however contrary they are to modern U.S. labor policy. At this point, the lurking health issues in *Lochner* were gone, removing any police power counterweight to freedom of contract. Justice Mahlon Pitney in *Coppage* did not treat the rejection of collective bargaining as a matter of partisan advantage, but rightly concluded that in all regimes of private property and freedom of contract, "the contract is made to the very end that each may gain something that he needs or desires more urgently than that which he proposes to give in exchange."[8] These exchanges for mutual gain often lead to greater disparities in wealth, while at the same time generating an overall social improvement in which the gains are shared by all parties to the transaction.

Justice Pitney's position was far preferable to Justice Holmes's view in dissent. Justice Holmes was evidently ambivalent about the wisdom of this labor legislation, but thought that the question was not for him to decide. He therefore would have sustained the statutes because workmen could think the new arrangement "fair," whether or not it led to mutual gains. He thus insisted that the scheme "may be enforced by law in order to establish the equality of position between the parties in which liberty of contract begins."[9] But this elegant formulation conceals an economic blunder by ignoring the simple point that mutual benefits arise from voluntary exchanges no matter how great the initial wealth differentials may be. Socially, why would we say that the only contracts that are allowed are those that give workers sufficient benefits to overcome some disparity? Individually, why would a poor person enter into any agreement that left him systematically worse off? Nor, of course, can any labor statute equalize either wealth or bargaining power. A labor statute can, however, give a union a monopoly position by imposing a duty to bargain on the company, only to compound the social losses by imposing higher administrative costs, yielding lower output overall. All too often the greatest union victories turn out to be the seeds of their long-term decline. The United Auto Workers secured hugely favorable contracts with Chrysler, Ford, and General Motors in 1979, only to lose over 75 percent of its membership—1.53 million members in 1979 to 701,818 in 2001, to 382,500 members in 2012—after reaching a low of 355,000 members in 2009.[10]

Justice Holmes's argument encapsulated the fundamental confusion of all progressive thinkers who equate large firm size with market power (which, if present, could be handled under the antitrust laws that the classical liberal judges, including Justice Peckham, sustained).[11] Large corporations that offer lower salaries and inferior working conditions won't be able to compete against more efficient, smaller competitors. But large corporations, with their extensive demand for labor, will tend to push the demand curves outward, thereby raising overall wages. The historical movement of wages and hours tracked this neoclassical view. Wages moved up and hours moved downward throughout this period as productivity improved and income rose. The picture was wholly consistent with the simple rules of supply and demand.[12]

Nonetheless, the progressive juggernaut counted among its successes the unanimous 1908 Supreme Court decision in *Muller v. Oregon*,[13] written by the influential conservative justice, David J. Brewer. *Muller* upheld a maximum hours statute that applied only to women, on the grounds that the delicate condition of women required specialized treatment.[14] The result may well have been attributed to the so-called Brandeis brief that offered a "scientific" survey of the existing literature on the subject. In actuality, the brief was little more than a disorganized recitation of countless public reports in support of the position, offered without a shred of independent analysis.[15] The result of this form of protectionism was of course to drive women out of markets in which they had previously been able to successfully compete. Kurt Muller "apparently fired" all of his female workers, only to replace them with Chinese males.[16] The passage of time has this irony. The Brandeis position on the need for special legislative protection for women has few supporters today. These statutes do not protect women, but exclude them from gainful occupations. What passed as advanced science in 1908 now counts as a per se form of sex discrimination that fails under modern readings of the Equal Protection Clause.[17]

Nonetheless, the die was cast. By the 1930s, the classical liberal position was in disarray. The Railway Labor Act of 1926,[18] the Norris-LaGuardia Act of 1932,[19] the National Labor Relations Act of 1935, and the Fair Labor Standards Act of 1938[20] all represented massive interferences in labor markets that received the blessing of the Supreme Court, on grounds similar to those stated in the early Justice Holmes dissents. The Fair Labor Standards Act of 1938 deals with minimum wage, maximum hours, and overtime. In addressing its constitutionality under the Commerce Clause in *United States v. Darby*,[21] Justice Stone took at face value the congressional claim that the FLSA was needed "to prevent the use of interstate commerce as the means of competition in the distribution of goods so produced, and as the means of spreading and perpetuating such substandard labor conditions among the workers of the several states." Just how competition among firms could decrease the standard of working conditions—when just the opposite is the expected economic result—has never been explained, then or now. The narrow definition of liberty and the broad account of the police power had done their jobs. The higher unemployment and disastrous breakdowns in heavily unionized industries—such as with automobiles and steel—were a legacy for another day.

Rate Regulation

It is also possible to trace out a similar arc for the protection of private property against confiscation under both the Takings and the Due Process Clauses of the Constitution. The basic problem with a so-called natural monopoly is that over the relevant portion of the supply curve, a single firm can add on additional units of output at a lower cost than a new entrant could supply them. This declining average-cost model means that a single firm is the most efficient producer. Yet at the same time, that producer has a strong incentive to raise its prices to monopoly levels. The regulation of natural monopolies could, in the short run, tend to reduce these costs to a competitive level, even at the risk of sacrificing innovation in the long run.[22]

The situation seemed to cry out for regulation, but the issue was how the new rates were to be set. Rate regulation is justified (uneasily) in classical liberal terms as a means to protect consumers against monopolistic expropriation. Yet unlimited rate regulation exposed railroads to the confiscation of the capital they had to invest before beginning operations. Low rates that covered the incremental cost of services would mean that it benefited a railroad to stay in business even if it could not recover its capital over the life of the investment. The various formulas for counteracting that risk were varied and complex. Sometimes public utility commissions scrutinized expenditures to see that they were necessary for operations; if so, under the rule in the 1898 decision in *Smyth v. Ames*, the rate of return had to be higher to compensate for the additional risks.[23] In dealing with this issue, the Court in *Board of Public Utility Commissioners v. New York Telephone*[24] insisted that all the accounts be balanced on an annualized basis, to prevent the ruse of cutting rates in one period on the dubious promise that they could be made up in the next. "Profits of the past cannot be used to sustain confiscatory rates for the future."[25]

In choosing rates, however, the Court by 1944 was prepared to allow the use of an alternative methodology that required the ratepayers to bear the risk of unwise investments. But that relaxation came only at the price of a lower rate of return, but one which was still sufficient to allow, in Justice Douglas's famous formulation in *Federal Power Commission v. Hope Natural Gas*, the regulated utility to "maintain its credit" and "attract capital" needed for it to remain in business.[26] So long therefore as the utility can maintain its bottom line, the Court should not scrutinize the calculations line by line to correct any errors made in the overall calculations.

In dealing with this issue, the justices before 1937 were aware that more was at stake in setting rates than the overall rate of return to the regulated industry. Also at stake were the relative prices charged to different customer groups, where the risk was that favorable rates to one group of customers could result in a dangerous form of cross-subsidization, which would allow various interest groups to foist the costs of their businesses onto others. The adverse economic consequence of that political intrigue is the distortion of the relative price of goods subject to state regulation. Thus in 1899 the Court through Justice Peckham struck down a Michigan statute that required the railroad to issue below market price one-thousand-mile tickets to preferred customers. "If the general power [to regulate] exist[s], then the legislature can direct the company to charge smaller rates for clergymen or doctors, for lawyers or farmers or school teachers, for excursions, for church conventions, political conventions, or for [anyone else]."[27] That theme was echoed in 1915. The Court, in *Northern Pacific Railway Co. v. North Dakota*,[28] made clear the limits of regulation: "But, broad as is the power of regulation, the State does not enjoy the freedom of an owner. . . . If [a common carrier] has held itself out as a carrier of passengers only, it cannot be compelled to carry freight. . . . In such a case, it would be no answer to say that the carrier obtains from its entire intrastate business a return as to the sufficiency of which in the aggregate it is not entitled to complain."[29] In the companion case of *Norfolk & Western v. Conley*,[30] the Court found that to subsidize rates for passengers' freight with unduly high rates on other freight was beyond the permissible limits of regulation by the state, given the distortions that take place between the two services. In all these cases, the ideal is to make sure that each line of business stands on its own bottom, so that it becomes impermissible, for example, to lower rates in a regulated industry on the ground that the firm could make up its losses on unregulated but profitable businesses. As Justice Holmes wrote in *Brooks-Scanlon Co. v. Railroad Commission*, "The plaintiff may be making money from its sawmill and lumber business, but it no more can be compelled to spend that than it can be compelled to spend any other money to maintain a railroad for the benefit of others who do not care to pay for it."[31]

This model of rate regulation has been compromised in the years since the Second World War. Thus in the 1953 decision in *Baltimore & Ohio Railway*, railroad rates set by the Interstate Commerce Commission were challenged on the ground that they required the B & O Railroad to carry fresh vegetables from Texas at reduced rates that did not allow them to recover their costs. The majority of the Court followed Justice Black when he threw up his hands saying that the matter of rate regulation over a complex network is so multifaceted that it becomes improper to look at a single rate in isolation. Justice Douglas, who had written the Court's decision in *Hope Natural Gas*, refused to rest content with the bottom-line formula of that case. Instead, he cited back to *Norfolk & Western* for the correct proposition that excessive discretion in the choice of rates could lead to a distortion of competition between rival markets, which indeed happened in this case under a rate structure that subsidized Texas produce at the expense of rivals in Arizona, California, and New Mexico. It was critical to allow the railroads to challenge those rates, moreover, because under settled rate regulation law, the disadvantaged producers had no standing to deal with the matter, as only the direct subjects of the rate regulation had standing to challenge the rates.[32]

Most of the rate cases in-between tended to move toward the rational basis side of the spectrum, by allowing rates to be set in the aggregate in ways that did not pay sufficient attention to the risks of cross-subsidies. Thus in the *Permian Basin Area Rate Cases*,[33] the Court upheld the Federal Power Commission's extensive discretion over the way in which rates were allocated across different firms operating in different portions of the market. For the most part, however, the Court in the modern era has waded only infrequently into matters of rate regulation. Most significantly in *Duquesne Light Co. v. Barasch*, Chief Justice Rehnquist adopted a defensible synthesis by letting public utility commissions adopt the *Smyth v. Ames* or the *Hope Natural Gas Standard,* so long as it followed a consistent methodology.[34] The cracks in that synthesis were evident, however, insofar as *Duquesne Light* allowed a *retroactive* disallowance of previously approved rates when there was a change in legislative policy.[35] Retroactivity is the sign of an unprincipled expansion of government power, which Rehnquist justified on the ground that the overall allowable rate of return under *Hope Natural Gas* was above the permissible level. But that logic misses the key importance of getting each regulatory decision right, so as to avoid rate instability that opens administrative agencies to political intrigue by introducing the kind of cross-subsidies that cannot survive in a competitive market. Indeed that logic, if extended, would allow a court to reduce the gains that a seller has on a contract of sale so long as the money paid gives a reasonable rate of return. It is easy to police retroactivity and wise to do so.

The far larger deviation from classical liberal principles arose in the ratemaking cases under the Telecommunications Act of 1996,[36] which imposed an elaborate regime of forced cooperation to allow new carriers to enter into competition with the incumbent Bell Operating Companies. Under the act, each of the new carriers had an exclusive franchise in its own territory under the litigation that broke up AT&T in 1982.[37] The statute was then intended to force the incumbent carriers either to interconnect with new entrants or to sell off pieces of their network to the newcomers at prices determined by the Federal Communications Commission (FCC). Those prices were based solely on "forward-looking" costs—technically called Total Element Long-Run Incremental Cost (TELRIC). That formulation assumed, however, that the network in place had adopted the best technology at that moment. In effect, the inevitable risk of technical deterioration in system value, from its inception to the time of ratemaking, fell on the incumbent carrier. Thus, if all the elements were sold off to new carriers, the incumbent carrier could never recover its costs of putting the system into place over its useful life. The propriety of the cost recovery rule never faced the constitutional challenge it deserved because the Supreme Court showed complete deference to the FCC regulations as a matter of administrative law. Thus, the FCC did not have to set rates based on these "historical" costs in the absence of a clear legislative mandate.[38] That same deference would surely have been given under the rational basis test if a constitutional challenge had been raised.

Here, the deviation from classical liberal principles is far more pro-found than it was in the earlier decisions, which paired a large rate base with a low rate of return and a small rate base with a high rate of return. In this context, the FCC imposed on the incumbent carriers the worst of both worlds by setting a narrow rate base with a low rate of return—the one impermissible combination. There is no argument for administrative deference in the face of clear conceptual error, even if it should be allowed in those issues on which it is hard to get clear answers, such as the allocation of joint costs between two different services that operate off a common platform. All too often, however, the Supreme Court treats all regulatory judgments as if they were cut from the same cloth. It is regrettable how easy it is to stray from sound constitutional principles by an indifference to technical issues of lasting importance—a problem that is repeated yet again in the takings cases considered in the next chapter.

22

Takings, Physical and Regulatory

T HE DIFFERENCES between the classical liberal and progressive positions are also evident whenever government takes or regulates private property, most notably, but not exclusively, in the context of land use. The operative constitutional provision provides, simply enough: "nor shall private property be taken for public use, without just compensation."[1] It should come as no surprise that this provision lies at the heart of the dispute between the classical liberal and progressive views of government. Strong property rights operate as a constraint against government power, for so long as the government must compensate when property is taken, its distinctive government power of eminent domain is hedged in by a price constraint that forces governments at all levels to compare the value of the property taken with the public resources needed to acquire it. As the price for condemnations goes up, the frequency of these condemnations goes down as well. Indeed, with takings, as with torts, the chief gain from strong sanctions lies not in the compensation that government must supply after the fact, but in the incentive that the just compensation imposes on both federal and state governments not to condemn or regulate at all.

The Original Understanding of the Takings Clause

This system will only work well if the courts articulate clear and powerful rules to govern this critical use of government power. Once again, it is no accident that the choice of the constitutional standard of review largely determines the effectiveness of this sanction on inefficient or excessive takings. It is therefore no surprise that when the Supreme Court invalidates a government initiative, it typically starts with a confident reiteration of this proposition from *Armstrong v. United States*:[2]

> The Fifth Amendment's guarantee that private property shall not be taken for a public use without just compensation was designed to bar Government from forcing some people alone to bear public burdens which, in all fairness and justice, should be borne by the public as a whole.

Justice Hugo Black applied this principle to require the government to compensate a subcontractor when it dissolved its valid lien that was given under Maine law for materials provided by a subcontractor for construction of navy personnel boats. The United States dissolved the lien by moving the unfinished boats to out-of-state naval shipyards. Why should the subcontractor foot the bill for assisting national defense that supplies him no special benefit? The *Armstrong* principle has strong constitutional legs. Virtually every property-protective decision cites the *Armstrong* proposition without qualification. In contrast, every decision that rejects property rights claims soft soaps the *Armstrong* principle by announcing, regrettably, that fixed rules must yield to "ad hoc" determinations that require the exercise of sound political discretion, which is then insulated from judicial review under the rational basis test.[3] In many cases, the line drawn is between those takings that involve a physical occupation of land and those that involve a regulation of how a property owner may use or dispose of that property. Under current law, the former are subject to examination under a strict scrutiny standard, while the latter are subject to the far more forgiving rational basis test.

The key question in this area of law is how this distinction maps onto the takings law proper. One historical reading of the Takings Clause, long championed by William Michael Treanor, insists that a close study of the historical record shows that the Takings Clause "required compensation when the government physically took private property, but not when government regulations limited the ways in which property could be used."[4] Before 1787, the books contained many statutory provisions that offer limited protection against the taking of certain protected types of tangible property. Thus a provision of the Massachusetts Body of Liberties from 1641 applies only to "Cattel or goods of what kinde soever."[5] Similarly a provision drafted by John Locke for the South Carolina Constitution only provided for protection against the seizure of "real property."[6] But as is the case with the Due Process Clause,[7] the Takings Clause replaces references to specific types of property with the broader protection of "private property"—which generally covers property interests of all types. On this score, the broader account of property offered in John Locke's *Second Treatise*, embracing "lives, liberties and estates," maps far better onto the Takings Clause than these earlier more asset-specific provisions.

One strength of the broader provision is that it maps onto a central feature of the Anglo-American property system, which recognizes partial interests in private property that fall short of outright, permanent, and perpetual ownership. Accordingly, the standard account of private property has both a physical and legal dimension. On the former, the boundaries of land go from the center of the earth to the top of the heavens, so no physical element is left without an owner. The incidents of ownership over that land include the right to exclude all others from its use, the right to use the land consistent with the like rights of neighbors, and the right to dispose of the land in whole or in part to any other person on whatever terms and conditions seem fit—subject, of course, to the same limitations on freedom of contract developed in the previous chapter. More critically, the system also recognizes that it is possible to create lesser interests in land, some of which are possessory, like life estates and leases, and others of which can only vest in the future, like reversions and remainders of different types. In addition, the property system develops extensive rules to govern servitudes, including easements, which make permissible entry into the land of others that would otherwise be a trespass, and covenants which force individuals to abstain from some particular use or development of land that they hold as a matter of ordinary common law property (e.g., covenants to prevent the obstruction of a view).

Conceptually the great vice of the Treanor position is that it assumes that none of the divided interests long protected under the private law receive any constitutional protection. Indeed, it is not clear that the materialman's lien that was dissolved in *Armstrong* counts as property under Treanor's definition. Rather, under Treanor's view, it appears that the government does not take property in cases where it forbids the owner from entering the property without choosing to enter that same property itself, because such aggressive regulation does not count as a case where the government "physically took" property. Yet that result is wholly inconsistent with the general anticircumvention principle, whereby close substitutes for takings should be treated as such in order to make sure that government actors do not break free of the fetters designed to bind them.[8] Absolute exclusion is "tantamount" to a physical taking, even if the government never sets foot on the property.

Treanor is aware that the historical evidence offers no single provision that has the breadth of the coverage found in the Takings Clause. He therefore seeks to shrink the gap between the historical record and his own narrow definition of physical takings by resort to two prominent strands of constitutional theory. The first is the "political process" theories of John Ely, developed in his well-known 1980 constitutional masterpiece, *Democracy and Distrust: A Theory of Judicial Review.* The second is found in the "fidelity in translation theories" of Lawrence Lessig.[9]

Ely's basic claim is that judicial review is most appropriate when breakdowns of the political process are most likely. Treanor claims that this is far greater in cases of actual occupation of property rather than in cases where only legal restrictions are imposed on its use or disposition. Under this approach, the target is the skewed substantive outcomes that are typically the products of skewed processes, which result in implicit or explicit wealth transfers from one group to another.[10] A simple modern example is a general master development plan that zones one parcel industrial and the one across the highway agricultural, thereby increasing the value of the first plot at the expense of the second. Actions of that sort are a constant peril to good government, and classical liberal theory seeks to rein them in without destroying the power of government to discharge its essential functions. But why is the likelihood of the breakdown of the political process confined to the occupation of property, and not cases of regulation? To be sure, there may be fewer cases in which the permanent occupation of private property can be justified under the sound rules of limited government. But there are surely some. It was commonplace during colonial times, as Treanor notes, for governments to take land without paying any cash compensation to its owner.[11] But the land taken was vacant, and the purpose was the construction of public works, such as building a public highway. The explanation for the practice was supplied by Treanor: "As historian Forrest McDonald has observed of this practice, 'New England colonial governments compensated landowners for taking part of their land by letting them keep the remainder of their land.'"[12] There is nothing in the Constitution requiring that all compensation be in cash. In-kind compensation does the job as well. Access to markets was key for farmers and miners. The surrender of some land increased the value of the retained land, so that the landowner was better off with smaller holdings made more valuable by their connection to the highway system. Why require explicit compensation when the in-kind compensation has made the landowner better off than before?

An identical conceptual frame can be used to deal with the land use regulations of modern times that Treanor does not discuss. In this context, the elaborate system of reciprocal covenants over a common may also provide the in-kind compensation that makes the payment of cash unnecessary and wasteful. But by the same token, the takings analysis of regulation also flips over for regulations that impose large losses on particular owners who receive only limited benefits in return. The question of whether these regulations work for mutual advantage depends critically on the level of judicial oversight supplied. Let that be lax and political forces will result in massive wealth transfers. Let it be assiduous, and the land regulations are far more likely to produce balanced gains across the board. There is, in principle, no reason why the taking of a restrictive covenant, worth millions, should be allowed without compensation when the related form of servitude, the possessory easement, requires full compensation from the state. Unfortunately, Treanor offers no explanation as to how Ely's political process story fails to map onto the distinction between physical and regulatory takings, but applies to both equally.

The translation approach from Lessig fares no better. The object of this inquiry is whether changed political circumstances allow the updating of original understandings to extend the scope of a particular clause. Treanor, following Lessig, notes, "contemporary takings jurisprudence means that courts today should protect those whose property interests are, given modern political realities, particularly unlikely to receive fair consideration from majoritarian decisionmakers."[13] But at this point, Lessig's effort to explain why legal norms should evolve is redundant because it covers the precise ground of the anticircumvention principle, which deals with just that risk. Indeed, Lessig's translation line is likely to yield inferior results because it purportedly depends on a global understanding of "modern political realities," which could easily vary from time to time and place to place. Again that ex ante evaluation of generalized probabilities and tendencies serves no useful purpose when it is possible, after the fact in any individual case, to make an assessment of whether a particular taking has been met with compensation, express or implied, or justified under some conception of the police power. I have long championed a consciously ahistorical application of the Takings Clause to regulatory issues. Oddly enough that approach makes more sense of the historical record than Treanor's self-conscious appeal to history.

The Classical Liberal Account of the Takings Clause

Philosophical Foundations

At this point, the key challenge is to give a sound explication of the clause that takes into account both the issues of circumvention on the one hand and police power justifications on the other. I have already conducted two extensive analyses of these problems in my books *Takings*[14] and *Supreme Neglect*,[15] so that it is not necessary to cite chapter and verse for each of the arguments developed in this section. In undertaking this task, the key insight is never to dismiss the insights of the Lockean tradition as an exercise in "possessive individualism" that ignores the effects of property rights on the larger fabric of society.[16] Classical liberalism is not a theory that glorifies private claims of personal or political advantage at the expense of others. To the contrary, it always seeks to channel government action where it is likely to do more good than harm, in part by aligning incentives so that the only way that political actors can advance their own self-interest is by undertaking actions that on balance improve the overall level of social welfare.

Nuisances and Land Use Regulation

This awareness of social consequence bears heavily on the use rights incident to private property. No system of private property lets a person do whatever he will with his land, come hell or high water. From Roman times forward, it has been recognized that limits on land use, uniformly applied, can improve the overall value of all parcels.[17] Clearly, allowing people to enter and use the land of others makes all private property collectively owned. Equally important, any system of private property necessarily restrains the commission of nuisances—usually non-trespassory invasions of waste, pollution, noise, and odors—that emanate from one person's land onto another's. The principle of long-run reciprocal advantage is best satisfied if all owners are presumptively prohibited from engaging in these activities. Here is how we know: when any single owner creates a subdivision, his optimal strategy is to attach a set of rights and duties to each parcel in ways that maximize the total sale value from all purchasers. You can examine a million subdivision agreements, all of which will vary in their restrictions on size, height, setbacks, and exterior design. But not one subdivision agreement will relax the common law prohibition against nuisance, so powerful is its contribution to effective land use regulation. All individuals in a state of nature are better off if they relinquish these rights to damage others in exchange for like protection for themselves.

The major function of the police power is to give the state the means to control these abuses by taking or regulating property without paying any compensation at all. Just that result is proper in disarming a criminal who threatens repeated violence or in abating a nuisance that threatens by filth and odors to invade the property of his neighbor's land. Reading the same ubiquitous police power into the Takings Clause is a sound interpretive step that adds yet another essential piece to the over-all picture, by allowing the government to adopt programs that aid in the effective enforcement of private rights when the high costs of private actions make them insufficient to deter or eliminate wrongful behavior. Many nuisances have multiple sources and/or multiple victims—think of emissions of exhaust from cars or methane gas from animals. Private rights of action often prove too cumbersome relative to direct control of these various forms of pollution by administrative regulation. At this point, the constitutional analysis has both means and ends dimensions. The proper ends under the police power are those of the private law of nuisance, no more and no less. The means are regulations that fit well with the chosen ends, by being neither overbroad nor underinclusive. It is not acceptable, either politically or constitutionally, to limit the pollution from one factory while allowing its next-door competitor to operate free of legal restraint. It is instead necessary to make sure that differential systems of enforcement do not result in the hidden wealth transfers that are prohibited under the Takings Clause. The evenhanded enforcement of the nuisance law is an essential ingredient of the proper constitutional plan.

It is mistaken, however, to think that the controls on these nuisances constitute the sole restrictions that improve real estate values across the board. In addition, the common law has developed a second class of restrictions dealing with what can be called noninvasive nuisances.[18] For example, no one can dig out his land to remove the lateral support of neighboring lands. In some instances, spite fences, erected solely to block a neighbor's view, are subject to action. But these cases are exceptional. For the most part, any additional restrictions needed to maximize land values are so varied that no one-size-fits-all prescription solves all problems. Accordingly, the standard solution allows, especially in the case of lands slated for subdivision, additional restrictive covenants that take into account the particular features of topography and design for each given parcel. These restrictions are usually made reciprocal across all owners. They also "run" with the land so that all successive owners are bound and benefited by the same covenants. One key element is to make sure that the value of the various holdings is constant regardless of the time that any particular owner acquires his or her interest.

What makes land use so difficult is that virtually every act done by one owner has some impact, positive or negative, on others. The common law rules had to be alert, therefore, to the risk that restrictions preventing small external harms could, on average, block land uses with high value to the owner. Hence, wisely missing from the common law list of nuisances are certain common activities: blocking views of neighbors, casting shadows, using bad design, or running a small business in a residential neighborhood. It hardly makes sense to impose uniform restrictions that cost each landowner $1,000 while providing only $100 in benefits to all neighbors. At that point, any uniform imposition only magnifies the social losses stemming from each individual application of the general rule. In the aggregate, these massive prohibitions cost far more than they are worth. If I cannot build to block your view, you cannot build to block mine. To be sure, the two views may not be of equal value, but, even when that is true, it only establishes that the gains that each party has in the original position are not equal. It does not make out a case for transfer payments between us. In both cases, each of us is better off with equal rights of land development than with none. So the original use rights remain. Any two (or more) parties that wish to alter the balance between them are free to do so by entering into restrictive covenants, which again run with the land, to pick up the slack.

This basic principle, moreover, applies to various instances protecting habitat and wetlands from private development. There is little doubt that dedicating lands to these activities counts as a taking of land for a public use. But it does not justify, as is commonly asserted, the regulation of these lands under the police power such that no compensation is provided to offset the losses that its restrictions impose on land use. The basic test that drives this result asks whether all the neighbors of a particular plot of land could employ the common law of nuisance to enjoin the use of a wetland or sensitive habitat, to which the answer has always been no. If not then the state cannot wield its power to force this change in land use unless it is prepared to pay its way. The failure to observe this distinction has led to serious mistakes, for example, in *Babbitt v. Sweet Home Chapter of Communities for a Great Oregon,*[19] which expanded the meaning of "take," defined in the Endangered Species Act to include actions that harass, harm, pursue, wound, or kill.[20] The most protean term on that list is "harm," which the regulations of the secretary of the interior defined to include "significant habitat modification or degradation where it actually kills or injures wildlife."[21]

Unfortunately, this definition tortures the meaning of "harm," by treating the failure to supply a benefit—prevention of "degradation" of habitat—as the equivalent of inflicting a harm. That equation is hopelessly broad. By its lights, I now harm all individuals to whom I do not at this instant lend a helping hand. By the same token, I also benefit all those individuals whom I now choose not to attack. The broad definitions attached to both harms and benefits are operative in all cases against all persons. The number of potential actions that it implies is beyond reckoning. The terms "harm" and "benefit" only have currency when it is possible at any given time to be in a situation where people are in a state of repose where they neither harm nor benefit each other. Cases of tort or restitution damages cannot be inevitable regardless of what people do.

More generally, our property baselines have to be defined, as they have always been defined, to make the necessity for legal intervention the exception and not the rule. The notions of harms and benefits make sense therefore only when defined in reference to our well-understood system of property rights. It is easy to say that any person who develops his own land may "harm" the environment, just as those actions may under a different understanding "benefit" others. Yet that conception of environmental harm is beside the point. Just as I do not harm any other person when I exclude him from my land, thus I do not harm the local environmental group when I prohibit it from using my garden for housing or feeding its animals, any more than I do from prohibiting it from using my phone for organizing its fundraising campaign. The core notion of harm relevant to legal disputes involves the use of force or fraud against others, and that notion does not include using my property for my own benefit. Private owners have done no wrong so there is no reason for them to be burdened with an obligation to "minimize and mitigate" their "impact" on endangered species,[22] as the law commonly requires, whenever they seek to use or develop their own land without creating a nuisance to others in the senses already developed. In these cases, the major political risk is that the government will overclaim private resources that have far less value in public hands than they do in private ones. Imposing a general environmental easement, which subjects all development to a potential mitigation obligation, lets the government operate as if there were no budget or scarcity restraints on their behavior. It also encourages perverse behavior by individuals that do possess valuable habitat, which it is in their interest to destroy if they can do so without government knowledge—"shoot, shovel and shut up."[23] Keep the traditional system of property rights in place, and these same landowners will develop the habitat so that they can sell it off to any government agency or private environmental group that is interested in preservation. Follow these rules, and the well-defined and exhaustive property rights are flexible enough to allow one piece of property to be used for development and the next to be used as a nature conservancy.

Coordination, Public Use, and Just Compensation

Any protean and cooperative development can only take place, moreover, if cooperation is possible among individuals, which is why the right to dispose of property—by sale, mortgage, lease, or joint tenancy—is an essential part of the overall system. Modern legal systems rely on a current version of the Statute of Frauds to put key transactions in writing, which can then be recorded in a centralized database, now commonly online, open to all to keep track of the various interests created such that potential buyers, tenants, and lenders can identify the proper person with whom to deal. With the law of nuisance to protect neighbors, a high velocity of voluntary exchanges produces contractual gains between the parties without creating dislocations among strangers. What's not to like?

To this question, the correct answer points to adverse neighborhood effects that share two characteristics. First, some activities are on
net disadvantageous to the members of the community. Second, the
huge transactional problems of organizing multiple owners may make
it impossible in practice to correct the errors these activities impose by
voluntary means. The relevant situations could easily involve difficulties
of coordination that respond to the ordinary prisoner's dilemma game.
It is in the interest of all landowners in a given area to limit their signs
to a certain size and to mount them flat against the wall. But if each
landowner knows that all the others follow those restrictions, it is in
his interest to erect a larger sign perpendicular to his building. Once
one person deviates from the ideal collective solution, others will follow.
Restrictive covenants between these parties are too difficult to negotiate,
so that a state regulation that replicates the result of the ideal contractual
system leaves everyone better off. One example is in placing signs flush
on building walls for all to see. Strong libertarians often have an exaggerated faith that human ingenuity can always overcome bargaining difficulties with clever contractual ploys. But in fact bargaining breakdown
is a pervasive feature of complex social situations. In some of these cases
the state imposes a collective solution that supplies each person with
compensation equal or greater in value to the rights surrendered. But
that outcome cannot be presumed; it must be demonstrated in particular
cases. Nothing says that implicit in-kind compensation is present whenever public solutions are imposed on private parties. Indeed just this
form of compensation is missing in the habitat preservation restrictions
imposed under the Endangered Species Act, which impose a concentrated burden on some property owners for the benefit of everyone in
society. In these cases, the rule in *Armstrong* requires compensation in
order to make good on the claim that the state takes property for public
use only on the payment of just compensation.

This overall account of taking must next ask what counts as a taking for a public use. Clearly any publicly run facility like a government
building or military facility counts. Much the same can be said of private
facilities like railroads that are open to public use by all comers and
that must charge nondiscriminatory rates. Indeed, the classical conception of public use also permitted a restricted class of takings for *private*
use in order to overcome a serious holdout problem that could arise if,
for example, a newly discovered mine was cut off from the only rail

connection by a tract of scrubland.[24] In essence, state power was allowed when high transaction costs of reassigning property rights blocked the sensible use or assembly of land resources. That definition, however, precludes the dangerous extension of that term in other situations.

The more ambitious systems of land planning cannot coexist with any sensible public use limitation. Thus in *Poletown Neighborhood Council v. City of Detroit*,[25] an entire community was ripped down to make way for a General Motors plant that never created the number of jobs that its backers had promised. Likewise, in *Hawaii Housing Association v. Midkiff*,[26] there was no serious holdout problem between landlord and tenant to justify a scheme whose sole purpose was to allow sitting tenants to use state force to require their landlords to sell, allowing the tenants to become outright owners of the property they lived on. The test used in that case was an extreme version of the rational basis test, holding that any "conceivable public purpose" was sufficient, which virtually any government action could satisfy. That decision raised little attention if only because the public at large does not identify with the expropriation of a landlord's interest. But in *Kelo v. City of New London*,[27] the public backlash was furious because the expropriation was of small individual homeowners to provide sites for a large urban renewal project that never got off the ground. Unfortunately, New London had no clue as to what use to make of the vacant land after the homes were razed: the property still sits vacant today in mute testimony to the hubris of land planners whose eyes are bigger than their stomachs.

It is examples like these then that make it imperative to keep a tight rein on public uses lest government power be used to move resources from A to B in ways that heighten the level of political intrigue, as particular groups vie to have the state exercise its condemnation power in their own direction. The situation is made worse when large public subsidies, such as the over $70 million that Connecticut showered on the City of New London, encourage wasteful public expenditures. These abuses remain even if full compensation is provided to landowners, which did not happen in *Kelo* where no weight was given to the subjective value of property to individuals who had made it clear that they would under no circumstances place their property on the market.

Quite simply, the just compensation requirement is not a sufficient check on political abuse. But once a forced exchange is found to meet the public use requirement, what form of compensation is constitutionally required? Sometimes that compensation is in cash, as when land is bought to construct a post office or a road. In other cases, however, the compensation supplied is *in kind*, as in the cases mentioned above: the acquisition of raw lands for highways or the imposition of some land use restrictions, like the sign ordinance just mentioned. The older law of trespass allowed one landowner to prevent all airplane flights overhead. A rule that recognizes that every landowner will be far better off with the benefits of air transportation than without it dispenses with cash compensation, except in those cases of low overhead flights that create disproportionate noise and inconvenience—where cash compensation is, and should be, paid. Likewise, large oil and gas pools often lie under the surface of many lands. Pooling production and guarding against waste can leave all owners better off than they would have been if each had drilled separately under his own land in ways that disrupted the integrity of the oil and gas field. Hence, a unitization scheme that places a large oil field under single management reduces the costs of production while increasing overall output, generating revenues to compensate each landowner for the loss or curtailment of drilling rights.

In sum, this system seeks to balance all the key components of a comprehensive system of land use regulation. It succeeds in ways that a hard-line libertarian system could not, because of that system's refusal to ever allow forced takings for public use, even when needed to overcome serious holdout problems. The Constitution does not say that private property may be taken for public use only with the consent of its owner. It says that it may be so taken when just compensation is provided. The classical liberal theory thus invites and requires a practice of forced exchanges, such as that developed above, which is out of place in a pure libertarian system.

The Modern Progressive Synthesis

Modern progressive theory, of course, gives little truck to libertarian qualms about the exercise of state power. Indeed, it lurches sharply to the other extreme because it harbors deep suspicions about the institution of private property, whose scope it seeks to sharply truncate. The first move in the progressive counterattack narrows the definition of private property, so that maximal constitutional protection is applied only to the right to exclude, not to the rights to use, develop, or dispose of land. The second is to expand the scope of public justifications far beyond the contours of the common law of nuisance. In working out its synthesis the key distinction lies between permanent physical occupations and regulatory takings. Let the government occupy land and there is in most instances a per se duty to compensate.[28] Limit the rights to use and dispose, and the more forgiving doctrines of rational basis take over. There are difficulties on both counts.

The Permanent Possession of Land

The scope of the per se compensation rule depends critically on what is meant by the permanent possession of land. The definition of "permanence" can operate as a powerful restriction on the rights of compensation when the state takes or damages land. The equivalence of taking by occupation and damaging by physical invasion is not one that should resonate even on Treanor's account of the Takings Clause. Indeed in dealing with this issue many state constitutions make clear the equivalence between the two. The Georgia Constitution speaks of the right of persons to "take or damage [private property] upon paying or tendering to the owner thereof just and adequate compensation."[29] The purported equivalence rests on two simple propositions. The first is that the individual landowner scarcely worries whether he is wiped out by occupation or destruction of property. Second, it should not matter to the state whether its gains come from the destruction of the land of others or from its occupation, which in many cases it does not care to exploit.

The issue comes to a head in the many cases in which the government releases water in its dam control operations and causes downstream damage. The supposed distinction between the tort of destruction and the permanent taking of land rests on the view that the venerable doctrine of sovereign immunity protects against the former but not the latter,[30] such that to allow recovery, "it is at least necessary that the overflow be the direct result of the structure, and constitute an actual, permanent invasion of the land, amounting to an appropriation of and not merely an injury to the property."[31]

The unprincipled line between permanent occupation and tort injury is being tested in *Arkansas Game & Fish Commission v. United States*, recently decided by the Supreme Court,[32] where the flood waters of the United States, before they retreated, caused permanent damage to the root systems of trees owned by the Arkansas Commission. A divided federal circuit panel, speaking through Judge Dyk, found that the "temporary" nature of the flooding eliminated any case for compensation under the established authorities.[33] The Supreme Court unanimously rejected that bright line rule on the ground that "most takings claims turn on situation-specific factual inquiries,"[34] without giving any real guidance on how that inquiry should be undertaken. Sadly, both the Federal Circuit and the Supreme Court misfired.[35] The Federal Circuit did not explain how the distinction between permanent and temporary takings rises to constitutional proportions. The Supreme Court remanded the case for further hearings without offering any direction on how the various factors should be weighed. What is needed is a third approach under which the key test proposition is that the government should never be able to do without compensation actions that are tortious when done by private parties. In this context, it means that the government cannot be enjoined from flooding other lands for what it regards as a public use, but it hardly follows that it should be able to flood lands of another with impunity so long as they are regarded as periodic or episodic. It is dangerous to accept any justification that the state needs discretion to manage public resources in ways that allow it to cause actionable harm to third parties. The whole point of the Takings Clause is to impose limits so that the external costs of government actions are incorporated in the decision-making calculus of public officials. Good government requires a rejection of the progressive view that dams and other public works should be free of judicial control, lest there be an excessive level of government action. The correct approach therefore does not seek to massage an untenable distinction. It rejects that distinction totally.

Regulatory Takings

The second half of the modern judicial synthesis grants large deference to government actors in cases of regulatory takings. In this area, the general skepticism about a rule-bound jurisprudence led Justice Brennan to note that the broad proposition in *Armstrong* did not prevent the need for "ad hoc" judgments in particular cases[36] of the sort extolled in *Arkansas Game & Fish*. That form of rule skepticism allowed Justice Brennan, in *Penn Central Transportation Co. v. City of New York*,[37] to sustain a landmark preservation statute that prevented Penn Central from using its air rights, a recognized property interest under New York law, for

constructing a new, elegant residential and office tower. Justice Brennan's position was that in most instances any diminution in land value
attributable to regulation should be treated as noncompensable under
his ad hoc balancing test, just as if it had been caused by the operation
of market forces.

The first difficulty in this analysis is that it does not explain why the
taking of air rights, by which the landowner is prohibited from building
on top of his structure, does not count as a physical taking of property
the surface owner is no longer able to enter. The situation in effect is the
exact duplicate of the hypothetical given above in which the government does not take property but refuses to allow its owner to enter. This
is not, moreover, the first case of divided interests in property where it is
often difficult to know whether a particular action amounts to a physical
or regulatory taking. The much-mooted 1922 takings case of *Pennsylvania Coal Co. v. Mahon*[38] involved a simple situation in which the state's
Kohler Act decreed that the coal company had to transfer to surface
owners the "support estate" that it had retained when it first conveyed
out the surface interest some forty years earlier.[39] In effect the landowners took the land knowing they assumed the risk that mining operations
could lead to the collapse of their homes. Justice Holmes held that the
regulation went "too far," but never bothered to explain why the case
only involved a regulation at all. The change in rules required a transfer
of a support interest that could be described as well as a physical interest
in land, especially as it required the coal company to keep pillars of coal
in place to support the surface and the structures on it. It was clear that
the transfer benefited all surface owners and hurt all mine owners so
that Pennsylvania could not identify any implicit in-kind compensation
for the transfer, let alone the "average reciprocity of advantage," that
Holmes in a famous aphorism thought insulated certain forms of government action from constitutional invalidation.

The distinction between regulation and occupation, then, is far
from watertight. Even if the distinction between occupation and regulation could be established, it would not have altered Brennan's analysis in *Penn Central*, where he showed not the slightest recognition that
market and regulatory forces always operate in opposite fashion. Government regulation reduces the size of the social pie that competition
expands. It is therefore a mistake to treat them as though they are in
any sense constitutional or social equivalents. Justice Brennan's stunted

approach, however, downgrades the protection of all rights to use and dispose of property except in cases of physical occupation. To make matters worse, in the ensuing decades the ability to protest a regulatory taking has become even more difficult because astute regulators are now able to interpose endless procedural obstacles to slow down real estate development. One such rule, holding that all landowners must exhaust local administrative procedures before they can go to court, gives local governments every incentive to extend administrative procedures ad infinitum.[40] Another rule says that issues that could be raised in state courts must be raised there, making it virtually impossible to have a federal court examine the merits of a federal constitutional takings claim.[41]

At the same time, the new synthesis mightily expands the justifications for state action. As already noted, "harm" goes far beyond the common law nuisance cases, so that the state may, but need not, impose restrictions dealing with views, height, density, setbacks, exterior design, wetlands, endangered species, and access to public ways. The initial thrust came in the 1926 zoning case of *Village of Euclid, Ohio v. Ambler Realty Co.*,[42] which upheld a zoning ordinance that prohibited industrial development on a large, integrated plot of land unwisely zoned for residential use. Potential adverse neighborhood effects were declared sufficient to justify an 80 percent loss in the parcel's value, while any positive effects of development on nearby businesses and residences were studiously ignored.

This indefinite system of property rights excites the worst fears of classical liberals. Neighbors with mixed motives are often in a position to veto or burden the development, sale, rental, or use of particular parcels. The ostensible minimum requirement that some viable economic use remain is easily circumvented. Let it be decreed, as in *Lucas v. South Carolina Coastal Council*,[43] that full compensation is required if, but only if, regulation prevents any new construction, and the regulators move into high gear to slip away from that restriction. Sensing constitutional oblivion, the regulators' next iteration imposes large-lot zoning. Once in place, all architectural designs have to be approved by multiple committees that can take months to meet. Nature studies have to be done on flora and fauna; height and setback restrictions may be imposed. Midway through the process, the permit requirements can be changed at will, and so on down the line. Each of these maneuvers eats away at the project's value, even if none is sufficient to sink the project by itself.

Meanwhile, the Supreme Court has yet to explain how the combined effect of these multiple regulations should be treated.

The passivity from the top leads to bolder community initiatives, including "deals" whereby the project will be approved only if the developer kicks in $10 million to help fund a new art club or after-school facility for children already in the neighborhood. These endless negotiations between developers, local governments, and community activists delay construction; they create large amounts of community animosity that yield marked reductions in land value without generating any offsetting social benefits. The strong territorial basis of local political systems lets anxious neighbors veto rights over projects that could provide housing or jobs for dozens or even hundreds of individuals whose voices are rarely if ever heard. Here is one example: the efforts of Related Realty to redevelop the large Kingsbridge Armory in the Bronx were vetoed by the New York City Council because Related Realty was not willing to require its tenants, including large retail companies, to pay "a living wage" to their employees.[44] Why land use restrictions should be used to support union demands in a devastated community was never explained.

Rent Control

The weak definition of property rights and the broad set of justifications have also kept in place too many rent control schemes. The state keeps the tenant in possession after the lease expires at a price that it thinks the tenant can afford, but far below the current price. The transaction should be stopped in its tracks by a sensible public use requirement, given that the transaction involves a transfer, piece by piece, to the tenant of the landlord's interest in his own property. The huge gap between the controlled and market rents encourages landlords to make nonstop efforts to pry out tenants who use their political clout to remain in possession. And all the while the courts claim that the tenants are not in physical occupation of the property, at which point the per se takings rule would apply. Instead, it is held, incorrectly, that it is permissible for a tenant to remain forever in possession because the original lease was "voluntary," even if only for a fixed term.[45] Current takings law reduces the critical temporal division of property to a matter of no significance. Similarly the distinction between permanent and temporary takings, which proved of no use in the flooding cases, has come to the rescue of various rent stabilization programs, since Justice Holmes in *Block v. Hirsh*[46] held that temporary rent control regimes could be justified in times of emergency when permanent ones might not be. But the line becomes an art form in New York City where since 1969 there has been a succession of three-year stabilization laws in which the "emergency" justification relates only to the shortage of rental vacancies, itself attributable to the rent stabilization laws rather than the dislocation of floods, plagues, or wars.[47] In effect, every known principle of landlord-tenant law is turned on its head to sustain a system whose economic dislocations and political costs are too well known to require extensive comment. This system would collapse instantly if the local government that championed the rent control had to make up in cash to the landlord the gap between market and regulated rent—which is precisely why that does not happen. For regulations and for land acquisition, the quantity demanded decreases as the price increases.

And Now?

As a matter of first principle, theories of limited government play no role whatsoever in the progressive view of economic liberty and land use regulation. Yet the question arises whether these practices are so entrenched that it becomes foolish to summon the justices to perform their constitutional duties. On this question I am of two minds, given the mountains of political and judicial support for the current consensus. Short of an economic meltdown, which may be coming, the status quo will persist no matter what a voice from the classical liberal fringe says. A monumental sea change in constitutional approach is not in the cards. Still, it is best to push hard, not only in the real property issues of this chapter but also on the labor market issues of the previous one. These are the two primary markets that must function well in any successful society. Yet both are hedged in with restrictions that create massive dislocations that have become more entrenched by the day. It may be impossible to return to a strong regime of property and contract rights, but the efforts have to be made, for otherwise we run the near certain risk of a prolonged social decline, as the government is authorized to enter into negative-sum transactions, where the gain to the state from either taking or regulating private property is smaller than the losses that it imposes on private owners. It is not enough in the current downturn for any classical liberal to say "don't blame me" for the current debacle. It is imperative to push hard for a restoration of the lost classical liberal synthesis. That classical liberal synthesis has, however, shown more staying power in dealing with various forms of personal liberties, to which the next chapter turns.

23

Personal Liberties and the
Morals Head of the Police Power

T HE PREVIOUS TWO CHAPTERS have examined all claims for economic liberties and property rights through a two-step analysis that first examines the scope of the underlying constitutional right, and then turns to the reasons the state advances to justify limiting that right. On economic liberties and property rights, the manifest trend has been to narrow the scope of the basic rights and to expand the scope of public justifications for their limitation in ways inconsistent with both the constitutional text and the classical liberal theory that undergirds it. This same two-step process of analysis also applies to a range of personal activities that, during the nineteenth century, were said to fall under the "morals" head of the police power.[1] These cases involved a wide range of activities that were thought to be sinful, most notably sexual practices such as adultery, prostitution, sodomy, homosexuality, abortion, and contraception. It also covered activities like gambling, cockfighting, and perhaps even bowling.

The Transformation of the Morals Regulation

In all these areas, the nineteenth-century justices had little or no patience at the constitutional level with freedom of contract arguments brought by individuals subject to various forms of criminal prosecution. To be sure, states could always decide to legalize certain activities, and in the case of lotteries, even run those activities themselves.[2] Yet the dominant, but not quite uniform attitudes of the time harshly condemned many of these practices. The critics often made explicit reference to an insistent social norm of disgust that works at cross-purposes with any theory of individual liberty.[3] State regulations could extend broadly to cover, for example, the full range of extramarital practices, allowing the state to exert extensive control over marriage. Thus *Reynolds v. United States*[4] upheld the ban on polygamy (leading to extensive forfeiture of property), as once practiced by some Mormons, on the ground that it offended common moral standards. The Court added, moreover, that it was appropriate for the jury to consider the consequences of polygamy to its "innocent victims," without mentioning who those might be.[5] In economic terms, it counts as an anticompetitive restriction that protects some religions at the expense of others.

Reynolds's strict moral judgment of sexual and marital practices became anachronistic in the last half of the twentieth century. In recent times, if anything, traditional judicial attitudes have flipped. Any questions of morality are regarded as matters of highly valued personal liberty, which the state can limit only upon a strong showing of interests that are narrowly crafted to deal with particular externalities of the sort that, ironically enough, are valid within the framework of a classical liberal theory. The spread of contagion, for example, falls within that category, for here the physical harm is one against which self-help measures often prove hopeless. It is therefore perfectly appropriate to allow for quarantines of infectious individuals, killing of diseased cattle, or withholding of contaminated goods from the stream of commerce—so long as these are not pretexts for anticompetitive activities, which is the underlying motivation in many cases. One early example of the potential for abuse was *Jew Ho v. Williamson*,[6] in which a purported quarantine applied only to the Chinese quarter of San Francisco. While Anglos were allowed to go in and out of the quarantined district at will, the local Chinese, who had borne the brunt of many a discriminatory law,[7] were required to stay put. On the other hand, consistent with classical liberal theory, taking personal offense at the knowledge that others may be engaged in some (by the observers' own lights) sordid practice is decidedly not a sufficient ground to stop the activity. Offense is self-generated, and whipping one's friends into a frenzy should never become the source of legal rights.

It is possible, therefore, to reconceptualize the understanding of the morals power so that its application becomes more consistent with classical liberal theory. But the historical evolution of the doctrine took quite a different path and was often justified for ad hoc reasons that resisted incorporation into the classical liberal approach. This chapter deals with four episodes in the theory of morals: contraception, abortion, homosexual sodomy, and gay marriage, all of which document the stunning transformation of the meaning of liberty under the Due Process Clause from constitutional pariah to constitutional darling.

Contraception

The customary judicial deference to traditional morals regulation first broke in an area where there was the least public resistance to the regulated practice—the use and sale of contraceptives. The decision illustrates a real tension for defenders of the classical liberal tradition. On the one hand, it seems as though there is no originalist support for the position that any portion of the Fourteenth Amendment is directed to the protection of these rights. The Privileges or Immunities Clause comes closest, but there is no historical source that regards freedom in matters of sexual relations as one of the traditional liberties that this clause protects. Indeed, the issue is not just one of noninclusion in the basic text. It is also a case in which the long historical reference to the morals head of the police power speaks in the opposite direction. Yet at the same time, so long as the use of contraceptive devices causes no harm to strangers, it looks like an activity that should be insulated from any government regulation, given that the mere offense that others take to practices contrary to their own moral and religious beliefs has no weight in the calculus.

As a matter of constitutional interpretation, it seems here that the authoritative history trumps the philosophical opposition to the state regulation of morals. Yet with the flagging faith in originalist-type arguments, it is no surprise that the constitutional dam on matters of morals broke in an area in which the Court was catching up with established mores, not blazing new paths of its own. In most states, the sale and use of contraceptives were legal, as legal rules keep up pretty well with changes in dominant social attitudes. Those who did not approve did not have to use them and could limit their access by their own children. But to every social consensus there is at least one outlier. In this instance, it was the Connecticut law that imposed punishment by fine or imprisonment on "[a]ny person who uses any drug, medicinal article or instrument for the purpose of preventing conception."[8] The statute then doubled down on the original prohibition by imposing like sanctions against "[a]ny person who assists, abets, counsels, causes, hires or commands another to commit any offense," which included persons who either sold or administered the devices in question.[9]

The controversial decision in *Griswold v. Connecticut*[10] struck down these statutes by an appeal to—take your pick—the penumbra and emanations of specific provisions of the Bill of Rights (Justice Douglas),[11] the Ninth Amendment (Justice Goldberg),[12] or old-fashioned substantive due process (Justice Harlan).[13] These judicial adventures were stoutly resisted by Justices Black and Stewart in dissent on the ground that *Griswold* simply brought the ghost of *Lochner* back to life. But this was not the case; nothing in *Lochner* purported to address the morals head of the police power. *Lochner* insisted only that the labor statute at issue was justified as a means to protect either the safety or health of the individual.

The many theories used to defend *Griswold* raised eyebrows, especially with the sudden revival of the Ninth Amendment, which simply provides: "The enumeration in the Constitution, of certain rights, shall not be construed to deny or disparage others retained by the people."[14] This amendment contains no internal substantive theory, but presupposes that some rights not covered in the other amendments of the Bill of Rights were, in good Lockean fashion, "retained" by the people at the formation of the original social contract.

Unfortunately, this amendment does not easily mesh with the specific constitutional guarantees on such matters as speech and property. But that point is of little consequence if the other substantive provisions directed to those areas are given a sensible reading. Thus, an alternative account of *Griswold* defends its outcome as a simple matter of freedom of contract under *Lochner*, but only if that decision is read *narrowly* to exclude the traditional broad references to the morals head of the police power. What justification can the state offer for restricting contractual arrangements, be they to purchase goods or advice, that do not pose any threat to the life or property of third parties, or even to the users of those contraceptives (which, in some instances at least, help prevent the transmission of sexual diseases)?

Unfortunately, that straightforward libertarian approach was blocked by what every member of the Warren Court perceived to be

Lochner's bad constitutional odor. Instead of a general appeal to personal freedom writ large, the case rummaged through the set of personal liberties until it defended its interventionist approach by a localized appeal to the notion of marital privacy: "Would we allow the police to search the sacred precincts of marital bedrooms for telltale signs of the use of contraceptives? The very idea is repulsive to the notions of privacy surrounding the marriage relationship."[15] But the argument fails for two reasons. First, many portions of this statute could still be enforced, including the prohibitions on sale and on third-party assistance in the use of contraceptive devices. Second, there is no apparent reason why the privacy argument, so construed, should be limited to marital couples, even if it includes them. Thus the marital limitation disappears as the toleration for what used to be called fornication increases, as it surely has, so that within a matter of years the Supreme Court no longer imposed the marriage limitation on sexual freedom.[16] The morals head thus shrunk as the classical liberal theory gained strength. And done properly, the Ninth Amendment could have remained a sideshow to the main event, as explicit constitutional provisions took over the space that it sought to occupy.

Abortion

Most of the extensive constitutional debate over *Griswold* stemmed from the collective astonishment over its bold rationales, not its substantive conclusion. Yet once exotic constitutional interpretation caught on, it took little imagination to see that it could spread to other, more controversial areas. As late as 1968, there was puzzlement in Hubert Humphrey's eyes when he was asked, as a Democratic nominee, to state his views on abortion. His reply, as I recall, was that it was a question for the states, not the federal government. The constitutional challenge to the practice was widely regarded as inconceivable. At least, that is, until the hyperactive 1972 Supreme Court Term, when *Roe v. Wade*[17] rudely shattered those complacent expectations.

As a political matter, one could not take comfort in the modest view that the *Roe* Court was just nudging the last recalcitrant state into conformity with the modern social consensus. Abortion was then, and remains now, a divisive social issue. Every state in the Union applied some criminal statutes to abortion, justified by what was perceived as the need to protect unborn life against material attack. The law on this subject was not always rigid, and it was common to make exceptions for abortion when it was necessary to save the life of the mother or when the child was conceived by rape or incest. Questions on the propriety of the abortion of offspring with known birth defects were hotly debated as well.

The public division over abortion existed for three good reasons. First, like in *Griswold*, the Court could offer no credible originalist argument for a practice that was universally illegal. Second, unlike in *Griswold*, there was no popular consensus in favor of a right to abortion, and much organized opposition to it. And third, the classical liberal position did not point in favor of a woman's right to have an abortion. As a very young legal scholar, I wrote an article on *Roe* in 1973 that the late Professor Philip Kurland of the *Supreme Court Review* entitled "Substantive Due Process by Any Other Name: The Abortion Cases."[18] Kurland chose a fine title for the article that he might have written, but only after it was published did I realize that the title did not accurately represent the views I had taken in the article. I did not share the same legal process concerns as the late John Hart Ely, who, in a far more famous article, "The Wages of Crying Wolf: A Comment on *Roe v. Wade*,"[19] stressed the real institutional risks to the Supreme Court of moving into such controversial waters when Justice Harry Blackmun manufactured a constitutional right to an abortion (at least in the first trimester). It was easy for conservatives to insist that the same liberals who despised *Lochner* on economic affairs were hypocritical to embrace its allegedly free-form logic on abortion.

Yet that line of attack ignores the key role that the police power played in the *Lochner* analysis, for there is good reason to believe that *Roe* is wrongly decided even if *Lochner* is right. To take the analysis from the top, a woman's choice to have an abortion implicates the now-rejected theory of freedom of contract the moment she hires a doctor, nurse, or anyone else to perform that operation. That one point surely counts in *Roe*'s favor. Yet at the same time, *Lochner*'s health and safety heads of the police power have real purchase in the context of abortion. Recall that during the so-called *Lochner* era, the state could abrogate the assumption of risk defense for industrial accidents under the Employer Liability Acts or impose a mandatory scheme of workers' compensation statutes that undid the entire negligence system.[20]

In this context, the thrust of my 1973 article was that protection of any right to abortion was suspect even under the narrow Millian "harm principle" articulated in his 1859 classic, *On Liberty:* "That the only purpose for which power can be rightfully exercised over any member of a civilized community, against his will, is to prevent harm to others."[21] The Supreme Court did not appreciate the scope of this police power argument when it insisted that abortions had to be constitutionally protected because the use of the term "person" in the Constitution did not include unborn persons in dealing with such issues as protection against unreasonable search and seizures, reapportionment of election districts, emoluments for public service, and a number of like provisions.[22] Translated to the abortion context, this argument, if correct, helps explain why a fertilized egg does not get explicit constitutional protection under the Fourteenth Amendment.

Yet conception is the only sharp break in the continuous process of reproduction. No later point, including the three trimesters, has that quality. If the verbal evasions in *Roe* are rejected, this sets up a person-against-person conflict which instantly highlights the distinction between *Griswold* and *Roe* and undermines the constitutional case for *Roe* on both moral and legal grounds. Indeed, it is possible to go further and insist that the case against abortion rights does not depend on such a strong finding about the status of the fetus. Even if the only person whose liberty is at stake is the mother's, the police power inquiry asks this follow-up question: does some combination of health, safety, and morals limit the mother's *prima facie* right, much as it does in other cases? The key point is that the termination of a pregnancy is not a close cousin to removing a wart, which even abortion proponents concede when they recognize the moral gravity of the abortion question. Hence, on this modified view, the ultimate constitutional question is whether the imperfect status of the fetus, which will in the ordinary course become a person, is *in and of itself* a sufficient reason for state intervention.

At this point, one response is to say that the key question is the level of scrutiny that is brought to the case. The state's interest in the protection of the fetus could survive rational basis review, but not any form of strict scrutiny. Yet why? The fetus is closer to a person than to a wart, which can never evolve into a person. It is for that reason, for example, that the government will appoint a guardian to protect the property interests of an unborn child, and indeed, in property matters, a future child who is not yet conceived. And it is surely telling that the deliberate killing of a fetus by a stranger who attacks the mother could be treated as an independent form of homicide, even if one short of murder, and not just part of the parental assault. It is worth noting, of course, that the state's interest in maternal care shows the special weight given to assisting the mother in protecting the fetus, which strengthens the case for allowing the state to protect the fetus against the mother as well. There could be an extended discussion about other hard cases: children born of rape or children suffering from serious genetic diseases such as Tay-Sachs or even spina bifida. Yet just the effort to carve out limited justifications for some abortions undermines the moral and legal grounds for *Roe*'s categorical right of abortion. Once health and safety are introduced into the mix, the shoe is now on the other foot. Why ignore the strong historical spread of abortion laws starting in the nineteenth century?

To be sure, these arguments do not clinch the case for making the state adopt a ban on abortion. The complications of seeking to enforce prohibitions on abortion, including (to consider health and safety from the other side) the risks of back-alley abortions and the increased criminal activity that might accompany a ban, probably lead to the conclusion that the state is under no duty to criminalize abortion the way it is probably under a duty to criminalize murder. Put the whole picture together and abortion does not present a real tension between a (supposed) claim of liberty on the one hand and a long set of historical practices on the other. Quite simply, abortion, unlike honest labor, did not count as a traditional liberty. Thus it is no great stretch to say that even a relatively narrow conception of the police power covers abortions, so that the widespread historical practice of criminalizing abortion (chiefly to punish those who perform abortions) does amount to a legitimate state function.

This view holds even if one treats the case, as writers like Catharine MacKinnon do, as one of sex discrimination,[23] not personal liberty. The concern here is not only with the want of any textual basis for this claim. It is also that any nondiscrimination principle, as we saw in connection with the dormant Commerce Clause and the economic liberties cases, is not absolute. Like any other constitutional claim, it must be rejected if it meets valid state justifications. At that point, the new home for *Roe* leads it to run into the same police power objections as before. It is not credible to suppose that men should be subject to a prohibition on having abortions. It is also easy to see why the prohibitions on performing an abortion on others can be sex-neutral. But if the protection of the life of the unborn child suffices to block a liberty claim, then it suffices to block the antidiscrimination claim as well. So in the end, the argument for abortion comes up short within the classical liberal framework.

What of the simple fact that abortion has been entrenched for over thirty-nine years, now with a clear majority of public support for the view that abortion is legally protected but morally complex? The issues here involve the vexing problems of the prescriptive constitution, discussed in Chapter 3, where a key question is how long usage affects a decision that was wrong at its inception. My own sense is that this awkward current accommodation has it about right today. The costs of legal enforcement of a prohibition on abortion are very high, and thus are eliminated in a world where no Supreme Court (especially the one that wrote *Roe*) could persuade the dissenters, both in and out of the Roman Catholic Church, that abortion is morally unproblematic. Women should be instructed on the grave issues of abortion but not told that they cannot have one on demand, at least early in pregnancy. There can be a large set of litigated cases as to whether the state may burden the right to an abortion by insisting that people receive counseling before having an abortion, or in requiring parental consent and the like. We can live with those disputes, fierce as they are, but it is risky to tamper with *Roe* itself in light of the enormous disruption of settled practice. Indeed, if the constitutional decision were reversed, legislation would reestablish the right for an abortion in at least one state, which then opens up a huge avenue for pro-abortion forces. It therefore makes sense to preserve (but not extend) the status quo. The situation is surely inelegant, but that is always what happens when text and history collide.

Homosexual Sodomy

A generation after *Roe*, the traditional morals head of the police power was under attack in the domain of homosexual behavior, where the change in social mores had led to a rapid reduction in the level of criminal punishment. However, in this instance, the political resistance to the legalization of the practice and the social disapproval of it were far greater than with contraception, although eventually becoming less than to abortion. It was only a matter of time, therefore, before the clash between conflicted modern mores and the Constitution would find its way into the courts. That conflict came to a head in the 1986 decision of *Bowers v. Hardwick*.[24] Here, tradition took precedence over liberty as Justice Byron White wrote for a five-to-four majority that, over a fierce dissent by Justice Harry Blackmun, upheld the prohibition on sodomy out of an uneasy respect for this dying tradition.[25] Justice White's majority opinion worked by a process of analogy and comparison to find some "fundamental" constitutional right, but quickly distinguished other claims that had been recognized under that rubric, including both marital privacy and the right to contraception. Correctly applying traditional doctrine, he concluded that "the proposition that any kind of private sexual conduct between consenting adults is constitutionally insulated from state proscription [by precedent] is unsupportable."[26] And so it was in light of the fact that the criminal prohibition against sodomy had an unbroken line of support from ancient times until the early 1960s, when the legislative bans started to loosen. Every original colony banned sodomy; when the Fourteenth Amendment was ratified, all but five of the thirty-seven states made the action criminal.[27]

Justice White's history was pretty solid. However inconsistent this historical record may be with libertarian theory, there are no credible grounds to believe that any portion of the Fourteenth Amendment was intended to remove the power of the state to enact and enforce such bans. As a matter of political theory, logic beats tradition; but as a matter of constitutional law, the opposite is equally true. At least it was, until the 2003 decision of the Supreme Court in *Lawrence v. Texas*,[28] at which point an overt libertarian streak on what are now termed "intimate" personal relationships toppled *Bowers* from its historically precarious perch. Justice Anthony Kennedy sought to redo Justice White's social history on morals regulation at and before the adoption of the Fourteenth Amendment. Much of that history shows that anti-sodomy laws were often applied to both men and women, or were not enforced except against children, or were repealed and reenacted. But none of this erratic practice undermines the central historical claim in *Bowers*, which was that the state's police power allowed (but did not require) states to control this form of behavior.

At heart, however, Justice Kennedy cared less about the history and more about the presumption of liberty that he believed should govern the case. Thus, he embraced the exact proposition that Justice

White had rejected seventeen years before: "[A]dults may choose to enter upon this relationship in the confines of their homes and their own private lives and still retain their dignity as free persons. . . . The liberty protected by the Constitution allows homosexual persons the right to make this choice."[29] Indeed, "[t]he instant case involves liberty of the person both in its spatial and in its more transcendent dimensions."[30] That liberty, of course, finds its home in the Due Process Clause of the Fourteenth Amendment.[31] At this point, the persistent conceptual reservations about substantive due process were cast decisively to one side. The thought that liberty should be limited only to acts of imprisonment was likewise never on the radar. Instead, the Due Process Clause covers "liberty of the person both in its spatial and more transcendent dimensions."[32] Cases for economic liberty need not apply for reconsideration.

With an introduction like that, there was no chance that the abstract category of state power to regulate morals could survive. Since the case was based on liberty, Justice Kennedy did not rely on a puny equal protection argument (embraced by Justice Sandra Day O'Connor, who had gone along with the *Bowers* majority)[33] that the statute should be struck down because sodomy between people of the opposite sex was allowed when sodomy between persons of the same sex was prohibited. Try that fix, and in the next iteration the Texas statute might prohibit both kinds of sodomy, which in a real sense makes the problem worse than ever. At this point the statute had to go down in flames once Texas conceded that its law did not address (morals to one side) any of the traditional concerns of the police power that fit under a libertarian theory: the protection of minors, the protection of people against coercion, or even public conduct or prostitution.[34] The key feature was that "full and mutual consent" eliminated all grounds for state intervention. Hence *Lawrence*, with its occasional hyperbole to individual rights and a narrow approach to possible defenses, tracks the standard libertarian arguments to a tee, even though written and endorsed by judges who had little patience with that basic approach in other contexts. In one sense, the inversion of logic between economic liberties and matters of intimate personal association is complete. The irony here is that Justice Kennedy took refuge not in classical liberal theory, but in his own view of a living constitution. "As the Constitution endures, persons in every generation can invoke its principles in their own search for greater freedom."[35] Lord knows what happens when the next generation of social conservatives takes over.

Gay Marriage

One question left open by *Lawrence* is whether Justice Kennedy's constitutional evolution had reached its end. In a sense, he thought it did when he basically drew, albeit not quite explicitly, the line between the criminalization of sodomy and the line against constitutional protection for gay marriage. After all, *Lawrence* "does not involve whether the government must give formal recognition to any relationship that homosexual persons seek to enter."[36] But why not? The decision against criminalization rested on an exalted view of all sexual relations that self-consciously held that those relations found in marriage could be duplicated by gay individuals who lived outside its protective sphere. The Kennedy argument did not rest on the need for an extensive state apparatus to enforce the criminal law in ways that necessarily intruded on personal privacy. If he had taken that position, he might have held the line of gay marriage on the view that the state faces no administrative or enforcement difficulties when it denies a couple a marriage license. But those administrative arguments ring hollow when set up against a liberty claim which has "transcendent dimensions."

No one can be sure as of this writing how the constitutional challenge to Prop 8—"Only marriage between a man and a woman is valid or recognized in California"[37]—now before the Supreme Court in *Hollingsworth v. Perry*[38] will shake out, assuming that the Supreme Court decides to hear it on the merits. And there are additional layers of complexity raised in the companion decision in *United States v. Windsor*[39] which challenges the federal definition of marriage as a union between one man and one woman in the Defense of Marriage Act. Nonetheless, as a matter of first principle, the logic of individual choice stressed in *Lawrence* surely permits individuals to decide to have sexual relationships outside as well as inside the institution of marriage. But by what logic can it be said that same-sex couples could be denied the same status before the law when it refuses to give them "formal recognition" of their relationship? It does not take an evolving view of the Constitution to see that this issue is ripe for the application of the general doctrine of unconstitutional conditions, which holds that the state cannot use its licensing power to favor one type of social arrangement relative to another unless it can posit some distinct justification for doing so.

This argument generalizes to the conclusion that the state licensing power has to be exercised in favor of all if it is done in favor of any. That position could easily be resisted by the traditionalists who used the word "meretricious" to describe the same conduct that Justice Kennedy found "transcendental" in *Lawrence*.[40] But he has forfeited the use of that argument, and thus runs into the buzzsaw that courts have taken it upon themselves to be arbiters of social values, which indeed they have to do once they treat strong classical liberal theory as a guide to their position. But once the historical barricades to constitutional interpretation are overrun, what possible grounds are there to stop with decriminalization when equal rights to marriage still beckon? At this point, all the arguments are prudential. We know from the successful passage of Proposition 8 in California that public opinion is deeply divided on the question of gay marriage. Indeed, all the political ugliness took place precisely because the California Supreme Court ignored the bounds of judicial prudence when it mandated recognition of gay marriage on state equal protection grounds.[41]

We thus stand again at the crossroads between the historical and prescriptive constitutions. Once the historically correct reading in *Bowers* is disregarded, the justices live in the world of the constitutional second-best, where they must decide whether to extend a dubious precedent to its next logical conclusion or to pull in their horns in order to avoid provoking a political melee. My own cowardly instincts are fully on display here. I would have voted with the majority in *Bowers* and with the dissent in *Lawrence*. But ten years later, I would keep the status quo because even in that short time I think that the outcome has been legitimated. But I would not make the constitutional leap on gay marriage in the face of divided public sentiment on a question that goes to the heart of the morals head of the police power.

I make this last point with some obvious reluctance because the case for gay marriage is far more powerful than the more popular cause of having the antidiscrimination laws cover sexual orientation as they do the well-accepted grounds of race, sex, age, and national origin. And why this inversion? Because labor markets are competitive, so there is no need for the state to intrude when thousands of employers compete vigorously to hire gay employees. Yet the state exerts its monopoly position when it either grants or denies a marriage license. That is real power. The key lesson to take away from this discussion of morals is that the same political dynamics that govern economic affairs are ultimately at work in social matters as well. The lesson—trust competition, and fear state monopoly—works well as a constitutional template, albeit one that was missed by the drafters of the Fourteenth Amendment, who had enough other issues to worry about in the aftermath of the Civil War.

SECTION II

SPEECH

24

Freedom of Speech and Religion
Preliminary Considerations

THE DIVISION between classical liberal and progressive thought also shapes the constitutional debates over the First Amendment rights relating to both speech and religion. As usual, the interpretive inquiry begins with the choice of the standard of review applicable to the particular cases. The first judicial instinct is to think (wrongly) that speech and religion deserve special protections that property rights and economic liberties do not. That approach seems misconceived from the get-go because the most reliable protections for speech and religion come from the security of a sound basic system of law unrelated to particular issues of either speech or religion. It is virtually impossible to envision how the state could interfere with, let alone terrorize, religious and political institutions if in all cases it systematically and unflinchingly protected property rights and economic liberties for its citizens and for other persons and institutions subject to its jurisdiction.

A Return to Classical Liberalism?

Most critically, the protection of freedom of speech and religion becomes *more* difficult to organize in any regime in which rights related to property and contract are systematically underprotected. Under these weaker constitutional regimes, it becomes necessary to demand special protections for religion or speech that are systematically denied for property and contract in everyday affairs. For example, it is easier for a church to resist an order from the state that it must, or must not, hire women or

gays as priests if all organizations have the right to associate, or not associate, with others in ways that they see fit. Put in the general prohibition
against discrimination, and any exemption from that norm is vulnerable to attack as an establishment of religion. Deny that exemption, and
the statute is exposed to the charge that it infringes the free exercise of
religion. The conflicts become acute if both protections are read broadly.
They become largely useless if watered down from face value. Neither of
these problems need arise if the two clauses are read consistently as part
of a classical liberal scheme, whose coherent theory of property rights
necessarily undergirds any claim of freedom, be it of speech or religion.

For interpretive purposes, however, it is important to accept the
differential mindset at face value, for it leads to the quick conclusion
that the rational basis test dominating the constitutional treatment
of property and contract does not take pride of place in dealing with
speech or religion. Deference is no longer the reflexive trope of choice
in dealing with such matters because modern courts strongly identify
with the underlying concerns addressed in the First Amendment but
not with rights of property and contract. The moment courts decide to
strengthen the constitutional guarantees, the classical liberal framework
that was rejected in property and contract cases supplies the roadmap
for constitutional discourse with its two key functions: broad definitions
of the basic rights and narrow treatment of state efforts to limit them.
These tendencies are of course not uniform in the cases, and progressive anxieties surface most clearly in cases where the speech in question
deals with corporate or business behavior on such key matters as labor
relations and participation in political activities, be it by corporations
or other political action committees (PACs). In this section, I shall trace
these crosscurrents, first in speech and then in religion.

The text of the First Amendment is short in length but categorical in
tone. In its entirety it states:

> Congress shall make no law respecting an establishment of religion, or
> prohibiting the free exercise thereof; or abridging the freedom of speech,
> or of the press, or the right of the people peaceably to assemble, and to
> petition the Government for a redress of grievances.[1]

One of the great defenders of that amendment, Justice Hugo Black,
took the position that the First Amendment, in dealing with speech, said
"what it meant and meant what it said," so that its protection should be

treated as well-nigh absolute in the domains to which it applied.[2] It is easy to take the same approach with respect to the even broader phrase "free exercise" in the Religion Clauses. But this approach misgauges the meaning of the constitutional text. In this instance, the term "freedom" calls to mind the classical liberal position that a person is free to do or say what he will so long as the exercise of his freedom does not systematically infringe on the like freedoms of others. The most obvious of these exceptions deal with trespass, fraud, defamation, monopoly, insults, bribery, the use and threat of force, and the protection of minors.

To protect *freedom* of speech or religion does not require the law to protect all forms of speech or religious activities regardless of context or content. It only requires that the protection of these freedoms be incorporated into a larger system in which the relationship of private to common property is essential to the overall enterprise. These freedoms are strongest when exercised by individuals on their own property, so long as they do not commit (like any other landowner) a nuisance against their neighbors. They are necessarily modulated in public commons to which all individuals have equal but limited access. And they are at their lowest ebb when individuals try to exercise the rights of speech or religion by trespassing on the lands of others.[3] Any use of the term "freedom" analytically links to the general classical liberal theory, and deviations from that theory in either direction will necessarily be flawed. There is no free pass for one kind of error relative to another. Any misguided constitutional protection of fraud is as much a violation of the rights of others as is a government suppression of true speech. Both need special justifications to overcome the general libertarian presumptions that make force and fraud the first limitations on private conduct.

In light of this basic connection, any discussion of speech and religion necessarily invites the two-part inquiry that was so essential in dealing with rights relating to contract and property: first, identify the scope of the right; then, examine the possible justifications for limitations on that right. Since the protection of speech and religion commands greater esteem and affection among judges and academics, we should expect that the overall analysis will, in many cases, reflect the classical liberal synthesis. But in those areas where progressive influences are more pronounced—union elections, campaign financing, and hate speech, for example—we should expect the case law to gravitate back to the older paradigm of narrow basic protection subject to broad exceptions.

Modern Approaches to Religion and Speech

Modern theories about freedom of speech tend to concentrate on a number of variables. Holmes's famous statement that "the best test of truth is the power of the thought to get itself accepted in the competition of the market"[4] shows an affection for market arrangements that was far from evident in Holmes's *Lochner* dissent[5] on maximum hour laws some fourteen years before. Just as the uncoordinated offers from many buyers and sellers allow prices and goods to be efficiently exchanged, so the presentation of different views in both private and public fora is more likely to pave the way for discussion and debate. Such discourse tends, on average, to move any society toward the best collective choice in any given situation in settings dealing with such critical matters as war and peace, where individuals who disagree cannot go their separate ways.

Yet there is a deserved element of caution. There are no guarantees in dealing with such a broad topic: competition in the marketplace of ideas is just "the best *test* of truth." But it is hard to find any other single general test that performs better, unless we know in advance which Solons should control matters necessarily in the public domain even in a regime of limited (but not zero) government. Even the best tests yield both false negatives and false positives. Although the marketplace of ideas is imperfect, it is far better than any alternative arrangement human institutions can devise. We know this from the way that freedom of speech is guarded in private associations that have to make collective decisions. Whether we are dealing with commercial, charitable, social, or religious organizations, all of them construct their boards and committees in ways that give everyone a right to speak before a vote is taken. How that speech is rationed, moreover, is usually decided by an appeal to pre-agreed-upon house rules of order. The bidding structures that operate in many markets usually do not apply, if only because the speech has value not only to the speaker but also to his or her audience. A bidding system for ordinary commodities works because it can safely ignore this interactive component. But in cases where deliberation matters, concentrating on the speaker to the exclusion of the audience fails to take into account these positive deliberative externalities. Hence, all rules are devised to take into account gains on both sides of an interchange. This system of internal ordering is not confined to deliberation or speech in private settings. The same two-sided relationship governs speech in all contexts, so that the models at work in private institutions are equally instructive when examining public discourse.

As some of these last refinements suggest, Holmes's marketplace image is incomplete. The notion of freedom of speech, linguistically, covers far more than these kinds of competitive exchanges. Quite simply, there is a lot of important nonmarket, noncompetitive talk. So why narrow the interpretation of an elusive word in a constitution so that it covers one, and only one, form of interaction? Is reading poetry, singing, acting, preaching, or praying any less a form of speech than politics or other deliberative forms of activity? Does one rule apply if the poem is a hymn to springtime and another if the poem is a veiled attack on some major political figure? Any consistent classical liberal is reluctant to anchor the protection of speech, including speech on religion, to any flimsy content-based ground that unduly constricts the scope of the constitutional guarantee.

Fortunately, modern writers both on and off the Court are sensitive to this risk. When Robert Bork wrote in 1971 that the constitutional function of speech was to protect political exchanges only,[6] his reward was an incessant and undignified political barrage that helped derail his Supreme Court nomination in the Senate. Apart from political atmospherics, the outcome was ironic because Bork—who eventually abandoned his earlier position in favor of a broader reading—was largely following the earlier work of Alexander Meiklejohn, who had famously proclaimed a close connection between freedom of speech and participation in the processes of political self-governance.[7] Clearly all this speech matters, and so too does the speech of outsiders designed to call attention to their abuse, in the exercise of what Vince Blasi has elegantly called the "checking" function.[8] The connection between this use of the term "checking" and the system of checks and balances is an apt reminder that both notions are cut from the same cloth.

None of these political participation defenses of freedom of speech should be understood to romanticize the issue. Freedom of speech is *not* part of a glorious script that always leads to positive deliberative outcomes. This point is especially salient under modern law because the perverse economic incentives set up by today's feeble protections of property and contract invite the formation of coalitions to gain undeserved political capital by browbeating—with constitutionally protected speech—any vulnerable opposition. Unfortunately, there is no sec-ond-best solution that cancels out the persistent grievous constitutional errors that have drained protection away from property and contract. However fractious and uninformative the meetings that take place in zoning boards across the land may be, preventing people—some people? which people? what times? what topics?—from having their say only makes matters worse. The only way to improve the public discourse is to correct the initial structural error by strengthening the rules of prop-erty and contract in ways that neutralize brazen appeals for partisan advantage in the political arena. In this sense, strong property rights and strong speech and religion rights should be understood as complements in a coherent whole.

One effort to combat narrow arguments that tie freedom of speech to political processes stresses the role that speech plays in individual self-realization of natural talents and abilities.[9] These theories of speech resonate with more general principles of individual autonomy, which are often used to limit the power of government to coerce individuals to take voluntary actions that are meant to assist other individuals. The no-duty-to-rescue doctrine in the general tort law is a reflection of that typical reluctance to interfere. Such theories are by no means limited to dealing with matters of speech. They surely apply to religious convic-tions, and they can easily be extended to all forms of human conduct, including the realization of self through honest labor. In each and every one of these guises, this notion of self-determination tends to support a uniform conception of limited government. The theory of self-realiza-tion must therefore explain why speech is a distinctive element in this particular program relative to other human endeavors, which it fails to do. The theory also runs the risk that some groups will invoke it in order to impose all sorts of affirmative obligations on other individuals or soci-ety at-large to supply the material support necessary for the former to reach self-realization—without sensing the limitations it imposes on the independence and, yes, autonomy of those individuals who bear that burden through either regulation or taxation. It will not be the first, or the last time that the refusal to extend that support will be characterized as harming those who are denied the requested subsidy. In addition, the theory of self-realization offers no clue as to the limitations that should be imposed on the exercise of the right of speech and, by extension, religion, and thus is incomplete at its very core.

There is a larger truth buried here. For the classical liberal, using these ungainly theoretical constructs to justify freedom of speech or freedom of religion makes no more sense than asking for a unified justification for any individual's basic freedom of action. What public-regarding justification could you offer for scratching your nose, drinking a cup of coffee, or playing a round of golf? None, really. The conventional wisdom on freedom of speech goes astray precisely because it places the burden of justification on the wrong party: the speaker. Conversely, under a consistent classical liberal position, the inquiry flips over so now we ask: what justification must the *government* advance to limit that speech in ways that disrupt the voluntary relationship between the speaker and his audience? The same types of arguments apply to the freedom of religion. It is instructive to follow the interpretive responses in both areas.

Free Speech and Free Exercise: Twins or Opposites?

The modern law eventually comes to a largely sensible resting place, in part by adopting a clever linguistic strategy that expands the reach of the Free Speech Clause by substituting for "speech" a broader term, "communication or expression." The late Thomas Emerson, who helped popularize the shift, made no bones about his constitutional orientation when he opened his book *The System of Freedom of Expression* with this salvo:

> A Libertarian approach to the First Amendment Freedom of Expression includes the right to form and hold beliefs on any subject and to communicate those beliefs to others by whatever medium one chooses whether by traditional means, oral or press, or by other means, music and art . . . [and i]ncludes the right to hear the opinions of others, the right to inquire, reasonable access to information, and the right of assembly and association.[10]

The words "expression" and "communication" are aimed at protecting all the close substitutes to speech that are not caught by the literal meaning of the term, including forms of symbolic speech like burning draft cards[11] and flags,[12] wearing black armbands to protest the Vietnam War,[13] and smearing paint all over one's face.[14] In dealing with these issues, the Court has taken the view that the conduct in question was closely akin to "pure speech," which "is entitled to comprehensive protection under the First Amendment."[15] To employ the copyright analogy, it would be foolish for anyone to say that the Intellectual Property Clause that gives protection to "authors" for their "writings"[16] does not cover art, movies, dance, and all the other activities that routinely receive copyright protection today. In the area of copyright, the same arguments that lead to the protection of writings lead to the protection of these other forms of creative expression. With speech, acceptance of the anticircumvention principle, articulated in Chapter 3, is needed to prevent the erosion of constitutional freedoms by legislative actions. After all, writing is a substitute for speech, gesticulation substitutes for both, and other physical actions (like wearing armbands) pick up the slack. Accordingly, ordinarily there is no good reason for limiting these collateral forms of communication, except on grounds that are appropriate for limiting speech itself under a restrained version of the police power. Hence, it is correct to treat actors (or nude dancers for that matter)[17] as engaged in speech. It is not possible to protect the speech of anyone who waves the flag, without protecting the flag-waving as well.

A similar line of argument applies to expression, or more accurately, "exercise" in religion. That term cannot be limited only to matters of ritual, when all aspects of human life can easily be subjected to religious creeds. The constitutional protection has to follow the underlying practices, lest there be yet another violation of the anticircumvention norm of constitutional interpretation. But in this context, all the pressure is moving in the opposite direction, so that there are constant attempts to limit the free exercise of religion to matters of ritual and not to more general matters of behavior that members of given faiths regard as essential to their own religious activities. Whenever, for example, there is a clash between religious liberty and the antidiscrimination laws, the government position has sought to limit constitutional protection to "a ministerial exception," narrowly construed.[18] It should be possible, consistent with classical liberal principles, to protect religious liberty to its full extent while also guarding against the risk of conferring state monopoly to given groups on religious matters. Competition among churches for the loyalty of present and prospective members is thus a given component of the free exercise of religion. The robust protection of religion, moreover, covers more than organized churches, so that individuals are entitled to act on the strength of whatever religious beliefs they have. Deists do not belong to any church, and they rely on reason and experience, not faith, to justify their positions. In secular terms, they are allowed to compete for members with other religions and thus their practices, like those of other religions, are protected against state regulation to the same degree as other religions. This injunction to respect all religions is, however, more difficult to honor than it seems, for in ordinary usage the term commonly includes those individuals who believe in some higher moral code without having any belief in God at all, as in the ethical or natural religions.[19] Fortunately, most of these questions lie at the fringe and not the core of the discussion on religions. But the concerns are clear. It is always dangerous to place a state thumb on the side of any substantive religious vision, which in a sense makes it more or less imperative to use the protection of religious freedom to protect atheists as well as deists.

The first interpretive step thus broadens the definitions of speech and religion and is consistent with the general classical liberal orientation. It shows that the constitutional law governing speech and religion is on a very different trajectory from the law governing property—where one common interpretive blunder equates private ownership with one of its constituent parts: the right to exclude. The differences remain even when the discussion turns to the potential justifications for state regulation.

Justifications for Limiting Free Speech and Religious Actions

In dealing with these justifications for the assertion of state power, the contrast between speech and religion on the one hand and property and contract on the other becomes still more pronounced. The core of the police power lies in the ability of the state to prevent the actions of individuals that cause harm to others. In working this definition, the first critical junction turns on the scope of the word "harm" as it is used in the standard formulation of the principle found in John Stuart Mill's *On Liberty*: "the only purpose for which power can be rightfully exercised over any member of a civilized community, against his will, is to prevent harm to others."[20] As became clear when discussing the regulation of private property and economic liberty, it is easy to drain the harm principle of all content by allowing it to embrace a broad class of supposed interests that advance overall social welfare even if they hurt the economic positions of some individuals, as all productive activity always does. It is possible, for example, to claim that the failure to rescue results in harms to others, at which point everyone could in principle be under a legal duty to assist all others, even in the absence of a special relationship or statutory duty.[21] Competitive harm could justify government regulation to control against "ruinous" forms of price competition in such key areas as agriculture and transportation. Similarly, land use regulations designed to deal with the protection of views or with aesthetic claims going to the character of a neighborhood have also been routinely held to fall within the definition. The question with both speech and religion is whether similarly broad accounts of the police power could be used to swallow the initial protection by including, for example, the offense that other individuals take to the message of speech or the content of religious beliefs.

A moment's reflection should indicate that the use of these broad accounts of harm spells the end of these fundamental protections, which would easily permit barriers to entry in both these markets. Thus with nude dancing or flag burning, the offense that other individuals take toward individuals engaging in these activities cannot count as a form of harm that allows these activities to be stopped, certainly when done on private places, and, with flags, in public places as well. By the same token, a broad definition of the "morals" head of the police power cannot be used toward that end. Thus in *Barnes v. Glen Theatre*, which upheld a prohibition against nude dancing, Justice Scalia stated that "[t]he purpose of Indiana's nudity law would be violated, I think, if 60,000 fully consenting adults crowded into the Hoosier Dome to display their genitals to one another, even if there were not an offended innocent in the crowd."[22] Clearly the rejection of the defense of consent is meant to go outside the traditional domains of police and safety to include, as Scalia himself notes, those acts which are found "'*contra bonos mores*,' i.e., immoral. In American society, such prohibitions have included, for example, sadomasochism, cockfighting, bestiality, suicide, drug use, prostitution, and sodomy."[23]

It is worth noting the highly diverse list of practices that are included on this list. Prohibition of cockfighting is for the protection of animals. Bestiality deals with degrading human practices as well as animal abuse. Sadomasochism and suicide prohibitions deal with the protection of self. Prostitution and sodomy involve consensual arrangements. It should be clear that all these forms of protection raise serious problems of their own, for some of them at least can be justified in part as health or safety measures. With regard to at least one practice, sodomy, the Supreme Court has backed off the precedent set in *Bowers v. Hardwick*,[24] so that any regulation dealing with sexual conduct is now in play precisely because it has at most a partial overlap with the traditional police power justifications, as Justice Blackmun's *Bowers* dissent vigorously protested.[25] These same morals justifications have an obvious role to play given the strong religious objections to homosexuality in general. But, here again, the classical liberal approach has to look with suspicion on any efforts to carry these generalizations into the secular sphere. The strong protection of religious rights necessarily must curtail the scope of the police power as well.

All this is not to say that the class of potential justifications in speech and religion cases is inconsequential, any more than this could be said in other areas. Private land use, for example, has long organized around the tort of nuisance, which is a complex but limited branch of the law dealing chiefly with non-trespassory invasions of one person's property on the land of another, but occasionally touching other kinds of non-invasive conduct, such as spite fences.[26] Just how do these rules apply in cases where zoning laws, for example, prevent the use of advertisements or for sale signs,[27] or the building of churches in certain neighborhoods?[28] The potential classical liberal justifications available to the state in speech cases can likewise run broadly. At a *minimum*, virtually every argument that could raise a valid claim against a speaker under the private law (including appeals to the law of nuisance and fraud) can in principle afford a parallel justification to the state. This list of defenses is larger than commonly supposed in both speech and religion cases.

At the top of the list, of course, are justifications that are intended to counter the private use of force and fraud, including defamation, invasion of privacy, and intentional infliction of emotional distress. These can prove exceedingly difficult to apply in religion cases where the line between true belief and religious hucksterism is hard to police.[29] Second, common law and equity courts also recognize a cause of action for the inducement of breach of contract, including bribes, but only in those cases where the inducer is on notice of the existence of the contract or the status of the public official. Third, there are all sorts of actions brought against persons who enter into contracts in restraint of trade. Fourth, there are the rules in place to govern the use of the commons—meaning any area that is open to the public, be it on a general or restricted basis. Fifth, there are rules that protect against the exploitation of infants. Finally, it is necessary to address the amorphous set of "morals" defenses which include, as noted, key questions such as marriage, prostitution, gambling, and the like. The subsequent chapters in the next two sections take up these topics, first for speech and then for religion.

25

Force, Threats, and Inducements

THE INITIAL ROUND of First Amendment litigation arose in the after-math of World War I, where the central issue on the table related to the interconnections of force, threats of force, and inducement. Frequently, force and persuasion lie at opposite poles in political discourse, as the former short-circuits the public debate that the latter fosters. In a deep sense, the First Amendment offers protection against the dangers of industrial policy in the domain of public discourse. It is not the function of government to pick winners and losers in political debate. Rather, it is to let all speak, no matter what the content of their message or its popularity with the public at large. A society needs its gadflies just as it needs its heroes. Letting all speak allows everyone to say their piece, no matter how fierce the level of objection. Indeed, the more potent or outlandish the argument, the greater the need for it to be made—no matter how much it hurts the feelings of those on the losing side of the debate. Entry into political debate does not require the majority's consent, let alone its blessing. Consistent with the narrow version of the harm principle, the offense or hurt that people experience from the publication of adverse sentiment should be regarded as "noncognizable" in the sense that no legal liabilities of any sort are generated. No one should take these private harms into account in any social cost-benefit analysis of political discourse.

There is, however, a second cut. That persuasion which is used to ask people to step up to their political or civic obligations is welcome. But the use or threat of force, which is banned in all other areas of life, receives no comfort or protection from the First Amendment. It is well understood that these actions are inconsistent with the operation of any voluntary market. Those markets depend on true information in order to guide exchanges that work for the benefit of both parties. Introduce force or the threat thereof, and its target no longer compares the value of what is surrendered to that which is received. He compares the value of what is surrendered to the threat of greater loss if he does not comply with the demands of others. All political and expressive markets are subject to the same constraint, so that it becomes necessary to police the delicate line between force in all its manifestations on the one side and persuasion on the other.

Nor do force and fraud mark the limits of the proper state control of speech. The same can be said of that limited form of persuasion which asks any person to *breach* his or her preexisting obligations. The closest private analogy to the constitutional issue is the tort of inducement of breach of contract, with special emphasis on the word "breach."[1] For example, inducing an employee to leave his job when he is free to do so has the positive result of fostering competition, a critical component of sound market operations. But urging an employee to leave his job when doing so would breach a contract has the negative result of undermining the entire system of voluntary association.

Unexpected Synergies

On this view, inducement of a breach of duty goes hand in hand with the use of force and fraud in order to achieve any set of ends. In fact, both analytically and historically, it is impossible to treat them separately since they are typically used in tandem. Any person who is intent on having his way will usually resort to both tactics. Even the most hardened gangster will mix carrots and sticks to gain compliance. The inexorably self-interested logic is that the first carrot is far more likely to have its desired impact of bending a target to the persuader's will than the hundredth stick. The rational agent therefore will use whatever mix of sticks and carrots maximizes the expected return from his efforts to secure his objective. This unified strategy causes genuine complications for the First Amendment because it shows how difficult it is to draw any sharp and principled line between action and speech. The problem is acute precisely because everyone agrees that the use of force should not be afforded the same First Amendment protection as speech, even if that force is meant to issue a warning to others, and thus has some expressive content: hanging a hated rival from the lamppost to express indignation at his political beliefs does not immunize the killer from liability for murder. Tort law calls this form of expression "actual malice" which, if anything, aggravates the wrong. No one would dare defend the opposite result, even one reluctant to embrace the general classical liberal theory on other matters.

That same classical liberal theory makes it impossible to adopt any truncated account of what it means to use force as once again the anti-circumvention principle comes into play. The need to guard against private abuses of power has always led everyone, everywhere, to treat the *threat* of force as a form of force, even if threats necessarily involve speech, gestures, or other forms of communicative conduct. Think of what the world would look like if that position were rejected. A robber goes to someone and says, "Your money or your life." Prudently, the victim surrenders the money to save his life, and in so doing obviates the actual use of force. No one would dare argue that this threat to use force should receive constitutional protection under the guarantee of freedom of speech just because no force has actually been used.

This set of examples raises the question of what circumstances and what threats are beyond the protection of the First Amendment. Just looking at coercion in isolation, this question gives rise to immense difficulties that pervade the criminal law of assault and battery and self-defense. It is delusive to think that any constitutional analysis could sidestep the necessary ambiguities that define this problem as a matter of first principle. The problem is acute because there is nothing in the logic of threats that makes them credible only if the threat of force is imminent. Threatening to use force next week if a check is not received in the mail tomorrow is the essence of the tort of intentional infliction of emotional distress,[2] which does not receive immunity from legal sanction solely because of its delayed consequences. To be sure, the immediacy of the threat is always relevant, but never dispositive: most extortionists are quite happy to give their target some time to raise the money.

This problem with threats—their immediacy and their severity—is compounded by positive inducements to secure compliance. These inducements, moreover, need not be combined with the threat of force but often work quite well without it, as in cases of bribery of public or private officials, or indeed any (tangible) inducement intended to make public or private officials disregard their duties to citizens in the first case or shareholders in the second. The potential range of police power justifications for state intervention therefore is quite large even if we seek to confine the analysis to those that make sense under any small government theory of constitutional law.

National Security in Wartime

All of these elements have surfaced in somewhat chaotic fashion in the first generation of freedom of speech cases that arose during and after World War I. Reduced to a sentence, these were all concerned with one constellation of issues: how much running room do you give individuals to urge and cajole before the state can pounce on them with a criminal prosecution?[3] The focal point of much of this litigation was the Espionage Act of 1917, passed during President Woodrow Wilson's second term, which made it a crime to willfully "make or convey false reports or false statements with an intent to interfere" with the military success of the United States, or "to promote the success of its enemies." It also made it criminal to willfully "cause or attempt to cause insubordination, disloyalty, mutiny, or refusal of duty, in the military or naval forces of the United States," and finally, to willfully "obstruct the recruiting or enlistment service of the United States."[4]

Here is the nub of the problem. No one can credibly claim that the statutory ends are illegitimate. Nor can they credibly claim that all forms of inducement—whether mixed with threats of force, as they often are (think picket lines)—are, or should be, categorically insulated from criminal prosecution. So, in the end, the entire matter necessarily boils down to one of the extent and degree of the government prohibition. The ultimate determinants of that calculation always bring the inquiry back to a choice between two kinds of error: overenforcement on the one hand and underenforcement on the other. In making that choice, all the traditional rules about anticipatory relief that arise, for example, in connection with issuing preliminary injunctions in nuisance and pollution cases involving threatened emissions, necessarily arise here as well. The likelihood of allowing serious harm lies on one side of the scale, and the dangers of attacking legitimate speech sit on the opposite side. The ever-present fixation on immediacy always cuts in favor of the accused: if there is a later stage at which dangerous activities could be stopped, with the possibility of damage actions or criminal sanctions, the balance of convenience shifts against immediate enforcement. Every one of the relevant First Amendment inquiries relates to using remedial choices for future and uncertain harms that arise daily in nonconstitutional settings. Yet the high stakes of constitutional adjudication give us no novel tools to put in the judicial tool kit. Carrying the traditional analysis of remedial uncertainty over to the First Amendment context does not bias or inform that inquiry.

So how do we draw the line on timing, and why? An earlier 1907 Holmes decision held that the publication of a cartoon and articles attacking the probity of the Colorado Supreme Court was not protected under the First Amendment because it "tend[ed]" to interfere with the administration of justice.[5] That "bad tendency" test helped shape the subsequent litigation under the Espionage Act, but it did not clinch the argument for state power. No ardent government prosecutor ever argued that simple disapproval of American involvement in foreign wars was criminal under the Espionage Act, even though it could lead thoughtful or impressionable individuals to resist induction into the military. But once the anti-government talk got so nasty and bellicose that participants in the war were branded agents of Satan and patriotism was equated to murder, the mood changed. At least one early lower court decision, *Shaffer v. United States*,[6] left the question of criminal incitement to the jury, which could vote to convict even though it was not obliged to do so.

The most famous case in this line was *Schenck v. United States*,[7] in which Justice Holmes also sustained a criminal conviction under the Espionage Act for mailing an inflammatory socialist leaflet denouncing American participation in the First World War. Two portions of this opinion deserve special attention.

First, Justice Holmes noted that "[t]he question in every case is whether the words used are used in such circumstances and are of such a nature as to create a clear and present danger that they will bring about the substantive evils that Congress has a right to prevent. It is a question of proximity and degree."[8] Note that he does not, nor should he, restrict those "substantive evils" to the use of force or fraud, which would ignore all cases of improper inducement. Nor is this test as tolerant of government action as the earlier bad tendency test in *Patterson*.

Holmes then utters in *Schenck* the famous line: "The most stringent protection of free speech would not protect a man in falsely shouting fire
in a theatre and causing a panic."[9] Yet even though this sentence proves
that the First Amendment is not absolute, it hardly proves that the broad
exception to it accepted in *Schenck* makes any sense. The shouting of
"fire" will cause panic precisely because no other actions are needed for
it to have its desired effect. Yet the contribution to any discourse on any
topic is negligible.

Neither of those propositions is true about the speech in *Schenck*.
Holmes gets a bit closer to the line in his previous sentence, which is
usually not quoted: "[The First Amendment] does not even protect a
man from an injunction against uttering words that may have all the
effect of force."[10] For that proposition he cites a labor injunction case,
Gompers v. Buck's Stove & Range Co.,[11] which held in principle that agreements to conduct boycotts through "verbal acts" may be "as much subject to injunction as the use of any other force whereby property is
unlawfully damaged,"[12] while undoing the contempt citation in the particular case for overbreadth. Those labor boycott cases are also stronger
against the defendants, all of whom had agreed to act in concert with
one another in pursuit of what was at the time an unlawful boycott.
Neither Holmes's hypothetical nor *Buck's Stove* supports his principled
exception to the First Amendment.

Holmes also pounces on what may have been a fatal concession
of the defense: "if an actual obstruction of the recruiting service were
proved, liability for words that produced that effect might be enforced."[13]
But Holmes misses on the causation and timing issues. The verb "produced" does not attach any weight to the set of decisions that must be
made by other individuals after they receive the leaflet through the mail.
This case therefore hardly looks like one that is covered by the common
law of attempts given the multiple decisions and actions by others that
must intervene—each of which offers a potential target for government
intervention that has far less adverse effects on political speech. The timing of the remedy is thus critical, and on that issue the First Amendment
cautions against resorting to overlong chains of causation to ground a
criminal conviction.

Holmes's decision in *Schenck* should be contrasted with Learned
Hand's famous 1917 opinion in *Masses Publishing Co. v. Patten* which revealed a visceral reluctance to punish actions of generalized incitement.[14]

Hand had previously considered the similar question (but not with criminal prosecutions) of whether the postmaster general could keep out of the mail periodicals that published lurid and vigorous attacks against U.S. military efforts. The case was difficult in principle because of two factors. The Masses (a revolutionary outfit as its name suggests) intended to disrupt the military effort and likely would have had some success. Learned Hand refused to grant the postmaster an injunction because he did not want to construe the term "cause" that broadly, lest he suppress too much criticism of the war effort. What is troublesome and perhaps wrong about his opinion is not the refusal to let the postmaster have his way, but his seizing the occasion for a metaphysical disquisition on causation when in fact it raises the same hard question that arises in all cases of anticipatory bans: which type of error produces greater harm, overenforcement or underenforcement?

The correct analysis, therefore, is not to parse, as Hand did, the words of the statute, or to put quotation marks around the word "cause," but to be candid in the overbreadth analysis. Two points cut that way. First, there is no particular person to whom this message is directed, so there is no way to be sure which of a thousand such influences impelled the action of, say, any draft resistor. Second, a more focused remedy is available against anyone who violates the law, or, perhaps anyone who counsels illegal activity in a more direct way. The simple linguistic ploys do not get at the hard issues.

The same year that gave us *Schenck*, 1919, also gave us *Debs v. United States*.[15] The still unrepentant Justice Holmes wrote for a unanimous court in upholding a conviction of the noted socialist presidential candidate Eugene V. Debs for a fiery speech that he made at the Ohio convention of the Socialist Party in June 1918, before the First World War had come to an end. Note the risks just from the trial itself: even an acquittal after prosecution is a harrowing experience, so that the defenders of free speech cannot rest easy with this result. What they want is immunity from suit under a doctrine too clear to admit exception.

So matters stood until *Abrams v. United States*, also decided in 1919,[16] which resulted in yet another conviction of Jewish socialist supporters of the Bolsheviks, who distributed incendiary leaflets supporting their cause. The views that Learned Hand had expressed in *Masses* did not, evidently, wean the Supreme Court off the pro-prosecution sentiment that Holmes had voiced in *Schenck*. So once again, the majority of the

Court sustained the jury verdict on the simple ground that nothing in the record could upset it. But Learned Hand did win over Justice Holmes, who wrote a memorable dissent that has since become a landmark of the law of free speech.

His analysis deserves close attention. As a matter of criminal law, the Court is surely correct to say that no one can defeat an allegation of criminal intent by alleging virtuous motive. An accused cannot escape the clutches of the Espionage Act by insisting that he wanted to save Russia, not hurt the United States. Holmes is wrong in contesting this point by claiming that the adverse consequence targeted by the government has to be "the proximate motive of the specific act."[17] That standard has never applied in other contexts, and it should not apply here.

Where Holmes reaches his rhetorical genius is on making the critical second-order judgment on questions of degree. He starts modestly enough by summarizing his earlier view in *Schenck*: "the United States constitutionally may punish speech that produces or is intended to produce a clear and imminent danger that it will bring about forthwith certain substantive evils that the United States constitutionally may seek to prevent."[18] Quite simply, he concludes that publication of pamphlets is never "forthwith" enough to justify the imposition of this punishment, given the First Amendment commitment to freedom of speech. That result should, however, apply as a matter of general criminal law wholly apart from the First Amendment, which shows the extent to which ordinary criminal law, when rightly construed, is respectful of the claims of freedom of speech. With the underbrush cleared away, Holmes then displays the full extent of his rhetorical genius by penning the following memorable passage:

> But when men have realized that time has upset many fighting faiths, they may come to believe even more than they believe the very foundations of their own conduct that the ultimate good desired is better reached by free trade in ideas—that the best test of truth is the power of the thought to get itself accepted in the competition of the market, and that truth is the only ground upon which their wishes safely can be carried out. That, at any rate, is the theory of our Constitution. It is an experiment, as all life is an experiment. Every year, if not every day, we have to wager our salvation upon some prophecy based upon imperfect knowledge. While that experiment is part of our system, I think that we should be eternally vigilant against attempts to check the expression

of opinions that we loathe and believe to be fraught with death, unless they so imminently threaten immediate interference with the lawful and pressing purposes of the law that an immediate check is required to save the country.[19]

In time, Holmes's insistence that the publication of general manifestos did not warrant criminal prosecution gained ground. That position led him in 1925 to join Justice Brandeis in protesting the "Red Scare" prosecutions for criminal anarchy in *Gitlow v. New York*,[20] given that the "Left Wing Manifesto" was not targeted to any particular audience. A similar state conviction was sustained in *Whitney v. California*[21] over the fierce, principled objections of Justices Holmes and Brandeis, who concurred on narrow technical grounds only.

The issues that were in full heat in the aftermath of World War I returned to prominence with the Red Scare during the 1950s, when once again the Communist threat gave rise to genuine concerns as to whether the First Amendment protected speech directed against the security and safety of the United States. At issue was the application of the Smith Act, which made it a crime "to knowingly or willfully advocate, abet, advise, or teach the duty, necessity or propriety of overthrowing or destroying any government in the United States by force or violence. . . ."[22] Additional provisions prohibited the publication or printing of materials that tended toward that end and organizing or helping groups achieve those ends.[23]

In *Dennis v. United States*,[24] the issue came to a head when the United States charged that the defendant had, during the period from April 1, 1945, to July 20, 1948, published pamphlets and otherwise engaged in instruction that incited individuals to take steps to overthrow the United States by force and violence. The district court charges took pains to note, "it is not the abstract doctrine of overthrowing or destroying organized government by unlawful means which is denounced by this law, but the teaching and advocacy of action for the accomplishment of that purpose, by language reasonably and ordinarily calculated to incite persons to such action."[25] In the Second Circuit, an older, but not necessarily wiser Learned Hand—author of the defense of free speech in *Masses*—affirmed the decision by making this inroad to the clear and present danger test derived from *Schenck*: "In each case, [courts] must ask whether the gravity of the 'evil,' discounted by its improbability, justifies such invasion of free speech as is necessary to avoid the danger."[26] That approach was explicitly endorsed by the Supreme Court, which placed ample reliance on the cautionary instructions given to the jury.

On balance, the case for this particular position seems thin, especially when the discounting is done correctly. The very length of the instructional period suggests that nothing serious was afoot. A prolonged immersion in such standards as the Communist Manifesto of 1848 should not provoke those dire predictions. Indeed, as Justice Black pointed out in his *Dennis* dissent,[27] this particular prosecution did not even charge the parties with an attempt to overthrow the government, precisely because no such attempt existed. Nor did they even say or write anything that in itself was designed to overthrow the government. All their speculations were to take effect, if at all, at some later date that in fact never came. The majority decision of Chief Justice Fred Vinson, and the concurrence of Justice Frankfurter, can be commended for their awareness of how close this case came to the line. No dictatorship could long flourish under their view. But that said, it seems as though they put the line in the wrong place, given that the traditional criminal law doctrines of conspiracy and attempt remain in force against defendants who shift their activities from the openness of the classroom to the secrecy of the criminal cell.

It is therefore no surprise that these criminal prosecutions petered out. In *Yates v. United States*,[28] the Court—speaking through Justice John Marshall Harlan—threw out a similar Smith Act prosecution by a six-to-one vote, by giving only lip service to *Dennis* and its distinction between teaching the forcible overthrow of government as an "abstract principle" and its concrete instantiation in an actual plot. In time, the whole bad tendency doctrine came clattering down as tolerance for contentious speech rose during the 1960s. In *Edwards v. South Carolina*[29] and *Cox v. Louisiana*,[30] the Court paid no attention to any version of the bad tendency doctrine when it invalidated the convictions of civil rights protest marchers before the statehouse and the courthouse respectively, even though the risk of force loomed larger in these cases than in the pamphleting cases that arose during and after World War I. Finally, the entire World War I edifice was dismantled in *Brandenburg v. Ohio*,[31] which arose from protests to the Vietnam War. No longer would "abstract objections" about the merits of the Vietnam War give rise to any criminal prosecutions. The verbal distinctions that had sustained conviction in *Dennis* were now put in service of the First Amendment. The willingness to stay the hand of government prosecutors against publications was a great victory in the battle for freedom of speech.

Yet in the midst of this self-congratulation, it is important to understand not only the importance of this line of free speech cases, but also its sensible *narrowness*. If some shadowy group meets in secret planning to bomb a military installation, the law of conspiracy will nail it every time. If it trains operatives to tackle recruits as they are entering a military facility, it will face the same fate. If one bribes a public official, the First Amendment offers no get-out-of-jail-free card. Once public discourse is no longer part of the equation, the law comes down hard (as it should) against intrigue and conspiracy.

This basic question about the threat and use of force arises not only in the area of national security but also bears on other difficult questions, such as whether picketing by labor unions in support of their bargaining demands should count as a disguised use of force or as a high-minded appeal to public sympathies. This question does not relate to whether one supports or opposes labor unions, but rather whether it is possible to disentangle exhortation and threats by strikers who have little or no sympathy with scabs.

The issues are so fact-intensive that there is no single principle that explains how these cases should be decided under common law, the labor statute, or the Constitution.[32] The correct approach in this and similar cases—pickets at abortion clinics offer another example—is to split the difference in the framing of the injunction. Ban the bullhorns and baseball bats; keep the picketers twenty feet from the entrance; let them use signs; watch over them with police. Intermediate cases need intermediate solutions, all of which begin with the recognition that preventing both the use of the threat of force and the inducement of breaches of public obligations are legitimate ends. Scrutiny on means is thus the order of the day. In the end it is not always possible to have clear remedial solutions. But once the ends are clear, the means can be adjusted. The Court's belated adoption of classical liberal principles has helped prevent the law from going too far astray. It is important that, going forward, it be kept on that straight if narrow path.

26

Fraud, Defamation, Emotional Distress, and Invasion of Privacy

O NE OF THE CENTRAL DIFFICULTIES in First Amendment law results from its collision with the ordinary law of tort, which is, to say the least, of ancient vintage. When courts chiefly focus on physical injuries, they necessarily explore the limitations on freedom of action, starting with the unwavering judicial commitment against the use of force.[1] But just as the tort law limits the freedom of action, so it also limits the freedom of speech, and for the same reason—that the harm some speech can generate outweighs its social value. The parallel between the two positions is well captured by the general prohibition against the use of force *and* fraud in libertarian thought—where the former regulates conduct and the latter regulates speech. In this regard, a strong presumption should be made in favor of the proposition that the *freedom* of speech does not extend to tortious actions, which include the four potential heads of liability raised in this chapter: fraud, defamation, intentional infliction of emotional distress, and, more haltingly, the invasion of privacy.

Fraud—Commercial and Social

There are strong social reasons to impose limitations on the use of fraud in human affairs. At a minimum it is clear that deliberately giving misinformation undermines the voluntary quality of individual actions, contracts, and relationships. The problem is not limited to commercial contexts, for fraud is a way in which to achieve advancements in a wide variety of other social settings as well. In some cases, fraud can be the source of physical injuries, as when a man goes over a cliff because he has been falsely told that a barrier will protect him from the fall. In commercial contexts fraud can take a variety of forms, including false statements designed to induce individuals to buy worthless shares of stock at high prices or to sell valuable assets at low prices. Resume fraud is a critical issue in employment contexts. In some instances, fraud is an avenue for social advancement or higher prestige by carefully cultivating a false, but attractive social image. The First Amendment has rarely, if ever, been invoked in connection to physical injury, but its relevance to personal and social interactions is indisputable. The clear line is that truthful statements should usually escape legal sanction, but fraudulent ones should not. All too often, however, First Amendment law takes a too suspicious view toward certain truthful statements, and a too sympathetic a view to false ones. This chapter traces out those developments in both commercial and social settings.

Fraud in commerce poses a grave threat to the operation of voluntary markets. In the normal case, the contracting mechanism works because each side makes its own valuation of the goods and services exchanged, so that both parties benefit from their gains from trade. Their joint gains open up new opportunities to third parties, so that the result of most business transactions is win/win both for the transacting parties and the public at large. When the incorrect estimations of value derive solely from the misleading acts of one party to the agreement, the willingness in common law to allow damages or rescission makes sense both as a commercial matter and within the framework of the First Amendment.

Indeed, the problem of fraud is so pervasive that private rights of action given to aggrieved parties after the fraud has taken place are generally regarded as insufficient. That scheme of remedies in commercial cases is therefore supplemented, and often replaced, by two additional systems of social control. In the first instance, extensive disclosure requirements are often imposed on institutional players. Most credit card and other loans are subject to extensive disclosure devices, of which the annual percentage rate is the simplest. Most sales of securities in public markets are made by prospectus whose contents are subject to oversight by the Securities and Exchange Commission. Fines and criminal sanctions make up the second supplementary system to combat fraud. After the fact, individual lawsuits are often difficult to maintain in dealing with, say, claims of fraud in the issuance of home mortgages. Here a system of fines and criminal sanctions are a helpful deterrent to supplement any additional private right of action that may be difficult to maintain. This grand question on the adequacy of private rights of action takes exactly the same form with fraud as it does with various forms of physical injury, as elaborate statutes such as the Clean Water Act[2] and the Clean Air Act[3] are an essential feature of any rational program of environmental protection. The key point in this analysis is that the same basic strictures that apply to other forms of activities carry over to speech and other forms of expression. The classical liberal theory thus supplies a seamless system that governs both the articulation of individual entitlements and social remedies.

The flip side to this concern with fraud is the proposition that people are allowed to say what they want so long as their statements do not mislead others (notwithstanding various proscribed threats, obscenities, and defamatory remarks). That general proposition applies to all forms of speech—political, commercial, and social. The key to understanding the First Amendment in these contexts is to show that its application rests on these private law conceptions, just as it did in dealing with various forms of speech that could be construed as threats to use force against private persons or to overthrow the government of the United States.

In light of this general orientation, the older view that commercial transactions should be outside the scope of the First Amendment[4] is not defensible in the long run. Unless it runs afoul of the standard prohibitions on speech, commercial speech is entitled to as much protection as any other. In practice, of course, there is at least one difference between political and commercial speech that can be understood and policed. No one should say that all speech in newspapers is commercial because it is funded by advertisements. But if push comes to shove, it is clearly more important to keep political and artistic speech alive than commercial speech, if only because the former holds open a greater possibility of checking government abuse than the latter. Hence, for structural reasons, it should not matter that many individuals would quite happily sacrifice their rights to political participation in order to buy an advertised flat-screen television at a bargain price. Systematic concerns have greater salience than individual purchasing decisions.

By the same token, however, it seems a mistake to demote commercial speech into some nether region along with defamation, fighting words, obscenity, and the like. Those forms of speech receive low levels of protection precisely because they fall into the traditional police power categories dealing with the control of force and fraud or, in the case of obscenity, with moral matters (especially when directed toward children). It is, however, unwise to consign commercial speech to this "low-value" category solely because it lacks the social punch found in many forms of political and artistic expression. Rather, in light of the substantial benefits that advertisement contributes to the smooth operation of competitive markets, it should be welcomed, not spurned, and thus afforded an intermediate level of protection, which attaches roughly equal weight to the risks of over- and under-inclusion.[5]

Even with that framework, the differences between commercial and political speech matter. The concrete nature of this speech makes it easier to identify claims that should be condemned on one of four traditional grounds: fraud, misrepresentation, concealment, or nondisclosure. Put otherwise, the class of protected opinion, which is broad in political and artistic contexts, is far narrower in commercial cases. To give but one example, trade disparagement and passing off have long been recognized as a commercial wrong, either by understating the value of a rival's goods or pretending that one's own goods are really those of a superior competitor.[6] Indeed, the Lanham Act, which deals with "the deceptive and misleading use of marks," is of unquestionable constitutionality,[7] notwithstanding the inevitable marginal cases that fall close to the line on both sides. Courts are well cognizant of the potential conflict in this area, as in copyright, between free expression and protected interests; it would be overkill to eliminate on constitutional grounds all protection of well-established intellectual property rights. Therefore it did not take any bold judicial initiative to hold that the fair use exception to the Copyright Act[8]—so essential to allowing criticism of published works—did not allow *The Nation* to publish huge extracts from the unpublished manuscript of ex-president Gerald Ford's memoirs.[9] When powerful interests lie on both sides of the scale, some rule of reason is needed govern the tension between them.

In light of these developments, the mixed emotions about commercial speech are best captured by an intermediate scrutiny standard on both the question of means and ends. The applicable inquiry typically boils down to a test derived from *Central Hudson Gas & Electric Corp. v. Public Service Commission*,[10] where the Public Service Commission (PSC) sought to prevent promotional advertising intended to stimulate demand for electricity in times of acute shortage. In dealing with this question, the Court in *Central Hudson* asked whether the expression was covered by the First Amendment, which it was, and whether it was misleading, which it wasn't.[11] That second prong makes it clear that fraud, or indeed any misrepresentation is, at the very least, subject to heightened scrutiny. Once that is done the question shifts to justification, so that the PSC had to show a "substantial" government interest.[12] Then the test goes to means, by asking "whether the regulation directly advances the governmental interest asserted, and whether it is not more extensive than is necessary to serve that interest."[13] The reach of the First Amendment allows only for tailored restrictions against force and fraud. Thus, it followed that the PSC could not block the company's speech to advance its business interest in energy conservation.[14] That conclusion seems appropriate given that rate regulators may still set the right prices for electricity under various conditions. For example, rate regulators could allow utilities to charge customers higher prices for consumption during peak periods.

A similar analysis applies to ordinary commercial advertisements on such key elements as price. The more accurate the information, the better the public decisions on key issues of the day. But the question of truth or falsity does not depend on how the advertisement is distributed. Therefore, one tell-tale sign that state regulation has gone overboard is any selective limitation on the mode of information distribution. Thus, the Supreme Court rightly struck down a Rhode Island statute that banned the use of off-premise advertisements for liquor in the absence of any credible showing of how this might pose a safety or health hazard.[15] Meanwhile, concerns with particular types of transactions can be addressed through more direct regulation. Any fears dealing with sales to minors, for example, may be better addressed through direct restrictions on sale or consumption, or even by tax increases that tend to have greater impact on teenagers who have limited income. The various permutations are endless, but a sensible classical liberal framework supplies the proper analytical approach.

The use of fraudulent behavior in social settings has generally not been subject to legal sanctions. But the issue received a most unsatisfactory resolution in *United States v. Alvarez*,[16] where the operative provision of the 2005 Stolen Valor Act (SVA) reads as follows:

Whoever falsely represents himself or herself, verbally or in writing, to have been awarded any decoration or medal authorized by Congress for the Armed Forces of the United States . . . shall be fined under this title, imprisoned not more than six months, or both.[17]

The SVA increased the statutory penalty to one year when the fraudulent representation involved the false claim of the receipt of the Medal of Honor, of the sort that Xavier Alvarez made in his first public meeting as a member of the Three Valley Water District Board in Southern California. At one level the claim could be treated as a "pathetic attempt" to gain personal respect, as Justice Kennedy claimed for a six-member majority.[18] But on this issue Justice Alito seemed to have the better argument by showing that large numbers of individuals had made these claims to the Veterans History Project and *Who's Who*.[19] In this setting, the use of a collective social sanction to pick up the slack where private rights of action leave off seems to be a sensible legal accommodation similar to that in cases of credit and security fraud. But the set of social sanctions against this form of fraudulent behavior broke down, so that the personal exposure of fraudulent speakers had not been able to stem the increasing tide of these misstatements. Yet Justice Kennedy went badly off the rails when he noted, "government has no power to restrict expression because of its message, its ideas, [or] its subject matter,"[20] but instead "demands that content-based restrictions on speech be presumed invalid" unless and until the government can justify those restrictions.[21]

The statement represents a complete inversion of sound constitutional principles. The notion of content-based laws has an honorable place to play in First Amendment law, where it is clear, for example, that time, place, and manner restrictions on expression must apply equally to persons on the opposite side of a political issue, lest one get an unfair advantage over another. The whole point of an antifraud regime is to destroy the undeserved parity between those who tell lies and those who do not. Indeed, the common position that fraudulent statements constitute a form of unfair competition that can be enjoined at the request of their victims makes clear that only by preventing fraud is it possible to get the correct parity between parties. Justices Breyer and Kagan thought that they could split the difference by drafting a narrower statute than the SVA, but offered no language that could do the job better than that which was found in the SVA.[22] At this point we see how the First Amendment can be turned on its head, given that false statements are not part of the freedom of speech that it protects. The problem here is not confined to these fraud cases, for the great criticism of the Supreme Court's treatment of defamation under the First Amendment is that it is also subject to this vice.

Defamation

The question of truth or falsity in public debate also plays a significant role in defamation cases, particularly in actions brought by public officials and public figures against media defendants—print, broadcast, and Internet—for defamation. The logic of the basic tort of defamation fits securely within the framework of classical liberal theory. The tort of defamation involves a minimum of three parties: the defendant makes a false statement of fact about the plaintiff to a third party, who in consequence of the false information alters his or her relationships in ways that deprive the plaintiff of beneficial commercial or social relationships. The action often gains real force because publications in media cases are directed toward third parties, all of whom may be persuaded to alter their behavior in ways that hurt the plaintiff's business or social prospects. In most situations, therefore, a plaintiff is entitled to sue for general damages, whereby she does not have to track down the individual perceptions of every person who could have voted for her in an election, watched a movie in which she starred, or avoided some business product that she promoted. Such cases are always fact-intensive insofar as the loss of business or friendship could have arisen from other causes, which a defendant may always introduce at trial to cut down on awarded damages.

However, if the abstract logic of defamation cases fits within the classical liberal framework, its implementation does not. Blackstone's influential early statement gave much shape to this area:

> The liberty of the press is indeed essential to the nature of a free state; but this consists in laying no *previous* restraints upon publications, and not in freedom from censure for criminal matters when published. Every free man has an undoubted right to lay what sentiments he pleases before the public: to forbid this, is to destroy the freedom of the press: but if he publishes what is improper, mischievous, or illegal, he must take the consequence of his own temerity.[23]

The first half of this proposition has remained rock-solid. The early restraint runs the risk of vast overbreadth. Applied consistently, it could also bankrupt newspapers and individuals who are subjected to these injunctions. The second half of the proposition is, however, far more problematic. On the plus side, it is just the availability of damage remedies that eases the sting where defamation has worked its harm. On the negative side, the woolly definition of matters "improper, mischievous, or illegal"[24] makes it all too likely that, in some instances at least, lawmakers and judges can and will use heavy damage judgments to cudgel unwelcome critics into submission.

Common law judges who worked on the subject before it came under First Amendment restraints in *New York Times Co. v. Sullivan*[25] acknowledged these twin risks.[26] Their ingenious accommodation allowed false statements of fact to generate liability wholly without proof that the defendant meant to harm the plaintiff or failed to take reasonable steps to avoid such harm. In this instance, private parties, public officials, and public figures (entertainers, authors, movie stars, magnates, and the like) were all subject to the same rule. The question in each case was whom the false statement harmed, not whom the defendant meant to hit.[27] This tough standard, however, was offset by rules that gave extensive protection to any defendant who presented a reasonably complete view of the facts of a case, or who relied on facts in common knowledge to back up their opinion about whether the plaintiff was a thief or an unscrupulous opportunist. That privilege of fair comment was absolute, and again it applied indifferently to all classes of plaintiffs.[28] And finally, the Supreme Court in *Near v. Minnesota*[29] adhered to the prohibition against prior restraints, i.e., those that prevent publication, in defamation cases, without committing itself to an examination of the state law rules in defamation cases.

In general, these rules worked well until they ran smack into the civil rights turmoil of the late 1950s and early 1960s.[30] In the landmark case of *New York Times Co. v. Sullivan*,[31] a Montgomery public safety commissioner claimed that an advertisement published in the *Times* by various civil rights groups had defamed him. Only about 394 copies of the *Times* were sold in Alabama, and the Alabama Supreme Court sustained an award of $500,000 in general damages, without any proof of malice—with prospects of still more adverse judgments against the *Times* as other southern officials in the nebulous class of potential plaintiffs lined up for blood. The simplest way to attack this miscarriage of justice was to dispose of the damage award on the ground that a local folk hero could hardly have suffered any damages at all. (It also would have helped if the *Times* could have removed the case to federal court, which was not possible because of the strategic naming of four Alabama clergymen whose names had appeared in the allegedly defamatory advertisement.)[32] That simple decision would have ended the threat to the *Times* and made it clear that the First Amendment (when applied to the states) limited the ability of legislatures and courts to work their judicial magic.

Nonetheless, all the justices of the Supreme Court were troubled with the strict liability standard used in common law defamation cases. Justice Black, joined by Justice Douglas, took a misshapen absolutist view, which would have undone a huge chunk of state defamation law, by affording the defendants an absolute privilege against any suit by public officials. But that view would tolerate the worst of frauds. Thus, Justice Brennan's view—requiring a showing of "actual malice"[33] on the part of the defendant in suits against public officials (soon extended to public figures like actors and athletes,[34] but not private figures, for whom a negligence standard was used for no particular advantage, but with far less controversy)[35]—backed off the absolutist position of Justice Black and Justice Douglas. "Actual malice" is something of a term of art because it is defined not as bad motive—e.g., race hatred—but exclusively as making a statement knowing that it was false, or in reckless disregard of its truth or falsity.[36] It is at this point that "First Amendment exceptionalism" creates constitutional protections for false statements that go beyond those afforded under classical liberal theory, which does not slight the role of individual reputation as an interest worthy of legal protection. It is incumbent therefore to ask whether this striking departure from the older rules improves the overall situation.

On balance, the old synthesis did better. One risk of the new rule is that weak protections for public officials against defamation could easily deter some able individuals from entering the political arena in either administrative or electoral roles. Another is that the extraordinary difficulty of figuring out which actors in a complex production process had what knowledge, or harbored what intention, adds to the costs of resolving disputes, even when the falsity of the statement is evident from facts clearly on the public record. One possible compromise would deny recovery of damages but force the media defendant to acknowledge and correct its false statement of fact in a manner, and with the same level of publicity, with which it had been originally imported. Under the retraction laws of many states, the publication of this corrected statement will be sufficient to negate any action for punitive damages, and the common practice is for most litigation to cease with that publication.[37]

But if the defendant remains adamant, as often happens, the plaintiff cannot typically get a declaration of truth even if he or she is prepared to waive claims to all damages. The press is more concerned with the (deserved) hit to its reputation, which is exactly why correction should be allowed as a remedy for ordinary individuals whose reputations have been grievously injured by the press. Just that result has been approximated in at least one decision. In the famous struggle between the then Israeli general Ariel Sharon and Time, Inc., Judge Abraham Sofaer ruled: "In New York, a plaintiff entitled only to nominal damages of one dollar is entitled to the vindication which a jury verdict can bring."[38] The cleaner solution would allow the finding of falsity without worrying about either nominal or punitive damages.[39] This model allows the truth to prevail. However, media defendants have resisted this approach fiercely because they do not wish to take the reputational hit similar to that which their stories often inflict on private parties who do not have the ability to fight back. It is also worth noting that large corporate parties are often mortally afraid to pursue any remedy against a media defendant for fear of being flayed in the public eye by the party whom they have sued.

The combined effect of the various defenses open under the *New York Times* solution has reduced suits against media defendants to a mere trickle in the last twenty years. Yet losses to individual plaintiffs' reputations matter, and a careful scrutiny of all aspects of the defamation suit under the older common law rules seems to set the better balance between the plaintiff's interest in reputation (i.e., the relational interests she has or hopes to acquire) and freedom of speech than the Supreme Court's current solution, which offers ordinary people too little, not too much legal protection. Sometimes government gets too small.

Intentional Infliction of Emotional Distress

From the earliest times, the common law has offered protection against assaults,[40] which by common account amount to direct offers of force against the person or property of another. More recently, both in

England and the United States, the common law has come to recognize that the intentional infliction of emotional distress, often by extreme and outrageous conduct, is wrongful even though it does not threaten the direct use of force.[41] In most situations, these childish pranks or worse involve no effort at publication communication, and hence raise no First Amendment concern. But in some cases, at least, the mixture of the profane and the macabre has just that effect by a mixture of defamation and poor taste.

This issue has come before the Supreme Court in a number of cases. Thus in *Hustler Magazine v. Falwell*,[42] *Hustler Magazine* ran a mock interview with Reverend Jerry Falwell in which he had his "first time" in a "drunken incestuous rendezvous with his mother in an outhouse," splashed over a small disclaimer announcing that the ad was just a parody.[43] Speaking through Chief Justice Rehnquist, the Supreme Court held that given the need for "breathing space" under the First Amendment, the suit could not proceed either under a theory of defamation or of intentional infliction of emotional distress.[44]

The argument for the first conclusion was that no one could believe that the statement was true—which is not to say that it could not, even if known to be false, cause others to avoid a particular party out of an abundance of caution or distaste, which was the common law rule.[45] The claim for intentional infliction of emotional distress was likewise dismissed on the ground that First Amendment values often require "public figures" to toughen their hides against malicious assaults.[46] More specifically, Rehnquist feared that the allowance of this action would open the doors toward lawsuits against political commentators such as the cartoonist Thomas Nast—even though he cited no case demonstrating that awful eventuality. The decision in *Hustler* may have been correct for the simple reason that Falwell used the *Hustler* story in his own fundraising efforts.[47] But it is surely incorrect insofar as it relies on the slippery slope argument to make a case. Slippery slope arguments have some traction when it is still unsettled whether a narrow decision imposing liability will lead to ever more aggressive applications of the basic rule. But in *Hustler* that risk has been negated by extensive experience, because the common law courts and juries have always been alert to the possible dangers. The only way to guard totally against overbreadth is to curtail the relief that is otherwise warranted. The breathing space argument thus fails to give equal weight to the second form of error—that individuals will be needlessly harmed by extreme and outrageous conduct.

The role of intentional infliction of emotional distress as a companion to defamation arose in more poignant circumstances in *Snyder v. Phelps*,[48] where once again the Supreme Court's overambitious First Amendment exceptionalism pushed free speech to its outer limits. The Westboro Baptist Church mounted a tasteless demonstration on public lands on the day of the funeral of Lance Corporal Matthew Snyder, in Westminster, Maryland. Out of sight and at a distance of about 1,000 feet, the demonstration falsely (and irrelevantly) accused him of being gay. As in *Hustler*, the defamation case was (wrongly) dismissed on the ground that no one would believe that rant, but the case for intentional infliction of emotional distress did reach the jury, which awarded very substantial damages: $2.9 million in actual and $8 million in punitive, which the district court trimmed to $2.1 million while leaving the verdict and actual damages intact. Relying on *Hustler*, the Supreme Court threw out the entire case.

On the facts of the case, the dismissal should have been cautiously, not eagerly embraced. The defendant's demonstration was out of sight of the funeral, and thus was in a sense no more offensive there than at Westboro's headquarters in Topeka, Kansas. Even tort law is reluctant to allow for these actions in the absence of any direct sensory observation.[49] But, whether as a matter of tort or First Amendment law, the case surely should have come out the other way if the demonstrators and its chants were done to harass individual attendees to their faces, or otherwise disrupt the funeral services. Let those lines be crossed and the balance no longer favors the supposed political message that is used as an excuse for inflicting gratuitous pain on people who are entitled to a moment of quietness. *Snyder* is not an occasion to celebrate the robustness of the First Amendment. It is a moment to lament the bad taste of those who push its protection to the limits. In a world where some form of balancing is inescapable, the Supreme Court missed the useful opportunity to set some limits on boorish behavior, just as the case should have induced the Court to retreat from its overly restrictive actual malice rule in defamation cases.

Invasion of Privacy

The uncertain fate of actions for invasion of privacy offers a different glimpse of the unity of the classical liberal conception with its dual emphasis on the twin wrongs of falsity and the breach of contract. In this connection, the key issue is whether the publication of truthful information acquired in lawful ways should be regarded as an actionable invasion of privacy that can allow its victims a right of action for damages or an injunction against future publication. The original impetus for a tort of invasion of privacy stemmed from the famous article that Samuel Warren and Louis Brandeis penned in the *Harvard Law Review* in 1890[50] to keep the press from prying into private affairs—in that instance, to curb the sensationalist coverage of Warren's daughter's wedding. This tort has some traction, as it should, when the invasion of privacy comes from one of two sources. The first is where the information is obtained in confidence from a plaintiff, at which point the common law rules on contract and trade secrets set the stage for their enforcement. The second is where a defendant enters the plaintiff's property or otherwise snoops on private conversations. This can occur even in the absence of a formal trespass, when the defendant goes where he knows that he is not wanted and when he publishes the materials in the paper[51] or worse, on YouTube.

The initial presumption in these cases, therefore, cuts against the Warren and Brandeis position, on the ground that no persons should be entitled to the same protection against the publication of truthful information as against false information. It is for that reason that over the years, the Warren and Brandeis position has been eviscerated by the creation of an extensive First Amendment "newsworthiness" exception. The first espousal of the "newsworthiness" exception in 1940 allowed a merciless dissection of the life of William James Sidis, a child prodigy turned eccentric genius, by James Thurber in a well-known *New Yorker* piece, the publication of which contributed to Sidis's early death.[52]

The initial libertarian impulse is to challenge this entire branch of the law of privacy. The hard question in this context is whether it is possible to carve out any narrow exceptions to the right to publish true facts in those few cases where the deleterious effects to the private individual far exceed any gains to public discourse. The presumption at first should be set against allowing these exceptions, but the one case that might well overcome that presumption is the public disclosure of embarrassing private facts, which receives some limited endorsement in the *Restatement (Second) of Torts*, Section 652D, as articulated by the late torts scholar William L. Prosser.[53] One attractive test of that position arose in *Briscoe v. Reader's Digest Association*,[54] where the California Supreme Court rejected *Reader's Digest*'s First Amendment claim of privilege for publishing the name of a rehabilitated truck hijacker some eleven years after the event, thereby causing his family to leave him. *Briscoe* was to find that there was no public interest in this disclosure, but it remains an open question as to whether this privilege should be granted in light of claims that the concealment of this information allows the plaintiff to continuously misrepresent his past to his family. I therefore have more sympathy for this case if the family already knew of the information, so that the public disclosure just subjected them to external abuse that they could not tolerate.

Whatever the soundness of this uneasy judgment, the nascent privacy privilege in *Briscoe* came to a crashing halt in *Cox Broadcasting Corp. v. Cohn*,[55] where the U.S. Supreme Court held that a Georgia law that prevented the publication of a rape victim's name fell before the First Amendment. In this case, keeping the information quiet is by no stretch of the imagination part of a scheme by any person to conceal her past from strangers, and the protection goes a long way to ease the reentry of these rape victims back into society. It is worth noting that most newspapers tend not to publish the names of rape victims, who in litigation are often called "Doe" or "Roe" (as in *Roe v. Wade*[56] on abortion, for example). It seems a bit odd that the Supreme Court has upheld a First Amendment privilege on these matters, as most newspapers protect the name of the rape victim, even when published elsewhere; many advocacy groups beg the victim to tell her story in public in order to increase awareness of the crime. It thus looks as though the private responses in the press have, except perhaps in celebrity cases, smoothed over the rough edges of the classical liberal conceptions.

The analysis in question has to change when the published information has been stolen by the defendant or knowingly received by him as stolen information. The most conspicuous case of this sort was the *Pentagon Papers Case*,[57] which denied a government injunction against the publication of the "History of U.S. Decision-Making Process on Viet Nam Policy"[58] that was released to the *New York Times* and *Washington Post* in violation of government policy. The Court denied the injunction by invoking the strong historical prohibition against the prior judicial restraint of publication. As is common in these matters, this approach downplays the difference between the critic who publishes his own statements and the receiver of stolen documents who publishes information that he knows has been taken illegally from others.

The closest analogy to these situations involves individuals who take from a third party property that they know has been stolen from the plaintiff. The good faith purchaser often receives protection against the true owner, but the bad faith purchaser, who has knowledge of the wrongful acquisition of the property, does not.[59] Why use a different rule in dealing with stolen information, including trade secrets, in which the original owner has a proprietary interest? The difficulties in the First Amendment arise with respect to the interests of third parties, which are at their highest when the publication is of stolen materials that pertain to matters of public interest.

In dealing with this case, the trade-off is clearly between national security on the one hand and the integrity of government secrets on the other. The case recently came to the fore in connection with former Justice David Souter's well-publicized 2011 commencement address at Harvard Law School, which purported to demonstrate the need to incorporate extratextual values into constitutional discourse to resolve conflicts internal to the text. Yet, given the existence of the police power, the only question here is how this task ought to best be done, not whether it has to be done at all. On that score, Justice Souter writes that the absolutist approach of Justice Black

> fails because the Constitution has to be read as a whole, and when it is, other values crop up in potential conflict with an unfettered right to publish, the value of security for the nation and the value of the president's authority in matters foreign and military. The explicit terms of the Constitution, in other words, can create a conflict of approved values, and the explicit terms of the Constitution do not resolve that conflict when it arises.[60]

Justice Souter is surely correct to pinpoint the conflict between the freedom to publish and the demands of national security, but it takes more than his general appeal to "values" to resolve the conflict he identifies. Ironically, Justice Souter's supposed slap at conservative originalist thinkers is beside the mark, for, as repeatedly stressed, any intelligent form of originalism has to incorporate the police power into its framework. The real question is just how far the police power's derogation of what might otherwise be a plenary right to publish goes and why.

That said, how well does Justice Souter pull off this originalist inquiry? Well enough, but not flawlessly. Justice Souter is within reason to defend the judicial line drawn in the *Pentagon Papers Case* between matters that merely embarrass the government and those (like publication of departure times for military vessels) that disclose government secrets that could imperil military operations. To claim that the presumption against prior restraint covers these cases is to turn the Constitution into some kind of suicide pact.

Perhaps the right answer to this question rests on nothing more than the simple observation that the illegal release of documents by government officials should be tolerated whenever government officials have improperly classified these documents as government secrets— at best a ticklish proposition that might often require ex parte and in camera judicial review, as in hearings under the Foreign Intelligence Surveillance Act (FISA).[61] This privilege, however, should not extend to those cases where the parties have not exhausted their efforts to obtain proper release through these conventional means. At this point, the desirable institutional strategy is to force the claim of privilege into recognized legal challenges, such as those under the Freedom of Information Act.[62] The advantage of this approach is that it does not allow the wrongful, unilateral actions of some parties to force public disclosure before the government has a chance to make its case before a neutral judicial figure. Occasionally, the issue of delay may well compromise some serious public interest when only immediate release can check government abuse. Yet that does not appear to be the case with the Pentagon Papers, whose general account of government actions contained no time-sensitive information. This process-based approach requires courts to develop rules for deciding when such challenges are appropriate, given that any unquestioned claim for total government secrecy is no more defensible in a constitutional setting than is a claim that government ownership of the roads allows the state the unfettered right to control the composition of traffic. The government never has the luxury of claims of outright ownership.

Whatever the difficulties in these cases, the balance in values should be quite the other way when it comes to the publication of stolen business trade secrets. Thus in *Ford Motor Co. v. Lane*,[63] the defendant blogger knowingly received trade secrets stolen from the Ford Motor Company that related to such vital features as the design of its new models and the details of its manufacturing operations. He then duly published those secrets on the web.[64] The district court held that the precedent in *Pentagon Papers* prevented it from enjoining publication of those documents unless the defendant breached some confidentiality agreement or fiduciary duty.[65] But the point makes no sense at all. Any third person that takes these documents should be held bound by the restrictions that he knew bound the party from which they came. The public interest supports efforts to keep those trade secrets secret in order that firms will invest the capital needed to generate them. Even where there might be some indication that the documents in question contain evidence of some private misconduct, the correct response is to turn those papers over to government officials for examination, not to release them publicly before any such finding has been made. It takes a peculiarly dogmatic mind to equate these business interests with those found in the Pentagon Papers.

In sum, the analysis of the First Amendment in connection with fraud, defamation, emotional distress, and privacy is consistent with the general theme of this book. There is no special set of tools in the constitutional arsenal that goes beyond those already available in private law for these same problems. The protection of freedom of speech should never be twisted to the strange proposition that all speech should be protected. Rather, the correct line of analysis understands that the presumption of liberty in the area of speech should be preserved as it is in the area of action, but that this presumption can be overridden in those cases where fraud, defamation, emotional harm, or breach of confidential arrangements enter into the equation. To the extent that modern constitutional law deviates from these principles, its conclusions lack strong justification, which results in erratic judicial performance in each of the substantive areas of law addressed in this chapter.

27

Government Regulation of the Speech Commons

T HE PREVIOUS CHAPTER linked the ordinary conceptions of fraud, defamation, emotional distress, and privacy to First Amendment theories of freedom of speech. Since the earliest of historical times, however, no legal system has ever confined itself to regulation of speech or other activities that take place between private individuals exclusively on private property. In addition, the law has had to undertake the difficult and extensive task of regulating the use and operation of common property under some amalgam of customary and statutory rules.[1] The rise of these public institutions often reverses the fundamental presumptions of the private law. Now exclusivity gives way to equal access.

From the Economic Commons to the Public Forum

A common law system of private property, for example, specifies that the ownership of land, chattels, and animals is established by the unilateral actions of individuals who are fortunate enough to first occupy land, grab chattels, or capture animals. The common thread that links these three cases together is the first possession rule. In sharp contrast, the basic regimes of common property, dating back to Roman law, never tolerate these claims for exclusive use, all of which would necessarily destroy a commons that achieves its greatest value when open to all. The early arrivals to a river or a highway thus obtain no long-term advantage over later arrivals, with whom they must share the river or road on fair, reasonable, and nondiscriminatory terms. In addition, when governments create new forms of common property by, for example, the exercise of their eminent domain power, these too are in general held in common.

The explanation for this role reversal from private to common property is not hard to see, particularly for streets and rivers, which operate as links between privately owned properties. The great risk of having a single owner control a highway or river is that he will exert his monopoly power to raise prices and to exclude disfavored rivals. In virtue of that power, the law has long imposed correlative duties of service on common carriers, namely those operating in monopoly positions under which they are required to take all customers on reasonable and non-discriminatory terms.[2] The former term is intended to make sure that the holder of that monopoly power does not receive a supracompetitive rate of return. The latter term is intended to make sure that no group is charged with a disproportionate share of the common costs. The same rules carry over to government when it exercises its monopoly position over public rivers and roads.

All private common carriers must take all comers, subject to capacity restraints, unless there is some good reason to decline to offer services, such as nonpayment of fees or misbehavior. The basic instinct here is that freedom of association is not the dominant concern in settings where customers do not have any deep or personal interconnections. Thus this common carrier restriction applies to the operation of a highway, but not to a private automobile that rides the public highways. The common carrier has to allow access to all individuals who in the exercise of their rights of association may choose not to associate with others. The equal access regime carries over to relatively modern technologies like railroads and telecommunications in an effort to counter those powerful tendencies.

One aspect of this doctrine's historical development in connection with access to public roads was that the state could not require a private carrier to take all customers. Instead, in *Frost v. Railroad Commission*, the Supreme Court held that the state could only impose on private carriers various rules that were necessary to preserve the competitive character of the roads in question.[3] Justice Sutherland struck down a protectionist statutory scheme mandating that "a private carrier may avail himself of the use of the highways only upon condition that he dedicate his property to the business of public transportation and subject himself to all the duties and burdens imposed by the Act upon common carriers."[4] In so doing he followed a unanimous decision the year before that the express statutory conversion of a private carrier into a common carrier "would be taking private property for public use without just compensation, which no state can do consistently with the Due Process Clause of the Fourteenth Amendment."[5] That position did not survive as a constitutional norm, as Justice Sutherland himself reversed course six years later by taking a rational basis approach to the same problem.[6]

The forces that influence the governance of common property may no longer raise constitutional issues in key economic matters, but these forces are still very much in play in the context of First Amendment issues, which have never been resolved under a rational basis standard. Indeed, in this area the history runs in the exact opposite direction. The nineteenth-century First Amendment cases, chiefly, had little patience with the historical differences between private and common property. But as the level of scrutiny rose, the modern First Amendment cases came increasingly to rely, often without explicit acknowledgment, on the basic distinctions developed in connection with common carriers.

For these purposes, the story begins with two 1890s Massachusetts decisions of Oliver Wendell Holmes, one dealing with employment law and the other with public streets and parks. In *McAuliffe v. City of New Bedford*,[7] the plaintiff was dismissed from his job for soliciting contributions for political purposes in violation of a categorical prohibition in the political code. Justice Holmes noted that under his employment contract, the plaintiff served at the pleasure of the town, which could dismiss him for good reason, bad reason, or no reason at all. That rule works well for private employers who almost always work without subsidies in competitive markets. But the transfer of that rule to the public realm is both pithy and unsatisfactory:

> The petitioner may have a constitutional right to talk politics, but he has no constitutional right to be a policeman. There are few employments for hire in which the servant does not agree to suspend his constitutional rights of free speech as well as of idleness by the implied terms of his contract. The servant cannot complain, as he takes the employment on the terms which are offered him. On the same principle the city may impose any reasonable condition upon holding offices within its control. This condition seems to us reasonable, if that be a question open to revision here.[8]

Note that in his opening salvo Holmes equated idleness with speech as grounds for potential dismissal, in ways that do not square with the elevated place that speech holds in the constitutional firmament. Perhaps that is why he blinked in the last sentence, smuggling in a reference to the reasonableness of the terms, which, strictly speaking, is never relevant to the employer's rights to fire under a contract at will. And well he should. Is it really the case that the mayor could require the converse of what the local ordinance said, namely, require the employee to contribute to the mayor's reelection campaign in order to keep his job?

In *Massachusetts v. Davis*,[9] the local ordinance provided that no one shall make any public address on any public grounds without a permit supplied by the mayor. No grounds were specified for issuing or denying a permit. Justice Holmes affirmed the conviction of a minister who preached a sermon by treating the case as if it were a rerun of *McAuliffe*.

> For the legislature absolutely or conditionally to forbid public speaking in a highway or public park is no more an infringement of the rights of a member of the public than for the owner of a private house to forbid it in his house. When no proprietary rights interfere, the legislature may end the right of the public to enter upon the public place by putting an end to the dedication to public uses.[10]

The Supreme Court then affirmed by taking refuge in a "right/privilege" distinction which was intended to cement political control over resources subject to public ownership: "The right to absolutely exclude all right to use necessarily includes the authority to determine under what circumstances such use may be availed of, as the greater power contains the lesser."[11] The Court also rejected the view that the state overstepped its proprietary position solely because preaching the gospel has been allowed "from time immemorial" on public property, thus adhering to the standard common law position against inferring easements from the state based on common practice.

The supposed inference that the "greater power contains the lesser" represents one of the great structural fallacies of constitutional law, which arises from its failure to incorporate the distinction between private and common property found everywhere else in the law. The maxim that the greater entails the lesser is in fact indispensable in competitive markets where multiple parties operate simultaneously on both sides of the market. In those settings, prices tend to converge with time. These markets could never efficiently determine those prices if either side were placed under a legal duty to deal with all other persons at prices set by government command. Just which buyers would be required to deal with which sellers, and why? The presence of numerous alternatives means that no party has the power to raise or lower prices, so that the competitive system works just fine without additional constraints on either side.

Yet once monopoly power is introduced in the provision of goods and services, the refusal to deal has far greater power, which is why the party who holds that power is now under the duty to deal with its customers on reasonable and nondiscriminatory terms. These concerns do not disappear solely because that extra power is vested in the state. Quite the contrary, these distinctive state powers introduce two complicating factors that run through all the cases. The first is monopoly power and the second is tax subsidy. The question of monopoly power is not unique to government. Nor is its ability to raise revenues by force from all members of society. Every person subject to any form of government coercion therefore has at least some stake in how government agencies operate. It is necessary therefore to combat the omnipresent risk that tax revenues will be used to hire workers on selective bases, which can skew wealth, privilege, and opportunity from one political faction to a second.

Some movement away from the contract at will model therefore seems virtually inescapable. Yet imposing a straitjacket on government employment comes with a heavy price tag, because many key government positions necessarily require making political choices to allow for implementation of general policies adopted by democratic procedures. A civil service regime cannot work for high-level employees, as noted in the discussion of the right of the president to remove senior officials from office.[12] But designing some substitute regime is, if anything, more difficult than in the case of public rivers and roads, where the risk of systematic exclusion also spells disaster to those who need access on a routine basis. The modern "public forum" cases, which make public spaces open to all comers on reasonable and nondiscriminatory terms, derive their strength from the common law rules developed in other contexts.

The proper objective is to find legal mechanisms to control against the favoritism and extortion that the powers to exclude and to tax necessarily create. The key question therefore is how to limit the discretion of public officials in ways that do not unduly impede their ability to discharge public functions. One way to control that discretion is to subject public officials to a set of all-or-nothing choices. By so doing, the state has less flexibility to burden some individuals for their political beliefs while granting favors to others on those same grounds. On this view, it is the exercise of a *selective* power to exclude that raises red flags. Should the incumbent mayor be able to exclude from the public square only speakers opposed to his reelection? Under the greater-includes-the-lesser argument, that should be permissible so long as the mayor is able to exclude all people from the public sphere. Yet this is exactly where Holmes goes wrong. The limits on state power are not tied only to cases where individuals have "proprietary" claims. It also extends to cases where they have limited rights to a share in the commons. The same with a decision to hire members of only one political party for routine service jobs or to require that they contribute handsomely to party coffers in order to keep their positions.

Manifestly, the correct analysis goes in the opposite direction. The ability to select some and exclude others is in practice the greater power, not the lesser one, which is why it is so rightly feared. Permit selective exclusions and some individuals can be denied driver's licenses on public roads that are routinely allowed to their political opponents. Yet once this prohibition is in place, the mayor will be tempted to conceal his political objectives by crafting neutral restrictions on the use of public property or on hiring city workers that to his knowledge will have a disparate impact that favors his particular cause. Facially neutral restrictions, made with foreknowledge of partisan advantage, also have the power to distort political power. Obviously, some discretion is needed to run any complex operation. It is necessary therefore to examine the reasons why these restrictions are imposed—such examination would bar spurious justifications for hiring persons who cannot pass well-designed competence evaluations, especially when there is clear opportunity to hire individuals from the opposite side of the political fence who do perform well. The strict scrutiny regime, which prevents states from excluding competitive rivals in dormant Commerce Clause cases, has strong parallels here.

In the end, therefore, any high level of judicial scrutiny will cabin the levels of public discretion that the greater/lesser principle appears to allow. That trend is visible in the government regulation of public spaces and, to a lesser extent, in employment markets. It is important briefly to examine both in turn.

Public Fora—The Modern Response

The break from the past in dealing with public fora took place in *Hague v. Committee for Industrial Organization*,[13] where Justice Owen J. Roberts, writing only for himself and Justice Black, took dead aim at *Davis* by writing: "Wherever the title of streets and parks may rest, they have immemorially been held in trust for the use of the public and, time out of mind, have been used for purposes of assembly, communicating thoughts between citizens, and discussing public questions. Such use of the streets and public places has, from ancient times, been a part of the privileges, immunities, rights, and liberties of citizens."[14] He cites no authority for the proposition that in the end carries the day, as it should have, given that a boss mayor overran the union headquarters with police, "searching individuals and confiscating circulars and handbills relating to CIO union activities."[15] Not a tough decision on the facts.

From this point forward it is just a matter of technique to decide what reasons for controlling the use of the commons pass muster and which do not. At this point, classical liberal principles help shape the inquiry. The first point is that "time, place, and manner" regulations, which balance legitimate government interests with rights of free assembly and speech,[16] usually can pass muster because they are not directed toward the content of a message, and thus are more difficult to press into the service of improper or partisan ends. In essence, this modern formulation traces the common law of nuisance insofar as it regulates or prohibits loudspeakers mounted on sound trucks[17] or the loud performances of a rock band, so long of course as the imposition of these restrictions is done in a fair and evenhanded way so as not to tilt the political scales in one direction or another.[18] And, as in all cases asking for private injunctions, the remedy has to be proportionate to the wrong. Thus, in *Schneider v. State*,[19] the Court held that the government could not issue a blanket prohibition against leafleting on public streets even with the admitted risk that this morning's leaflets can become this afternoon's trash. Sanctions for those who litter may be less than complete, but they avoid the risk of dangerous overbreadth, which matters in a regime in which both communication and cleanliness count as legitimate interests.

The situation gets more complicated of course when the use or occupation of a public facility by one individual or group could preclude its simultaneous use or occupation by another, and in these situations, the first-come, first-serve rules are also put in abeyance. Thus, in _City of Cincinnati v. Discovery Network_,[20] the question was how the city could allocate the space for news racks on public streets. The Court held that the legitimate state interest in controlling clutter and appearance on public roads did not justify an explicit preference in the placement of news racks on public property, or for larger papers at the expense of smaller commercial publications, just because the city thought that these marginal publications had lower speech value. Instead, the older common carrier model was applied to this case, so that the city was forced to adopt some neutral system of allocation—bids, lotteries, rotation—that did not afford the initial occupants priority over latecomers to public resources. Economically speaking, a bid system for the available spots does have the advantage of maximizing revenues from public sources in ways that a lottery or a rotation cannot. But the lottery is easier to run, and the rotation ensures that everyone has a shot of getting at least some fraction of the available spaces.

This analysis is the same that should be applied to the broader spectrum of governmental regulation of public spaces. Indeed a general solution need not, and should not, be limited to cases where the only interest at stake is private speech. Exactly the same systems of allocation of public space should apply as well in nonspeech contexts, as they did under _Frost_. Treating the speech issues as a subset of a larger problem means that evenhanded treatment between rival participants is only the first step in the process. The second step tries to maximize overall value of all common resources, whether or not speech related, by preventing public giveaways to private parties under the inverse of the Takings Clause: "nor shall public property be given to private parties, without just compensation."[21]

The same logic applies to issuing parade permits for use of public facilities. As a matter of first principle, these should be granted to all groups on equal grounds, leaving it to those groups to decide whom to admit into their ranks and whom to exclude. The application of the modern antidiscrimination laws to these activities was given short shrift, notwithstanding their widespread use in ordinary employment markets. Thus, in _Hurley v. Irish-American Gay, Lesbian and Bisexual Group_,[22] the issue was whether the South Boston Allied War Veterans Council had to let the GLIB march under its own banner in the Veterans Council's larger St. Patrick's Day celebration. The Massachusetts Supreme Judicial Court held that the state antidiscrimination law[23] could require the council to include the GLIB contingent's float to express solidarity with other gay, lesbian, and bisexual groups.[24] That argument is wrong for the reasons noted in *Frost*: wholly apart from the free speech issue, state control of public roads does not allow it to turn a private float into a quasi-public institution.

The Supreme Court unanimously reversed the decision, making only passing reference to the common carrier arguments that are the strongest foundation for the result. Justice Souter's decision contains no discussion of *Frost* and no reference to the doctrine of unconstitutional conditions. But he does note that cable companies have "a monopolist opportunity to shut out some speakers," which in turn "gives rise to the Government's interest in limiting monopolistic autonomy."[25] But consistent with this basic model, he stressed that the operators of the parade had discretion in deciding whom to include and whom to exclude, with an eye to making all the floats part of an ensemble, so that "each is understood to contribute something to a common theme."[26] The state works as a common carrier even if the Veterans Council does not. Consistent therefore with the basic structure of unconstitutional conditions, Massachusetts in *Hurley* could not use its monopoly power over the state highways to overcome the rights of association guaranteed to all groups under the First Amendment, so long as the parade was both "peaceful and orderly."[27] "[A] speaker has the autonomy to choose the content of his own message," which the state power could not overcome,[28] no matter what its own views of political morality. The forms of forced association that apply to labor relations on private property do not apply to expressive organizations that conduct their activities on public property.

The same rules have been extended on numerous occasions to efforts of universities and other institutions to close their facilities to students who represent views that the majority find unacceptable. At this point, the exquisite First Amendment scales treat these operating institutions as "limited public forums" that can exclude these groups from the classroom during class time, but must follow a strict nondiscrimination policy in allocating general facilities to other organizations. So long as other groups are allowed on campus, no state college could exclude the Students for a Democratic Society from using its premises, unless SDS was committing some independently illegal act.[29]

    That same legal principle fared less well in *Christian Legal Society Chapter of California, Hastings College of Law v. Martinez,*[30] where by a five-to-four vote, the Supreme Court sustained Hastings Law School in its refusal to treat CLS as a "Registered Student Organization" because of its unwillingness to adhere to Hastings policy prohibiting discrimination "on the basis of race, color, religion, national origin, ancestry, disabilities, age, sex or sexual orientation."[31] CLS offended that policy by insisting that members and officers abstain from extramarital sexual relations. It also barred from membership any person who engaged in "unrepentant homosexual conduct."[32] Its meetings were open to all comers. The upshot was that Hastings was held entitled to bar CLS from sharing on equal terms with sixty other student groups the use of the Hastings name, logo, bulletin boards, email systems, and campus offices, or receive funding for activities and travel. The case raises complications not present in *Hurley,* where there was no doubt that any individual group of students could displace the faculty on academic decisions. Rather than any such demands, CLS sought only to take advantage of the same benefits that were accorded other groups in the use of Hastings facilities. Nonetheless, Justice Ginsburg wrote as if the unconstitutional conditions doctrine did not exist, by taking the view that Hastings only withheld a benefit, but did not require CLS to admit any students. But it is exactly that use of state monopoly power that the doctrine of unconstitutional conditions is meant to counteract, given that no monopolist has, or should have, the power to refuse to deal without cause. Accordingly, the case should have been treated as one in which all the facilities in question counted as a "limited public forum" when not dedicated to academic uses. Hastings, as the decider in this case, can surely exclude all outsiders from its buildings, but it cannot discriminate against insiders solely on the grounds of their religious views, let alone require that CLS admit into its membership and leadership positions individuals strongly opposed to its worldview.

Employment Relations

As one might predict, the rules governing employment relations are more tolerant of employer discretion given the massive complexities in running any public office. To point out just three landmarks along the road, in *Pickering v. Board of Education,*[33] the Court held that a board of education could not dismiss a teacher who criticized the board's handling of financial matters in a newspaper letter. The role of "citizen" was sufficiently distinct from that of employee. There was no obvious connection between the protest in the papers and the performance in the schools. At the other extreme, the Supreme Court addressed an issue that had received cavalier treatment in their earlier case of *United Public Workers of America v. Mitchell*.[34] *Mitchell* upheld the 1939 Hatch Act,[35] which on a categorical basis prohibits government civil servants from holding public office, participating in elections, or otherwise engaging in political campaigns. The statute is a bulwark against the pervasive risk of partisan politics taking over the civil service, and thus in fact meets the test of reasonableness that Holmes alluded to in *McAuliffe*. From there it was but a short step to uphold various remedial strategies, with extensive judicial oversight, intended to limit the City of Chicago (during the first Richard Daley administration, no less) from exerting undue influence over rank and file employees.[36]

The landscape gets a lot clearer when no issues of political speech are involved in a dispute. The First Amendment quickly yielded to the management needs of a district attorney's office in *Connick v. Meyers*,[37] holding that a lawyer who did not like her reassignment could not send the office into turmoil by attempting to rally her coworkers to the cause. And on a five-to-four vote, the Supreme Court held in *Garcetti v. Ceballos*[38] that a Los Angeles County attorney could not in that work-related context claim the benefit of the First Amendment. On multiple occasions, both in private to his superiors and publicly in court, Ceballos had protested what he considered to be police misconduct in a controversial case. The Court held that disciplinary action against Ceballos for speech made as part of his official duties was not subject to First Amendment protection.[39]

In all these borderline cases, the line between official duties and public protest seems to get the situation about right. Any dual capacity situation is difficult. So greater scrutiny is needed than the at-will rule supplies. That additional oversight, moreover, is supplied by a metric that allows the employer to do what others do on discipline issues, so long as there is no covert form of favoritism. The case law on this topic can literally fill volumes, and there may be mistakes on points of detail. But the overall structure has endured with high levels of judicial oversight precisely because it started from a set of sound premises, all of which have been rejected in ordinary cases of property and contract.

Taxation and Other Burdens

The concerns with discretion in the exercise of government power also extend to that largest of social commons—the entire public. The basic theory of classical liberal taxation, which has been decisively rejected in economic areas, is that the state should seek to raise revenues to discharge its public functions in ways that require the lowest exercise of discretion in imposing the tax. A flat tax on either income or investment, with no special exemptions or exclusions, is the best way to achieve that ideal.[40] That position has been decisively rejected in all tax cases, where a takings challenge to progressive taxation has been cast aside under some variation of the rational basis test.[41] But owing to the higher level of scrutiny of government under the First Amendment, the classical liberal vision now finds a limited home in dealing with the First Amendment issues related to the taxation of newspapers.

In *Minneapolis Star & Tribune Co. v Minnesota Commissioner of Revenue*,[42] the change in context from property to speech led to a sea change in constitutional approach. At issue in the case was a progressive use tax on the cost of ink and paper for newspaper production, where higher rates were charged to larger papers. The *Minneapolis Star* was one of 16 out of 374 paid circulation papers in the state subjected to the higher taxes, which required it to pay over $600,000 in 1974. The Supreme Court recognized that Minnesota's tax did not single out particular newspapers for their political views, which had happened in the earlier Louisiana case of *Grosjean v. American Press Co.*,[43] where the allies of Huey Long imposed a 2 percent license tax on a group of Louisiana newspapers whose circulation exceeded 20,000. Clearly, the effort to use selective taxes to target these abuses is a per se violation of any sound tax theory, notwithstanding any principle that the greater power comprehends the lesser.

The harder question raised by *Minnesota Star* is whether to target *any* tax, regardless of legislative intention, that has just this divisive effect. *Minneapolis Star* contained no perceptible evidence that the flat tax generated any negatives in the overall operation of the economic system. As Justice O'Connor stressed in her opinion, the flat tax makes it far harder, if not impossible, to exact selective retribution of your enemies in the press, because of the need to impose a like tax on your friends. The insistence on this single form, however, imposes no revenue constraint on the state, which can set the tax as high or low as it chooses, without having differential rates or selective exemptions. Nor does this solution put courts in a position where they have to make speculative estimations of the incidence of a given tax, for those calculations don't matter given the simplified form. That same logic could of course apply to the taxation of all income from all goods and services. It is only the current low level of scrutiny courts apply to taxation that allows the creation of today's steeply progressive tax that now exempts close to half the population from any income tax at all, thereby creating a vocal built-in constituency for the expansion of all public entitlement programs.

The basic logic on selective exemptions does not only apply to the press, but to any cases in which either a selective tax subsidy or a selective tax penalty distorts the relative preferences between different political outlooks. Thus, in *Speiser v. Randall*,[44] Justice Brennan held that real estate property taxation exemptions could not be given to those World War II veterans who signed an oath swearing allegiance to the United States. This kind of direct loyalty oath, based on the political viewpoint of the speaker, ran into even heavier resistance as the "Red Scare" started to recede. To allow its operation created genuine splits in the population along political lines. By this logic, a tax exemption for all veterans has no such political punch and thus would survive in a world where only restrictions based on speech were forbidden. A broader classical liberal theory would, however, reject even that distinction.

Next, in less dramatic form, the challenged scheme in *Arkansas Writers' Project, Inc. v. Ragland*[45] exempted from the regular sales tax only certain types of publications—"general circulation" magazines were not excluded. As a matter of ordinary taxation theory, the exemptions should be allowed to all sales transactions or none. But once again, the unconstitutional conditions doctrine only applied to distinctions that were speech related. Here it was hard to find any animus against a broad category of general purpose publications. But once again, so what? There is no danger from a uniform rule that simplifies administration by reducing discretion while also keeping the tax base intact.

The use of classical liberal theory produces, when the standard of scrutiny is high, a hard-fought synthesis that covers both regulation and taxation, albeit only in the sphere of speech. Yet the moment the worm turns and the progressive conceptions of good government take over, the law moves in exactly the opposite direction, as is evident in the First Amendment treatment of both labor laws and campaign finance, which are the topics of the next chapter.

28

Progressive Regulation of Freedom of Speech

Labor, Communications, and Campaign Finance

M ost First Amendment law applies in contexts that are broadly consistent with classical liberal principles. Nonetheless, First Amendment law is not somehow insulated from the progressive critique that exerts so much influence on issues dealing with separation of powers, federalism, property rights, and economic liberties. This chapter systematically explores three important areas where traditional First Amendment principles have come into conflict with major progressive reforms. These include the application of antitrust and labor laws to speech activities, the licensing procedures followed by the Federal Communications Commission, and campaign finance regulation.

The Progressive Influence on Free Speech

In each of the three areas discussed above, the expansion of government regulation necessarily imposes further restrictions on speech rights, not only for the media, but also for ordinary businesses and associations. But the current legal trend all too often makes light of these restrictions by insisting that they are somehow only "incidental" to some legitimate form of economic regulation that does not single out speech generally, or the press in particular, for unduly severe regulation.[1] That part of the law is widely regarded as noncontroversial, but in fact presents constitutional difficulties that are much more acute than the current sunny view of the topic suggests.

The risk in all of these cases is that the low standard of review courts use today in cases involving taxation, commerce, private property, and other economic liberties will carry over to speech-related issues. Courts have treated economic liberties this way since the New Deal era because of a deep conviction that government regulatory power is justified by the abundance of the neutral scientific and technical expertise needed to implement a political vision adopted after extensive public participation. Generalized judicial fears about inequality of bargaining power in the private sphere and the undue influence of wealth in public affairs have led to a persistent progressive effort to limit the influence of money on politics. There is much to be said about using a uniform standard of review in connection with speech and religion on the one hand, and private property and economic liberties on the other. To the progressive mindset, that involves lowering the level of scrutiny for speech restrictions on large organizations to the same level as scrutiny used for regulation of such organizations in economic areas. This move gets the situation backwards, however, for the proper equivalence runs in the opposite direction. Standards should be toughened for these economic rights, not reduced for matters of public political speech.

Antitrust and Labor

One central challenge in First Amendment law is the extent to which organizations that engage in various speech activities, broadly conceived, should be subject to the general law of the land. This is clearly unproblematic in connection with the general rules against force and fraud, for which speech acts are used as evidence of intent in such crimes as murder, rape, arson, and theft. The legal system could not operate if the external evidence of these mental states was systematically excluded from evidence, which of course it is not.[2] By the same logic, the usual antitrust prohibitions against various monopoly practices should not be derailed because they rely on speech acts to prove the mental elements when parties collude to raise prices, restrict output, divide territories, and take other steps that reduce overall social welfare. Thus in *Associated Press v. United States*,[3] the question was whether the Associated Press engaged in illegal exclusive dealing practices, in violation of the Sherman Act, when it gave existing members rights to determine whether their direct competitors could be admitted as AP members. There are respectable antitrust arguments that cut in both directions. The exclusion of direct competitors has the advantage of inducing higher levels of participation by existing members who do not have to share their benefits with newcomers. But as the size of the association becomes larger, further exclusion runs the risk of excessively concentrating the control of news firms in local markets to the detriment of the overall economy.

It is no part of this constitutional inquiry to resolve the underlying antitrust dispute on its merits. But it is noteworthy that its correct resolution is wholly consistent with the First Amendment objective of pursuing competition in the marketplace of ideas. So long, therefore, as the antitrust laws make sense (especially in their horizontal application, i.e., to firms at the same level of production within the industry) in the general case of all businesses, nothing in the logic of freedom under the First Amendment forces courts to apply a hard-line libertarian view of antitrust law to the press—one that finds cartelization entirely proper so long as it involves neither force nor fraud. The preference of competition to monopoly is sufficient to insulate the antitrust laws from charges that their reliance on speech and intent evidence to detect monopoly violates the First Amendment. Just as there is no blanket freedom of action or contract, there is no blanket freedom of speech. All are subject to justifications that pass muster under the police power.

The analysis takes a different direction with respect to the earlier 1937 Supreme Court decision in *Associated Press v. NLRB*,[4] which asked whether the NLRB's prohibition against the dismissal of workers for their union activities under the NLRA was inconsistent with the press's guarantee of freedom of speech. In rejecting this contention, the Supreme Court stressed bluntly: "The publisher of a newspaper has no special immunity from the application of general laws. He has no special privilege to invade the rights and liberties of others. He must answer for libel. He may be punished for contempt of court. He is subject to the anti-trust laws."[5] Unfortunately the two halves of the proposition do not cohere. The first, which is correct, is that the First Amendment protection of freedom of the press gives the press no license to violate the rights and liberties of others. But the definition of protected constitutional rights cannot be left for the legislature to determine as it pleases by application of "general laws." Instead the laws that govern must conform to the proper extrinsic standard. The rules dealing with libel, contempt of court, and, as we have just seen, antitrust laws, are all comfortably housed in a classical liberal regime. Their enforcement only brings the common law and the constitutional law into a welcome and closer alignment.

From start to finish, the NLRA is a fish of a different stripe. Its basic rules on collective bargaining were routinely justified at the time as an advancement of the principle of freedom of association by, among others, its key backer, Senator Robert Wagner of New York. The senator sought to clothe the act in libertarian garments: "It is the next step in the logical unfolding of man's eternal quest for freedom. . . . Only 150 years ago did this country cast off the shackles of political despotism. And today, with economic problems occupying the center of the stage, we strive to liberate the common man. . . ."[6] But his contention turns the definition of freedom upside down, as is all too common in labor analysis of freedom of association.[7]

A system of freedom of association is not specific to one group of individuals in one set of roles. It is a principle that applies to all persons at all times and gives to each of them the right to choose to associate or not with others. Justice Brennan, in *Roberts v. United States Jaycees*, wrote, "Freedom of association . . . plainly presupposes a freedom not to associate."[8] But this principle does not apply with full force only to intimate associations, as Justice Brennan insisted. Rather, it applies indifferently to all types of associations for all purposes. In this regard, the earlier cases that struck down federal and state precursors of the NLRA on freedom of contract and association grounds had it about right.[9] Employers could not be forced to negotiate with workers against their own will and their rights of association deemed forfeited, given that the workplace is a voluntary association of its own members. The only basic exception to the rule of freedom of association applies to groups, like common carriers, that can exert some degree of monopoly power. In this context, however, Congress expanded this exception when it granted immunity from the antitrust laws to unions in 1914 in sections 6 and 20 of the Clayton Act.[10] From that date on, the risk of monopoly lay not with the firms that were subject to unionization efforts, but with the unions. Under the NLRA, unions gained additional powers—most notably, the ability, once recognized, to force management against its will to the bargaining table.

From these basic principles it follows that the imposition of the NLRA, or for that matter, the Fair Labor Standards Act, which is subject to the same analysis,[11] requires a wholly different analysis from the antitrust laws to which it has too often been falsely compared. In this instance, the imposition of unionization on press employers will necessarily limit their ability to deploy resources as they see fit. They must bear the expense of negotiation with unions; they must pay monopoly premium wages; they must face the risk of strikes; and they have to yield to work rules that can inhibit the flexibility of their workforce or prevent the purchase and use of new equipment.

It hardly answers the challenge of these major economic impediments to say that they impose only an "incidental" burden on the freedom of speech. It is perfectly well understood that the only way for unions to succeed is to limit the options of the firms they target. A generation before the approval of the NLRA, no question could arise as to whether the press needed special protection under the First Amendment. These organizations would get all the protection they needed under the general law. But once the general law fumbled the issue of freedom of association in basic business contexts, the question of whether the First Amendment carved out speech-related institutions for special treatment became insistent. Yet the current law does not even begin to address this question.

Nor, it turns out, does national labor law deal effectively with other issues relating to freedom of speech—in this instance, of the employers who are subject to extensive obligations under the collective bargaining process. The process operates to make the union and its employees a part owner of the employer's firm. This fundamental reversal of entitlements makes it impossible to follow ordinary common law rules with respect to other aspects of their tripartite employer-employee-union relationship. Employers, for example, no longer have the absolute right to exclude union organizers during organizational campaigns, but are forced to allow them at least limited access to the covered employees.[12] In similar fashion, the usual rules that allow each side in any disagreement to engage in free and uninhibited speech no longer apply to labor, where the entire matter of employer speech is regulated by Section 8(c):[13]

> *Expression of views without threat of reprisal or force or promise of benefit.* The expressing of any views, argument, or opinion, or the dissemination thereof, whether in written, printed, graphic, or visual form, shall not constitute or be evidence of an unfair labor practice under any of the provisions of this subchapter, if such expression contains no threat of reprisal or force or promise of benefit.

By design, the final clause of this statutory provision places gentle handcuffs on employer speech. Outside the labor context, a threat of reprisal constitutes bad action if it involves the threat of force. But in this context, the threat of reprisal clearly refers either to the firing of—or other such actions—taken against pro-union workers during the organization drive. That is exactly what should happen in any free-market setting where employment is terminable at will by either party: The only contracts that should be formed are those that work to the mutual benefit of both sides, and neither is under the duty to bargain.

But once the duty to bargain is recognized, this provision has to be included for that labor scheme to survive. Similarly, normally the promise of a benefit is a good thing, but in the labor context, collective bargaining cannot survive if at the first sign of trouble an employer can offer workers benefits sufficient to undermine the union's organizational efforts. Hence such offers are regarded as unfair labor practices under the law.[14] Yet by the same token, it is equally well accepted that predictions of what will happen if a union is chosen are neither promises nor threats and thus remain legal under the NLRA. The fine line between threats and predictions is a grammarian's paradise, at which point all well-tutored employers necessarily speak in the passive voice about what will happen to the firm if unionized—not what they will choose to do. More to the point, it does not count as a threat to let workers know the fate of other unionized plants. Such information often leads to worker opposition to unionization from those employees who think that the risk of closure or downsizing from collective bargaining or strikes does not justify the gamble for a wage premium. The counterspeech that meets the requirements of Section 8(c) has given management enough running room so as to contribute to the sharp erosion of union membership.

But from a conceptual point of view, the key point remains: Once the NLRA is thought justified for whatever reasons, all these complementary adjustments have to be put in place for the system to go into effect, including those that allow the employer to speak to its employee in choreographed opposition to any union organization drive. It is for just this reason that Craig Becker, now co-general counsel for the AFL-CIO, ran into such a firestorm of opposition when President Barack Obama nominated him to the NLRB in 2010.[15] In his well-known article on the subject, Becker advocated removing employer speech rights during organization campaigns.[16] That proposal makes perfect sense so long as employers are free to refuse to deal with unions. But once unions have the right to force bargaining in good faith, they become in effect part owners of the firm, and that assertion of power justifies letting employers seek to persuade workers to stay out of the union orbit.

The entire matter would be handled far more efficiently by returning to the earlier rule that allowed employers, with the much-maligned Yellow Dog contract, to tell workers they could not remain members of a union so long as they worked for the firm. At that point the interdependence is over, so that employers should truly have no say over unionization drives. But that simple solution could not survive the progressive reforms that in the end have introduced so much unnecessary brinksmanship into labor relations. No system of unionization is consistent with orthodox conceptions of freedom of speech that have long worked well in other political or social contexts. The current legal solution shows all too well that the ability to protect speech is effectively compromised when other property rights are overridden, which is what happens when employers (both individual and corporate) are forced to bargain with unions against their will. That whole process puts an inchoate lien on the assets of the firm, which only confirms a central tenet of classical liberal theory that in labor relations as elsewhere, as the old refrain goes, private property is the guardian of every other liberty.[17]

Telecommunications Law

The tension between government regulation and the First Amendment also took an unfortunate turn in modern communications law. In this particular area, the general law governing speech should apply to broadcasts over the airwaves, cable, or Internet, just as it applied to newspapers, pamphlets, and books in days of old. The anticircumvention principle does not lose its bite in the modern technological age. But these earlier systems of regulation all were directed to the private production of information, so that government officials could not point to the state ownership of the means of production as an additional source of their own powers.

Nonetheless, the same structural defects that have rendered the FCC unable to give a proper response to the property rights issue have also dogged its efforts to develop as a licensor a coherent account of free speech.[18] The basic difficulty starts with the broad delegation of authority as it applies to speech. In addressing this issue, Justice Frankfurter was confident that the FCC's broad delegation standard could accommodate all the demands of free speech. Writing in *National Broadcasting Co. v. United States*, he stated: "The standard it provided for the licensing of stations was the 'public interest, convenience, or necessity.' Denial of a station license on that ground, if valid under the Act, is not a denial of free speech."[19]

Frankfurter's bold and confident progressive rejection of the "traffic officer" model[20] does not mesh well with traditional protections for freedom of speech. Here are just two examples of the problem. One basic legal norm is that government may not force the press to give equal time to its opposition. Thus in *Miami Herald Publication Co. v. Tornillo*,[21] the Supreme Court had no trouble in dispensing with a Florida "right to reply" statute that required writers of editorials to publish letters disagreeing with their point of view, noting the risk that this rule could encourage editors to "conclude that the safe course is to avoid controversy."[22] The conclusion did not depend on the additional costs, if any, of publishing these letters, because a newspaper is no "passive receptacle" of the opinions of others, but an expression of its own editorial views. Any legal duty to publish replies operates as a tax on the freedom of speech. The correct response is to encourage the new entry of outlets for rival views. It was, as the Court rightly concluded, ultimately pointless to compare the cost considerations for new entry in 1971 to those in 1791.[23] Government-mandated cross-subsidies are a form of disguised taxation that is inconsistent with the freedom of speech.

Tornillo, however, makes no reference to the 1969 Supreme Court decision in *Red Lion Broadcasting Co. v. Federal Communications Commission*,[24] in which the Supreme Court upheld the so-called "fairness doctrine," which gave (before its repeal by the FCC in 1987)[25] dissenting voices in broadcast the same right of reply that was denied in *Tornillo*. Justice Frankfurter's rhetoric about the spectrum in *NBC* resonated clearly in *Red Lion*:

> Because of the scarcity of radio frequencies, the Government is permitted to put restraints on licensees in favor of others whose views should be expressed on this unique medium. But the people as a whole retain their interest in free speech by radio and their collective right to have the medium function consistently with the ends and purposes of the First Amendment.[26]

This two-step argument misses the central point. Scarcity is endemic to all social institutions, which is why we create and protect property rights in the first place: development by the designated owner cannot take place without the systematic exclusion of others. In this key respect, the FCC rules *retard* entry by imposing a nondelegable duty on each broadcast operator to determine its broadcast content. By that one stroke, the law introduces a strong quasi-monopoly element into speech law that makes it impossible for any government licensee to behave like a prudent owner—by leasing out time segments on its station to persons or organizations with different points of view. When the Cosmopolitan Broadcasting Corporation opted for this sensible business model, it promptly lost its license because of its failure to discharge its statutory obligation to determine content on its assigned frequency.[27] The ownership model blocks any such government imposition.

Thus the larger question: Why stifle any system of property rights allocation that brings more voices to the public sphere by allowing the owner of a frequency to let others express their own views as lessees or assignees of particular frequencies? The technological transformation between 1969 and the present makes it all too clear that the dominant constraint today is good content, not available bandwidth. Any First Amendment doctrine that lashes itself to some perceived levels of scarcity is too rigid to work well over time. The property rights system that creates incentives for open entry and technical innovation across a wide range of unregulated areas having little to do with speech can work its magic by decentralizing the control over broadcast speech. The progressive approach does not work because its central planning model reduces the number of independent voices on political and similar cultural issues.

The second major error of Frankfurter's formulation deals with public morals and decency. Currently the FCC does not regulate the Internet and cable, and these media are replete with all sorts of vulgar speech that some people, a shrinking fraction, believe offends every social norm of decent behavior, which is a good reason to change the channel or turn off the set. It is inconceivable that the government today could ban the use of four-letter words on cable and the Internet, which have thrived in large measure because of their greater artistic freedom. As if in a time warp, the 1934 Communications Act allows the FCC to construe "indecent language" in broadcasting in ways that are consistent with the mores of 1934. That extra FCC power over broadcasts follows from the federal ownership of the spectrum, so that when a licensee "accepts that franchise it is burdened by enforceable public obligations."[28] One such condition makes it illegal to "utter[] any obscene, indecent, or profane language by means of radio communication," which was added into the law by a 1948 amendment.[29] It is therefore little short of amazing that as late as 2009 in *Federal Communications Commission v. Fox Television Stations, Inc.*,[30] the Supreme Court undertook an extensive investigation to decide whether "fleeting expletives, the use of 'F- and S-Words,'" are subject to government regulation. How this prohibition makes sense when just about every sentient being is glued to hit shows that flout every grim Victorian prohibition is never explained. The obvious distinction between *Tornillo* and *Red Lion* goes utterly unexplored. Justice Frankfurter's optimism in *NBC* on the compatibility of free speech with government licensure has proved erroneous, but appears to be immune to political or constitutional correction.

Campaign Finance Regulation

General Considerations

The third topic that demonstrates the distinct influence of progressive policies on First Amendment law is the highly contentious issue of campaign finance reform, the centerpiece of which, the Court's five-to-four defense of corporate speech in *Citizens United v. Federal Election Commission*,[31] has generated a firestorm of popular resentment.[32] The standard progressive position on campaign finance leaves the government with broad powers to regulate how money is raised and spent in political campaigns. These activities are regarded less like the traditional stump speech, which deserves protection, and more like the standard forms of corporate misbehavior, which must be checked by decisive government action. As the "sober-minded" Elihu Root stressed, the grand objective is to keep money out of public life,[33] so that corporate dollars do not influence legislators to "vote for their protection and the advancement of their interests as against those of the public." This bipolar worldview ignores the common situation in which clashing corporations fall on both sides of any issue. It also warps an understanding of the central concerns in this area.

To attack this issue correctly, it is essential to identify the conditions under which it makes sense for businesses to contribute to political causes. The simple self-interested calculus states that individuals and firms alike will invest in political activities only to the extent that their expected return will exceed their expected costs. Under this test, the level of expenditures—whether to influence legislative or administrative activities, or for the election of particular candidates—will increase as the power of political bodies increases. One prime objective of a classical liberal system is to constrain unneeded political discretion at every point, by its strong preference for flat taxes on a single tax base and by subjecting all legislative and administrative action to constitutional oversight that supplies just compensation for government-imposed limitations on private property and economic liberties, unless they fall within the well-defined categories of police power justification. The comprehensive combination of tax and compensation rules helps align the incentives of political actors with overall social welfare by shrinking the opportunity for factional gains. As individuals and firms have less to gain, and less to lose, through the political process, they will reduce their levels of partisan investments.

In that highly constrained world, there is little need for anxiety about giving extensive protection to political speech under the First Amendment. Even in a classical liberal regime, people will continue to have decided preferences over war-and-peace and a raft of other issues that of necessity require collective deliberation. They should be able to voice their views as they think appropriate, which they can only do if they are allowed to cooperate through ordinary contractual means with other individuals and groups to make their views known. Any speaker is allowed to rent out a private hall for political activities and should be able to hire independent contractors and employees to aid in that venture, just as he or she is allowed to do so for all of his or her commercial ventures. Put otherwise, a right of association is part and parcel of the right to speech for all individuals and groups, regardless of their size and power. There is no teleological theory that says that only self-appointed members of the press (of which Citizens United was apparently not one) are entitled to participate in political debate with an added advantage over proprietary firms that have multiple objectives.

Again the key point is that incumbents who specialize in speech should not be allowed to erect barriers against potential competition no matter where it comes from. Indeed these collateral rights of association are required under the anticircumvention principle which is an essential part of the ordinary rules of constitutional construction, subject to the standard caveats about monopolization, which in this context is a risk associated with specialty business, whether or not in corporate form.[34] On this view, there is no need to torture the constitutional guarantee of "the right of the people peaceably to assemble," which in general is better reserved for public meetings by way of protest or demonstration.[35] Similarly, any persons should be able to solicit contributions from others to support legislation or to elect political candidates by use of the same contractual devices.

The constant threat of favoritism and corruption is best addressed indirectly by limiting the powers of public officials once elected. But that basic structural safeguard cannot prevent corruption by itself. Even a classical liberal state has to provide for defense, public records, infrastructure, and a wide range of similar functions. Corruption in the bidding process for obtaining work in these activities is a constant threat, which is why it may well be necessary in a small government to adopt anticorruption statutes such as the Tillman Act,[36] which (before *Citizens United*) prohibited all contributions by corporations to candidates, and the comparable provisions of the National Labor Relations Act, which does the same for unions.[37] Both of these statutes are supplemented by the prohibitions on political contributions by civil service federal employees in the Hatch Act of 1939,[38] whose constitutionality was sustained in *Oklahoma v. United States Civil Service Commission*.[39] This legislation, which is itself not beyond criticism, is directed toward low-hanging fruit. Its general effectiveness thereby places the burden on the next generation of reformers to show that the marginal benefits of the new statutory prohibitions exceed their marginal cost.

Weak private property rights in the modern progressive state and the corresponding power of government to license public property increase the total level of rent-seeking political activity. But prohibitions on these speech activities cannot undo the fundamental mistake of building a legal system that offers weak constitutional protection for property rights and economic liberties. More specifically, no respectable constitutional theory should accord pride of place to corporate contributions over union contributions, or the reverse. In corporate contexts, there is no clear correlation between the source of the funds and the position taken on legislation. Many of the protracted political struggles are business versus business, and take place, for example, between tobacco companies and health care organizations, or content providers and telecommunications carriers, or coal and natural gas companies. In other contexts, there are many situations in which the interests of large corporations diverge from those of small ones. But no sound account of freedom of speech tries to draw inferences from the particular lineup of players on particular issues. Wholly apart from these differences, individual corporations are wise to hedge their bets by giving some support to both major political parties. To complicate the system further, corporate/union alliances are common on both sides of such sensitive issues as international trade and immigration. There is therefore no reason to believe that any effort to restrict some forms of campaign contribution will have a desirable systematic skew against "the" corporate interest.

Against this complex background, the Supreme Court has swayed to and fro in its attitude toward political contributions. The Court's first major foray into the matter resulted in its 1976 decision in *Buckley v. Valeo*,[40] which sought to split the baby by allowing any individual to spend as much money as he or she wished on political campaigns, but accepted sharp limits on the amount of contributions that political candidates themselves could accept and further validated statutory requirements for the disclosure of campaign contributions.

A general theory of freedom surely allows any person to spend his or her own money on gaining election, subject to the usual restraints against force, fraud, bribery, and corruption. It is very difficult to find a strong justification for the limits on campaign contributions, which are the lifeblood of most campaigns. Oddly enough, the strongest rationale for contribution limitations may be to protect potential donors from implied threats of political retribution, which are ever more credible in a state that affords the legislature extensive powers.

Finally, the use of disclosure legislation is decidedly a double-edged sword. It surely allows informed voters to judge a potential candidate by his or her associates. But it also exposes both candidates and their supporters to threats of harassment by their political opponents. How to balance these considerations admits no easy categorical answer, which is why the Supreme Court was right in *John Doe No. 1 v. Reed*[41] to reject a facial challenge to a Washington State statute that imposed disclosure requirements on those who signed petitions for a ballot referendum. But the risk of abuse and retaliation could well be deserving of constitutional protection in some contexts, including the "Preserve Marriage,

Protect Children" petition at issue in that case. Again the point here is not viewpoint specific. The as-applied challenge could easily succeed when brought by supporters of gay marriage, where parties on both sides of the debate could be entitled to the protection of anonymity. As one appellate court put the issue: "Campaign finance disclosure laws must strike a balance between protecting individual speakers from invasions of privacy and harassment on the one hand, and enabling transparency and accountability in political campaigns on the other."[42] On this point, nothing about the First Amendment allows courts or legislatures to escape the chronic problems of over- and underinclusive legislation.

These general principles also counsel against adopting the ever more convoluted schemes of campaign finance regulation that have sprouted up in recent years. The classical liberal tradition starts from the premise that it is *not* the role of government to redress inequalities of wealth that were achieved by honest means. Attacking those gains reduces the incentive to create them in the first place and could easily lead to the adoption of substantive rules that favor massive wealth transfers by allowing the political majority to fund its own campaigns out of resources taken from the same persons whom it purports to tax. Majoritarian politics are necessary to allow full participation by all persons who have an immense stake in the system even if they have no wealth of which to speak.

But unbridled majoritarianism will overstep its bounds, as Madison predicted in his analysis of faction in *The Federalist No. 10*, if majorities are allowed to discharge debtors from their obligations or to confiscate wealth through political action, which is why protection of both contracts and property from majorities is part and parcel of the overall political system. Any effort to force the rich to subsidize the poor increases the risk. Indeed, legislative action to redress the inequality of wealth creates its own distortion by allowing one candidate running off public funds to be *better off* than wealthier candidates who have to diminish their own personal wealth to pursue public office. That subsidy distorts elections by allowing marginal candidates who cannot raise support from their own base to feast off the wealth of supporters and opponents alike to run their own campaigns. It would surely be a mistake, for example, to assume that the base of individuals supporting transfer payments to the poor and lower middle class consists only of members of those groups when these causes rank high in the firmament of progressive causes everywhere.

Yet it is striking that recent Supreme Court discussions of the issue tend to ignore the warnings of *The Federalist No. 10* on the risks of faction in examining legislation that imposes government controls over campaign finances. It is for good reason that the general anticircumvention principle should block the legislature from diluting the advantages that personal wealth lets certain people bring to political campaigns—often on both sides of a controversial issue. If the government cannot block the rich from speaking publicly in their defense, it cannot tax or otherwise burden their speech when they wish to speak in their own defense by diverting public funds into the coffers of their opponents (some of whom may be rich as well). It therefore follows that First Amendment protection properly limits legislation that either burdens or taxes individual wealth by giving subsidies to those individuals' competitors.

These principles help shape the basic argument about both federal and state efforts to redress financial disparities among candidates. Thus in *Davis v. Federal Election Commission*[43] the Court struck down that portion of the McCain-Feingold Act that allows any candidate whose opponent expends over $350,000 of his or her personal funds to triple his or her normal contribution amount, while the high spender remains subject to the original contribution limitation. The Supreme Court was right to treat the relaxation of the financial burden on opponents as an implicit tax on one's own contribution.

The candidate has to make personal financial sacrifices while the public, including those citizens who favor the burdened candidate, must subsidize the rival. In light of the risks that this program of cross-subsidy could easily reduce the willingness of some people to enter the political campaign circuit by offering support to their rivals, there is no reason to think that this proposal will even nudge public campaigns in the right direction. Rich people who are campaigning, for example, against progressive taxation are not seeking to twist the political system improperly in their favor. What they are trying to do is to prevent majoritarian policies from moving in the opposite direction, in an age in which the total amounts of transfer payments away from the rich have increased.[44] To be sure, some rich candidates could seek special subsidies for their own preferred industries, which run quite in the opposite direction. But the burden here is on the proponents of new legislation to show a compelling state interest—which cannot be done for proposals whose benefits are unproven.

Similarly in *Arizona Free Enterprise Club's Freedom Club PAC v. Bennett*,[45] the Supreme Court struck down the Arizona Citizens Clean Elections Act,[46] which imposed a complex financing regime for all state primary and general elections. Under the scheme, candidates received a lump sum payment from the state, which was augmented by additional moneys from the state to the extent that expenditures made by or on behalf of private candidates exceeded the base amount received by the publicly financed candidate. The basic purpose of this scheme, as in *Davis*, was to neutralize private expenditures by providing countervailing payments to those candidates who took public support. Thus the first part of the system made it clear that it made no sense for any candidate to use private funds if he or she intended to spend any sum less than the state authorized amount. Why spend your own money when the state will pay you an equivalent sum? Any private expenditure therefore could only give an added advantage of amounts in excess of that base sum. Yet each additional dollar of private expenditure triggered an equivalent increase in the public funding for rivals, so that the added dollars provided no comparative advantage over publicly funded candidates.

A divided Supreme Court struck down this scheme on the grounds that the state desire to equalize wealth was not a compelling state interest. Justice Kagan's dissent insisted that the Arizona statute results in "more speech and thereby broadens public debate"[47] which insulated it from constitutional challenge. But the Constitution does not protect "more speech" or "more public debate." It protects freedom of speech, which is as much offended by government cross-subsidies as by direct prohibitions on speech. As in all economic settings, the key question is one of relative prices, which are distorted whether the speech of one party is suppressed or that of a direct opponent is subsidized. This principled fear of the distortive effects of cross-subsidies is as powerful with speech as it is with international trade.

Given the danger of these interventions, Justice Kagan's appeal to the ubiquitous but undefined fear of political corruption justifying these restrictions falls flat. In particular, she overstates her case when she insists that when "candidates for public office accept large campaign contributions in exchange for the promise that, after assuming office, they will rank the donors' interests ahead of all others. As a result of these bargains, politicians ignore the public interest, sound public policy languishes, and the citizens lose confidence in their government."[48]

But this chain of inference is comprised of missing links. The point of having political platforms is to commit a candidate to a program that will be followed in office. It cannot be corruption to keep to those campaign pledges, whether made to voters at large or to political donors more specifically. Nor does the commitment to the program amount to a vague "promise to put donor's interests ahead of all others." There is no promise, express or implied, to put donors first. There is only a political promise to follow the program, which is needed for politicians to make credible commitments to voters as well as their financial backers. If the program is in fact sound, it should garner support. If it is not, there are at least no surprises and unexplained reversals of position. But however it comes out, the last thing that any court can do is to posit the unsoundness of political programs that have achieved support from a donor base. Other means remain available to deal with quid pro quo corruption or influence peddling. Nor is there any reason to believe political candidates who receive public funding will operate under any constraints that will mythically lead them to support the public good. Defenders of campaign finance regulation cannot make their case by conjuring up horror stories from unregulated campaign contributions while ignoring the alternative perils that lurk in their own publicly run systems. These restrictions on individual expenditures and contributions should therefore be struck down in the absence of a clear justification.

Corporate Speech

The puzzles of individual campaign contributions present major problems on which it is impossible to dispel some core honest disagreement. It is possible, however, to be more confident that it is unwise to direct specific regulations to corporate speech. As a matter of general legal theory, a corporation is often characterized as though it were a creature of the state. That attitude dates back to Chief Justice Marshall's famous words in *Dartmouth College v. Woodward*:[49]

> A corporation is an artificial being, invisible, intangible, and existing only in contemplation of law. Being the mere creature of law, it possesses only those properties which the charter of its creation confers upon it, either expressly, or as incidental to its very existence.

That language seems to suggest that the state's unlimited powers in establishing corporations eliminate any First Amendment objection to the regulation of corporate speech. Indeed Justice Rehnquist cited just this passage in his lonely dissent in *First National Bank of Boston v. Bellotti*,[50] to support the astonishing proposition that "[i]t cannot be so readily concluded that the right of political expression is equally necessary to carry out the functions of a corporation organized for commercial purposes,"[51] from which he claimed that political activities should not be treated "as necessarily incidental" to the essential business functions of a corporation.[52]

Rehnquist's hasty dismissal of the doctrine of unconstitutional conditions is wrong for two reasons. First, it misstates the issue in *Dartmouth College*. Marshall held that Dartmouth College was entitled under the Contracts Clause—"No State shall . . . pass any . . . Law impairing the Obligation of Contracts"[53]—to use its corporate charter to shield it from a takeover attempt by New Hampshire, which wanted to turn the college into a public institution. The case thus holds that the Contracts Clause binds the state to its own contracts. *Dartmouth College* did not, however, ask whether, as the quoted passage suggests, a state can impose any conditions it likes on the formation of new corporations. Marshall's dictum on this point rests on an erroneous view of a corporation, which is better understood not as some disembodied entity, but as a "nexus of contracts" that allows individuals to coordinate their business activities.[54] Limited liability then shields the private wealth of shareholders from the debts of the corporation, which increases their willingness to contribute.

The key inquiry is what price, if any, the state can exact for the privilege. Surely the state cannot condition the receipt or retention of a corporate charter on the willingness to maintain separate campuses for its white and black students, as the Supreme Court mistakenly held in *Berea College v. Kentucky*.[55] More precisely, the only conditions that the state should be allowed to attach to the privilege of incorporation are those that improve the *efficiency* of the overall system. States can ask corporations to take out liability insurance when necessary to protect strangers against the wrongful conduct of corporate agents, to register in all states in which they wish to do business, and to submit to local jurisdictions for their activities within the state. But nothing whatsoever says that the shareholders and employees of a corporation should forfeit their right to freedom of association—or, more to the point, to participate in political action that protects them as ordinary individuals. Nor does anyone believe that the constitutional protections of freedom of the press apply to newspapers and periodicals only to the extent they operate in individual or partnership form. The constitutional protections of freedom of speech apply independent of form to individuals, partnerships, and corporations alike.

At this point, the argument should proceed in the usual two-step fashion. First, what is the value of the individual or group interest that the regulation places at risk? Second, what are the justifications for the regulation? Thus in *Bellotti*, the Supreme Court struck down a Massachusetts law that prohibited corporations from contributing funds to a group dedicated to blocking a Massachusetts referendum to authorize a graduated state personal income tax. Progressive taxation is a constitutional nonstarter in a classical liberal system, but is a fair proposal under modern constitutional principles. Surely opposition, or support, for that proposal counts as high-value political speech. Yet what compelling interest justifies their deprivation? Preventing corruption is highly implausible in any referendum that involves no payments to any public official. Silencing corporate speech by government fiat should never be allowed. Bank shareholders protect their individual interests against the corporate board through their own internal procedures. If individuals cannot be barred from contributing to these campaigns, neither can corporations. *Bellotti* was correctly decided.

The Supreme Court took a very different tack in *Austin v. Michigan Chamber of Commerce*,[56] by upholding Michigan's Campaign Finance Act,[57] which allowed corporations to support political candidates only by using funds designated for that purpose. Once again, the statute imposes an explicit limitation on speech that would not be tolerated against individuals who are never required to use only segregated funds for political purposes. Nonetheless, Justice Thurgood Marshall (who dissented in *Bellotti*) justified the law by appealing to two considerations:

> The first is the State's interest in sustaining the active role of the individual citizen in the electoral process, and thereby preventing diminution of the citizen's confidence in government. The second is the interest in protecting the rights of shareholders whose views differ from those expressed by management on behalf of the corporation.

Both arguments are fatally flawed. Corporations are not citizens, but their shareholders are often citizens of the state, or citizens of other states who themselves are entitled to support candidates for public office in states where they do not reside. Nor is it clear that a broader base of political participation somehow reduces citizen confidence, when it is equally plausible to insist that political confidence diminishes when the state muzzles potential speakers. Therefore, as long as the mechanisms of corporate governance can address minority shareholder rights, both arguments in *Austin* fail. Nor does the equation shift by making any special claim of corporate "corruption," or worse, "the appearance of corruption."[58] The applicable constitutional standard for political speech calls for an "exacting scrutiny," under which a restriction is upheld "only if it is narrowly tailored to serve an overriding state interest."[59] Generalized suspicions of corporate irregularity do not come close to meeting that standard.

Unfortunately, *Austin* paved the way for the Supreme Court's decision in *McConnell v. Federal Election Commission*,[60] which upheld the complex set of limitations on corporate speech contained in the Bipartisan Campaign Reform Act (BRCA) (often called "McCain-Feingold").[61] That act first limits the amount of "soft-money contributions," covering general expenditures for party activities that fall short of specific endorsements for a particular candidate. These were largely left unregulated under the Federal Election Campaign Act of 1976. McCain-Feingold also limits the amount of advertising that may be done, both by and on behalf of political parties, within thirty or sixty days of an election.[62]

These are substantial limitations on freedom of speech that would, without question, be struck down if imposed on individuals. Yet the justifications offered by both Justices Stevens and O'Connor, like those in *Austin*, fall far short of making out any "exacting" claim of a compelling state interest. The two justices were content to assert that the record is "replete" with instances in which money purchases access to political actors.[63] But their one specific illustration was a clever ruse that the milk industry used to amass hefty sums to aid Richard Nixon's reelection campaign in order to protect their minimum price supports.[64] They might have noted that the issue would have dissipated if in 1934, in *Nebbia v. New York*,[65] the Supreme Court had not allowed the state to set minimum prices for milk, backed by criminal sanctions.

As this one example shows, Justices Stevens and O'Connor were unable to reach any general conclusion whether corporate contributions count as good or bad from any neutral social perspective. Nor is it possible to develop one, so long as the current constitutional framework is indifferent to the legislative choice between competition and monopoly, which creates the inexcusable levels of political discretion. But in today's environment, it cannot be the case that every popular effort on matters of taxation, employment, regulation, or free trade should receive assistance from the Supreme Court, which refuses to take any constitutional stand against the risks of faction which itself moves the country ever further from a sustainable competitive equilibrium. The same progressive naiveté on the dangers of partisan politics drove the unfortunate dilution of First Amendment rights in *Austin* and *McConnell*.

This house of intellectual cards came under attack in *Federal Election Commission v. Wisconsin Right to Life*.[66] WRTL ran advertisements urging viewers to contact their United States senators to let them know where they stood on the issue of abortion. One could call this abstract speech, or perhaps disguised electioneering efforts that fall within the scope of McCain-Feingold. But it is just those ad hoc determinations that make it unwise to let the act chill speech that is directed to one of the major social issues of our time. A conservative five-to-four majority did some high-stepping to hold that *McConnell* did not preclude an "as-applied" challenge to the prohibition of an "electioneering communication" and advertisements that were "the 'functional equivalent' of express campaign speech."[67] The court reasoned that strict scrutiny (honored only in name in *McConnell*) placed the burden of proof on the government to show that this mixed form of speech fell within the statutory prohibition.

After *WRTL*, the relevant law was in an evident state of disarray, for that case's evasive and ad hoc techniques offered, at most, inadequate and erratic constitutional protection of corporate speech. It was therefore no surprise that *WRTL*'s middle position disintegrated in *Citizens United*, which held that McCain-Feingold could not block an airing of the film *Hillary: The Movie* within thirty days of a Democratic primary in which she was running for the Democratic presidential nomination. The film represents political speech that lies at the core of the First Amendment, so it should attract the exacting scrutiny so obviously missing in *McConnell*. But the coalition that carried *WRTL* took the case one step further by overruling *McConnell*.

On the doctrinal side, the First Amendment protects the freedom of speech in general terms that do not exclude corporations from its coverage. In his dissent, Justice Stevens made the narrow historical argument that corporations did not achieve full legal personhood at the time of the nation's founding,[68] but he would never invoke that argument to suggest that corporations are not citizens of the state in which they are incorporated or where they have their principal place of business. Nor would it make the slightest sense to admit that large partnerships (let alone large limited partnership) are entitled to speech protection that is systematically denied to corporations because of the unrelated feature of limited liability.

The corruption rationales are, moreover, as weak in this case as in *Austin* and *McConnell*. And what has become still clearer is that all too often the political constraints on corporations that were belittled by Justice Marshall have an enormous impact on corporations. The simple point here is that corporations that sell in consumer markets run the risk of instant retribution for taking high-profile stands that cut against their customer base. John McKay, the CEO of Whole Foods, learned that lesson the hard way when his critique of the Obama health care plan created an instant consumer backlash. Here is one brutal assessment of the overall position: "While the word 'corporation' may conjure up images of Microsoft and British Petroleum, the truth is that the vast majority of corporations in the United States are small business corporations or ideological corporations." In addition, it should come as no surprise that "[m]ost corporations also are in business to make a profit, and therefore cannot afford to alienate customers or encounter negative press."[69] Corporations that have the right to take political stands are all too often buffeted by demands from activist groups on all sides to take up their causes. This is a right that most businesses do not value or want to exercise. The only groups that really want the power to take political positions as corporations are labor unions, chambers of commerce, and advocacy groups like WRTL and Citizens United that do not run the risk of alienating consumers.[70] If corporations want to brave that backlash, by all means let them if the alternative requires a huge administrative apparatus that imposes high compliance costs on pain of criminal liability.

RELIGION

29

Free Exercise

THE TWO RELIGION CLAUSES of the First Amendment read as follows: "Congress shall make no law respecting an establishment of religion, or prohibiting the free exercise thereof."[1] As noted in Chapter 24, those two commands cut in opposite directions. The constant danger runs as follows. Any protection of religious liberty above and beyond the protection given to other activities could be read as an establishment of religion, while any restriction on activity of religious institutions could be read as limiting the free exercise of its members. Each clause always lurks in the wings when the other is under consideration. Indeed, many cases raise difficult interpretive questions under both at the same time. Nonetheless, it is necessary to break down the larger issue into its component parts, and on this score it is better to begin with the Free Exercise Clause[2] than with the Establishment Clause.[3] The simple reason is that the Free Exercise Clause deals with the issue of individual liberty, which, rightly understood, rests on a view of individual entitlements that precedes the creation of the state. In contrast, for its part, the Establishment Clause necessarily presupposes public institutions that have as their function, among others, the protection of religious liberty by first collecting tax revenues that are then spent on a wide range of public goods.

Neutrality versus Accommodation

The basic insight in dealing with the Free Exercise Clause is that the freedom of religion it protects is a subset of a larger conception of individual freedom, which works off a bottom-up Lockean theory with no explicit

religious agenda. Authoritative pronouncements from on high are perfectly appropriate within a religion, but they are useless to resolve the
claims between members of that religion and other individuals or groups
in society. Many faiths have accounts of religious freedom that privilege
their own position against all outsiders. But for constitutional purposes,
these deeply held preferences must be disregarded to find a theory of
religious freedom that covers all instances of its free exercise. The only
workable account of religious freedom suitable for doctrinal purposes
must be indifferent to the truth or falsity of any given set of religious
beliefs. After all, inconsistent religious views of the world can all be
wrong, but they cannot all be right. At this point, the focus turns to
the standard libertarian justifications, developed elsewhere, that can be
invoked for limiting the free exercise of religion, which again turns the
inquiry back to the use of force and fraud. Only after these questions of
religious liberties among strangers are resolved is it possible to examine
how the Free Exercise Clause operates in settings with more pervasive
state control, including first the public commons and thereafter matters
of education and employment.

It is also important to recognize that today this inquiry takes place
in a second-best world in which it is already conceded that restrictions
on private property and economic liberty receive only a low rational
basis review, which tolerates large amounts of redistribution through
taxation and regulation. The ordinary rights of an earlier era become
extraordinary rights today, so that any distinctive exercise of rights of
association, for example, could be attacked as a religious preference
and hence an establishment of religion. Think of a rule that exempts
the clergy from sex discrimination prohibitions. Conversely, whenever
religious individuals are subjected to norms that limit their freedom of
association, is there a denial of the free exercise of religion? Think of
a rule that subjects religious organizations to the same restrictions on
sex discrimination as all other employers. Put in other words, the challenge is to mesh any heightened standard of protection for religious liberty in a world that affords only weak protection for private property,
as under zoning laws, and associational freedom, as with employment
discrimination laws. The tension between special exemptions and uniform rules runs throughout this area.[4] The central choice, as it turns
out, is whether the neutral application of some general law to religious
institutions is permissible regardless of its disparate impact on religious
groups—which, as with dietary restrictions, is almost always known to

the legislature. Or must there be some accommodation to special religious beliefs, so that parity need not be achieved when there is need to counteract the known disparate impacts of general legal regulation. The best way to sort out these issues is to start with the government's regulation of private behavior, after which it is possible to ask what changes when the government acts not only as regulator, but also as employer, educator, or property owner. This approach favors analytic clarity over historical continuity by stressing distinctions that Supreme Court case law sometimes overlooks, downplays, or rejects.

The Government as Regulator

The Supreme Court's initial foray into the Free Exercise Clause was its 1879 decision in *Reynolds v. United States*.[5] A unanimous Court upheld a bigamy prosecution of Mormons in Utah, though the Free Exercise Clause, by binding Congress which administered the territory, necessarily applied. Thus Chief Justice Morrison Waite construed the clause by adopting a narrow definition of the basic right and a broad account of the permissible state justifications—the antithesis of a classical liberal position. Put otherwise, a strong dosage of judicial deference was thus built into the ground floor. Waite wrote:

> [T]he only question which remains is, whether those who make polygamy a part of their religion are excepted from the operation of the statute. . . . [W]hile [the laws] cannot interfere with mere religious belief and opinions, they may with practices. Suppose one believed that human sacrifices were a necessary part of religious worship; would it be seriously contended that the civil government under which he lived could not interfere to prevent a sacrifice? Or if a wife religiously believed it was her duty to burn herself upon the funeral pile of her dead husband; would it be beyond the power of the civil government to prevent her carrying her belief into practice?
>
> So here, as a law of the organization of society under the exclusive dominion of the United States, it is provided that plural marriages shall not be allowed. Can a man excuse his practices to the contrary because of his religious belief? To permit this would be to make the professed doctrines of religious belief superior to the law of the land, and, in effect, to permit every citizen to become a law unto himself. Government could exist only in name under such circumstances.[6]

The various arguments and analogies that Chief Justice Waite packed into this short passage have set the law on free exercise on the wrong course from the beginning, from which it has never fully recovered. Waite's initial query was whether any individuals should be "excepted" or "excuse[d]" from a law of general applicability.[7] That presumption, however, is at its peak with respect to those norms that are designed to serve classical liberal ends of stopping the use of force and fraud. But the moment the laws in question interfere with basic freedoms of association, that presumption no longer retains the power that it has with respect to the core applications of the criminal law. As noted in Chapter 23, that presumption has shifted in connection with morals offenses, most notably on such issues as prostitution and fornication, which involve sexual activities outside of marriage. But there is a real question as to whether the Utah legislation falls within that category, or whether it is better understood as the effort of one religious group to block practices that are inconsistent with its own beliefs. Unlike gay marriage, which until late has never been sanctioned, polygamous marriages date back to Biblical times—Jacob first married Leah and then Rachel. In total Jacob had four wives.[8] Health and safety regulation is always open to challenge as a disguised form of anticompetitive labor regulation. The same principle should apply to marriage restrictions.

Chief Justice Waite therefore erred in setting the initial presumption not in favor of liberty, but in favor of the overall use of state power. He then compounds that error by insisting that although laws "cannot interfere with mere religious belief and opinions, they may with practices."[9] That narrow reading conflicts with the textual commitment to the free *exercise* of religion, in which religious practices are necessarily included. To make his position credible, Waite then appeals to the example of human sacrifice. This case is, however, easily distinguishable from polygamy, for constraints against human sacrifice are manifestly consistent with the general classical prohibition on force and fraud. Waite then adds a second case that is far closer to the line—the prohibition of suicide in connection with discharging religious duty. It is worth noting that classical liberal writers condemned suicide because, although individuals were custodians of their own bodies, one's body was itself a gift from God that could not be used to violate fundamental norms of humanity. John Locke wrote "[man] has not liberty to destroy himself,"[10] to which Immanuel Kant added that suicide violates the categorical imperative because no person should be used "merely as means, but must in all his actions be always considered as an end in himself."[11]

More modern discussions on this same topic often reach the same conclusion on the more functional ground that no rational person would take his own life, so that the fact of suicide itself is evidence of some underlying incapacity or external coercion—a presumption that loses some, perhaps much, of its power in cases of voluntary euthanasia at the end of life.[12] Recent Supreme Court cases have continued to uphold the prohibition in recognition of these practical concerns.[13] Clearly some measure of constitutional deference on this issue is required given the serious cross-currents over the prospect of diminished capacity and undue influence. Nor do these interests exhaust the realm of justifications for social control. There is little doubt that the state can stop religious sacrifice of animals to the extent that these cause pollution to public waterways, for the antinuisance rationale applies to all liberties. But here state efforts to control these externalities have to be justified by showing at the very least the existence of such harm. It is not sufficient to do so because of a dislike of religious slaughter for its own sake, especially if it is engaged in by an unpopular sect.[14]

The leap, therefore, from murder and suicide, or from the creation of common law nuisances to plural marriage is a non sequitur, for it offers no independent moral theory to explain why the state's judgment should be dispositive against a constitutional challenge, except for the fact that the opposition to plural marriage is accepted by all dominant religions. There is no harm to others here, or even harm to self. Whether the topic is religion or speech, any collective disapproval about the desirability of particular practices should carry no weight, unless it is tied to harms to the parties involved, as measured by their own lights. Thus, it is permissible to show that polygamy is abusive to some, or indeed all, women. It would also be relatively simple to justify a prohibition against plural marriages for young girls. But even here, the age prohibition is sensible whenever young girls under parental control are shipped off to husbands against their will in monogamous relationships, so the case against polygamy collapses down into the usual and proper concern with the protection of minors. In the end, Waite's chilling conclusion is that any uniform and general law made by the majority can be imposed on a minority, on whose members alone it has a substantial negative impact. In this instance, the denial of the free exercise claim does look like a violation of the Establishment Clause.

That evident tension between the free exercise of religion and neutral laws surfaced again in *Prince v. Massachusetts*,[15] where the Court,
speaking through Justice Wiley Rutledge, upheld the application of a
child labor law against a woman who was the guardian of her nine-
year-old niece. The aunt violated those laws by taking the child with her
to help sell copies of two Jehovah's Witnesses publications—*The Watch-
tower* and *Consolation*—on the public streets. This child labor statute was
not directed to long hours in factories; it instead prohibited girls under
eighteen and boys under twelve from selling any wares on the street.
The stated justification for this prohibition was that this child labor law
served its stated end "that children be both safeguarded from abuses and
given opportunities for growth into free and independent well developed men and citizens."[16] In addition, the five-member majority of the
Court held, citing *Reynolds*, that her religious motivations did not trigger
an equal protection claim since all children were subject to the same
regulations prohibiting them from selling religious tracts on public highways. The absence of a suspect classification led again to a deferential
standard of review. In contrast with the Equal Protection Clause, however, the Free Exercise Clause is not a simple demand for parity. It is an
explicit substantive constitutional guarantee, which was held to apply
against the states. On that question, warning bells should ring when the
state conveniently exempts from the general child labor law altar boys
and youthful choristers who ply their efforts inside religious "edifices"[17]
and not "on the public streets."[18]

Unfortunately, *Prince* made no effort to explain why the Jehovah's
Witnesses' religious activities were less deserving of protection than others simply because they operated only on the public highways. Of course
the police power can apply to the religious activities of children, but
not under some rational basis review. The specific religious guarantee
calls for a higher level of scrutiny that in turn demands some particularized showing of a likelihood of child abuse or neglect, which is not
likely on the facts in *Prince*. It surely does not do for the Supreme Court
to cite a case that found the state to be acting within its police power
when it prohibited child labor in "hazardous employment"[19] working
on machine tools with no hint of any religious issue. Even if the Jehovah's Witnesses were not singled out for special treatment, the disparate
impact of the child labor law, which may well have been its design,
operates as an indefensible burden on religious liberty, for the simple

reason that it puts Massachusetts's thumb on the scale in favor of some religions and against others. The simple requirement of formal equality in the application of any law is never sufficient to protect against state abuse. Disparate impact matters as well.

The majority in *Prince* entertained no doubt about the ability of the state to require children to receive some schooling, notwithstanding any conflict between religious belief and state programs.[20] That position coexisted uneasily with the earlier Supreme Court decision in *Pierce v. Society of Sisters*, which allowed parents (under the Due Process Clause, which had teeth before its modern evisceration) to provide for a religious education of their children outside the public school system.[21] Nonetheless, *Prince* held that parents could be required to supply some form of education for children. *Prince* in turn was limited in *Wisconsin v. Yoder*,[22] which held that Amish parents could refuse, on religious grounds, to send their children to public school without providing some alternative education. Once again, the case presents a square claim of the free exercise of religion against the state, which claims to protect all minors from parental misconduct. But for formal education and similar issues, the correct constitutional framework is easier than commonly supposed. For a long time, the state required no child to have an education.[23] Yet there was no evidence that this gap in state activity resulted in either stunted children or an ignorant populace, given the strong desire of parents to provide education for their own children. The Amish practice is not the result of an isolated decision by quirky parents. It was made as part of an overall system of faith, which in the years of its operation probably has produced fewer casualties than the public education system in many an inner-city locale. As with the child labor cases, citizenship and civic responsibility sound like lofty ideals, but the correct standard throughout always looks for some particularized form of abuse directed against the individual children, just as should have been done in *Prince*. The basic presumption in favor of religious autonomy can never be displaced by diffuse and unsubstantiated police power claims.

Reynolds and *Prince* also influenced the misguided Supreme Court decision in *United States v. Lee*,[24] once again in connection with the Amish. Social Security law exempts from taxation all self-employed persons whose well-established religious tenets make them "conscientiously opposed to acceptance of the benefits" from any private or public retirement or disability system.[25] The statutory exemption is narrowly drafted to prevent opportunism and abuse. No one disputed that the Amish qualified. The exemption, however, did not allow Lee to opt out of the Social Security system for his Amish employees. He refused to pay the payroll tax because the Amish treat it as "sinful" not to take care of their own "elderly and needy."[26] A unanimous Court accepted that the collection of the tax burdened the Amish. It also expressed no doubt as to the sincerity of Lee's belief and explicitly acknowledged that "compulsory participation in the social security system interferes with their free exercise rights."[27]

At this point, the issue concerns the justification for the burdens so imposed. Chief Justice Warren Burger put the point as follows: "The social security system in the United States serves the public interest by providing a comprehensive insurance system with a variety of benefits available to all participants, with costs shared by employers and employees."[28] As with the comparisons to human sacrifice and suicide in *Reynolds*, however, the argument proceeded by a flawed analogy from paying taxes to support wars regarded as sinful to paying money into the Social Security system. Somehow the government could not function "if denominations were allowed to challenge the tax system because tax payments were spent in a manner that violates their religious belief."[29]

Once again, basic economic theory exposes the flaw. In this instance, the appeal to the "public interest" is not invoked to control the dangers of monopoly power, as it is in the ratemaking cases. Nor is there a state interest in supplying public goods, namely those which, when supplied to one person, must necessarily be supplied to all.[30] Public goods must be funded by coercive taxes, for otherwise everyone has a temptation to free-ride on the payments of their fellow citizens. But the Social Security system is not concerned with paying for public goods, such as street lights, the court system, or national defense. It is a different beast entirely because its payments go into individual bank accounts, which are as exclusive as property rights possibly can be. Social Security can exempt all the Amish, whether self-employed or not, from both contributions and payments without worrying about any free-rider problems. After all, the Amish are not insisting on their right to collect benefits without paying taxes—a claim that the Court rightly rejected in *Bowen v. Roy*[31] where the Roys claimed that their Native American religious beliefs prevented them from supplying the Social Security numbers of their family members who received benefits under the Aid to Families with Dependent Children and Food Stamp programs. With the Amish entirely removed from the system, progressive social policies may determine how the remainder is divvied up under the weak standard of rational basis review. But the protection of religious liberties need not be consigned to the same fate. Given Amish beliefs, *Lee's* confused account of the public interest leads to a forced wealth transfer from the Amish to the individuals receiving Social Security benefits. This outcome is not correct.

Nor did the Court do better in the subsequent decision in *Bob Jones University v. United States*,[32] which allowed the Internal Revenue Service (IRS) to deny Bob Jones University tax-exempt status because of its decision on religious grounds to ban interracial dating among its students. In a world without taxation, Bob Jones is within its rights to have such a mandate under classical liberal principles of freedom of association, given the wealth of other educational choices available to students who find the policy morally unacceptable. But the state cannot lead them to shut the program down because of the offensive premises on which it rests. All things considered, the country is healthier when more options are made available. Whether the program lives or dies should depend on whether students wish to enroll, not on whether the IRS disapproves of their behavior. The imposition of a tax regime, therefore, should not alter the relative balance between Bob Jones and other universities that take a different view on interracial dating. Unfortunately, the IRS's redefinition of "charitable" distorts that balance in favor of Bob Jones's many rivals. When the question is instead whether the state can fund programs for maternal health but not for abortion, the forceful liberal response attacks the state-induced distortion between two alternatives with equal constitutional status.[33] Yet in *Bob Jones*, the Supreme Court held that the state had a "compelling" state interest in barring discrimination—a holding on which it relied in its prior decisions in *Reynolds, Prince,* and *Lee*—cases for which no kind words should be uttered.[34] Yet how can the interest be compelling for tax purposes given the evident constitutional difficulties of any direct effort to prohibit religious institutions from refusing to allow their students to engage in interracial marriage, or for that matter from allowing only men to serve as priests? The parallels here to the protection of freedom of speech are strong, where the government cannot condition the receipt of government benefits on signing loyalty oaths.[35]

The issue in this instance is not which set of restrictions we dislike most. It is whether either set should be allowed when the state has a duty to remain neutral across different ideological beliefs.

The same flawed logic that runs from *Reynolds* to *Bob Jones* led to the 1990 watershed decision of *Employment Division, Department of Human Resources v. Smith*,[36] which asked whether Oregon could deny unemployment benefits to members of the Native American Church who used peyote for religious purposes. At first look, the case did not seem to deal with the regulation of private conduct, but rather with the withholding of state benefits. However, the decision to withhold benefits turned on whether Oregon could apply its general criminal ban to this religious subgroup, consistent with the Free Exercise Clause. So the Court returns to *Reynolds*'s insistence that valid general laws preclude the need for granting accommodations for actions that look more like polygamy than ritual slaughter or spousal suicide. Where, then, is the tangible risk of harm in this highly regimented use of peyote in controlled settings? Is there any evidence that ingesting peyote functions as a precursor to violent or other antisocial activities?

In upholding the ban, Justice Scalia retreated from the broad claim in *Reynolds* that all forms of conduct fell outside the protection of the First Amendment. He acknowledged that "[i]t would doubtless be unconstitutional, for example, to ban the casting of 'statues that are to be used for worship purposes,' or to prohibit bowing down before a golden calf."[37] But in his view, this case went one step further because Smith sought to escape the application of "a generally applicable law" against the use of peyote, without examining the weight of the countervailing religious interest.[38] In so doing he ignored the disparate impact of the law on Smith whose religion both commanded and restrained his use of peyote.

Scalia then distinguished *Yoder*, which had evinced a more liberal spirit, as falling in a class of cases best understood as offering greater constitutional protection for conduct that combined the exercise of religion with other constitutionally protected activities such as freedom of speech and of the press.[39] He thus pointed to cases like as *Cantwell v. Connecticut*,[40] which invalidated a state law that gave the local administrator of a licensing system complete discretion to forbid any religious or charitable solicitations. But this point too lacks any theoretical heft. Both speech and free exercise are embodiments of the same classical liberal approach to freedom. Each has the same internal conceptual integrity. There are no cases in which two supposed half violations equal one whole. Instead, there are cases where some practices violate both the Free Exercise and the Free Speech Clauses, instead of just one. Nor should it change the case if smoking peyote for religious purposes becomes expressive conduct in this select group of religious devotees.

Smith provoked a sharp bipartisan outcry for failing to make a modest accommodation to satisfy religious beliefs. A unified Congress first passed the Religious Freedom Restoration Act,[41] which purported to undo the rigid tests in *Smith*, only to have it struck down by the Supreme Court in *City of Boerne v. Flores*.[42] *Boerne* took it as a given that *Smith* established the outer limit of individual protections under the Free Exercise Clause. At this point, the issue concerned the simple question of whether the Congress could expand the substantive scope of the Equal Protection Clause beyond the contours laid out in *Smith*. If it could, then Congress would have the power to act under Section 5 of the Fourteenth Amendment that reads simply: "The Congress shall have the power to enforce by appropriate legislation, the provisions of this article." Yet once the Court's interpretation of the Equal Protection Clause is dispositive, it is no longer appropriate for the Congress to impose limitations on the states that the Equal Protection Clause does not require. Stated otherwise, it is easy for Congress to impose limits on its own powers if it believes that the Court's interpretation of any clause supplies anyone with insufficient protection against its own actions. But the Congress cannot adopt the strategy to impose additional restrictions on the behavior of the states, which are coordinate sovereigns within the system.

Once rebuffed in *Boerne*, Congress responded with the Religious Land Use and Institutionalized Persons Act (RLUIPA),[43] which in effect applied, in defiance of *Smith*, a far higher level of scrutiny to general laws in two designated areas of concern. One prong of RLUIPA stipulates: "No government shall impose a substantial burden on the religious exercise of a person residing in or confined to an institution...."[44] It then requires strict scrutiny of such legislation through its means and ends provisions: the law shall not be sustained unless the burden furthers "a compelling governmental interest" and does so by "the least restrictive means."[45] In *Cutter v. Wilkinson*[46] the Supreme Court upheld that portion of RLUIPA on the ground that an accommodation of religious practices does not necessarily run afoul of the Establishment Clause—a clear retreat from *Smith*. That same formula—compelling state interest coupled with least restrictive means—also controls the land use provisions of RLUIPA and has yet to be reviewed by the United States Supreme Court. However, in the lower court decisions on the subject, the constitutionality of the statute has been presumed,[47] leaving open the issue of statutory construction of whether the religious land use provisions of the statute apply to eminent domain proceedings, to which the correct answer seems to be no, given that land use regulation does not cover the taking of property.

The authority of *Smith* was further shaken in *Hosanna-Tabor Evangelical Lutheran Church & School v. EEOC*,[48] which asked whether to read in a statutory "ministerial exception" to insulate the church from the Americans with Disabilities Act of 1990 (ADA).[49] The case arose when the Lutheran Church chose to dismiss Cheryl Perich, a "called" teacher, rather than return her to the classroom after a medical leave for narcolepsy. "Called teachers" are called by God. Unlike "lay" teachers, they must be Lutherans and go through special training before assuming their positions. A unanimous Supreme Court held that a ministerial exception was indeed necessary to save the ADA from an attack under the Free Exercise Clause, and thus blocked the application of the ADA to this case. The Court held that it was for the church, and not the ADA, to determine who counted as a minister under its own internal rules.

This case could never arise under a classical liberal theory because the principles of freedom of contract would require the repeal of the ADA in all cases of private employers,[50] thereby obviating the need to create ad hoc accommodations in some. But under the prevailing principle of *Smith*, it might have appeared that a neutral rule of general application could survive constitutional challenge. Nonetheless, Chief Justice Roberts made short shrift of *Smith* by claiming that "a church's selection of its ministers is unlike an individual's ingestion of peyote. *Smith* involved government regulation of only outward physical acts. The present case, in contrast, concerns government interference with an internal church decision that affects the faith and mission of the church itself."[51]

His purported distinction makes no sense at all. First, *Hosanna Tabor* appears to apply only to called teachers, not lay teachers. Yet the ability of a church to control its own internal deliberations depends as much on controlling the second as it does on controlling the first. In the 1979 case of *NLRB v. Catholic Bishop of Chicago*,[52] the Supreme Court held that the National Labor Relations Act does not apply to teachers in church schools in the absence of a clear congressional statement that it does so. *Chicago Bishop* made no reference to the ministerial exception that loomed so large in *Hosanna Tabor.* Yet now it is unclear whether on the applicable balance of interest that the ADA applies to lay teachers. There is no need for that guarded caution in an otherwise commendable decision.

Second, *Smith* should not survive *Hosanna Tabor.* The inhalation of peyote in *Smith* was described by the chief justice as dealing with "only outward physical acts."[53] That is an odd way, to say the least, to describe conduct that is an essential part of a religious ritual. If that core religious practice lies outside constitutional protection, why then protect instructional activities that are at least one step further removed from core religious practices? It is as though the United States could ban, under some general law, the use of religious wafers in Catholic Communion, but could not require them to permit unions to organize the nuns, and perhaps the lay teachers, in parochial schools. All these distinctions are beside the point. The only defensible line is that the internal affairs of religious institutions are beyond the scope of the government's power to regulate employment relations.

Whether the law will continue to move toward that position remains to be seen. The current flashpoint is the massive litigation efforts brought by the Roman Catholic Archbishop of Washington and the University of Notre Dame[54] for a declaration that the Patient Protection and Affordable Care Act is unconstitutional insofar as it mandates that these institutions, as employers, supply contraception to their employees, or ensure that their insurers do so at no extra expense.[55] The scope of these limited protections is further truncated by the narrow definition of a "religious employer" under the regulations, so that it covers only nonprofit organizations for whom inculcation of religious values is their purpose, and then, furthermore, only if they serve or employ "primarily" persons who share in their religious tenets. By this definition, most Roman Catholic hospitals, shelters, schools, and universities are not covered. It is particularly odious that the price for gaining the contraceptive exemption is denying services to non-Catholic individuals. To the extent that principles of institutional autonomy apply in the religious context, the contraception mandate should be dead on arrival on constitutional grounds, even for cases of "lay" as opposed to the "called" employees, who alone fit within the ministerial exception read into the ADA. At least so I thought until I read an open letter signed by well over a hundred prominent law professors who think that one of the many virtues of the contraceptive mandate is to advance religious liberty. At the beginning of their letter, the signatories write:

> Nothing in our nation's history or laws permits a boss to impose his or her religious views on non-consenting employees. Indeed, this nation was founded upon the basic principle that every individual—whether company president or assistant janitor—has an equal claim to religious freedom.[56]

In a footnote, the signatories insist that *Hosanna Tabor* "is easily distinguishable, because the case merely held that a house of worship is exempt from certain employment laws when hiring and firing ministers. In contrast, the no-copay contraception rule exempts houses of worship altogether, and affects the rights of all employees, including those who do not share the faith of their employers."[57]

They then conclude with this message:

> Religious freedom must not provide a justification to deprive women of legal rights they should enjoy as employees and citizens. To the contrary, the First Amendment specifically preserves space for their religious liberty, and secures their right to act as individuals who exercise their own conscience on matters pertaining to their faith, body, and health.[58]

The letter is wrong in its analysis of both the Free Exercise Clause and the applicable precedent. On the former, the "boss cannot just impose his or her religious views on non-consenting employees." The word "impose" suggests that any employer can tell workers what to do, which is never the case so long as they have the right to quit their jobs. In this case, moreover, that issue does not even arise, because there is nothing that any religious employer has done to prevent its workers from obtaining contraception from other providers at their own expense. Workers are not coerced, moreover, when an employer fails to supply a benefit that some workers want. The term "coercion" is, however, correctly used to describe a mandate to supply workers with benefits that violate an employer's faith. The principle of freedom of association only makes sense when both sides are free to associate on whatever terms they both see fit. The coercion here is on the behalf of the dissident employees, not against them.

Nor do the precedents help salvage the contraceptive mandate. *Smith* is clearly in disarray after *Hosanna Tabor*, which deals not only with the hiring and firing of ministers, but also with the management of the internal affairs of a church. How *Hosanna Tabor* can be limited to hiring and firing, when the ADA applies to all employer decisions, seems odd indeed. Any government action covered by the ADA appears to be covered by *Hosanna Tabor*. To be sure, the conceptual equivocations in *Hosanna Tabor* make the outcome of future litigation on the mandate uncertain, which only confirms the uneasy position of religious liberty under our current constitutional order.

Free Exercise and the Exercise of Government Powers

In free exercise cases thus far considered, the government acted solely pursuant to its general power to regulate. In those cases, its power is at low ebb, given that it seeks to interfere in private relationships that are entered into for mutual gain. But the situation becomes more complicated in religion cases, as it was in speech cases, when the government can also properly rely on some independent relationship that it has with the parties whose conduct it regulates—such as when using its power as a landowner, educator or employer. The key question asks how these additional powers change the balance of advantage in dealing with free exercise cases in a number of discrete contexts.

Religious Qualifications for Public Office. Part of this question is addressed by explicit constitutional guarantees, such as Article VI, clause 3, which says flatly that "no religious Test shall ever be required as a Qualification to any Office or public Trust under the United States."[59] The clause was a conscious break from the then current English policy, directed toward Roman Catholics and nonconformists, which allowed for such practices until the passage of the Test Act of 1828[60] and the Catholic Relief Act of 1829.[61] It is therefore no surprise that the Supreme Court has, for example, struck down a Maryland law requiring that a person have a belief in God in order to "hold public office."[62] Even though Article VI, clause 3 could not apply to state officials, the provision was struck down under the Free Exercise Clause as applied to the states in yet another application of the ubiquitous doctrine of unconstitutional conditions. In the same vein, a plurality of the Supreme Court held that Tennessee could not exclude any priest or minister from seeking to become a delegate at a state constitutional convention, again as an impermissible burden on the free exercise of religion.[63] That question is, of course, not resolved by the Test Act cases, for what is at stake is not the need of a nonbeliever to swear a religious oath, but the converse situation: can the state show a sufficient risk that religious officials will put their religious duties before their secular ones to disqualify them on conflict of interests grounds? Here again choosing the right level of scrutiny resolves the problem. Politics is never a pristine business, so in the absence of any demonstrable connection in an individual case, the generalized police power justification should be emphatically rejected.

Public Lands and Roads. Generally speaking, the power over public lands cannot be exercised in ways that force individuals to forsake their religious liberties any more than it can require them to relinquish their rights to political speech—no matter how much individual citizens might prefer personal mobility to either political participation or religious conviction. For all the mistakes in *Prince v. Massachusetts*,[64] the five-member majority did not think the government's case became stronger because the defendant and her niece proselytized on the public highway. Similarly, an anti-littering ordinance that could not stop leaflet distribution on private property could not stop it on public highways either, whether done by Jehovah's Witnesses (again) or labor picketers.[65] A similarly tough attitude applies to ordinances prohibiting the posting of signs on public property for fear of visual clutter.[66] The proper response is to prosecute those who litter or to wait until some localized situation justifies action against the party who litters.

This situation, however, becomes more complex in cases of government lands, not highways, to which no one has a guaranteed right of access. In *Lyng v. Northwest Indian Cemetery Protective Association*,[67] the United States Forest Service sought to build roads on public lands that were the burial grounds of the Yurok, Karok, and Tolawa Indians. Yet the tribes' effort to block construction under a free exercise claim failed on the simple ground that the government could do what it wanted with "what is, after all, its land."[68] That result presumes that the Indian use rights had no protected status against the state, which is in line with the strong positive streak of general American law,[69] which does not allow one to use prescriptive rights against the government.[70] However, those prescriptive rights would apply to private owners and should defeat the government's claims to exceptional status, as that claim is inconsistent with basic classical liberal principles. There is simply no reason to carve out a different rule on the odd ground that established burial grounds go unnoticed by public authorities. The road could simply be relocated.

Education

It is also important to ask what additional powers the government has when it takes on the role of an educational provider. The heavy managerial responsibilities that the government must bear favor the granting of those powers. But two reasons fall on the other side of the balance. First, the government has real market power, given that for most children public schools are often the only option. Second, the government raises tax revenues from the very parties whose options it seeks to limit. Once again, the Jehovah's Witnesses provide the litmus test for both speech and religion claims on the simple question of whether the state can require children to recite the Pledge of Allegiance in school when it violates their good faith belief that such behavior is a form of idolatry. In *Minersville School District v. Gobitis*,[71] Justice Felix Frankfurter invoked a broad police power claim that "national cohesion" was necessary to "national security."[72] Citing *Schneider v. State*, he concluded oddly that littering "presents a totally different order of problem from that of the propriety of subordinating the possible ugliness of littered streets to the free expression of opinion through distribution of handbills."[73] He was right that the stakes are higher, but wrong to conclude that coercing schoolchildren to violate their religious norms best combats the intolerance of the Nazis and Fascists with whom we would soon be at war.

It is not surprising, then, that three years later *West Virginia State Board of Education v. Barnette*,[74] with Frankfurter now in dissent, overturned *Gobitis* by reading into the Constitution, as Frankfurter protested, "the general libertarian views in the Court's opinion," with which as a matter of personal conviction "I should whole heartedly associate myself."[75] Fortunate it was that Justice Robert Jackson writing for the majority did follow Frankfurter's personal views. Never did the narrow accounts of the police power look so good. Private schools, which do not have the power of the state behind them and which in any event face competition from other schools, do have the power to either require the Pledge or to prohibit its use. Once again, the public trump card of ownership and management of the schools does not flip the balance for either speech or religion claims. What remains is to decide what lesser restrictions on religious dress and symbols are appropriate. It is doubtful that any school could prohibit a student from wearing a cross or star around his neck, for "[i]n the absence of a specific showing of constitutionally valid reasons to regulate their speech, students are entitled to freedom of expression of their views."[76] But the class of valid reasons is often quite broad: thus it is equally clear that it could prevent students from asserting the right to say prayers out loud during the middle of a final examination; the formula adopted that asks for "reasonable accommodations without undue hardship,"[77] which derives from the civil rights laws, appears to be the best solution at any high level of generalization. That is the implicit norm of most secular schools, and it is for all its evident weaknesses the best guideline for public action.

Employment

Sherbert v. Verner[78] presents, in stark form, the legal tangles that arise with the unemployment benefits of the modern welfare state. To guard against abuse, these statutes usually deny compensation to any individual who refuses suitable work without good cause. Ms. Sherbert, a Seventh-Day Adventist, was dismissed from her previous job because of her refusal to work on the Sabbath. She claimed that she was entitled to unemployment benefits because she was unable to find a suitable job that did not require Saturday work. Her stark choice: abandon her faith to keep her job or forgo a job to keep the faith. Justice Brennan found this choice intolerable because it "puts the same kind of burden upon the free exercise of religion as would a fine imposed against appellant for her Saturday worship."[79]

This is not so. To see why, consider the position of Sherbert vis-à-vis her employer. *Sherbert* arose before the passage of the modern antidiscrimination law, when her employer had no legal duty to accommodate her religious preferences, whether or not it compromised either the firm's profitability or the comfort level of other workers. Why, then, make other unemployment insurance participants pay higher premiums to subsidize Ms. Sherbert's religious preferences? This issue would have disappeared if she could have paid a higher premium or received a lower wage to cover her increased risk of joblessness. Or the system could have equalized the risk by letting her only receive benefits when she couldn't work for other reasons. Needless to say, a fine on all

Saturday worship is not needed to prevent some cross-subsidy of her religion by others.

It is also instructive to look at Sherbert's case after the passage of the Civil Rights Act of 1964, with its ban against discrimination "because of such individual's . . . religion."[80] In its original form, it did not address "cost-justified" discrimination based on religion. But it is one thing not to hire Sherbert for a Monday-through-Friday job because of her religion, and quite another not to hire her because, unlike all other employees, she refuses to work on Saturdays. That hole was plugged by the act's 1972 amendment that covered "all aspects of religious observance and practice, as well as belief, unless an employer demonstrates that he is unable to reasonably accommodate to an employee's or prospective employee's religious observance or practice without undue hardship on the conduct of the employer's business."[81] Surprisingly, the Supreme Court has construed this reasonable accommodation and undue hardship tandem narrowly so that anything more than a "de minimis cost" is today treated as an "undue hardship,"[82] which makes sense for an employer that has to revise its workforce without running afoul of collective bargaining agreements and a host of other employment laws. The obvious tension with *Sherbert* was left unexplored: if the antidiscrimination law doesn't require the cross-subsidy, why does the Constitution? *Sherbert* looks wrongly decided. Perhaps it ought not be overruled, but neither should its reach be extended. In an age of flex-time employment, few people face Sherbert's alleged dilemma.

Sherbert sets the stage for the controversial decision in *Goldman v. Weinberger*,[83] which asked whether an Orthodox Jew who worked as a clinical psychologist in the Air Force could be disciplined for wearing a yarmulke that did not conform to the military's uniform dress code. Justice Rehnquist rejected the strict scrutiny standard in favor of granting hands-off discretion to the military, fearing the slippery slope argument that allowing yarmulkes today means accepting turbans and dreadlocks tomorrow. Should the military be required to engage in the unappetizing task of having to make exceptions for the dress of one religion but not another, or may it avoid that line-drawing problem by imposing an overbroad ban on Goldman's yarmulke that imposes only a trivial burden on the military? Unlike *Sherbert*, no reassignment of workers will obviate the problem. But in thinking about the military setting, it is instructive that most private employers are willing to make this kind of routine accommodation, which in all likelihood is required under current law. Yet there are limits: no Roman Catholic may, as a right, insist on wearing at work a large anti-abortion button with a picture of an unborn fetus that causes massive workplace disruptions and productivity losses.[84] The dress codes will clearly differ for combat, and could be revised here in the face of problems of performance or morale. But the basic presumption in favor of free exercise should apply in the absence of a particularized showing of a substantial government burden. Some might argue that to give Goldman this break is to establish his religion. The next chapter looks at the other side of the problem: does any special accommodation offend the Establishment Clause by giving a preference to members of some religions that is denied to others?

30

The Establishment Clause

Theoretical Foundations

IN THIS CHAPTER, we leave the question of free exercise to tackle the daunting interpretive problems surrounding the Establishment Clause. Per usual, the written portion of the clause covers only a fraction of the relevant issues, because it says nothing about either the reach of the clause or the possible justifications for limiting its scope. As a brute historical matter, the Establishment Clause was intended to place a ban on the ability of Congress (to whom the First Amendment is exclusively directed) to establish a national church, based on the model of the Anglican Church in England. Such an official church would have a privileged position that would allow it to rely on tax revenues collected from believers and nonbelievers alike. A national church would also have the exclusive right to perform special state functions in which no rival church could participate. Further, establishing a national church would necessarily override the free exercise of religion whenever it mandated church attendance by nonbelievers.[1]

Given these obvious evils, it is worth noting that the text of the Establishment Clause does not read like a universal condemnation of established churches. Rather, the Establishment Clause reads like an anticompetitive provision: *Congress* may not establish a church that horns in on a well-recognized state prerogative. At the time of the founding, many states had established churches. Proposals, most notably in Virginia, to transfer general taxes to a favored religious institution gave rise to impassioned and successful opposition from both James Madison and Thomas Jefferson.[2] With the abolition of the last remaining established church in Massachusetts in 1833, the views of Madison and Jefferson had gained universal acceptance,[3] without any judicial intervention.

The abolition of state churches appears at first blush to make moot any dispute over the incorporation of the Establishment Clause so that it binds the states. But that is not the case. Thus, the issue of incorporation first proved salient in *Everson v. Board of Education*[4] and thereafter in the vast tangle of law that followed the case. Incorporation was of concern because of the wide range of unresolved collateral issues raised by government activities that fell short of a formal designation of one established church. On the one side, there is what might be termed the problem of "partial" or "limited" establishment, whereby the state confers on one or more churches some preference or advantage over others. *Everson* itself, for example, dealt with state support for busing school students to parochial schools,[5] but the larger basic issue clearly extends far beyond that one context. In addition, there are all sorts of historical practices—both symbolic and financial—that acknowledge the central role of religion in private and public life. Any tough look at religious preferences has to be squared with the inverse concern that certain state practices could easily put some or all religious individuals and organizations at a disadvantage, relative to other secular groups that are freed of such impediments. The full range of justifications for state interaction are thus in place. Now that the Establishment Clause has been read through the Fourteenth Amendment to apply to the states, these issues are constantly on the federal judicial agenda.

The key question, therefore, is how to organize the inquiry. In this instance, the best approach is to follow the line of organization that was used in connection with the Free Exercise Clause. The first order of business is to select the proper overarching intellectual framework, which involves understanding what is at stake in the recurrent choice between the strict separation of church and state, on the one hand, and reasonable accommodations between church and state, on the other. Once that relationship is developed, it is instructive to see how these two views play out.

In this chapter, I examine the philosophical bases for the long-standing debate between two approaches to establishment: separation and accommodation. Once those preliminaries are completed, I shall look at the different types of government actions to which they could apply.

Accordingly, I shall first examine direct forms of regulation that have been challenged as Establishment Clause violations. Next, I shall look at the various government tax and subsidy programs that have been challenged on the same grounds. Lastly, I shall analyze the Establishment Clause challenges to various uses of public or common property. In this instance, it is best to start with the standard public forums such as streets and parks and then move to limited public forums such as schools and government bases. The margin for error in these cases is often much smaller than it is in such areas as freedom of speech because of the profound tension between the Free Exercise and the Establishment Clauses, both of which exert strong pressures, albeit in opposite directions.

Separation versus Accommodation

The initial inquiry asks whether Establishment Clause cases should be viewed through the lens of separation or the lens of accommodation. In their ideal formulations, separation means that religious and secular institutions should have nothing to do with each other, a position that, taken literally, no one defends. Accommodation takes the view that cooperation between religious and nonreligious institutions can be sources of mutual gain. One simple example is the separationist demand to keep all religious symbols off of public property, while accommodationists want to allow all to enter on roughly even terms.

It is easy for people to run the two together in ways that make this debate appear unduly abstract or conceptual. In *Zorach v. Clauson*,[6] Justice William O. Douglas upheld a New York law that allowed students to have released time from regular classes to receive religious instruction on off-school premises. In so doing, he distinguished the earlier case of *McCollum v. Board of Education*,[7] which had found an establishment of religion when the state used its power to permit students to attend classes taught by parochial school instructors on public school premises during the school day. In his view, "we cannot expand [*McCollum*] to cover the present released time program unless separation of Church and State means that public institutions can make no adjustments of their schedules to accommodate the religious needs of the people."[8] But Justice Douglas never explained how the two strands, separation and accommodation, work together.

Just how do they mesh? On this issue, the correct analysis begins in what today is regarded as an improbable location—at the points of overlap and conflict between a libertarian theory that treats individual autonomy as the ultimate good and a classical liberal theory that also starts with a baseline of individual autonomy, but allows deviations from that baseline to the extent that they work to the universal advantage of all players subject to a common legal regime. To make that analogy relevant, it is necessary to decompose both church and state into the individuals who are situated on either or both sides of the line. The approach is parallel to one that examines partnerships and corporations to evaluate the consequences of legal rules by looking not at these entities as such, but at their flesh and blood members. It then becomes painfully obvious that all members of any given church are members of the larger society. But at the same time, not all members of society are members of a particular church, just as the members of one church are surely not members of a second.

This imperfect overlap of benefits and burdens generates a wide range of conflicts of interest among these various constituent groups, with serious implications for analyzing both legislative enactments and their executive implementation. Thus, a measure that improves the welfare of all church members could easily result in losses to all citizens who were not church members. That imbalance could occur whether the gains to church members were, in the aggregate, larger or smaller than the losses to the common citizens. Similarly, other measures could benefit the members of one church at the expense of another, with little consequence on individuals who are not members of either. Think of a shift of a government contract from Church A to Church B. Or consider that the ratio of benefits and burdens could change, with religious groups coming out the losers compared to nonreligious individuals.

This array of possibilities restates the simple point that both legislative and executive action often lead to all sorts of wealth transfers between groups: some explicit, but more implicit. The difference between explicit and implicit is important because the former are easier to identify and to eliminate. But, by the same token, a doctrine that looks only to explicit forms of transfer is systematically underinclusive. That is the case with rules that ignore disparate impact, often intentionally, in connection with the dormant Commerce Clause doctrine, the Takings Clause, and the Free Exercise Clause. It is also the case here.

Sniffing out implicit transfers of wealth or opportunities may avoid the underinclusion question, but only at the cost of reducing the reliability of the overall system. This, in turn, could lead to sweeping condemnation of practices that should be regarded as proper. The expansion of the doctrine to cover these cases must, therefore, be precise enough to avoid introducing new levels of error. And it must unearth implicit transfers that are worth correcting.

I believe that it is worthwhile to make that effort in virtually all areas of constitutional endeavor. Those transfers that generate negative sum games should not be allowed in principle, because the gains to the winning faction are smaller than the losses its political prowess inflicts on others. In contrast, positive sum games should be encouraged, taking care to distinguish between two types. First, in some cases the winners receive enough in benefits that they could, in principle (in ways that track the Kaldor-Hicks standard of social welfare), compensate the losers and still be left better off than before. Yet for logistical reasons that often involve the number of parties, that payment of compensation does not take place. Alternatively, these good measures could generate strong social improvements (in ways that track the standard Pareto measures of social utility), which produce benefits to all concerned so that the compensation, be it in cash or in kind, makes all parties better off.

In outlining these possibilities, I have stressed both the transfers that take place from one church to another and the transfers that take place between churches as a group and nonreligious individuals or organizations. This view is at odds with a minority position that sees the Establishment Clause as limiting preferences between churches, but having nothing to say about the preferences that churches as a group receive relative to nonchurch groups. Thus, Professor Robert Cord notes that Madison thought it appropriate to set aside a day to allow people to offer praise to "their Heavenly benefactor."[9] Madison was also part of a congressional committee in favor of setting up the chaplaincy system in the United States Senate,[10] rightly upheld in *Marsh v. Chambers*,[11] which noted that the program was put into place at the very time that the First Amendment was adopted.[12] And Joseph Story gave the Establishment Clause a narrow reading by claiming that the purpose of the clause was to protect against "all rivalry among Christian sects."[13] That view would leave all non-Christian religions out in the cold, with no textual warrant for the exclusion. Elsewhere, Story wrote more broadly that the

Free Exercise Clause was not offended "by aiding with equal attention the votaries of every sect to perform their own religious duties, or by establishing funds for the support of ministers, for public charities, for the endowment of churches, or for the sepulture of the dead."[14] He did not, however, write in a context where the claims of nonbelievers were at issue, so he did not have to address any broader claim of the reach of the Establishment Clause.

As an overarching issue, the narrow view of the Establishment Clause is vulnerable to attack for two reasons. First, as a textual matter, the word "church" does not appear in the First Amendment. What is at stake is a law "respecting an establishment of religion,"[15] which looks textually as if it rejects *both* the favoritism of one religion over another and the favoritism of all religious institutions over their nonreligious rivals. The word "respecting" suggests no need to establish any church or engage in religious practice proper to trigger potential application of the Establishment Clause. The word "an" is an effort to protect all permutations and possibilities. The drafting looks as though it treats the explicit subsidy of a religion as the core wrong, only to guard thereafter against its circumvention by measures that give differential benefits to religion, without endowing them with formal titles or special charters. The analogy to the Takings Clause is the destruction of property to which the government does not take title.

Second, as a functional matter, the broader coverage is critical because the political process risks of illicit transfers are present with equal force in dealing with either direct regulation or hidden subsidy. It may well be that particular measures fall into a class of "justified establishments," as it were. But it seems hard to infer that these precedents would justify massive transfers from the congressional coffers to all religions, much less only to Christian religions. The effort to stabilize relationships among religious factions is in line with Madison's concern with political factions. But this only addresses one line of cleavage. The larger problem is all variations on the theme, to which the limited reach of the Establishment Clause cannot apply. Whatever the real doubts on original position, the prescriptive constitutional interpretation has taken hold. Thus, the narrower reading is not likely to resurface after decades in which the broader definition has reshaped our law. That variation on original intention, if it were, is fully justified because it gives ample voice to the theory of limited government that animates the entire Bill of Rights.

The Libertarian versus the Classical Liberal

Once that broad range of the Establishment Clause is accepted, it is possible to state the tension between the libertarian and classical liberal positions with greater clarity, both generally and as it applies to religious activities. The strong libertarian sees the many virtues of a separationist position, but remains deeply suspicious of allowing any further legislative or executive matter that might pass for social improvement. That concern stems from two related philosophical commitments. The first is analytical: many libertarians of the Kantian persuasion reject any formal analytical apparatus that invokes a notion of positive and negative sum games. They think that any effort to introduce consequentialism into the analysis of social problems detracts from the strong, indeed bedrock, moral sense of right and wrong, which alone can guide these inquiries.

The second, softer version of this position is that, whatever the theoretical virtues of that expanded inquiry, any effort to enter some version of a cost/benefit universe is so fraught with error and confusion that the game is not worth the candle. The supposed social improvements will turn out to be illusory, and the inevitable valuation difficulties and administrative tangles will make a bad situation worse. Therefore, even *if* the theoretical case can be made out, it is best to avoid the siren call of marching down that road.

This debate ranges over all areas of law. A strong libertarian, for example, is deeply suspicious of using the constitutional takings power to condemn real property for government use. "Purchase what you want in the voluntary market!" is his response. Similarly, the stout libertarian is more suspicious of a wide range of regulations, e.g., zoning, that transfer wealth from A to B.[16] As a basic theoretical matter, this position is untenable because it does not attach any systematic weight to powerful holdout positions that have routinely led to forced exchanges in such key areas as private necessity (e.g., I may dock my boat at your pier without your consent in times of necessity) and the standard common law doctrine that denies to any common carrier the right to refuse to deal with ordinary customers without cause—a doctrine that has immense application to government control over a wide variety of legal commons. That disregard of the holdout issue is, moreover, not tenable as a constitutional position, given that the Takings Clause authorizes takings, at least for public use, upon payment of just compensation. In my view, however, that constitutional position can be made to work in practice precisely because it is possible to develop rules of valuation for all sorts of settings that undermine the indeterminacy argument raised against a wide array of taxes and regulations.

Indeed, just that view carries over to the Religion Clauses, but with limited focus. The current two-tier system of American constitutional law has essentially given up the ghost of trying to fight any generalized redistribution from any well-defined person of group A to any well-defined person of group B through state coercion. Doctrinally, that conclusion is buttressed by a minimum rational basis standard that permits any weak justification to carry the day. To the extent that decisions over the Religion Clauses retreat to "rational basis" analysis, there are, in effect, no functional restraints on what a legislature or administrative agency can do to transfer income or wealth to and from religious groups as a class. But note that there is no explicit just compensation component in either of the Religion Clauses; nonetheless, their explicit, deeper, and narrower commitment to free exercise and against establishment is not so easily bypassed or whittled away. It becomes critical to look at these matters more closely.

Within this context, the current appeal of the strong autonomy position under the Establishment Clause finds voice in the separationist tradition. In particular, there is Jefferson's "wall of separation" between church and state, which he put thusly:

> Believing with you that religion is a matter which lies solely between Man & his God, that he owes account to none other for his faith or his worship, that the legitimate powers of government reach actions only, & not opinions, I contemplate with sovereign reverence that act of the whole American people which declared that *their* legislature should "make no law respecting an establishment of religion, or prohibiting the free exercise thereof," thus building a wall of separation between Church & State.[17]

It should quickly be apparent that even if the powers of government reach "actions only, not opinions," religious behavior necessarily covers both actions and opinions, so that the boundary line between the two spheres of authority is a good deal more difficult to draw than Jefferson's cryptic account suggests. It is instructive to take the "wall" analogy seriously. The success of the operation lies in the sphere of autonomous control that church and state alike exert over their jurisdictions. At this point, the analysis is surely more complex because even if state is accurately in the singular (i.e., without considering federalism), church must be plural in an age that accepts established churches that are, of course, never exclusive. But, oddly enough, the strict rule of separation generalizes to multiple churches, none of which, alone or in combination, can turn to the state for some special advantage, either unique or collective. Likewise, on the other side, those who are hostile to religion cannot turn to the state in order to impose special limitations on religion. This strong view helps to illuminate both the free exercise and the establishment pieces of the puzzle. The first keeps the state at bay. The second keeps churches at bay. The simplicity of the rule becomes a cardinal virtue of the system: the lower the levels of discretion, the more likely it is that the ideal division will be achieved.

However attractive this vision is as a first step to the overall analysis, it does not tell the whole story. It is easy to point to cases where the rules on individual autonomy work, as well as to cases where the rules break down. Take the "wall" analogy, for example, in the context of real property from which it derives. An owner's development of his real estate and his enforcement of contracts for the sale of property and services are applications of the autonomy principle without which the entire economy grinds to a halt. Yet at the same time, these rigid boundaries create in every known society a regime of live-and-let-live, such that reciprocal, low-level interferences are tolerated precisely because these accommodations work, in the long term, to the mutual advantage of both sides.[18] This is a case where the measurement and valuation issues seem trivial relative to the observed gains. The rule works for two parties, and it works well for n parties in complex real estate configurations where the transaction costs of a sensible renegotiation become ever greater.

Under the Religion Clauses, this generalized analysis of property rights applies only to transfers across religious lines, either between churches or between all churches and all nonchurch institutions in whatever form or configuration appears to make sense. Once implicit wealth transfers across religious lines become the proper target of the Establishment Clause, all the elements of the puzzle fit into place without giving undue weight to any one particular element. In some instances, the case law takes the view that no public institution should coerce individuals to engage in religious activities; in the eyes of others, coercion is not sufficient to capture the entire field. The question of allocating government subsidies from tax dollars to religious or nonreligious activities is also in the mix. But government involvement need not be limited to coercion and subsidy: a third strand stresses that the endorsement or discouragement of religious activities in a wide number of places could affect the ultimate distribution of benefits and burdens. This should alert us to the opposite risk of complex legislative schemes that require religious individuals to subsidize their nonreligious brethren. In principle, the correct result is that *none* of these elements alone is the trigger to the analysis. What matters is how these operate in particular contexts, either alone or in tandem, to work the transfer of wealth or personal opportunities along the forbidden axes within or across religions.

The Lemon *Test*

Some effort to grasp the nettle is found in the highly criticized but oft-quoted test that the United States Supreme Court announced in *Lemon v. Kurtzman*,[19] which invalidated both a Rhode Island and a Pennsylvania statute that purported to give block grants equal to a fixed percentage of salary to reimburse nonpublic elementary and secondary schools for the cost of "teachers' salaries, textbooks, and instructional materials in specified secular subjects."[20] At this point, the Court announced a three-part test that has been honored as much in the breach as in the observance:

> First, the statute must have a secular legislative purpose; second, its principal or primary effect must be one that neither advances nor inhibits religion; finally, the statute must not foster an "excessive government entanglement with religion."[21]

For the moment, put aside the soundness of the particular decision to see how the test might fit into the debate between separationists and accommodationists. The words "redistribution of wealth or opportunity across religious lines" do not appear in this text, but the test nonetheless contains some hints of the many relevant factors. The need for a secular purpose is deficient insofar as it remains unclear whether that purpose must be exclusive, dominant, primary, or just one of multiple purposes. Yet for all that ambiguity, it remains likely that any legislation lacking any secular legislative purpose is likely to skew matters heavily toward religious groups in ways that are inconsistent with the anti-redistributive purpose of the Establishment Clause. Treat it, therefore, as a piece of evidence rather than some invariable truth. Any examination of its "principal" or "primary" effect looks less at intention and more at the skew. The reference here to "neither advances nor inhibits religion" is once again suggestive of a concern to prevent redistributions of wealth or opportunities in either direction, so that there is an establishment of sorts whenever nonreligious institutions are required, expressly or implicitly, to subsidize religious ones, or the reverse. And the last requirement about excessive entanglement is best understood as an effort to keep some degree of separation of church from state in order to reduce the odds of any unintended redistribution. If, however, the ultimate test that remains is redistribution, then this formula surely fails to capture all the elements, even if it is suggestive of some. In addition, it tends to lead to highly particularized inquiries that make the law unworkable in practice, thereby encouraging an artificial segregation of parochial school activities into permitted and prohibited categories. It is no wonder that the *Lemon* test is extolled in one case and ignored in the next.[22]

To get this analysis correct, however, no shortcuts will do. It is necessary to do what in management circles is called an (intellectual) 360-degree review, which is intended to evaluate the program as a whole to see its overall effects. When the dust settles, relatively simple rules calling for block grants, tax deductions, or vouchers dominate the vagaries of the *Lemon* test. In order to handle the matter, the next chapter looks at two sides of the establishment problem: direct regulation of religion and government subsidies. Chapter 32 then looks at the application of the Establishment Clause in connection with the commons.

31

Regulation and Subsidy under the Establishment Clause

I N VIRTUALLY ALL AREAS of law, the Constitution has to deal with the twin questions of takings and givings. The first of these topics includes direct government regulation of private activities, and the second covers the use of government grants, subsidies, or licenses that either allow or promote those activities on which the government chooses to shower its largess. The direct regulation of religious activities covers a wide range of possible situations, of which perhaps the most instructive are the Sunday Closing or Sunday Blue Laws.

Direct Regulation

The initial foray in the regulatory arena was the 1961 decision of the Supreme Court in *McGowan v. Maryland*,[1] which upheld a criminal conviction of a department store for sales of various articles in violation of the Maryland Sunday Closing Laws. Those laws forbade the sale of many (but not all) articles of commerce on Sunday, or the Sabbath Day. On the same day, in *Braunfield v. Brown*,[2] the Court also rejected a free exercise challenge to Pennsylvania's Sunday Closing Law in a case brought by Orthodox Jewish merchants. In principle, either plaintiff could have brought the other case, but, without question, the claim made by the Jewish merchants had more potency than that made by the all-purpose department store. The Jewish merchants claimed their religious beliefs required they close on Saturday, to keep the Jewish Sabbath, while rival merchants prepared to stay open on Saturday had to close only one day, and not two. The mainline merchants in *McGowan* wished to stay open on all seven days, but suffered from no added burden from the law because of any religious beliefs.

As a matter of general theory, a free exercise claim raises the question of whether a special exemption should be given to a law of general applicability. In *McGowan*, with a Christian twist, the law in question forbade persons to "profane the Lord's day" by engaging in "Sabbath Breaking"[3] and scheduled its exemptions in the statute in the afternoon and late evening when Christian services were not in session. The hodgepodge provisions of the Maryland law thus sought to create a universal day of rest for all persons, including those who had already rested on a Sabbath day of their own choosing. As a commercial actor, McGowan was in no position to raise the free exercise claim, but could raise the Establishment Clause claim. Yet even the latter was more forcefully presented by the Jewish merchants who suffered a distinctive harm by having to remain closed for two days instead of one. Indeed, in principle, it is possible to craft a ruling that restores the interreligious balance by allowing any religious individuals to close on either Saturday or Sunday as they see fit, thereby losing some perceived benefit of social solidarity by having all businesses closed on the same day. Taken as a whole, the Sunday Closing Laws indisputably manifest an effort by believers to impose their views on members of other faiths as well as nonbelievers. To be sure, nothing in either statute requires Jews or nonbelievers to practice the Christian faith. Much in the statutes, however, prevents them from exercising their own personal beliefs without imposing like burdens on statutory beneficiaries. The statutes, therefore, operate differently from a scheme that requires all businesses to close every Tuesday for a day of rest, or even one that prohibits all persons from working more than six days per week. In both those cases the generalized prohibition, much like maximum hour laws, might well be attacked under a more robust doctrine of freedom of contract. But neither proposed statute would generate the differential impact along religious lines in ways that trigger both free exercise and establishment challenges. In *McGowan* and *Braunfield*, the identification of the Sabbath as an essential portion of the program brings the cases within the ambit of both the Free Exercise Clause and the Establishment Clause.

At this point, the analysis turns to the state justification for the Sunday Closing Laws, recognizing that no proposal could come close to the kinds properly regarded as acceptable under a classical liberal theory. The Court in both *McGowan* and *Braunfield* identified the appropriate state interest as the need to have a

> uniform day of rest for all citizens; the fact that this day is Sunday, a day of particular significance for the dominant Christian sects, does not bar the State from achieving its secular goals. To say that the States cannot prescribe Sunday as a day of rest for these purposes solely because centuries ago such laws had their genesis in religion would give a constitutional interpretation of hostility to the public welfare rather than one of mere separation of church and State.[4]

But why give this collectivist justification the slightest weight at all? Clearly these statutes are not designed to control force or fraud. The cases involve a hopelessly wide definition of a negative externality. The statutes here have nothing to do with the law of nuisance. Instead, they presuppose that, in Maryland or Pennsylvania, people on one side of town are unable to rest when they choose because people on the other side of town have chosen to shop. The statutes, of course, do not prevent people from doing heavy work around the house, even if they cannot engage in commercial activity. In essence, the Court conjures up an indefensibly broad definition of a negative externality that levers an enormous wealth transfer to Christians who keep the Sunday Sabbath from everyone else. The obvious and intended disparate impact of the legislation needs no comment. It was well known and understood by all parties in question. Because the legislation does not force individuals to pray on a day that is set aside for rest, one element of indefensible coercion is removed from the equation, but nothing eliminates the implicit cross-subsidy from Orthodox Jewish merchants to their competitive rivals. The Free Exercise and Establishment Clauses should work in tandem to invalidate the statute.

Ironically, the repeal of the Sunday Closing Laws has given rise to a strict reading of the Establishment Clause. The *Estate of Thornton* arose under a Connecticut provision, which, after the liberalization of that state's Sunday Closing Law, provided that no employer could dismiss a worker who refused to work on his or her Sabbath Day.[5] The law functioned alongside the Civil Rights Act of 1964, which forbids employment discrimination on grounds of religion (including dismissal over religious beliefs for which reasonable accommodations may be made). The problem arose because the repeal of the Sunday Closing Law now exposed Sabbatarians to the risk of being forced to choose between their jobs and their religious beliefs. At this point, the balance of interests is much closer than it was in *McGowan*, which resulted in huge system-wide wealth transfers among groups. Nonetheless, in an opinion mentioning neither *McGowan* nor *Braunfeld*, the Court held, probably correctly, that the statute offended the Establishment Clause. Chief Justice Warren Burger observed that the law "arms Sabbath observers with an absolute and unqualified right not to work on whatever day they designate as their Sabbath" and "thus commands that Sabbath religious concerns automatically control over all secular interests at the workplace," including those of the employer and co-employees.[6] In a classical liberal regime of freedom of contract, that result is surely correct. It is for the parties to decide on a decentralized basis how to trade off religious beliefs with economic success, so long as the state has nothing to do with it. But the case is at least a bit closer than Chief Justice Burger suggests given that the Civil Rights Act has truncated the freedom of contract by making religion a forbidden ground of dismissal, at least in those cases where reasonable accommodations are possible. At this point, the Civil Rights Law has compromised the employer interest that Connecticut invoked in *Estate of Thornton*. Once that interest has been limited, it is at most only a second-best judgment as to whether Connecticut's putting its statutory thumb on the employee's scale should be regarded as an unacceptable preference. Second-best choices are always difficult, but it is doubtful that this type of statute would ever be passed in a state that did not have a Sunday Closing Law to begin with; thus, the decision in *Estate of Thornton* is barely correct. The larger lesson, of course, is that the application of the Establishment Clause is always more tricky in a highly regulated environment than it is in a market-driven one.

Subsidies

Theoretical Complications

The operation of subsidies is always more difficult to deal with than direct regulation. Subsidies can come in all sizes and forms, making it difficult to figure out their incidence and effect. Imagine that a town decides to repair a public road on which a church is located along with other business establishments. If the church is the largest landowner along that stretch of road, does this count as a subsidy? What result if the road is paid for out of general revenues charged to all residents in the city? And what if church lobbying efforts were instrumental in securing the repairs? Questions like these arise in a wide range of trade contexts, dealing with such matters as whether the United States, in violation of its international trade agreements, had provided a subsidy to Boeing Aircraft by footing the cost of infrastructure, reimbursing research costs, or providing research grants.[7]

Rather than start in a netherworld from which there is no escape, it is easiest to begin with those cases that involve direct benefits to religious organizations. Such direct benefits could be either in the form of direct payments or tax benefits, such as exemptions from real estate taxation. As ever, the key element in this normative analysis is to determine from all available evidence whether there is an implicit transfer of wealth, either between religious and nonreligious persons, or between members of different religious groups. There is no shortcut to this analysis, for the existence of an implicit transfer depends both on the source of the funds and on the identification of the transferees. In dealing with taxes outside the area of religion, the correct rule with special assessments is to use a matching system of benefits to costs in the absence of a precise dollar measurement of various in-kind benefits. By giving each person the same fraction of the total benefits as cost, everyone, even if acting solely out of self-interest, will vote only for those programs that provide net social benefits.

In the context of religion, transfers across individuals on grounds of wealth no longer matter, but this same matching principle applies with transfers across religious and nonreligious groups alike. Thus, the danger of an imbalance can result from an overtaxation, on the one side, or a reduction of benefits on the other. The words "coercion" and "endorsement" do not quite capture the full range of the inquiry. What is needed is a serious effort at exposing the hidden transfers.

Public Aid to Religious Education

The first modern case that raised the matter of government benefits was *Everson*, which asked whether New Jersey could pay for the transportation of all schoolchildren to public and private schools alike, by reimbursing parents for their transportation expenses.[8] In examining this provision, Justice Hugo Black stressed that these children were entitled to ordinary police and fire protection, as well as the usual set of sewer connections for their schools.[9] In one sense, these services illustrate the reason why an ardent separationist position cannot prevail. There is no possible separability for the state provision of public goods, which under the standard economic definition must be supplied to all people whenever they are supplied to some. The state, which exercises a monopoly of force within the jurisdiction, cannot create a protective void by refusing to extend those needed public services to religious persons and institutions.

Oddly enough, however, the provision of these services is more difficult to grasp than the reimbursement of transportation expenses. As to the latter, we can make the safe assumption that the parents of both religious and nonreligious schoolchildren contributed to the public treasuries in rough proportion to the money that they receive back from the state for their transportation expenditures. The constant pressure for public aid to parochial schools stems from the irrefutable fact that tax dollars from parochial school parents support public school students. Without the state's aid, there is a heavy tax on the one side and the receipt of a subsidy on the other. The parochial school supports should be viewed with presumptive validity to the extent that they seek to redress, but not to reverse, this initial financial imbalance. Allowing the state to pay for these transportation expenses for both classes of students has that restorative feature. In dissenting from this arrangement, Justice Jackson insisted that "[t]he prohibition against establishment of religion cannot be circumvented by a subsidy, bonus or reimbursement of expense to individuals for receiving religious instruction and indoctrination."[10] He was right in his concern with circumvention, but wrong on the particulars, given that without the reimbursement, the only wealth transfer is a subsidy that moves from parochial school families to public school ones, not the other way.

To turn to the other side of the equation, classic public goods like police and fire protection or sewer hookups are more difficult to analyze, because the extensive joint and common costs of providing classic economic public goods are not uniquely allocable to any one person. Nonetheless, that complication does not need to derail the *Everson* result. At this point, the proper procedure is to ask whether the same group of persons who pay the taxes are recipients of the nonexclusive state benefits. This question can be answered in the affirmative, because these public services are routinely applied to churches and other religious institutions. It is just too expensive and impractical to ask churches and other charities to set up parallel networks when they have neither the power of taxation nor eminent domain. So including the costs of parochial school transportation is permitted, as long as the parents of religious school students are also taxpayers.

Not surprisingly, in the years since *Everson*, the Supreme Court has vacillated in the types of benefits that the state can provide to students in parochial schools. *Lemon* itself illustrates the problem.[11] Recall that in *Lemon* the Court invalidated Rhode Island and Pennsylvania statutes that paid grants equal to a fixed percentage of salary to reimburse nonpublic elementary and secondary schools for "the cost of teachers' salaries, textbooks, and instructional materials in specified secular subjects."[12] The obvious concern was with entanglement. But the solution, which was to invalidate what are in essence block grants, gets the institutional analysis exactly backwards. If it is well understood that some equalization is needed, the simplest way to provide it is on a matching fund basis, without any attempt to tie any given expenditure to any given outcome. That approach reduces the level of state administrative oversight and increases local flexibility in using the funds received. The huge battle could then be over the size of the transfer payment, not the terms and conditions that create such high levels of state intrusion and lead to such odd decisions.

Once this simple principle is abandoned, the cases are sure to turn out discordant. Thus, it has been held that states can lend books to parochial students,[13] but not maps, magazines, or tape recorders.[14] Similarly, notwithstanding *Everson*, the Supreme Court has held that the state cannot reimburse parochial schools for the transportation expenses incurred on field trips, given that these are administered by the school district.[15] The key element of distinction derives from the third, or entanglement, factor of the *Lemon* test, which starts from the premise that excessive parochial teacher involvement opens up the possibility of hijacking public funds for religious purposes.

Block grants do much to remove government entanglement in the operation of all schools, both secular and parochial. They also avoid all the endless borderline cases that arise when public moneys allow, in line with *Everson*'s parity principle, both public school and parochial school teachers to offer additional instruction on such matters as remedial reading in parochial school classrooms, including those shorn of all religious symbols.[16] In *School District of Grand Rapids* and *Aguilar*, Justice William Brennan thought that the school environment itself created powerful, if subtle cues to students that could impermissibly promote religion in a way inconsistent with the entanglement prong of the *Lemon* test. These decisions represent a low point in general Establishment Clause jurisprudence. The evidence of subtle coercion was based exclusively on *a priori* grounds, without any documented instances of overt abuse over the many years that both programs had been in effect. Yet many non–Roman Catholic parents send their children to parochial schools, and they do not show lasting scars from standing in silence while other students recite their prayers. No one assumes that incurable student fragility in examining students' First Amendment rights of speech and the press. Why, then, assume their vulnerability and naiveté in dealing with the analogous First Amendment issue?

At a more general level, the *Lemon* test, with its preoccupation on motive and entanglement, forces courts to micromanage too many relationships between church and state. With such a heavy level of scrutiny, it becomes difficult to equalize the imbalance except at prohibitive cost, loss of time, and social disruption—i.e., removing the students from their religious classroom environment into alien and confusing settings to avoid an Establishment Clause violation. In similar fashion, any supposed constitutional insistence that cash go directly to students, and not to schools, again forces the inefficient distribution of funds, without addressing the fundamental cash transfers from religious students who do not use the public school system to nonreligious students who do. Direct payment to schools results in a vast administrative simplification, so long as the size of the check depends on the ability of the parochial school to attract enrollees. The great vice comes from paying money directly to schools independent of their performance.

In this environment, the real source of anxiety is not in the name of the payee on the check, but in the risk of the cross-subsidy of religious education by nonreligious parents, which could happen when parochial schools attempt to do two tasks instead of just one. But it is both futile and foolish to impose a constitutional safeguard that looks at each itemized expenditure separately to decide whether it meets constitutional standards. If states do not use block grants, they alternatively could preserve the requisite level of flexibility by allowing parents a tax deduction for certain expenses arising from sending students to parochial schools. In *Mueller v. Allen*,[17] the four liberal dissenters (Marshall, Brennan, Blackmun, and Stevens) rejected this approach by denouncing these tax deductions as an illicit subsidy to religious institutions, without taking into account the equalization issue. Justice Rehnquist had the better argument in treating these payments (95 percent of which went to parochial school students) as corrective measures against a preexisting cross-subsidy in favor of public school parents. The large number of parochial school children also leads to a large reduction in requisite public school expenditures, further exacerbating the overtax on parents who send their children to parochial schools while supporting, through direct taxes, parents of public school children.

This same set of issues arose a generation later in *Zelman v. Simmons-Harris*[18] where, unlike in *Mueller*, vouchers (not tax deductions) were provided for students to attend any private school of their own choice. As with *Mueller*, 96 percent of the students (and 82 percent of the schools) were parochial. The direct nature of the grant to the student (which is then paid to the school) neutralizes the entanglement issue and corrects the cross-subsidy that would otherwise exist in favor of public school students. Programs of this sort are, of course, vastly superior to any system whereby the state pays parochial (or indeed any charter) schools some lump sum regardless of their ability to attract students, for any program that gives payments without regard to performance is subject to all sorts of potential abuse. The combination of public funding—which removes expenditures from the public school system—and private choice has benefits far beyond the elimination of cross-subsidies. It also introduces a measure of competition into education, which is otherwise dominated by a public school monopoly, run all too often for the benefit of unionized teachers rather than students. Indeed, the difficult theoretical question with *Zelman* is not whether vouchers should be *allowed*, but whether they should be *required* in order to offset the powerful redistributive tendencies in favor of public school students under the current regime. In principle, the answer is yes, and for good reason: the introduction of competitive forces at an earlier date would have helped stem the decline of public education, which exhibits all the sluggish features of any state monopoly.

Overall, the bottom line seems clear, and it calls for an extensive revision of the *Lemon* rule. The sound prescription covers block grants, tax deductions, or vouchers to all private schools, parochial schools included. These techniques share the simplicity of a charitable deduction and do a far better job of righting the balance between church and state than any futile attempt to trace individual expenditures to some proper source under the complex *Lemon* formula.

Tax Exemptions for Religious Institutions

The difficulties with lump sum grants to private schools have their analogue with tax exemptions that the federal and state governments confer on religious institutions. In *Walz v. Tax Commission of New York*,[19] the issue came to a head when a local real estate owner challenged a New York City practice of granting property tax exemptions to properties solely used for religious purposes. The obvious criticism of this position is that so long as these institutions receive public services, the fatal mismatch between the properties taxed and the properties benefited creates the illicit wealth transfer that runs afoul of the cross-subsidy test under the Establishment Clause. The actual impact of the exemption is, however, impossible to determine without some knowledge of the religious composition of the city's taxpayers. If all city residents, without exception, belong to one church, the issue would be wholly academic. These residents could pay for their church services either by direct taxes on their own property or by increasing their dues to cover the direct levies imposed on the church. The same dollars from the same people apply to all expenses. That result holds with multiple churches, so long as the proportion of city residents in each church tracks their proportion in the general population. The pro rata distribution precludes wealth transfers across groups.

Unfortunately, these restrictive assumptions hold in only a few cases. Commonly, different ethnic and social groups have different attachments to religious and nonreligious institutions, giving rise to massive cross-subsidies. The situation becomes still more muddied, because the New York City code provision afforded the same exemption to all sorts of other groups, including hospitals, playgrounds, libraries, and medical associations—all of which had secular purposes. But drowning religious subsidies in a sea of other transfer payments is a diversion from the central question, for the creation of other legitimate cross-subsidies does not negate the explicit subsidy that religious groups receive from nonbelievers. In *Walz*, Chief Justice Burger ignored the entire literature on the "tax expenditure" budget, the central thesis of which is that a specialized form of tax relief is on par with a direct transfer payment in its economic effect.[20] Denying that proposition ignores the major risk of the circumvention of basic constitutional protections. The distinction between "mere passive state involvement" and "the affirmative involvement characteristic of outright governmental subsidy" is at best arid.[21] The government that collects the taxes is the one that "actively" grants the tax subsidy.

Yet beneath all the linguistic fog lie real concerns, including a reversal of the subsidy's direction. The usual real estate bill itemizes the purposes for which the taxes are to be used, of which educational expenditures are by far the largest. Why should churches be forced to support their competitors by making expenditures from which they receive no return benefits? A sounder approach, therefore, might be prepared to split the difference: churches continue to pay for those services, such as trash removal and police protection, that they receive on the same basis as everyone else, but they are exempt from taxes that support their rivals, and perhaps for those services from which they gain no benefit at all. The blithe attitude taken toward this topic in *Walz* prevents consideration of these intermediate solutions, which could reduce the massive dislocations that would surely arise by eliminating the exemption without inserting any substitution. Right now, many other institutions with charitable exemptions—such as large universities in small towns—often pay voluntary fees in lieu of taxes to ease the municipal burden for their direct services on such mundane matters as fixing potholes and removing trash.[22] Religious organizations could be asked to do the same. Much of the reluctance to overturn the exemption rests on the reliance interest that these institutions place on the old order insulating them from any and all burdens. Taking a middle position that seeks to match the benefits and burdens of any tax regime is consistent with classical liberal theory. It should also make for a smoother transition towards a more equitable division of the burdens of public services. An explicit analysis trumps a set of verbal generalizations.

32

The Commons

THE ESTABLISHMENT CLAUSE also presents major issues in connection with the proper utilization of the commons, that is, those places to which all have access but are allowed only limited use. Here, again, the ultimate objective is to prevent skewed uses of these public spaces that do not reflect a user's contribution to the creation and maintenance of these spaces. The commons, of course, did not start with religious activities, but in connection with the manifold activities of everyday life. The widespread presence of public beaches, buildings, squares, parks, and athletic fields shows the futility of a hard-line separationist position that seeks to exclude all religious persons from using these places. It is not feasible (or correct) to prevent a church outing, including one sponsored by the Boy Scouts, from having a picnic in Central Park. The simple solution for the common facility is to allow religious persons access on the same terms and conditions as everyone else. Accommodation is not an option—it is an inevitability.

Theoretical Framework

Management becomes far more difficult with demands for disproportionate use of the commons of the sort that necessarily displace everyone else; parades, as opposed to beach outings, are one such example. Similar issues come with special demands to structures or exhibits that hog more than their fair share of public lands. Should these public spaces be available for religious displays, including everything from the Ten

Commandments, to a crèche, to a picture of the Reverend Martin Luther King? Do these rules for open fields then apply to a public building with a particular use, such as a courthouse or military base? The diversity of common property, along with the inherent difficulty in managing it, counsels a level of caution before making constitutional judgments. As anyone who lives as a joint-tenant or tenant-in-common with family, friends, and roommates knows, these collective operations rarely admit unique solutions, even if no issue of religious preference raises its head. The lack of unique solutions should not force the law to adopt the per se rule of the separationist model. But neither should it lead to a rule of total judicial deference to whatever decisions a government body chooses to make. The search for the middle ground is tenable, again by seeking to prevent the redistribution of common resources between groups. The key principle is to prevent mismatches between the resources that one group commits to the common venture and the benefits (tangible and symbolic) that the group derives from that venture.

To see how the inquiry can be narrowed, consider what should be done when two religious groups seek to make use of the same public square for a religious display, either temporary or permanent. Immediately, we can eliminate two of the four possibilities. Neither religious group may use the commons for its displays or activities to the exclusion of the other; to allow such would be an unacceptable implicit wealth transfer from religious group A to religious group B, or vice versa. Accordingly, there are only two permissible permutations: one that allows both groups to use the facility in some equal, shared way, while the other is one that keeps both parties from using the public space— leading to what Richard John Neuhaus condemned as the "naked public square."[1] The question is how to choose between them. The same principles can then apply on a pro rata basis when multiple groups seek access to common resources.

In dealing with all these variations, two methods present themselves. The first method relies on naked intuition to decide which of these two choices seems preferable. Invoking *Lemon v. Kurtzman*,[2] a separationist could easily desire a rule that keeps all explicit religious activities off the public square in order to prevent any unwanted entanglement or excessive administrative burden. Let private parties provide the space for various services or displays as the owners of these various resources choose. The alternative—the accommodationist position—claims that the joint gains from higher utilization of public spaces, which are, of course, supported in large measure by taxes paid by religious individuals, generates sufficient gains across the board to justify incurring these greater administrative costs.

Choosing between these two alternatives is not easy, if only because many public sites—e.g., highway medians—should be kept off-limits to religious activities for all sorts of logistical reasons. Other locations might be suitable only for a narrow class of uses. But rather than generalize from these cases, it is useful to address this problem by asking first how private institutions manage their private commons. A private commons issue arises whenever the owner of private property creates a common space for use by its customers or tenants. Stores, schools, and apartment houses all create lobbies, hallways, and recreational areas, indoors and outside, which are open equally to all persons invited to use the premises. These organizations face the question of what religious and secular symbols to place in the building and around the grounds on a permanent basis and, during the holiday season, what displays to erect and which activities to permit. If two rival religious groups make requests in this private setting, what rule is the conscientious proprietor likely to follow in response to their expressed wishes?

There is no uniform answer to this wide set of interrelated questions. But there are pronounced tendencies. In most settings and most of the time, the presumption is that the facility will be offered up to both groups on something that approaches even terms. Whether that elusive evenness is measured by the number of groups that use the facility, the size of their respective memberships, or the nature of their proposed activities or displays varies across cases, and is usually a subject of intense, often heated, negotiations. However, for the most desirable locations, high utilization by all groups, with a healthy dose of compromise, is generally the equilibrium position. Private schools have lobby sings in which representatives from all religious groups participate. Religious themes are part of the overall system. For balance, they sing holiday songs without any religious significance at all. There is a full understanding that this decision does not rest on unanimous consent, for some minority groups oppose all special uses. But in private settings, rarely will minority groups hold a veto position, though they will almost always be granted an exit position if they choose not to participate in all or part of the activities. In some instances, the opposition becomes so fierce that some people would rather leave the organization than abide by its decisions. But the same is true with respect to collective decisions to stop the celebrations. Collective decisions in private settings always produce losers. The same must be expected, only more so, in public spaces, where the numbers of persons are greater and their tastes more heterogeneous than the self-selected members of a school or a club. With these preliminaries in mind, it is possible now to analyze cases in order to determine whether, and if so when, the established decisions go wrong.

Parks and Streets

The leading case on the use of parks and roads is *Lynch v. Donnelly*,[3] which presents the simple question of whether the city of Pawtucket, Rhode Island, in conjunction with the local merchants, could erect a Christmas display in a park owned by a nonprofit organization in the middle of the downtown area. The display contained a wide range of seasonal objects, including Santa Claus, reindeer, candy-striped poles, a Christmas tree, and a crèche portraying the birth of Christ.[4] The modest cost of putting up the display was borne by the city.[5] A highly fractured Court allowed the display of the crèche.[6]

Each of the opinions issued in *Lynch* is unsatisfactory in some way. Writing for the Court, Chief Justice Burger mounted a two-pronged attack. He first insisted that it would be "ironic" to place undue weight on the crèche "at the very time people are taking note of the season with Christmas hymns and carols in public schools and other public places."[7] Thereafter he sought to minimize the problem by noting that the crèche was embedded in a larger display of other seasonal objects so that it need not be regarded as religious, at least in this context.[8] What a peculiar form of social blindness to a depiction of one of the holiest events in the Christian religion! The display may have had a modest secular purpose, but it also had a dominant religious one, which it seemed to advance with explicit cooperation between the government and the local merchants. Under *Lemon*, the crèche seemed to be a sure loser, which explains why Chief Justice Burger downgraded its religious significance. It was no wonder that he also embraced the part of *Lemon* that turned the wall of separation into a "blurred, indistinct, and variable barrier depending on all the circumstances of a particular relationship."[9]

Justice O'Connor, for her part, did no better. In her view, entanglement was not the only way for governments to run afoul of the Establishment Clause; either the endorsement or disparagement of religion could do this as well. At this point, she reversed course by finding that "Pawtucket did not intend to convey any message of endorsement of Christianity or disapproval of non-Christian religions."[10] The last half of the proposition is more likely to be correct than the former, but both were contested by Justice Brennan's dissent, which found that all elements of the *Lemon* test were satisfied.[11] Yet by the same token, he surely exaggerated the negative effect that this display would have on most persons who used the public square. These same displays are common in the lobbies of shopping centers and in store windows. No one makes that big of a deal about these displays until they are litigated. Perhaps, as Justice Brennan suggested, Pawtucket had endorsed the display because it did nothing to "disclaim" it.[12] But if so, this suggestion trivializes the entire operation because next year a boilerplate disclaimer, satisfying no one, could be displayed at the base of the crèche, which would have about the same effect as government warnings about the dangers of smoking that are placed on cigarette packages.

The simplest way to resolve this case is for the nonprofit organization not to use city funds to erect the crèche, at which point the controversy would be resolved, though not necessarily for the thousands of other crèches erected in public spaces. As to them, as usual, the villain of the piece stems from the futile effort to force this case into the unworthy clutches of the *Lemon* test. A better approach is to return to the fundamentals of the commons. The case takes on one posture if the city gives the merchants a lock on the site for its Christmas display, considering that no single group should ever have exclusive of use of the commons. In this case, if some other group wished to come forward, the Christmas display would have to yield ground, and the two groups should work toward a common solution. At this point, the entanglement question could be avoided by asking the city to determine the size of any particular exhibit, after which it could devise some allocation of available space for the various entrants.

That solution is not unlike the decision the Court reached in *City of Cincinnati v. Discovery Network, Inc.*,[13] involving the allocation of newspaper kiosks on public streets. The common thread is that the initial incumbent does not have a perpetual right of renewal. When done correctly, the city can then simply state that it is operating like a common carrier, which no more commits itself to the viewpoints it expresses than it does when it opens up a soapbox for political oratory in the public park. On this view, if one group wants to put up a purely religious display, let it. And then let someone else do the same for their religious or ethical cause. The Court, however, veered away from this solution when it banned a freestanding display of the crèche, but bent back in the proper direction by allowing a Christmas tree to stand next to a menorah,[14] leaving one to wonder what it would do if a nativity scene was paired with a depiction of Moses receiving the Ten Commandments at Mount Sinai. Some discretion has to be given to governments in the management of common spaces. So long as they do not use their power to shift the balance of power between religious groups, they should be insulated from searching judicial review. Hypersensitivity is never allowed to shut down raucous speech in public places. Likewise, it should not be used to remove signs depicting the full richness of our religious and social traditions from the public square.

That same theme surged to the forefront in the subsequent case of *Van Orden v. Perry*,[15] where the question was whether the placement in 1961 of a Ten Commandments monument, six feet high and three and one-half feet wide, on the Texas State Capitol grounds constituted an establishment of religion. In line with the basic theory, the key question should be whether the parties who sponsored that monument had monopoly power with respect to these grounds. With seventeen monuments and twenty-one historical markers,[16] the safe answer to that question is no, but the reasons given by the Court were elusive. A bare and fractured Court was right to give short shrift to the *Lemon* test. The Court was also right, on balance, to let the status quo remain in place on an implicit theory of constitutional prescription. But by the same token, it was wrong to rely on the unsatisfactory ground that this monument was "passive,"[17] as if any of the other seventeen monuments could have been active. At least, however, that was more persuasive than Justice O'Connor's dissent, which found this particular setting to be offensive even though the inclusion of the Ten Commandments on a Supreme Court frieze is not.[18]

The tides of war changed in *McCreary County v. ACLU*,[19] and for good reason. In that instance, the Ten Commandments stood along with several other documents inside two Kentucky courthouses where they were treated as part of the "precedent legal code."[20] Here, the dissenters in *Van Orden* became the majority, rehabilitating the *Lemon* test one more time to find that these displays violated the Establishment Clause. Their decision was correct, but not on those grounds.[21] The key point is that a single state hand placed all the relevant documents, so that the diversity of views that counters state monopoly power was conspicuously absent. Citing the code as legal authority in courthouses across the state gave it an authoritative position with a lot more pop than that for monuments located in various parks. Surely no one could think that the two cases had to come out the opposite way: that Texas should have lost and Kentucky should have won. The area is obscure and its relevant distinctions are not perfect, but the classical liberal concern with state monopoly power shows that, in this instance, the line was drawn in the right place.

The law in this area next took a turn for the worse in *Pleasant Grove City, Utah v. Summum*,[22] in refusing to come to grips with the commons problem at law. Pleasant City maintained a 2.5-acre public park, which was home to about fifteen public displays, eleven of which were donated by private parties. Most of the monuments bore some thematic relationship to city history including the historic granary, a wishing well, and a fire station. Another included the Ten Commandments. Summum, a Utah religious organization, sought to add its own monument, "the Seven Aphorisms of Summan," to the collection, on a scale similar to that of the Ten Commandments. At this point, the correct analysis should ask why the city could exclude this monument so long as there was space on the grounds, when it is difficult to find a reason for exclusion unless some alternative applicant came forward when space was constrained. Thus, the city should be required to accept this monument unless it could show cause as to why it should be excluded as inappropriate for the venue, which it never attempted to do.

Instead, Justice Alito, writing for a unanimous court, took a wrong turn by insisting that the permanent monuments, unlike temporary displays, "represent government speech,"[23] to which the First Amendment rights of freedom of speech do not attach.[24] That position does not seem credible in connection with the Ten Commandments, which the government could not endorse on its own. Nor does it seem to represent some immutable state of affairs, for, although the Washington Monument is "closely identified" with the government,[25] no one would make that mistake with a private monument when its donor's name is permanently affixed to the base of the display. If the government can distance itself from temporary speakers on public property, it can do so with permanent speech by making a single, permanent disclaimer. Treating this as a case of government speech thus short-circuits the question of how

Pleasant Grove can be squared with *Van Orden*, where the decentralized mode of ownership and display helps neutralize the risks of monopoly power. Yet the issue is never faced in Justice Alito's opinion and is mentioned only in passing in Justice Scalia's brief concurring opinion.[26]

The lack of a forthright approach to the commons issue shows how the important distinction between public commons and a government building can matter in understanding the interaction between religious symbols and government actions. What makes those issues so difficult is that this nation has long survived ceremonial invocations such as "In God we Trust" (when many of us do not) or "God Save this Honorable Court" (even by those who think that it is beyond redemption). As Justice Douglas wrote in *Zorach v. Clauson*,[27]

> Prayers in our legislative halls; the appeals to the Almighty in the messages of the Chief Executive; the proclamations making Thanksgiving Day a holiday; "so help me God" in our courtroom oaths—these and all other references to the Almighty that run through our laws, our public rituals, our ceremonies would be flouting the First Amendment. A fastidious atheist or agnostic could even object to the supplication with which the Court opens each session: "God save the United States and this Honorable Court."[28]

Any aggressive application of the endorsement test would render these expressions vulnerable, which is one reason why those like Justice O'Connor, who relied on the test, are determined not to put real teeth in it. These modest statements are such a part of the conventional social background that they fly beneath the constitutional radar. A second argument, and one with greater purchase, is that they have been around so long and have done so little demonstrable harm that it is not worth a major public battle to remove them. Whatever the textual arguments, in these contexts at least, the prescriptive constitution should prevail. The costs of transition back to some unrealized past are simply too high. The status quo is once again king.

Schools and Universities

Limited Public Fora

The discussion of ceremonial functions is just the tip of a larger iceberg, because like all other portions of the First Amendment, the Establishment Clause raises knotty questions in organizing the use of limited public fora—that is, locations that are open to all but over which the state exerts a strong management function. As in speech cases, the operative distinction is this: for those management and instructional activities that are at the core of teaching functions, the doctrine of unconstitutional conditions does not have much traction. The state is given a larger, but by no means absolute level of discretion in these cases. But universities and schools also operate as facilities managers whose role more closely mirrors the control that the state has over public highways. These facilities can be kept off-limits to nonstudents or opened to them as the institution sees fit. They cannot, however, limit the use of these facilities or operations to nonreligious institutions and must, as in speech cases, convert themselves into a common carrier whose duty is to treat all entrants equally. Thus, in *Widmar v. Vincent*,[29] the Court refused to allow the University of Missouri at Kansas City to deny religious groups access to its facilities after hours when these same facilities were open to nonreligious groups. The state could not appeal to its interest in promoting the greater separation of church and state, but had to accommodate both groups equally. Likewise, in *Lamb's Chapel v. Center Moriches Union Free School District*,[30] the Court treated the Central Moriches school district as a limited public forum that, once it opened its door to other groups, could not refuse to let Lamb's Chapel use its facilities after hours to run a religiously oriented film series that stressed the importance of family values. Finally, in *Rosenberger v. Rector and Visitors of the University of Virginia*,[31] a majority of the Court concluded that the university had to defray the printing costs to third-party contractors for a Christian magazine, just as it did for all other campus publications. The issue here was funding, not editorial content, which made the case resemble *Everson v. Board of Education*,[32] albeit at the university level. Once again, fees collected from all students could not be denied to some solely because of the viewpoints expressed.

School Prayer

The role of the Establishment Clause shifts in dealing with universities and schools insofar as they have distinctive management functions that to some extent must reflect the preferences of the communities of which they are a part. That difference becomes most apparent in connection with *Engel v. Vitale*,[33] in which Justice Black (who had written *Everson*) struck down, on Establishment Clause grounds, an official prayer in

New York schools. The prayer read, "Almighty God, we acknowledge our dependence upon Thee, and we beg Thy blessings upon us, our parents, our teachers and our country."[34] Striking the strong separationist theme, he wrote:

> [T]he constitutional prohibition against laws respecting an establishment of religion must at least mean that in this country it is no part of the business of government to compose official prayers for any group of the American people to recite as a part of a religious program carried on by government.[35]

To reinforce that notion, he referred back to the contentious disputes in England over the Book of Common Prayer, which each religious sect in turn sought to turn to its own advantage.[36] But the differences between the two cases are more instructive than the similarities. The English Book of Common Prayer was a centralized command that all had to obey. The bland New York prayer was recommended by the state, but could be rejected or altered by individual districts,[37] which introduced a key element of decentralization into the process. In addition, after *West Virginia State Board of Education v. Barnette*,[38] opt-out rights for individual students were fully respected. Justice Black had many suggestions as to how prayer could be conducted before school hours, or in separate rooms, to avoid constitutional challenges.[39] But in this instance these incomplete logistical proposals seem largely beside the point, for the political checks, both then and now, look to be strong enough to guard against serious abuse. Ironically, working through these management proposals could be counterproductive if they further enmesh the courts in the operation of local schools.

There are always differences between saying prayers in schools and saying them in Congress, but it is never clear which way they cut. Children may benefit more from them, or their parents may be more zealous in guarding them against evil. But whatever the distinctions, it seems that some deference should be owed to the sentiments of the majority on matters like these, for we are dealing not with state regulation of private firms, but state management of public institutions. The lone dissent of Justice Potter Stewart[40] returned to the same set of everyday occurrences that motivated Justice Douglas to strike a more accommodationist note in *Zorach*.[41] In the firestorm of controversy that followed, the School Prayer Amendment was introduced, first in 1962 and then on multiple occasions between 1973 and 1997. Its text reads:

Constitutional Amendment—Declares that: (1) to secure the people's right to acknowledge God according to the dictates of conscience, neither the United States nor any State shall establish any official religion, but the people's right to pray and to recognize their religious beliefs, heritage, or traditions on public property, including schools, shall not be infringed; and (2) neither the United States nor any State shall require any person to join in prayer or other religious activity, prescribe school prayers, discriminate against religion, or deny equal access to a benefit on account of religion.[42]

Whether this effort to balance competing interests would allow teachers to lead students in prayer is ironically not decided by the School Prayer Amendment, which leaves open the critical question of whether the "people's right" to engage in prayer allows the state to orchestrate the service—a most unwise idea if it goes beyond the well-defined institutional arrangements in place in *Engel*.

Whatever the ultimate merits of this untested amendment, the decisions after *Engel* reveal how closely contested these cases are on the merits. Thus, the level of state control was raised a notch in *Abington School District v. Schempp*,[43] where the law required that certain passages from the "Holy Bible" be read aloud each day in school, along with the Lord's Prayer—both without comment.[44] That practice was rightly struck down since it lacks the broad base of support that was present in *Engel*. It is not clear whether it would survive under the now dormant School Prayer Amendment, given that it injects school personnel in the performance of religious tasks. Subsequently, the Supreme Court ventured onto thinner ice in *Wallace v. Jaffree*,[45] when the Court refused to allow schools to set aside one minute at the start of each day for silent reflection and prayer—a practice that has no explicit link to any religion and is congenial with a wide range of ethical beliefs. Christian groups that were still stewing over their defeat in *Engel*[46] supported the moment of silence. The key point in *Jaffree* was that prayer was controlled from below and not above. It seems consistent with the most sensible aspects of the School Prayer Amendment.[47] In striking down this law, Justice Stevens overemphasized the motivation behind the statute, at least in the absence of any evidence that teachers systematically urged students to use this occasion for school prayer.[48] Ordinary instruction in both public and private schools offers so many open avenues for the infusion of religious content that it seems unwise to block this one while permitting others to go unattended.

The real dangers of this aggressive brand of judicial oversight are most manifest in *Lee v. Weisman*,[49] which again shows the authoritarian overlay in an aggressive reading of the Establishment Clause. By long-established and inclusive custom, middle schools in Providence, Rhode Island, asked a rotation of religious leaders of different faiths to give nondenominational prayers at graduation ceremonies, which refer to God as a free spirit but not as the representative of any religion.[50] Rotation in office (not feasible for permanent religious displays) is a sensible way to attack this problem when it is impossible, as with crèche displays, to accommodate all parties in the same space at the same time. When faced with these generalized prayers, not many people choose to leave the premises or sit in silent protest. There seems little doubt that to avoid this litigation, the school board would have been quite happy to let Deborah Weisman refuse to stand during the ceremony or to leave the premises, both of which (as accommodations do) leave her in a less than ideal position.

Any comprehensive analysis, however, has to look at both sides of the coin, including the accumulated preferences of all the other parents and children who were pleased with an arrangement that seems to have worked well for years. In one sense, *Lee* could be viewed as a less dramatic rerun of the flag-salute cases such as *Barnette*,[51] where, of course, the stakes were far higher. But the Establishment Clause claim is both far stronger and far more problematic than the Free Exercise Clause. In *Barnette*, the Court rightly secured the opt-out rights of one person under the banner of free exercise.[52] In *Lee* it unwisely accepted the far stronger establishment claim that once a single person objects, everyone has to follow her command—even on ceremonial occasions that seem clearly distinguishable from the daily prayers at issue in cases like *Engel, Schempp,* and *Wallace.* All the efforts to develop compromises, to create sensible rotations, and to follow speech guidelines count for nothing, even when public schools imitate principles that are commonly and uneventfully applied in private school settings. At this point, the law moves far beyond the limited public forum issues in cases like *Widmar, Lamb's Chapel,* and *Rosenberger.*

It does not do, as Justice Kennedy wrote for the majority in *Lee,* to hold that special protection is needed for individual members of minority groups because attendance at public school is compulsory and attendance at graduation highly desired.[53] That same "psychological" coercion is present for the majority of the school populations whose wishes are systematically ignored so that a single outlier can determine the overall policy. *Lee* is a poignant reminder of the dangers of using a strict separationist policy for public institutions when all private institutions show a greater measure of flexibility.

Another troublesome implication of *Lee* is that it sets up a credible challenge against the use of the words "under God" in the Pledge of Allegiance, at least to the extent they are used in school contexts. The Court averted that challenge in *Elk Grove Unified School District. v. Newdow*,[54] where the Supreme Court, on narrow standing grounds, vacated the decision of the Court of Appeals for the Ninth Circuit, which had held that the inclusion of the words "under God," added to the pledge in 1954, was inconsistent with the Establishment Clause.[55] At the Supreme Court, the case was sidetracked on the correct ground that Mr. Newdow did not have standing to raise this issue since the child's mother had exclusive custodial rights over the daughter via a decree entered in California.[56] As someone who wrote (with Neal Katyal, a former acting solicitor general) a brief urging just that position,[57] I believe that the procedural disposition prevented a major culture war.

Under current law, using the words "under God" in an official pronouncement could well violate the Establishment Clause. If the issue had been raised in 1954, perhaps it would have been worth fighting, for the great danger in this initiative is in turning over the control of national symbols to a small minority of the population. Thus, the Establishment Clause claim differs fundamentally from the free exercise claim that was accepted in *Barnette*, which allowed Jehovah's Witnesses not to recite the Pledge against their conscience. But with the Establishment Clause claim, a single dissident parent, as in *Lee*, shuts down the operation for everyone else, which creates much more serious issues. The state has, after all, essential management functions in the operation of public schools, which should surely be responsive to the collective wishes of the students who attend these schools and the parents who pay for them. Just how far one goes is always an issue. In support of his own case, Newdow went so far as to insist that the words "under God" were little different from the words "under Jesus."[58] His implicit subtext was that if using the word "Jesus" violates the Establishment Clause, then so do the words "under God," with their theistic bent. But small differences again matter, just as they do between *Engel* and

Schempp. The looser term "God" covers a wider social consensus, with a more apparent compromise; conversely, the term "Jesus" indicates the control of a dominant religious faction that belies the claim of an "indivisible" nation.[59] The line is again far from perfect. But whatever doubts may have existed in 1954, too much water has passed over the dam and the words should remain part of the Pledge under our prescriptive constitution. It is preferable that *Newdow* be removed without an opinion that, in upholding the Pledge of Allegiance, could go too far. The issue has remained inert now for nearly ten years. May it continue to rest in obscurity.

Curricular Decisions

The shift from ceremonial to curricular issues raises still more difficult questions. It is at this point that it seems virtually impossible to present a "neutral" educational curriculum in virtually any substantive area that does not divide people along religious lines. The only systematic way to avoid this problem is to get rid of public education in its entirety—noting it was not a common practice at the Founding—so that private organizations (including those funded by vouchers) could decide on the curriculum they choose for the students who attend. The inevitable specter of state coercion is diffused by the decentralization of educational decisions, which is in line with the classical liberal condemnation of government monopoly in the realm of ideas, as well as in the markets for goods and services. With voluntary sorting not being possible, deliberation is the fallback position, where cooler heads will not always prevail.

At this point, it is imperative to ask how to treat government commands to follow certain educational practices. Contrary to the prevailing practices, these are situations in which the decisions of local school boards should receive far greater deference than those of states themselves. The state yields centralized commands. Local governments create diversity and competition, which increase the likelihood that disgruntled parents who dislike some decisions can vote with their feet by moving to some other school district.[60] In the absence of some strong substantive theory of what the right answer is in particular cases, the correct judicial response is, in general, to "defer" to the decisions of political branches on matters of curriculum.

The few cases that deal with this matter usually address the question of evolution, where the oversimplified proposition that man descends from apes is in mortal conflict with biblical views on the creation of the earth and the origin of man. Substantively, the achievements of Darwinian theories of evolution stand as one of the great monuments to human intelligence, to which theories of creationism offer only feeble responses. Therefore, it seems almost too easy to conclude that any state that uses legislation to ban the teaching of evolution for religious reasons no longer deserves the deference accorded to curricula and, accordingly, that the ban should be struck down, as it was in *Epperson v. Arkansas*.[61] The case was only marginally closer when, in *Edwards v. Aguillard*,[62] Louisiana decided that any school teaching evolution had to also teach creationism; it then made its preferences clear by requiring schools to create curriculum guides for creationism, but not evolution.[63] Justice Scalia sought to defend this statute in the name of academic freedom,[64] which is odd because no individual teacher could opt out of the general state command.[65] He also treats the question of the validity of evolutionary theory as more contested than it actually is.[66] The decision to override this legislative preference does not, of course, prevent private schools from teaching creationism and excluding evolution. But market forces operate quietly, but effectively, when these opinions are shown to have no validity or influence in the wider world outside religious circles.

Over a wide range of issues, the Supreme Court has not maintained a consistent path in Establishment Clause cases, chiefly because liberals and conservatives cannot agree on the fundamentals. For the most part, on this question, the conservatives show more classical liberal tendencies than the liberals, and thus have the better of the argument. But the tortuous path of decisions leaves much to be desired. Improvements, moreover, are only likely to come from courts that explicitly embrace classical liberal theory. Amid all the complexity of the constitutional doctrine, a resolution depends on an outlook developed elsewhere in the law. The legal doctrine should encourage those accommodations that work for mutual gain to all parties. By the same token it must be always on the alert for implicit wealth transfers that warring factions generate through either legislative or administrative action. It may seem odd, but should also seem inevitable, that the key to unlocking the law of religious freedom and state establishment ultimately depends on fashioning legal rules to encourage positive sum games and to clamp down on negative sum games. But that in fact is just how it is.

SECTION IV

EQUAL PROTECTION

33

Race and the Fourteenth Amendment

B Y NO STRETCH of the imagination does the Constitution of 1787 represent the last word on race, sex, and citizenship. This chapter traces the law of race through modern times, chiefly through the lens of the multiple layers of interpretation of the Fourteenth Amendment. The law as it relates to both citizenship and sex will be discussed in that order in the following two chapters.

The Early History: Privileges and Immunities

The treatment of race in the 1787 Constitution was, in any point of view, both limited and decidedly negative. The Fugitive Slave Clause did not use the word "slave," but it did require all persons in free states to return to their owners any person "held in Service or Labour" in another state.[1] Next, the elaborate compromise around the Three-Fifths Clause settled key issues of taxation and representation between free and slave states by counting slaves as three-fifths of a person for these purposes.[2] Article I, Section 9 made it impossible for states to stop "[t]he Migration or Importation of such Persons as any of the States now existing shall think proper to admit,"[3] which meant that the international slave trade could operate for twenty years, in a provision that was, for good measure, not subject to amendment under Article V. The conscious limitation of federal power under the Commerce Clause was in part designed to make sure that Congress could not tamper with slavery in those states where it was allowed. And even the Privileges and Immunities Clause of Article IV, Section 2 was intended in part to prevent discrimination against citizens of slave states by free states. The simple explanation is that, at the time, the Constitution could not have secured consent without these short-term compromises.

These provisions did not represent anything close to a moral consensus on the question of slavery. The intellectual attack on slavery dates back to at least Justinian's Institutes, which treated the institution of slavery as one of the regrettable consequences of political power. Thus Justinian wrote these three brief but compelling passages:

> [W]ars arose, and then followed captivity and slavery, which are contrary to the law of nature; for by the law of nature all men from the beginning were born free.[4]

> [S]lavery is an institution of the law of nations, against nature subjecting one man to the dominion of another.[5]

> All this originated in the law of nations; for by natural law all men were born free—slavery, and by consequence manumission, being unknown.[6]

The Romans of course then developed a highly sophisticated law of slavery.[7] Yet by 1772, Lord Mansfield (William Murray) handed down his short decision in *Somersett's Case* deciding that slavery had been abolished in England,[8] even as it survived until 1833 in the rest of the British Empire.[9] It is worth noting that James Madison of Virginia, writing in *The Federalist Papers*, did not have the heart to defend the Three-Fifths Clause, but detached himself from the compromise by the rhetorical device of introducing some fictional "Southern brethren" to provide the required explanation.[10] That transparent rhetorical strategy could not conceal the affront that the Constitution inflicted on the fundamental libertarian premise that all persons have equal and full rights before the law.

The intellectual attacks on slavery took their toll on the institution. But riches and power of this sort are not often voluntarily surrendered. So it took a bloody Civil War to undo the fatal decision to legitimize slavery under the 1787 Constitution. The legal and social course of race relations took many an odd turn in the post–Civil War period. At root, the evolution of the law regarding race represents a hard-fought struggle to reach an ideal state in which all natural persons became legal persons with full and equal rights, such as those that they were said to enjoy in the state of nature. Achieving that objective meant removing the total disabilities on slaves and the partial disabilities on women (respecting their capacity to vote, to hold property, and to enter into contracts) that historically marked every legal system. The highly visible abolitionist movement of the antebellum period was one manifestation of the trend insofar as it demanded what its name suggested—the abolition of slavery. But rhetoric matters. One standard move of the abolitionists was to insist that the end of slavery need *not*, indeed *did not* confer on former slaves the full panoply of political and civil rights held by members of the white race.[11] Those political rights included the right to vote and to hold public office, while civil rights (at least in the original meaning) covered those rights to own and dispose of real and personal property. *Dred Scott v. Sandford* held that freed slaves could never become citizens of the United States within the meaning of the Constitution.[12] That decision was oddly consistent with the stated abolitionist view. It also helped precipitate the Civil War.

During the war, the ambiguous position of former slaves was not resolved in Lincoln's Emancipation Proclamation, which likewise finessed the point of full rights for slaves by announcing without clarification that they should be "forever free."[13] In a controversial use of his power as Commander-in-Chief, Lincoln freed the slaves held in the Confederate States, but only in those which did not rejoin the Union as of January 1, 1863. "Emancipation," which derives from the Latin word *mancipatio*—a formal method to transfer ownership of slaves—literally means a conveyance out of slavery. Because it only eliminated the servile status, emancipation does not (and could not) confer either citizenship or full civil or political rights on ex-slaves.

Emancipation thus left slaves in limbo, but not for long. The political environment in the post–Civil War years bore no relationship to what it was in the antebellum years. In December, 1865, eight months after the South surrendered, the Thirteenth Amendment abolished the status of slavery and involuntary servitude in the United States: "Section 1. Neither slavery nor involuntary servitude, except as a punishment for crime whereof the party shall have been duly convicted, shall exist within the United States, or any place subject to their jurisdiction."[14] But in and of itself, the Thirteenth Amendment did not confer citizenship on freed slaves. That development required the ratification of the Fourteenth Amendment in 1868:

Section 1. All persons born or naturalized in the United States, and subject to the jurisdiction thereof, are citizens of the United States and of the State wherein they reside. No State shall make or enforce any law which

shall abridge the privileges or immunities of citizens of the United States;
nor shall any State deprive any person of life, liberty, or property, without due process of law; nor deny to any person within its jurisdiction the
equal protection of the laws.[15]

It was a constitutional revolution for both individual rights and federal structure. The first sentence overrules *Dred Scott.*[16] It goes beyond
the limited objectives of the pre–Civil War abolitionists. With one bold
stroke, the Fourteenth Amendment makes all individuals who were
born in the United States citizens, notwithstanding their inferior status
at the time of their birth. That one sentence then connects to all the
scattered constitutional provisions that enumerate the advantages and
obligations of citizenship. The Fourteenth Amendment thus renders former slaves eligible to run for public office and, by overruling *Dred Scott,*[17]
establishes that former slaves can sue or be sued in federal court under
Article III, subject to the same jurisdictional limitations applicable to all
other citizens.[18] Former slaves were thus protected under the Privileges
and Immunities Clause of Article IV, which ensures that "[t]he Citizens
of each State shall be entitled to all Privileges and Immunities of Citizens
in the several States,"[19] such that former slave states had to give equal
treatment to former slaves living in other states.

In most contexts, however, the Citizenship Clause is essential for
determining the rights that citizens in good standing have against the
United States and the states. In solving that question, the key interpretive point is that of the three substantive protections that follow the
definition, only the first, the Privileges or Immunities Clause, applies
exclusively to citizens. The Due Process Clause and the Equal Protection Clause both extend to all persons, which includes aliens as well as
citizens. The insistent question, then, is how to account for that difference in language. One possibility is to argue that the choice of language
carries no significance, but only reflects the usual political conflict surrounding the drafting of a constitutional amendment, and the resulting
confusion of language. That argument can never be discounted in its
entirety, but it does not appear to be true to a text that draws the same
distinction elsewhere in the document. It seems odd, therefore, that two
words would be used without importance if either of them would have
sufficed for all three guarantees.

Any effort to understand the progression of the Fourteenth Amendment is fraught with difficulty. Yet on this score the simplest observation

is, in the end, the most compelling. The only sensible reading of the amendment begins with the recognition that the smaller set of citizens receives rights more extensive than those rights accorded to the larger set of aliens. Accordingly, it becomes necessary to develop a two-tier theory of rights that meets this structural imperative. The best explanation for this difference hearkens back to the broad and narrow accounts of liberty in the Due Process Clauses of the Fifth and Fourteenth Amendments, as discussed earlier in Chapter 21. The basic tier given to everyone covers freedom from imprisonment, except when convicted through those processes that were due. That reading puts no strain whatsoever on the Due Process Clause of the Fourteenth Amendment, which, as its natural meaning suggests, deals chiefly with a range of procedural protections against imprisonment, fines, and the death penalty. It does not ask whether certain economic liberties are conferred on all persons. Those liberties are restricted to citizens protected under the Privileges or Immunities Clause. Stated otherwise, this view avoids the difficulty in explicating the arguably oxymoronic phrase "substantive due process."

As a natural law matter, this inelegant solution flies in the face of the universality of natural rights. But within a particular state, the ability of the sovereign to dictate the rules of the game explains the slippage that takes place between a general normative theory and a system of positive rights against a given sovereign. That same troubled relationship between sovereign power (and the widespread application of sovereign immunity) and the defense of natural rights is found everywhere in the law today.

At this point, what reading should be given to the phrase "privileges or immunities," which lacks an obvious analogue in plain English? On this question, the key task is to situate the term historically, largely outside the racial context, by looking at its use in early English charters, the Privileges and Immunities provision in Article IV of the Articles of Confederation, and the Privileges and Immunities Clause of Article IV of the Constitution. Thus, the Virginia Charter of 1606 states that "all . . . Persons being our Subjects, which shall dwell and inhabit within every or any of the said several Colonies and Plantations, . . . shall have and enjoy all Liberties, Franchises, and Immunities . . . as if they had been abiding and born, within this our Realm of England. . . ."[20] The template of the Privileges and Immunities Clause of Article IV of the United States Constitution was Article IV of the Articles of Confederation which states that "the free inhabitants of each of these States, paupers, vagabonds, and fugitives from justice excepted, shall be entitled to all privileges and immunities of free citizens in the several States; . . ."[21]

Yet just what does the phrase comprehend? The most salient previous account was offered in 1823 by Justice Bushrod Washington, riding on circuit in *Corfield v. Coryell*.[22] The precise substantive question in *Corfield* was whether an out-of-state plaintiff could dredge for oysters in the coastal waters of New Jersey. The particular answer to that question was no—the out-of-state person did not share in the common resources of the state. But in rejecting that claim, Washington outlined key "fundamental" rights that the Privileges and Immunities Clause did reach:

> Protection by the government; the enjoyment of life and liberty, with the right to acquire and possess property of every kind, and to pursue and obtain happiness and safety; subject nevertheless to such restraints as the government may justly prescribe for the general good of the whole. The right of a citizen of one state to pass through, or to reside in any other state, for purposes of trade, agriculture, professional pursuits, or otherwise; to claim the benefit of the writ of habeas corpus; to institute and maintain actions of any kind in the courts of the state; to take, hold and dispose of property, either real or personal; and an exemption from higher taxes or impositions than are paid by the other citizens of the state; . . . to which may be added, the elective franchise, as regulated and established by the laws or constitution of the state in which it is to be exercised.[23]

Washington's formulation in effect duplicates the basic constitutional approach—strong rights of property and contract, subject to general police power that allows for the regulation of these activities for the benefit of the population as a whole. Indeed there is also evidence that the scope of the Privileges or Immunities Clause was meant to incorporate all the substantive guarantees contained in the first eight amendments of the Bill of Rights. Thus, during the ratification debates over the Fourteenth Amendment, Senator Jacob Howard first read the quoted passage from *Corfield*, only to say that "to these should be added the personal rights guaranteed and secured by the first eight amendments of the Constitution," which he then enumerated.[24] Read in combination, the broad definitional scope of privileges and immunities necessarily imposes a massive limitation on state powers, because no state may "make or enforce any law" that limits this capacious list. This robust provision thus limits the role of the Due Process and Equal Protection

Clauses, which must not be read to extend to aliens all the enumerated rights that the Privileges or Immunities Clause confers on citizens. The Due Process Clause focuses on key procedural protections. Similarly, the Equal Protection Clause—"nor shall any state . . . deny to any person within its jurisdiction the equal protection of the laws"—normalizes the protection that all persons "within its jurisdiction"—that is, subject to the exercise of its sovereign power—receive in the application of civil and criminal law.[25] The guarantee against favoritism in public administration was an enormous issue in the South during Reconstruction. Rightly understood, it should cover both cases of improper prosecution and failure to prosecute.

Offering any complete capsule account of the permissible grounds of distinction is never easy, for surely nothing in the Equal Protection Clause was meant to upset well-established patterns of substantive criminal law, with its distinction by sex (in case of rape) and by age (in dealing with juvenile offenders). But the first cut ignores the loose ends and gets to the core concerns of the perceived breakdown in the regularity of the criminal process. Differential prosecution based on race, or indeed any other similar characteristic such as religion or origin, or, alternatively, the failure to prosecute crimes similarly based are forbidden under the Equal Protection Clause. Of course the government can limit the prosecution of bank fraud to participants in the banking system. But they cannot make the imposition of liability turn on any personal characteristic unrelated to the substantive offense.

On this account the denial of equal protection does not depend on some expansive modern vision of "state action" or the performance of some particular action. The differential enforcement of the civil and criminal code counts as a denial of rights, then as now, even if such differentiation arises only from some omission. The Equal Protection Clause is not limited to race, for it would not do to subject Protestants, women, or persons with disabilities to double the fines for burglaries given to everyone else.

All generalized protections of property and contract therefore are confined to citizens. But the question then is how should we interpret these protections? The congressional debates over the meaning of the terms "privileges and immunities" did not so much dispute the views of Bushrod Washington. Rather, they focused on whether that provision should be read narrowly as a nondiscrimination clause. On that view, the Privileges or Immunities Clause did not enshrine any explicit substantive rights, but only operated like the Privileges and Immunities Clause of Article IV in preventing any state from discriminating between whites and blacks under its own laws. The difficulty with that reading is that the Privileges or Immunities Clause of the Fourteenth Amendment is not worded as a nondiscrimination provision tied to race or any other classification of persons. Nor, for that matter, are the first eight amendments of the United States. Rather, the text of the Privileges or Immunities Clause reads as a substantive guarantee of the full panoply of rights, including those relating to liberty and property. In particular, the language of the Fourteenth Amendment stands in stark contrast to the Civil Rights Act of 1866[26] which, inter alia, makes just that move when it guarantees to all persons born in the United States the right "to make and enforce contracts, to sue, be parties, and give evidence, to inherit, purchase, lease, sell, hold, and convey real and personal property, and to full and equal benefit of all laws and proceedings for the security of person and property, as is enjoyed by white citizens. . . ." The phrase "as is enjoyed by white citizens" clearly imposes a nondiscrimination constraint that operates for the benefit of nonwhite citizens, which clearly targets the recently freed slaves. That statute of course moves one step beyond the abolition of slavery accomplished by the Thirteenth Amendment in 1865. Many of the speeches at the time took just this view,[27] despite the view's failure to line up with either the text or the context of the Fourteenth Amendment, adopted in 1868. But as matters turned out, neither of these two readings was accepted by the Supreme Court when the issue arose in the epic decision of *Slaughter-House Cases*.[28]

On their face, the *Slaughter-House Cases* had nothing to do with race. The question was whether Louisiana violated the privileges or immunities of its citizens when the Louisiana legislature created a legal monopoly for the slaughtering of all animals within Orleans Parish. Did those butchers who were excluded from the state-approved facility face a loss of their privileges to enter into that trade? The substantive issue would require the Court to decide whether the facility was meant to exclude nonfavored parties or whether it was set up as a health measure to prevent the spread of waste. That question, however, was never answered, as the *Slaughter-House* decision was sidetracked on an issue that no one had debated at all: did any traditional account of privileges or immunities apply at all? Justice Samuel Freeman Miller held that it did not. He also held that the words "citizens of the United States" did not refer to all the rights of the persons made citizens in the first clause of the Fourteenth Amendment, but only protected the distinctive rights of these persons in their role as citizens of the United States asserting federal rights. This narrow class of federal rights prevented the states from blocking ordinary citizens from petitioning the United States government for grievances, as protected under the First Amendment, or using navigable waters for interstate travel.[29] Bushrod Washington's famous enumeration was quoted in full only to be dismissed as rights "which the State governments were created to establish and secure."[30] Unceremoniously, the federal government was shunted aside from protecting citizens from flagrant abuse of the criminal justice process, notwithstanding the language in Section 5 of the Fourteenth Amendment that gives Congress the power "to enforce, by appropriate legislation, the provisions of this article." Justice Miller defended his decision on the structural ground that the Fourteenth Amendment was not intended to make the United States the "perpetual censor" of the states on all matters great and small, including those unrelated to the emancipation of the slaves.[31]

To many modern progressives, withdrawing the Privileges or Immunities Clause from economic issues was a godsend, and they protested the subsequent decisions of the Supreme Court that smuggled them back in through the newly discovered doctrine of substantive due process, which raised, under a different clause, the same issues that had been mishandled in the *Slaughter-House Cases*. Thus, when the same government grant came back to the Supreme Court a dozen years later, the dissenting justices in *Slaughter-House*, led by Justice Joseph Bradley, insisted that Bushrod Washington's list of privileges and immunities had its proper home in the Due Process Clause of the Fourteenth Amendment, but, with an instructive slip of the pen, only as it applied to citizens, as per the Privileges or Immunities Clause.[32] This is a classical illustration of how one error in dealing with a clause of the Constitution is introduced, albeit imperfectly, to offset a prior mistake.

The Rise of Separate but Equal

For these purposes, however, the real significance of *Slaughter-House* lies not in how it was circumvented in the economic liberty cases, but how it was applied in the area of race. The key decision for this purpose is

United States v Cruikshank,[33] in which, three years after *Slaughter-House*, the Supreme Court blocked federal prosecution of a group of whites charged with conspiracy in the murder of more than a hundred black citizens during the Colfax Massacre in Louisiana.[34] The opinion is replete with references to the limited scope of national citizenship under *Slaughter-House*. *Cruikshank* held that the prosecutions were beyond the power of the federal government, thereby liberating the killers. In the domain of race relations, *Slaughter-House* sharply curtailed federal criminal oversight of local governments. Ironically, one of its findings was that no part of the Bill of Rights, including the Second Amendment right to bear arms, was binding on the states.[35] Since the Court found there were no federal rights at stake, it necessarily followed that the federal government had no "appropriate" role to play in dealing with state activities. The original design of the Fourteenth Amendment that had contemplated active federal oversight of state activities was reduced to a dead letter, and there was effectively no federal oversight over state enforcement of criminal laws in the South, ushering in the disasters of a segregated South that lasted at the very least until *Brown v. Board of Education* in 1954.

The next major step in insulating Jim Crow laws from federal oversight took place in *Plessy v. Ferguson*, which in one grand pronouncement upheld three separate pillars of the old South: segregation in transportation, segregation in schools, and a prohibition of racial intermarriage.[36] In so doing, the eight-member majority, speaking through Justice Henry Billings Brown, a Republican from Detroit who was born in New England, rejected the equal protection challenge on the ground that the states had broad authority to organize their internal affairs as they wished under their extensive police power.[37] The most important point here is that the Court's approach flew in the face of the ordinary views of liberty and property, which would allow a railroad to integrate its cars without regard to race. Indeed the standard view was that all common carriers had to take their customers on reasonable and nondiscriminatory terms, so that if there was any legal pressure on the system it was toward integration, not segregation. Furthermore, the prohibition against racial intermarriage cuts to the core of freedom to contract where it counts the most—on matters of personal association.

The treatment of segregated schools poses a greater challenge in light of the historical evolution of the Equal Protection Clause. The list

of privileges and immunities as of 1823 involved a list that was com-
piled before the rise of public schools in the immediate post–Civil War
years. As a general matter, the distribution of all public benefits and
burdens was not captured by the Privileges or Immunities Clause or for
that matter by the individual guarantees in the first eight amendments
of the Bill of Rights. This is why, in 1865, the Reconstruction Congress could contemplate "forty acres and a mule" for freed slaves in the
Confederacy and debate the desirability of a race-specific benefits program before segregated galleries.[38] These programs could be legislatively
enacted, but were not thought to be either required or prohibited under
the Constitution. Therefore, as a textual matter, it was inconceivable
under the original understanding of the Equal Protection Clause that its
terms, which applied to all persons, could nevertheless be used to create
these highly specific rights against the government for some targeted
group of citizens.

The implicit assumption that the Equal Protection Clause did not
apply to the distribution of government benefits shaped the doctrine in
the post–Civil War period. Thus, as Jim Crow set in, Justice Brown in
Plessy could rely comfortably on the pre–Civil War decision of Justice
Lemuel Shaw of the Massachusetts Supreme Judicial Court in *Roberts
v. City of Boston*,[39] which exhibited exceptional deference to the school
committee, even in the face of an explicit Massachusetts constitutional
guarantee that "all persons without distinction of age or sex, birth or
color, origin or condition, are equal before the law."[40] The presumption
of judicial deference doomed the case. But in all likelihood, Justice Shaw
had a different agenda in Massachusetts, as Boston schools were in fact
desegregated by the school committee in 1855, six years after the case
was decided.

The situation in the South was far different, and it is worth recall-
ing that the Louisiana legislation upheld in *Plessy* was the latest step in
a backsliding in the states that had started in the aftermath of *Slaughter-House*. Regrettably enough, one person who did not see this pattern
was former Supreme Court justice David Souter, who was so committed
to his defense of the "living constitution" that he wanted to celebrate the
bold shift from *Plessy* to *Brown*, some fifty-eight years later.[41] Yet to make
that case, the before-and-after differences have to be highlighted. In his
view, *Plessy* was to be expected: "the members of the Court in Plessy
remembered the day when human slavery was the law in much of the

land. To that generation, the formal equality of an identical railroad car meant progress."[42] But that apologia ignores the path of history, not to mention Justice John Marshall Harlan's stirring dissent that embraced a "color-blind constitution" and predicted, correctly, that in time *Plessy* would come to be regarded as "pernicious" as the *Dred Scott* decision.[43]

Nor does Souter's account acknowledge the internal confusion between coercion and freedom that undergirded Justice Brown's opinion. To make his case, Brown relied on the *Civil Rights Cases* of 1883, which struck down a statute that mandated integration of private facilities on the ground that the statute did not address any state action under the Fourteenth Amendment. To Brown, freedom of association was the ideal: "If the two races are to meet upon terms of social equality, it must be the result of natural affinities, a mutual appreciation of each other's merits and a voluntary consent of individuals."[44] True enough. How that statement supports a state mandate that separates the races, however, was never explained.

Justice Souter's misuse of social history invites a cautionary note regarding constitutional interpretation. At times, justices are so anxious to prove the necessity of a "living constitution" that they are prepared to excuse horrific decisions in order to explain why only evolving social perceptions, not textual interpretation or objective facts, lead to advancement in constitutional law. This is dangerous talk. There are in fact strong, powerful principles that are lasting, of which freedom of voluntary association is surely one. I shall outline what I think is the proper defense of *Brown v. Board of Education* shortly. But for the moment, it is sufficient to stress that this brief excursion into historical relativism only makes it easier for the next generation of illiberal judges to find other excuses to limit associational freedom.

Notwithstanding its threadbare intellectual foundations, *Plessy* proved to be no aberration. In 1908, in *Berea College v. Kentucky,*[45] the Supreme Court upheld the state of Kentucky's right to require a private institution wanting to practice integration to teach its black and white students on separate campuses located miles from each other. Again, it is critical to recognize the antilibertarian doctrinal weapons the Supreme Court utilized to achieve this result. First, it accepted a broad definition of the state's police power (which had been relied on in the Kentucky courts) to justify this limitation on personal freedom and private property rights. Second, it concluded that the state could condition the incorporation of the college on its willingness to comply with whatever conditions it sought to impose, including those that related to separation. This reflected the then common view that the doctrine of unconstitutional conditions had no strength, under the prevailing doctrine that the greater power to issue corporate charters included the lesser power to condition them on teaching black and white students on separate campuses.[46] If we can deny you the charter, we can condition it on racial separation. To the objection that Berea College had been chartered before the Kentucky law was passed came the answer that any prior grant from the state is subject to the state's implied power to "alter, amend or repeal" the private charter.[47] Once again, the lone dissenter in the case was Justice John Marshall Harlan, who saw the evident tension between the narrow definition of the liberty that the majority adopted in *Berea College* and the broader definition that Justice Peckham had adopted in *Allgeyer v. Louisiana*[48] prior to his opinion in *Lochner*.[49] Harlan also bolstered his argument by reference to *Adair v. United States*,[50] which held that the principle of liberty of contract precluded the use of mandatory collective bargaining on interstate rails. Justice Peckham joined the majority in *Berea College* for the simplest of reasons—he was a northern Copperhead (i.e., sympathizer to the South) and a lifelong racist, who deserted his classical liberal principles when they mattered most.[51]

The Road to Brown v. Board of Education

The question that remained was how to get out of the constitutional hole the early cases and doctrine had dug for the nation. The first step took place in *McCabe v. Atchison, Topeka & Santa Fe Railway Co.*,[52] which put modest teeth in the separate but equal doctrine announced in *Plessy* by holding that facilities offered to blacks must be equal in quality to those offered to whites. That case enshrined the doctrine while limiting its application. And there is no evidence that it had much effect on the segregated South. The next step took place in *Buchanan v. Warley*,[53] which struck down a Kentucky ordinance under which black persons were forbidden to buy homes in blocks that had a majority of white owners, just as it forbade white persons from purchasing land in blocks the majority of whose residents were black. Clearly the ordinance was designed to meet the equal protection objection by building in a formal parity of these restrictions between the races. But any belief in the ability to dispose of property as a fundamental right would brush off that objection. The dual restriction only compounds the injustice, for the one error does not offset the other.

These decisions of course fall a long way short of the greatest of the decisions, *Brown v. Board of Education*,[54] which held, under the Equal Protection Clause, that segregated schools had "no place" under the Constitution.[55] In its immediate aftermath, *Brown* generated a legion of uneasy supporters who worried about the weakness of its analytical foundations. And as a textual matter it is manifestly, if regrettably, incorrect under the original understanding of the Fourteenth Amendment. Public education was not treated as one of the privileges or immunities of citizens of the United States, and the issue of the public administration involved in the equal protection of laws, devoted as it was largely to criminal protection, had nothing to do with the operation of the educational system. But clearly that rigid historical and textual view turns a blind eye to all of the other major constitutional errors that allowed the segregated system as a whole to take the monstrous form it did.

It may well have been analytically inappropriate for Chief Justice Earl Warren to write an opinion that glossed over all the serious doctrinal pitfalls in the most ambitious Supreme Court decision ever written. But what choice did he have? The only viable alternative would have been to write a candid opinion which said that this mode of correction was needed to undo the errors of the previous case law. He even could have sought to update the original conception of privileges and immunities to cover public educational institutions. In retrospect that line of argument seems stronger today than it was at the time. It is highly doubtful that any system of pernicious segregation could have survived if the earlier flawed constitutional decisions had not excluded all blacks from the polls, had not gutted federal intervention to prevent massive abuse of state power, and had not refused to enforce faithfully the contract and property rights of all black citizens. That history was water over the dam even in 1954. On balance, candor would not have been a virtue, but would have been an open admission of weakness that would have delegitimized the decision and posed even greater difficulties in the painful campaign of constitutional self-correction that took place in the aftermath of *Brown*. Perhaps, therefore, by summoning a firm moral tone that appealed to empty generalities, Chief Justice Warren took the prudent course of action.

Yet the unwillingness of Warren to be candid about his ground for intervention has not been without costs in both the short and long runs. In the immediate aftermath of *Brown*, the Supreme Court wrote its brief and doctrinally suspect 1955 decision in *Bolling v. Sharpe*,[56] which ordered desegregation in the District of Columbia School District under the Due Process Clause of the Fifth Amendment. Because the Equal Protection Clause only binds the states, the Court in *Bolling* was driven to the odd doctrinal position of reverse incorporation by reading the equal protection guarantee back into the Due Process Clause of the Fifth Amendment. The Court then backtracked on *Brown I* in *Brown II*, when it only stated delphically that the pace of desegregation should proceed at "all deliberate speed,"[57] so that most of the real support behind integration came from the active intervention of the Department of Justice, which was able to withhold federal funds from school districts that did not comply with the desegregation mandate.[58] For its part, the Supreme Court became restive with the slow pace of integration and thus held in 1968 that freedom-of-choice plans were insufficient to meet the mandates of *Brown*.[59] Yet its own efforts to impose strong mandatory busing remedies in the 1970s had, at most, limited effect.[60] The constraints on judicial coercion over local school decisions became all too evident.

Affirmative Action in Modern Times

Fortunately, the social situation regarding affirmative action, however confused and divided, is improved today. Now that the political system has been largely nursed back to health, the color-blind principle should be restricted to the equal enforcement of criminal and civil law in the judicial setting, which were its original objects. As for the public deliberation over how school systems should operate, the color-blind principle is far too restrictive in light of the huge forces of identity politics, which exert great pressure below the surface in all communities and among all groups. Those race-conscious programs do not represent some per se political evil. Often they are hard-fought compromises wrought by individuals who are only trying to work their way through a complex social thicket in which a purposeful policy of inclusion has displaced the strong separatist tendencies of a bygone generation. Here, as with so many other state-run programs, the deferential business judgment rule of corporate law that insulates directors from liability to unhappy shareholders offers a suitable private law analogy. School boards and the local parents who interact with them are not saints, but they should be left with sufficient flexibility so that their decisions are not subject to any per se rule of invalidation, but rather are sustained if made in good faith and supported by reasonable investigation on reasonable grounds.

That same position applies to the larger question of whether the government ought to be allowed to engage in conscious affirmative action programs. On this score, the key point to note is that, in theory, the ideal of freedom of association should apply in all private settings, including the employment relationship covered by Title VII of the Civil Rights Act. It is perfectly understandable why the drafters of the 1964 act sought to impose a color-blind norm in this area in response to the rampant discrimination in the South and elsewhere in labor relationships. But once again, that justification did not rest on a sound set of abstract first principles, all of which point in the opposite direction, except in the odd situations where some employer might be said to exert monopoly power in the labor market. Rather, the need for some color-blind rule was driven by the historical necessity to combat the vicious combination of public and private forces that created segregated institutions backed by the barrel of a gun. But unlike the situation with public accommodations, where the color-blind standard has worked without difficulty, labor markets are more complicated. Under the original plan of the 1964 act, the dominant view was that the effects of past discrimination should work themselves out naturally over time. As then Professor Michael Sovern wrote in 1966: "To violate Title VII, one must treat differently because of race itself and not merely because of an applicant's lack of qualifications which he was prevented from acquiring because of his race."[61] But before the ink could dry on the page, it became clear that the original and aloof stance of letting time heal all wounds would not work in the face of massive civil unrest, as full-scale race riots hit Detroit, Los Angeles, New York, and Washington, D.C., in the years after the passage of the Civil Rights Act.[62] Stronger medicine was needed, and, on that question, the color-blind principle had as its major consequence the slowing down of private and public affirmative action programs until the ingenious (if textually indefensible) decision of Justice Brennan, in *United Steelworkers of America v. Weber*,[63] opened up the possibilities for affirmative action in the teeth of a color-blind textual provision that repeatedly extends its protection to "any individual"[64]—without reference to race or sex.[65] At present, the two-tiered situation in which Title VII continues to apply to discrimination against minorities and women, but not to discrimination in their favor, remains the law of the land—with the blessing of most businesses who need the freedom of action that *Weber's* broad exception to the Civil Rights Act of 1964 supplies. Without it, a dual standard of strict scrutiny would strangle labor markets, as every hiring decision would be subject to judicial challenge.

The great damage Justice Brennan did in this area was to devise an opinion stating that strict judicial scrutiny of the then standard forms of occupational testing that had a disparate impact against members of minority groups held firm even for public and private employers that had active and bona fide affirmative action programs.[66] In so doing, he gave too much weight to coercive action and made it more difficult to unleash broad business support for corrective race-conscious action to take place in the workplace. The carrot of affirmative action has been effective. The stick of disparate impact cases has not. Those two prongs have made it difficult for decades to work sensible political compromises on the testing of public employees in a race-conscious environment.

In this heated context everything gets turned upside down. One area of extreme contention concerns the application of race-conscious tests for public employment. Thus in *Ricci v. DeStefano*,[67] the New Haven firefighters case, the conservatives were willing to accept the detailed compromises in tests when shown that they have been prepared with wide community input and extensive expert assistance. Liberals invoke the misguided disparate impact standard and thus remain convinced, wrongly, that a civil rights violation lurks behind every testing situation, including those in which affirmative action programs are strongly in place. The same good faith standard that should apply to the efforts spent on working school assignments should apply to these testing rules, in cooperative deliberations that seem wholly untainted by illegitimate racial attitudes.

A larger issue looms with respect to various race-conscious programs in both K-12 and higher education. With respect to the former, traditional segregation is no longer in the picture. The current battles regarding primary schools are not over keeping formal segregation, but over whether local school districts can adopt various race-conscious techniques to facilitate integration in the face of housing patterns that push toward de facto segregation. In dealing with these issues, it is troublesome to note that just as segregation has been vanquished, integration has not been secured. It is far easier to remove a legal barrier than it is to reconstruct a just society by dictates from either the Congress or the courts. At this point, we have witnessed a profound role reversal. The aggressive intervention of the Equal Protection Clause has now become the rearguard weapon of choice of conservatives who still believe in the color-blind principle. At this same time, liberal groups almost wish, at least silently, that *Brown* were no longer on the books. Thus in *Parents Involved in Community Schools v. Seattle School District No. 1*,[68] Chief Justice Roberts invoked *Brown*'s color-blind principle to thwart efforts at conscious community building in both Seattle and Louisville. The liberals rightly complained that this wooden application of the earlier decision ignored all the underlying social and political realities in both communities. To make out that case, of course, it is necessary in retrospect to stress the breakdown of the proper political order in the South under Jim Crow, which cried out for a color-blind remedy. The short-term cost of taking the color-blind position was low, because as of 1954 there was little danger that southern school districts would show excessive preference for black students or affirmative action programs. The advocates of the 1964 civil rights legislation were right to keep the affirmative action option off the table, given the risk that it could spark major resistance to the civil rights cause. But the stakes were much different fifty years later, in *Seattle School District No. 1*, when affirmative action remedies were thought by many to be a key component to any system of education in primary and secondary schools.

Similar issues of changed expectations also have arisen in higher education. In the 2003 litigation in *Grutter v. Bollinger*,[69] the Court upheld a program that treated race as one significant factor among others in determining admission to the University of Michigan Law School. The view was that thoughtful administration of the admissions system could lead to strengthening an entering class of students one person at a time. In the companion case of *Gratz v. Bollinger*,[70] the Court struck down the admissions program to the Arts and Sciences program at the University of Michigan because of its rigid formula giving preference points to African-American applicants based on race. In an important sense, these decisions are exactly backwards, for the use of discretion opens up the system to intrigue that admissions systems helped to control by using numerical criteria as a key part of the admissions process. The bottom line is that these affirmative action programs survived, albeit in less than ideal form.

At present, affirmative action is now heading back to the Supreme Court because of disputes over the affirmative action program in the University of Texas system. Before *Brown v. Board*, Texas was at the forefront of state segregationist activities, so much so that in the 1950 decision in *Sweatt v. Painter*,[71] the Supreme Court had little trouble in exposing the fig leaf of separate but equal in law school education. In response to its earlier history, Texas adopted an aggressive affirmative action program, justified, uneasily as ever, on the twin pillars of the correction of past discrimination and the need for greater diversity going forward. That program was struck down in *Hopwood v. Texas*,[72] which prompted Texas to go into high gear to get around the judicial system. Its preferred approach was to pass legislation making it mandatory for campuses in the University of Texas system to admit, automatically, all Texas high school seniors who finished in the top 10 percent of their class, in order to boost minority representation, by tapping a larger fraction of entering students from heavily minority school districts. As a result, 90 percent of all seats were filled by this practice, and the remaining 10 percent were filled by what has been called in *Fisher v. University of Texas*,[73] "Academic and Personal Achievement Indices," which let the schools make "a holistic, flexible, and individualized"[74] evaluation of any applicant who did not secure admission under the 10 percent plan.

The Texas legislative scheme can be attacked from both sides. For those who take the color-blind injunction seriously for higher education, the Texas program should be dead-on-arrival, given its transparent race-conscious justification, which could never survive the searching inquiry required under an orthodox strict scrutiny standard. The larger holistic approach is driven by the same set of social imperatives that were found in *Grutter*. Yet by the same token, anyone who thinks that the system requires flexibility will prefer the current Texas system if they cannot go back to the pre-*Hopwood* program. Knocking out the present system in favor of a strictly enforced color-blind norm would cause a huge upheaval in a system that surely needs marginal adjustments, which are better supplied by administrators on campus.

Overall, the twisted history and multiple rationales offered for both diversity and affirmative action should create massive uneasiness on all sides of the political spectrum. To regain our social bearings, as a nation, we should hope to return to classical liberal principles. These principles point out one fundamental distinction in government arrangements that should carry the day: management and regulation work in different ways. When the state is exercising its managerial functions, it should get the benefit of a relatively relaxed standard of oversight that otherwise should be denied to it in its regulatory function. The classical liberal approach on these matters may restrict the domain of government activities, but it does not impose a stranglehold on the brave individuals who have the thankless and controversial task of balancing competing interests. As has often been said, the sign of a good contract is that everyone is happy, and the sign of a good settlement is that everyone is sad. Unfortunately, on race relations we cannot write on a blank slate and thus are typically in settlement mode. We therefore must remain context-sensitive. The strong doctrinaire flavor of *Brown* served well in its time, but its rigid color-blind formulas were a second-best default rule that does not work as well in modern times where governments must be given some discretion in sorting out competing claims. Racial success going forward depends on finding the right social balance between classical liberal theory and a social history that at every turn flouted its fundamental principles.

34

Citizenship and the Fourteenth Amendment

AS THE LAST CHAPTER revealed, the Citizenship Clause of the Fourteenth Amendment was truly transformative on the issue of race.
Two other major substantive areas remain: the role of citizenship in
American constitutional law and the role of sex discrimination under
the Equal Protection Clause. This chapter tackles the question of citizenship, which raises three separate issues. The first issue deals with
the simple question of how citizenship is acquired and lost. The second
deals with the troubled distinction between citizenship and alienage in
the aftermath of the decline of the Privileges or Immunities Clause of
the Fourteenth Amendment. The third deals with the efforts of modern
progressives to impress their notions of positive rights on both the Citizenship and Equal Protection Clauses of the Fourteenth Amendment.

The Acquisition and Loss of Citizenship

The Citizenship Clause of the Fourteenth Amendment makes it clear
that both natural born and naturalized persons can become citizens of
the United States. The Citizenship Clause, however, is not the exclusive source of citizenship. Sensibly enough, Congress also has the power
to confer citizenship on individuals who do not meet these conditions,
including individuals born overseas to one or two American parents.[1] Yet
the Citizenship Clause is silent on the processes by which citizenship is
acquired or, once validly acquired by birth or naturalization, how it is lost.

The decision whether to permit aliens entry into the United States
and the terms on which they are admitted is a political and not a

constitutional decision, to be decided at the federal and not the state level.[2] So too is the decision whether to confer citizenship on those who have been allowed to enter. The situation could scarcely be otherwise, either for entry or citizenship, for this nation, like all others, could not maintain its internal integrity if the United States were treated as a large common carrier whose borders were open to all persons as of right, except when good cause is shown to keep them out. The boundary lines between nations are more rigid than those between neighboring landowners. Thus, in upholding the right of Congress to deny citizenship to a person who refuses to declare in advance that he would bear arms in the defense of the United States, the Supreme Court stated in no uncertain terms, "[n]aturalization is a privilege, to be given, qualified, or withheld as Congress may determine, and which the alien may claim as of right only upon compliance with the terms which Congress imposes."[3] That power is not only tied to conditions that might go to the loyalty of potential citizens, but under current law, Congress's power to apply any kind of conditions it chooses. Specifically, this includes the power to admit or exclude aliens on the basis of their race and national origin. Today the doctrine of unconstitutional conditions imposes no constraints on the discretion conferred on Congress.

More concretely, the power of Congress "[t]o establish an uniform Rule of Naturalization"[4] does not impose a moral imperative on the United States to develop a naturalization regime that treats all like cases alike, under some expansive but fictive Equal Protection Clause made applicable to the federal government. It only means that any rule touching this subject should have geographic uniformity so that the same set of rules applies to all entrants to the United States, regardless of where they gain access to the country. The substantive freedom on eligibility for citizenship is revealed by its historical progression. Citizenship was limited to "free white persons" in 1790, extended to persons of African descent in 1870, to indigenous people of the Western Hemisphere in 1940, and to persons of Chinese descent in 1943.[5] Other categories have been added since. Clearly there can be no right of outsiders to enter at will, for that would render sovereign boundaries ineffectual. But who should be permitted entry, and whether they shall be granted citizenship, raises profound questions of national policy that are not touched by the Fourteenth Amendment, which relates only to the activities of the states and thus does not limit Congress on the issue, that is, at least until the Supreme Court in *Bolling v. Sharpe* found an equal protection component in the Due Process Clause of the Fifth Amendment in order to outlaw segregation in the District of Columbia.[6] In exercising this power, Congress has adopted elaborate rules for revoking citizenship based on incomplete or misleading disclosures on applications. Open or closed borders are thus a policy matter only, as are the conditions that can be attached by agreement to the naturalization of any alien. The natural law ideal of unlimited movement of all individuals across open borders cannot be preserved in any system composed of sovereign nation states.

All of these developments should be a source of genuine intellectual unease. The basic premise of any classical liberal system, or indeed any system that stresses the natural rights of all peoples, has no place for territorial limitations on what can be acquired.[7] But in this context, those principles form the basis of unattainable ideals. Nations are not simply private property writ large, but because they act in that manner on the international stage, the privileges and immunities afforded to citizens are broader than the basic rights given to all persons.

The constitutional issues become more serious when the question turns to the grounds on which citizenship can be revoked for persons born in the United States or those who have been properly naturalized. Although the Constitution specifies how citizenship is acquired, except for congressionally imposed conditions, it says nothing about how it can be lost. At one time, the dominant legal view was that any citizen by birth or naturalization could lose that status by committing actions inconsistent with allegiance to the United States. These notably included voting in foreign elections and serving in the armed forces of a foreign nation.[8] In *Perez v. Brownell*, Justice Felix Frankfurter, writing for a five-member majority, held that Congress had the power to make these adjustments to prevent "embarrassments in the conduct of foreign relations. . . ."[9] His rationale seems patently overbroad if it allows Congress to strip any person of his or her citizenship by a simple declaration. Surely, in the teeth of the Citizenship Clause of the Fourteenth Amendment, a Jim Crow Congress could not forfeit the citizenship of all former slaves by issuing such a declaration.

Given this serious problem, *Perez* was overruled by a five-four decision in *Afroyim v. Rusk*.[10] In *Afroyim*, Justice Hugo Black (who had dissented in *Perez*) promptly lurched too far toward the opposite extreme when he wrote:

> [T]he Fourteenth Amendment was designed to, and does, protect every
> citizen of this Nation against a congressional forcible destruction of his
> citizenship, whatever his creed, color, or race. Our holding does no more
> than to give to this citizen that which is his own, a constitutional right
> to remain a citizen in a free country unless he voluntarily relinquishes
> that citizenship.[11]

Yet why should any citizen who engages in hostile actions toward the
United States keep any purported benefits of citizenship simply by refusing to renounce his status?[12] These actions are inconsistent with the obligations of citizenship and should give the government the added option
to try those individuals for treason. Once someone has engaged in such
conduct and is given an option to return to the United States for trial,
which for good reason is never accepted, the government should be able
to treat them as enemy combatants. As such, they would be subject to
trial by a military tribunal if in custody, or exposed to efforts to capture
or kill if outside custody.

Once again, think of the private analogies. In ordinary partnerships
and associations, forfeiture of membership is never flatly prohibited, but is
always allowable for cause. That option should be the case for citizenship
as well. The Citizenship Clause thus raises thorny questions that it does
not resolve. But hardcore criminal attacks against the lives and property
of American citizens on behalf of foreign governments or other outlaw
organizations surely justify a forfeiture of citizenship, without doing violence to the basic constitutional structure, even if ordinary crimes, however horrendous, do not. In effect, it seems quite pointless to argue that
an individual such as Anwar al-Awlaki should be able to plot against the
United States from a remote post in Yemen, but then be able to protect
himself from physical attack because he is a naturalized citizen. Whether
naturalized or not, all citizens should be subject to the risk of excom-
munication when they engage in dangerous activities that amount not
merely to voting in a foreign election, but to prosecuting mayhem against
the United States. There is of course a deep sense in which citizenship is
a privilege. But it should never be an irrevocable one.

Alienage and Equal Protection

The second question is how the Citizenship Clause relates to the Privileges or Immunities Clause. As a matter of original design, limiting
strong constitutional rights to citizens makes perfect structural sense in

light of the vast powers that the national government has over aliens admitted within the borders. Nonetheless, on the issue of government powers over aliens, it has long been settled that even though nations can deny aliens citizenship, they cannot strip them of all personal rights to liberty and property. One standard formulation of international law states the proposition as follows:

> Every State is by the Law of Nations compelled to grant to aliens at least equality before the law with its citizens, as far as safety of person and property is concerned. An alien must in particular not be wronged in person or property by the officials and courts of a State. Thus the police must not arrest him without just cause. . . .[13]

The obligation of nations under international law, of course, carries over to states within the nation, which is why both the Due Process and Equal Protection Clauses of the Fourteenth Amendment fit so well into the basic scheme. They are written in ways that preserve these very rights against arbitrary arrest and arbitrary seizure of property. But privileges and immunities raise very different questions. There are no such rights to economic liberties or to acquire property against the federal government. It therefore makes sense that these rights, which are protected by the Privileges or Immunities Clause, only apply to citizens. The basic logic of the Fourteenth Amendment thus squares with the structure of the United States Constitution and the standard norms of international law.

Slaughter-House changed all that. Once the Privileges or Immunities Clause disappeared from view, the slack was taken up by broader readings of the Due Process Clause and, especially, the Equal Protection Clause. The simple pragmatic reason for this turnabout is that states do not have the power to admit or exclude aliens into the United States. The fact that this power remains securely lodged in the hands of the federal government allows the courts to extend aliens additional protection without fear of opening the floodgates to foreigners. Within this national cocoon, the question that then arises is, what rights should be afforded to aliens and why? The classical liberal vision of universal rights eventually takes over this corner of the law.

Ironically, the evisceration of the Privileges or Immunities Clause in *Slaughter-House*[14] led to an *increase* in the level of protection that is now afforded to aliens. Without privileges and immunities in the picture, the only question is whether the decisions of state and local governments to place aliens into a special class turns on whether we think there is a sensible normative basis for this distinction in the particular context to which it applies. Often none is available. Thus in an era when economic liberties received extensive protection, the Supreme Court in *Truax v. Raich*[15] struck down a statute that required private employers to maintain a workforce of at least 80 percent American citizens. If the Privileges or Immunities Clause governed, aliens would be outside the scope of constitutional protection, so the difficult interpretive question would have been whether a restriction on the ability of aliens to work for citizens abridged the privileges of the citizen employers, even if it did protect the aliens they wished to hire. The correlative nature of the rights and duties would present a real obstacle to constructing any consistent protection of the economic liberties of citizens without extending that protection to aliens as well, given the frequent prospect of trade and cooperation between citizens and aliens. We cannot be sure how those connections would have been worked out because the question was treated as moot once the oversight of economic liberties switched to some combination of the Equal Protection and Due Process Clauses.[16] Once the switch is made, the remainder of the analysis turns on the traditional police power question of whether these restrictions relate to matters of safety or health or, more improbably, to the general welfare or the preservation of morals. In principle, it might be possible to make such an argument under the first two heads of the police power. However, the evident protectionist purpose of the statute—never acceptable under serious judicial scrutiny—makes clear it should be struck down within the traditional classical liberal framework.

The 1937 New Deal transformation of the law, moreover, does not change that particular concern even as the focal point shifts from competitive processes to the protection of politically vulnerable minority groups from unfair discrimination. Put otherwise, the "discrete and insular minorities" focus first articulated in *United States v. Carolene Products Company*[17] exerts a powerful influence. The confluence of these various strands is evident in *Takahashi*,[18] where the question was phrased as whether the Equal Protection Clause rendered unconstitutional a California law passed at the height of the anti-Japanese sentiment during the Second World War in 1943 that barred a Japanese alien from working as a commercial fisherman in public waters off the California coast solely because his race made him ineligible for citizenship. Justice Black, who had upheld the internment of American *citizens* of Japanese origins in *Korematsu v. United States*,[19] did a complete turnaround regarding Japanese *aliens* faced with state law restrictions of the same vintage. He placed heavy reliance on *Truax* when he insisted that the plenary power of naturalization at the federal level did not allow states to engage in like forms of discrimination in the teeth of both the Equal Protection Clause and the 1866 Civil Rights Act.[20]

Historically, his decision was demonstrably incorrect. *Truax* took great pains to insist that it extended its protection only to private businesses, but did not touch either public property or public employment.[21] The first of these points, public property, was nothing more than a continuation of earlier doctrine that the ability to fish in state waters was a common right that Justice Washington had *excluded* from the list of privileges and immunities in *Corfield v. Coryell*.[22] That theme was adopted in *Truax*: "the regulation or distribution of the public domain, or of the common property or resources of the people of the state, the enjoyment of which may be limited to its citizens as against both aliens and the citizens of other states."[23] No qualifications. The constitutional claim in *Truax* arose solely because the discrimination in question was directed to "the conduct of ordinary private enterprise."[24] The nineteenth-century synthesis that denied constitutional protections against the government distribution of benefits continued to hold sway.

The same categorical approach ruled out any constitutional protection for aliens seeking any and all types of public employment. Less than a month after *Truax*, the Court in *Heim v. McCall*[25] sustained (in a taxpayer standing suit, no less) a provision of the New York labor law that gave an employment preference to "citizens over aliens," including, in this instance, workers who constructed key elements of New York City's subway system.[26] In light of the expenditure of government revenues on a public project, it followed early precedent that held "it belongs to the state, as the guardian and trustee for its people, and having control of its affairs, to prescribe the conditions upon which it will permit public work to be done on its behalf, or on behalf of its municipalities."[27] Again, no qualifications or subtleties.

Yet once *Takahashi* used equal protection arguments to pry open state common property to aliens, it was only a matter of time before that same approach carried over to the distribution of government benefits that heretofore fell outside the scope of the Fourteenth Amendment.

Thus in *Graham v. Richardson*,[28] the question was whether Arizona and Pennsylvania could condition the payment of welfare benefits to aliens on residency within the United States for some particular number of years. Justice Blackmun held that *Takahashi* and *Truax* governed so that discrimination against aliens now was treated as "inherently suspect and subject to close judicial scrutiny."[29] Claims of a "special public-interest doctrine" intended "to preserve limited welfare benefits for its own citizens" failed to pass constitutional muster.[30] This stunning reversal in judicial sentiment was evident, because now aliens were regarded as a "discrete and insular" minority entitled to special protection under *Carolene Products*.[31] With one effortless step, the basic distinction between citizen and alien built into the fabric of the Fourteenth Amendment suddenly became vulnerable under its Equal Protection Clause.

Needless to say, the purported insulation of public hiring decisions regarding aliens from all constitutional scrutiny could not survive once welfare benefits were subject to equal protection review. Like clockwork, two years after *Graham* the other shoe fell in *Sugarman v. Dougall*,[32] which involved a challenge to hiring restrictions that New York City imposed on aliens. *Carolene Products* was again invoked to justify a high level of judicial scrutiny where none before had existed.[33] At this point the Court concluded that there was at best a poor fit between the alienage classification and New York City's legitimate objectives, chiefly that of exploiting some close "identity between a government and the members, or citizens, of the state,"[34] for "[t]he civil servant participates directly in the formulation and execution of government policy,"[35] which is limited to "state elective or important nonelective executive, legislative, and judicial positions."[36] Once again, both the constitutional text and its underlying theory were ignored. To his credit, Justice Rehnquist in his dissent takes the history more seriously. But in so doing he only rejects Justice Blackmun's majority decision to employ the de facto strict scrutiny standard[37] without acknowledging how deeply the citizen/person distinction is built into the structure of the Fourteenth Amendment. Rather than retain the historical carte blanche position, Justice Rehnquist applied a rational basis analysis to the public employment of aliens.[38] He did not want to unravel recent history by accepting that the deeper reach of the Privileges or Immunities Clause renders the Equal Protection Clause inapplicable to public employment.

The standard of review in alienage cases raised its most vexing questions in connection with K-12 education. In *Plyler v. Doe*,[39] the question was whether Texas could deny its illegal ("undocumented") children the same education it provides to children who are either citizens of the United States or aliens who are legally within the state. The clear textual argument is that the citizen/alien classification cannot be regarded as arbitrary when it is built into the very fabric of the Fourteenth Amendment. But against the background of *Takahashi* and *Sugarman*, Justice Brennan, writing for the majority in a five-four decision, resorted to an acontextual equal protection analysis. Alienage was not a suspect classification, like race, nor was education a fundamental right like speech or, more to the point, voting.[40] Nonetheless alienage could be treated as a disfavored classification, and education an important interest. By cobbling the two together, he could overturn the Texas decision to exclude aliens from the educational system, while recognizing that these same children could be unceremoniously deported by the federal government.[41]

Having reached this point in his analysis, it was simple for Justice Brennan to dismiss Texas's supposed financial and institutional justifications as short-sighted, given his deeply held conviction that many of these alien children become a greater burden on the American system if allowed to reach maturity without a useful education.[42] The cost of educating undocumented alien children need not be greater than the cost of educating legal aliens—at least if special education programs are kept out of the mix. Of course, the probability of illegal alien children remaining in the United States as adults is surely lower than it is for legal aliens, but no one knows by how much.[43]

The dissent by Chief Justice Warren Burger raised all these points.[44] But since the Equal Protection Clause was unmoored from the rest of the Fourteenth Amendment, the underlying empirical concerns remain uncertain. However, as a juridical matter, how Texas should govern appears to be a classic question of state management of public resources, where the case for judicial deference to legislative action is strong no matter how foolish their decisions. The federal courts that embellish equal protection law rights do not have to raise funds or administer complex government systems. Once again, creating positive rights through judicial manipulation of the Fourteenth Amendment is not the correct approach.

In sum, it is critical to take stock of these developments in light of the originalist claims to constitutional interpretation. On this score, the history points to a position at total variance with the common practice. Yet it is hard to gainsay the proposition that the types of protection offered in recent decisions reflect a highly desirable normative framework. Before the adoption of the Fourteenth Amendment, aliens received many types of local benefits as a matter of common practice. There is no reason why those protections could not also be given after its passage. This demonstrates a situation where the explicit constitutionalization of the citizen/alien distinction moves the overall legal system away from an implicit universalism of rights particularly characteristic of the classical liberal constitution. Viewed as a question of how to apply the prescriptive constitution, the modern view that treats seriously claims of aliens against state and local governments has much to commend it. The near-strict scrutiny standard goes perhaps one step too far. But enter the prescriptive constitution: it is better that we stick with the modern view than return to the historically correct, but intellectually impoverished and socially deleterious view that denied aliens the use of common property, the ability to acquire private property, and all access to employment in either the public or the private sector.

The Progressive View of Citizenship and Equal Protection

This account of both citizenship and equal protection carefully seeks to limit constitutional benefits to the core rights protected under classical liberal systems. The progressive vision of citizenship and equal protection does not reject any of these considerations, but takes the argument one step further. In the judicial arena, the early action occurred through the Equal Protection Clause, where there was a brief but powerful flurry of action to treat wealth, like race, as a suspect classification. Thus in *McDonald v. Board of Election Commissioners*,[45] Chief Justice Warren hinted that higher judicial scrutiny is warranted "where lines are drawn on the basis of wealth or race, two factors which would independently render a classification highly suspect and thereby demand a more exacting judicial scrutiny."[46] It takes no imagination to see that this position either trivializes the sorry history about race or exaggerates the role of wealth. But either way, this bold and uninformed pronouncement is light years away from the concern of the Equal Protection Clause, which is to prevent inconsistent enforcement of the criminal law by prosecuting some but not others on the basis of race. Differences in wealth always emerge from the operation of voluntary transactions, for nowhere does it say that transactions that work for mutual gain always generate equal increments in wealth for the parties. Nor need it follow that all individuals will enter into the same number of wealth enhancing transactions. The effort to impose some general "patterned principle" of ideal wealth distribution through constitutional means would generate, at the state level no less, a continual requirement of judicial oversight that would ultimately frustrate the essential function of wealth creation. It is hard enough for any classical liberal to accept a state that allows the government to engage in forced redistribution. But it defies comprehension to convert a clause intended to limit state power into one that compels the redistribution of wealth on a nonstop basis. Few propositions are less informed than Chief Justice Warren's remarks. Indeed the perverse enormity of his vision quickly chased away both liberal and conservative writers.[47] How the states acting unilaterally could achieve redistribution was an open question, given that many of the greatest wealth disparities lay across state lines.

In the end, however, judicial developments did not follow a single path. Even if the equalization of wealth were confined to individual states, the logistical difficulties of judicial enforcement and the unanticipated consequences of policing these wealth differentials led the Supreme Court to retreat from this mission in *San Antonio Independent School District v. Rodriguez*,[48] albeit only by a five-to-four vote. There, the Court refused to order an equalization of the property tax to overcome income disparities among districts, including those that involved poorer districts with a majority of Mexican-American students, by refusing to allow wealth transfers across school district lines.[49]

The wisdom of that decision seems beyond question. A program of district equalization had been adopted on a state level, most notably in California two years before *Rodriguez* was decided.[50] In practice its profound transformations in educational policy have done little to calm the fears of those opposed to massive forms of wealth transfer.[51] Yet by the same token, most people sense that a perpetuation of wealth differences across class and race over time could contribute to higher levels of social instability. Ironically, of course, nearly a decade after *Rodriguez* the Court decided *Plyler*, where it refused to allow discrimination against alien school children. This counteracted some of the adverse effects of *Rodri-guez*, but was on balance far less disruptive to overall system operation.

What then can be done for education without resorting to this high level of constitutional adventurism? At this point, the best answer is not further regulation, but deregulation. The many private individuals and foundations that seek to address these inequalities have met only scant success. Additionally, efforts to use financial sticks and carrots to deal with these inequalities offer no guarantees whatsoever that the transfer of funds will work to benefit students if strong teachers' unions can expropriate those budget increments. Irrespective of the theoretical appeal of major wealth transfers, the surer path to overall improvement rests on tough-minded steps that most legislatures and courts are reluc-tant to take. The first step is to make it official government policy that all teachers are hired on competitive contracts and must agree to work without union representation. The willing acceptance of any monopoly union is tantamount to a violation of the public trust by inflating wages above a fair, competitive, and sustainable level. The state should never tolerate monopoly unions when competitive conditions are available, to which the majority of state budgets offer ample testimony.[52] The second step is to remove all the barriers to entry for both charter schools and voucher programs to create strong competitive pressures on public insti-tutions. The third and final step is to not allow public school districts to collude in setting wages for teachers.

Now that the equal protection arguments for mandated redistribu-tion have faltered, a similar fate likely awaits the parallel efforts to build a case for wealth redistribution under the Citizenship Clause. Nonethe-less, progressive writers have seized upon this clause to implement a program of massive state intervention. For example, Bruce Ackerman offers a "Citizenship Agenda" that does far more with the Privileges or Immunities Clause than Bushrod Washington ever dreamed of doing in *Corfield*.[53] In contrast to Washington, Ackerman's urgent message is for the courts to "expand and deepen the privileges of national citizenship. Women's suffrage during the Progressive Era, Social Security during the New Deal, the antidiscrimination laws of the civil rights era—all provide notable examples."[54] Similarly, Professor Goodwin Liu (now a justice on the California Supreme Court) thinks that some distinctive notion of national citizenship is the engine for implementing an agenda of educational equality in the United States, chiefly by forcing major federal expenditures to more needy communities.[55] In this vision, it is not enough to make slaves free and citizens equal. It becomes imperative to use the Citizenship Clause of the Fourteenth Amendment as the tool to make "national citizenship meaningful and effective."[56] Liu argues "the grant of congressional power to enforce citizenship rights implies a constitutional duty of enforcement."[57]

This last proposal turns the Fourteenth Amendment upside down by converting a constitutional provision that limits the use of state power into one that drives federal expenditures in the area of education. How much more could be done, given the all-pervasive federal involvement in the area, is an open question. The current state programs, with at most mixed success, already aim to redirect wealth to many districts that need it; further constitutional intervention is at best pointless.[58] Nor is there any sense that the transfer of wealth could by any measurable standard improve the situation. Liu's program is the classic illustration of the effort to create an aggressive regime of positive rights from afar, which simply cannot work in any government with limited resources—including our own. The overall lesson should be clear. Citizenship rights are critical; the protection of aliens is critical as well. The classical liberal framework does, in this as in all other areas, a better job at reaching the right results than the modern progressive maneuvers, which use the label as a covert way to create another unsustainable system of positive rights.

35

Equal Protection and Sex Discrimination

T HE PREVIOUS ANALYSIS of race and citizenship sets the stage for dealing with the third major classification under the Equal Protection Clause—that states may classify individuals on account of sex or, as is more commonly said today, gender. This choice of terms is not without consequences for the shape of equal protection law. Traditionally, "gender" was used to classify nouns in foreign languages. That classification process often looks inherently arbitrary, which in turn suggests, perhaps indirectly, that sex differences relevant to human reproduction do not carry over to other areas of life. The use of the term "sex," in contrast, suggests that these human differences are not only immutable (at least in the overwhelming number of cases), but also shape the entire range of social behaviors for all men and women alike. Taken as a whole, the use of the term "sex" tends to legitimate classifications that the term "gender" tends to brand as suspect. As I think that biological influences are pervasive in all areas of human life, I shall use the earlier term "sex" throughout this chapter.[1]

Sex Differences and Classical Liberal Theory

Paradoxically, the terminological dispute described above should, in principle, have little to do with the analysis of the Equal Protection Clause. Confine that clause to the ordinary enforcement of criminal and civil law, and (with the key exception of sex-based offenses, such as statutory rape)[2] the same rules should apply to men as to women, just as they do to aliens as to citizens, or to blacks as to whites. That limited (but vital) role for equal protection principles is to make sure that state legislation does not deviate from these bedrock principles. It is not a charter for the creation of positive rights against the government.

Accordingly, any distinction based on sex is easily handled within classical liberal theory, which regards sex as wholly irrelevant to the basic private law fields of property, contract, and tort, and similarly to any political right such as participation in public affairs. Those key issues surely could have had traction under the Privileges or Immunities Clause, but historically, all the nineteenth-century liberalization of women's rights in both private and public law were regarded as exclusively legislative endeavors—changes that took place with great rapidity and imperfect execution in the years following the Civil War.[3]

The initial entry of sex into constitutional law came from the opposite direction. The early twentieth-century expansion of state regulation in economic areas consciously appealed to sex differences. As already noted, cases like *Muller v. Oregon*[4] in 1908 justified imposing a minimum wage law precisely because it worked exclusively to protect women. Only later generations rightly perceived this "protection" as a denial to women of the freedom of contract that the law left undisturbed for men, which thus posed a serious threat to equality of opportunity under the law.[5] Thus it was no surprise that in 1948—the same year that *Takahashi v. Fish and Game Commission*[6] was decided—Justice Felix Frankfurter in *Goesaert v. Cleary* allowed Michigan to ban a woman from tending a bar, unless she was "the wife or daughter of the male owner," by indicating that "the Constitution does not require legislatures to reflect sociological insight."[7] No classical liberal could ever accept that limitation on occupational freedom without a strong showing of danger to women's health and safety not shared by men, so that the issue would be regarded more as a freedom of contract issue and less as an equal protection one. But within a generation the modern transformation of equal protection law took place with respect to sex classifications. The following are some benchmarks along the way.

Estate Administration

As the sociological pressures mounted, the legal tide began to turn against Frankfurter. By 1971 in *Reed v. Reed,*[8] the Supreme Court wrote a short opinion that ignored *Goesaert* and concluded, simply, that the Equal Protection Clause "does . . . deny to States the power to legislate that different treatment be accorded to persons placed by a statute into different classes on the basis of criteria wholly unrelated to the objective of that statute."[9] With those words it struck down an Idaho statute providing that, in choosing the administrator of an estate, the probate court should categorically prefer men to women if both stood in the same relationship to the deceased (e.g., as children of parents). Idaho's purported justification of administrative simplicity was dismissed out of hand: "To give a mandatory preference to members of either sex over members of the other, merely to accomplish the elimination of hearings on the merits, is to make the very kind of arbitrary legislative choice forbidden by the Equal Protection Clause."[10] Move the Equal Protection Clause beyond the protection of the criminal law, and it is hard to resist this conclusion. If any arbitrary choice is needed, it could be made at a very low cost by lot.

Spousal Benefits for Military Personnel

Reed is of little practical consequence in the area of estate administration. Legislatures at that time were busy removing all male preferences from those statutes dealing with community property by allowing, for example, either spouse, acting alone, to enter into transactions with a third party.[11] Nonetheless, the case had immense importance in launching a new category of equal protection inquiry that quickly went beyond the relatively mundane task of setting default rules for choosing estate administrators. Within two years, the level of scrutiny was ratcheted up in *Frontiero v. Richardson*.[12] Writing for a plurality of four, Justice Brennan struck down a federal statutory presumption that permitted the wives of military men to receive automatically a dependency allowance, but required the husbands of military women to prove dependence by showing that they received at least one-half of their support from their service member wives.[13] At the time, there were approximately 1,500,000 married men in the armed services, but only about 4,000 married service women.[14] The case came to the Supreme Court without any precise statistics of the percentage of female service members who had dependent husbands, but the government did note in its Supreme Court brief that "97.7 percent of married men between the ages of 25 and 44, whose wives were present, were in the civilian labor force."[15] The clear inference was that of these 4,000 married servicewomen, over 3,900 women were likely to have independent husbands. Yet at the same time, the percentage of servicemen with independent wives was likely to be far lower. Based on this information, a divided three-judge panel held that if it required parity,

> [t]he Court would be faced with a Hobson-like choice in fashioning a remedy: either strike down the conclusive presumption in favor of married service men, forcing the services to invest the added time and expense necessary to administer the law accurately, or require the presumption to be applied to both male and female married members, thereby abandoning completely the concept of dependency in fact upon which Congress intended to base the extension of benefits.[16]

Right on! Essentially what the majority held was that the rule adopted by Congress minimized the sum of decision and error costs, which is generally regarded as the best procedure to use in making decisions under conditions of uncertainty. At the time, it would have been too costly to wade through the hundreds of thousands of dependency claims by females when the background rate of dependency was quite high. On the other hand, it would be unwise to set a presumption in favor of dependency for husbands that would likely be wrong well over 95 percent of the time. As a matter of sheer technique, it is not possible to fault the statutory design. Drawing lots may work in *Reed*, but not here. The administrative and error costs of any parallel rule for male and female military personnel are far higher. The techniques adopted show no sign of bias and should satisfy the strictest standard of judicial scrutiny.

In reversing the decision below, Justice Brennan had no interest in the statistical techniques used to evaluate these critical ratios. He knew that the only way to achieve equalization was to extend the benefit of the presumption to a few husbands of service women so as not to wreck the lives of thousands of women whose husbands were in the military. To reach that result, he engineered yet another doctrinal tour-de-force. It had already been established that an Equal Protection Clause analysis applied to the federal government through the medium of the Due Process Clause in cases of egregious violations, such as with racial segregation in District of Columbia schools.[17] To exploit that sentiment, Brennan referenced the infamous statement of Justice Bradley in *Bradwell v. State*,[18] which sustained the Illinois statute that banned women from the practice of law on these grounds:

> The natural and proper timidity and delicacy which belongs to the female sex evidently unfits it for many of the occupations of civil life.

The constitution of the family organization, which is founded in the divine ordinance, as well as in the nature of things, indicates the domestic sphere as that which properly belongs to the domain and functions of womanhood. The harmony, not to say identity, of interest and views which belong, or should belong, to the family institution is repugnant to the idea of a woman adopting a distinct and independent career from that of her husband.[19]

This passage has of course been criticized countless times. But silly as its characterization of women may be, it is a simple non sequitur to take the next step of insisting that "stereotyped distinctions between the sexes" reduced women during the nineteenth century to a social position that was, "in many respects, comparable to that of blacks under the pre-Civil War slave codes,"[20] or to pay little respect to the political process that had done so much to erase earlier inequalities by, for example, actively recruiting women into military service. To Justice Brennan (and Justices Douglas, White, and Marshall), the upshot of this history was that the strict scrutiny standard applied to race should carry over to sex, albeit in a somewhat attenuated form given the obvious difficulties that stood in the way of treating them identically for all purposes. "Separate but equal" was a catchphrase for Jim Crow segregation on matters of race. But on matters of sex, the once odious "separate but equal" standard, when properly applied, becomes the gold standard in dealing with such issues as single-sex bathroom facilities and college athletic teams.

In essence, the strict scrutiny approach of the *Frontiero* plurality quickly morphed into a (tough) intermediate scrutiny standard that had more strength than the rational basis standard in *Reed*, but less perhaps than the anticipated strict scrutiny standard of the Equal Rights Amendment that looked at the time on its way to adoption. The defender of a sex-based classification bears the heavy burden of "exceedingly persuasive justification for the classification."[21] Accordingly, a statute's proponent must show that "the classification serves important governmental objectives, and that the discriminatory means employed are substantially related to the achievement of those objectives."[22] But even that standard should never make it appropriate to strike down a statutory framework that actually gets the economics right. Unlike so many forms of economic regulation, there is no convincing story in *Frontiero* of untoward political influence that warps the statutory scheme. There is in effect no reason for bad judicial economics to correct a sound political process that has moved light years away from *Bradwell*. Allow the social patterns on dependency or enlistment to change, and the law could change as well. On matters of sex as well as race, a higher level of discretion should be afforded to government in the operation of its own benefit programs than in its regulation of private businesses.

One question is just how far this development should go. The language quoted above comes from *Mississippi University for Women v. Hogan*[23] where the Court by a five-to-four vote required Mississippi to open its all-female nursing school to otherwise qualified men. With the benefit of hindsight, many men have entered the nursing profession, making it clear that sex differences pose no insuperable obstacle to its operation. The only real question is whether the state should be granted deference in the organization of its own institutions, so long as a respectable number of private institutions maintain that distinction. The case is a far cry from race discrimination with invidious animus, given, as Justice Powell's dissent notes, that all of the state's twenty-four other university and junior colleges were coeducational, including two that offered nursing curricula.[24] The decision to make this institution coed therefore reduces the diversity of the types of educational institutions offered by the state, without offering any compelling explanation for a result that might well have been introduced politically if the case had come out the other way. Yet the rationale offered here clearly must fall under the standard derived from *Reed* and *Frontiero*.

This line of cases explains the many difficulties with the Equal Rights Amendment that were lurking in the background when *Frontiero* was decided. That amendment removed the pesky term "protection" to read: "Equality of rights under the law shall not be denied or abridged by the United States or by any State on account of sex."[25] But the proposed amendment (which uses the now-unfashionable term "sex") was silent on two key, interrelated questions. What standard of review should apply to sex classifications? And what police power exceptions are consistent with the ERA's basic structure? Following the near-strict scrutiny approach of Brennan in *Frontiero* necessarily requires some understanding of the systematic differences between men and women on measures concerning physique, attitudes, and aptitudes across and within fields, which could easily influence the distribution of occupational choices. Men may be more likely to become construction workers than women, and female doctors more likely to become pediatricians than male doctors, but less likely to become neurosurgeons.[26] And of course male/female differences in the military, which I shall address presently, are both large and persistent.

Within a market setting, these differences count as a social advantage because they increase the prospective gains from trade through specialization. The correct classical liberal response is to remove all bans on women in practicing law or tending bar and allow voluntary sorting to give voice to any differential preferences and abilities between men and women. If Justice Bradley's dire evaluation had proven correct, few women would have succeeded at the practice of law. But even if he were dead right on sex differences, he offered no reason for not letting women decide for themselves whether to compete with men in the practice of law. The same result applies to any occupational restriction directed only toward men. The verdict of history offers the best falsification of Bradley's cramped worldview. Yet by the same token, it is useful to recall Robert Nozick's injunction against using "patterned principles" to test for the justice of certain social arrangements.[27] In any voluntary market with open entry, we should expect to see differences in occupational choices by subgroups, even if we cannot always predict what they might be. Indeed, the one sure sign that markets are not operating well is lockstep percentages of men and women across occupational fields with widely different qualifications. While the state should not prohibit women from entering into any profession, neither should it insist on parity of representation in any field, nor bar any private program of affirmative action by imposing a misguided sex-blind norm on private institutions.

Safety and Insurance Regulation

There is still the question of how this position plays out with regard to other forms of sex-based regulation, where the appropriate level of judicial scrutiny is higher than it is for the government acting in its management function. In *Craig v. Boren*,[28] an Oklahoma statute prohibited the sale of "non-intoxicating" 3.2 percent beer to men under the age of twenty-one and to women under the age of eighteen. Justice Brennan struck the statute down under his near-strict scrutiny standard. Obviously, the historical discrimination against women played no part in this statutory scheme. The statute is best understood as a health and safety measure justified in large measure by the fact that the arrest rate for eighteen-to-twenty-year-olds driving under the influence of alcohol for men was about 2.0 percent, while for women of the same age, it was 0.18 percent—an eleven-fold difference.[29] As a first approximation, 98 percent of good male drivers in the eighteen-to-twenty age range are subject to limitations that do not apply to female drivers of the same age. Yet that is exactly how it should be, so long as there is any correlation between arrest rates and injury or death rates. The state interest in safety is very strong. To ignore this correlation is to needlessly keep women in that age group from drinking when it does no harm or allow men to drink at an age when it could cause great harm. It is not possible to determine ex ante which men fall within the dangerous class, and to enforce a prohibition on male drivers only after they have committed a drinking and driving offense could easily be too little, too late. As Justice Brennan noted, the Oklahoma statute could be criticized for not going far enough, because it allows men between the ages of eighteen and twenty to consume alcohol that they did not purchase.[30] But from the tenor of his decision, that broader statute could also fail under his extended equal protection analysis, as it involves a greater intrusion on the activities of these men.

Indeed, the analysis could go further. Many states have statutes that require prior government approval of insurance rates.[31] If one such state took into account the aggregate experience of male and female drivers, it would have to permit differential premium rates that *Craig* seems to prohibit. The consequence would be that as a group, female drivers would have to subsidize male drivers, resulting in an excess number of accidents from having too many men on the road. So long as there are differences between men and women, as well as differences within the classes of men and women, it is unwise to use the Equal Protection Clause as a club to block the rational pricing of insurance products. This is exactly what happens if the epithet "stereotypical" is hurled against sound insurance practices, that is, those that accurately price the underlying risk. The great irony here is that the usual rational basis test in such cases as *Williamson v. Lee Optical, Inc.,*[32] used in that case to sustain anticompetitive regulations, has never treated either under- or overinclusiveness as a reason for striking down a law. In *Craig*, the state interest in saving lives was considered far stronger than the state interest in *Lee Optical*, which was protecting ophthalmologists or optometrists from competition with opticians in grinding lenses and fitting glasses. Think of it this way: even under the older *Lochner*[33] rules congenial to classical liberals, this statute would pass constitutional muster with flying colors. It should have done so here. Rational basis still imposes some limitations: if Oklahoma had decided to prevent eighteen-to-twenty-year-old women from drinking 3.2 percent beer while allowing men at that age bracket to do so, then by all means it should have been struck down. But *Craig v. Boren* is a country mile from that reversed outcome. The inversion is thus complete in that the modern liberal tradition now strikes down laws that easily pass muster under a classical liberal account of the police power.

Statutory Rape

The strong effort of the Brennan wing of the Supreme Court did eventually run into resistance. In *Michael M. v. Superior Court*,[34] a bare majority of the Supreme Court finessed the heightened scrutiny standard in *Craig* to uphold the traditional application of statutory rape statutes only to males when both parties were under the age of consent. In this context, the sensible approach to the Equal Protection Clause is to treat like cases alike. But in sexual matters, the entire pattern of social interaction has a deep asymmetry whereby it is more costly, if only from the risk of pregnancy, for an underaged female to engage in sexual intercourse than it is for an underaged male. No classical liberal theory could ignore these deeply-entrenched differences in determining an acceptable legal code. One can argue whether the deepest fears relate to unwanted pregnancy and the complications of an unwanted abortion or from social, or even the possible, but unproved physical pressures that boys and young men can impose on underaged females. But the exact balance does not matter. It is very difficult to identify any dislocation in the political process that results from the continued use of widespread historical norms and practices, which legislatures can modify if they so choose.

Many have praised Edmund Burke for his view that gradual changes are preferable to sharp discontinuities in various areas of life.[35] His views have real punch in this context, especially as a constitutional matter. But as a legislator, I would think long and hard before removing the protections for young girls or imposing like sanctions on older women with respect to younger men, who are not likely to have the same adverse psychological response to sexual relations. Sexual dimorphisms—i.e., systematic differences between the sexes on matters of either structure or behavior—are most decisive on matters related to sex and reproduction. It seems foolish to mandate that legislatures ignore basic facts that ordinary people understand about the asymmetrical roles of males and females. The female imperative is to be selective in her choice of mates, given her investment in producing a single offspring at a time. On the other hand, males have less incentive to be selective, given their ability to father many offspring at the same time. So long as human behaviors are influenced by these biological dynamics, the traditional laws are not just a matter of "outmoded sexual stereotypes,"[36] but profound behavioral adaptations to the requirements of natural selection. Durability is a good test of social soundness that should be disregarded only with caution. There are profound sexual differences that attentive and responsible parents address in raising their children, and these easily could be reflected in law. These differences could lead many sensible persons to retain the current differential set of sanctions for statutory rape. Once again, on the matter of criminal regulation, a classical liberal approach is more flexible, and less dogmatic, than the modern liberal alternative.

Military Operations

These concerns with custom, continuity, and the soundness of the political process apply with equal force to military matters where the issue refers not to the organization of the state criminal code, but to the management and operation of federal and state military operations. As a general matter, neither judges nor legislatures are skilled in organizing and running armies. Legislative interference in military operations, however, is virtually impossible to stop. But the strongest possible presumption should be set against judicial interference in military affairs. Indeed that strong presumption especially should be in effect to guard against the Court using equal protection arguments to address the deployment or organization of military forces. Very few, if any, would want to suggest that women have no place in modern military services. Women fill, for example, vital positions in the Israeli army, taking key noncombat roles providing intelligence, legal, and supply services. That specialization increases the overall power of the military for a nation that does not have the luxury of making logistical sacrifices in support of the abstract ideal of gender parity.

The same logic surely applies within the American military force, albeit with less urgency. In battle, our enemies and our friends worry about the size and strength of our battalions, not the internal sex-specific distributional requirements we impose on ourselves. It was for that reason that race segregation within the military made so little sense: the army works better with cohesive units. Thus, Harry Truman ended the practice of racial segregation in 1948 by executive order, not litigation, when reform was long overdue.[37] But sex discrimination is another issue altogether. The common wisdom of all militaries, our own included, builds in that distinction on the ground floor. Even the champions of women in the military never demand strict parity. Their claim is always for greater participation, which in particular cases may be fully justified. But an equal protection argument is simply unable to calibrate the distinctions that should and should not be drawn between men and women in the service. It is for this reason that highly dubious policies like "Don't ask, don't tell"[38] for gay and lesbian soldiers should not have been undone by constitutional decree, no matter how explicit and inexcusable the policy was. It is far better to get rid of it by nonconstitutional means, which happened in September, 2011.[39] Indeed, even here it is clear that the legislative change of policy, even if sorely overdue, required some careful and thoughtful management to ensure a successful transition. Judicial intervention from on high was the last thing needed.

It is also necessary to consider other activities that relate indirectly to the organization of military operations. Here the same line has held, but uneasily. In *Rostker v. Goldberg*,[40] a judicial majority upheld the Military Selective Service Act[41] insofar as it authorized the president to establish a draft registration system for males but not females. Unfortunately, both the majority and the minority started from the wrong premise by assuming that a "heightened level" of scrutiny should be brought to the uniform practice of military recruitment. But why? Everyone concedes that the military does not have to be sex-blind in the persons whom it drafts. Why then must the military waste resources on activities with a low rate of return in order to engage in a draft registration system that yields a high rate of return? There seems to be little or no reason to abandon the draft insofar as it helps with the deployment of men, or to add in a draft that is little more than a nuisance for the deployment of women. A high level of scrutiny is, I believe, inappropriate for cases in which the government is trying to operate an essential service that cannot be delegated to private industry.

That general approach should transfer to the operation of state academies, one of whose missions is to train individuals for military service. Yet when put to the test, Justice Ginsburg in *United States v. Virginia*[42] again demanded an "exceedingly persuasive justification"[43] for allowing the state to continue to operate the Virginia Military Institute as a single-sex facility, as it had done since its founding in 1839. Tradition did not matter; nor was any deference given to the decisions of democratic institutions; nor did Justice Ginsburg point to any breakdown in the political process in the state of Virginia, all of whose other institutions were coed. As a political and business judgment, Virginia could have decided that the gains from admitting a few female students into its military academy did not justify the disruption of its own established practices. But in this complex administrative area, judicial deference was nowhere in evidence. Instead, armed with the heightened scrutiny test derived from such decisions as *Mississippi University for Women*,[44] a far more straightforward equal protection challenge, Justice Ginsburg easily mowed down the (true) assertion that VMI's "adversative method"[45] worked best in an all-male environment. In seeking to evaluate this collective institution, Ginsburg lapsed back into an individualistic model for collective decision-making that should shame even the most ardent libertarian. In her view, the only fact of relevance was that admission may have been "desirable to some women,"[46] no matter how few. But in a social calculus, any gains to a small fraction of individuals, regardless of sex, must be offset by the losses to other individuals, including men whose education may be less effective in a coed environment, especially one organized under judicial oversight.

With her partial social calculus in play, it was easy to order that some women be admitted to the school. But at this point, the equal protection claim dissolves. Heightened scrutiny does not require 50 percent female admissions, nor does it determine how women shall be taught or integrated with the rest of the force. It would be impossible, for example, to require all women to meet the traditional physical standards required of men in training or on maneuvers. Nor can they all be required to use the same caliber of firearms with equal effectiveness. If those issues are left untouched, then why break down the entry barrier? Usually decrees of specific performance are limited to cases like the transfer of the ownership of land where the court need not engage in continuous supervision of activities. But in these intense environments, judicial oversight is not possible on such operational details. One virtue of legislation in contexts of this sort is that it sets the framework for making the inelegant compromises necessary to make complex interventions succeed. If United States service academies can make coed education work, so might VMI. Yet on the other hand, a single all-male institution increases the systemic level of diversity in the United States and affords a measuring rod against which the performance of the coed academies could be benchmarked. Forced homogeneity is no social virtue.

In sum, it is critical to stress just how far the new equal protection jurisprudence of sex discrimination in the public sphere deviates from sound classical liberal principles. But there is no other conclusion once we recall that across all categories and all systems, the administration in corporate, charitable, and religious organizations is tested by some variation of the business judgment rule that leaves scope for the good faith decisions of those in charge. We do not have here, as in key cases dealing with race, a total breakdown in political institutions that cries out for judicial remediation. Rather, we have a system in which the unwillingness of the justices to understand the uses and limits of their powers pays disrespect to democratic values in those fields where they should be the highest. The Court's current jurisprudence is truly a regrettable reversal of sound principles. The willingness of the justices to curb massive forms of economic favoritism and abuse that legislatures impose on private individuals is negligible. Yet their willingness to take over the operation of public institutions is subject to few binding limitations. It is all backwards under any sound classical liberal theory of governance.

PART FOUR

CONCLUSION

Conclusion

The Classical Liberal Alternative

THE CENTRAL MISSION of *The Classical Liberal Constitution* is to go against the grain of modern Supreme Court jurisprudence and much of the legal scholarship that has grown up around that body of work. The motivation for this argument should be apparent from the major disarray that infects every area of modern American life: steady decline in the average standard of living; constant battles over debt limits and fiscal cliffs; uncertainty over key elements of the tax structure; massive overregulation of the most productive sources in society (health care and financial services); government-inspired brinksmanship in labor negotiations; and runaway redistribution programs that undercut the economic production that makes these programs viable. All of these major programs could not have happened under the original constitutional structure, faithfully interpreted in light of changed circumstances. The confluence of these events cannot be dismissed as the result of random noise or simple mistakes. Rather, they are the ultimate consequence of the profound progressive break with the classical liberal tradition that was the guiding genius in the drafting and interpretation of the Constitution.

These errors originate with *both* traditions that dominate modern American constitutional law—one conservative and the other progressive. The purpose of this book has been to demonstrate that in most major areas of modern constitutional law, the classical liberal approach offers a coherent third alternative that avoids the pitfalls of these two worldviews, while incorporating the best of each. The need for this third approach should be evident from the deep conceptual flaws of both modern approaches. I shall begin with a discussion of conservative originalism, and then move on to modern progressivism.

Conservative Originalism

The Positive Case

The conservative side begins with a strong attachment to constitutional originalism that stresses the importance of keeping true to the original public meaning of key constitutional texts. It is easy to identify the strong and sensible motivation behind this general view. What judges say is of great significance, especially in a system that operates under an invariant rule of judicial supremacy. Without demonstrated fidelity to constitutional text, nothing whatsoever in the American constitutional system prevents insulated and unelected justices from invoking the "living constitution" to impose their personal, usually politically liberal, preferences on the United States in ways that short-circuit the mechanisms of democratic accountability that lie at the heart of our system of government. This criticism is dead on with respect to much of modern progressive thought both on and off the Supreme Court. For example, reading the Cruel and Unusual Punishment Clause to impose a uniform code of criminal sentencing on the states and federal government for the most serious offenses has exactly that feel.[1] That same form of judicial adventurism can also alter the fundamental power relationships between the national and state governments, as through the inexorable expansion of the commerce power to cover all productive activities, no matter how local. Faithful adherence to the "original public meaning" of a document preserves legitimacy by removing the justices from political temptation.

The initial difficulty with this broad account starts from the simple proposition that conservative originalists cannot remain faithful to the twin commitments of fidelity to text on the one hand and judicial restraint on the other. It is therefore a hopeful sign that on many key issues, including federalism, campaign finance regulation, and takings for public use, conservative originalists have begun to move away from the mantra of judicial restraint. That move is strictly necessary because the Constitution is written in broad bold strokes, which at some points confer vast powers on government and at others impose major limitations on their exercise. That general proposition applies with equal force to the key features of both constitutional structure and the articulation of individual rights. The last thing therefore that the Constitution represents is a full-throated endorsement of popular democracy. No faithful construction of the Constitution should water down its various protections in order to achieve that result under the dubious, all-purpose banner of judicial restraint. The true test is to find the proper balance between legislative choice and constitutional constraint.

That Manichean approach to law is not the sign of intellectual confusion, but of an acute awareness that government has to be strong enough to discharge the limited tasks assigned to it, but not so strong as to wipe out the individual rights of the people whom it has been entrusted to protect. It is often too easy today to forget that the central function of government is to deal with what the ancients called "self-preservation," or the right to be free from both the use and threat of force. It is for that reason that the original defenders of the social contract started with the fundamental proposition that society depends upon the mutual renunciation of force, which cannot be achieved in any stable way by a complex web of bilateral or multilateral agreements.

The Two Sides of Judicial Restraint

From this simple observation, it becomes clear that the very origins of government do not lie in individual consent, but in that form of constructive consent that imposes on all individuals that master bargain, which government then must enforce by creating public institutions with sufficient resources and authority to enforce that bargain. The consistent application of a nontextual norm of judicial restraint allows the key political actors in that system too much discretion for the system to operate at maximum efficiency. On the structural side, the willingness not to enforce the explicit limitations on the powers to tax and spend, or on federal power dealing with commerce, has led to an intolerable expansion of government power. By the same token, ingenious efforts to limit the guarantees of private property and economic liberties have compounded that difficulty at both the state and federal levels.

Here then is the nub of the organizational difficulty. The government that must be strong enough to control violence should not be made so strong that its powers are directed to preserve and protect a wide range of private monopolies in such key markets as agriculture, labor, and real property. The advocates of judicial restraint should not acquiesce by twisting the words "commerce among the several states" to permeate all local activities ranging from local commerce to agriculture, manufacture, and mining. The expansion of federal regulation vastly increases the risk of monopoly institutions with no countervailing benefit in maintaining social order or the enforcement of voluntary transactions. By the same token, the constant effort to water down the meaning of private property so that it covers, at most, the exclusive right of possession (and with rent control, no less) create undue state power over rights of use and disposition that turn sensible zoning laws into instruments of local monopoly control. Fidelity to text should block both these moves that have flourished under the misguided banner of judicial restraint.

All of this is not to say that there is no place for judicial restraint. Indeed, in my view, the critical distinction is that which derives from corporate law, which allows the directors and officers of a corporation broad discretion in the operation of their business under the business judgment rule, which is suspended only when there is some clear conflict of interest between these individuals and the shareholders that justifies some higher level of scrutiny. At that point, a higher level of scrutiny is needed to see whether the corporation has dealt fairly with the parties who trade with it and whether those parties have received fair value for their contribution to the exchange.[2] Likewise, when the government engages in taking or regulation, it should be subject to that "fair value" limitation which embodies a high level of scrutiny insisting that the state show a strong justification for its action or otherwise supply just compensation for what it has taken. But when the government is engaged in running its many enterprises, it must have at least some of the discretion that is afforded the directors and officers of corporations, a position that is reflected in the "discretionary function" exception that is so central to the Federal Torts Claims Act.[3] It is this line between takings by way of occupation or regulation and everyday management operations—not any distinction between preferred freedoms and ordinary rights—that should drive the analysis. On this view, therefore, the conservative hostility to affirmative action in public schools and universities, which translates into a strict scrutiny test, is a mistake[4]—just as the liberal insistence that sex differences do not matter in the organization of military academies gives rise to the opposite answer.[5] This lower level of scrutiny along the lines of the business judgment rule is not entirely toothless and would not allow overt and invidious discrimination. Indeed, the necessity of lowering scrutiny levels is a good reason to prefer the devolution of government management responsibilities onto private parties, so that vouchers and charter schools become preferable to public schools in the K-12 space, and private universities become preferable to state ones. But once these issues are locked into the public sphere, the strict scrutiny that should be applied to taxation and regulation can no longer be used to decide cases where business judgment determinations are the very actions in which government officials are required to engage.

Implied Terms: Anticircumvention and the Police Power

The difficulties with conservative originalism do not rest on its overreliance on the institutional norm of judicial restraint in some cases and the aggressive assertion of judicial power in others. These institutional errors stem in large measure from the questionable methods of interpretation that conservative originalists too often bring to difficult texts. The motivation to avoid arbitrary exercises of judicial power does not justify its cramped mode of interpretation which, ironically, is not faithful to the dominant interpretive norms of the Founding period. The simple point here is that in no legal system at any time could the question of construction be reduced to a search for original public meaning of terms that are found in the constitutional text. To be sure, finding that meaning is an important part of the overall inquiry, where the insistence on public meaning short-circuits the appeals to subjective understandings of constitutional text by individual judges. The subjective theory of interpretation is widely regarded as inappropriate for dealing with ordinary contract questions, because it provides no answer to the challenge of what should be done when two sets of intention are at variance with each other. The situation does not become any easier on that score when the relevant parties are not only the drafters of the original constitutional texts, but members of the state conventions (that ratified the original Constitution) and the state legislatures that have approved the various amendments.

But solving one problem, even imperfectly, is not to solve them all. As indicated earlier, three additional problems have to be addressed to get a fuller understanding. The first one deals with the problem of circumvention of particular text by clever legislative strategies. This problem arises constantly in ordinary litigation. If the law prohibits an individual from forcing poison down the throat of another person, it cannot be that the killer can conceal the poison in a drink he sets before his victim. It will not do to say that the victim was the author of his own doom because he drank the poison. So too that if there is a prohibition on the taxation of exports, it cannot be permissible to tax the exporter based on the value of the goods moved through interstate commerce. This principle is not imposed solely as a matter of ordinary linguistic interpretation. It is imposed because of the full knowledge that persons who are constrained by law will do what they can to evade its operation. Unless countermeasures are taken to prevent the adoption of these close substitutes, the entire scheme will fall to pieces. It is for that reason that freedom of speech covers not just speech, but writing and all other forms of expression. It is for that reason that the government that cannot ban trade or speech also cannot subject it to special taxation. The scope of the guarantee makes sense only if it applies indifferently to all forms of communications.

The second gap in the originalist view is that it offers no basis for the implication of additional constitutional terms that are dependent on either government structure or the nature of individual rights. The Constitution does not once mention sovereign immunity, yet the maintenance of the federal/state system depends in large measure on the view that the adoption of a federalist system did not strip the states of their previous immunities. Similarly, the entire edifice of the police power does not have a single word of textual support, yet it must be read into the Constitution in order to place its individual guarantees into perspective. Here again the analysis starts with analogous provisions of private law. "Thou shalt not kill" is one of the fundamental propositions of civilized rights. But unless one allows an exception in cases of self-defense—if need be through interpretation—the rule will be hopelessly overbroad. Similarly, it cannot be that the government must pay compensation for property taken when it disarms a violent criminal.

Yet once even a single justification is allowed to qualify the constitutional text, it is off to the races. Self-defense is not the only way to defeat or undermine a charge of murder; provocation has to be considered. Nor is self-defense absolute; the question of retreat and excessive or disproportionate force must be considered as well. The key lesson on interpretation is that a bare text raises more questions than it answers, which makes it imperative to isolate the general theory that animates the text—usually the protection of personal autonomy, liberty, and property—and then construct the defenses that are consistent with that worldview. Admitting self-defense into the system does not allow A to kill B because of the color of his tie—or his skin. It is only through the use of a general theory that these questions can be answered, and that theory requires an understanding of how the private law deals with ordinary disputes as one essential guide to figuring out what the government can do as of right, and what it may do only if it provides just compensation.

The Prescriptive Constitution

Finally, there is the nasty question of prescriptive transformation of the Constitution by long usage. This notion also depends on the parallel uses of prescription in the law of easements, whereby long usage of a right of way translates what began as a trespass into a vested right. The doctrine always has pitfalls along the way, but in the end, no system of interpretation can do without this notion. An erroneous element is built into the system at an early stage. Other institutions are built up around it. Slowly it becomes both difficult and dangerous to disentangle them. In the face of these transformations, a slavish emphasis on original public meaning tends to reduce the case of prescriptive adjustments to zero.

More specifically, the case in favor of judicial supremacy is weak even if it is clear that the legislature and the executive cannot force the federal courts to hear issues that are not within their original constitutional mandate. Similarly, the ability of the Supreme Court to review state law judgments that call into question provisions of the United States Constitution may be essential to keep the union intact. The original Constitution was too wary of judicial power to allow the first and too wary of federal power to allow the second. Quite simply, the designers of the original system were bold experimentalists who worked from past historical precedents that did not give a good indication of the strains that would emerge once the federal system was up and running. But unless we have some doctrine of provision, the devout originalist has to abandon both *Marbury v. Madison*[6] and *Martin v. Hunter's Lessee*,[7] notwithstanding the essential role that they play in organizing our collective life. Similarly, the entire edifice of the dormant Commerce Clause is a judicial invention that allows courts to work in a constructive fashion to create a national common market free of obstructive state interference, a risk that would have rated low at the time of the Founding. Yet no one, I hope, would urge that it be dismantled on the ground that only the Commerce Clause properly authorizes actions by Congress without imposing any limitations on the power of the states.

The use of the prescriptive constitution is necessarily tricky because the long passage of judicial decisions is not a sufficient condition for their continued adoption. The Court was right to overrule *Plessy v. Ferguson*[8] and its separate but equal doctrine in *Brown v. Board of Education*.[9] And in my view one should do everything possible to curb or to at least cut back the affirmative scope of the federal government under the Commerce Clause on the ground that the new powers are chiefly used to create national cartels through state power that are also antithetical to the basic provisions of classical liberal theory. It is quite impossible to ignore the normative questions implicit in any challenge to a long-standing rule. And it is equally critical to make those judgments within the one normative theory that drives the original constitutional structure, namely the protection of private property and economic liberties within a framework of limited government. One risk of modern originalism is that it becomes so text-bound that it ignores the relationships between text, structure, and basic normative theory.

Modern Progressivism

Linguistic Ambiguity and Judicial Deference

The list of serious shortfalls of conservative originalism does not, however, legitimate the powerful strands of progressive thought that have dominated much of American constitutional law since the New Deal. The progressives have launched many misguided attacks on originalism to show how difficult it is to find shared meanings in ordinary texts or to anticipate the many changes in technology and political theory since the Founding period. In making ambiguity the interpretive norm, they do serious danger to the rule of law, which can only function if words are clear enough so that they can receive the same meaning by the authors of the text and the multiple and diverse parties who are bound by it. Ambiguity in some cases is to be expected, but usually only in complicated cases with mixed motives and uncertain extent. It is always a dangerous move to find that certain directives are so uncertain that it is necessary to defer to legislative and administrative bodies for their elaboration. A substantial degree of deference is appropriate where the government is running a business. But far less is required when the government takes it upon itself to tell other people how to run their own businesses.

Too often progressives show an uncritical affection for administrative expertise and impartiality in cases where both are hard to come by. They are clearly wrong on both accounts. One reason why some progressives will say that "Originalism is Bunk," to use the infelicitous title of Mitchell Berman's article,[10] is that for all its weakness as a general theory, originalism reaches powerful conclusions that are at war with the progressive vision of strong government at every level coupled with sharp limitations on private property and economic liberties.

In some instances, the effort is made to ease that stark conflict by appealing to a notion of "Living Originalism," made popular by Jack Balkin,[11] that seeks to subvert the doctrine while paying homage to it. To be sure, no one quarrels with any constitutional claim that the Commerce Clause allows the regulation of the telegraph, the telephone, the railroad, the automobile, and the airplane, even though none were in existence at the time the Constitution was ratified. But there is no sleight of hand in that conclusion. Defining the scope of the power as "Commerce . . . among the several States"[12] does not limit the federal power to the forms of interstate commerce in use at the time of the Founding.

But by the same token, however, these changes in technology, large or small, should not be allowed to mask a fundamental shift in constitutional theory when two additional moves are made. The first says that local commerce is necessarily entwined with interstate commerce, without explaining why it is not possible to distinguish between the local subways that lead to the Port Authority Terminal on Eighth Avenue and Forty-Second Street and the interstate buses that depart hourly from it to distant points. If interstate commerce reaches new technologies that cross state lines, it also excludes those new technologies that stay within state lines. Second, there is nothing about the transformation of technology that makes manufacturing, mining, or agriculture part of interstate commerce solely because they rely on inputs that could come from out of state or ship finished products to buyers who exist out of state. The relationship of manufacture to trade is the same now as it always has been.

Monopoly versus Competition

Nor is this conclusion upset by any pragmatic considerations that arise from any real or supposed increase in the value of interstate trade. In this regard, the removal of barriers to trade increases the efficiency of markets by allowing competition in places where it was once difficult or impossible to achieve. The real driver of the doctrinal transformation stems not from the fact of that increased competition, but from the fear of that competition. The progressive movement can find many ways to gild the lily, by pointing to higher purposes—certainly higher than any lowly consideration of economic efficiency—to justify its multiple interferences with market behavior. But it is all window dressing for the single constant that marks all of its legislative innovations at the federal and state levels: the unspoken but persistent preference for government monopolies over private competition. It does not matter whether one looks to the various Agricultural Adjustment Acts or to the manifold restrictions on labor markets running through the 1914 Clayton Act, the 1926 Railway Labor Act, the 1935 National Labor Relations Act, and the 1938 Fair Labor Standards Act.[13] They are all designed to restrict free entry and to empower certain preferred groups to gain monopoly profits in their relative market niches. State laws, such as endless zoning and occupational restrictions, tend to move strongly in the same direction.

Of course there are exceptions to this rule in some small fraction of cases. But the unwillingness to require the state to justify its limitations makes it impossible to challenge the manifold restrictions that prefer less output to more, so long as the preferred clientele gets a larger share of that smaller pie. Done once, it produces some lucky winners. Done repeatedly, it produces only losers, and a general decline in levels of income and wealth on a nationwide scale.

The Rise of Rational Basis

It takes a certain degree of intellectual ingenuity to convert the Constitution into a doctrine that tolerates all these monopoly interventions. But through two words—rational basis—the progressives have introduced a battering ram that too many conservative judges are prepared to use as well. The United States has the "Power To lay and collect Taxes, Duties, Imposts and Excises, to pay the Debts and provide for the common Defence and general Welfare of the United States."[14] The purposes stated are meant to impose limitations on what Congress may do. There are, for example, all sorts of close cases on what counts as "general Welfare of the United States." But the right answer to hard questions will be beyond reach if the entire clause is enveloped in an interpretive gauze that transforms the three specific heads of legitimate purposes into an open-ended list simply because it is just too hard to police these categories. Nor does the Takings Clause provide that a taking for "public use"[15] means a taking for any "conceivable public purpose"[16] that tickles the fancy of a state legislature or administrative body.

Private Law and Political Faction

One reason for this evisceration, moreover, is the conscious departures of progressive justices from the private law notions that are the essential building blocks of any constitutional order. In misunderstanding or mocking these foundations, they are all too often joined by conservative justices, who also suffer from an overexposure to public law and an attention deficit with respect to private law. Here, the basic point is that the elaborate set of private law institutions that create multiple interests in land is a highly efficient device that leads to its effective articulation. The willingness of the system to encourage voluntary transfer and the creation of divided interests in real property is accompanied by a set of institutions—a writing requirement under the Statute of Frauds and a recordation system—that maximize the gains from trade by facilitating voluntary transactions. The well-defined rights created by this system reduce the risk of their expropriation by clever government action. But once the public law conceptions of property are allowed to displace these norms, the door is opened wide to all sorts of factional intrigue as political actors find it easier to block productive use and voluntary exchange by a set of insufferable land use regulations whose cumulative impact is to shrink the size of these resources. The exact strategies hardly matter. What matters is that a detailed knowledge of private transactions is no part of public law before the United States Supreme Court.

The issues involved do not only deal with property cases, but with all sorts of institutional arrangements. The doctrine of standing is in such disarray today, because the judges who articulate it have from the beginning had no solid understanding of the role of the principles of equitable jurisdiction that were consciously built into the definition of judicial power under Article III.[17] Thus all structural issues are stripped

from the Supreme Court because the justices insist on some particularized injuries that are the hallmark of actions at law and the antithesis of
those numerous equitable devices that are used to allow for the effective
aggregation of individual claims. Nor does it help if the original errors
on standing are compounded by the misuse of notions of *damnum absque
iniuria* (harm without legal injury) that also derive from the private law,
where they insulate ordinary competition from judicial sanction. Finally,
no court could hope to correctly interpret the law of takings by equating
private ownership with the right of exclusive possession, and by ignoring every doctrinal development dealing with divided interests in land
and with easements and servitudes over the rights of other parcels. Yet
all of these errors are repeated time after time in cases dealing with the
protection of air rights, mineral rights, easements, and covenants, which
all too often are articulated in an unrecognizable form of dealing with
constitutional issues.

From Limited Government to Positive Rights

The last of the major progressive sins is the constant willingness to let
the legislature create an endless stream of positive rights as part of the
modern social democratic state. The original notion of negative rights
cannot cover the entire waterfront, but it does set the stage for a proper
appreciation of the role of government. The protections against force
and fraud create norms that function well among all persons. Their protection does not depend on any particular level of social wealth, and
it applies to all persons equally. The rights work in small and in large
societies. Once the issue turns to Social Security, Medicare, Medicaid,
unemployment benefits, food stamps, and other programs, the rights
become harder to define in rational and sustainable ways. The levels of
payment are highly contingent on wealth, and the principles that might
work in smaller societies cannot work in larger ones. Confining these
tasks to the state level places an effective brake on their size because
of the threat of exit. Placing them at the federal level guarantees their
expansion to higher levels.

It is therefore nothing short of amazing how willing progressive
judges and scholars are to read positive rights into a Constitution
drafted with the opposite ends in mind. The Privileges and Immunities Clause no longer is intended to guarantee rights of trade and
occupational liberties across state boundaries. Justices instead become

concerned with the extension of welfare benefits. The Equal Protection Clause is no longer focused on ensuring that the criminal justice system is fair for both future victims and future offenders. It now becomes the all-purpose provision to attack traditional forms of classification as invidious discrimination. It has even been argued that the Thirteenth Amendment, whose first section reads, "Neither slavery nor involuntary servitude, except as a punishment for crime whereof the party shall have been duly convicted, shall exist within the United States, or any place subject to their jurisdiction,"[18] should be interpreted as a platform for positive rights on the ground that those who do not have certain minimum levels of wealth are in a condition of involuntary servitude, which now "exists" for millions of people.[19] To be sure, the progressive movement has not been able to find positive rights in the Constitution. But it has been able to remove any and all constitutional barriers to their legislative creation, which results in a huge expansion of the size of government. In a word, the progressive synthesis is unsustainable: there are too many positive rights on a productive base whose size is shrunk by progressive legislation.

To the Future

It should be clear then that both the progressives and conservatives work on models that are too divorced from constitutional text, constitutional theory, and private law. The consequences of these repeated errors are not just judicial curiosities. These epic mistakes in constitutional and political judgment have long-term adverse effects on the power of a nation to regenerate and recreate itself. So long as conservative justices cloak themselves in the language of judicial restraint on structural and economic issues, they will not address the legislative and administrative excesses at both the federal and state levels. So long as progressives continue to embrace policies that first tolerate and then encourage the massive expansion of transfer payments off an ever-decreasing productive base, they will also reinforce the economic and political risks.

The political forces in favor of the current situation are living proof of the Madisonian fear of factions. Its intellectual origins are best summarized in words that have heroic significance to modern progressives in the pithy but ill-chosen words of Oliver Wendell Holmes in his powerful but misguided dissent in *Lochner v. New York:*

> The Fourteenth Amendment does not enact Mr. Herbert Spencer's Social Statics. . . . [A] Constitution is not intended to embody a particular economic theory, whether of paternalism and the organic relation of the citizen to the state or of *laissez faire*.[20]

Holmes is partly correct to insist that the Constitution does not follow Mr. Herbert Spencer's Social Statics. But in its crucial provisions that have survived to the present day, the Constitution was intended to embody the theory of classical liberal thought. Holmes therefore commits a constitutional blunder of epic proportions when he claims that "a" constitution is not intended to embody a particular economic theory. No constitution could hope to survive if not driven by some general guiding theory. One can look to the length and breadth of the doctrine and find not a single syllable that is conducive to thinking that our Constitution (which is not just "a" constitution) embodies paternalism and the organic relation of the citizen to the state.

Whether our Constitution embraces a theory of laissez-faire depends on how that doctrine is defined. If it is meant to take, as Holmes seems to address, the extreme libertarian position that rules out taxation, eminent domain, and the provision of public goods, then ours surely is not a laissez-faire constitution. But that caricature gives far too much running room to the critics of laissez-faire. In a historical account of the doctrine, the late Jacob Viner offered this more astute version of laissez-faire:

> I will carefully avoid using the term laissez faire to mean what only unscrupulous or ignorant opponents of it and never its exponents make it mean, namely, philosophical anarchism, or opposition to any governmental power or activity whatsoever. I will in general use the term to mean what the pioneer systematic exponents of it, the Physiocrats and Adam Smith, argued for, namely, the limitation of governmental activity to the enforcement of peace and of "justice" in the restricted sense of "commutative justice," to the defense against foreign enemies, and to public works regarded as essential and as impossible or highly improbable of establishment by private enterprise or, for special reasons, unsuitable to be left to private operation.[21]

Viner goes on to note that both Smith and the Physiocrats were prepared to extend the role of government somewhat beyond these limits, but the reference to "commutative" justice was meant to exclude wholesale programs of income redistribution through government action, actions that Viner defended, at least on the far smaller scale of 1960.[22] But otherwise, Viner's account of laissez-faire squares with the classical liberal position defended throughout this book. He makes it crystal clear that the defenders of laissez-faire, both before and after Adam Smith, harbored a deep distrust of all forms of monopoly behavior, a view that was shared by the old guard justices before the progressive revolution took hold.

To be sure, this account does not discuss separation of powers, federalism, or the pervasive role of the doctrine of unconstitutional conditions. But Viner and his ilk were not lawyers charged with putting the system into play. They were general theorists who sought to outline its basic functions. But on that level their positions are far more coherent than the received dogmas of modern American constitutional law. They well understood that classical liberal theory stood or fell as an intellectual whole. Toward that end, Viner quotes an 1843 passage from the *Edinburgh Review* which is prescient in its rejection of the modern distinction between preferred freedoms and ordinary rights: "Be assured that freedom of trade, freedom of thought, freedom of speech, and freedom of action, are but modifications of one great fundamental truth, and that all must be maintained or all risked; they stand and fall together."[23] This entire sweep of intellectual history is rejected in Holmes's famous quip. We are all the losers of Holmes's fundamental misunderstanding of the classical liberal constitution. We will all be losers if we continue to think that progressive and conservative thought are the only available choices. The blunt truth is that a strong embrace of the classical liberal constitution offers the only sure path to rejuvenation of America's constitutional and political institutions.

Notes

Introduction

1. Thomas Paine, *Common Sense* (1776). The words appear at the outset of the second full paragraph of this work, available online at http://www.early-america.com/earlyamerica/milestones/commonsense/text.html.
2. Michael W. McConnell, "Active Liberty: A Progressive Alternative to Textualism and Originalism?," 119 *Harv. L. Rev.* 2387, 2391 (2006) (reviewing Stephen Breyer, *Active Liberty: Interpreting Our Democratic Constitution* (2005)).
3. Cass R. Sunstein, "Incompletely Theorized Agreements," 108 *Harv. L. Rev.* 1733 (1995).
4. John Locke, *The Second Treatise of Government* (C. B. Macpherson ed., 1980) (1690).
5. See, e.g., James M. Landis, *The Administrative Process* 8 (1938).
6. See Walter Berns, *Freedom, Virtue, and the First Amendment* (1957). One lead is here: http://www.citizenship-aei.org/2011/09/event-re-cap-walter-berns-and-the-constitution.
7. Pub. L. No. 79-404, 60 Stat. 237 (1946) (codified as amended at 5 U.S.C. §§ 551–559, 701–706 (2006)).
8. For a modern version, see Peter L. Strauss, "Formal and Functional Approaches to Separation-of-Powers Questions—A Foolish Consistency," 72 *Cornell L. Rev.* 488 (1987).
9. For the leading early exposition of these views, see James Bradley Thayer, "The Origin and Scope of the American Doctrine of Constitutional Law," 7 *Harv. L. Rev.* 129 (1893).
10. U.S. Const. art. I, § 2, cl. 3: "Representatives and direct Taxes shall be apportioned among the several States which may be included within this Union, according to their respective Numbers, which shall be determined by adding to the whole Number of free Persons, including those found to Service for a Term of Years and excluding Indians not taxed, three fifths of all other Persons."
11. Id. art. IV, § 2, cl. 3: "No person held to service or labour in one state, under the laws thereof, escaping into another, shall, in consequence of any law or

regulation therein, be discharged from such service or labour, but shall be delivered up on claim of the party to whom such service or labour may be due."

12. Lon L. Fuller, *The Morality of Law* (1964).

13. See *United States v. Lopez*, 514 U.S. 549 (1995), subject now to the strictures in *Nat'l Fed'n of Indep. Bus. v. Sebelius*, 132 S. Ct. 603 (2012), with sharply divided views on the power of Congress to regulate economic "inactivity," discussed *infra* Chapter 12 ("Constitutional Pushback: 1995 to Present, From *Lopez* to *NFIB*"). For Justice Thomas's originalist position, see United States v. Lopez, 514 U.S. 549, 584 (1995) (Thomas, J. concurring) (urging the Court to be "more faithful to the original understanding of that Clause."): *United States v. Morrison*, 529 U.S. 598, 627 (2000) (Thomas, J. concurring) (same).

14. See Mark Tushnet, *Taking the Constitution Away from the Courts* 181 (1999).

15. Larry D. Kramer, *The People Themselves: Popular Constitutionalism and Judicial Review* (2004).

16. Stephen Breyer, *Active Liberty: Interpreting Our Democratic Constitution* (2005).

17. See Cass R. Sunstein, *One Case at a Time* (1999); Cass R. Sunstein, "Burkean Minimalism," 105 *Mich. L. Rev.* 353 (2006). For his latest views on the question, see Cass R. Sunstein, *Beyond Judicial Minimalism* (2008), available at http://papers.ssrn.com/sol3/papers.cfm?abstract_id=1274200.

18. James B. Thayer, "The Origin and Scope of the American Doctrine of Constitutional Law," 7 *Harv. L. Rev.* 129, 144 (1893).

19. Robert H. Bork, *The Tempting of America: The Political Seduction of the Law* (1990).

20. U.S. Const. art. I, § 1.

21. *New York Central R.R. v. Winfeld*, 244 U.S. 147, 169 (1917) (Brandeis, J., dissenting) ("The contention that Congress has, by legislating on one branch of a subject relative to interstate commerce, pre-empted the whole field, has been made often in this court."). Note the sentence itself recognizes that the issue itself had long predated the invocation of the term, which it had. See, e.g., Stephen Gardbaum, "The Breadth vs. the Depth of Congress's Commerce Power: The Curious History of Preemption during the *Lochner* Era," in *Federal Preemption: States' Powers, National Interests* 48 (Richard A. Epstein & Michael S. Greve eds., 2007).

22. U.S. Const. art. VI, cl. 2.

23. For an exhaustive account of the complexities of the new federalism, see Michael S. Greve, *The Upside Down Constitution* (2012).

24. On which see Daniel A. Farber, *Retained by the People* (2007).

25. *Lochner v. New York*, 198 U.S. 45, 53 (1905).

1. The Classical Liberal Synthesis

1. See *Palko v. Connecticut*, 302 U.S. 319, 325 (1937).

2. See U.S. Const. art. I, § 8, cl. 15–16; id. art. II, § 2, cl. 1.

3. Id. art. I, § 10, cl. 3.

4. Id. art. IV, § 2, cl. 3 (the Fugitive Slave Clause).

5. President Gerald Ford, Address to a Joint Session of Congress (Aug. 12, 1974), available at http://www.fordlibrarymuseum.gov/grf/quotes.asp.

6. Mass. Const. art. I (annulled by Amendments, art. VCI).

7. See Jonathan Haidt, et al., "Group Report: What Is the Role of Heuristics in Making Law?" in *Heuristics and the Law* 141 (Gerd Gigerenzer & Christoph Engel eds., 2006). For a more general statement of Haidt's view, see Jonathan Haidt, *The Happiness Hypothesis* (2006).

8. See, e.g., Robert Nozick, *Anarchy, State, and Utopia* (1974).

9. See James Buchanan & Gordon Tullock, *The Calculus of Consent* (1962).

10. *Federalist No. 10*, at 46 (James Madison) (Clinton Rossiter ed., 1999).

11. See *Federalist No. 44*, at 250–251 (James Madison) (Clinton Rossiter ed., 1999).

12. For a list of such options, see the Home Affordable Modification Program (HAMP), available at http://www.freddiemac.com/singlefamily/service/mha_modification.html, which has largely failed. See also Jon Prior, "SIG-TARP: HAMP's Failure 'Devastating,' Permanent Mods Flat in December," *Housing Wire* (Jan. 11, 2011), available at http://www.housingwire.com/news/sigtarp-hamps-failure-devastating-permanent-mods-flat-december.

13. *Federalist No. 51*, at 293 (James Madison) (Clinton Rossiter ed., 1999).

14. Herbert Storing, *What the Antifederalists Were For* 5 (1981).

15. See id. at ch. 3.

16. Id. at 53.

17. *Federalist No. 78*, at 434 (Alexander Hamilton) (Clinton Rossiter ed., 1999).

18. *Federalist No. 10, supra* note 10, at 45 (James Madison).

19. Alexander Hamilton, Federal Convention, June 18, 1787, in 1 Farrand, *Records* 282–283, reproduced in *The Founder's Constitution* ch. 8, n.10 (Philip Kurland & Ralph Lerner eds., 1987).

20. James Madison, *Notes of Debates* 39; for this and other sources, see Randy E. Barnett, *Restoring the Lost Constitution: The Presumption of Liberty* 34–38 (2003).

21. For discussion, see Noble E. Cunningham, Jr., *The Jeffersonian Republicans: The Formation of Party Organization, 1789–1801* (1953).

22. See Aristotle, *The Politics of Aristotle* 157, at IV.2.1289a (Ernest Barker trans., 1952); for explication, see "Aristotle's Political Theory," in *Stanford Encyclopedia of Philosophy*, available at http://plato.stanford.edu/entries/aristotle-politics/#return1-supplement1.

23. See, e.g., Quentin Skinner, *Liberty before Liberalism* 28–31 (1998) (discussing the views of Harrington, Milton, Nedham, and Sydney).

24. U.S. Const. art. IV, § 4: "The United States shall guarantee to every State in this Union a Republican Form of Government, and shall protect each of them against Invasion; and on Application of the Legislature, or of the Executive (when the Legislature cannot be convened) against domestic Violence."

25. *Pacific States Tel. & Tel. Co. v. Oregon*, 223 U.S. 118 (1912). For a defense of referenda, see Robert D. Cooter, *The Strategic Constitution* (2000).

26. For a critique, see David P. Currie, *The Constitution in the Supreme Court: The First Hundred Years, 1789–1888*, at 252–257 (1985).

27. Storing, *supra* note 14, at 83 n.7. For two leading defenses of republicanism, see Cass R. Sunstein, "Beyond the Republican Revival," 98 *Yale L.J.* 1539 (1987); Frank I. Michelman, "Law's Republic," 97 *Yale L.J.* 1493 (1988). For a historical account of republican liberty, see Mortimer Sellers, *The Sacred Fire of Liberty: Republicanism, Liberalism and the Law* (1998).

28. *Federalist No. 1*, at 1 (Alexander Hamilton) (Clinton Rossiter ed., 1999).

29. See, Sunstein, *supra* note 27.

30. *Federalist No. 10*, *supra* note 10, at 80 (James Madison).

31. Senator Arlen Specter, Remarks at the Federalist Society National Convention, Washington D.C. (Nov. 17, 2006) (audio available at http://www.fed-soc.org/audio/2006lawcon/SpecterAddress-11-17-06.mp3).

32. 5 U.S. 137 (1803).

33. For an account of the brutal and near hysterical political squabble, see Larry D. Kramer, *The People Themselves: Popular Constitutionalism and Judicial Review* 114–121 (2004).

34. U.S. Const. art. I, § 2, cl. 1.

35. *Federalist No. 68*, at 380 (Alexander Hamilton) (Clinton Rossiter ed., 1999).

36. U.S. Const. amend. XV.

37. Id. amend. XIX.

38. Id. amend XXVI.

39. Id. amend. XVII.

40. Id. amend. XXIV.

41. Id. art. I., § 7, cl. 2.

42. The chief exponent of this unwise proposal is Sanford Levinson, *Framed: America's 51 Constitutions and the Crisis of Governance* (2012).

43. John Rawls, *A Theory of Justice* (1971); this theme occurs before the Founding as well in, for example, Adam Smith, *A Theory of Moral Sentiments* 134 (D. D. Raphael & A. L. Macfie eds., 1976) (1759), which stresses the critical role for the "impartial observer."

44. Tariff Act of 1930 (Smoot-Hawley Tariff), Pub. L. No. 71-361, 46 Stat. 590 (codified as amended at 19 U.S.C. §§ 1202–1683g (2006)). "The Economists' Tariff Protest of 1930" can be found at 4(3) *Econ. Journal Watch* 345 (Sept. 2007), available at http://econjwatch.org/articles/economists-against-smoot-hawley. The lead authors of that letter included Paul H. Douglas, then at the University of Chicago, and Irving Fisher, then at Yale University. For a balanced modern appraisal of its harm, see "The Battle of Smoot-Hawley: A Cautionary Tale about How a Protectionist Measure Opposed by All Right-Thinking People Was Passed," *The Economist* (Dec. 18, 2008), available at http://www.economist.com/node/12798595.

45. Tom Doggett, "Senate Vote Marks Start of End for Ethanol Subsidies," Reuters (Jan. 16, 2011), available at http://www.reuters.com/article/2011/06/16/us-usa-senate-ethanol-idUSTRE75F5IN20110616.

46. Charles Beard, *An Economic Interpretation of the Constitution* (1913).

47. For discussion, see Forrest McDonald, *We the People, The Economic Origins of the Constitution* (1958).
48. U.S. Const. art. I, § 10, cl. 2.
49. Id. art. IV, § 2, cl. 1.
50. Id. art. I, § 2, cl. 3.
51. *Federalist No. 54*, at 304 (James Madison) (Clinton Rossiter ed., 1999).
52. U.S. Const. art. IV, § 2, cl. 3: "No person held to service or labour in one state, under the laws thereof, escaping into another, shall, in consequence of any law or regulation therein, be discharged from such service or labour, but shall be delivered up on claim of the party to whom such service or labour may be due."
53. See John R. Vile, *The Constitutional Convention of 1787: A Comprehensive Encyclopedia of America's Founding* 180–181 (2005).
54. See id.
55. See id. Alexander Hamilton also had a plan that included two houses, one whose members were elected for three-year terms and the second whose members served for life or at least on good behavior. Hamilton, *supra* note 19, at 282–83.
56. U.S. Const. art. I, § 2.
57. Id. art. I, § 3.
58. Id. art. II, § 1.
59. See Lynn Baker, "The Spending Power and the Federalist Revival," 4 *Chapman L. Rev.* 195 (2001).

2. The Progressive Response

1. Pub. L. No. 93-205, 87 Stat. 884 (codified as amended at 16 U.S.C. §§ 1531–1544 (2006)).
2. Created in 1970 by executive order. Reorganization Plan No. 3 of 1970, 3 C.F.R. § 199 (1970), reprinted as amended in 42 U.S.C. § 4321 (2006).
3. Pub. L. No. 91-596, 84 Stat. 1590 (codified as amended at 29 U.S.C. §§ 651–678 (2006)).
4. Employee Retirement Income Security Act of 1974, Pub. L. No. 93-406, 88 Stat. 829 (codified as amended in scattered sections of 26 and 29 U.S.C.).
5. Stephen Breyer, *Active Liberty: Interpreting Our Democratic Constitution* (2005).
6. Id. at 19–20.
7. Id. at 33.
8. Id. at 20, 25.
9. Id. at 7–8.
10. Robert Stern, "The Commerce Clause and the National Economy, 1933–1946," 59 *Harv. L. Rev.* 645 (1946) (part 2 at 883).
11. Id. at 946.
12. See, e.g., *United States v. Socony-Vacuum Oil Co.*, 310 U.S. 150 (1940) (allowing treble damages under the Sherman Act against oil company practices that the government had previously urged Socony to undertake). For a fuller

account, see Daniel Crane, "The Story of *United States v. Socony-Vacuum*: Hot Oil and Antitrust in the Two New Deals" in *Antitrust Stories* (Daniel Crane & Eleanor Fox eds., 2007).

13. 304 U.S. 144, 152 n.4 (1938).

14. See Clayton Act, ch. 323, § 6, 38 Stat. 730, 731 (1914) (codified at 15 U.S.C. § 17 (2001)).

15. See *Euclid v. Ambler Realty Co.*, 272 U.S. 365 (1926).

16. *Block v. Hirsh*, 256 U.S. 135 (1921).

17. 295 U.S. 495 (1935). For an exhaustive account of the Schechters' travails, see Amity Shlaes, *The Forgotten Man* (2007). To his credit, Justice Brandeis was a member of the unanimous court that struck this statute down.

18. E.g., Agricultural Adjustment Act of 1933, ch. 25, Title I, 48 Stat. 31 (codified at 7 U.S.C. §§ 601–27).

19. Michael Wachter, "Labor Unions: A Corporatist Institution in a Competitive World," 155 *U. Pa. L. Rev.* 581, 583 (2007).

20. Adolf Berle & Gardner Means, *The Modern Corporation and Private Property* 357 (1932).

21. Adolf A. Berle, Jr., "For Whom Corporate Managers Are Trustees: A Note," 45 *Harv. L. Rev.* 1365, 1372 (1932).

22. Woodrow Wilson, *Congressional Government: A Study in American Politics* 187 (1956) (first published in 1885).

23. James Landis, *The Administrative Process* 11–12 (1938).

24. Daryl J. Levinson & Richard H. Pildes, "Separation of Parties, Not Powers," 119 *Harv. L. Rev.* 2311 (2006).

25. See *Federalist No. 51* (James Madison) (Clinton Rossiter ed., 1999).

26. For the move, see Joseph F. Mahoney, "Backsliding Convert: Woodrow Wilson and the 'Seven Sisters,'" 18 *Am. Q.* 71 (1966). The "seven sisters" refers to the large oil companies of the time.

27. See *infra* Chapter 15 ("The Dormant Commerce Clause").

28. *Baldwin v. G.A.F. Seelig, Inc.*, 294 U.S. 511 (1935).

29. *W. Lynn Creamery v. Healy*, 512 U.S. 186 (1994).

3. Constitutional Interpretation

1. Antonin Scalia, "Common Law Courts in a Civil Law System: The Role of the United States Federal Courts in Interpreting the Constitution and Laws," in *A Matter of Interpretation: Federal Courts and the Law* 17, 38 (Amy Gutmann ed., 1997).

2. U.S. Const. art. 1, § 8, cl. 11. See generally Theodore M. Cooperstein, "Letters of Marque and Reprisal: The Constitutional Law and Practice of Privateering," 40 *J. Maritime L. & Commerce* 221 (2009).

3. For further discussion, see *infra* Chapter 20 ("Procedural Due Process: Implementing the Classical Liberal Ideal").

4. See, Chapter 20 *infra*.

5. For discussion, see Richard A. Epstein & Michael S. Greve, "Conclusion: Preemption Doctrine and its Limits," 309, 312–315, in R. Epstein & M. Greve eds. *Federal Preemption: States' Powers, National Interests* (2007).

6. For the parallels, with references to Roman law, see Richard A. Epstein, "A Common Lawyer Looks at Constitutional Interpretation," 72 *Bost U. L. Rev.* 699 (1992).

7. 25 U.S. 419 (1827).

8. Id. at 445.

9. *Lochner v. New York*, 198 U.S. 45, 53 (1905).

10. Thomas M. Cooley, *A Treatise on the Constitutional Limitations Which Rest Upon the Legislative Power of the States of the American Union* (1868). He does not use the words "police power" but the interaction between legislative power and constitutional limitations lies at the center of his inquiry.

11. Christopher G. Tiedeman, *A Treatise on the Limitations of the Police Power in the United States* (1886).

12. Ernst Freud, *The Police Power, Public Policy and Constitutional Rights* (1904).

13. *Near v. Minnesota*, 283 U.S. 697 (1931).

14. *New York Times v. United States*, 403 U.S. 713, 734 (1971).

15. Ludwig Wittgenstein, *Philosophical Investigations*, ¶ 70 (G. E. M. Anscombe trans., 1958): "Someone says to me 'Shew the children a game.' I teach them gaming with dice, and the other says 'I didn't mean that sort of game.' Must the exclusion of a game with dice come before his mind when he gave me the order."

16. Justinian Digest, IX, 2, which can be found in F. H. Lawson, *Negligence in the Civil Law* (1950).

17. Richard A. Epstein, "A Common Lawyer Looks at Constitutional Interpretation," 72 *B.U. L. Rev.* 699 (1992) (developing the parallels in detail).

18. Louis Michael Seidman, "Let's Give Up on the Constitution," *New York Times*, December 30, 2013. For a more complete statement of Seidman's views, see Louis Michael Seidman, *On Constitutional Disobedience* (2013).

19. Jack M. Balkin, *Living Originalism* 3 (2011).

20. Antonin Scalia, "Originalism: The Lesser Evil," 57 *U. Cin. L. Rev.* 849 (1988).

21. For more detailed discussion, see *infra* at Chapters 9 through 13.

22. For discussion, see, e.g., Thomas W. Merrill, "Bork v. Burke," 19 *Harvard J.L. & Pub. Pol.* 509 (1996); Cass R. Sunstein, "Burkean Minimalism," 105 *Mich. L. Rev.* 353 (2006).

23. "English Bill of Rights: An Act Declaring the Rights and Liberties of the Subject and Settling the Succession of the Crown," available at http://15.law.yale.edu/17th_century/england.asp.

24. Scalia, *supra* note 20, at 862.

25. 408 U.S. 238 (1932).

26. 428 U.S. 153 (1976).

27. U.S. Const. amend. V.

28. 132 S. Ct. 2455, 2463 (2012) (internal quotation marks omitted).

29. Id. at 2460 (internal citations and quotation marks omitted).
30. 543 U.S. 551 (2005).
31. 130 S. Ct. 2011 (2010).
32. 433 U.S. 584 (1977).
33. 554 U.S. 407 (2008).
34. The point was missed by everyone involved in the case until it was discovered by Dwight Sullivan, who summarized the situation as follows: "Section 552(b) of the National Defense Authorization Act for Fiscal Year 2006, 119 Stat. 3136, 3264 (2006), provides '[u]ntil the President otherwise provides pursuant to' UCMJ [Uniform Code of Military Justice] article 56, 'the punishment which a court-martial may direct for an offense under' the amended UCMJ article 120 'may not exceed the following limits: . . . For an offense under subsection (a) (rape) or subsection (b) (rape of a child), death or such other punishment as a court-martial may direct.'" Dwight Sullivan, "The Supremes Dis the Military Justice System," CAAFlog (Jun. 28, 2008), available at http://caaflog.blogspot.com/2008/06/supremes-dis-military-justice-system.html.
35. 132 S. Ct. 2455 (2012).
36. 128 S. Ct. 2783 (2008).
37. D.C. Code § 7-2507.02 (2012).
38. 128 S. Ct. 2821–2822.
39. U.S. Const. amend. II.
40. 307 U.S. 174 (1939).
41. Ch. 757, 48 Stat. 1236 (1934).
42. U.S. Const. art. I, § 8, cl. 16, 17.
43. *Miller*, 307 U.S. at 178.
44. See Chapter 11 ("The Commerce Clause: Transformation and Consolidation: 1937 to 1995").
45. U.S. Const. art. I, § 8, cl. 18.
46. 32 U.S. 243 (1833).
47. *Heller*, 128 S. Ct. at 2823.
48. Id. at 2790.
49. § XIII, in 5 Thorpe 3082, 3083 (emphasis added), quoted in *Heller*, 128 S. Ct. at 2802.
50. *Miller*, 307 U.S. at 178
51. *Heller*, at 2800.
52. Id.
53. *Heller*, 128 S. Ct. at 2800, citing Eugene Volokh, "Necessary to the Security of a Free State," 83 *Notre Dame L. Rev.* 1, 5 (2007).
54. Id at 2816.
55. Id. at 2621.
56. *Heller v. District of Columbia*, 670 F.3d 1244 (D.C. Cir. 2011).
57. 638 F.3d 458, 475 (4th Cir. 2011).
58. Id. 475.
59. 701 F.3d 81 (2d Cir. 2012) (Wesley, J.).

60. N.Y. Penal Law § 400.00(2)(f) (McKinney 2013).

61. 702 F.3d 933 (7th Cir. 2012) (Posner, J.).

62. Id. at 941.

63. 720 Ill. Comp. 5/24-1, 5/24-1.6 (West 2013).

64. 702 F.3d 941.

65. 130 S. Ct. 3020.

66. For more detailed accounts of the Fourteenth Amendment, see *infra* Chapters 33 ("Race and the Fourteenth Amendment") and 34 ("Citizenship and the Fourteenth Amendment").

67. 83 U.S. 36 (1873).

68. 130 S. Ct. 3028–3031.

69. Id. at 3031–3036.

70. Id. at 3036.

71. Id. at 3036–3042.

72. 92 U.S. 542 (1876).

73. Id. at 553.

74. 6 F. Cas. 546 (C.C.E.D.Pa. 1823) (No. 3,230).

75. 5 U.S. 137 (1803), discussed *infra* Chapter 4 ("The Origins of Judicial Review").

76. 14 U.S. 304 (1816), discussed *infra* Chapter 4 ("The Origins of Judicial Review").

77. 262 U.S. 447 (1923).

78. 163 U.S. 537 (1896), discussed *infra* Chapter 33 ("Race and the Fourteenth Amendment").

79. 83 U.S. 36 (1873).

80. 92 U.S. 542 (1876).

4. The Origins of Judicial Review

1. 5 U.S. 137 (1803).

2. 60 U.S. 393 (1857).

3. 163 U.S. 537 (1896).

4. 323 U.S. 214 (1944).

5. 317 U.S. 111 (1942).

6. 410 U.S. 113 (1973).

7. 545 U.S. 469 (2005).

8. For an earlier statement of this position, see Richard A. Epstein, "Substantive Due Process by Any Other Name: The Abortion Cases," 1973 *Sup. Ct. Rev.* 159.

9. See *infra* Chapter 15 ("The Dormant Commerce Clause").

10. For the canonical critique of the decision, see Alexander M. Bickel, *The Least Dangerous Branch* 1–14 (1962).

11. Id. at 12–14.

12. Id. at 7–10.

13. Thomas Jefferson, Letter to Abigail Adams, Sept. 11, 1804, 8 *Writings of Thomas Jefferson* 310 (M. Ford ed., 1897).
14. Lincoln First Inaugural Address, Mar. 4, 1861, in 6 *Messages and Papers of the Presidents* 5 (J. Richard ed., 1900).
15. See, e.g., *Underhill v. Hernandez*, 168 U.S. 250, 252 (1897) ("[T]he courts of one country will not sit in judgment on the acts of the government of another, done within its own territory.").
16. U.S. Const. amend. V.
17. Id. art. I, § 9, cl. 2.
18. See *Federalist No. 78* (Alexander Hamilton) (Clinton Rossiter ed., 1999).
19. U.S. Const. art. III, § 1.
20. John Locke, *Second Treatise of Government*, §§ 149, 227 (1690), available at http://www.ilt.columbia.edu/academic/digitexts/locke/second/locke2nd.txt.
21. Baron de Montesquieu, *The Spirit of Laws* (J. V. Prichard ed., Thomas Nugent trans., 1914), available at http://www.constitution.org/cm/sol.txt.
22. For discussion of this and other similar issues, see Philip Hamburger, "Law and Judicial Duty," 72 *Geo. Wash. L. Rev.* 1, 22–23 (2003).
23. 77 Eng. Rep. 638 (C.P. 1610).
24. Id. at 652.
25. 1 William Blackstone, *Commentaries of the Law of England* 91 (1965).
26. Id. at 160.

5. Marbury *and* Martin

1. John Manning, "Separation of Powers as Ordinary Interpretation," 124 *Harv. L. Rev.* 1939, 1944 (2011).
2. U.S. Const. art. III, §§ 1–2.
3. *Marbury v. Madison*, 5 U.S. 137 (1803).
4. U.S. Const. art. III, § 1, cl. 2. It was later held that the grant of original jurisdiction in these cases did not preclude appellate jurisdiction over persons regarding whom the Supreme Court had original jurisdiction. See *United States v. Ravara*, 2 U.S. 297, 298–299 (1793).
5. Philip Hamburger, *Law and Judicial Duty* ch. 13 (2008).
6. See William W. Crosskey, 2 *Politics and the Constitution in the History of the United States* 969–971 (1953).
7. Id.; Hamburger, *supra* note 5, at 422–435.
8. *Marbury*, 5 U.S. at 180.
9. Id. at 177.
10. Id.
11. *Federalist No. 78*, at 433 (Alexander Hamilton) (Clinton Rossiter ed., 1999).
12. Id. at 433–434 (Alexander Hamilton), citing Montesquieu, *The Spirit of Laws* 156 (Thomas Nugent trans., 1899), available at http://archive.org/details/spiritoflaws01montuoft.

13. U.S. Const. art. III, § 3.
14. Id. art. I, § 9, cl. 3.
15. Id. at cl. 5.
16. See Crosskey, *supra* note 6, at 969–971.
17. U.S. Const. art. III, § 2, cl. 2.
18. See, e.g., Henry Hart, "The Power of Congress to Limit the Jurisdiction of Federal Courts: An Exercise in Dialectic," 66 *Harv. L. Rev.* 1362, 1365 (1953). But see Herbert Wechsler, "The Courts and the Constitution," 65 *Colum. L. Rev.* 1001, 1005–1007 (1965) (arguing that the federal courts, including the Supreme Court, "do not pass on constitutional questions because there is a special function vested in them to enforce the Constitution or police the other agencies of government. They do so rather for the reason that they must decide a litigated case that is otherwise within their jurisdiction and in so doing must give effect to the supreme law of the land. That is, at least, what Marbury v. Madison was all about.").
19. 1 Stat. 577, ch. 66. The act expired on March 3, 1801, the last day of the John Adams administration.
20. As reported by 1 Horace Greeley, *The American Conflict, A History of the Great Rebellion in the United States of America* 106 (1864).
21. 2 *Messages and Papers of the Presidents* 582 (J. Richardson ed., 1896).
22. *Federalist No. 78*, at 433 (Alexander Hamilton) (Clinton Rossiter ed., 1999).
23. David P. Currie, "The Constitution in the Supreme Court: The Powers of the Federal Courts, 1801–1835," 49 *U. Chi. L. Rev.* 646, 686 (1982).
24. 358 U.S. 1 (1958).
25. *Marbury*, 5 U.S. at 177.
26. 347 U.S. 483 (1954), discussed *infra* Chapter 33 ("Race and the Fourteenth Amendment").
27. 14 U.S. (1 Wheat.) 304 (1816).
28. Treaty of Paris art. 5, U.S.-Gr. Brit., Sep. 13, 1783, 8 Stat. 80.
29. U.S. Const. art. VI, § 2.
30. *Martin*, 14 U.S. at 348.
31. See, e.g., Brief for Senator Arlen Specter, as Amicus Curiae Supporting Petitioners at 4, *Boumediene. v. Bush*, 553 U.S. 723, 128 S. Ct. 2229 (2008) (Nos. 06-1195 and 06-1196) (the "[Supreme] Court should hold that the MCA's attempt to curtail the Guantanamo detainees' access to habeas corpus is constitutionally infirm").
32. See, for an attack on these aggressive uses of constitutional law to redistribute wealth, Ralph K. Winter, Jr., "Poverty, Economic Equality, and the Equal Protection Clause," 1972 *Sup. Ct. Rev.* 41 (1972).

6. Standing

1. *Marbury v. Madison*, 5 U.S. 137 (1803).
2. U.S. Const. art. I, § 3, cl. 6.

3. Id.

4. Id. art. I, § 5, cl. 1.

5. Id. art. I, § 6, cl. 1.

6. Id. art. IV, § 3.

7. *Coleman v. Miller*, 307 U.S. 433 (1939).

8. For an example of the modern view, see Jeremy Waldron, "The Core of the Case against Judicial Review," 115 *Yale L.J.* 1346 (2006).

9. Letter of the Supreme Court to President George Washington (1793), *Documents in Early American History*, available at http://courses.missouristate.edu/ftmiller/letteradvisoryopin.htm.

10. 2 U.S. 402 (1792).

11. Id. at 413.

12. U.S. Const. art. III, § 2, cl. 1.

13. *In re Chrysler LLC*, 576 F.3d 108 (2d Cir. 2009). This decision was later dismissed as moot for reasons that were never explained. *Ind. State Police Pension Trust v. Chrysler LLC*, 130 S. Ct. 1015 (mem) (2009).

14. For an account of the tangled history, see Lyle Denniston, "U.S. Says TARP Issue Out of Court's Reach," *SCOTUSblog* (Jun. 8, 2009), available at http://www.scotusblog.com/2009/06/us-says-tarp-issue-out-of-courts-reach.

15. 262 U.S. 447 (1923) (consolidated actions).

16. 67 Pub. L. No. 97, 42 Stat. 224 (1921), ch. 135.

17. U.S. Const art. I, § 8, cl. 1, discussed *infra* Chapter 13 ("Enumerated Powers: Taxing and Spending").

18. William A. Fletcher, "The Structure of Standing," 98 *Yale L.J.* 221, 229 (1988).

19. David P. Currie, "Misunderstanding Standing," 1981 *Sup. Ct. Rev.* 41, 43 (1981).

20. 504 U.S. 555 (1992).

21. Id. at 560–561 (alterations in original) (internal citations omitted). There are some doubts whether the word "legally" belongs before "protected" in this formulation. See *Judicial Watch, Inc. v. U.S. Senate*, 432 F.3d 359, 363 (D.C. Cir. 2005) (refusing to allow a challenge to the three-fifths filibuster rule in the Senate on the ground that there was no connection between delays in filling seats and delays in deciding cases). The simpler ground on the merits is that these rules are matters for the Senate to decide for itself.

22. See, e.g., *Restatement (Second) of Torts* § 693.

23. *Pruitt v. Allied Chem. Corp.*, 523 F. Supp. 975 (E.D. Va. 1981) (allowing suits by marina, boat, tackle, and bait shop owners, but not their wholesalers and retailers, for kepone spill in James River and Chesapeake Bay).

24. *Lujan*, 504 U.S. at 559.

25. U.S. Const. art. III, § 2, cl. 1.

26. For the early history of advisory opinions in England and the United States, see Philip Hamburger, *Law and Judicial Duty* 151–154, 371–377, 522–526, 597–600 (2008).

27. See generally, Note, "The Mootness Doctrine in the Supreme Court," 88 *Harv. L. Rev.* 373 (1974).

28. *S. Pac. Terminal Co. v. ICC,* 219 U.S. 498, 515 (1911).

29. 410 U.S. 113 (1973).

30. Id. at 125–127.

31. 330 U.S. 75 (1947).

32. Cass R. Sunstein, "What's Standing after *Lujan*? Of Citizen Suits, "Injuries," and Article III," 91 *Mich. L. Rev.* 163, 187 (1992) (emphasis added). For similar work in this vein, see Cass R. Sunstein, "Standing and the Privatization of Public Law," 88 *Colum. L. Rev.* 1432 (1988). See also Steven L. Winter, "The Metaphor of Standing and the Problem of Self-Governance," 40 *Stan. L. Rev.* 1371 (1988).

33. Anon. 87 Eng. Rep. 791 (K.B. 1703). For a discussion of these private rights of action in modern times, see *Cort v. Ash,* 422 U.S. 66 (1975).

34. For the canonical account of the English history, see F. W. Maitland, *Equity: A Course of Lectures* (A. H. Chaytor & W. J. Whittaker eds., 1909). For the ultimate American acceptance of the need for equity courts, see Hamburger, discussed *supra* Chapter 5 (*"Marbury* and *Martin"*).

35. For discussion, see id.

36. See, e.g., *Brushaber v. Union Pac. R.R.,* 240 U.S. 1 (1916) (suit against board of trustees to enjoin income tax proper).

37. 101 U.S. 601 (1879).

38. Id. at 609; see also *Miller v. Grandy,* 13 Mich. 540, 550 (1865).

39. See John F. Dillon, *Municipal Corporations* § 1580 et seq. (5th ed., 1911), for the relevant authorities.

40. U.S. Const. art. I, § 8, cl. 1.

41. 259 U.S. 20 (1922).

42. *Commonwealth of Massachusetts v. Mellon,* 262 U.S. 447, 480 (1923).

43. Id. at 487.

44. 198 U.S. 45 (1905), discussed *infra* Chapter 21 ("Freedom of Contract").

45. For the thesis, see Sunstein, "Standing and the Privatization of American Law," *supra* note 32, at 1433. At other times Sunstein appears to back off this thesis in favor of a view that attributes the success of standing to an uneasy alliance between conservative and liberal judges, where the former tend to reify a narrow version of common law rights, and the latter want to insulate political decisions from judicial oversight. See also Steven L. Winter, "The Metaphor of Standing and the Problem of Self-Governance," 40 *Stan. L. Rev.* 1371 (1988). For the critique of the "fragile" empirical foundations of the thesis, see Daniel E. Ho & Erica L. Ross, "Did Liberal Justices Invent the Standing Doctrine? An Empirical Study of the Evolution of Standing, 1921–2006," 62 *Stan. L. Rev.* 1, 1–2 (2010). Note that Ho and Ross do not systematically separate out constitutional from administrative standing cases.

46. See 302 U.S. 464, 479 (1938); see also *Tenn. Elec. Power Co. v. Tenn. Valley Auth.,* 306 U.S. 118 (1939); *Ashwander v. Tenn. Valley Auth.,* 297 U.S. 288 (1936).

47. 306 U.S. 118 (1939).
48. Id. at 140.
49. 297 U.S. 288, 320–322 (1936).
50. 309 U.S. 470 (1940).
51. 73 Pub. L. No. 416, ch. 652, 48 Stat. 1064 (1934).
52. This entire system of FCC licensing has massive substantive drawbacks when measured against a system of private property rights over the spectrum. For the classic exposition, see Ronald H. Coase, "The Federal Communications Commission," 2 *J. Law & Econ.* 1 (1959). The difficulties include the want of standards to decide who should get the license and the inability to switch uses of the bandwidth without government approval.
53. Administrative Procedure Act, 79 Pub. L. No. 404, 60 Stat. 237 (1946).
54. APA, 5 U.S.C. § 702.

7. Modern Standing Law

1. See Daniel E. Ho & Erica L. Ross, "Did Liberal Justices Invent the Standing Doctrine? An Empirical Study of the Evolution of Standing, 1921–2006," 62 *Stan. L. Rev.* 1, 2–3 (2010).
2. 418 U.S. 166 (1974).
3. 418 U.S. 208 (1974).
4. See, for elaboration, *Ass'n of Data Processing Serv. Orgs. v. Camp*, 397 U.S. 150, 153 (1970); for application, *Clarke v. Sec. Indus. Ass'n*, 479 U.S. 388 (1987) (allowing security industry to protest bank entry into the brokerage business).
5. 467 U.S. 340 (1984).
6. 369 U.S. 186 (1962). For the discussion of the political question doctrine, see *infra* Chapter 8 ("The Political Question Doctrine").
7. *Baker*, 369 U.S. at 208.
8. *Marbury v. Madison*, 5 U.S. 137, 163 (1803).
9. 330 U.S. 1 (1947).
10. 392 U.S. 83 (1968).
11. Pub. L. 89-10, 79 Stat. 27, 20 U.S.C. ch. 70.
12. *Flast,* 392 U.S. at 102–103.
13. Id. at 103.
14. See *supra* Chapter 6 ("Standing: Background and Origins"). The now-discarded limitations on direct taxes were put into the original Constitution precisely to prevent Congress from imposing taxes that transferred wealth from rich to poor states. See *Pollock v. Farmers' Loan & Trust Co.*, 157 U.S. 601 (1895) (holding that the income tax on property was a direct tax that had to be apportioned among the states under U.S. Const. art. I, § 9, cl. 4). That decision was overturned by the Sixteenth Amendment. Note that *Pollock* was a suit, like *Brushaber*, that allowed shareholders of a corporation to sue its directors to demand that they resist the imposition of an illegal tax.

15. 454 U.S. 464 (1982).
16. Id. at 472. See, for a defense of this position, R. Lea Brilmayer, "The Jurisprudence of Article III: Perspectives on the 'Case or Controversy' Requirement," 93 *Harv. L. Rev.* 297 (1979), and, for a response, Mark H. Tushnet, "The Sociology of Article III: A Response to Professor Brilmayer," 93 *Harv. L. Rev.* 698 (1980). My sympathies lie with Tushnet, notwithstanding the major differences in our substantive views of constitutional law.
17. 551 U.S. 587 (2007).
18. Id. at 619.
19. 131 S. Ct. 1436 (2011).
20. Id. at 1441.
21. Id. at 1447 (quoting *Flast*, 392 U.S. at 106).
22. Id. at 1450.
23. 405 U.S. 727 (1972).
24. 504 U.S. 555, 560 (1992). For discussion, see Cass R. Sunstein, "What's Standing after *Lujan*? Of Citizen Suits, Injuries, and Article III," 91 *Mich. L. Rev.* 163 (1992).
25. Endangered Species Act of 1973, 93 Pub. L. No. 205, 87 Stat. 884, as amended 16 U.S.C. § 1531 et seq.
26. Id. § 1536.
27. "Any person may commence a civil suit on his own behalf (A) to enjoin any person, including the United States and any other governmental instrumentality or agency . . . who is alleged to be in violation of any provision of this chapter." 16 U.S.C. § 1540(g).
28. *Lujan*, 504 U.S. at 560–562.
29. For the modern framework, see, e.g., *Fed. R. Civ. P.* 19(a). For a general discussion, see Fleming James, Jr., et al., *Civil Procedure* § 10.11 (5th ed. 2001).
30. See e.g., *Lumley v. Wagner*, 42 Eng. Rep. 687 (Ex. 1852) (denying specific performance but allowing an injunction against working for third parties).
31. See, *Lumley v. Gye*, 118 Eng. Rep. 749 (K.B. 1853). For the modern formulation, see *Restatement Second of Torts*, § 766 (1977).
32. *Chevron U.S.A., Inc. v. Natural Res. Def. Council, Inc.*, 467 U.S. 837 (1984) (announcing rule of deference without citing or discussing § 706 of the APA).
33. APA 5 U.S.C. § 706: "To the extent necessary to decision and when presented, the reviewing court shall decide all relevant questions of law, interpret constitutional and statutory provisions, and determine the meaning or applicability of the terms of agency action."
34. See *Allen v. Wright*, 468 U.S. 737 (1984) (in which standing was denied on the ground that the claimed decline in educational advantage could not be traced to the racial exclusion of these schools—i.e., the causation prong).
35. *Simon v. E. Ky. Welfare Rights Org.*, 426 U.S. 26 (1976) (indigent organizations lack standing to challenge hospital charitable exemptions).
36. 549 U.S. 497 (2007).

37. 42 U.S.C. § 202.

38. 262 U.S. 447 (1923).

39. 549 U.S. at 520 n.17.

40. Pub. L. No. 67-97, 42 Stat. 224 (1921).

41. 42 U.S.C. § 7521(a)(1) (2006) (emphasis added).

42. Richard A. Epstein, "Carbon Dioxide: Our Newest Pollutant," 43 *Suffolk L. Rev.* 797 (2010).

43. See, e.g., *Steel Co. v. Citizens for a Better Environment*, 523 U.S. 83 (1998) (dealing with provisions for citizen suits under the Emergency Planning and Community Right-To-Know Act).

8. The Political Question Doctrine

1. 5 U.S. 137 (1803).

2. Id. at 166.

3. Id.

4. *German Alliance Ins. Co. v. Lewis*, 233 U.S. 389, 406 (1915).

5. *Baker v. Carr*, 369 U.S. 186, 217 (1962). For similar sentiments, see *Japan Whaling Ass'n v. Am. Cetacean Soc'y*, 478 U.S. 221, 330 (1986) ("exclud[ing] from judicial review those controversies which revolve around policy choices and value determinations constitutionally committed for resolution to the halls of Congress or the confines of the Executive Branch"). The interpretation of treaties did not fall into that class.

6. *Int'l Ass'n of Machinists and Aerospace Workers (IAM) v. OPEC*, 649 F.2d 1354 (9th Cir. 1981). Then Professor Antonin Scalia was counsel for OPEC in this case.

7. U.S. Const. art. IV, § 4.

8. Id. art. II, § 2, cl. 1. "The President shall be Commander in Chief of the Army and Navy of the United States, and of the Militia of the several States, when called into the active Service of the United States." See also art. I, § 8, cl. 15: "Congress shall have the Power . . . To provide for calling forth the Militia to execute the Laws of the Union, suppress Insurrections, and repel invasions."

9. 48 U.S. 1 (1849).

10. E.g., id. at 39: "Certainly, the question which the plaintiff proposed to raise by the testimony he offered has not heretofore been recognized as a judicial one in any of the State courts."

11. Id. at 40. For some of the complexities, see David P. Currie, *The Constitution in the Supreme Court: The First Hundred Years 1789–1888* at 252–257 (1985).

12. 48 U.S. at 38–39.

13. 223 U.S. 118 (1912).

14. For one review, see Robert Cooter, *The Strategic Constitution* (2000).

15. 369 U.S. 186 (1962).

16. 2 Will. 4, c. 45 (1832).

17. 369 U.S. at 222.

18. Id. at 226.

19. U.S. Const. amend 14, § 5.

20. 369 U.S. at 302–303.

21. 377 U.S. 533 (1964).

22. Id. at 562.

23. *Gaffney v. Cummings*, 412 U.S. 735, 754 (1973).

24. See, for example, *Veith v. Jubelirer*, 541 U.S. 267 (2004), with a sharp division of opinion on the justiciability of these cases.

9. The Commerce Power

1. U.S. Const. art. 1, § 8, cl. 3.

2. *Federalist No. 45* (James Madison) (Clinton Rossiter ed., 2009).

3. John Locke, *The Second Treatise of Government* ¶ 123, at 67 (C. B. McPherson ed., 1980) (1690).

4. 1–3 Adam Smith, *The Wealth of Nations* 109 (Andrew S. Skinner ed., Penguin Classics, 1986 [1776]).

5. Jack Balkin, *Living Originalism* 151 (2011).

6. See Vicki Been, "'Exit' as a Constraint on Land Use Exactions: Rethinking the Unconstitutional Conditions Doctrine," 91 *Colum. L. Rev.* 473 (1991). For comments on the limits of the exit power, see Richard A. Epstein, "Exit Rights under Federalism," 55 *Law & Contemp. Prob.* 147 (1992).

7. See Michael Heller, *The Gridlock Economy: How Too Much Ownership Wrecks Markets, Stops Innovation, and Costs Lives* (2008).

8. Treaty of Westphalia, Holy Rom. Emp.-Fr., art. LXIX, LXXXIX (Oct. 14, 1648), available at http://avalon.law.yale.edu/17th_century/westphal.asp.

9. One early reference is to Sir Matthew Hale, *De Portibus Maris* (Concerning the Gates of the Sea). Hale lived from 1609 to 1676 and was published posthumously in the 1780s. Hale's views on regulation were adopted in *Allnutt v. Inglis*, 104 Eng. Rep. 206 (K.B. 1810), from which they were incorporated into American constitutional law in *Munn v. Illinois*, 94 U.S. 113, 126–129 (1876). For a discussion, see Richard A. Epstein, *Principles for a Free Society: Reconciling Individual Liberty with the Common Good* 282–285 (1998).

10. See *infra* Chapter 10 ("The Commerce Clause in Transition: 1865–1937").

11. 22 U.S. 1 (1824).

12. 9 Johns. 507 (N.Y. 1812).

13. *Gibbons*, 22 U.S. at 194.

14. Id. at 190.

15. Id. at 194.

16. Id. at 203.

17. Id. at 193–194.

18. *Federalist No. 11* (Alexander Hamilton) (Clinton Rossiter ed., 1999). For elaboration, see Richard A. Epstein, "A Most Improbable 1787 Constitution: A Mostly Originalist Critique of the Constitutionality of the ACA" 28, 32–37, in *The Health Care Case: The Supreme Court's Decision and Its Implications* (Nathaniel

Persily, Gillian E. Metzger & Trevor Morrison eds., 2013). See also, the discussion of *Hammer v. Dagenhart*, 247 U.S. 251 (1918), which is discussed further in ch. 10, infra.

19. Joseph Story, *Commentaries on the Constitution of the United States* (Ronald D. Rotunda & John E. Nowak eds., abridged ed., 1987) (1833) [hereinafter Story, Commentaries].
20. *Corfield v. Coryell*, 6 F. Cas. 546 (E.D. Pa. 1823).
21. Id. at 550.
22. See *infra* Chapter 15 ("The Dormant Commerce Clause").
23. *Gibbons*, 22 U.S. at 190.
24. 48 U.S. 283 (1849).
25. Id. at 400.
26. U.S. Const. art. I, § 9, cl. 1.

10. The Commerce Clause in Transition

1. 128 U.S. 1 (1888).
2. Id. at 21–23.
3. Id at 21.
4. 156 U.S. 1, 14 (1895).
5. Id. at 13.
6. 175 U.S. 211 (1899).
7. 21 U.S.C. §§ 1–15.
8. 268 U.S. 295 (1925).
9. *Coronado Coal*, 268 U.S. at 310.
10. 310 U.S. 469 (1940).
11. *The Daniel Ball*, 77 U.S. 557 (1870).
12. Id. at 565.
13. See *Second Employer's Liability Cases (Mondou v. N.Y., New Haven, & Hartford R.R.)*, 223 U.S. 1 (1912). See also, in the same vein, *S. Ry. Co. v. United States*, 222 U.S. 20 (1911), upholding the Safety Appliance Act.
14. 258 U.S. 495 (1922).
15. 118 U.S. 557 (1886).
16. Ch. 104, 24 Stat. 379 (1887).
17. *Houston E. & W. Tex. Ry. Co. v. United States (Shreveport Rate Cases)*, 234 U.S. 342 (1914) (consolidating several appeals).
18. Id. at 351–352.
19. 37 U.S. 72 (1838).
20. See *Wis. R.R. Comm'n v. Chicago, Burlington & Quincy R.R.*, 257 U.S. 563 (1922).
21. 188 U.S. 321 (1903).
22. *Brooks v. United States*, 267 U.S. 432, 436 (1925).
23. See, e.g., Louis Kaplow, "Extension of Monopoly Power through Leverage," 85 *Colum. L. Rev.* 515 (1985), and for a recent guide, Warren S. Grimes, *Tying:*

Requirements Ties, Efficiency and Innovation, Testimony on Single-Firm Conduct and Antitrust Law, before Department of Justice and Federal Trade Commission (2006), available at http://www.justice.gov/atr/public/hearings/single _firm/comments/219982.htm.

24. See *Hipolite Egg Co. v. United States*, 220 U.S. 45 (1911).

25. *Hoke v. United States*, 227 U.S. 308 (1913).

26. Without going into exhaustive detail, the basic position is this: "The WTO's agreements permit members to take measures to protect not only the environment but also public health, animal health and plant health. However, these measures must be applied in the same way to both national and foreign businesses. In other words, members must not use environmental protection measures as a means of disguising protectionist policies." World Trade Organization, *What We Stand For*, available at http://wto.org/english/thewto_e/ whatis_e/what_stand_for_e.htm.

27. 247 U.S. 251 (1918).

28. See Benjamin Powell, *No Sweat: How Sweatshops Improve Lives and Economic Growth* (2011), for the frightening and gory details.

29. *Bailey v. Drexel Furniture Co. (Child Labor Tax Case)*, 259 U.S. 20 (1922).

11. The Commerce Clause

1. Federal Trade Commission Act of 1914, 15 U.S.C. § 41 (2006).

2. Radio Act of 1927, Pub. L. No. 632, 44 Stat. 1172.

3. 256 U.S. 135 (1921).

4. 272 U.S. 365 (1926).

5. See Department of Commerce, Standard State Zoning Enabling Act; Department of Commerce, Standard City Planning Enabling Act. Both acts are available at http://www.planning.org/growingsmart/enablingacts.htm.

6. New York 1916 Zoning Resolution, discussed in New York City Department of City Planning, *About Zoning*, available at http://www.nyc.gov/html/dcp/ html/zone/zonehis.shtml.

7. Pub. L. No. 73-90, 48 Stat. 195 (1933).

8. 295 U.S. 495 (1935). For an exhaustive account of the Schechters' travails, see Amity Shlaes, *The Forgotten Man: A New History of the Great Depression* (2007). To his credit, Justice Brandeis was one member of the unanimous court that struck this statute down.

9. 295 U.S. at 521–523.

10. Id. at 546.

11. *Kidd v. Pearson*, 128 U.S. 1 (1888).

12. *Houston E. & W. Tex. Ry. Co. v. United States*, 234 U.S. 342 (1914).

13. *Coronado Coal Co. v. United Mine Workers*, 268 U.S. 295 (1925).

14. *Schechter Poultry*, 295 U.S. at 548.

15. For a sympathetic account of the Supreme Court's action to give guidance to the Roosevelt Administration, see Barry Friedman, *The Will of the People* (2009).

16. Pub. L. No. 74-198, 49 Stat. 449 (codified as amended at 29 U.S.C. §§ 151–169 (2006)).

17. 301 U.S. 1 (1937).

18. Agricultural Adjustment Act of 1933 (Emergency Agricultural Relief Act), ch. 25, Pub. L. No. 73-10, 48 Stat. 31; Agricultural Adjustment Act of 1935, §§ 1–62, 49 Stat. 750; Agricultural Adjustment Act of 1937, ch. 296, 50 Stat. 246; Agricultural Adjustment Act of 1938 (Cooley Tobacco Act), ch. 30, Pub. L. No. 75-430, 52 Stat. 31.

19. 317 U.S. 111 (1942).

20. Pub. L. No. 75-718, 52 Stat. 1060 (codified as amended at 29 U.S.C. § 201).

21. 312 U.S. 100 (1941).

22. Ch. 372, 49 Stat. 449 (1935).

23. 29 U.S.C. § 160.

24. *Jones & Laughlin*, 301 U.S. at 31.

25. 37 U.S. 72 (1838), discussed in chapter 10, supra.

26. 312 U.S. at 116.

27. 247 U.S. 251 (1918).

28. 312 U.S. at 114.

29. Id. at 123.

30. Id. at 124.

31. 317 U.S. at 114–116.

32. 315 U.S. 110 (1942).

33. *Wickard*, 317 U.S. at 127.

34. Sherman Antitrust Act, ch. 647, 26 Stat. 209 (1890) (codified as amended at 15 U.S.C. §§ 1–7 (2006)).

35. See *supra* note 18.

36. *Gibbons v. Ogden*, 22 U.S. 1, 196 (1824).

37. Id. at 194 (emphasis added).

38. *Wrightwood Dairy Co.*, 315 U.S. at 119.

39. Laurence H. Tribe, *American Constitutional Law* § 5-4, at 808 (3d ed., 2000), quoting *Gibbons*, 22 U.S. at 194.

40. 317 U.S. at 120.

41. 22 U.S. at 194–95.

42. *Wickard*, 317 U.S. at 122 (emphasis added).

43. *Shreveport Rate Cases*, 234 U.S. at 351 (emphasis added).

44. See Tribe, *supra* note 39, at 810.

45. Michael S. Greve, *The Upside-Down Constitution* 203 (2012).

46. Id. at 346.

47. Wagner Act of 1935, Pub. L. No. 74-198, 49 Stat. 449 (codified as amended at 29 U.S.C. §§ 151–169 (2006)).

48. See Richard E. Schumann, *Compensation from World War II through the Great Society* (Bureau of Labor Statistics, Jan. 30, 2003), available at http://www.bls.gov/opub/cwc/cm20030124ar04p1.htm. Schumann explains, "[T]he transition to a peacetime economy was complicated by a number of problems,

including providing economic opportunity for both returning servicemen and the current workforce. . . . The result was a wave of strikes precisely when the public was anxious to see more consumer goods in stores and showrooms. Congress reacted to the wave of strikes in 1946–1947 by passing the Labor-Management Relations (Taft-Hartley) Act in 1947."

49. See *supra* Chapter 10 ("The Commerce Clause in Transition: 1865–1937") for discussion of *Hammer.*

50. See Jack Balkin, *Living Originalism* 164 (2011).

51. *Federalist No. 45* (James Madison) (Clinton Rossiter ed., 1998).

52. 2 *The Debates in the Several State Conventions on the Adoption of the Federal Constitution as Recommended by the General Convention at Philadelphia* 424 (Jonathan Elliot ed., 2d ed., 1836), quoted in Balkin, *supra* note 50, at 143.

53. Id. at 424–425.

54. Balkin, *supra* note 50, at 145.

55. *The Debates, supra* note 52, at 448.

56. Balkin, *supra* note 50, at 165.

57. See Chapter 12's discussion of the Patient Protection and Affordable Care Act.

58. Balkin, *supra* note 50, at 165.

59. 402 U.S. 146 (1971).

60. 379 U.S. 241 (1964).

61. 379 U.S. 294 (1964).

62. See *infra* Chapter 33 ("Race and the Fourteenth Amendment").

63. For one careful analysis of the post-1975 effects, see John J. Donohue III & James J. Heckman, "Continuous versus Episodic Change: The Effect of Federal Civil Rights Policy on the Economic Status of Blacks," 29 *J. Econ. Literature* 1603 (1991). See also Richard A. Epstein, "The Paradox of Civil Rights," 8 *Yale L. & Pol'y Rev.* 299 (1990). For an earlier empirical study, see James J. Heckman & Brook S. Payner, "Determining the Impact of Federal Antidiscrimination Policy on the Economic Status of Blacks: A Study of South Carolina," 79 *Am. Econ. Rev.* 138, 140–142 (1989).

64. Pub. L. No. 75-718, ch. 676, 52 Stat. 1060.

65. 312 U.S. 100 (1941).

66. FLSA Amendments of 1961, Pub. L. No. 87-30, 75 Stat. 65.

67. FLSA Amendments of 1966, Pub. L. No. 89-601, 80 Stat. 830.

68. FLSA Amendments of 1974, Pub. L. No. 93-259, 88 Stat. 68.

69. 392 U.S. 183 (1968).

70. 426 U.S. 833 (1976).

71. 469 U.S. 528, 538–539 (1985).

72. For the canonical works, see Herbert Wechsler, "The Political Safeguards of Federalism: The Role of the States in the Composition and Selection of the National Government," 54 *Colum. L. Rev.* 543 (1954); Jesse H. Choper, *Judicial Review and the National Political Process* (1980).

73. 421 U.S. 542 (1975).

12. Constitutional Pushback

1. 514 U.S. 549 (1995).

2. Id. at 551–552, 567–568.

3. See id. at 552–559.

4. Id. at 558–559 (citations omitted).

5. See Laurence H. Tribe, *American Constitutional Law* 831–832 (3d ed., 2000) (discussing the significance of *Lopez*).

6. *Lopez*, 514 U.S. at 569 (Kennedy, J., concurring).

7. 529 U.S. 598 (2000).

8. Pub. L. No. 103-322, 108 Stat. 1902 (1994) (codified as amended in scattered sections of 16, 18, and 42 U.S.C.).

9. 545 U.S. 1 (2005).

10. Cal. Health & Safety Code § 11362.5 (2005).

11. 21 U.S.C. § 801 (2006).

12. On which see Richard A. Epstein & Paula Stannard, "Constitutional Rate-making and the Affordable Care Act: A New Source of Vulnerability," 38 *Am. J.L. & Med.* 243 (2012).

13. For discussion, see Richard A. Epstein, *Mortal Peril: Our Inalienable Right to Health Care?* 27–41 (1997).

14. For an expose of one such incident, see David A. Hyman, "Lies, Damned Lies, and Narrative," 73 *Ind. L.J.*, 797, 813–832 (1998) (detailing the difference between the events and the public story in the death of Terry Takewell in relation to the passage of The Emergency Medical Treatment and Active Labor Act).

15. Victoria Craig Bunce, *Health Insurance Mandates in the States 2011—Executive Summary* (Council for Affordable Health Insurance, 2011), available at http://www.cahi.org/cahi_contents/resources/pdf/MandatesintheStates2011ExecSumm.pdf. For updates, see *Trends in State Mandated Benefits*, available at http://www.cahi.org.

16. Elise Gould, *The Erosion of Employment-Based Insurance* (Economic Policy Institute, Nov. 1, 2007), available at http://www.epi.org/page/-/old/briefing papers/203/bp203.pdf; Elizabeth Mendes, *Fewer Americans Have Employer-Based Health Insurance* (Gallup Wellbeing, Feb. 14, 2012), available at http://www.gallup.com/poll/152621/fewer-americans-employer-based-health-insurance.aspx.

17. *Nat'l Fed. of Ind. Bus. (NFIB) v. Sibelius*, 132 S. Ct. 2566, 2609 (2012).

18. Ezra Klein, "Reagan's Solicitor General: 'Health Care Is Interstate Commerce. Is This a Regulation of It? Yes. End of Story,'" *Wonkblog* (*Wash. Post*, Mar. 28, 2012), available at http://www.washingtonpost.com/blogs/wonkblog/post/reagans-solicitor-general-health-care-is-interstate-commerce-is-this-a-regulation-of-it-yes-end-of-story/2011/08/25/gIQAmaQigS_blog.html.

19. 95 U.S. 168 (1869).

20. 322 U.S. 533 (1944).

21. *NFIB*, 132 S. Ct. at 2586.
22. See Richard A. Epstein, "Judicial Engagement with the Affordable Care Act: Why Rational Basis Analysis Falls Short," 19 *Geo. Mason L. Rev.* 931, 936–949 (2012).
23. *NFIB*, 132 S. Ct. at 2612.
24. Id.
25. Id. at 2615 (emphasis added).
26. For further discussion, see *infra* Chapter 13 ("Enumerated Powers: Taxing and Spending").
27. For an academic version of the same argument that also overstates the prisoner's dilemma component in this case, see Leslie Meltzer Henry & Maxwell Stearns, "Commerce Games and the Individual Mandate," 100 *Geo. L.J.* 1117 (2012).
28. For details, see *Health Indiana Plan—Health Insurance for Adults* (City of Bloomington) (2013), available at http://bloomington.in.gov/documents/viewDocument.php?document_id=2334.
29. Einer Elhauge, "If Health Insurance Mandates Are Unconstitutional, Why Did the Founding Fathers Back Them?," *The New Republic* (Apr. 13, 2012), available at http://www.tnr.com/article/politics/102620/individual-mandate-history-affordable-care-act.
30. Id.
31. 1 Stat. 605 (1798), available at http://history.nih.gov/research/downloads/1StatL605.pdf.
32. Militia Acts of 1792, ch. 28 & 3, 1 Stat. 271.
33. U.S. Const. art. I, § 8, cl. 16.
34. See Andrew Koppelman, "'Tough Luck' Becomes Law," *Salon* (Jun. 27, 2012), available at http://www.salon.com/2012/06/27/tough_luck_becomes_law.
35. 661 F.3d 1, 21 (D.C. Cir. 2011).

13. Enumerated Powers

1. 132 S. Ct. 2566 (2012).
2. U.S. Const. art. I, § 8, cl. 1. For a lengthier treatment of these issues, see Richard A. Epstein, "Standing and Spending—The Role of Legal and Equitable Principles," 4 *Chap. L. Rev.* 1 (2001).
3. See, e.g., Richard A. Posner, "Taxation by Regulation," 2 *Bell J. Econ. & Mgmt. Sci.* 22 (1971); George J. Stigler, "The Theory of Economic Regulation," 2 *Bell J. Econ. & Mgmt. Sci.* 3 (1971).
4. *NFIB*, 132 S. Ct. at 2636.
5. Id. at 2658.
6. 262 U.S. 447 (1923). For discussion, see *supra* Chapter 6 ("Standing: Background and Origins").
7. See Mancur Olson, *The Logic of Collective Action* 14–15 (1965), for the standard early account.
8. For an early discussion, see Story, *Commentaries* 337–341.

9. Story, *Commentaries* 479.

10. See *supra* Chapter 12 ("Constitutional Pushback: 1995 to Present, from *Lopez* to *NFIB*").

11. *Federalist No. 41*, at 211–213 (James Madison) (Clifton Rossiter ed., 1999).

12. See Alexander Hamilton, *Report on Manufactures*, Communicated to the House of Representatives, Dec. 5, 1791, at 40 (Gov't. Print. Off., 1913).

13. For an account, see John C. Eastman, "Restoring the 'General' Welfare Clause," 4 *Chap. L. Rev.* 63 (2001), which offers a narrow reading without noting the relevance of the phrase "of the United States."

14. 30 *Annals of Cong.*, Senate, 14th Cong. 2nd Sess. 211 (1817), discussed in Eastman, *supra* note 13, at 69.

15. President James Buchanan to House of Representatives (Feb. 24, 1859), in 7 *A Compilation of the Messages and Papers of the Presidents 1789–1897*, at 3079 (James D. Richardson ed., 1897), discussed in Eastman, *supra* note 13, at 70.

16. Michael Greve, *The Upside-Down Constitution* 163 (2012).

17. 297 U.S. 1 (1936).

18. Pub. L. No. 73-10, 48 Stat. 31.

19. 301 U.S. 548 (1937).

20. Pub. L. No. 74-271, 49 Stat. 620 (codified as amended at 42 U.S.C. § 1101).

21. *NLRB v. Jones & Laughlin Steel Corp.*, 301 U.S. 1 (1937).

22. *Steward Machine*, 301 U.S. at 599.

23. Id. at 602 (quoting Franklin Pierce, Veto Message (May 3, 1854)), reprinted in 5 *A Compilation of the Messages and Papers of the Presidents 1789–1897*, at 248–249 (James D. Richardson ed., 1897), which followed the same cautious view on the spending power as Madison and Buchanan, *supra* note 13.

24. 285 U.S. 262, 311 (1932).

25. *Steward Machine*, 301 U.S. at 589–590.

26. Matthew Hale, "De Portibus Maris," in 1 *A Collection of Tracts Relative to the Law of England* 77-78 (Francis Hargrave ed., 1787).

27. 12 East 527, 104 Eng. Rep. 206 (K.B. 1810).

28. Id. at 538, 104 Eng. Rep. at 21.

29. 94 U.S. 113, 127–128 (1876).

30. 483 U.S. 203 (1987).

31. 23 U.S.C. § 158 (1982 ed., Supp. III).

32. 128 U.S. 1 (1888).

33. *Cal. Retail Liquor Dealers Ass'n v. Midcal Aluminum, Inc.*, 445 U.S. 97, 110 (1980).

34. 483 U.S. at 212.

35. 247 U.S. 251 (1918).

36. *Bailey v. Drexel Furniture Co.*, 259 U.S. 20 (1922).

37. 483 U.S. at 207 (some internal quotations and citations omitted).

38. Id. at 208 & 208 n.3.

39. Id. at 211–212.

40. E.g., *Nevada v. Skinner*, 884 F.2d 445, 448 (9th Cir. 1989) (upholding the national speed limit); *California v. United States*, 104 F.3d 1086 (9th Cir. 1997)

(upholding federal requirements on California to provide services to illegal aliens); *Koslow v. Pennsylvania*, 302 F.3d 161, 174 (3d Cir. 2002) (upholding a provision requiring a state to waive immunity under the Eleventh Amendment in order to receive certain federal funds).

41. 132 S. Ct. at 2599.
42. Id.
43. Stanley Surrey & Paul R. McDaniel, *Tax Expenditures* 3 (1985).
44. 132 S. Ct. at 2593–2600.
45. Kaiser Commission on Medicaid and the Uninsured, *Financing New Medicaid Coverage under Health Reform: The Role of the Federal Government and States* (May 2010), available at http://www.kff.org/healthreform/upload/8072.pdf.
46. Id.
47. Kaiser Commission on Medicaid and the Uninsured, *Expanding Medicaid under Health Reform: A Look at Adults at or below 133% of Poverty* (Apr. 2010), available at http://www.kff.org/healthreform/upload/8052-02.pdf.
48. See *NFIB*, 132 S. Ct. at 2566; *Florida v. U.S. Dep't Health & Human Servs.*, 648 F.3d 1235, 1268 (11th Cir. 2011).
49. *NFIB*, 132 S. Ct. at 2604.
50. Id. at 2602 (internal citations and quotation marks omitted).
51. *Jefferson Parish Hosp. Dist. No. 2 v. Hyde*, 466 U.S. 2 (1985); Louis Kaplow, "Extension of Monopoly Power through Leverage," 85 *Colum. L. Rev.* 515 (1985). For a recent guide, see Warren S. Grimes, *Tying: Requirements Ties, Efficiency and Innovation*, Testimony on Single-Firm Conduct and Antitrust Law, before Department of Justice and Federal Trade Commission (2006), available at http://www.justice.gov/atr/public/hearings/single_firm/comments/219982.htm.
52. *NFIB*, 132 S. Ct. at 2604.
53. *Lorain Journal Co. v. United States*, 342 U.S. 143 (1951).
54. 132 S. Ct. at 2605.

14. The Necessary and Proper Clause

1. U.S. Const. art. I, § 8, cl. 19.
2. *Federalist No. 33*, at 202 (Alexander Hamilton) (Clinton Rossiter ed., 1999); *Federalist No. 44*, at 284 (James Madison) (Clinton Rossiter ed., 1999).
3. For a recent defense of this position, see the views of Robert Natalson in Gary Lawson, Geoffrey P. Miller, Robert G. Natalson, & Guy I. Seidman, *The Origins of the Necessary and Proper Clause* 119 (2010).
4. 17 U.S. 316, 423 (1819) ("[S]hould Congress, under the pretext of executing its powers, pass laws for the accomplishment of objects not intrusted to the government, it would become the painful duty of this tribunal, should a case requiring such a decision come before it, to say that such an act was not the law of the land.").
5. 22 U.S. 1, 188 (1824) ("In the last of the enumerated powers, that which grants, expressly, the means for carrying all others into execution, Congress

is authorized 'to make all laws which shall be necessary and proper' for the purpose. But this limitation on the means which may be used, is not extended to the powers which are conferred.").

6. See Gary Lawson & Patricia B. Granger, "The 'Proper' Scope of Federal Power: A Jurisdictional Interpretation of the Sweeping Clause," 43 *Duke L.J.* 267, 326–330 (1993) (stressing the word "proper").

7. Lawson, et al., *supra* note 3, at 120–121.

8. William Baude, "Rethinking the Federal Eminent Domain Power," 122 *Yale L.J.* 1738 (2013).

9. 91 U.S. 367, 371 (1875); Baude, *supra* note 8 at 1791.

10. U.S. Const. art. I, § 8, cl. 7.

11. Baude, *supra* note 8 at 1774-1785.

12. Id. at 1742, 1764-1765.

13. Id. at 1763.

14. An Act providing for the Cessions of Castle Island, in the harbor of Boston, to the United States, and for other purposes therein mentioned, 1798 *Mass. Acts* 217, ch. 16 (Jun. 25, 1798), cited in Baude, *supra* note 8, at 1762 n122.

15. 17 U.S. 316 (1819).

16. See David P. Currie, *The Constitution in Congress: The Federalist Period 1789–1801* (1997).

17. 79 U.S. 457, 537 (1871).

18. For discussion, see *supra* Chapter 13 ("Enumerated Powers: Taxing and Spending").

19. "Jefferson's Opinion on the Constitutionality of a National Bank: 1791," *The Avalon Project: Documents in Law, History and Diplomacy* (2008), available at http://avalon.law.yale.edu/18th_century/bank-tj.asp (emphasis in original).

20. "Hamilton's Opinion as to the Constitutionality of the Bank of the United States: 1791," *The Avalon Project: Documents in Law, History and Diplomacy* (2008), available at http://avalon.law.yale.edu/18th_century/bank-ah.asp (emphasis added). Marshall then adopted this interpretation in *McCulloch*, 17 U.S. at 413–414.

21. See, for discussion, Randy E. Barnett, *Restoring the Lost Constitution: The Presumption of Liberty* 171–173 (2004).

22. *McCulloch*, 17 U.S. at 406–407.

23. Id. at 407 (emphasis in original).

24. Id. at 421.

25. See Julian E. Zelizer, *The American Congress: The Building of Democracy* 155–156 (2004).

26. Fed. Reserve Bank of Phila., *The First Bank of the United States: A Chapter in the History of Central Banking* 10 & n.26 (Jun. 2009), available at http://www.philadelphiafed.org/publications/economic-education/first-bank.pdf; see also Zelizer, *supra* note 25, at 156.

27. For discussions, see Ralph C. H. Catterall, *The Second Bank of the United States* (1902); Bray Hammon, *Banks and Politics in America from the Revolution to the Civil War* (1957).

28. James Bradley Thayer, *John Marshall* 68 (1901); Felix Frankfurter, "John Marshall and the Judicial Function," 69 *Harv. L. Rev.* 217, 219 (1955). For a similar outlook from one of Frankfurter's ablest clerks, see David P. Currie, *The Constitution in the Supreme Court: The First Hundred Years, 1789–1888* 160–62 (1985).

29. 75 U.S. 603 (1870).

30. 79 U.S. 457 (1871).

31. U.S. Const. art. I, § 10, cl. 1.

32. Id. art. I, § 8, cl. 5.

33. Id. art. I, § 8, cl. 3.

34. *Legal Tender Cases*, 79 U.S. at 536.

35. *Federalist No. 44, supra* note 2 (Clinton Rossiter ed., 1999).

36. 12 U.S.C. ch. 3.

37. 34 F.2d 910, 914 (2d Cir. 1929).

38. See, for discussion, John Taylor, *Getting Off Track: How Government Actions and Interventions Caused, Prolonged, and Worsened the Financial Crisis* (2009).

39. 148 *Cong. Rec.* E192 (2002) (statement of Rep. Paul).

40. See Milton Friedman & Anna Jacobsen Schwartz, *A Monetary History of the United States: 1867–1960* (1963).

41. 188 U.S. 321 (1903).

42. Id. at 358.

43. For discussion, see Jonathan Harrison, "Enumerated Federal Power and the Necessary and Proper Clause," 78 *U. Chi. L. Rev.* 1101, 1102–1103 (2011).

44. 301 U.S. 1 (1937).

45. NLRA, 74 Pub. L. No. 198, 49 Stat. 449 (codified as amended at 29 U.S.C. §§ 151–169 (2006)).

46. *Jones & Laughlin*, 301 US. at 41, 42.

47. See *NLRB v. Fansteel Metallurgical Corp.*, 306 U.S. 240 (1939).

48. Michael C. Harper & Samuel Estreicher, *Labor Law: Cases, Materials and Problems* 104 (4th ed., 1996).

49. 80 Pub. L. No. 101, 61 Stat. 136 (codified as amended at 29 U.S.C. §§ 141–157 (2006)).

50. 545 U.S. 1 (2005).

51. Id. at 22, 26–27.

52. 132 S. Ct. 2566 (2012).

53. Id. at 2579.

54. Id. at 2592.

55. 130 S. Ct. 1949 (2010).

56. 132 S. Ct. at 2592 (emphasis in original) (citing *Comstock*, 130 S. Ct. at 1954–1955). The due process objections to this procedure had been addressed in *Kansas v. Hendricks*, 521 U.S. 364, 356–358, and *Kansas v. Crane*, 534 U.S. 407 (2002).

57. *Comstock*, 130 S. Ct. at 1962, 1964.

58. *NFIB*, 132 S. Ct. at 2592 (emphasis in original) (citing *Jinks v. Richland Cnty.*, 538 U.S. 456, 459, 462 (2003)).

59. *NFIB*, 132 S. Ct. at 2592 (emphasis in original) (citing *Sabri* v. *United States*, 541 U.S. 600, 602, 605 (2004)).

15. The Dormant Commerce Clause

1. 25 U.S. 213, 306–307 (1827).
2. U.S. Const. art. VI, § 2, discussed *supra* Chapter 5 (*"Marbury* and *Martin"*).
3. 22 U.S. 1, 221 (1824).
4. Id. at 225–226 (Johnson, J., concurring).
5. 75 U.S. 168 (1869).
6. U.S. Const. art. III, § 2.
7. 336 U.S. 525 (1949).
8. 317 U.S. 111 (1942).
9. *H. P. Hood & Sons*, 336 U.S. at 539.
10. *Pike v. Bruce Church, Inc.*, 397 US. 137, 142 (1970).
11. Id.
12. *W. Lynn Creamery, Inc. v. Healy*, 512 U.S. 186, 194–197 (1994).
13. *Camps Newfound/Owatonna, Inc. v. Town of Harrison*, 520 U.S. 564, 580–581 (1997).
14. 27 U.S. 245 (1829).
15. *Corfield v. Coryell*, 6 F. Cas. 546 (E.D. Pa. 1823) (No. 3230), discussed in greater detail *supra* Chapter 9 ("The Commerce Power: Theory and Practice, 1787–1865").
16. 53 U.S. 299 (1851).
17. 303 U.S. 177 (1938).
18. 325 U.S. 761 (1945).
19. See, e.g., *Kassel v. Consol. Freightways Corp. of Del.*, 450 U.S. 662 (1981) (Powell, J., plurality).
20. See Tandem Truck Safety Act of 1984, Pub. L. No. 98-544, 98 Stat. 2829.
21. 340 U.S. 349 (1951).
22. See also *WTO Agreements and Public Health*, at 11, available at http://www.wto.org/english/res_e/booksp_e/who_wto_e.pdf: "The basic WTO principle is non-discrimination: WTO Members cannot discriminate between their trading partners nor between imported and locally-produced goods that are otherwise similar. Since the inception of GATT more than 50 years ago, Article XX of GATT guarantees Members' right to take measures to restrict imports and export of products when those measures are necessary to protect the health of humans, animals and plants (Article XX(b))."
23. 432 U.S. 333 (1977).
24. 477 U.S. 131 (1986).
25. Id. at 144 (citations omitted) (internal quotation marks omitted).
26. 437 U.S. 117 (1978).
27. Id. at 128.

28. 453 U.S. 609 (1981).

29. Id. at 617 (quoting *Complete Auto Transit, Inc. v. Brady*, 430 U.S. 274, 279 (1977)).

30. 512 U.S. 186 (1994).

31. See *supra* note 28.

32. See *Carmichael v. S. Coal & Coke Co.*, 301 U.S. 495, 522 (1937) ("The only benefit to which the taxpayer is constitutionally entitled is that derived from his enjoyment of the privileges of living in an organized society, established and safeguarded by the devotion of taxes to public purposes.").

33. 519 U.S. 278 (1997).

34. Id. at 295–296.

35. Id. at 299.

36. 682 F.3d 1144 (9th Cir. 2012). For the record, I have signed on to a petition for certiorari asking the Supreme Court to overturn this decision.

37. 6 F. Cas. 546 (E.D. Pa. 1823) (No. 3230).

38. 426 U.S. 794 (1976).

39. 447 U.S. 429 (1980).

40. 467 U.S. 82 (1984).

41. See Donald H. Regan, "The Supreme Court and State Protectionism: Making Sense of the Dormant Commerce Clause," 84 *Mich. L. Rev.* 1091, 1194 (1986).

42. For similar arguments, see the discussion of *Hammer v. Dagenhart*, 247 U.S. 251 (1918), *supra* Chapter 10 ("The Commerce Clause in Transition: 1865–1937"); the Medicaid extension, *supra* Chapter 13 ("Enumerated Powers: Taxing and Spending"); and free speech, *infra* Chapter 24 ("Freedom of Speech and Religion: Preliminary Considerations").

43. 437 U.S. 617 (1978).

44. Id. at 627.

45. 505 U.S. 144 (1992).

46. Pub. L. No. 99-240, 99 Stat. 1842 (codified at 42 U.S.C. §§ 2021(b)–(j)).

47. David DeMille, "White House Is 'Done with Yucca,'" *The Spectrum* (Jan. 30, 2010), available at http://www.thespectrum.com/article/20100130/NEWS 01/1300311/White-House-is-done-with-Yucca.

48. 511 U.S. 383 (1994).

16. Basic Principles and Domestic Powers

1. For discussion, see Christopher R. Berry & Jacob E. Gersen, "The Unbundled Executive," 75 *U. Chi. L. Rev.* 1385 (2008), and for criticism of that position, see Steven G. Calabresi & Nicholas Terrell, "The Fatally Flawed Theory of the Unbundled Executive," 93 *Minn. L. Rev.* 1696 (2009).

2. 28 U.S.C. § 595 (1978).

3. For a contemporary account, see Carroll Kilpatrick, "Nixon Forces Firing of Cox; Richardson, Ruckelshaus Quit," *Wash. Post*, Oct. 21, 1973, at A01, available

at http://www.washingtonpost.com/wp-srv/national/longterm/watergate/articles/102173-2.htm.

4. 487 U.S. 654, 697–734 (1988).

5. In 1999, the statute lapsed due to Congress's failure to pass a reauthorization. The Office of the Special Prosecutor was terminated and replaced by the U.S. Department of Justice Office of Special Counsel, which operates with relative autonomy within the departmental structure.

6. U.S. Const. art. II, § 1, cl. 1.

7. Id. art. II, § 4; id. art. I, § 3, cl. 6.

8. Id. art. II, § 1, cl. 7.

9. Id.

10. Eric A. Posner & Adrian Vermeule, *The Executive Unbound: After the Madisonian Republic* (2010), critically reviewed in Richard H. Pildes, "Law and the President," 125 *Harv. L. Rev.* 1381 (2012).

11. Posner & Vermeule, *supra* note 10, at 15.

12. U.S. Const. art. II, § 2. cl. 1 ("The President . . . shall have Power to Grant Reprieves and Pardons for Offenses against the United States, except in Cases of Impeachment.").

13. Id. art II, § 2, cl. 3.

14. Pildes, *supra* note 10, at 1408.

15. Id. at 1406 (citing Daryl Levinson, "Parchment and Politics: The Positive Puzzle of Constitutional Commitment," 124 *Harv. L. Rev.* 657 (2011)).

16. John Locke, *Second Treatise of Government* ¶144 (C. B. Macpherson ed., 1980) (1690) (emphasis omitted).

17. *Federalist No. 70* (Alexander Hamilton) (Clinton Rossiter ed., 1999).

18. *Federalist No. 71* (Alexander Hamilton) (Clinton Rossiter ed., 1999).

19. Id.

20. U.S. Const. art. II, § 3.

21. Id. art. II, § 2, cl. 2.

22. Id. art. II, § 2, cl. 1.

23. Id. art. II, § 3.

24. Id. art. II, § 2, cl. 1.

25. Id. art II, § 2, cl. 2.

26. Id. art II, § 2, cl. 1.

27. Id. art. II, § 2, cl. 2.

28. Id. art. III, § 1.

29. For various arguments on this point, see *Reforming the Court: Term Limits for Supreme Court Justices* (Roger C. Cramton & Paul D. Carrington eds., 2006).

30. U.S. Const. art. II, § 2, cl. 2.

31. Id. art. III, § 1.

32. For an exhaustive account on the subject, see Michael B. Rappaport, "The Original Meaning of the Recess Appointments Clause," 52 *U.C.L.A. L. Rev.* 1487 (2005); T. J. Halstead, *Recess Appointments: A Legal Overview* (Cong. Research Serv., RL33009, 2005), available at http://fpc.state.gov/documents/organization/50801.pdf.

33. U.S. Const. art. II, § 2, cl. 3.

34. Rappaport, *supra* note 32, at 1519; Halstead, *supra* note 32, at 4.

35. Amelia Frenkel, "Defining Recess Appointments Clause 'Vacancies,'" 88 *N.Y.U. L. Rev.* 729 (2013).

36. Id. at 734.

37. *Noel Canning v. NLRB,* 705 F.3d 490 (D.C. Cir. 2013)

38. Id. at 499.

39. See 157 Cong. Rec. S5297 (daily ed. Aug. 5, 2011).

40. See 157 Cong. Rec. S8789 (daily ed. Dec. 23, 2011).

41. *NLRB v. Noel Canning,* cert. granted 2013 Lexis 4876 (2013). To follow the progress of the case, see http://www.scotusblog.com/case-files/cases/national-labor-relations-board-v-noel-canning/.

42. "Bush Appoints Bolton as U.N. Ambassador," *NBC Politics* (Aug. 1, 2005), available at http://www.msnbc.msn.com/id/8758621/ns/politics/t/bush-appoints-bolton-un-ambassador.

43. Peter Kirsanow, "Obama's Recess Appointments to the NLRB," *Nat'l Rev.* (Mar. 29, 2010), available at http://www.nationalreview.com/corner/197104/obamas-recess-appointments-nlrb/peter-kirsanow.

44. Helene Cooper & Jennifer Steinhauer, "Bucking Senate, Obama Appoints Consumer Chief," *N.Y. Times* (Jan. 4, 2012), available at http://www.nytimes.com/2012/01/05/us/politics/richard-cordray-named-consumer-chief-in-recess-appointment.html?_r=1&pagewanted=all.

45. John Yoo, "Obama Oversteps His Limits with Cordray Recess Appointment," *Ricochet* (Jan. 4, 2012), available at http://ricochet.com/main-feed/Obama-Oversteps-His-Limits-with-Cordray-Recess-Appointment.

46. U.S. Const. art. II, § 2, cl. 2.

47. 424 U.S. 1 (1976).

48. Pub. L. No. 92-225, 86 Stat. 3 (codified as scattered sections of 2 U.S.C.).

49. U.S. Const. art. II, § 2, cl. 2.

50. Kenneth A. Shepsle, "Congress Is a "They," Not an "It": Legislative Intent as Oxymoron," 12 *Int'l Rev. L. & Econ.* 239 (1992), at least in those cases short of unanimity of opinion.

51. For a discussion of the immense bottlenecks that have emerged in recent years, see Anne Joseph O'Connell, "Vacant Offices: Delays in Staffing Top Agency Positions," 82 *S. Cal. L. Rev.* 913 (2009).

52. 487 U.S. 654 (1988).

53. Pub. L. No. 95-521, §§ 601–602, 92 Stat. 1824, 1867–1874 (codified as amended at 28 U.S.C. §§ 49, 591–598 (2006)).

54. 520 U.S. 651 (1997).

55. Id. at 663.

56. 501 U.S. 868 (1991).

57. 204 F.3d 1125 (D.C. Cir. 2000).

58. Id. at 1143 (quoting *Butz v. Economou,* 438 U.S. 478, 513 (1978)).

59. For a voluminous documentation of the point, see Steven G. Calabresi & Christopher S. Yoo, *The Unitary Executive: Presidential Power from Washington to Bush*

(2008). For my response to their arguments, see Richard A. Epstein, "Executive Power in Political and Corporate Contexts," 12 *U. Pa. J. Const. L.* 277 (2010).

60. U.S. Const. art. II, § 3.
61. 272 U.S. 52 (1926).
62. Id. at 131.
63. 14 Stat. 430 (1867).
64. For a discussion, see *Myers*, 272 U.S. at 164–171.
65. Id. at 173–174, 263 & n.34, 278 n.63.
66. Pendleton Civil Service Act, ch. 27, 22 Stat. 403 (1883).
67. U.S. Const. art. II, § 2, cl. 2.
68. Id. art. I, § 8, cl. 18.
69. *Myers*, 272 U.S. at 175 (internal citations omitted).
70. 116 U.S. 483 (1886).
71. Id. at 485.

17. Delegation and the Rise of Independent Agencies

1. See John Locke, *Second Treatise of Government* §§ 143–144 (C. B. Macpherson ed., 1980) (1690).
2. For an account see David P. Currie, *The Constitution in Congress: The Federalist Period 1789–1801,* at 146–151 (1997).
3. U.S. Const. art. I, § 8, cl. 7.
4. Id. art. I, § 8, cl. 3.
5. See Currie, *supra* note 2, at 148.
6. U.S. Const. art. I, § 1.
7. See Daryl J. Levinson & Richard H. Pildes, "Separation of Parties, Not Powers," 119 *Harv. L. Rev.* 2311 (2006), to which see my reply, Richard A. Epstein, "Why Parties and Powers Both Matter: A Separationist Response To Levinson and Pildes," 119 *Harv. L. Rev. F.* 210 (2006), available at http://harvardlawreview.org/media/pdf/epstein.pdf.
8. 293 U.S. 388 (1935).
9. 295 U.S. 495 (1935).
10. 73 Pub. L. No. 67, § 9(c), 48 Stat. 195, 200 (1933).
11. For the institutional background, see Daniel A. Crane, "The Story of *United States v. Socony-Vacuum*: Hot Oil and Antitrust in the Two New Deals," in *Antitrust Stories* 91 (Eleanor M. Fox & Daniel A. Crane eds., 2007).
12. 293 U.S. at 431–433.
13. For the numbers, see Louis Jaffe & Nathaniel Nathanson, *Administrative Law, Cases and Materials* 52 (4th ed., 1976).
14. 73 Pub. L. No. 73-67, § 3(a)(2), 48 Stat. 195, 196.
15. 295 U.S. at 553.
16. For repeated and justified harping on this cartel theme, see Michael S. Greve, *The Upside-Down Constitution* (2012).
17. Pub. L. No. 77-421, 56 Stat. 23 (codified at 50 U.S.C. §§ 901–05) (repealed 1956).

18. Pub. L. No. 77-421, §§ 1(a), 2(a), 56 Stat. 23, 24.
19. See *Amalgamated Meat Cutters & Butcher Workmen of North America, AFL-CIO v. Connally*, 337 F. Supp. 737 (D.D.C. 1971).
20. 462 U.S. 919 (1983).
21. Id. at 959–967 (Powell, J., concurring).
22. U.S. Const. art. I, § 7, cl. 2.
23. Id. For Chief Justice Burger's discussion, see 462 U.S. at 945–951.
24. *Chadha*, 462 U.S. at 944.
25. Id. at 979–996 (White, J., dissenting).
26. Id. at 969–970, 974.
27. Pub. L. No. 99-177, 99 Stat. 1037 (1985).
28. *Bowsher v. Synar*, 478 U.S. 714, 727–728 (1986).
29. Id.
30. Id. at 722.
31. See, e.g., *Humphrey's Executor v. United States*, 295 U.S. 602 (1935) (holding that the president could only remove a commissioner from the Federal Trade Commission for a cause specified by Congress in the Federal Trade Commission Act).
32. 15 U.S.C. § 41.
33. 47 U.S.C. § 154(c).
34. 15 U.S.C. § 78d(a).
35. 29 U.S.C. § 153(a).
36. 47 U.S.C. § 303; see also *Nat'l Broad. Co. v. United States*, 319 U.S. 190, 193–194 (1943) (the commission investigated whether certain regulations were in the "public interest, convenience, or necessity").
37. On the ICC generally, see "125 Years since the Interstate Commerce Act: A Symposium in the Form of a Final Convocation," 95 *Marquette L. Rev.* 1123 (2012).
38. 295 U.S. 602 (1935).
39. Id.
40. Id. at 628.
41. U.S. Const. art. I , § 8, cl. 18.
42. Compare Lawrence Lessig & Cass R. Sunstein, "The President and the Administration," 94 *Colum. L. Rev.* 1 (1994), with Steven G. Calabresi & Saikrishna B. Prakash, "The President's Power to Execute the Laws," 104 *Yale L.J.* 541 (1994). My sympathies, it should be evident, run with Calabresi and Prakash.
43. See, e.g., Peter L. Strauss, "The Place of Agencies in Government: Separation of Powers and the Fourth Branch," 84 *Colum. L. Rev.* 573, 578 & n.16 (1984) (internal citation omitted).
44. See, e.g., *Smyth v. Ames*, 169 U.S. 466 (1898) (striking down Nebraska rate restriction on railroad rates under "fair value" standard); *Chicago, M. & St. P. Ry. v. Minnesota*, 134 U.S. 418, 458 (1890) (allowing judicial review of state railroad rates); see also *Sw. Bell Tel. Co. v. Pub. Serv. Comm.*, 262 U.S. 276, 306–308 (1923) (Justice Brandeis's criticism of fair value rule).

45. Sustained at the federal level in *Crowell v. Benson*, 285 U.S. 22, 38 (1932).

46. For a discussion, see *State ex. rel. R.R. & Warehouse Comm'n v. Chicago, M. & St. P. Ry. Co.*, 37 N.W. 782 (Minn. 1888). That decision sustained the use of the commission system but denied judicial review of ratemaking decisions for their fairness, which was later held to be required under the United States Constitution.

47. For the ultimate constitutionality of these schemes after some initial hesitation, see *New York Cent. R.R. Co. v. White*, 243 U.S. 188 (1917).

48. For discussion of Article I courts and judges, see Richard H. Fallon, Jr., et al., *Hart and Wechsler's The Federal Courts and the Federal System* 339–349 (6th ed., 2009); see also "Federal Tribunals in the United States," *Wikipedia*, available at http://en.wikipedia.org/wiki/Article_I_and_Article_III_tribunals#Article_I_tribunals.

49. See *N. Pipeline Constr. Co. v. Marathon Pipe Line Co.*, 458 U.S. 50, 87 (1982) (limiting the jurisdiction of Article I bankruptcy courts). For the technical statutory fix that followed, see the Bankruptcy Amendments and Federal Judgeship Act of 1984, 98 Stat. 333 (1984).

50. *Thomas v. Union Carbide Agric. Prods. Co.*, 473 US. 568 (1984).

51. *Commodities Futures Trading Comm'n v. Schor*, 478 U.S. 833 (1986).

52. See the various essays in *Reforming the Court: Term Limits for Supreme Court Justices* (Roger C. Cramton & Paul D. Carrington eds., 2006).

53. See discussion, *supra* Chapter 11 ("The Commerce Clause: Transformation to Consolidation, 1937–1995"), at notes 50–55 and accompanying text.

54. For a discussion of the rule of first possession, see Richard A. Epstein, "Possession as the Root of Title," 13 *Ga. L. Rev.* 1221 (1979). For key authorities, see *Pierson v. Post*, 3 Cai. R. 175 (N.Y. 1805); *J. Inst.* 2.1.12; *G. Inst.* 2.66.

55. See *"Tribune Co. v. Oak Leaves Broad. Station,"* 68 *Cong. Rec.* 216 (1926) (reprinting Ill. Cir. Ct. decision of Nov. 17, 1926). For rival interpretations of the complex interaction between this case and the legislative movement, see Charlotte Twight, "What Congressmen Knew and When They Knew It: Further Evidence on the Origins of U.S. Broadcasting Regulation," 95 *Public Choice* 247 (1996); Thomas W. Hazlett, "Oak Leaves and the Origins of the 1927 Radio Act: Comment," 95 *Public Choice* 277 (1998).

56. *Hoover v. Intercity Radio Co.*, 286 F. 1003, (D.C. Cir. 1926).

57. *United States v. Zenith Radio Corp.*, 12 F.2d 614 (N.D. Ill. 1926).

58. For a clear account see *National Broad. Co. v. United States*, 319 U.S. 190, 210–215 (1943); Ronald Coase, "The Federal Communication Commission," 2 *J. L. & Econ.* 1 (1959); Thomas W. Hazlett, "The Rationality of U.S. Regulation of the Broadcast Spectrum," 33 *J. L. & Econ.* 133 (1990).

59. Radio-Communications Act of Aug. 13, 1912, 37 Stat. 302, 47 U.S.C. § 51 et seq.

60. 47 U.S.C. §§ 81–83, 85–119 (repealed 1934).

61. See Jeremy Waldron, *The Dignity of Legislation* 17 (1999). The mere title of this book reveals the gulf that separates our respective worldviews.

62. *Nat'l Broad. Co. v. United States,* 319 U.S. at 215–216.
63. See *Cosmopolitan Broad. Co. v. FCC,* 581 F.2d 917 (D.C. Cir. 1978).
64. Bureau of Labor Statistics, *Union Members Summary* (Jan. 22, 2010), available at http://www.bls.gov/news.release/union2.nr0.htm.
65. 130 S. Ct. 2635 (2010).
66. Noel Canning v. NLRB, 705 F.3d 490 (D.C. Cir. 2013). The case is discussed in more detail in Chapter 16 *supra* at 257.
67. For my elaboration, see Richard A. Epstein, "A Common Law for Labor Relations: A Critique of the New Deal Labor Legislation," 92 *Yale L.J.* 1357 (1983).
68. 130 S. Ct. 3138 (2010).
69. Sarbanes-Oxley Act of 2002, Pub. L. No. 107-204, 116 Stat. 745 (codified in scattered sections of 15 and 18 U.S.C.).
70. *Alaska Airlines v. Brock,* 480 U.S. 678, 684 (1987): "Unless it is evident that the Legislature would not have enacted those provisions which are within its power, independently of that which is not, the invalid part may be dropped if what is left is fully operative as a law" (internal quotation marks omitted).
71. Julia Schiller, "Deterring Obstruction of Justice Efficiently: The Impact of Arthur Andersen and the Sarbanes-Oxley Act," 63 *Ann. Surv. Am. L.* 267 (2007).

18. Foreign and Military Affairs

1. U.S. Const. art. II, § 2, cl. 2.
2. See id. art. I, § 8, cl. 3 (giving Congress the power "to regulate commerce with foreign nations, and among the several states, and with the Indian tribes").
3. 15 U.S.C. §§ 61–66 (2006).
4. U.S. Const. art. I, § 8, cl. 3 (the Commerce Clause is sometimes also broken down into the Interstate Commerce Clause or the Foreign Commerce Clause).
5. Id. art. I, § 8, cl. 9.
6. See, e.g., *Weiner v. United States,* 357 U.S. 349 (1958) (upholding presidential removal power from the 1948 War Claims Commission).
7. U.S. Const. art. I, § 8, cl. 10.
8. Id. art. I, § 8, cl. 11.
9. Id. art. I, § 8, cl. 12.
10. Id. art. I, § 8, cl. 13.
11. Id. art. I, § 8, cl. 14.
12. Id. art. I, § 8, cls. 15–16.
13. *Campbell v. Clinton,* 203 F.3d 19 (D.C. Cir. 2000).
14. Id. at 24 (Silberman, J., concurring in his own opinion on political question grounds).
15. 299 U.S. 304 (1936).
16. Id. at 311–313.

17. Id. at 312.
18. Id. at 312, 314.
19. Id. at 315–316.
20. See *NLRB v. Jones & Laughlin Steel Corp.*, 301 U.S. 1, 76 (1937) (McReynolds, J., dissenting) Justice Sutherland joined this dissent.
21. *Curtiss-Wright*, 299 U.S. at 318.
22. Id. at 318.
23. Id. at 319.
24. U.S. Const. art. II, § 2, cl. 1.
25. *Federalist No. 69* (Alexander Hamilton) (Clinton Rossiter ed., 1999).
26. See U.S. Const. art. II, § 2, cl. 1; id. art. I, § 8, cl. 15.
27. *Federalist No. 64* (John Jay) (Clinton Rossiter ed., 1999).
28. *Youngstown Sheet & Tube Co. v. Sawyer*, 343 U.S. 579 (1952) (commonly referred to as the *Steel Seizure Case*).
29. See, e.g., Labor Management Relations (Taft Hartley) Act, Pub. L. No. 80-101, 61 Stat. 136 (1947).
30. *Youngstown*, 343 U.S. at 637 (Jackson, J., concurring) ("When the President takes measures incompatible with the expressed or implied will of Congress, his power is at its lowest ebb, for then he can rely only upon his own constitutional powers minus any constitutional powers of Congress over the matter.").
31. Pub. L. No. 88-408, 78 Stat. 384 (1964).
32. On these and other issues, see Saikrishna Prakash, "Unleashing the Dogs of War: What the Constitution Means by 'Declare War,'" 93 *Cornell L. Rev.* 45 (2007).
33. Pub. L. No. 93-148, 87 Stat. 555 (1973).
34. "Mr. M[adison] and Mr. Gerry moved to insert *'declare,'* striking out *'make'* war; leaving to the Executive the power to repel sudden attacks." 2 *The Records of the Federal Convention of 1787*, at 318 (Max Farrand ed., 1966) (James Madison's Convention notes from August 17, 1787). *The Prize Cases*, 67 U.S. 635 (1863) (noting that the president has independent authority to repel aggressive actions by third parties).
35. See Pub. L. No. 93-148, § 4, 87 Stat. 555, 555–556 (1973).
36. Id. at § 5(b), 556.
37. John Hart Ely, "Suppose Congress Wanted a War Powers Act That Worked," 88 *Colum. L. Rev.* 1379 (1988).
38. John C. Yoo, Memorandum for William J. Haynes II, General Counsel of the Department of Defense (Mar. 14, 2003), available at http://gulcfac.typepad.com/georgetown_university_law/files/march.14.memo.part1.pdf.
39. See John C. Yoo, *The Powers of War and Peace: The Constitution and Foreign Affairs after 9/11* (2005).
40. See Prakash, *supra* note 32, at 56–58, 87, 92; Harold Hongju Koh, *The National Security Constitution: Sharing Power after the Iran-Contra Affair* 74–77 (1990).
41. Pub. L. No. 95-511, 92 Stat. 1783 (1978) (codified at 50 U.S.C. §§ 1801–1885c).

42. Pub. L. No. 107-40, 115 Stat. 224 (2001).

43. Id. at § 2(a).

44. U.S. Const. art. II, § 2, cl. 1.

45. Id. art. I, § 8, cl. 14.

46. See Id. art. I, § 8, cl. 18.

47. John C. Yoo, Memorandum for William J. Haynes II, *supra* note 38, at 4–5.

48. Id. at 13.

49. See *Youngstown*, 343 U.S. at 635–647 (Jackson, J., concurring).

50. John C. Yoo, Memorandum for William J. Haynes II, *supra* note 38, at 13 n.13.

51. See *Hamdan v. Rumsfeld*, 548 U.S. 557, 592 (2006) (noting in *dicta* the general distinction between the scope of a military campaign (for Congress) and the particular tactics chosen (for the president): "Congress cannot direct the conduct of campaigns") (quoting *Ex parte Milligan*, 71 U.S. 2, 139 (1866) (Chase, C. J., concurring)).

52. For the rejection of his position, see, e.g., *Hamdan v. Rumsfeld*, 548 U.S. at 575–589.

53. US. Const. art. I, § 9, cl. 2.

54. Riding circuit refers to a practice in which Supreme Court justices used to travel around the country serving as temporary judges on various circuit courts.

55. *Ex Parte Merryman*, 17 F. Cas. 144 (C.C.D. Md. 1861) (Taney, Circuit Justice).

56. U.S. Const. art IV, § 4 ("The United States shall guarantee to every State in this Union a Republican Form of Government, and shall protect each of them against Invasion; and on Application of the Legislature, or of the Executive (when the Legislature cannot be convened) against domestic Violence.").

57. See Habeas Corpus Act, 12 Stat. 755 (1863).

58. See *INS v. St. Cyr*, 533 U.S. 289 (2001); Gerald Neuman, "Habeas Corpus, Executive Detention, and the Removal of Aliens," 98 *Colum. L. Rev.* 961 (1998).

59. See *St. Cyr*, 533 U.S. at 301 n.16 (2001) (citing *Sommersett v. Stewart*, 20 How. St. Tr. 1, 79–82 (K.B. 1772); *Case of the Hottentot Venus*, 104 Eng. Rep. 344, 344 (K.B. 1810); *King v. Schiever*, 97 Eng. Rep. 551 (K.B. 1759)).

60. See, e.g., *Boumediene v. Bush*, 553 U.S. 723 (2008).

61. See, e.g., *Rasul v. Bush*, 542 U.S. 466 (2004).

62. *Rasul*, 542 U.S. at 488–505 (Scalia, J., dissenting).

63. 28 U.S.C. § 2241(a).

64. *Johnson v. Eisentrager*, 339 U.S. 763, 770 n.4 (1950).

65. *Curtiss-Wright*, 299 U.S. at 318 ("Neither the Constitution nor the laws passed in pursuance of it have any force in foreign territory unless in respect of our own citizens.").

66. *United States v. Verdugo-Urquidez*, 494 U.S. 259 (1990).

67. 605 F.3d 84 (D.C. Cir. 2010).

68. *Al-Maqaleh v. Gates*, 604 F. Supp. 2d 205, 209 (D.D.C. 2009).

19. From Structural Protections to Individual Rights

1. For this tripartite classification, see *Roberts v. United States Jaycees*, 468 U.S. 609 (1984). Expressive associations include civic groups with a social mission. Intimate associations cover marriage and religious groups. Expressive associations may, under current law, be subject to antidiscrimination law. Intimate associations may not.
2. See, e.g., *Morey v. Doud*, 354 U.S. 457, 475 (1957).
3. See *Garcia v. San Antonio Metro. Transit Auth.*, 469 U.S. 528 (1985), discussed *supra* Chapter 11 ("The Commerce Clause: Transformation to Consolidation, 1937–1995").
4. 429 U.S. 190, 197 (1976) (gender discrimination).
5. See, e.g., *Reed v. Campbell*, 476 U.S. 852 (1986).
6. Gerald Gunther, "Foreword: In Search of Evolving Doctrine on a Changing Court: A Model for a Newer Equal Protection," 86 *Harv. L. Rev.* 1, 8 (1972). Ironically, a third tier, closer to strict scrutiny than rational basis, was introduced in the sex discrimination cases, *infra* Chapter 35 (and also discussed above). No proposition is entirely uniform. See, e.g., *Mathews v. Lucas*, 427 U.S. 495, 510 (1976) (insisting that an analysis under the rational basis test is "not a toothless one," albeit in the context of a suit about social security benefits, not economic liberties).
7. 60 U.S. 393 (1856).
8. *Slaughter-House Cases*, 83 U.S. 36 (1873).
9. 304 U.S. 144 (1938).
10. 300 U.S. 379 (1937).
11. 261 U.S. 525 (1923).
12. *United States v. Carolene Prods. Co.*, 304 U.S. at 153 n.4.
13. John Hart Ely, *Democracy and Distrust: A Theory of Judicial Review* 75–77 (1980).
14. Id. at 80.

20. Procedural Due Process

1. U.S. Const. art. I, § 9, cl. 3.
2. Id. art. I, § 10, cl. 1.
3. 59 U.S. 272 (1856).
4. Id. at 276.
5. Nathan S. Chapman & Michael W. McConnell, "Due Process as Separation of Powers," 121 *Yale L.J.* 1672, 1677 (2012).
6. For iteration of this point and an excellent summary of the early due process law, see Gary Lawson, *Federal Administrative Law* 671, 674–677 (5th ed., 2009).
7. *Dr. Bonham's Case*, 8 Co. Rep. 107a, 114a C.P. (1610).
8. Id. at 118a.
9. See James R. Stoner, Jr., *Common Law and Liberal Theory: Coke, Hobbes, and the Origins of American Constitutionalism* 49–51 (1992).

10. 1 William Blackstone, *Commentaries on the Laws of England* 91 (1765). For discussion, see R. H. Helmholz, *"Bonham's Case,* Judicial Review, and the Law of Nature,"* 1 *J. Legal Analysis* 325 (2009).

11. John Hart Ely, *Democracy and Distrust: A Theory of Judicial Review* 18 (1980).

12. See the statement in Lon L. Fuller, *The Morality of Law* 39 (1964).

13. For a detailed defense of this position, see Richard A. Epstein, *Design for Liberty: Private Property, Public Administration and the Rule of Law* 66–76 (2011).

14. U.S. Const. art. IV, § 1.

15. 118 U.S. 356 (1886).

16. Id. at 369.

17. See, e.g., *Johnson v. Eisentrager,* 339 U.S. 763, 778 (1950); *Boumediene v. Bush,* 553 U.S. 723 (2008).

18. *Eisentrager,* 339 U.S. at 781.

19. See 28 U.S.C. § 1332 (c)(1) ("a corporation shall be deemed to be a citizen of every State and foreign state by which it has been incorporated and of the State or foreign state where it has its principal place of business").

20. John Locke, *Second Treatise of Government* ch. 9 ¶ 123, 124 (1690).

21. 1 Blackstone, *supra* note 10, at 125.

22. See *Restatement (Second) of Torts* § 559 ("A communication is defamatory if it tends so to harm the reputation of another as to lower him in the estimation of the community or to deter third persons from associating or dealing with him.").

23. 1 Blackstone, *supra* note 10, at 130.

24. 2 Blackstone, *supra* note 10, at 2.

25. 262 U.S. 390 (1923).

26. Id. at 399.

27. Locke, *supra* note 20.

28. See, e.g., *Tarleton v. M'Gawley,* 170 Eng. Rep. 153 (K.B. 1793); *People's Express Airlines, Inc. v. Consol. Rail Corp.,* 495 A.2d 107 (N.J. 1985).

29. 341 U.S. 123 (1951).

30. Id. at 137–138

31. See *Ellsworth v. Martindale-Hubbell Law Directory, Inc.,* 280 N.W. 879, 881–882 (N.D. 1938).

32. 341 U.S. at 161.

33. See Locke, *supra* note 20, ch. 5 ("Of Property").

34. Charles A. Reich, "The New Property," 73 *Yale L.J.* 733 (1964).

35. Id. at 733.

36. *W. River Bridge Co. v. Dix,* 47 U.S. 507 (1848).

37. 409 U.S. 488 (1973).

38. 182 F.2d 46 (D.C. Cir. 1950).

39. Id. at 57–58.

40. 367 U.S. 886 (1961).

41. Id. at 896.

42. 408 U.S. 564 (1972).

43. See, e.g., *Slochower v. Bd. of Higher Educ.,* 350 U.S. 551 (1956).

44. For an extensive treatment of the subject, see Richard A. Epstein, *Bargaining with the State* (1993).

45. *Wieman v. Updegraff,* 344 U.S. 183, 192 (1952).

46. *Perry v. Sindermann,* 408 U.S. 593 (1972).

47. Id. at 597.

48. 416 U.S. 134 (1974).

49. 5 U.S.C. § 7501.

50. *Kennedy v. Sanchez,* 349 F. Supp. 863 (N.D. Ill. 1972).

51. *Arnett v. Kennedy,* 416 U.S. at 154.

52. Id. at 171.

53. 470 U.S. 532 (1985).

54. Id. at 541.

55. *In re Winship,* 397 U.S. 358 (1970) (Brennan, J.).

56. *Apprendi v. New Jersey,* 530 U.S. 466 (2000).

57. *Hecht Co. v. Bowles,* 321 U.S. 321, 329 (1944).

58. *Amoco Prod. Co. v. Vill. of Gambell,* 480 U.S. 531, 542 (1987). For discussion, see Jared A. Goldstein, "Equitable Balancing in the Age of Statutes," 96 *Va. L. Rev.* 485 (2010).

59. *eBay, Inc. v. MercExchange, LLC,* 547 U.S. 388, 391 (2006) (patent injunction). See also *Winter v. Nat. Res. Def. Council, Inc.,* 555 U.S. 7, 129 S. Ct. 365 (2008) (refusing to enjoin naval operations to protect whale watching).

60. 211 U.S. 306 (1908).

61. 198 U.S. 45 (1905).

62. 283 U.S. 589 (1931).

63. 395 U.S. 337 (1969).

64. Id. at 345.

65. 402 U.S. 535 (1971).

66. 400 U.S. 433 (1971).

67. Id. at 434.

68. 397 U.S. 254 (1970).

69. 424 U.S. 319 (1976).

70. Id. at 335.

21. Freedom of Contract

1. 198 U.S. 45 (1905). For an exhaustive defense of the *Lochner* decision, see David Bernstein, *Rehabilitating Lochner: Defending Individual Rights against Progressive Reform* (2011), favorably reviewed in 125 *Harv. L. Rev.* 1120 (2012). Representative of the scorn heaped on the case, see Jack M. Balkin, "'Wrong the Day It Was Decided': *Lochner* and Constitutional Historicism," 85 *B.U. L. Rev.* 677 (2005).

2. U.S. Const. amend. XIV, § 1 ("[N]or shall any State deprive any person of . . . liberty . . . without due process").

3. 165 U.S. 578, 589 (1897).

4. See WTO Agreements and Public Health, discussed *supra* Chapter 10, at note 26; Chapter 15 ("The Dormant Commerce Clause") at note 22.

5. See Roscoe Pound, "Liberty of Contract," 18 *Yale L.J.* 454 (1909).

6. 208 U.S. 161 (1908).

7. 236 U.S. 1 (1915).

8. Id. at 17.

9. Id. at 27.

10. These figures are found on the World Socialist website. Jerry White, "UAW Membership Continues to Plummet," *World Socialist* (Apr. 1, 2010), available at http://www.wsws.org/articles/2010/apr2010/uawm-a01.shtml. There was a modest rebound to 376,612 UAW members in 2010. "UAW Membership Increases," UAW News Releases (Mar. 28, 2013) (Mar. 31, 2011), available at http://www.uaw.org/articles/uaw-membership-increases-0.

11. See, e.g., *Addyston Pipe & Steel Co. v. United States*, 175 U.S. 211 (1899).

12. For some of these numbers, see Richard A. Epstein, *How Progressives Rewrote the Constitution* 3–6 (2006).

13. 208 U.S. 412 (1908).

14. Id.

15. Brief of Respondent, *Muller v. Oregon*, 208 U.S. 412 (1908), available at http://www.law.louisville.edu/library/collections/brandeis/node/235.

16. See Bernstein, *supra* note 1, at 62.

17. See *infra* Chapter 35 ("Equal Protection and Sex Discrimination").

18. Railway Labor Act of 1926, Pub. L. No. 69-257, 44 Stat. 577 (current version at 45 U.S.C. §§ 151–188 (2006)).

19. Norris-La Guardia Act of 1932, Pub. L. No. 72-65, 47 Stat. 70.

20. Fair Labor Standards Act of 1938, Pub. L. No. 75-718, 52 Stat. 1060 (current version at 29 U.S.C. ch. 28, § 207 et seq. (2006)).

21. 312 U.S. 100, 109–110 (1941).

22. See Harold Demsetz, "Why Regulate Utilities?," 11 *J.L. & Econ.* 55 (1968); Richard A. Posner, "Natural Monopoly and Its Regulation," 21 *Stan. L. Rev.* 548 (1969).

23. 169 U.S. 466 (1898).

24. 271 U.S. 23 (1926).

25. Id. at 32.

26. 320 U.S. 591, 603 (1944).

27. *Lake Shore & Mich. S. Ry. Co. v. Smith*, 173 U.S. 684, 695 (1899).

28. 236 U.S. 585 (1915).

29. Id. at 595–596.

30. 236 U.S. 605 (1915).

31. 251 U.S. 396, 399 (1920).

32. *S. Pac. v. Darnell-Taenzer*, 245 U.S. 531, 533–534 (1918).

33. 390 U.S. 747 (1968).

34. 488 U.S. 299 (1989).

35. Id.

36. Telecommunications Act of 1996, Pub. L. No. 104-104, 110 Stat. 56 (codified at 47 U.S.C. § 151 et seq. (2006)).
37. *United States v. Am. Tel. & Telegraph Co.*, 552 F. Supp. 131 (D.D.C. 1982), *aff'd sub nom. Maryland v. United States*, 460 U.S. 1001 (1983).
38. *Verizon Commc'ns Inc. v. FCC*, 535 U.S. 467, 495 (2002). For earlier litigation under the Telecommunications Act of 1996, see *AT&T Corp. v. Iowa Utils. Bd.*, 525 U.S. 366, 394–395 (1999).

22. Takings, Physical and Regulatory

1. U.S. Const. amend. V.
2. 364 U.S. 40, 49 (1960).
3. See *Penn Cent. Transp. Co. v. City of New York*, 438 U.S. 104, 124 (1978).
4. William Michael Treanor, "The Original Understanding of the Takings Clause and the Political Process," 95 *Colum. L. Rev.* 782 (1995). For an updated defense of the Treanor thesis, see Matthew P. Harrington, "Regulatory Takings and the Original Understanding of the Takings Clause," 45 *Wm. & Mary L. Rev.* 2053 (2004).
5. Treanor, *supra* note 4, at 785.
6. Id.
7. See *supra* Chapter 20 ("Procedural Due Process: Implementing the Classical Liberal Ideal").
8. See Richard A. Epstein & Michael S. Greve, "Federal Preemption: Principles and Politics," *Federalist Outlook* 4 (Jun. 2007), available at http://www.aei.org/files/2007/06/04/20070604_Federalistg.pdf.
9. See Lawrence Lessig, "Fidelity in Translation," 71 *Tex. L. Rev.* 1165 (1993).
10. Treanor, *supra* note 4, at 818–819.
11. Id. at 788.
12. Id. at 788, quoting Forrest McDonald, *Novus Ordo Seclorum: The Intellectual Origins of the Constitution* 23 (1985).
13. Treanor, *supra* note 4, at 856.
14. Richard A. Epstein, *Takings: Private Property and the Power of Eminent Domain* (1985).
15. Richard A. Epstein, *Supreme Neglect: How to Revive Constitutional Protection for Private Property* (2008).
16. See, e.g., C. B. Macpherson, *The Political Theory of Possessive Individualism* (1962).
17. For a more detailed explanation, see Richard A. Epstein, "Covenants and Constitutions," 73 *Cornell L. Rev.* 906 (1988).
18. See Richard A. Epstein, "Nuisance Law: Corrective Justice and Its Utilitarian Restraints," 8 *J. Legal Stud.* 49, 66 n.46 (1979).
19. 515 U.S. 687 (1995).
20. Endangered Species Act of 1973, 87 Stat. 884, 16 U.S.C. § 1531 (1988 ed. and Supp. V).
21. 50 CFR § 17.3.
22. 16 U.S.C. § 1539(a)(2)(A).

23. See Ronald Bailey, "Shoot, Shovel, and Shut Up: Celebrating 30 Years of Failing to Save Endangered Species," *Reason Magazine* (Dec. 31, 2003), available at http://reason.com/archives/2003/12/31/shoot-shovel-and-shut-up.

24. See, e.g., *Strickley v. Highland Boy Gold Mining Co.*, 200 U.S. 527 (1906).

25. 304 N.W.2d 455 (Mich. 1981). Fortunately in Michigan, *Poletown* has been overruled by *County of Wayne v. Hathcock*, 684 N.W.2d 765 (Mich. 2004).

26. 467 U.S. 229 (1984).

27. 545 U.S. 469 (2005).

28. See *Loretto v. Teleprompter Manhattan CATV Corp.*, 458 U.S. 419 (1982).

29. Ga. Code Ann. § 22-1-6.

30. See *Keokuk & Hamilton Bridge Co. v. United States*, 260 U.S. 125 (1922).

31. *Sanguinetti v. United States*, 264 U.S. 146, 149 (1924) (Sutherland, J.).

32. 133 S. Ct. 511 (2012).

33. 637 F.3d 1366, 1377 (Fed. Cir. 2011).

34. *Ark. Game & Fish*, 133 S. Ct. at 518.

35. For an extended critique of both decisions, see Richard A. Epstein, "The Takings Clause and Partial Interests in Land: On Sharp Boundaries and Continuous Distributions," 78 *Brook. L. Rev.* 589 (2013).

36. 438 U.S. 104, 124 (1978).

37. Id.

38. 260 U.S. 393 (1922).

39. For a detailed discussion, see William Fischel, *Regulatory Takings: Law, Economics and Politics* (1995).

40. See, e.g., *Williamson Cnty. Regional Planning Comm'n v. Hamilton Bank*, 473 U.S. 172 (1985).

41. *San Remo Hotel, L.P. v. City and Cnty. of San Francisco*, 545 U.S. 323 (2005).

42. 272 U.S. 365 (1926).

43. 505 U.S. 1003 (1992).

44. Eliot Brown, "Council Torpedoes Kingsbridge Armory, Again," *N.Y. Observer* (Dec. 21, 2009), available at http://www.observer.com/2009/real-estate/kingsbridge-armory-torpedoed-council-again ("The Council voted on Monday afternoon, 48–1, to override the mayor's veto, as the body, and particularly most of the Bronx delegation, had become insistent that all retailers inside the mall pay a living wage to their employees, which would have been a new standard in the city.").

45. *Yee v. City of Escondido*, 503 U.S. 519 (1992).

46. 256 U.S. 135 (1921).

47. Kim Velsey, "Rental Relief! Mayor Bloomberg Renews NYC Rent Regulation Law," *N.Y. Observer* (Mar. 27, 2012), available at http://observer.com/2012/03/rental-relief-mayor-bloomberg-renews-nyc-rent-regulation-law.

23. *Personal Liberties and the Morals Head of the Police Power*

1. For an extensive discussion, see William J. Novak, *The People's Welfare: Law and Regulation in Nineteenth Century America* (1996).

2. See generally *Stone v Mississippi*, 101 U.S. 814 (1880).

3. For explication, see Jonathan Haidt, "The Emotional Dog and Its Rational Tail: A Social Intuitionist Approach to Moral Judgment," 108 *Psychol. Rev.* 814 (2001).

4. 98 U.S. 145 (1878).

5. Id. at 168.

6. 103 F. 10 (C.C.N.D. Cal. 1900) (No. 12,940).

7. See, e.g., *Yick Wo v. Hopkins*, 118 U.S. 356 (1886) (dealing with discriminatory rules for laundry permits).

8. Conn. Gen. Stat. § 53-32 (1958).

9. Id. § 54-196.

10. 381 U.S. 479 (1965).

11. See id. at 484 ("The foregoing cases [dealing with religion, speech, association, and quartering soldiers] suggest that specific guarantees in the Bill of Rights have penumbras, formed by emanations from those guarantees that help give them life and substance.").

12. Id. at 486–499.

13. Id. at 499–502.

14. U.S. Const. amend. IX.

15. *Griswold*, 381 U.S. at 485–486.

16. See *Eisenstadt v. Baird*, 405 U.S. 438 (1972).

17. 410 U.S. 113 (1973).

18. Richard A. Epstein, "Substantive Due Process by Any Other Name: The Abortion Cases," 1973 *Sup. Ct. Rev.* 159.

19. John Hart Ely, "The Wages of Crying Wolf: A Comment on *Roe v. Wade*," 82 *Yale L.J.* 920 (1973).

20. See *Second Employers' Liability Cases*, 223 U.S. 1 (1912); *N.Y. Cent. R.R. Co. v. White*, 243 U.S. 188 (1917) (dealing with workers' compensation).

21. John Stuart Mill, *On Liberty* 68 (1982) (1859).

22. *Roe*, 410 U.S. at 157–159.

23. Catharine A. MacKinnon, *Sexual Harassment of Working Women: A Case of Sex Discrimination* 28 (1979).

24. 478 U.S. 186 (1986).

25. On its prevalence, see William J. Novak, *The People's Welfare: Law and Regulation in Nineteenth-Century America* 274 (1996).

26. *Bowers*, 478 U.S. at 191.

27. Id. at 192–193.

28. 539 U.S. 558 (2003).

29. Id. at 567.

30. Id. at 562.

31. Id. at 578.

32. Id. at 562.

33. Id. at 579.

34. Id. at 578.

35. Id. at 579.

36. Id. at 578.

37. Cal. Const. art. I, § 7.5.

38. 671 F.3d 1052 (9th Cir. 2012).

39. 699 F.3d 169 (2d Cir. 2012).

40. Id. at 562.

41. *In re Marriage Cases*, 183 P. 3d 384 (Cal. 2008). For a longer account of equal protection as it relates to sex, see *infra* Chapter 35 ("Equal Protection and Sex Discrimination").

24. Freedom of Speech and Religion

1. U.S. Const. amend. I.

2. Hugo Black, "The Bill of Rights," 35 *N.Y.U. L. Rev.* 865 (1960).

3. See, e.g., *PruneYard Shopping Ctr. v. Robins*, 447 U.S. 74 (1980).

4. *Abrams v. United States*, 250 U.S. 616, 630 (1919).

5. See *Lochner v. New York*, 198 U.S. 45, 75–76 (1905) (Holmes, J., dissenting).

6. Robert H. Bork, "Neutral Principles and Some First Amendment Problems," 47 *Ind. L.J.* 1 (1971).

7. Alexander Meiklejohn, Free Speech and Its Relation to Self-Government (1948).

8. Vince Blasi, "The Checking Value in First Amendment Theory," 1977 *Am. B. Found. Res. J.* 521 (1977).

9. See, e.g., Martin Redish, "The Value of Free Speech," 130 *U. Pa. L. Rev.* 591 (1982).

10. Thomas Emerson, *The System of Freedom of Expression* 1 (1970).

11. *United States v. O'Brien*, 391 U.S. 367 (1968).

12. *Texas v. Johnson*, 491 U.S. 397 (1989).

13. *Tinker v. Des Moines Indep. Cmty. Sch. Dist.*, 393 U.S. 503 (1968).

14. Emerson, *supra* note 10, at 5–6.

15. *Tinker*, 393 U.S. at 505–506.

16. See U.S. Const. art. I, § 8, cl. 8 ("Congress shall have the power . . . To promote the Progress of Science and useful Arts, by securing for limited Times to Authors and Inventors the exclusive Right to their respective Writings and Discoveries.").

17. *Barnes v. Glen Theatre, Inc.*, 501 U.S. 560, 575 (1991) (distinguishing activities prohibited for causing harm to others from activities prohibited as "immoral"); see also *City of Erie v. Pap's A.M.*, 529 U.S. 277 (2000).

18. *Hosana-Tabor Evangelical Lutheran Church & Sch. v. EEOC*, 132 S. Ct. 694, 706–708 (2012), discussed *infra* Chapter 29 ("Religion: Free Exercise").

19. See, e.g., *Webster's Dictionary*, available at http://www.webster-dictionary.net/definition/religion.

20. John Stuart Mill, *On Liberty* (1982) (1859).

21. For the classic common law statement of the no-duty-to-rescue rule, see *Buch v. Armory Mfg.*, 44 A. 809 (N.H. 1897). The basic rule remains in place today notwithstanding extensive academic criticism, if only because the alternatives are worse. *Restatement (Second) Torts* § 315.

22. *Barnes*, 501 U.S. at 575.
23. Id.
24. 478 U.S. 186 (1986).
25. Id. at 210 n.5 (attacking the decision on the grounds that justifications like those were rejected in *Loving v. Virginia*, 388 U.S. 1 (1967)).
26. For discussion, see *supra* Chapter 22 ("Takings, Physical and Regulatory").
27. See, e.g., *Metro Media v. City of San Diego*, 453 U.S. 490 (1981) (striking down a statute that prohibited noncommercial signs on an owner's own premises while allowing commercial signs).
28. See Religious Land Use and Institutionalized Persons Act of 2000, 42 U.S.C. §§ 2000cc–2000cc-5 (2006), discussed *supra* Chapter 29 ("Religion: Free Exercise").
29. For some sense of the difficulties, see *Ballard v. United States*, 322 U.S. 78 (1946).

25. Force, Threats, and Inducements

1. For the leading case, see *Lumley v. Gye*, 118 Eng. Rep. 749 (K.B. 1853).
2. See *St. Rubbish Collectors Ass'n v. Siliznoff*, 240 P. 2d 282 (Cal. 1952) (holding that threats at meetings were actionable only if they applied in the future).
3. For an exhaustive analysis of these cases from a strong free speech perspective, see Geoffrey R. Stone, *Perilous Times: Free Speech in Wartime* 135–233 (2004).
4. Espionage Act, ch. 30, tit. I, § 3, 49 Stat. 219 (1917).
5. See *Patterson v. Colorado*, 205 U.S. 454, 463 (1907).
6. 255 F. 886 (9th Cir. 1919).
7. 249 U.S. 47 (1919).
8. Id. at 52.
9. Id.
10. Id.
11. 221 U.S. 418 (1911).
12. Id. at 439.
13. 249 U.S. at 52.
14. 244 F. 535 (S.D.N.Y. 1917).
15. 249 U.S. 211 (1919).
16. 250 U.S. 616 (1919).
17. Id. at 627.
18. Id.
19. Id. at 630.
20. 268 U.S. 652 (1925).
21. 274 U.S. 357 (1927).
22. Smith Act, tit. I, § 2(a)(1), 54 Stat. 670, 671 (1940) (current version at 18 U.S.C. § 2385).
23. Id. at 2(a)(2) & 2(a)(3).
24. 341 U.S. 494 (1951).

25. *Dennis*, 341 U.S. at 501–503.
26. *United States v. Dennis*, 183 F.2d 201, 212 (2d Cir. 1950).
27. *Dennis*, 341 U.S. at 579.
28. 354 U.S. 298 (1957).
29. 372 U.S. 229 (1963).
30. 379 U.S. 536 (1965).
31. 395 U.S. 444 (1969).
32. For different views, see *Teamsters, Local 695 v. Vogt, Inc.*, 354 U.S. 284 (1957); *Thornhill v. Alabama*, 310 U.S. 88 (1940); and *Vegalahn v. Guntner*, 44 N.E. 77 (Mass. 1896) (split decision with a Holmes dissent skeptical of the injunction).

26. Fraud, Defamation, Emotional Distress, and Invasion of Privacy

1. See, e.g., *Beach v. Hancock*, 27 N.H. 223 (1853).
2. 33 U.S.C. §§ 1251–1387 (2006).
3. 42 U.S.C. §§ 7401–7671 (2006).
4. See *Valentine v. Chrestensen*, 316 U.S. 52 (1942).
5. See Ronald H. Coase, "Advertising and Free Speech," 6 *J. Legal Stud.* 1 (1977). For respectful criticism that classes commercial speech as low value, see Geoffrey R. Stone, "Ronald Coase's First Amendment," 54 *J. L. & Econ.* S367 (2011).
6. See *Dicke v. Fenne*, 82 Eng. Rep. 411 (K.B. 1639) (holding actionable defendant's statement that he could give "a peck of malt to his mare, and she would piss as good beer as [the plaintiff] doth brew"); *Millington v. Fox*, 40 Eng. Rep. 956 (Ch. 1833) (granting injunctive relief against defendant's use of plaintiff's identifying stamp on its similar products).
7. Pub. L. No. 79-489, 60 Stat. 427 (codified as amended at 15 U.S.C. §§ 1051–1141 (2006)). For a discussion of the constitutional issues that arise with expanded trademark protection, see Robert C. Denicola, "Trademarks as Speech: Constitutional Implications of the Emerging Rationales for the Protection of Trade Symbols," 1982 *Wis. L. Rev.* 158 (1982).
8. Copyright Revisions Act of 1976, 17 U.S.C. § 107 (2006).
9. *Harper & Row, Publishers, Inc. v. Nation Enters.*, 471 U.S. 539 (1985).
10. 447 U.S. 557 (1980).
11. Id. at 566–567.
12. Id. at 566.
13. Id.
14. Id. at 571–572.
15. *44 Liquormart, Inc. v. Rhode Island*, 517 U.S. 484 (1996).
16. 132 S. Ct. 2537 (2012).
17. Stolen Valor Act of 2005, Pub. L. No. 109-437, 120 Stat. 3266 (2006) (codified at 18 U.S.C. § 704 (2006)).
18. *Alvarez*, 132 S. Ct. at 2542.
19. Id. at 2558.

20. Id. at 2543.

21. Id. (quoting *Ashcroft v. ACLU*, 535 U.S. 564, 573 (2002)).

22. Id. at 2551–2556 (Breyer, J., concurring).

23. 4 William Blackstone, *Commentaries on the Law of England* 151, 152 (1769).

24. Id.

25. 376 U.S. 254 (1964).

26. *Post Publ'n Co. v. Hallam*, 59 F. 530 (6th Cir. 1893). For earlier English views on the scope of the fair comment privilege, see *Carr v. Hood*, 170 Eng. Rep. 981 (K.B. 1808). For English commentary on the topic, see George Spencer Bower, *A Code on the Law of Actionable Defamation* (1908).

27. See, e.g., the influential English decision *E. Hulton & Co. v. Jones* [1910], A.C. 20.

28. For the classic discussion, see Van Vechten Veeder, "Freedom of Public Discussion," 23 *Harv. L. Rev.* 413 (1910).

29. 283 U.S. 697 (1931).

30. For the classic discussion of the connection, see Harry Kalven, Jr., *The Negro and the First Amendment* (1965).

31. 376 U.S. 254 (1964).

32. See id. at 256; 28 U.S.C. § 1441(b) (1958) (allowing removal to federal court only where no defendant "is a citizen of the State in which such action is brought").

33. 376 U.S. at 267.

34. *Curtis Publ'g Co v. Butts*, 388 U.S. 130 (1967).

35. See *Gertz v. Robert Welch, Inc.*, 418 U.S. 323 (1974); see also *Gertz*, 418 U.S. at 369 (White, J., dissenting) (for a strong defense of the older strict liability common law rules).

36. *Sullivan*, 376 U.S. at 279–280.

37. See, e.g., Cal. Civ. Code § 48a (West 2010) (establishing procedures for requesting and publishing retractions).

38. *Sharon v. Time, Inc.*, 599 F. Supp. 538, 586 (S.D.N.Y. 1984).

39. See Pierre N. Leval, "The No-Money, No-Fault Libel Suit: Keeping *Sullivan* in Its Proper Place," 101 *Harv. L. Rev.* 1267 (1988) (arguing for the recognition of a no-damages libel suit, where the plaintiff would sue for a judgment of the issue of falsity without having to prove "actual malice").

40. *I. de S. & Wife v. W. de S.*, Y. B. Lib. Ass. folio 99, placitum 60 (1348).

41. See, e.g., *Wilkinson v. Downton*, 2 Q.B. 57 [1897] (involving violent physiological responses and nervous shock to a practical joke when a woman was falsely told that her husband had been badly injured); *Restatement (Second) of Torts* § 46.

42. 485 U.S. 46 (1988).

43. Id. at 48.

44. Id. at 56–57.

45. *Burton v. Crowell Publ'g Co.*, 82 F.2d 154 (2d Cir. 1936) (holding actionable an inadvertent obscene photograph).

46. *Hustler*, 485 U.S. at 56–57.

47. *Hustler Magazine, Inc. v. Moral Majority, Inc.*, 606 F. Supp. 1526, 1530 (C.D. Cal. 1985) (noting that "sending along an actual copy of the parody was part of Falwell's 'marketing approach' to fund-raising").

48. 131 S. Ct. 1207 (2011).

49. See, e.g., *Thing v. La Chusa*, 771 P.2d 814 (Cal. 1989).

50. Samuel Warren & Louis Brandeis, "The Right to Privacy," 4 *Harv. L. Rev.* 193 (1890).

51. *Roach v. Harper*, 105 S.E.2d 564 (Va. 1958).

52. See, e.g., *Sidis v. F-R Publ'g Corp.*, 113 F.2d 806, 810 (2d Cir. 1940).

53. William L. Prosser, "Privacy," 48 *Cal. L. Rev.* 383 (1960).

54. 483 P. 2d 34 (Cal. 1971).

55. 420 US. 469 (1975), reiterated in *The Florida Star. v. B.J.F.*, 491 U.S. 524 (1989).

56. 410 U.S. 113 (1973).

57. *New York Times Co. v. United States (Pentagon Papers Case)*, 403 U.S. 713 (1971).

58. Id. at 714.

59. For a modern statement of the rule see Uniform Commercial Code, §§ 8-301–8-302. For discussion see Saul Levmore, "Variety and Uniformity in the Treatment of the Good-Faith Purchaser," 16 *J. Legal Stud.* 43 (1987); Alan Schwartz & Robert E. Scott, "Rethinking the Laws of Good Faith Purchase," 111 *Colum. L. Rev.* 1332 (2011).

60. David Souter, Commencement Address, Harvard Univ. (May 27, 2010), available at http://news.harvard.edu/gazette/story/2010/05/text-of-justice-david-souters-speech.

61. Foreign Intelligence Surveillance Act of 1978, Pub. L. No. 95-511, 92 Stat. 1783 (codified as amended in scattered sections of 50 U.S.C.).

62. 5 U.S.C. § 552 (2006).

63. 67 F. Supp. 2d 745 (E.D. Mich. 1999) For my views on this topic, see Richard A. Epstein, "Privacy, Publication, and the First Amendment: The Dangers of First Amendment Exceptionalism," 52 *Stan. L. Rev.* 1003 (2000).

64. 67 F. Supp. 2d at 747.

65. Id. at 753.

27. Government Regulation of the Speech Commons

1. For discussion, see Richard A. Epstein, "On the Optimal Mix of Common and Private Property," 11 *Soc. Phil. & Pol.* (No. 2) 17 (1994).

2. See chapter 21, supra.

3. See 271 U.S. 583 (1926).

4. Id. at 592.

5. See *Mich. Pub. Util. Comm'n v. Duke*, 266 U.S. 570, 577–578 (1925) (Butler, J.).

6. See *Stephenson v. Binford*, 287 U.S. 251 (1932).

7. 29 N.E. 517 (Mass. 1892).

8. Id. at 517–518.

9. 39 N.E. 113 (1895).

10. Id. at 113.

11. *Davis v. Massachusetts*, 167 U.S. 43, 48 (1897).

12. See *supra* Chapter 16.

13. 307 U.S. 496 (1939).

14. Id. at 515.

15. *Hague v. Committee for Industrial Organization*, 101 F.2d 774, 778 (3d Cir. 1939).

16. See *Cox v. New Hampshire*, 312 U.S. 569, 574 (1941).

17. *Kovacs v. Cooper*, 336 U.S. 77 (1949).

18. *Ward v. Rock against Racism*, 491 U.S. 781 (1989).

19. 308 U.S. 147 (1939).

20. 507 U.S. 410 (1993).

21. I develop this theme in Richard A. Epstein, "The Public Trust Doctrine," 7 *Cato J.* 411 (1987).

22. 515 U.S. 557 (1995).

23. Mass. Gen. Laws ch. 272, § 98 (1992).

24. *Irish-American Gay, Lesbian and Bisexual Group of Boston v. City of Boston*, 636 N.E.2d 1293, 1295–1298 (Mass. 1994).

25. *Hurley*, 515 U.S. at 577.

26. Id. at 576.

27. Id. at 568.

28. Id. at 573.

29. *Healy v. James*, 408 U.S. 169 (1972).

30. 130 S. Ct. 2971 (2010).

31. Id. at 2979.

32. Id. at 2974.

33. 391 U.S. 563 (1968).

34. 330 U.S. 75 (1947).

35. 5 U.S.C. § 7324 (1939).

36. *Elrod v. Burns*, 427 U.S. 347 (1976).

37. 461 U.S. 138, 142 (1983).

38. 547 U.S. 410 (2006).

39. Id. at 421.

40. For my defense, see Richard A. Epstein, "Can Anyone Beat the Flat Tax?," 19(1) *Soc. Philo. & Pol.* 140 (2002).

41. See, e.g., *Brushaber v. Union Pac. R.R.*, 240 U.S. 1 (1916).

42. 460 U.S. 575 (1983).

43. 297 U.S. 233 (1936).

44. 357 U.S. 513 (1958).

45. 481 U.S. 221 (1987).

28. *Progressive Regulation of Freedom of Speech*

1. See, e.g., *Cohen v. Cowles Media Co.*, 501 U.S. 663 (1991).

2. See, e.g., *Wisconsin v. Mitchell*, 508 U.S. 476, 486 (1993).

3. 326 U.S. 1 (1945).

4. 301 U.S. 103 (1937).

5. Id. at 132–133.

6. Quoting 79 *Cong. Rec.* 7565 (1935), reprinted in 2 *NLRB, Legislative History of the National Labor Relations Act, 1935,* at 2321 (1949).

7. See Archibald Cox, "Rights under a Labor Agreement," 69 *Harv. L. Rev.* 601 (1956).

8. 468 U.S. 609, 623 (1984) (noting the tension between the principle of freedom of association and a general antidiscrimination law).

9. See *Adair v. United States,* 208 U.S. 161 (1908) (federal); *Coppage v. Kansas,* 236 U.S. 1 (1915) (state).

10. Clayton Antitrust Act of 1914, 15 U.S.C. § 17 and 29 U.S.C. § 52 (2006).

11. See *Okla. Press Pub'g Co. v. Walling,* 327 U.S. 186 (1946) (Fair Labor Standards Act).

12. 29 U.S.C. § 158(a)(1), which makes it an unfair labor practice for an employer to "interfere with, restrain, or coerce employees in the exercise of the rights guaranteed in [29 U.S.C. § 157: Right of employees as to organization, collective bargaining, etc.]."

13. 29 U.S.C. § 158(c).

14. See, e.g., *NLRB v. Exch. Parts Co.,* 375 U.S. 405 (1964).

15. Steven Greenhouse, "Former N.L.R.B. Member Takes Post in a Big Union," *N.Y. Times* (May 22, 2012), at B2, available at http://www.nytimes.com/2012/05/23/business/craig-becker-appointed-to-afl-cio-role.html?_r=0.

16. Craig Becker, "Democracy in the Workplace: Union Representation Elections and Federal Labor Law," 77 *Minn. L. Rev.* 495 (1993); for a detailed response, see Richard A. Epstein, "The Deserved Demise of EFCA (and Why the NLRA Should Share Its Fate)," in *Research Handbook on the Economics of Labor and Employment Law* 177, 180–185 (M. Wachtler & C. Estlund eds, 2012).

17. See James W. Ely, *The Guardian of Every Other Right: A Constitutional History of Property Rights* (3rd ed., 2008).

18. See *supra* Chapter 17 ("Delegation and the Rise of Independent Agencies").

19. *Nat'l Broad. Co. v. United States,* 319 U.S. 190, 227 (1943).

20. Id. at 215.

21. 418 U.S. 241 (1974).

22. Id. at 257.

23. Id. at 248, 251.

24. 395 U.S. 367 (1969).

25. Upheld in *Syracuse Peace Council v. FCC,* 867 F.2d 654 (D.C. Cir. 1989).

26. 395 U.S. at 390.

27. *Cosmopolitan Broad. Corp. v. FCC,* 581 F.2d 917 (D.C. Cir. 1978).

28. *CBS v. FCC,* 453 U.S. 367, 395 (1981) (quoting *Office of Commc'n of the United Church of Christ v. FCC,* 359 F.2d 994, 1003 (D.C. Cir. 1966)).

29. 18 U.S.C. § 1464 added by 62 Stat. 769 (80th Cong. Sess. 2, 1948).

30. 556 U.S. 502 (2009).

31. 558 U.S. 310 (2010).

32. For one such popular denunciation, see Jamie Raskin, "'Citizens United' and the Corporate Court," *The Nation* (Sept. 13, 2012), available at http://www.thenation.com/article/169915/citizens-united-and-corporate-court#.

33. Elihu Root, *Addresses on Government and Citizenship* 143 (R. Bacon & J. Scott eds., 1916), quoted in *McConnell v. FEC*, 540 U.S. 93, 115 (2003) (internal citation omitted).

34. See *NAACP v. Alabama ex. rel. Patterson*, 357 U.S. 449, 460 (1958).

35. For the broader reading of that clause, see John D. Inazu, *Liberty's Refuge: The Forgotten Freedom of Assembly* (2012).

36. Pub. L. No. 59-36, 34 Stat. 864 (1907) (codified as amended at 2 U.S.C. § 441b(a) (2006)).

37. Labor Management Relations (Taft-Hartley) Act of 1947, Pub. L. No. 80-101, § 304, § 313, 61 Stat. 136, 159 (superseded by Federal Election Campaign Act Amendment of 1976, Pub. L. No. 94-283, § 112, § 321, 90 Stat. 475, 490) (codified as amended at 2 U.S.C. § 441b(a) (2006)).

38. Pub. L. No. 76-252, 53 Stat. 1147 (codified as amended in scattered sections of 5 and 18 U.S.C.).

39. 330 U.S. 127 (1947).

40. 424 U.S. 1 (1976).

41. See 130 S. Ct. 2811, 2821 (2010).

42. See *Ctr. for Individual Freedom v. Madigan*, 697 F.3d 464, 499 (7th Cir. 2012).

43. 554 U.S. 724 (2008).

44. See, e.g., Fabrizio Perri & Joe Steinberg, *Inequality and Redistribution during the Great Recession*, Economic Policy Papers (Federal Reserve Bank of Minneapolis, Feb. 2012), available at http://www.minneapolisfed.org/pubs/eppapers/12-1/epp_12-1_inequality.pdf (finding that redistribution through taxes and transfer programs reached historically high levels in 2010).

45. 131 S. Ct. 2806 (2011).

46. Ariz. Rev. Stat. Ann. § 16-940 et seq. (West 2006 & Supp. 2010).

47. *Bennett*, 131 S. Ct. at 2829.

48. Id.

49. 17 U.S. 518, 636 (1819).

50. 435 U.S. 765, 823 (1978).

51. Id. at 825.

52. Id.

53. U.S. Const. art. I, § 10, cl. 1.

54. See, e.g., Henry N. Butler, "The Contractual Theory of the Corporation," 11 *Geo. Mason U.L. Rev.* 99 (1989).

55. 211 U.S. 45 (1908).

56. 494 U.S. 652 (1990).

57. Mich. Comp. Laws § 169.254(1) (1979).

58. *Austin*, 494 U.S. at 658.

59. *McIntyre v. Ohio Elections Comm'n*, 514 U.S. 334, 347 (1995).

60. 540 U.S. 93 (2003).

61. Pub. L. No. 107-155, 116 Stat. 81 (2002) (codified in scattered sections of 2, 18, 28, and 47 U.S.C.).
62. Section 323(b).
63. *McConnell*, 540 U.S. at 150.
64. Id. at 119–120 n.6.
65. 291 U.S. 505 (1934.
66. 551 U.S. 449 (2007).
67. Id. at 456–457.
68. *Citizens United v. FEC*, 130 S. Ct. 876, 949–950 (2010) (Stevens, J., dissenting).
69. See John Mackey, Opinion, "The Whole Foods Alternative to ObamaCare," *Wall St. J.* (Aug. 11, 2009), at A15, available at http://online.wsj.com/article/SB10001424052970204251404574342170072865070.html.
70. See, e.g., James Bopp, Jr. & Kaylan Lytle Phillips, "The Limits of *Citizens United v. Federal Election Commission*: Analytical and Practical Reasons Why the Sky Is Not Falling," 46 *U.S.F. L. Rev.* 281, 300–302 (2011); see generally Richard A. Epstein, "*Citizens United v. FEC:* The Constitutional Right That Big Corporations Should Have but Do Not Want," 34 *Harv. J.L. & Pub. Pol'y* 639 (2011).

29. Free Exercise

1. U.S. Const. amend. I.
2. Id.
3. Id.
4. For an early defense of the neutrality position, see Philip Kurland, "Of Church and State and the Supreme Court," 29 *U. Chi. L. Rev.* 1 (1961). For a defense of the view that the Free Exercise Clause allows for religious exemptions to accommodate religious beliefs, see Michael W. McConnell, "The Origins and Historical Understanding of Free Exercise of Religion," 103 *Harv. L. Rev.* 1409 (1990).
5. 98 U.S. 145 (1879).
6. Id. at 166–167.
7. Id.
8. *Genesis* 29:28, 30:4, 30:9.
9. Id. at 166.
10. See, e.g., John Locke, *Second Treatise of Government* ch. 2 ¶ 6 (C. B. Macpherson ed., 1980) (1690).
11. Immanuel Kant, *Fundamental Principles of the Metaphysics of Morals* (Thomas Kingsmill Abbott trans., Merchant Books, 2009) (1785).
12. For my own views, see Richard A. Epstein, *Mortal Peril: Our Inalienable Right to Health Care?* 306–308 (1997).
13. See, e.g., *Vacco v. Quill*, 521 U.S. 793 (1997); *Washington v. Glucksberg*, 521 U.S. 702 (1997).
14. *Church of the Lukumi Babalu Aye, Inc. v. City of Hialeah*, 508 U.S. 520 (1993).
15. 321 U.S. 158 (1944).

16. Id. at 165.
17. Id. at 170.
18. Id. at 171 (Murphy, J., dissenting).
19. *Sturges & Burn Mfg. Co. v. Beauchamp*, 231 U.S. 320 (1913).
20. *Prince*, 321 U.S. at 166 (citing *Pierce v. Society of Sisters*, 268 U.S. 510 (1925)).
21. *Pierce v. Society of Sisters*, 268 U.S. 510 (1925); see also *Meyer v. Nebraska*, 262 U.S. 390 (1923) (holding that the state could not prohibit the education of children in languages other than English).
22. 406 U.S. 205 (1972).
23. Edwin G. West, *Education with and without the State*, HCO Working Paper 61 (World Bank, 1996), *available at* http://www.schoolchoices.org/roo/west1. htm (cross-country comparison of historical and modern systems of education); Edwin G. West, *Education and the Industrial Revolution* (2d ed., 2001) (noting the spread of education during the Industrial Revolution prior to government intervention).
24. 455 U.S. 252 (1982).
25. 26 U.S.C. § 1402(g)(1) (1960).
26. *Lee*, 455 U.S. at 255.
27. Id. at 257.
28. Id. at 258.
29. Id. at 260.
30. For the standard account, see Mancur Olson, *The Logic of Collective Action: Public Good and the Theory of Groups* (1965).
31. 476 U.S. 693 (1986).
32. 461 U.S. 574 (1983).
33. *Harris v. McCrae*, 448 U.S. 297, 329 (1980) (Brennan, J.). For my own conflicted views, see Richard A. Epstein, *Bargaining with the State* 285–294 (1993).
34. *Bob Jones*, 461 U.S. at 603.
35. See the discussion of *Speiser v. Randall*, 357 U.S. 513 (1958), *supra* Chapter 27 ("Government Regulation of the Speech Commons").
36. 494 U.S. 872 (1990).
37. Id. at 877-878.
38. Id. at 878.
39. Id. at 881–882.
40. 310 U.S. 296 (1940).
41. Religious Freedom Restoration Act of 1993, 42 U.S.C. § 2000bb et seq. (2006).
42. 521 U.S. 507 (1997).
43. Religious Land Use and Institutionalized Persons Act of 2000, 42 U.S.C. §§ 2000cc–2000cc-5 (2006).
44. Id. § 2000cc-1(a).
45. Id. § 2000cc-1(a)(1)–(2).
46. 544 U.S. 709 (2005).

47. *St. John's United Church of Christ v. City of Chicago*, 502 F.3d 616, 640 (7th Cir. 2007) (holding that the O'Hare Modernization Act falls outside RLUIPA).

48. 132 S. Ct. 694 (2012).

49. Pub. L. No. 101-336, 104 Stat. 327 (codified as amended at 42 U.S.C. §§ 12,101–213 (2006)).

50. For the case, see Richard A. Epstein, *Forbidden Grounds: The Case against Employment Discrimination Laws* 480–494 (1992).

51. *Hosana Tabor*, 132 S. Ct. at 707.

52. 440 U.S. 490 (1979).

53. *Hosana Tabor*, 132 S. Ct. at 697.

54. *Roman Catholic Archbishop of Washington v. Sebelius*, No. 12-815 (D.D.C. filed May 21, 2012); *University of Notre Dame v. Sebelius*, No. 12-253 (N.D. Ind. filed May 21, 2012).

55. 42 U.S.C. § 300gg-13(a)(4); Group Health Plans and Health Insurance Issuers Relating to Coverage of Preventive Services under the Patient Protection and Affordable Care Act, 76 Fed. Reg. 46,621 (Aug. 3, 2011) (to be codified at 26 C.F.R. pt. 54, 29 C.F.R. pt. 2590, & 45 C.F.R. pt. 147) (interim final rules providing for an exemption for direct payment for contraceptives as preventive care for employers while still requiring insurers to include contraception as covered preventive care for women). See also Certain Preventive Services under the Affordable Care Act, 77 Fed. Reg. 16,501 (proposed Mar. 21, 2012) (to be codified at 26 C.F.R pt. 54, 29 C.F.R. pt. 2590, & 45 C.F.R. pt. 147) (proposing similar requirements as interim final rules).

56. The letter was read into the Congressional Record on the floor of the House of Representatives the day it was released. 158 Cong. Rec. E1369-72 (daily ed. Aug. 1, 2012) (statement of Rep. Laura Richardson).

57. Id.

58. Id.

59. U.S. Const. art. VI, cl. 3.

60. Sacramental Test Act, 1828, 9 Geo. IV, c. 17.

61. Catholic Relief Act, 1829, 10 Geo. IV, c. 7.

62. *Torcaso v. Watkins*, 367 U.S. 488, 489 (1961). The offending law was Article 37 of the Declaration of Rights of the Maryland Constitution.

63. *McDaniel v. Paty*, 435 U.S. 618 (1978).

64. 321 U.S. at 170.

65. See, e.g., *Schneider v. State*, 308 U.S. 147 (1939).

66. *Members of the City Council v. Taxpayers for Vincent*, 466 U.S. 789 (1984).

67. 485 U.S. 439 (1988).

68. Id. at 453.

69. See *Johnson v. M'Intosh*, 21 U.S. 543 (1823) (where an earlier Indian title in land was inferior to a subsequent government title).

70. For discussion, see Ira C. Lupu, "Where Rights Begin: The Problem of Burdens on the Free Exercise of Religion," 102 *Harv. L. Rev.* 933 (1989).

71. 310 U.S. 586 (1940).

72. Id. at 595.

73. Id.

74. 319 U.S. 624 (1943).

75. Id. at 646.

76. See *Tinker v. Des Moines Sch. Dist.*, 393 U.S. 503, 511 (1969).

77. Civil Rights Act of 1964, 42 U.S.C. § 2000e et seq. (2006).

78. 374 U.S. 398 (1963).

79. Id. at 404.

80. Civil Rights Act of 1964, 42 U.S.C. § 2000e et seq. (2006).

81. Id.

82. *Trans World Airlines, Inc. v. Hardison*, 432 U.S. 63, 84 (1977).

83. 475 U.S. 503 (1986).

84. *Wilson v. U.S. W. Commc'ns*, 58 F.3d 1337 (8th Cir. 1995).

30. The Establishment Clause

1. For a discussion of these practices, see *Everson v. Bd. of Educ.*, 330 U.S. 1 (1947).

2. See, e.g., *id.* at 12–13; Hening, 12 *Statutes of Virginia* 84 (1823); James Madison, *Memorial and Remonstrance against Religious Assessments*, reprinted in 2 *Writings of James Madison* 183 (Gaillard Hunt ed., 1900).

3. For a discussion and references, see *Abington Sch. Dist. v. Schempp*, 374 U.S. 203, 254–258 (1963) (Brennan, J., concurring).

4. *Everson*, 330 U.S. 1.

5. Id. at 3.

6. *Zorach v. Clauson*, 343 U.S. 306 (1952).

7. *McCollum v. Bd. of Educ.*, 333 U.S. 203 (1948).

8. *Zorach*, 343 U.S. at 315.

9. See Robert C. Cord, *Separation of Church and State: Historical Fact and Current Fiction* 35 (1982).

10. Id. at 23.

11. 463 U.S. 783 (1983).

12. Id. at 788.

13. Cord, *supra* note 9, at 13.

14. *Terrett v. Taylor*, 13 U.S. 43, 49 (1815).

15. U.S. Const. amend. I.

16. See, e.g., Ellen Frankel Paul, *Property Rights and Eminent Domain* (2008).

17. Letter from Thomas Jefferson to Messrs. Nehemiah Dodge, Ephraim Robbins, and Stephen S. Nelson, Comm. of the Danbury Baptist Ass'n in the State of Conn. (Jan. 1, 1802), available at http://www.loc.gov/loc/lcib/9806/danpre.html (emphasis in original).

18. See *Restatement (Second) of Torts* § 822 cmt. g (based on *Bamford v. Turnley*, 122 Eng. Rep. 25, 26 (K.B. 1860)).

19. 403 U.S. 602 (1971).

20. Id. at 607.

21. Id. at 612–613 (internal citations omitted).

22. For discussion of these cases, see *infra* Chapters 31 ("The Establishment Clause: Regulation and Subsidy") and 32 ("Establishment: The Commons").

31. Regulation and Subsidy under the Establishment Clause

1. 366 U.S. 420 (1961).

2. 366 U.S. 599 (1961).

3. *McGowan*, 366 U.S. at 445.

4. Id. at 445; see *Braunfield*, 366 U.S. at 607 (pointing out that, as the Court similarly found in *McGowan*, "we cannot find a State without power to provide a weekly respite from all labor and, at the same time, to set one day of the week apart from the others as a day of rest, repose, recreation and tranquillity [sic]").

5. *Estate of Thornton v. Caldor, Inc.*, 472 U.S. 703 (1985). The Connecticut statute was: Conn. Gen. Stat. § 53-303e(b).

6. *Estate of Thornton*, 472 U.S. at 709.

7. "EU Accuses U.S. of Paying Billions in Boeing Subsidies," *USA Today* (Mar. 23, 2007), available at http://www.usatoday.com/travel/flights/2007-03-23-eu-boeing-subsidy-ap_N.htm.

8. *Everson v. Bd. of Educ.*, 330 U.S. 1 (1947).

9. Id. at 17.

10. Id. at 24.

11. *Lemon v. Kurtzman*, 403 U.S. 602 (1971).

12. Id. at 607.

13. *Bd. of Educ v. Allen*, 392 U.S. 236 (1968).

14. *Meek v. Pittenger*, 421 U.S. 349 (1975).

15. *Wolman v. Walter*, 433 U.S. 229 (1977).

16. See *Sch. Dist. of Grand Rapids v. Ball*, 473 U.S. 373 (1985), overruled by *Agostini v. Felton*, 521 U.S. 203 (1997); *Aguilar v. Felton*, 473 U.S. 402 (1985) also; strik. 521 U. S. 203, overruled by *Agostini*, 521 U.S. at 203.

17. 463 U.S. 388 (1983).

18. 536 U.S. 639 (2002).

19. 397 U.S. 664 (1970).

20. On tax expenditures, see *supra* Chapter 13 ("Enumerated Powers: Taxing and Spending"), at note 42.

21. *Walz*, 397 U.S. at 691.

22. See, e.g., Karin Fischer, "Brown U. to Pay Its Hometown $31.5-Million to Help Close Budget Gap," *The Chronicle of Higher Education* (May 1, 2012), available at http://www.chronicle.com/article/Brown-U-to-Pay-Its-Hometown/131757.

32. The Commons

1. See Richard John Neuhaus, *The Naked Public Square: Religion and Democracy in America* (2d ed., 1986).

2. 403 U.S. 602 (1971).

3. 465 U.S. 668 (1984).

4. Id. at 671.

5. Id.

6. Id. at 687.

7. Id. at 686.

8. See id. at 686.

9. Id. at 679 (quoting *Lemon*, 403 U.S. at 614).

10. *Lynch*, 465 U.S. at 691.

11. See id. at 694–704.

12. Id. at 706.

13. 507 U.S. 410 (1993), discussed *supra* Chapter 27 ("Government Regulation of the Speech Commons").

14. *Cnty. of Allegheny v. ACLU*, 492 U.S. 573 (1989).

15. 545 U.S. 677 (2005).

16. Id. at 681.

17. Id. at 686.

18. Id. at 740.

19. 545 U.S. 844 (2005).

20. Id. at 853.

21. Id. at 870–874.

22. 555 U.S. 460 (2009).

23. Id. at 472.

24. Id. at 469.

25. Id. at 472.

26. Id. at 482–483.

27. 343 U.S. 306 (1952).

28. Id. at 312–313.

29. 454 U.S. 263 (1981).

30. 508 U.S. 384 (1993).

31. 515 U.S. 819 (1995).

32. 330 U.S. 1 (1947).

33. 370 U.S. 421 (1962).

34. Id. at 422.

35. Id. at 425.

36. Id. at 426–427.

37. Id. at 422–423.

38. See 319 U.S. 624 (1943).

39. *Engel*, 370 U.S. at 423 n.2.

40. Id. at 444–450 (Stewart, J., dissenting).

41. *Zorach*, 343 U.S. at 306.

42. H.R.J. Res. 78, 105th Cong. (1997).

43. 374 U.S. 203 (1963).

44. Id. at 205.

45. 472 U.S. 38 (1985).
46. See, e.g., Brief for Christian Legal Society & Nat'l Ass'n of Evangelicals as Amici Curiae Supporting Appellants, *Wallace*, 472 U.S. 38 (No. 83-812); Brief for Moral Majority, Inc. as Amicus Curiae, *Wallace*, 472 U.S. 38 (Nos. 83-812, 83-929).
47. See H.R.J. Res. 78, *supra* note 42.
48. See *Wallace*, 472 U.S. at 55–60.
49. 505 U.S. 577 (1992).
50. Id. at 581.
51. 319 U.S. at 624.
52. Id.
53. See *Lee*, 505 U.S. at 594–597 (noting the significance of graduation ceremonies and the psychological pressures facing young students who are in the minority).
54. 542 U.S. 1 (2004).
55. *Newdow v. U.S. Cong.*, 328 F.3d 466 (9th Cir. 2002).
56. *Newdow*, 542 U.S. at 17–18.
57. See Brief for Joseph R. Grodin as Amicus Curiae in Support of Neither Party, *Newdow*, 542 U.S. 1 (No. 02-1624).
58. Brief for Respondent at 33–34, Newdow, 542 U.S. 1 (No. 02-1624).
59. See *Newdow*, 542 U.S. at 42 (O'Connor, J., concurring).
60. For the general point, see Charles M. Tiebout, "A Pure Theory of Local Expenditures," 64 *J. Pol. Econ.* 416 (1956) (extolling competition between local governments).
61. 393 U.S. 97 (1968).
62. 482 U.S. 578 (1987).
63. Id. at 581, 588.
64. See id. at 636–646 (Scalia, J., dissenting).
65. See id. at 588 (discussing the statute's provisions).
66. Id. at 634.

33. Race and the Fourteenth Amendment

1. "No person held to Service or Labour in one State, under the Laws thereof, escaping into another, shall, in Consequence of any Law or Regulation therein, be discharged from such Service or Labour, but shall be delivered up on Claim of the party to whom such Service or Labour may be due." U.S. Const. art. IV, § 2, cl. 3.
2. "Representatives and direct Taxes shall be apportioned among the several States which may be included within this Union, according to their respective Numbers, which shall be determined by adding to the whole Number of free Persons, including those bound to Service for a Term of Years, and excluding Indians not taxed, three fifths of all other Persons." U.S. Const. art. I, § 2, cl. 3.

3. Id. art. I, § 9, cl. 1.

4. *The Institutes of Justinian*, Book I, tit. II, § 2 (J. B. Moyle trans., 5th ed., 1913).

5. Id., Book I, tit. III, § 2.

6. Id., Book I, tit. V.

7. For the classic exposition, see W. W. Buckland, *The Roman Law of Slavery: The Conditions of the Slave in Private Law from Augustus to Justinian* (Cambridge University Press, 1908).

8. *R. v. Knowles, ex parte Somersett*, 20 State Tr. 1 (1772).

9. Slavery Abolition Act 1833, 3 & 4 Will. IV c. 73 (1833), with minor exceptions.

10. *Federalist No. 54* (Clinton Rossiter ed., 1999).

11. For discussion, see Andrew Kull, *The Color-Blind Constitution* 4–6 (1992).

12. 60 U.S. 393 (1856).

13. For the full text of the Emancipation Proclamation, see *American Treasures of the Library of Congress*, available at http://www.loc.gov/exhibits/treasures/trt026.html.

14. U.S. Const. amend. XIII.

15. Id. amend. XIV, § 1.

16. 60 U.S. 393.

17. Id.

18. See U.S. Const. art. III, governing the judiciary, where the term "citizen" appears five times in § 2.

19. Id. art. IV, § 2, cl. 1.

20. Virginia Charter of 1606, reprinted in 7 *The Federal and State Constitutions Colonial Charters, and Other Organic Laws of the States, Territories, and Colonies Now or Heretofore Forming the United States of America* 3784 (Francis Newton Thorpe ed., 1909). My thanks to Daniel Hulsebosch for pointing out this and similar sources.

21. Articles of Confederation of 1778, art. IV, § 1, available at http://memory.loc.gov/cgi-bin/ampage?collId=llsl&fileName=001/llsl001.db&recNum=127.

22. 6 F. Cas. 546 (C.C.E.D. Pa. 1823).

23. Id. at 551–552.

24. *Congressional Globe*, 39th Cong., 1st Sess. 2765–2766 (1866). Good authority has it that until today "[n]o one has ever contradicted Senator Howard's explanation of the meaning of the text." Michael Stokes Paulsen, et al., *The Constitution of the United States* 1351 (2010).

25. U.S. Const. amend. XIV, § 1.

26. Act of Apr. 9, 1866, ch. 31, § 1, 14 Stat. 27–30, 27.

27. David P. Currie, *The Constitution in the Supreme Court: The First Hundred Years, 1789–1888*, at 347–348 (1985); William Nelson, *The Fourteenth Amendment* 163–164 (1988).

28. *Slaughter-House Cases*, 83 U.S. 36 (1873).

29. Id. at 79–80 ("The right to peaceably assemble and petition for redress of grievances, the privilege of the writ of *habeas corpus*, are rights of the citizen guaranteed by the Federal Constitution. The right to use the navigable

waters of the United States, however they may penetrate the territory of the several States, all rights secured to our citizens by treaties with foreign nations, are dependent upon citizenship of the United States, and not citizenship of a State.").

30. Id. at 76.

31. Id. at 78.

32. *Butchers' Union Co. v. Crescent City Co.*, 111 U.S. 746, 764 (1884) (Bradley, J., dissenting) ("I then held, and still hold, that the phrase has a broader meaning; that it includes those fundamental privileges and immunities which belong essentially to the citizens of every free government, . . . Mr. Justice Washington enumerates. . . .").

33. 92 U.S. 542 (1875).

34. See generally Charles Lane, *The Day Freedom Died: The Colfax Massacre, the Supreme Court, and the Betrayal of Reconstruction* (2008).

35. *Cruikshank*, 92 U.S. at 551–555.

36. 163 U.S. 537 (1896).

37. Id. at 550–551.

38. Comm'n for Positive Educ., *The Forty Acres Documents: What Did the United States Really Promise the People Freed from Slavery?* (1994) .

39. 59 Mass. 198 (1849).

40. Id. at 206.

41. Text of Justice David Souter's Speech, *Harvard Gazette* (May 27, 2010), available at http://news.harvard.edu/gazette/story/2010/05/text-of-justice-david-souters-speech.

42. Id.

43. *Plessy*, 163 U.S. at 559 (Harlan, J., dissenting).

44. *Plessy*, 163 U.S. at 551.

45. 211 U.S. 45 (1908).

46. See discussion of *Davis v. Massachusetts, supra* Chapter 27 ("Government Regulation of the Speech Commons").

47. *Berea College*, 211 U.S. at 57.

48. 165 U.S. 578 (1897).

49. *Lochner v. New York*, 198 U.S. 45 (1905).

50. 208 U.S. 161 (1908).

51. See, e.g., James W. Ely, Jr., "Rufus W. Peckham and Economic Liberty," 62 *Vand. L. Rev.* 591 (2009).

52. 235 U.S. 151 (1914).

53. 245 U.S. 60 (1917).

54. 347 U.S. 483 (1954).

55. Id. at 495.

56. 347 U.S. 497 (1954).

57. *Brown II*, 349 U.S. 294, 301 (1955).

58. For discussion, see Gerald Rosenberg, *The Hollow Hope: Can Courts Bring About Social Change?* 43–46 (1993).

59. See *Green v. County Sch. Bd.*, 391 U.S. 430 (1968).
60. See *Swann v. Charlotte-Mecklenburg Bd. of Educ.*, 402 U.S. 1 (1971).
61. See Michael L. Sovern, *Legal Restraints on Racial Discrimination in Employment Law* 71 (1966).
62. See Robert M. Fogelson, "Violence and Grievances: Reflections on the 1960s Riots," 26 *J. of Soc. Issues* 141 (1970).
63. 443 U.S. 193 (1979).
64. Id. at 218.
65. Civil Rights Act of 1964, 42 U.S.C. § 2003.
66. *Connecticut v. Teal*, 457 U.S. 440 (1982).
67. 557 U.S. 557 (2009).
68. 551 U.S. 701 (2007).
69. 539 U.S. 306 (2003).
70. 539 U.S. 244 (2003).
71. 339 U.S. 629 (1950).
72. 236 F.3d 256 (5th Cir. 2000).
73. *Fisher v. Univ. of Texas*, 631 F.3d 213 (5th Cir. 2011), *cert. granted*, 132 S. Ct. 1536 (2012).
74. Id. at 221.

34. Citizenship and the Fourteenth Amendment

1. *Rogers v. Bellei*, 401 U.S. 815 (1971).
2. See, e.g., *Hines v. Davidowitz*, 312 U.S. 52, 66 (1941) (stating that "the regulation of aliens is so intimately blended and intertwined with responsibilities of the national government that where it acts, and the state also acts on the same subject," federal law is supreme and state law must yield to it).
3. *United States v. Macintosh*, 283 U.S. 605, 615 (1931).
4. U.S. Const. art. I, § 8, cl. 4.
5. 8 U.S.C. § 703 (repealed 1952). For a brief account, see *Takahashi v. Fish & Game Comm'n*, 334 U.S. 410, 412 n.1 (1948) (noting the gradual expansion of eligibility for citizenship on the basis of race or nationality).
6. 347 U.S. 497 (1954). See also *Adarand Constructors v. Pena* 515 U.S. 200 (1995)(applying *Bolling* to affirmative action programs).
7. For discussion, see Richard A. Epstein, "The Natural Law Bridge between Private Law and Public International Law," 13 *Chi. J. Int'l L.* 47 (2012).
8. See *Perez v. Brownell*, 356 U.S. 44, 48–56 (1958) (discussing legislative and judicial history of "denationalization").
9. Id. at 57–58.
10. 387 U.S. 253 (1967).
11. Id. at 268.
12. U.S. Const. art. III, § 3, cl. 1 reads: "Treason against the United States, shall consist only in levying War against them, or in adhering to their Enemies, giving them Aid and Comfort. No Person shall be convicted of Treason unless

on the Testimony of two Witnesses to the same overt Act, or on Confession in open Court." Note that the use of the term "person" in this context must be limited to citizens lest every foreign combatant be guilty of treason against the United States.

13. 1 L.F.L. Oppenheim, *International Law* 547–548 (H. Lauterpacht ed., 5th ed., 1937).
14. *Slaughter-House Cases*, 83 U.S. 36 (1873).
15. 239 U.S. 33 (1915).
16. See *West Coast Hotel v. Parrish*, 300 U.S. 379 (1937) (upholding Washington State's minimum wage law for women only against a Fourteenth Amendment Due Process Clause challenge).
17. 304 U.S. 144, 152, n.4 (1938).
18. 334 U.S. at 412.
19. 323 U.S. 214, 218–220 (1944).
20. *Takahashi*, 334 U.S. at 415–416.
21. *Truax*, 239 U.S. at 40.
22. 6 F. Cas. 546, 551–552 (C.C.E.D. Pa. 1823).
23. 239 U.S. at 39–40.
24. Id. at 40.
25. 239 U.S. 175 (1915).
26. Id. at 189.
27. Id. at 191 (citing *Atkin v. Kansas*, 191 U.S. 207, 222–223 (1903)).
28. 403 U.S. 365 (1971).
29. Id. at 372.
30. Id. at 374.
31. 304 U.S. at 152, n.4, cited in *Graham*, 403 U.S. at 372.
32. 413 U.S. 634 (1973).
33. Id. at 642, criticized in id. at 655–656 (Rehnquist, J., dissenting).
34. Id. at 641.
35. Id.
36. Id. at 647.
37. Id. at 655.
38. Id. at 653–654.
39. 457 U.S. 202 (1982).
40. Id. at 223.
41. Id. at 226.
42. Id. at 230.
43. While the relative probability of illegal versus legal aliens remaining in the United States is unknown, for statistics and general discussion of the 2007 census data see Steven A. Camarota, *Immigrants in the United States, 2007: A Profile of America's Foreign-Born Population* (Center for Immigration Studies, Nov. 2007), available at http://www.cis.org/articles/2007/back1007.pdf.
44. 457 U.S. at 242. For a critique of the willingness to abandon the traditional two-tier classifications under the Equal Protection Clause, see Dennis J.

Hutchinson, "More Substantive Equal Protection? A Note on *Plyler v. Doe*," 1982 *Sup. Ct. Rev.* 167.

45. 394 U.S. 802 (1969).

46. Id. at 807 (internal citation omitted).

47. For the liberal point of view, see Frank I. Michelman, "Foreword: On Protecting the Poor through the Fourteenth Amendment," 83 *Harv. L. Rev.* 7 (1969); for the conservative, see Ralph Winter, "Poverty, Economic Equality, and the Equal Protection Clause," 1972 *Sup. Ct. Rev.* 41.

48. 411 U.S. 1 (1973).

49. Id. at 12, 55.

50. *Serrano v. Priest*, 487 P. 2d 1241 (Cal. 1971).

51. For discussion, see Jeffrey I. Chapman, *Proposition 13: Some Unintended Consequences* (Public Policy Institute of California, 1998), available at http://www. ppic.org/content/pubs/op/OP_998JCOP.pdf.

52. See Chris Edwards, "Public Sector Unions and the Rising Costs of Employee Compensation," 30 *Cato J.* 109–112 (Winter 2010) (discussing the public sector union premium and the pressure on states' budgets).

53. Bruce Ackerman, "The Citizenship Agenda," in *The Constitution in 2020*, at 109–110 (Jack M. Balkin & Reva B. Siegel eds., 2009).

54. Id. at 110.

55. Goodwin Liu, "National Citizenship and the Promise of Equal Educational Opportunity," in *The Constitution in 2020*, *supra* note 53, at 119.

56. Id.

57. Id. at 127.

58. See No Child Left Behind Act, 20 U.S.C. §§ 6301–04 (2001) (outlining federal spending on education for disadvantaged schools and children). For an empirical evaluation of No Child Left Behind and its mixed results, see Thomas S. Dee & Brian Jacob, *The Impact of No Child Left Behind on Student Achievement*, Working Paper No. 15531 (Nat'l Bureau of Econ. Research, 2009).

35. Equal Protection and Sex Discrimination

1. See, e.g., Richard A. Epstein, "Gender Is for Nouns," 41 *DePaul L. Rev.* 981 (1992).

2. See discussion *infra* under head "Statutory Rape."

3. For discussion see, e.g., Norma Basch, *In the Eyes of the Law: Women, Marriage, and Property in Nineteenth Century New York* (1982) ; Carole Shammas, "Re-Assessing the Married Women's Property Acts," 6 *J. Women's Hist.* 9 (1994), available at http://courses.knox.edu/hist267/shammasproperty. pdf (comparing the Married Women's Property Acts to emancipation proclamations).

4. 208 U.S. 412 (1908). For further discussion, see *supra* Chapter 21 ("Freedom of Contract").

5. See, e.g., Sylvia A. Law, "Rethinking Sex and the Constitution," 132 *U. Pa. L. Rev.* 955 (1984).

6. 334 U.S. 410 (1948).

7. *Goesaert v. Cleary*, 335 U.S. 464, 466 (1948).

8. 404 U.S. 71 (1971). Ruth Bader Ginsburg was on the brief for Sally M. Reed.

9. Id. at 75–76.

10. Id. at 76.

11. See, e.g., Cal. Civ. Code § 5125 (1975); Idaho Code § 32-912 (1974); N.M. Stat. Ann. §§ 57-4A-7, 57-4A-8 (1973); Wash. Rev. Code § 26.16.030 (1972).

12. 411 U.S. 677 (1973).

13. Id. at 678–679.

14. Brief for Appellee at 4 *Frontiero v. Laird*, 411 U.S. 677 (1973) (No. 71-1694), 1972 WL 137566 at *8 n.5, *9 n.7.

15. Id. at *9 n.6.

16. *Frontiero v. Laird*, 341 F. Supp. 201, 208 (M.D. Ala. 1972).

17. *Frontiero*, 411 U.S. at 680–682, n.5, n.7 (citing *Bolling v. Sharpe*, 347 U.S. 497 (1954)).

18. 83 U.S. 130 (1873) (following *Slaughter-House Cases*, 83 U.S. 36 (1873), in the *United States Reports*).

19. Id. at 141 (Bradley, J., concurring).

20. *Frontiero*, 411 U.S. at 685.

21. *Miss. Univ. for Women v. Hogan*, 458 U.S. 718, 724 (1982) (citations omitted) (internal quotation marks omitted).

22. Id.

23. Id.

24. Id. at 735.

25. H.R.J. Res. No. 208, 92nd Cong., 2d Sess. (1972).

26. For an assessment, see Victor R. Fuchs, "Women's Quest for Economic Equality," 3 *J. Econ. Persps.* 25 (1989).

27. Robert Nozick, *Anarchy, State, and Utopia* 168 (1974).

28. 429 U.S. 190 (1976).

29. Id. at 201.

30. Id. at 204.

31. E.g., Assem. B. 2578 (Cal. 2010).

32. 348 U.S. 483, 487–488 (1955).

33. *Lochner v. New York*, 198 U.S. 45 (1905).

34. 450 U.S. 464 (1981).

35. See, e.g., 5 Edmund Burke, *The Works of the Right Honourable Edmund Burke* 522–523 (2010).

36. *Michael M.*, 450 U.S. at 496.

37. Exec. Order No. 9981, 13 *Fed. Reg.* 4313 (Jul. 26, 1948).

38. 10 U.S.C. § 654 (repealed 2011).

39. Don't Ask, Don't Tell Repeal Act of 2010 (H.R. 2965, S. 4023).

40. 453 U.S. 57 (1981).
41. 50 U.S.C. § 451.
42. 518 U.S. 515 (1996).
43. Id. at 534.
44. Id. at 533.
45. Id. at 542.
46. Id. at 520.

Conclusion

1. See the discussion of *Miller v. Alabama*, 132 S. Ct. 2455 (2011), discussed *supra* Chapter 3 ("Constitutional Interpretation").
2. See, e.g., *Weinberger v. UOP, Inc.*, 457 A.2d 701 (Del. 1983).
3. 28 U.S.C. § 2680(a).
4. See *Parents Involved in Comm. Sch. v. Seattle Sch. Dist. No. 1*, 551 U.S. 701 (2007); *Gratz v. Bollinger*, 539 U.S. 244 (2003) (both discussed *supra* Chapter 33 ("Race and the Fourteenth Amendment")).
5. See *United States v. Virginia*, 518 U.S. 515 (1996) (discussed *supra* Chapter 35 ("Equal Protection and Sex Discrimination")).
6. 5 U.S. 137 (1803). For discussion, see *supra* Chapter 4 ("The Origins of Judicial Review") and Chapter 5 ("Judicial Review: *Marbury* and *Martin*").
7. 14 U.S. 304 (1816). For discussion, see *supra* Chapter 5 ("Judicial Review: *Marbury* and *Martin*").
8. 163 U.S. 537 (1896). For discussion, see *supra* Chapter 33 ("Race and the Fourteenth Amendment").
9. 347 U.S. 483 (1954). For discussion, see *supra* Chapter 33 ("Race and the Fourteenth Amendment").
10. Mitchell Berman, "Originalism Is Bunk," 84 *N.Y.U. L. Rev.* 1 (2009).
11. Jack M. Balkin, *Living Originalism* (2011).
12. U.S. Const. art. I, § 8, cl. 3.
13. For discussion of the latter three acts, see *supra* Chapter 21 ("Freedom of Contract").
14. U.S. Const. art. 1, § 8, cl. 1.
15. Id. amend. V. For analysis and discussion of the Takings Clause, see *supra* Chapter 22 ("Takings, Physical and Regulatory").
16. *Hawaii Hous. Auth. v. Midkiff*, 467 U.S. 229, 241 (1984).
17. For discussion, see *supra* Chapter 6 ("Standing: Background and Origins") and Chapter 7 ("Modern Standing Law").
18. U.S. Const. amend. XIII, § 1.
19. See, e.g., "Symposium, Thirteenth Amendment: Meaning, Enforcement, and Contemporary Implications," 112 *Colum. L. Rev.* 1447 (2012); Douglas J. Colbert, "Liberating the Thirteenth Amendment," 30 *Harv. C.R.-C.L. L. Rev.* 1 (1995); Baher Azmy, "Unshackling the Thirteenth Amendment: Modern Slavery and a Reconstructed Civil Rights Agenda," 71 *Fordham L. Rev.* 981 (2002).

20. 198 U.S. 45, 75–76 (1905) (Holmes, J., dissenting). For discussion of *Lochner* and related cases, see *supra* Chapter 21 ("Freedom of Contract").
21. Jacob Viner, "The Intellectual History of Laissez Faire," 3 *J. Law & Econ.* 45, 45 (1960).
22. Id. at 67–68.
23. 77 *Edinburgh Rev.* 224 (1843) (quoted in Viner, *supra* note 21, at 55 n.41).

Index of Cases

General Index